Teacher's Resources

Fashion Marketing & Merchandising

Mary G. Wolfe
St. Michaels, Maryland

Publisher
The Goodheart-Willcox Company, Inc.
Tinley Park, Illinois
www.g-w.com

Contents

Introduction

Fashion Marketing & Merchandising is a comprehensive text designed to introduce students to fashion marketing and merchandising concepts. Besides the student text, *Fashion Marketing & Merchandising* learning package includes the *Student Workbook, Teacher's Resource Guide, Teacher's Resource CD,* **Exam**View® *Assessment Suite CD,* and *Teacher's* PowerPoint® *Presentations.* Using these products can help you develop an effective fashion marketing and merchandising program tailored to your students' unique needs.

Using the Text

The text *Fashion Marketing & Merchandising* is divided into eight parts with a total of 30 chapters. The material is organized and presented in a logical sequence of topics for the study of fashion marketing and merchandising. Although the text was written to be studied in its entirety, individual chapters and sections are complete enough to be studied independently.

The text is straightforward and easy to read. An expanded table of contents is included to give students an overview of the wide variety of topics they will be studying. The extensive glossary helps students learn terms related to fashion marketing and merchandising. A complete index helps them find information they want quickly and easily.

Each chapter includes several features designed to help students study effectively and review what they have learned.

Objectives. A set of behavioral objectives is found at the beginning of each chapter. These are performance goals that students will be expected to achieve after studying the chapter. Review the objectives in each chapter with students to help make them aware of the skills they will be building as they read the chapter material.

Fashion Terms. A list of vocabulary terms appears at the beginning of each chapter. Terms are listed in the order in which they appear in the chapter. These terms are in bold italic type throughout the text so students can recognize them while reading.

Discussing these words with students will help them learn concepts to which they are being introduced. To help students become familiar with these terms, you may want to ask them to

- look up, define, and explain each term
- relate each term to the topic being studied
- match terms with their definitions
- find examples of how the terms are used in current newspapers and magazines, reference books, the Internet, and other related materials

Summing It Up. A chapter summary is located at the end of each chapter. This section is a review of the major concepts covered in the entire chapter.

Fashion Review. Review questions at the end of each chapter are included to cover the basic information presented. This section consists of a variety of true/false, completion, multiple choice, and short essay questions. It is designed to help students recall, organize, and use the information presented in the text. Answers to these questions appear in the *Teacher's Resources.*

Fashion in Action. Suggested activities at the end of each chapter offer students opportunities to increase knowledge through firsthand experiences. These activities encourage students to apply many of the concepts learned in the chapter to real-life situations. Suggestions for both individual and group work are provided in varying degrees of difficulty. Therefore, you may choose and assign activities according to students' interests and abilities.

Using the *Student Workbook*

The *Student Workbook* designed for use with *Fashion Marketing & Merchandising* helps students recall and review material presented in the text. It also helps them apply what they have learned about fashion merchandising.

The activities in the guide are divided into chapters that correspond to the chapters in the text. The text provides the information students will need to complete many of the activities. Other activities will require creative thinking and research beyond the textbook.

You may want to use the exercises in the *Student Workbook* that relate directly to text material as introductory, review, or evaluation tools. Ask students to do the exercises without looking in the book. Then they can use the text to check their answers and answer questions they could not complete. The pages of the *Student Workbook* are perforated so students can easily turn completed activities in to you for evaluation.

The *Student Workbook* includes different types of activities. Some have specific answers related to text material. Students can use these activities to review as they study for tests and quizzes. Answers to these activities appear in *Teacher's Resources*.

Other activities, such as case studies and surveys, ask for students' thoughts or opinions. Answers to these activities cannot be judged as right or wrong. These activities allow students to form ideas by considering alternatives and evaluating situations thoughtfully. You can use these thought-provoking exercises as a basis for classroom discussion by asking students to justify their answers and conclusions.

The use of each activity in the *Student Workbook* is described in the *Teacher's Resources* as a teaching strategy under the related instructional concept. Activities are identified by name and letter.

Using the *Teacher's Resource Guide*

The *Teacher's Resource Guide* for *Fashion Marketing & Merchandising* suggests many methods of presenting the concepts in the text to students. It begins with some helpful information such as teaching suggestions and evaluation forms.

Chapter-by-Chapter Resources

Like the *Student Workbook*, the *Teacher's Resource Guide* is divided into chapters that match the chapters in the text. Each chapter contains the following features:

Objectives. These are the objectives that students will be able to accomplish after reading the chapter and completing the suggested activities.

Teaching Materials. A list of materials available to supplement each chapter in the text is provided. The list includes the names of all the activities contained in the *Student Workbook* and the masters contained in the *Teacher's Resources*.

Introductory Activities. These motivational exercises are designed to stimulate your students' interest in the chapter they will be studying. The activities help create a sense of curiosity that students will want to satisfy by reading the chapter.

Strategies to Reteach, Reinforce, Enrich, and Extend Text Concepts. A variety of student learning strategies is described for teaching each of the major concepts discussed in the text. Each major concept appears in the guide in bold type. The student learning experiences for each concept follow. Activities from the *Student Workbook* are identified for your convenience in planning daily lessons. They are identified with the letters *WB* following the title and letter of the activity. (*Needs for Clothing*, Activity A, WB.)

The number of each learning strategy is followed by a code in bold type. These codes identify the teaching goals each strategy is designed to accomplish. The following codes have been used:

RT identifies activities designed to help you *reteach* concepts. These strategies present the chapter concepts in a different way to allow students additional learning opportunities.

RF identifies activities designed to *reinforce* concepts to students. These strategies present techniques and activities to help clarify facts, terms, principles, and concepts, making it easier for students to understand.

ER identifies activities designed to *enrich* learning. These strategies help students learn more about the concepts presented by involving them more fully in the material. Enrichment strategies include diverse experiences, such as demonstrations, field trips, guest speakers, panels, and surveys.

EX identifies activities designed to *extend* learning. These strategies promote thinking skills such as critical thinking, creative thinking, problem solving, and decision making. Students must analyze, synthesize, and evaluate to complete these activities.

Answer Key. This section provides answers for review questions at the end of each chapter in the text, activities in the *Student Workbook*, the reproducible masters in the *Teacher's Resources*, and the chapter tests.

Reproducible Masters. Several reproducible masters are included for each chapter. These masters are designed to enhance the presentation of concepts in the text. Some of the masters are designated as *transparency masters* for use with an overhead projector. These are often charts or graphs that can serve as a basis for class discussion of important concepts. You can also use them as student handouts. Some of the masters are designed as *reproducible masters*. You can give each student a copy of these activities, which encourage creative and critical thinking. They can also serve as a basis for class discussion. Some masters provide material not contained in the text that you may want students to know.

Chapter Test Masters. Individual tests with clear, specific questions that cover all the chapter topics are provided. True/false, multiple choice, and matching questions measure student learning about facts and definitions. Essay questions are also provided in the chapter tests. Some of these require students to list information, while others encourage students to express their opinions and creativity. You may wish to modify the tests and tailor the questions to your classroom needs.

Using the *Teacher's Resource CD*

The *Teacher's Resource CD* includes all the contents of the *Teacher's Resource Guide*. Using the navigational buttons and a single mouse click, you can access the Teacher's Resources, Transparencies in PowerPoint, Lesson Plans, and Related Web Sites. The CD format allows you to view and print resource pages exactly as they appear in the *Teacher's Resource Guide* from your computer. The *Fashion Marketing & Merchandising Teacher's Resource CD* contains the following items:

- *Teacher's Resources.* This section of the TRCD contains the *Fashion Marketing & Merchandising Teacher's Resource Guide* in PDF format. This allows you to see each page exactly as it appears in the guide and print it from your computer. To produce overhead transparencies, print transparency master pages onto acetate film designed for your printer.
- *Transparencies in PowerPoint.* All blackline transparencies from the *Teacher's Resource Guide* are presented in PowerPoint format and listed by chapter.
- *Lesson Plans.* Quickly prepare customized daily lesson plans using our new click-and-print format. Begin with publisher-prepared resources and add your own time-tested resources. Lesson plans can be saved and modified using Microsoft Word.
- *Related Web Sites.* A direct Internet link is provided for numerous content-related Web sites.

Using the *ExamView® Assessment Suite CD*

This software suite includes the *ExamView Test Generator*, *Test Player*, and *Test Manager*. The *Test Generator* allows you to quickly and easily create and print tests from a test bank of hundreds of questions. The database includes all the questions from the chapter tests in the *Teacher's Resources* plus 25 percent additional questions for more complete coverage of chapter concepts. You can choose to generate a test with randomly selected questions or you can choose specific questions from the database. If you wish, add your own questions to create customized tests to meet your classroom needs. You may want to

make different versions of the same test to use during different class periods. Answer keys are generated automatically to simplify grading. The *Test Player* is used to deliver tests on a local area network (LAN). The *Test Manager* allows you to track results of paper and online tests created with the *Test Generator*.

Using the *Teacher's PowerPoint® Presentations*

The *Teacher's PowerPoint Presentations CD* is an excellent tool for reviewing key concepts in each chapter. The slides also include discussion questions and reflection/critical thinking questions. These PowerPoint presentations are not the same as those included on the *Teacher's Resource CD*.

There is a separate presentation for each of the 30 chapters in the text, with over 500 slides. The presentations were created in PowerPoint 2000, but you do not have to be running PowerPoint to use them. A download link for PowerPoint Viewer is supplied on the CD. If you want to make changes to the slides, you will need to have PowerPoint on your computer.

Using Other Resources

Much student learning in this class can be reinforced and expanded by exposing your students to a variety of viewpoints and teaching methods. By providing guest speakers, panel presentations, field trip experiences, and access to media resources related to fashion merchandising, you can greatly enhance student learning.

Current magazines and journals are good sources of articles on various aspects of fashion merchandising. Having copies in the classroom will encourage students to use them for research and ideas as they study fashion merchandising. Information can also be obtained from the Internet and World Wide Web†. Other information may be obtained through various professional organizations. The following may be able to provide you with some resources. (*An asterisk indicates that specific supplementary teaching materials are noted in these *Teacher's Resources*.)

*1SYNC
Princeton Pike Corporate Center
1009 Lenox Drive, Suite 115
Lawrenceville, NJ 08648
Phone: 866-280-4013   Fax: 609-620-4601
www.1sync.org

*Acrylic Council
1251 Avenue of the Americas
New York, NY 10020
Phone: 212-944-8480
www.fabriclink.com/acryliccouncil

*AIM USA
(See Automatic Identification Manufacturers)

*American Apparel Contractors Association
140 Mareanna Drive
P.O. Box 720693
Atlanta, GA 30358
Phone: 404-843-3171   Fax: 404-256-5380
www.usawear.org

*American Apparel & Footwear Association
1601 N. Kent Street, Suite 1200
2 Arlington, VA 22209
Phone: 800-520-2262   Fax: 703-522-6741
www.apparelandfootwear.org

*American Apparel Producers' Network (AAPN)
P.O. Box 720693
Atlanta, GA 30358
Phone: 404-843-3171   Fax: 413-702-3226
www.aapnetwork.net

American Arbitration Association
335 Madison Avenue, 10th Floor
New York, NY 10017-4605
Phone: 800-778-7879   Fax: 212-716-5905
www.adr.org

American Assoc. of Family & Consumer Sciences
400 N. Columbus Street, Suite 202
Alexandria, VA 22314
Phone: 800-424-8080   Fax: 703-706-4663
www.aafcs.org

*American Association of Textile Chemists &
Colorists
P.O. Box 12215
Research Triangle Park, NC 27709
Phone: 919-549-8141   Fax: 919-549-8933
www.aatcc.org

America at Retail Forecasters
Anne Murphy & Associates
100 Bleeker Street, Suite 21F
New York, NY 10012
Phone: 201-224-8229

*American Fiber Manufacturers Assoc., Inc.
1530 Wilson Blvd., Suite 690
Arlington, VA 22209
Phone: 703-875-0432   Fax: 703-875-0907
www.fibersource.com or
www.afma.org

*American Institute of Small Business
426 Second Street
Excelsior, MN 55331
Phone: 800-328-2906
www.aisb.biz

*American Marketing Association
311 South Wacker Drive, Suite 5800
Chicago, IL 60606
Phone: 800-262-1150   Fax: 312-542-9001
www.marketingpower.com

*American Society for Quality (ASQ)
P.O. Box 3005
Milwaukee, WI 53201-3005
Phone: 800-248-1946   Fax: 414-272-1734
www.asq.org

*American Wool Council
c/o American Sheep Industry Association
6911 South Yosemite Street
Englewood, CO 80112-1415
Phone: 303-771-3500   Fax: 303-771-8200
www.americanwool.org or
www.sheepusa.org

*American Yarn Spinners Association, Inc. (AYSA)
2500 Lowell Road
Gastonia, NC 28053
Phone: 704-824-3522   Fax: 704-824-0630
www.textileweb.com/storefronts/aysa.html

*AmericasMart, Atlanta
240 Peachtree Street, Suite 2200
Atlanta, GA 30303-1327
Phone: 800-285-6278   Fax: 404-220-3030
www.americasmart.com

*Apparel Magazine
Edgell Communications
4 Middlebury Blvd.
Randolph, NJ 07869
Phone: 973-252-0100
www.apparelmag.com

*Automatic Identification Manufacturers
125 Warrendale-Bayne Road
Warrendale, PA 15086
Phone: 800-338-0206   Fax: 724-934-4495
www.aimglobal.org

*Avery Dennison, Marketing Department
7722 Dungan Road
Philadelphia, PA 19111
Phone: 800-233-4177   Fax: 215-728-8921
www.averydennison.com

*BASF Corporation, Fibers Division
P.O. Drawer D
Williamsburg, VA 23187
Phone: 804-887-6000
www.basf.de/basf/html

Burda Patterns, Inc.
901 Wayne Street
Niles, MI 49121
Phone: 800-241-6887   Fax: 616-687-1500

*Burlington Industries, Inc.
  3330 West Friendly Avenue
  P.O. Box 21207
  Greensboro, NC 27420
  Phone: 919-379-2000
  www.burlington.com

*Business & Legal Reports, Inc.
  39 Academy Street
  Madison, CT 06443-1513
  Phone: 800-727-5257   Fax: 814-942-1736
  www.blr.com

*Butterick Company, Inc.
  161 Avenue of the Americas, 8th Floor
  New York, NY 10013
  Phone: 800-766-3619   Fax: 814-942-1736
  www.butterick.com

*California Market Center
  110 East Ninth Street, Suite A727
  Los Angeles, CA 90079-2827
  Phone: 800-225-6278   Fax: 213-630-3708
  www.californiamarketcenter.com

*Cambridge Educational
  2572 Brunswick Pike
  Lawrenceville, NJ 08648
  Phone: 800-468-4227   Fax: 800-329-6687
  www.cambridgeeducational.com

*Canadian Apparel Federation
  124 O'Connor Street, Suite 504
  Ottawa, Ontario K1P 5M9 – Canada
  Phone: 613-231-3220   Fax: 613-231-2305
  www.apparel.ca

*Canadian Textile Institute
  222 Somerset Street, West, Suite 500
  Ottawa, Ontario K2P 2G3 – Canada
  Phone: 613-232-7195   Fax: 613-232-8722
  www.textiles.ca

*Caribbean-Central American Action (CCAA)
  1818 N Street NW, Suite 310
  Washington, DC 20036
  Phone: 202-466-7464   Fax: 202-822-0075
  www.c-caa.org

Chamber of Commerce of the U.S.A.
  1615 H. Street, NW
  Washington, DC 20062
  www.uschamber.com

*Charlotte Merchandise Mart
  800 Briarcreek Road
  Charlotte, NC 28205
  Phone: 704-333-7709   Fax: 704-375-9410
  www.carolinasmart.com

*Chicago Apparel Center
  Suite 470, The Merchandise Mart
  200 World Trade Center
  Chicago, IL 60654
  Phone: 800-677-6278   Fax: 312-527-7980
  www.merchandisemart.com

*Liz Claiborne, Inc.
  1441 Broadway, 18th Floor
  New York, NY 10018
  Phone: 212-626-3485   Fax: 212-626-3416
  www.lizclaiborne.com

*Color Association of the United States
  315 West 39th Street, Studio 507
  New York, NY 10018
  Phone: 212-947-7774   Fax: 212-594-6987
  www.colorassociation.com

Color Me a Season, Inc.
  2901 Camby Road
  Antioch, CA 94509
  Phone: 800-692-6567   Fax: 925-778-0184
  www.colormeaseason.com

*Consumer Goods Technology
  Edgell Communications
  10 West Hanover Avenue, Suite 107
  Randolph, NJ 07869-4214
  Phone: 973-895-3300   Fax: 973-895-7711

Consumer Product Safety Commission
  1111 – 18th Street, NW
  Washington, DC 20207
  Phone: 800-638-2772
  www.cpsc.gov

*Cotton Board
  871 Ridgeway Loop, Suite 100
  Memphis, TN 38120-4019
  Phone: 901-683-2500   Fax: 901-685-1401
  www.cottonboard.org

*Cotton Incorporated
  1370 Avenue of the Americas, 34th Floor
  New York, NY 10019
  Phone: 212-413-8300   Fax: 212-265-5386
  www.cottoninc.com
  (World Headquarters: 6399 Weston Parkway,
  Cary, NC 27513 – Phone: 919-678-2220)

Council of Better Business Bureaus
  4200 Wilson Boulevard, Suite 800
  Arlington, VA 22203
  Phone: 800-477-6583
  www.bbb.org

*Council of Fashion Designers of America
  1412 Broadway, Suite 2006
  New York, NY 10018
  Phone: 212-302-1821   Fax: 212-768-0515
  www.cfda.com

*The Curriculum Center for Family and Consumer
   Sciences
   Texas Tech University
   P.O. Box 41161
   Lubbock, TX 79409-1161
   Phone: 806-742-3029   Fax: 806-742-3034
   www.hs.ttu.edu/ccfcs

*Custom Tailors and Designers Association of America
   The Talley Management Group, Inc.
   19 Mantau Road
   Mt. Royal, NJ 08061
   Phone: 856-423-1621   Fax: 856-423-3420
   www.ctda.com

*Dallas Market Center (Int'l. Apparel Mart)
   2100 Stemmons Freeway
   Dallas, TX 75207
   Phone: 800-325-6587   Fax: 214-655-6238
   www.dallasmarketcenter.com

*Dan River, Inc.
   2291 Memorial Drive
   P.O. Box 261
   Danville, VA 24543
   Phone: 800-274-2439
   www.danriver.com

*Department of Commerce
   14th Street & Constitution Avenue, NW
   Washington, DC 20202-0498
   Phone: 800-872-5327
   www.commerce.gov

*D.E. Visuals
   3595 NW 83rd Avenue
   Sunrise, FL 33351-6141
   Phone: 800-736-6438   Fax: 954-741-1746

Direct Marketing Association
   11 West 42nd Street
   New York, NY 10036-8096
   Phone: 212-768-7227
   www.thedma.com

Direct Selling Association
   1667 K Street NW, Suite 1100
   Washington, DC 20006-1660
   Phone: 202-452-8866   Fax: 202-452-9010
   www.dsa.org

*Edgell Communications
   4 Middlebury Blvd., Suite 1
   Randolph, NJ 07869
   Phone: 973-252-0100   Fax: 973-252-9020
   www.edgellcommunications.com

ESP/Ellen Sideri Partnership Inc.
   12 West 37th Street
   New York, NY 10018
   Phone: 212-629-9200   Fax: 212-629-0040
   www.espwired.com

*Family, Career, and Community Leaders of America,
   Inc. (FCCLA)
   1910 Association Drive
   Reston, VA 20191-1584
   Phone: 703-476-4900   Fax: 703-860-2713
   www.fcclainc.org

*The Fashion Center
   249 West 39th Street
   New York, NY 10018
   Phone: 212-764-9600   Fax: 212-764-9697
   www.fashioncenter.com

*The Fashion District of Los Angeles
   110 East Ninth Street, Suite C625
   Los Angeles, CA 90079
   Phone: 213-488-1153   Fax: 213-488-5159
   www.dpoa.com

*The Fashion Group International
   597 Fifth Avenue, 8th Floor
   New York, NY 10017
   Phone: 212-593-1715   Fax: 212-593-1925
   www.fgi.org

Fashion Institute of Design & Merchandising
   919 S. Grand Avenue
   Los Angeles, CA 90015
   Phone: 800-711-7175   Fax: 213-624-4777
   www.fidm.edu

Fashion Institute of Technology
   227 West 27th Street
   New York, NY 10001-5992
   Phone: 212-217-7999   Fax: 212-217-7909
   www.fitnyc.suny.edu

*Federal Citizen Information Center
   P.O. Box 100
   Pueblo, CO 81002
   Phone: 888-878-3256
   www.pueblo.gsa.gov

Federal Trade Commission (Public Reference Section)
   Sixth Street & Pennsylvania Avenue, NW
   Room 130
   Washington, DC 20580
   Phone: 202-326-2222
   www.ftc.gov

Federation Francaise de la Couture
   100-102, Faubourg Saint-Honore
   75008 Paris, France
   Phone: 331-4266-6444   Fax: 331-4266-9563
   www.modeaparis.com

Fiber Economics Bureau, Inc.
   1530 Wilson Blvd., Suite 690
   Arlington, VA 22209
   Phone: 703-875-0432   Fax: 703-875-0907
   www.fibersource.com

*Forstmann & Company
P.O. Box 128
Dublin, GA 31040
Phone: 912-272-4711
www.forstmann.com

*Fur Information Council of America (FICA)
8424A Santa Monica Blvd., #860
West Hollywood, CA 90069
Phone: 323-848-7940   Fax: 323-848-2931
www.fur.org

*GAP, Inc.
One Harrison
San Francisco, CA
Phone: 415-952-4400   Fax: 415-995-6491
www.gap.com

*Garment Industry Development Corporation
275 – 7th Avenue, 9th Floor
New York, NY 10001
Phone: 212-366-6160   Fax: 212-366-6162
www.gidc.org

Gerber Garment Technology, Inc.
24 Industrial Park Road West
P.O. Box 769
Tolland, CT 06084-0769
Phone: 800-826-3243   Fax: 203-871-6007
www.gerbertechnology.com

*Goodheart-Willcox Publisher
18604 West Creek Drive
Tinley Park, IL 60477-6243
Phone: 800-323-0440   Fax: 708-687-5068
www.g-w.com

Handweavers Guild of America
1255 Buford Highway, Suite 211
Suwanee, GA 30024
Phone: 678-730-0010   Fax: 678-730-0836
www.weavespindye.org

*Hartmarx Corporation
101 N. Wacker Drive
Chicago, IL 60606
Phone: 312-372-6300   Fax: 312-444-2710
www.hartmarx.com

Home Sewing Association
P.O. Box 1312
Monroeville, PA 15146
Phone: 412-372-5950   Fax: 412-372-5953
www.sewing.org

Home Shopping Network, Inc.
2501 – 118th Avenue North
St. Petersburg, FL 33716-1900
Phone: 813-572-8585   Fax: 813-572-8854
www.hsn.com

Hong Kong Trade Development Council
219 East 46th Street
New York, NY 10017
Phone: 212-838-8688   Fax: 212-838-8941
www.hktdc.com

*IMG Fashion
420 West 45th Street
New York, NY 10036
Phone: 212-253-2692   Fax: 212-772-0899
www.img-fashion.com

Indiana University of Pennsylvania
Human Development & Environmental Studies
207 Ackerman Hall
911 South Drive
Indiana, PA 15705-1037
Phone: 724-357-2336   Fax: 724-357-5941
www.iup.edu

*Insight Media
2162 Broadway
New York, NY 10024-0621
Phone: 800-233-9910   Fax: 212-799-5309
www.insight-media.com

*International Apparel Federation
5 Portland Place
London W1B 1PW, England
www.iafnet.org

*International Association of Clothing Designers &
Executives
835 NW 36th Terrace
Oklahoma City, OK 73118
Phone: 405-602-8037   Fax: 405-602-8038
www.iacde.com

International Colour Authority
33 Bedford Place
London WC1B 5JU, England
www.internationalcolourauthority.com

*International Fabricare Institute
14700 Sweitzer Lane
Laurel, MD 20707
Phone: 800-638-2627   Fax: 240-295-0685
www.ifi.org

*International Organization for Standardization
Geneva, Switzerland
www.iso.org

*International Textile & Apparel Association, Inc.
(ITAA)
P.O. Box 1360
Monument, CO 80132
www.itaaonline.org

*International Textile Manufacturers Federation (ITMF)
AM Schanzengraben 29
Postfach CH-8039
Zurich, Switzerland
Phone: +41-44 283 63 80   Fax: +41-44 283 63 89

Internet Fashion Mall
575 Madison Avenue, 7th Floor
New York, NY 10022
Phone: 800-859-1440   Fax: 212-891-6033
www.fashionmall.com

Invista
4123 East 37th Street North
Wichita, KS 67220
Phone: 877-446-8478
www.invista.com

Iowa State University
Apparel Merchandising, Design & Production
31 MacKay Hall
Ames, IA 50011-1120
Phone: 515-294-2695   Fax: 515-294-6364
www.iastate.edu

*JIST Publishing
8902 Otis Avenue
Indianapolis, IN 46216-1033
Phone: 800-648-5478   Fax: 800-547-8329
www.jist.com

June Tailor, Inc.
P.O. Box 208
Richfield, WI 53076
Phone: 800-844-5400   Fax: 800-246-1573
www.junetailor.com

*Kalorama Information
641 – 6th Avenue, 3rd Floor
New York, NY 10011
Phone: 800-298-5699   Fax: 212-807-2716
www.MarketResearch.com

*Kellwood Company
600 Kellwood Parkway
Chesterfield, MO 63017
Phone: 314-576-3100   Fax: 314-576-3462
www.kellwood.com

*Kmart, International Headquarters
3100 West Big Beaver Road
Troy, MI 48084-3163
Phone: 248-643-5200   Fax: 248-643-5513
www.kmart.com

*Lands' End Direct Merchants
5 Lands' End Lane
Dodgeville, WI 53595
Phone: 800-356-4444   Fax: 608-935-4135
www.landsend.com

*Learning Seed
330 Telser Road
Lake Zurich, IL 60047
Phone: 800-634-4941   Fax: 800-998-0854
www.learningseed.com

Leather Apparel Association
19 West 21st Street, Suite 403
New York, NY 10010
Phone: 212-727-1210   Fax: 212-727-1218
www.leatherassociation.com

Leather Industries of America (LIA)
3050 K Street, NW, Suite 400
Washington, DC 20007
Phone: 202-342-8497   Fax: 202-342-8583
www.leatherusa.com

The Limited Stores
Three Limited Parkway
Columbus, OH 43230
Phone: 614-415-7000
www.limited.com

The McCall Pattern Company
11 Penn Plaza
New York, NY 10001
Phone: 800-782-0323   Fax: 212-465-6963
www.mccall.com

*Meridian Education Corporation
90 MacCorkle Avenue, SW
South Charleston, WV 25303
Phone: 800-727-5507   Fax: 888-340-5507
www.meridianeducation.com

*Miami International Merchandise Mart
777 NW 72nd Avenue
Miami, FL 33126
Phone: 305-261-2900   Fax: 305-261-3659
www.mimm.com

*MindPerk
2133 East 9400 South #129
Sandy, UT 84093
Phone: 800-457-2523
www.mindperk.com

*Models Mart
159 West 25th Street, Suite 1001
New York, NY 10001
Phone: 800-223-1254   Fax: 212-741-6410
www.models-mart.com

*Mohair Council of America
233 W. Twohig
P.O. Box 5337
San Angelo, TX 76902
Phone: 800-583-3161   Fax: 915-655-4761
www.mohairusa.com

*Nancy's Notions, Ltd.
333 Beichl Avenue
P.O. Box 683
Beaver Dam, WI 53916-0683
Phone: 800-833-0690   Fax: 800-255-8119
www.nancysnotions.com

*Nasco
901 Janesville Avenue
Fort Atkinson, WI 53538-0901
Phone: 800-558-9595   Fax: 920-563-8296
www.eNASCO.com

*National Association of Display Industries, Inc.
(NADI)
4651 Sheridan Street, Suite 470
Hollywood, FL 33021
Phone: 954-893-7300   Fax: 954-893-7500
www.nadi-global.com

*National Association of the Sewn Products Industry
(SEAMS)
4921-C Broad River Road
Columbia, SC 29212
Phone: 803-772-5861   Fax: 803-731-7709
www.seams.org

*National Association of Store Fixture Manufacturers
(NASFM)
4651 Sheridan Street, Suite 470
Hollywood, FL 33021
Phone: 954-893-7300   Fax: 954-893-7500
www.nasfm.org

National Business Education Association
1914 Association Drive
Reston, VA 22091-1596
Phone: 703-860-8300   Fax: 703-620-4483
www.nbea.org

*National Cotton Council of America
1918 N. Parkway
P.O. Box 820285
Memphis, TN 38182-0285
Phone: 901-274-9030   Fax: 901-725-0510
www.cotton.org

National Council on Economic Education
1140 Avenue of the Americas
New York, NY 10036
Phone: 800-338-1192
www.nationalcouncil.org or
www.ncee.net

National 4-H Council
7100 Connecticut Avenue
Chevy Chase, MD 20815
Phone: 301-961-2800
www.fourhcouncil.edu

*National Retail Federation
325 – 7th Street, NW
Suite 1000, Liberty Place
Washington, DC 20004
Phone: 800-673-4692   Fax: 202-737-2849
www.nrf.com

National Textile Association
6 Beacon Street, Suite 1125
Boston, MA 02108
Phone: 617-542-8220   Fax: 617-542-2199
www.nationaltextile.org

National Textile Center
1121 N. Bethlehem Pike, Suite 60 #317
Spring House, PA 19477-1102
Phone: 215-540-0760   Fax: 215-689-4835
www.ntcresearch.org

Neighborhood Cleaners Association, International
252 W. 29th Street
New York, NY 10001
Phone: 800-888-1622   Fax: 212-967-2240
www.nca-i.com

Pacific Northwest International Trade Association
200 SW Market Street, Suite 1770
Portland, OR 97201
Phone: 503-224-8684   Fax: 503-323-9186
www.portlandalliance.com

Parsons The New School For Design
66 Fifth Avenue, 7th Floor
New York, NY 10011
Phone: 212-229-5600
www.parsons.newschool.edu

*Pendleton Woolen Mills
220 NW Broadway
P.O. Box 3030
Portland, OR 97208-3030
Phone: 800-760-4844   Fax: 503-535-5599
www.pendleton-usa.com

*JCPenney, Catalog Division
5500 South Expressway
Atlanta, GA 30390-0370
Catalog phone: 800-222-6161
Customer service phone: 800-709-5777
www.jcpenney.com

*Peter Glenn Publications
824 E. Atlantic Ave., 2nd Floor
Delray Beach, FL 33483
Phone: 888-332-6700
www.pgdirect.com

*Pineapple Appeal
P.O. Box 197
Owatonna, MN 55060
Phone: 800-321-3041   Fax: 507-455-2307
www.pineappleappeal.com

*QVC, Inc.
    1365 Enterprise Drive
    West Chester, PA 19380
    Phone: 610-701-1000   Fax: 610-701-1380
    www.qvc.com

*Retail Ad World Magazine
    Visual Reference Publications, Inc.
    305 Fifth Avenue, 11th Floor
    New York, NY 10001
    Phone: 800-251-4545   Fax: 212-279-7014
    www.vizzbiz.com

Retail Council of Canada
    121 Bloor Street East, Suite 1210
    Toronto, Ontario M4W 3M5, Canada
    Phone: 888-373-8245   Fax: 877-790-4271
    www.retailcouncil.org

*Retail Industry Leaders Association
    1700 N. Moore Street, Suite 2250
    Arlington, VA 22209
    Phone: 703-841-2300   Fax: 703-841-1184
    www.retail-leaders.org

*Retail Reporting Corporation
    302 Fifth Avenue
    New York, NY 10001
    Phone: 800-251-4545   Fax: 212-279-7014
    www.retailreporting.com

*Retailing Today Magazine
    425 Park Avenue
    New York, NY 10022
    Phone: 212-756-5000   Fax: 212-756-5290
    www.retailingtoday.com

*The School Company
    P.O. Box 5379
    Vancouver, WA 98668
    Phone: 800-543-0998   Fax: 800-518-2514
    www.schoolco.com

*Sears Roebuck & Company
    3333 Beverly Road
    Hoffman Estates, IL 60179
    Phone: 847-286-8316   Fax: 847-286-8351
    www.sears.com

Sew News Magazine
    741 Corporate Circle, Suite A
    Golden, CO 80401
    Phone: 800-590-3465
    www.sewnews.com

*Shoe Trades Publishing Company
    61 Massachusetts Avenue
    Arlington, VA 02474
    Phone: 781-648-8160   Fax: 781-646-9832
    www.shoetrades.com

Simplicity Pattern Company, Inc.
    2 Park Avenue, 12th Floor
    New York, NY 10016
    Phone: 888-588-2700
    www.simplicity.com

Singer Sewing Company
    1224 Heil Quaker Blvd.
    P.O. Box 7017
    LaVergne, TN 37086
    Phone: 800-474-6437
    www.singerco.com

Small Business Administration
    (See U.S. Small Business Administration)

*ST Publications, Inc.
    407 Gilbert Avenue
    Cincinnati, OH 45202-2285
    Phone: 800-925-1110   Fax: 513-421-5144
    www.stpubs.com

*STORES Magazine
    (See National Retail Federation)

Superintendent of Documents
    U.S. Government Printing Office
    732 North Capitol Street NW
    Washington, DC 20401
    Phone: 202-512-0000
    www.gpoaccess.gov

Symbol Technologies, Inc.
    One Symbol Place
    Holtzville, NY 11742-1300
    Phone: 800-722-6234   Fax: 631-738-5990
    www.symbol.com

*Tandy Leather Company
    3847 East Loop 820 South
    Fort Worth, TX 76119
    Phone: 800-433-3201   Fax: 817-451-5254
    www.tandyleather.com

*Teacher's Media Company
    101 Castleton Street
    P.O. Box 40
    Pleasantville, NY 10570
    Phone: 800-431-1934   Fax: 914-769-2109
    www.teachersmediacompany.com

*Textile/Clothing Technology Corporation
    211 Gregson Drive
    Cary, NY 27511-7909
    Phone: 800-786-9889   Fax: 919-380-2181
    www.tc2.com

Textile Distributors Association
    1040 West 40th Street, 18th Floor
    New York, NY 10018
    Phone: 212-869-2346
    www.penrose-press.com

Textile Industries Magazine
2100 Powers Ferry Road
Atlanta, GA 30339
Phone: 770-955-5656   Fax: 770-952-0669
www.textileindustries.com

*Textile World Magazine
2100 Powers Ferry Road, Suite 300
Atlanta, GA 30339
Phone: 770-755-5656   Fax: 770-952-0669
www.textileworld.com

*Thomson Course Technology (Crisp Learning)
1200 Hamilton Court
Menlo Park, CA 94025
Phone: 800-422-7477   Fax: 859-647-5963
www.courseilt.com

*Uniform Code Council
7887 Washington Village Drive, Suite 300
Dayton, OH 45459
Phone: 937-435-3870
www.uc-council.org

*Union of Needletrades, Industrial and Textile
Employees
275 – 7th Avenue
New York, NY 10001
Phone: 212-265-7000
www.unitehere.org

University of Delaware
Fashion & Apparel Studies Department
Allison Hall West, Room 211
Newark, DE 19716
Phone: 302-831-8714   Fax: 302-831-6081
www.udel.edu/fash/

*U.S. Department of Commerce
14th Street & Constitution Avenue, NW
Washington, DC 20230
Phone: 202-482-2000   Fax: 202-482-2331
www.commerce.gov

*U.S. Small Business Administration
409 – 3rd Street, SW
Washington, DC 20416
Phone: 800-827-5722
www.sba.gov

*VIDCAT
P.O. Box 1492
New York, NY 10056
Phone: 866-843-2282   Fax: 212-683-2713
www.vidcat.com

*VMS, Inc.
805 Airway Drive
Allegan, MI 49010-8516
Phone: 800-343-6430   Fax: 269-673-9509
www.VMS-online.com

*Voluntary Interindustry Commerce Solutions (VICS)
1009 Lenox Drive, Suite 202
Lawrenceville, NJ 08648
Phone: 609-620-4590
www.vics.org

Vogue Patterns Company
(*See* Butterick Co., Inc.)

*Women's Wear Daily
7 West 34th Street
New York, NY 10001-8191
Phone: 800-289-0273   Fax: 212-630-4201
www.wwd.com

*The Wool Bureau, Inc.
The Woolmark Company
330 Madison Avenue, 19th Floor
New York, NY 10017-5001
Phone: 212-986-6222   Fax: 212-557-5985
www.wool.com

†Note: The addresses, phone numbers, fax numbers, and Web site addresses listed may have changed since the publication of these *Teacher's Resources.*

Teaching Techniques

You can make fashion merchandising exciting and relevant by using a variety of teaching techniques. The following are some principles that will help you choose and use different teaching techniques in your classroom:

- Make learning stimulating. One way to do this is to involve students in lesson planning. When possible, allow them to select the modes of learning they enjoy most. For example, some students will do well with oral reports; others prefer written assignments. Some learn well through group projects; others do better working independently. You can also make courses more interesting by presenting a variety of learning activities and projects from which students may choose to fulfill their work requirement.

- Make learning realistic. You can do this by relating the subject matter to issues that concern young people. Students gain the most from learning when they can apply it to real-life situations. Case studies, role-playing, and drawing on personal experiences all make learning more realistic and relevant.

- Make learning varied. Try using several different techniques to teach the same concept. Make use of outside resources and current events as they apply to material being presented in class. Students learn through their senses of sight, hearing, touch, taste, and smell. The more senses they use, the easier it will be for them to retain information. Bulletin boards, films, tapes, and transparencies all appeal to the senses.

- Make learning success-oriented. Experiencing success increases self-esteem and confidence. Guarantee success for your students by presenting a variety of learning activities. Key these activities to different ability levels so each student can enjoy both success and challenge. You also will want to allow for individual learning styles and talents. For instance, some students excel at organizing material, while others are artistic or analytical. Build in opportunities for individual students to work in ways and at projects that let them succeed and shine.
- Make learning personal. Young people become more personally involved in learning if you establish a comfortable rapport with them. Work toward a relaxed classroom atmosphere in which students can feel at ease when sharing their feelings and ideas in group discussions and activities.

Following are descriptions of various teaching techniques you may want to try. Keep in mind that not all methods work equally well in all classrooms. A technique that works beautifully with one group of students may not be successful with another. The techniques you choose will depend on the topic, your teaching goals, and the needs of your students.

One final consideration concerns student rights to privacy. Some activities, such as autobiographies, diaries, and opinion papers, may violate students' rights to privacy. You can maintain a level of confidentiality by letting students turn in unsigned papers in these situations. You may also encourage students to pursue some of these activities at home for personal enlightenment without fear of evaluation or judgment.

Helping Students Gain Basic Information

You can group teaching techniques according to different goals you may have for your students. One group of techniques is designed to convey information to students. Two of the most common techniques in this group are reading and lecture. Using a number of variations can make these techniques seem less common and more interesting. For instance, students may enjoy taking turns to read aloud as a change of pace from silent reading. You can energize lectures with the use of flip charts, overhead transparencies, and other visual materials. Classroom discussions of different aspects of the material being presented get students involved and help impart information.

Other ways to present basic information include the use of outside resources. Guest speakers, whether speaking individually or as part of a panel, can bring a new outlook to classroom material. You can videotape guest lectures to show again to other classes or to use for review. You may also purchase or rent videos from educational sources or have students do Internet research.

Helping Students Question and Evaluate

A second group of teaching techniques helps students develop analytic and judgmental skills. These techniques help your students go beyond what they see on the surface. As you employ these techniques, encourage students to think about points raised by others. Ask them to evaluate how new ideas relate to their attitudes about various subjects.

Discussion is an excellent technique for helping students consider an issue from a new point of view. To be effective, discussion sessions require a great deal of planning and preparation. Consider the size of the discussion group and the physical arrangement. Since many students are reluctant to contribute in a large group, you may want to divide the class into smaller groups for discussion sessions. You will enhance participation if you arrange the room so students can see one another.

Discussion can take a number of forms. Generally it is a good idea to reserve group discussions involving the entire class for smaller classes. Buzz groups consisting of two to six students offer a way to get willing participation from students who are not naturally outgoing. They discuss an issue among themselves and then appoint a spokesperson to report back to the entire class.

Debate is an excellent way to explore opposite sides of an issue. You may want to divide the class into two groups, each to take an opposing side of the issue. You can also ask students to work in smaller groups and explore opposing sides of different issues. Each group can select students from the group to present the points for their side.

Helping Students Participate

Another group of teaching techniques is designed to promote student participation in classroom activities and discussion. There are many ways to involve students and encourage them to interact. Case studies, surveys, opinionnaires, stories, and pictures can all be used to boost classroom participation. These techniques allow students to react to or evaluate situations in which they are not directly involved. Open-ended sentences very often stimulate discussion. However, it is wise to steer away from overly personal or confidential matters when selecting sentences for completion. Students will be reluctant to deal with confidential issues in front of classmates.

The "fishbowl" can be a good way to stimulate class discussion. A larger observation group encircles an interactive group of five to eight students. The encircled students discuss a given topic while the others listen. Do not permit observers to talk or interrupt. Students can reverse positions at the end of a fishbowl session so some of the observers become participants.

One of the most effective forms of small group discussion is the cooperative learning group. Match small groups of learners to complete a particular task or goal. Assign each person in the group a role. Measure the success of the group not only in terms of outcome, but in the successful performance of each member in his or her role.

In cooperative learning groups, students learn to work together toward a group goal. Each member is dependent on others for the outcome. This interdependence is a basic component of any cooperative learning group. The value of each group member is affirmed as learners work toward their goal.

The success of the group depends on individual performance. Mix groups in terms of abilities and talents so there are opportunities for the students to learn from one another. Also, as groups work together over time, rotate roles so everyone has an opportunity to practice and develop different skills.

The interaction of students in a cooperative learning group creates a tutoring relationship. While cooperative learning groups may involve more than just group discussion, discussion is always part of the process by which cooperative learning groups function.

Helping Students Apply Learning

Some techniques are particularly good for helping students use what they have learned. Simulation games and role-playing allow students to practice solving problems and making decisions under non-threatening circumstances. Role-playing allows students to examine others' feelings as well as their own. It can help them learn effective ways to react or cope when confronted with similar situations in real life.

Role-plays can be structured, with the actors following written scripts, or they may be improvised in response to a classroom discussion. Students may act out a role as they themselves see it being played, or they may act out the role as they presume a person in that position would behave. Students do not rehearse roles, and they compose lines on the spot. The follow-up discussion should focus on the participants' emotions and the manner in which the characters resolved the problem. Role-playing helps students consider how they would behave in similar situations.

Helping Students Develop Creativity

You can use some techniques to help students generate new ideas. For example, brainstorming

encourages students to exchange and pool their ideas and to come up with new thoughts and solutions to problems. Do not allow evaluation or criticism of ideas. The format of spontaneously expressing any opinions or reactions that come to mind lets students be creative without fear of judgment.

You also can promote creativity by letting students choose from a variety of assignments related to the same material. For example, suppose you wanted students to know what type of information to look for on garment labels. You could ask them to contact a government agency to find out what the law requires on different labels. You might give them the choice of writing a case study involving the misreading of a label or a problem resulting from inadequate label information. Designing a product label or collecting a variety of garment labels and making a display would be options, too. Your students might even write a short story about caring for a closet full of clothes without labels. Any teaching techniques you use to encourage students to develop their ideas will foster their creativity.

Helping Students Review Information

Certain techniques aid students in recalling and retaining knowledge. Games can be effective for drills on vocabulary and information. Crossword puzzles and mazes can make the review of vocabulary terms more interesting. Structured outlines of subject matter can also be effective review tools. Open-book quizzes, bulletin board displays, and problem-solving sessions all offer ways to review and apply material presented in the classroom.

Teaching Students of Varying Abilities

The students in your classroom represent a wide range of ability levels. Students with special needs who are mainstreamed require unique teaching strategies. You must not overlook gifted students. You need to challenge them up to their potential. All the students in between will have individual needs to consider also. Often you will have to meet the needs of all these students in the same classroom setting. It is a challenge to adapt daily lessons to meet the demands of all your students.

To tailor your teaching to mainstreamed and lower-ability students, consider the following strategies:

- Before assigning a chapter in the text, discuss and define the key words that appear at the end of each chapter. These terms are defined in the glossary at the back of the text. Ask students to write out the definitions and tell what they think the terms mean in their own words. You might want to invite students to guess what they think words mean before they look up the definitions. You also can ask them to use new words in sentences and to find the sentences in the text where the new terms appear.

- When introducing a new chapter, review previously learned information students need to know before they can understand the new material. Review previously learned vocabulary terms they will come across again.

- Use the "Introductory Activities" section in the *Teacher's Resources* for each chapter. Students who have difficulty reading need a compelling reason to read the material. These introductory activities can provide the necessary motivation. Then students will want to read the text to satisfy their curiosity.

- Break the chapters up into smaller parts and assign only one section at a time. Define the terms, answer the "To Review" questions, and discuss the concepts presented in each section before proceeding to the next. It often helps to rephrase questions and problems in simple language and to repeat important concepts in different ways. Assign activities in the *Student Workbook* that relate to each section in the book. These reinforce the concepts presented. In addition, many of these activities are designed to improve reading comprehension.

- Ask students, individually or in pairs, to answer the "To Review" questions at the end of each chapter in the text. This will help them focus on the essential information contained in the chapter.

- Use the buddy system. Pair nonreaders with those who read well. Ask students who have mastered the material to work with those who need assistance. It also may be possible to find a parent volunteer who can provide individual attention where needed.

- Select a variety of educational experiences to reinforce the learning of each concept. Look for activities that will help reluctant learners relate information to real-life situations. It helps to draw on the experiences of students at home, in school, and in the community.

- Give directions orally as well as in writing. You will need to explain assignments as thoroughly and simply as possible. Ask questions to be certain students understand what they are to do. Encourage them to ask for help if they need it. You will also want to follow up as assignments continue to be sure no one is falling behind on required work.

- Use the overhead projector and the transparency masters included in the *Teacher's Resources*. A visual presentation of concepts will increase students' ability to comprehend the material. You may want to develop other transparencies to use in reviewing key points covered in each chapter.

- If you have advanced or gifted students in your class, you will need to find ways to challenge them. These students require assignments that involve critical thinking and problem solving. Because advanced students are more capable of independent work, they can use the library, Internet, and outside resources to research topics in depth. The "Additional Enrichment Activities" section in each chapter of the *Teacher's Resources* suggests research projects that may be appropriate for gifted students. You may be able to draw on the talents of advanced students in developing case studies and learning activities to use with the entire class.

Evaluation Techniques

You can use a variety of evaluation tools to assess student achievement. Try using the reproducible forms *Evaluating Individual Participation*, *Evaluating Individual Reports*, and *Evaluating Group Participation* included with the introductory material in the front of the *Teacher's Resources*. These rating scales allow you to observe a student's performance and rank it along a continuum. This lets students see what levels they have surpassed and what levels they can still strive to reach.

In some situations, it is worthwhile to allow students to evaluate their work. When evaluating an independent study project, for example, students may be the best judge of whether they met the objectives they set for themselves. Students can think about what they have learned and see how they have improved. They can analyze their strengths and weaknesses.

You may ask students to evaluate their peers from time to time. This gives the student performing the evaluation an opportunity to practice giving constructive criticism. It also gives the student being evaluated the opportunity to accept the criticism from his or her peers.

Tests and quizzes are also effective evaluation tools. You may give these in either written or oral form. In either case, however, you should use both objective and subjective questions to adequately assess student knowledge and understanding of class material.

Communicating with Students

Communicating with students involves not only sending clear messages, but also receiving and interpreting feedback. The following suggestions will encourage productive communication with your students:

- Recognize the importance of body language and nonverbal communication both in presenting material and interpreting student responses. Use eye contact, relaxed but attentive body position, natural gestures, and an alert facial expression as you present material. Look for the same body language from students as an indication of their attention. Voice is also an important nonverbal communicator. Cultivating a warm, lively, enthusiastic speaking voice will make classroom presentations more interesting. By your tone, you can convey a sense of acceptance and expectation to which your students will respond.

- Use humor whenever possible. Humor is not only good medicine, it opens doors and teaches lasting lessons. Laughter and amusement will reduce tension, make points in a nonthreatening and memorable way, increase the fun and pleasure in classroom learning, and break down stubborn barriers. Relevant cartoons, quotations, jokes, and amusing stories all bring a light touch to the classroom.

- Ask questions that promote recall, discussion, and thought. Good questions are tools that open the door to communication. Open-ended inquiries that ask what, where, why, when, and how will stimulate thoughtful answers. You can draw out students by asking for their opinions and conclusions. Questions with yes or no answers tend to discourage rather than promote further communication. Avoid inquiries that are too personal or that might put students on the spot.

- Rephrase student responses to be sure both you and they understand what has been said. Paraphrasing information students give is a good way to clarify, refine, and reinforce material and ideas under discussion. For example, you might say, "This is what I hear you saying...correct me if I'm wrong." Positive acknowledgment of student contributions, insights, and successes encourages more active participation and open communication. Try comments like, "That's a very good point. I hadn't thought of it that way before" or "What a great idea."

- Listen for what students say, what they mean, and what they do not say. Really listening may be the single most important step you can take to promote open communication. As students answer questions and express their ideas and concerns, try not only to hear what they say but to understand what they mean. What students leave unsaid can also be important. Make room for silence and time to think and reflect during discussion sessions.

- Share your feelings and experiences. The measure of what students communicate to you will depend in part on what you are willing to share with them. Express your personal experiences, ideas, and feelings when they are relevant. Do not forget to tell them about a few of your mistakes. Sharing will give students a sense of exchange and relationship.

- Lead discussion sessions to rational conclusions. Whether with an entire class or with individual students, it is important to identify and resolve conflicting thoughts and contradictions. This will help students to think clearly and logically. For example, in a discussion of retail buying, students may want higher quality goods and lower costs. Pointing out and discussing the inconsistency in these two positions will lead to more logical approaches to both buying and pricing of goods.

- Create a nonjudgmental atmosphere. Students will only communicate freely and openly in a comfortable environment. You can make them comfortable by respecting their ideas, by accepting them for who they are, and by honoring their confidences. It is also important to avoid criticizing a student or discussing personal matters in front of others.

- Use written communication to advantage. The more ways you approach students, the more likely you are to reach them on different levels. Very often, the written word can be an excellent way to connect. Written messages can take different forms—a notice on the chalkboard, a note attached to homework, a memo to parents (with good news as well as bad), or a letter exchange involving class members.

- Be open and available for private discussion of personal or disciplinary problems. It is important to let students know they can come to you with personal concerns as well as questions regarding course material. You generally need to handle these discussions and disciplinary actions confidentially and in a private setting.

Promoting Your Program

You can make fashion merchandising one of the most important course offerings in your school. You cover material that every student and teacher can use to advantage, including general business principles and small consumer knowledge. It pays to make the student body and faculty aware of your program. With good public relations you can increase your enrollment, gain support from administrators and other teachers, and achieve recognition in the community. The following suggestions can help you promote your program:

- Create visibility. It is important to let people know what is going on in fashion merchandising classes. Ways to do this include announcements of projects and activities at faculty meetings and in school bulletins or newspapers, displays in school showcases or on bulletin boards, and articles and press releases in school and community newspapers. Talk up your program with administrators, other teachers, and students. Invite them to visit your classes.
- Interact within the school. Fashion merchandising is related to many fields of learning. You can strengthen your program and contribute to other disciplines by cooperating with other teachers. For example, you can work with math teachers to present information on pricing. The more interaction you can generate, the more you promote the fashion merchandising program.
- Contribute to the educational objectives of the school. If your school follows stated educational objectives and strives to strengthen specific skills, include these overall goals in your teaching. For example, if students need special help in developing verbal or writing skills, select projects and assignments that will help them in these areas. Show administrators examples of work that indicate student improvement in needed skills.
- Serve as a resource center. Fashion merchandising information is of practical use and interest to almost everyone. You can sell your program by making your department a resource center of materials related to fashion merchandising. Invite faculty members, students, and parents to tap into the wealth of information available in your classroom.
- Generate involvement and activity in the community. Real merchandising education takes place in the community. You are teaching concepts students can apply immediately where they live. You can involve students in community life and bring the community into your classroom through field trips, interviews with businesspeople and community leaders, surveys, and presentations from guest speakers. You may be able to set up cooperative projects between the school and community organizations around textile or apparel manufacturing, retailing, fashion promotion, entrepreneurship, and other topics.
- Connect with parents. If you can get them involved, parents may be your best allies in teaching and selling fashion merchandising education. Let parents know when their children have done good work. Call on them to share their experiences or to form a panel to discuss specific topics. Moms and dads have been through much of what you are preparing students to do. Parents can be a rich source of real-life experience. Keep them informed on classroom activities and invite them to participate as they are able.
- Establish a student sales staff. Enthusiastic students will be your best salespeople. Encourage them to tell their parents and friends what they are learning in your classes. You might create bulletin boards or write letters to parents that focus on what students are learning in your classes. Ask students to put together a newsletter highlighting their experiences in fashion merchandising class. Students could write a column from your department for the school paper.

We appreciate the contributions of the following Goodheart-Willcox authors to this introduction: "Teaching Techniques" from *Changes and Choices*, by Ruth E. Bragg; and "Evaluation Techniques" from *Contemporary Living*, by Verdene Ryder.

Goodheart-Willcox Welcomes Your Comments

We welcome your comments or suggestions regarding Fashion Marketing & Merchandising and its ancillaries as we are continually striving to publish better educational materials. Please send any comments you may have to:

Editorial Department
Goodheart-Willcox Publisher
18604 West Creek Drive
Tinley Park, IL 60477-6243

or to send a memo to the editor, visit our Web site at

www.g-w.com

Evaluating Individual Participation

Name_____ **Date** _____ **Period** _____

The rating scale below shows an evaluation of your class participation. It indicates what levels you have passed and what levels you can continue to try to reach.

Attentiveness

1	2	3	4	5	6	7	8	9	10
Completely inattentive.		Seldom attentive.		Somewhat attentive.		Usually attentive.		Extremely attentive.	

Contribution to Discussion

1	2	3	4	5	6	7	8	9	10
Never contributes to class discussion.		Rarely contributes to class discussion.		Occasionally contributes to class discussion.		Regularly contributes to class discussion.		Frequently contributes to class discussion.	

Interaction with Peers

1	2	3	4	5	6	7	8	9	10
Often distracts others.		Shows little interaction with others.		Follows leadership of other students.		Sometimes assumes leadership role.		Respected by peers for ability.	

Response to Teacher

1	2	3	4	5	6	7	8	9	10
Unable to respond when called on.		Often unable to support or justify answers when called on.		Supports answers based on class information, but seldom offers new ideas.		Able to offer new ideas with prompting.		Often offers new ideas without prompting.	

Comments:

_____

_____

_____

_____

_____

Evaluating Individual Reports

Name_____ Date _____ Period _____

The rating scale below shows an evaluation of your oral or written report. It indicates what levels you have passed and what levels you can try to reach on future reports.

Report topic_____ Oral_____ Written _____

Choice of Topic

1	2	3	4	5	6	7	8	9	10
Slow to choose topic.		Chooses topic with indifference.		Chooses topic as assigned, seeks suggestions.		Chooses relevant topic without assistance.		Chooses creative topic.	

Use of Resources

1	2	3	4	5	6	7	8	9	10
Unable to find resources.		Needs direction to find resources.		Uses limited number of resources.		Uses assigned number of resources from typical sources.		Uses additional resources from a variety of sources.	

Oral Presentation

1	2	3	4	5	6	7	8	9	10
No notes or read completely. Poor subject coverage.		Has few good notes. Limited subject coverage.		Uses notes somewhat effectively. Adequate subject coverage.		Uses notes effectively. Good subject coverage.		Uses notes very effectively. Complete coverage.	

Written Presentation

1	2	3	4	5	6	7	8	9	10
Many grammar and spelling mistakes. No organization.		Several grammar and spelling mistakes. Poor organization.		Some grammar and spelling mistakes. Fair organization.		A few grammar and spelling mistakes. Good organization.		No grammar or spelling mistakes. Excellent organization.	

Evaluating Group Participation

Group _____
Members:

_____   _____

_____   _____

_____   _____

The rating scale below shows an evaluation of the efforts of your group. It indicates what levels you have passed and what levels you can try to reach on future group projects.

Teamwork

1	2	3	4	5	6	7	8	9	10
Passive membership. Failed to identify what tasks needed to be completed.		Argumentative membership. Unable to designate who should complete each task.		Independent membership. All tasks completed individually.		Helpful membership. Completed individual tasks and then assisted others.		Cooperative membership. Worked together to complete all tasks.	

Leadership

1	2	3	4	5	6	7	8	9	10
No effective leadership.		Group fragmented by several members seeking leadership roles.		Sought leadership from outside group.		One member assumed primary leadership role for the group.		Leadership responsibilities shared by several group members.	

Goal Achievement

1	2	3	4	5	6	7	8	9	10
Did not attempt to achieve goal.		Were unable to achieve goal.		Achieved goal with outside assistance.		Achieved assigned goal.		Achieved goal using added materials to enhance total effort.	

Members cited for excellent contributions to group's effort are:

_____   _____

_____   _____

Members cited for failing to contribute to group's effort are:

_____   _____

_____   _____

PART ONE

Basic Fashion and Business **Concepts**

The Meaning of Clothing and Fashion

Objectives

After studying this chapter, students will be able to

⊖ explain the basic reasons people wear clothes.

⊖ state why people make various clothing choices.

⊖ describe fashion in terms of art and science, and private and public awareness.

⊖ summarize economic and political influences on fashion.

⊖ define basic fashion terms.

Teaching Materials

Text, pages 16–32
   Fashion Terms
   Fashion Review
   Fashion in Action

Student Workbook
   A. *Needs for Clothing*
   B. *Fashion Facts*
   C. *A Fashion Mirror*
   D. *Express Your Thoughts*
   E. *Fashion Term Matching*

Teacher's Resources
   Clothing as Protection, reproducible master 1-1
   The Significance of Uniforms, reproducible master 1-2
   The Reasons for Wearing Clothing, transparency master 1-3
   Protective Clothing Innovations, reproducible master 1-4
   U.S. Economic and Social Influences on Fashion, reproducible master 1-5
   Chapter 1 Test

Introductory Activities

1. Discover students' feelings and knowledge about the meaning of clothing and fashion. Have students tell what they think clothing has meant to cultures throughout history. Discuss areas of art, crafts, and rituals.

2. Ask students if they think clothing is more important to people today than it was 50 years ago, 100 years ago, and 1,000 years ago. Ask them if they think clothing is more important to the people in the U.S. than it is in other countries.

3. Ask students to write down as many fashion terms as they can in two minutes and save the list. After the chapter has been studied, ask them to put a line across the bottom of their old list and write as many more fashion terms as they can. This should indicate to them where their knowledge was and where they are going.

Teaching Strategies to Reteach, Reinforce, Enrich, and Extend Text Concepts

The Reasons for Wearing Clothing

4. **ER** *Clothing as Protection*, reproducible master 1-1. Students are asked to write as many ways as they can think of in which clothing has been and is worn for protection from weather, environmental dangers, occupational hazards, and enemies. Then each category can be discussed as a class.

5. **RF** Discuss how clothing adornment and identification affect the mental attitudes and morals of people.

6. **RF** *The Significance of Uniforms*, reproducible master 1-2. Students are asked to list five activities for which uniforms are worn, describe each uniform, and explain the meaning, feeling, or special importance conveyed by each uniform. Follow with class discussion.

7. **RT** Assemble a file of colored pictures from magazines that show people dressed in various ways. Ask students to describe the probable psychological feelings of adornment or identification that are present in each case.

8. **ER** From a social studies book or a magazine such as *National Geographic*, have students view photos of cultural adornment.

9. **EX** Show the class photos of fashions from several past decades or centuries. Have the class discuss how adornment changes over time.

10. **EX** Have students debate the pros and cons of required school uniforms.

11. **RT** Have students discuss written and unwritten rules of appropriate attire for your school.

12. **RT** Discuss clothing in relation to modesty and then status.

13. **RT** *The Reasons for Wearing Clothing*, transparency master 1-3. Refer to the transparency as you summarize the universal reasons people wear clothes.

14. **RF** *Needs for Clothing*, Activity A, WB. Students are asked to write out the main needs for people to wear clothing, describe each need in their own words, and list articles of clothing that satisfy each particular need.

15. **EX** *Protective Clothing Innovations*, reproducible master 1-4. Use this for a class discussion about these and other innovations that are occurring with clothing.

Why People Select Certain Clothes

16. **RT** Ask students to discuss the meaning of values and attitudes, how attitudes are formed from values, and how clothing selection is affected by values and attitudes.

17. **ER** Have students discuss how various advertising of clothing plays to consumers' desires for economy, status, easy care, adventure, and comfort. If possible, show examples.

18. **RT** Ask students to explain different ways that conformity and individuality are shown with clothing.

19. **RT** Ask students to explain wants and needs in relation to clothing. Include a discussion of illustration 1-15 in the textbook.

20. **RF** *Fashion Facts*, Activity B, WB. Students are asked to answer questions related to fashion.

Ongoing Fashion Perspectives

21. **RT** Hold a class discussion about why fashion is both an art and a science.

22. **RT** Have students explain both private and public aspects of fashion.

23. **RF** *A Fashion Mirror*, Activity C, WB. Students are asked to explain fashion as "a mirror of our times" and show how specific current fashions indicate economic conditions, political issues, technology, newsworthy events, and popular entertainment.

24. **EX** Show students a video related to this chapter. Suggestions are *The Way We Dress: The Meaning of Fashion*. It is available from Nasco, Learning Seed, Insight Media, D.E. Visuals, and Meridian Education Corporation; *Why We Wear What We Wear* from Nasco and Teacher's Media Company; *How The World Dresses; Clothing and Global Culture* from D.E. Visuals, Learning Seed, VMS, Inc., and The Curriculum Center for Family and Consumer Sciences; and *Why Shirts Have Buttons; The Origins of Clothing* from D.E. Visuals, VMS, Inc., Learning Seed, and The Curriculum Center for Family and Consumer Sciences.

25. **ER** Display posters in the classroom related to this chapter. Suggestions are *2000 Years of Clothing* from Learning Seed and VMS, Inc.; *Fashion Show Through Time Posters* from Nasco and Teacher's Media Company. A PowerPoint Presentation, *Fashion Trends Through Time* is also available from Nasco and Teacher's Media Company.

26. **RF** *Express Your Thoughts*, Activity D, WB. Students are asked to think about and write their reaction to given statements.

27. **EX** *U.S. Economic and Social Influences on Fashion*, reproducible master 1-5. Pass copies of this to students and conduct a class discussion about each decade. Find the correlations between the events, behavior, and apparel over the years.

Fashion Terminology

28. **RF** Have students name specific garments until they can think of no more, then garment parts, and then accessories.

29. **RT** Explain to the students how a style, fashion, and design are different from one another. Show pictures from magazines or catalogs to illustrate your points.

30. Have a class discussion of John Fairchild's quote about certain people having [the condition of] style: "Style is an expression of individualism mixed with charisma. Fashion is something that comes after style."

31. **RF** Have students distinguish between *high fashion* and *mass fashion*.

32. **RT** Have students look up the word *homogenized* in the dictionary. Then have them relate that to an understanding of mass (volume) fashion.

33. **RF** Ask students to describe an example of a current fad, ford, and fashion look. Then discuss fads and fashion looks of past eras, showing pictures.

34. **RT** See how many fashion classics the students can name. Then, as a class, discuss others (such as loafer shoes, khaki pants, shirtwaist dresses, pleated plaid skirts, pullover sweaters, cardigan sweaters, navy blazers, corduroy pants, jumpers, button-down shirts, tuxedos, blue jeans, Chanel suits, polo shirts, trench coats, plain pumps, baseball caps, and beige pantyhose.). Show pictures of as many as possible.

35. **RF** *Fashion Term Matching*, Activity E, WB. Students are asked to match fashion terms with their definitions.

36. **RF** Show students a video about clothing terms as well as social aspects of fashion. *Fashion, Fads and Freedom* can be obtained from Learning Seed, VMS, Inc., and The Curriculum Center for Family and Consumer Sciences.

37. **ER** Make card games that increase fashion vocabulary available for the students. *The Clothes Game* and *Fashions from the Past* are both available from Nasco.

Additional Enrichment Activities

Research

38. Have students do research about personality studies that have shown what personality traits are indicated by the way people dress. Then have students share their information with the class.

39. Have students research and give an oral report to the class about the three components of attitudes: affective component, cognitive component, and behavioral component. Have them relate this information to consumer clothing decisions and the decisions of fashion businesses.

40. Have students research what clothing selections are most desirable and satisfactory for young children, middle/junior high school students, young adults, middle-aged people, and elderly people. Have students lead the class in a discussion about how clothing needs and values change as people's ages change.

Projects

41. Invite a fashion professional to speak to the class about why an understanding of the reasons various consumers make specific decisions about the apparel they buy and wear is essential for success in the fashion industry.

42. On tracing paper placed over a fashion drawing, have students sketch different designs of sleeves, collars, bodices, pants, skirts, and other garment parts. Have students include different lengths, shapes, and fullness of their garment parts. Then ask them to cut out their different garment parts to combine them in different ways into new designs. Also have them create new designs of the same style, such as a jumper, pantsuit, or shirtwaist dress using different collars or sleeves.

Answer Key

Text

Fashion Review, page 32

1. weather, environmental dangers, occupational hazards, and enemies (Student response. One example for each category:) Weather: coats, gloves, long underwear, wide-brimmed hats, windbreakers, water-repellent jackets. Environmental dangers: shoes, space suits, sterile gloves and face masks. Occupational hazards: hard hats, safety goggles, protective helmets, gloves, pads, special shoes and boots. Enemies: body shields and suits of armor, army helmets, camouflaged fabric, bulletproof vests, reflective vests/jackets.

2. Attractive decoration of the body provides a psychological feeling of well-being.

3. When people dress like others of a group, clothing fulfills the need to belong.

4. Besides achieving group identity, the clothes help the group members maintain a certain discipline of behavior.

5. the culture and social system

6. (Student response. Examples might include the following:) fur coats, expensive jewelry, designer labels, service stripes, school letter

7. They are the basis of a person's decisions, lifestyles, codes of ethics, and feelings or reactions.

8. Peer group pressure encourages people to conform and to gain a feeling of belonging. On the other hand, people also communicate their individuality by using self-expression in their clothing.

9. Personality traits affect the amount of decoration, comfort, economy, and other factors in peoples' clothing choices.

10. (Student response.)

11. As an art, fashion thrives on creative, innovative, forward-thinking ideas. As a science, fashion uses chemistry and technology to design, mass-produce, distribute, and sell fashion goods.

12. Personal fashion choices are a result of individual responses, yet can be constantly seen outwardly by others.
13. Styles are often brighter and more adventurous in good times, since people are willing to try new, different fashions.
14. They are produced in such large quantities and accepted by such a mass of people that they all seem to be alike.
15. (Student response.)
16. They are too unconventional and startling to be considered fashions.
17. (Student response.)
18. Good taste in fashion is often considered to be a well-designed outfit with fashion acceptance worn by someone on whom it looks appropriate.

Student Workbook

Needs for Clothing, Activity A

1. physical
2. psychological
3. social

(Descriptions and examples are student response.)

Fashion Facts, Activity B

1. Culture is a set of social norms or values; various cultures view beauty differently from others, which affects their thoughts about fashion.
2. Since uniforms are alike and specific to everyone in a certain group of people, they provide group identity, a sense of belonging, a position of authority, and/or decreased barriers among all those wearing them.
3. They indicate appropriate attire but do not specify exact items (style, color, etc.) that must be worn.
4. They specify a certain range of clothing options that results in group identity and similar behavior within the group.
5. Several human needs are fulfilled to different degrees at the same time.
6. (Student response.)
7. They can then produce and stock the items that will be preferred, and ultimately bought, by that group of consumers.
8. Ads try to create a stronger desire for particular products, playing to consumers' desires for economy, status, easy care, adventure, and comfort.
9. (Student response.)
10. (Student response.)
11. (Student response.)
12. (Student response.)
13. (Student response.)

A Fashion Mirror, Activity C

1. It reflects economic conditions, political issues, technology, current events, and popular entertainment, indicating the way we think and live at a given point in time.
2. (Student response.)
3. (Student response.)

Fashion Term Matching, Activity E

1.	G	9.	K
2.	D	10.	N
3.	O	11.	L
4.	J	12.	F
5.	A	13.	C
6.	M	14.	H
7.	E	15.	B
8.	I		

Teacher's Resources

Chapter 1 Test

1.	G	16.	T
2.	E	17.	F
3.	H	18.	T
4.	I	19.	F
5.	D	20.	T
6.	C	21.	C
7.	A	22.	D
8.	J	23.	A
9.	B	24.	C
10.	F	25.	D
11.	T	26.	A
12.	T	27.	A
13.	T	28.	D
14.	F	29.	B
15.	F	30.	B

31. because it reflects economic conditions, political issues, technology, current events, and popular entertainment, indicating the way we think and live at a given point in time
32. Fashions are the currently popular styles of objects or activities; the prevailing types of clothing bought and worn by large segments of the public. Fads are temporary, passing fashions that have great appeal to many people for a short period of time. Classic styles continue to be popular over an extended period of time, even though fashions change.
33. High fashion items are the very latest, unusual, (innovative) fashions of fine quality and high price, sold to a limited number of people. Mass fashion items are mass-produced in volume and widely sold at lower prices.

Clothing as Protection

Name_____ **Date** _____ **Period** _____

Write as many examples as you can think of that represent clothing as protection (past and present) for each of the following categories. Then have a class discussion of each category.

Protection from weather:	Protection from environmental dangers:
Protection from occupational hazards:	**Protection from enemies:**

The Significance of Uniforms

Name_____ **Date** _____ **Period** _____

List five jobs or activities for which uniforms are worn. Then describe how each uniform looks. Finally, explain what meaning, feeling, or special importance is conveyed by the uniform.

Job or Activity	Uniform Description	Meaning, Feeling, or Special Importance
1. _____	_____	_____
_____	_____	_____
_____	_____	_____
	_____	_____
	_____	_____
2. _____	_____	_____
_____	_____	_____
_____	_____	_____
	_____	_____
	_____	_____
3. _____	_____	_____
_____	_____	_____
_____	_____	_____
	_____	_____
	_____	_____
4. _____	_____	_____
_____	_____	_____
_____	_____	_____
	_____	_____
	_____	_____
5. _____	_____	_____
_____	_____	_____
_____	_____	_____
	_____	_____
	_____	_____

The Reasons for Wearing Clothing

Physical need:	**Protection**
Psychological needs:	**Adornment** **Identification**
Social needs:	**Modesty** **Status**

Protective Clothing Innovations

- Apparel has been created from aerospace technology that maintains the wearer's body temperature at a constant level. "Intelligent tissues" have capillaries that expand and contract with changes in the surrounding air temperature.

- For outdoor people, insect-repellent apparel defends wearers against mosquitoes, ticks and other insects that might carry diseases. It is also lightweight for hiking.

- With a button hidden in a sleeve, the wearer of a trendy battery-powered jacket can give an attacker a shock. A sharp stinging sensation forces the assailant to let go and become disoriented. The wearer is protected by a rubber lining and can escape.

- A carbon-incapsulated fiber used in uniforms can prevent chemical infusion. It is used in long underwear for those who work with dangerous chemicals or combined with a gas mask in a full suit for those threatened by chemical warfare.

- An impenetrable plasma layer coating can be applied to fully constructed garments to protect against chemical, nuclear, or biological weapons. This stops liquid from going through garments to the skin. It also has applications as a stain repellent finish for all types of clothing!

- A nuclear radiation blocking fabric, utilizing nanotechnology, fuses a lightweight, nontoxic, lead-free material between two outer layers for garment manufacturing. It was created to protect medical professionals from X-rays, and weighs only 15 percent of the old, leaded, anti-radiation apparel.

U.S. Economic and Social Influences on Fashion

Decade	Events	Behavior	Apparel

1920s	After World War I
	Increasing prosperity
	Voting rights for women
	Modern art, music,
	    literature Improvements
	    in machines
		The roadster car
		Daring looks and
		    behavior—women
		    smoking, short hair,
		    Charleston dance
		Factory production of
		    apparel replaced some
		    homemade
			Birth of sportswear
			Paris influence
			Chemise dresses, short
			    skirts
			Luxurious silks, satins,
			    crepes
			T-strap shoes, cloche hats
			Long strands of beads

1930s	Depression—
	    unemployment and
	    poverty
	Big bands and swing music
	Movies
		Frugality and conservatism
		Take the bus or streetcar
		Make do with what you
		    have
		Splurge only when able
			The housedress
			Hollywood influence of
			    stars and designers
			Soft looks, loose, light
			    fabrics
			Long hemlines, bias cuts
			Big hats, fur-collared coats

1940s	World War II—cut off from
	    French fashions
	Government restrictions
	Shortage of materials
	Radio and crooning
	    records—Crosby,
	    Sinatra
		Strong nationalism
		"Rosie the Riveter"—
		    women take men's jobs
		Common cause philosophy
		Glamour, pinup girls
		Shoulder length, pageboy
		    hairdos
			U.S. designers emerge
			Uniform-style suits
			Peplum jackets, padded
			    shoulders
			Pants for women
			Knee-length straight skirts
			Small hats perched in front
			Dior post-war "New Look"

1950s	Baby boom
	Prosperity; higher incomes
	    and living standards
	Korean Conflict
	Firms expand, go public,
	    diversify
	Imports start to rise
	Good transportation &
	    communications;
	    planes, TV
	Research and development
		Move to the suburbs
		Buy new homes,
		    appliances, furnishings
		Better quality of family life
		Station wagons
		More leisure time for sports
		    and recreation
		Rock and roll craze, sock
		    hops
		Conformity
			Volume clothing production
			Better fibers and finishes
			Proliferation of sportswear
			Classics; shirtwaist dresses
			At-home attire
			Sack dress; chemise
			Mink stoles
			Wash 'n' wear fabrics
			Men: Ivy League look, gray
			    flannel suit, skinny ties,
			    button-down shirts, car
			    coat

(Continued)

Decade	Events	Behavior	Apparel
1960s	Prosperity & big business Shopping centers & boutiques Kennedy/King assassinations Vietnam war & civil rights New technology for stretch fabrics & knitting methods London influence—Beatles, Twiggy, Mod, Carnaby	New sexual freedom Anti-establishment attitudes Generation gap Divorce, "free love," singles Drug experimentation The Volkswagen "Bug" Hippie era, flower children Experimentation in fashion	Resurgence of top designers Jackie Kennedy "costume" look—pearls, pill box hat Wild colors and patterns Ethnic and unisex clothes Fun furs; Nehru jackets Long straight hair; wigs Miniskirts; go-go boots
1970s	Women's liberation—equal rights More women working Stabilizing economy Energy crisis Watergate and political unrest Recessions mixed with consumerism Influential movies	Individualism New conservatism Urban renewal projects Equal Rights Amendment Minority organizations Compact/subcompact cars Self interest—take care of #1 Disco dancing, clubs Roller skating	Polyester double knits Women's pantsuits Men's leisure suits Designer jeans T-shirts, tank tops, boots Eclecticism Classic look—blazers, investment dressing Separates, not coordinates
1980s	Music videos and MTV Nuclear weapons buildup Two-income families Yuppie materialism (young urban professionals) New baby boom Explosion of imports Ecology interest Recession & unemployment Fitness craze	Home computers purchased Back to nature; health foods Nuclear freeze movement Day care centers Graffiti art Resurgence of patriotism Health education Convertibles and luxury foreign cars Recycling of paper & bottles	Stirrup pants; cropped tops Punk hairdos Androgynous dressing Classic tailored suits with bow at neckline Ripped jeans Animal-rights against furs Cotton pullover sweaters Warm-ups, aerobic exercise clothing Oversized silhouettes

(Continued)

Decade	Events	Behavior	Apparel
1990s	Microcomputer explosion More imports Women executives Corporate downsizings AIDS and cancer research Heavy credit purchases Internet and other computer uses Anti-government factions and bombings Questionable ethics of public officials	"Couch potatoes" stay home Sex and drug education Family vans and 4-wheel drive vehicles Entrepreneurship Eating out and convenience foods Easy access to material goods Vegetarianism Everyone too busy	Natural fibers that wrinkle "Safe styles" manufactured Black (colorless) clothes Short skirts Thrift store "chic," grunge look Tighter fit tries to return Casual office attire Polyester—microfibers and regenerated plastic bottles Return of 1970s fashion influences
2000s	Internet shopping Energy crisis Medical breakthroughs Historical movies World unrest/terrorism Natural disasters	Discount pricing Lack of modesty sometimes flaunted TV ads against teen smoking, sex, drugs, etc. Patriotism vs. pacifism	All hemlines acceptable Retro looks Clunky shoes Shirts, worn-out jeans and comfort Less consumerism

The Meaning of Clothing and Fashion

Name_____

Date_____ Period_____ Score_____

Chapter 1 Test

Matching: Match the following terms and identifying phrases.

_____ 1. Physical safeguards.

_____ 2. Things a person must have for existence or survival.

_____ 3. The prevailing opinion of what is attractive and appropriate for a given person and occasion.

_____ 4. Ideas, beliefs, and material items that are important to an individual.

_____ 5. The process of establishing or describing who someone is or what they do.

_____ 6. An article of wearing apparel, such as a dress or sweater.

_____ 7. An individual's feelings or reactions to people, things, or ideas.

_____ 8. Things that are desired for personal satisfaction.

_____ 9. Written or unwritten rules of appropriate attire.

_____ 10. The total characteristics that distinguish an individual, especially behavioral and emotional tendencies.

A. attitudes

B. dress codes

C. garment

D. identification

E. needs

F. personality

G. protection

H. taste

I. values

J. wants

True/False: Circle *T* if the statement is true or *F* if the statement is false.

T   F   11. In ancient times, clothing of simple design was made from items found in nature.

T   F   12. Occupational clothing includes special garments to protect workers from dangers encountered on the job.

T   F   13. Adornment can help attract the opposite sex and create envy in rivals.

T   F   14. Peoples' ideas about beauty and adornment remain constant throughout their lives.

T   F   15. Standards of modesty in the United States have remained constant through the last 100 years.

T   F   16. Wearing service stripes on a military sleeve or a school letter on an athletic jacket can raise the wearer's status.

T   F   17. Clothing can show who a person is or is not, but cannot indicate who that person would like to be.

(Continued)

Name_____

T   F   18. Advertising can influence people's values and attitudes.

T   F   19. Conformity is the quality that distinguishes one person from another or makes each person unique.

T   F   20. If standards of dress change quickly, the basic social structure of the society has probably changed.

Multiple Choice: Choose the best response. Write the letter in the space provided.

_____ 21. Clothing can provide protection _____.
  A. for adornment and identification
  B. through modesty and status
  C. against weather, environmental dangers, occupational hazards, and enemies
  D. All of the above.

_____ 22. A pair of blue jeans is an example of _____.
  A. a classic style
  B. occupation clothing that is now fashionable
  C. a garment
  D. All of the above.

_____ 23. Beauty is a quality that _____.
  A. gives pleasure to the senses and a good emotional reaction
  B. shows the underlying motivations for a person's actions
  C. contributes to a person's needs
  D. looks the best in avant-garde clothes

_____ 24. Culture is _____.
  A. how people dress like others from their country
  B. a standard of decency
  C. a nation's set of social norms or values
  D. changeable as fashion changes

_____ 25. Uniforms _____.
  A. are articles of clothing that are alike and specific to everyone in a certain group of people
  B. are symbols of group identity, providing a sense of belonging among the members
  C. can show a position of authority as well as decrease racial and religious barriers
  D. All of the above.

_____ 26. Fashion professionals who make or sell clothing items try to identify the values and attitudes of their customers so they can _____.
  A. produce and stock the items that will be preferred and bought by those consumers
  B. evaluate the balance of conformity and individuality in all consumers' clothing
  C. learn more about avant-garde designs in relation to good taste
  D. All of the above.

_____ 27. Fashion is both an art and a science because it _____.
  A. thrives on creative design ideas as well as technological advancement
  B. has both private and public viewpoints
  C. has both economic and political influences
  D. All of the above.

(Continued)

Name_____

_____ 28. Economic and political factors are shown in the way people dress because _____.
A. clothing usually gives a serious, conservative image in an era of hard times
B. clothing is usually fun, provocative, brighter, and more adventurous in good times
C. people tend to lose interest in their appearance in hard times and are more willing to try new, different fashions in good times
D. All of the above.

_____ 29. An apparel style _____.
A. includes the articles added to complete or enhance apparel outfits
B. is a particular design, shape, or type of garment that always has the same unique characteristics
C. is how attractive an outfit is
D. All of the above.

_____ 30. An apparel design is _____.
A. an homogenized craze
B. a unique version of a style that uses different fabrics, colors, trims, and combinations of ideas
C. an avant-garde style that has not yet become popular
D. a fashion look that becomes a ford or a best-selling runner

Essay Questions: Provide complete responses to the following questions or statements.

31. Why is fashion considered to be "a mirror of our times"?

32. Describe what fashions, fads, and classic styles are.

33. Describe the characteristics of high fashion and mass fashion items.

Fashion Movement

Objectives

After studying this chapter, students will be able to

- explain the role of fashion leaders and followers in fashion movement.
- state the theories of fashion movement.
- describe the stages and time spans of fashion cycles.
- analyze the main principles of fashion movement.
- compare factors that speed up or slow down fashion movement.
- relate the importance of fashion change.

Teaching Materials

Text, pages 33–47
  Fashion Terms
  Fashion Review
  Fashion in Action
Student Workbook
  A. *Fashion Myths and Truths*
  B. *Working with Fashion Movement*
  C. *Relating to Fashion Leaders and Followers*
  D. *Analyzing Today's Fashion Trends*
  E. *Some Terms to Ponder*
Teacher's Resources
  Trickle-Down Acceptance, transparency
    master 2-1
  How Fashions Trickle Down and Up,
    reproducible master 2-2
  *Adding to the Fashion Merchandise Acceptance
    Curve*, transparency master 2-3
  Fashion Cycle Lengths, transparency master 2-4
  Fashion Movement Discussion, reproducible
    master 2-5
  Chapter 2 Test

Introductory Activities

1. Ask students to describe their ideas of how fashion change takes place. During the discussion, reinforce ideas that are correct.
2. *Fashion Myths and Truths*, Activity A, WB. Students are asked to indicate if they think given statements are myth or truth. After students have worked on this independently, use it for discussion that introduces the chapter since the correct answers are explained on the back of the page.

Teaching Strategies to Reteach, Reinforce, Enrich, and Extend Text Concepts

Understanding Fashion Movement

3. **RT** Hold a class discussion about the perpetual, ongoing process of fashion movement. Include the benefits and reasons for fashion movement.
4. **RF** Ask students to explain the obsolescence factor and why most apparel is discarded before it is worn out.
5. **ER** *Working with Fashion Movement*, Activity B, WB. After reading about fashion movement and cycles in the text, students are asked to write out some answers and then work with examples on a merchandise acceptance curve.
6. **ER** Assemble a file of fashion leaders from the past to the present along with pictures of the fashions they introduced or influenced.
7. **ER** *Relating to Fashion Leaders and Followers*, Activity C, WB. Students are asked to respond to a statement and question about fashion leaders and followers, and then study and report on a fashion leader of the past.

8. **ER** Have students find a current newspaper or magazine article that spotlights a fashion leader who they think is introducing (or reinforcing the rise of) a new fashion trend. Have students write their reactions to or comments about the fashion leader and the possible upcoming trend. Then have them cut out or photocopy the article and attach it to their paper.

9. **RF** Have students discuss why most consumers are fashion followers or fashion laggers. Relate the discussion to social risk, fashion interest, and financial means.

Theories of Fashion Movement

10. **RT** *Trickle-Down Acceptance*, transparency master 2-1. Use this transparency as an overhead or handout for class discussion about the trickle-down theory. It shows that by the time fashion followers and laggers have fully accepted most fashion trends, fashion leaders have moved on to new trends.

11. **RF** *How Fashions Trickle Down and Up*, reproducible master 2-2. Use this as a handout to show and discuss the trickle-down and trickle-up theories. This especially relates each fashion level to the main socioeconomic groups as well as categories of retail stores where those consumers shop.

12. **RF** *Analyzing Today's Fashion Trends*, Activity D, WB. Students are asked to analyze new fashion trends and relate them to the trickle theories.

The Fashion Cycle

13. **RF** Going around the class, have each student describe a currently popular apparel item and explain where it is in the fashion cycling process.

14. **RT** Explain to students why the consumer use cycle has a different shape from that of the consumer buying cycle.

15. **RT** Hold a class discussion about why an understanding of the fashion cycle is important in fashion merchandising.

16. **ER** *Adding to the Fashion Merchandise Acceptance Curve*, transparency master 2-3. Use this as an overhead to show and discuss the consumers who accept fashions at the various places on the fashion cycle and the types of retail stores that stock items at those stages. This can also be reproduced and distributed to the students, if appropriate.

17. **RF** Divide the class into five groups of students. Have each group take on the identity of a different stage of the fashion cycle. In order of the cycle, the groups are to explain as many aspects as possible about their stage to the other members of the class. (For fun, the first and last stages can be sitting on the floor or on their knees, the rise and decline groups can give their reports bent over, and the peak stage can stand on their tiptoes to represent the degree of acceptance.) Make sure that promotional activities are also discussed for each stage.

18. **ER** From a book of historic costume, show pictures of fashions from 20, 50, 100, and 150 years ago. See if the styles of those times look funny, odd, charming, and gorgeous, respectively, as suggested by the chart 2-9 of the text.

19. **ER** Show the class a video about historic fashions. *History of Apparel Design: 1930 to the 21st Century* is available from Nasco, VMS, Inc., Meridian Education Corporation, D.E. Visuals, and The Curriculum Center for Family and Consumer Sciences. *Fashion Show Through History* is available from Nasco, VMS, Inc., and Meridian Education Corporation; *Fashion Frenzy, 100 Years of Clothing History* from Nasco, VMS, Inc., Teacher's Media Company, and Meridian Education Corporation; and *The History of Clothing* from Teacher's Media Company.

20. **RT** *Fashion Cycle Lengths*, transparency master 2-4. Use this as an overhead to discuss varying lengths of the main categories of fashion cycles.

21. **RF** Again using transparency master 2-1, *Trickle Down Acceptance*, have students identify long-run fashions (trends A and D) and short-run fashions (trends B and E).

22. **EX** *Some Terms to Ponder*, Activity E, WB. Students are asked to study definitions for new terms. Then they should paraphrase each definition in their own words and tell about any fashion looks that fit the term.

Principles of Fashion Movement

23. **RF** Have five students hold separate discussions, each about one of the principles of fashion movement. Class members should also try to think of specific fashions or trends (such as skirt hem lengths, shoulder pads, or width of neckties) that have illustrated each principle in the past.

24. **EX** *Fashion Movement Discussion*, reproducible master 2-5. Use this for a class discussion about fashion movement.

Factors That Speed or Slow Fashion Movement

25. **RT** Have class members explain each of the factors that accelerate and decelerate fashion movement and give examples of each.

The Importance of Fashion Change

26. **RT** Conduct a class discussion about why fashion is one of the greatest economic forces in present-day life.
27. **ER** Show the class a video about how the fashion industry creates a psychological need for new clothing (as well as autos). *What Consumers Consume* is available from D.E. Visuals.
28. **ER** Have students look up the word *dynamic* in the dictionary or on the Internet ("marked by continuous productive activity, change, or energy"). Then discuss why fashion is a dynamic industry. Also discuss why being a part of the fashion industry can be very exciting.

Additional Enrichment Activities

Research

29. Have students do research about the popularity of a particular fashion trend of the past. Then have them document as close as possible the times of the introduction, peak, and obsolescence of the fashion. They should draw a merchandise acceptance cycle for the fashion and share their information with the class.
30. Have students research and give an oral report to the class about a major world event that distinctly influenced fashions of the times.

Project

31. Have students talk to their grandparents or other older relatives, neighbors, and friends about how and why their personal fashions changed over the decades. If old photos can be obtained or photocopied, students should mount their findings with explanatory captions on a section of a bulletin board.

Answer Key

Text

Fashion Review, page 47

1. because new designs are constantly being created and consumers steadily replace their old clothes with new ones
2. Everyone, from the original designer to the final consumer, encourages fashion movement.
3. The old items look outdated because new fashion ideas have become popular.
4. Many fashion trends can coexist at the same time.
5. members of royalty
6. general insecurity, uncertain about their tastes, lack of interest in fashion, want to imitate those they envy, out of habit or custom, and/or don't have the time or money to be fashion leaders
7. the trickle-down theory, the trickle-up theory, the trickle-across theory
8. The new style is introduced. It increases in popularity. It is worn by many people. It decreases in popularity. Finally, it is discarded for a newer style.
9. the degree to which it is gaining or losing acceptance
10. A classic would be a long-run fashion. A fad would be a short-run fashion.
11. in about the span of a generation.
12. radical social/political change, a natural disaster, unexpected weather change
13. They "vote" by purchasing or not purchasing the fashions.
14. It helps to generate more sales of already accepted fashions.
15. People do not like drastic changes away from accepted, comfortable ideas.
16. (List four:) modern communications and mass media; good economic conditions; increased competition; technological advances; social and physical mobility; more leisure time available; higher levels of education; changing roles of women; seasonal changes
17. (List four:) bad economic conditions, cultural customs, religion, laws or other government regulations, disruptive world events
18. It reaches more people, is more sophisticated, utilizes new technology, and is more businesslike.

Student Workbook

Working with Fashion Movement, Activity B

1. Because people desire new fashions, the fashion industry creates new fashion products, and advertising and promotion encourage consumers to want new items.
2. They have the confidence and credibility to wear new fashions before they are generally accepted, and are noticed, which influences the dress of others.
3. They are affected by the obsolescence factor, which causes them to become outdated and unfashionable as time passes.
4. (See curves in 2-10 of the text.)

Teacher's Resources

Chapter 2 Test

1. F	16. T
2. C	17. F
3. J	18. T
4. A	19. F
5. H	20. T
6. D	21. D
7. I	22. C
8. G	23. C
9. E	24. A
10. B	25. B
11. T	26. A
12. F	27. C
13. T	28. A
14. F	29. D
15. F	30. D

31. (The correct answer is shown in the text illustration 2-6.)
32. (The correct answer is shown in the text illustration 2-10.)
33. (List three:) Consumer acceptance or rejection establishes fashions. Price does not determine fashion acceptance. Sales promotion does not determine fashion. Fashion movement is evolutionary, not revolutionary. Fashion extremes cause reversals to a new direction.
34. (List three:) bad economic conditions, cultural customs, religion, laws or other government regulations, disruptive world events

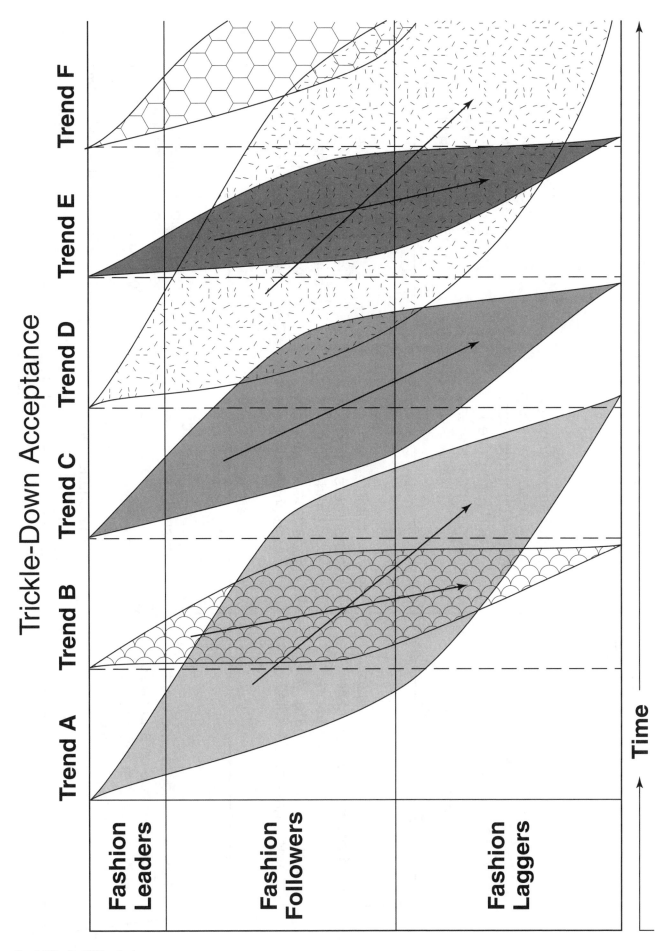

Trickle-Down Acceptance

Trend A Trend B Trend C Trend D Trend E Trend F

Fashion Leaders

Fashion Followers

Fashion Laggers

Time

How Fashions Trickle Down and Up

DOWN

UP

Wealthy people with economic freedom who are fashion leaders desiring upscale copies of the lower-class fashion look.

Fashion followers and laggers of unusual dress patterns who wear copies of looks from both lower- and upper-class consumers.

People (such as youth), because of circumstances, are forced to experiment with their apparel and become fashion innovators of unusual "looks."

Upper socioeconomic consumers who shop at designer boutiques and high-priced department stores.

Middle-level consumers who shop at mid-priced department, specialty, and chain stores.

Lower-income consumers who shop at low-end chains, discounters, and inexpensive mass merchandisers.

Fashion innovators and leaders who want distinctive, high fashion items with individual character.

Fashion followers who want good copies, updated styles, and classic looks that are current and appropriate, yet functional and durable.

Fashion laggers who want inexpensive copies and basic, suitable, and durable mass (volume) fashion.

Adding to the Fashion Merchandise Acceptance Curve

Note the consumers who accept fashions at the various places on the fashion cycle and the types of retail stores that stock items at those stages:

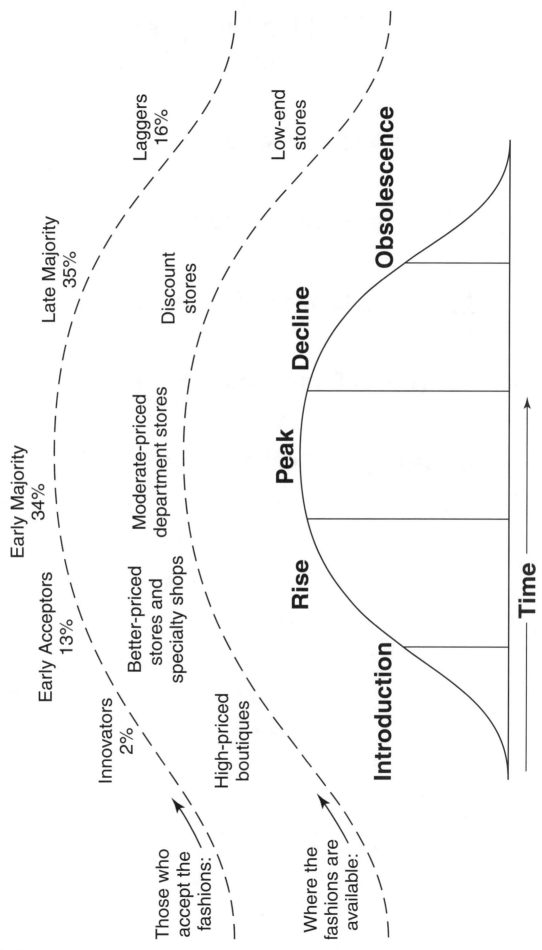

Fashion Cycle Lengths

Flop cycle: **No acceptance**

Fad cycle: **Short acceptance**

Normal cycle: **Medium acceptance**

Ford cycle: **Strong acceptance**

Classic cycle: **Continuing acceptance**

Fashion Movement Discussion

- For any particular style, there is a "latent period" between its previous fashion cycle and its next fashion cycle. Most styles are almost nonexistent during their latent periods.

- Neither fashions nor the fashion industry would exist without change. Change is the most important factor.

- Fashions occur by both imitation and differentiation, which are opposite each other, but both very relevant.

- Mass market trickle-across takes place faster these days because of instant global communication, fast production methods, and retail availability in many forms (stores, catalogs, Internet, etc.).

- Some wealthy people become "fashion victims." Since money does not buy taste or style, they may blindly follow fashion leaders who do not think, act, or look like them. That makes those who were "taken in" look even more like victims.

- Why are fashion leaders also sometimes called "fashion motivators"?

Fashion Movement

Name_____

Date_____ **Period**_____ **Score**_____

Chapter 2 Test

Matching: Match the following terms and identifying phrases.

_____ 1. The direction in which fashion is moving.

_____ 2. Individuals who are the last to adopt accepted styles.

_____ 3. Styles that are popular for a brief period of time, usually for only one selling season.

_____ 4. The ongoing rise, peak, and fall in popularity of specific styles or shapes.

_____ 5. The rejection of recently used items in favor of newer ones, even though the old items retain their utility value.

_____ 6. The few "fashion forward," trendsetting individuals with enough confidence and credibility to start new fashions.

_____ 7. Market state of having been supplied with the most it will absorb of a fashion.

_____ 8. A style that takes a long time to complete the fashion cycle.

_____ 9. Ongoing change in what is considered to be fashionable.

_____ 10. Individuals who wear a fashion look only when it is firmly accepted.

A. fashion cycle

B. fashion followers

C. fashion laggers

D. fashion leaders

E. fashion movement

F. fashion trend

G. long-run fashion

H. obsolescence factor

I. saturation

J. short-run fashions

True/False: Circle *T* if the statement is true or *F* if the statement is false.

T   F   11. Consumer desire for new fashions causes garment silhouettes and details to constantly change.

T   F   12. Most apparel items wear out before they go out of fashion.

T   F   13. Fashion movement involves many trends that coexist at any given time.

T   F   14. Fashion leaders wear styles after the fashions have become well-established.

T   F   15. The trickle-across theory is the world's oldest and most accepted theory of fashion movement.

T   F   16. The trickle-across theory claims that fashion moves horizontally through groups at similar social levels.

T   F   17. The increase in popularity of a fashion is almost always faster than its drop in popularity.

(Continued)

Name_____

T   F   18. As fashions come and go, they seem to be extreme and daring when first introduced, smart and stylish when they are popular, and dowdy and out-of-date after their peak.

T   F   19. Fashion cycles do not overlap.

T   F   20. Consumers "vote for" fashions by purchasing them and "vote against" them by not purchasing them.

Multiple Choice: Choose the best response. Write the letter in the space provided.

_____ 21. Fashion leaders are people who _____.
   A. like to be noticed and are especially responsive to change
   B. are not afraid to wear something before everyone else does
   C. usually have jobs, social status, or fame that puts them in the public view
   D. All of the above.

_____ 22. The majority of people follow rather than lead in fashion because _____.
   A. their extreme interest in fashion causes them to conform to standards set by others
   B. they have extra time and money to purchase all kinds of clothes, especially accepted fashions
   C. they are insecure and uncertain about their own tastes
   D. All of the above.

_____ 23. The trickle theory that suggests fashion trends start at the top of a "social ladder" and gradually progress downward through lower levels is the _____ theory.
   A. trickle-up
   B. trickle-across
   C. trickle-down
   D. trickle-in-and-out

_____ 24. Upscale fashion designs that imitated "grunge" fashions were an example of _____.
   A. the trickle-up theory
   B. long-run fashions
   C. fashion saturation
   D. the trickle-down theory

_____ 25. The bell-shape of the fashion cycle is known as the _____.
   A. trickle-theory curve
   B. merchandise acceptance curve
   C. path of least resistance
   D. culmination curve

_____ 26. At the beginning stage of the fashion cycle, new "looks" _____.
   A. seem unusual and are only accepted by a small number of fashion leaders
   B. are produced in large quantities in anticipation of an immediate rush of sales
   C. are purchased in large numbers by retail fashion buyers
   D. All of the above.

_____ 27. During the second stage of the fashion cycle, _____.
   A. consumers start to lose interest in the trends
   B. the price of most of the fashions goes up because of the increased demand
   C. retail fashion buyers order the items in quantity so they have the maximum amount in stock
   D. promotion mainly stresses color and price

(Continued)

Name_____

_____ 28. Specific fashion cycles _____.
   A. have been less distinct recently than in past centuries
   B. almost always have the same shaped acceptance curve
   C. are separate and do not overlap
   D. All of the above.

_____ 29. Breaks in fashion cycles occur periodically, which can be caused by _____.
   A. radical social/political change
   B. a natural disaster
   C. an unexpected change in a weather pattern
   D. All of the above.

_____ 30. Factors that accelerate (speed up) fashion movement include _____.
   A. higher levels of education, changing roles of women, more leisure time, and seasonal change
   B. modern communications and mass media plus technological advances
   C. good economic conditions, increased competition, and social and physical mobility
   D. All of the above.

Essay Questions: Provide complete responses to the following questions or statements.

31. Draw the fashion merchandise acceptance curve and label it with the five stages of the fashion cycle in the proper places.

32. Draw overlapping fashion cycles for a flop, fad, fashion, and classic and label each.

33. List, in any order, three of the five basic principles of fashion movement.

34. List three factors that tend to slow down (decelerate) fashion movement.

CHAPTER 3

Basic Economic Concepts

Objectives

After studying this chapter, students will be able to

- ⊖ identify economic products as either goods or services.
- ⊖ describe the role of profit, competition, and supply and demand in the free-market system.
- ⊖ distinguish between the main competitive market structures.
- ⊖ list the basic forms of business organizations.
- ⊖ describe the concept of business cycles.
- ⊖ explain the concepts of marketing and merchandising.

Teaching Materials

Text, pages 48–63
  Fashion Terms
  Fashion Review
  Fashion in Action
Student Workbook
  A. *Understanding Free-Market Concepts*
  B. *Economic Terms Crossword*
  C. *Questionable Thoughts*
  D. *Gaining Some Business Economic Background*
  E. *Economic Questions*
Teacher's Resources
  Economics Opinion Poll, reproducible master 3-1
  Goods vs. Services, transparency master 3-2
  Market Structure Comparison, transparency 3-3
  The Business Cycle, transparency master 3-4
  Relating to Markets and Marketing, reproducible master 3-5
  A Free-Market Business, reproducible master 3-6
  Chapter 3 Test

Introductory Activities

1. Discover students' feelings and knowledge about basic economic concepts. Have them write down these single and combined terms, followed by the first word they think of when they hear them, such as goods and services, recession, profit, monopoly, competition, economies of scale, supply and demand, business cycle, resources, and target market. Have a short general discussion about the concepts in relation to our free-market economic system. After finishing the chapter, have the students correct the misconceptions that were in their original lists and correctly describe each concept when called on.

2. *Economics Opinion Poll*, reproducible master 3-1. Have students fill out this survey about economic issues. It may be used to stimulate their thinking and also as a basis for discussion.

Teaching Strategies to Reteach, Reinforce, Enrich, and Extend Text Concepts

The Free-Market System

3. **ER** *Goods vs. Services*, transparency master 3-2. Use this transparency as an overhead or reproduce it for each student. Use it for class discussion to clarify the differences between goods and services. Discuss how all goods and services are products.

4. **ER** Ask students to find and compare at least three definitions of the United States economic system from economics texts, dictionaries, and/or encyclopedias. Then ask them to list and define key terms found in the definitions. Discuss with the class similarities and differences in the definitions.

5. **RT** Have students discuss how individuals make key economic decisions in a free-market economic system. Discuss how the desire for profit motivates the production of goods and services. Also, clarify the relationship between profit and competition.

6. **RF** Show a video, such as *Simple Supply and Demand* from Teacher's Media Company. Then hold a class discussion about how consumers create a demand for products and how businesses create the supply to meet that demand. Discuss how prices are affected by supply and demand. Also have students explain how and why a free-market system uses a minimum amount of resources to achieve a maximum standard of living for consumers.

7. **ER** Have students bring to class articles from newspapers or magazines (about apparel if possible) that illustrate the economic system in operation. Discuss the articles as a class in relation to how competition helps to control or lower prices, improve services and products, and increase the choices of goods and services. Then display the articles on a bulletin board.

Competitive Market Structures

8. **RT** *Market Structure Comparison*, transparency master 3-3. Use this as an overhead or reproduce it to distribute to all students. Have three students stand in a line across the front of the classroom. Ask the first one to thoroughly explain pure competition, the next one to explain oligopolies, and the last one to explain monopolies.

9. **RF** Hold a class discussion in which certain types of fashion items are named and then placed along the continuum shown in 3-9 of the text, between the extremes of pure competition and monopoly.

Basic Forms of Business Organizations

10. **RT** Go through a PowerPoint CD about basic forms of business organizations. An example is *Business Characteristics* from D.E. Visuals. Then, as a class, discuss the advantages and disadvantages of sole proprietorships, partnerships, and corporations using 3-11 of the text.

11. **EX** Have students assess why some corporations, such as Levi-Strauss, Blue Bell, and Palm Beach, have bought back their corporate stock to become private, allowing them to be freer to make long-term decisions.

12. **ER** Divide the class into five groups. Have them separately study and report on public corporations, private corporations, S corporations, and nonprofit corporations. Have the fifth group research and report on C corporations and limited liability companies (LLCs and LLPs).

13. **EX** Hold a class discussion about fashion companies doing IPOs (initial public offerings)—"going public"—by selling stock to investors. Talk about pros and cons discussed in the text as well as how this creates intense pressure to grow, stringent disclosure requirements, management's fear of losing control, and tight scrutiny of inventory and merchandising strategies by stockholders.

Business Cycles

14. **RF** Have the class discuss what happens to national income, employment, and production during economic expansions and recessions. Explain how different business cycles have different rates of growth and decline.

15. **RT** *The Business Cycle*, transparency master 3-4. Use this as an overhead or reproduce it to distribute to all students. Hold a class discussion about the "ups and downs" of the business cycle and where the U.S. economy is currently placed on it.

16. **RF** Referring to 3-12 in the text, have students explain why fashion purchases increase faster than the general economy in an expansionary period and drop off faster in a downswing of the economy.

17. **ER** *Understanding Free-Market Concepts*, Activity A, WB. Students are asked to answer questions and solve problems related to free-market concepts.

18. **RF** Show students a video about the basics of economics, such as *An Introduction to Economics*, or have them work with simulations, such as *Economics Made Easy*. Many resources are available from video services.

The Concept of Marketing

19. **RF** Have students view a video that discusses target markets as well as the marketing mix of product, price, place, and promotion. *Introduction to Marketing*, *That's Marketing! Understanding Consumer Behavior,* and other marketing videos are available from D.E. Visuals, Cambridge Educational, Learning Seed, Nasco, and Insight Media.

20. **RF** While referring to 3-16 of the text, have students name a specific apparel item or business and tell where they think it would fall on the marketing triangle. Discuss how the diagonal side of the triangle is comprised of approximate equilibrium points of supply matching demand.

21. **EX** *Relating to Markets and Marketing*, reproducible master 3-5. Use this master as a basis of discussion about markets and marketing. With students participating in order around the room, have each one read a bulleted item and comment about the wisdom of the phrase they have just read.

The Concept of Merchandising

22. **RF** Hold a class discussion about the meaning of the concept of merchandising, especially related to retailing. Explain how marketing is a wide category with a longer time span while merchandising is a specific category with more immediate timing.
23. **RF** Have students explain how marketing and merchandising complement each other (how they work together).
24. **RF** Have students discuss the merchandise blends of different specific stores that sell apparel items.
25. **RF** *Economic Terms Crossword*, Activity B, WB. Students are asked to complete a crossword puzzle that uses words from the entire chapter.
26. **RF** *Questionable Thoughts*, Activity C, WB. Students are asked to write multiple choice questions by section for the entire chapter. With the correct answers recorded on another piece of paper, the students should exchange workbook pages with a classmate to answer each other's questions.
27. **RF** *GainingSomeBusinessEconomicBackground*, Activity D, WB. Students are asked to answer questions and describe the target market for two advertisements they are to find.
28. **RF** *Economic Questions*, Activity E, WB. Students are asked to answer questions and solve problems that tie together this and earlier sections of the chapter.

Additional Enrichment Activities

Research

29. *A Free-Market Business*, reproducible master 3-6. Have students do research about a business and fill out the information asked for on the questionnaire. This can be done in groups of students or individually.
30. Have students research the U.S. business cycles of the last twenty years. Then they should decide where we are right now in a cycle, according to the leading economic indicators talked about in the news. They should share this information with the rest of the class, relating today's retail sales to the business cycle.

31. Have students research the structure and workings of either a communist or socialist economy. They should write a paper or give an oral report that contrasts the economy researched with the free-market system of the U.S.
32. Have students research how many billions of dollars and how many millions of employees are involved with the fashion business. Students might seek specific facts from library and Internet sources or from industry and government groups listed in the Resource List at the beginning of this guide (such as the American Apparel and Footwear Association, American Fiber Manufacturers Association, Department of Commerce, and National Retail Federation).

Projects

33. Have students make an appointment and interview a business person who plays a major role in a sole proprietorship, partnership, or corporation. Students should prepare well-thought-out questions based on this chapter before meeting with the person. After organizing the resulting information, students should make an informative oral report to the class. They should also send a thank-you note to the person they interviewed.

Answer Key

Text

Fashion Review, page 63

1. (Student response.) goods = fabrics, garments, accessory items; services = alterations, retail selling, laundering/dry cleaning, wardrobe consulting
2. People freely choose how to spend their money. Their choices determine which products are offered in the market and the prices of these products.
3. $2 profit on each shirt ($10 received minus $8 cost).
4. $3 profit on each shirt ($10 paid to manufacturer + $5 overhead = $15 cost per shirt to the retailer; $18 selling price – $15 cost = $3 profit).
5. The more competitors there are in an industry, the lower the prices will be.
6. Competition encourages higher quality goods and better service from businesses.
7. If supply is short, people will pay a higher price than if supply is great; if demand is high, people will pay a higher price than if demand is low.
8. the way people live, based on the kinds and quality of goods and services they can afford

9. No company in an industry is large or powerful enough to influence or control prices that would distort the free-market system.
10. A monopoly controls the products and prices; there is no competition.
11. They are easy and inexpensive to form for people who want to have their own business.
12. (Student response.) Corporations are usually bigger companies, have unlimited life spans, offer limited liability for the owners, and can raise money by selling stock.
13. (Student response.)
14. Public corporations offer their stock to the general public, while the stock of private corporations is not available to the general public.
15. S corporations are small, have no more than 35 shareholders, and are taxed like sole proprietorships or partnerships; nonprofit corporations exist to provide a social service rather than to make a profit.
16. Fashion products are affected more strongly than other products because they are less necessary.
17. A marketing-oriented approach plans all operations around satisfying customer wants and needs; a product-oriented approach focuses on making and trying to sell merchandise that is easy and economical to produce without checking the preferences of consumers.
18. Product—the right goods or services that are in demand. Price—the level that maximizes total profits. Place—how and where products are offered to customers. Promotion—spreading information to the marketplace.
19. planning, buying, and selling
20. Merchandising is a major segment of marketing; it matches the company's products to the market requirements that have been determined by marketing efforts.

Student Workbook

Understanding Free-Market Concepts, Activity A

1. They can sell their products to the others and buy what the others have.
2. Benefits are things that are useful or promote well-being. (Student response.)
3. (Student response.)
4. a. $100/dozen selling price − $60/dozen cost = $40 profit per dozen.
   b. $40/dozen profit × 3,000 dozens sold = $120,000 total profit.
5. $300,000 income (3,000 dozen sold at $100/dozen) − $300,000 costs (5,000 dozen made at $60/dozen) = $000 profit
6. It directly affects their profits.

7. a. raising the price because there is less supply
   b. lowering the price because there is more supply
   c. lowering the price because there is less demand
8. a. $30 selling price − $20 cost = $10 profit per pair.
   b. $10 profit × 75 pairs of jeans = $750 monthly profit.
9. a. $40 selling price − $28 cost = $12 profit; $12 profit × 180 pairs of boots = $2,160 total profit.
   b. $32 selling price − $28 cost = $4 profit × 100 pairs = $400 profit on the 100 pairs sold at $32. $25 selling price − $28 cost = $3 loss × 80 pairs = $240 loss from the 80 pairs sold at $25; $400 − 240 = $160 total profit.
10. a. Supply is lower and demand is higher.
    b. $55 selling price − $30 cost = $25 profit per pair × 150 pairs sold = $3,750 total profit.
    c. $25 profit per pair × 50 pairs = $1,250 unrealized profit.
11. It uses resources efficiently, supplies goods that are in demand, and raises the standard of living for consumers.
12. It offers the highest quality products for the lowest prices.

Economic Terms Crossword, Activity B

Gaining Some Business Economic Background, Activity D

1. legal responsibility for debts and obligations
2. a person who has controlling authority or is in a leading position; the person primarily or ultimately liable for legal obligations
3. a. unlimited personal liability for business debts
   b. unlimited liability with other partners for all business debts
   c. limited liability—can only lose the amount of the investment
4. fluctuations in the level of economic activity over periods of several years
5. an economic decrease in national income, employment, and production
6. small apparel items, such as inexpensive accessories that will give a new look to their old garments
7. an economic growth in national income, employment, and production
8. more costly apparel items such as dresses, coats, and suits
9. It is reported monthly; it predicts economic activity (ups and downs in the business cycle) 3 to 9 months in advance.
10. It measures the total value of goods and services produced in an economy over a certain period of time, usually one year. Its growth rate over time measures the economic health of a country and shows patterns of expansion and recession.
11. the block of consumers that a company wants as customers and toward whom it directs its marketing efforts
12. (Student response.)

Economic Questions, Activity E

1. a. $10 fixed costs + $50 unit costs = $60 total production costs per dozen dresses.
   b. $500,000 fixed costs ÷ 25,000 dozen dresses = $20 fixed costs per dozen; $20 fixed costs + $50 unit costs = $70 total cost per dozen dresses.
2. (Student response.)
3. a. $150,000 income − $30,000 fixed costs − $110,000 total unit costs = $10,000 profit.
   b. $300,000 income − $30,000 fixed costs − $220,000 total unit costs = $50,000 profit.
   c. Fixed costs are spread across twice as many sales.
4. Economies of scale emphasize producing more products economically rather than only producing what the market desires, as for the marketing-oriented approach.

5. To be successful, firms must have products that are desirable to consumers; having a lot of products doesn't do any good if consumers don't want them.
6. the making and selling of apparel and accessories that are desirable to customers
7. the right products being at the right place at the right time in the right quantity at the right price with the right appeal
8. Lower-priced products almost always sell in higher quantities (have higher sales volume), while products with high prices have smaller sales volumes.

Teacher's Resources

Chapter 3 Test

1.	C	16.	F
2.	E	17.	T
3.	I	18.	F
4.	D	19.	F
5.	G	20.	T
6.	A	21.	B
7.	J	22.	B
8.	H	23.	D
9.	B	24.	A
10.	F	25.	D
11.	T	26.	B
12.	F	27.	B
13.	T	28.	D
14.	F	29.	A
15.	F	30.	C

31. Pure competition is a market structure in which no company in an industry is extremely large or powerful enough to influence or control prices. Monopoly is a market structure in which there are no direct competitors in an industry; one company controls it.
32. (See 3-11 in the text under "Corporation.")
33. product: bringing the goods and/or services that are in demand into existence and to the market; price: pricing the products at the level that maximizes overall profits; place: how and where products are offered to customers; the distribution of selling and delivery into the hands of customers; promotion: nonpersonal activity to a large audience that furthers the sale of goods or services

Economics Opinion Poll

Name_____ **Date** _____ **Period** _____

To conduct this survey of opinions and attitudes about economic issues, read and think about the following statements. Place a check in the column that best describes your opinion. You will not be graded on your answers. Then, at the bottom of the page, rewrite the statements with which you disagree, stating what you think is true.

Agree	Disagree	Unsure	
_____	_____	_____	1. Consumers have no real choice in today's marketplace.
_____	_____	_____	2. The more choices there are in the marketplace, the harder it is for consumers to find what they want.
_____	_____	_____	3. Consumers have a major voice in a free-market economy.
_____	_____	_____	4. Consumer behavior makes a major impact on the overall economy.
_____	_____	_____	5. Advertising is an obstacle to consumers looking for value in the marketplace.
_____	_____	_____	6. A business with high profits is considered to be more successful than a business with low profits.
_____	_____	_____	7. The fashion industry includes all the businesses connected with the designing, manufacturing, promotion, selling, and distribution of textile and apparel products.
_____	_____	_____	8. The influence of fashion merchandising is a major indicator of the health of the United States economy, shown through retail sales figures.
_____	_____	_____	9. The same marketing approaches are required for goods as for services.
_____	_____	_____	10. The relationship between supply and demand affects the types and quantities of products offered in the marketplace.
_____	_____	_____	11. An economy is not an inanimate machine, but acts like a living organism.

_____

_____

_____

_____

_____

_____

_____

_____

Good vs. Services

Goods	Services
• Are tangible objects that can be recognized with the senses and physically examined.	• Usually intangible, involving actions rather than objects (consumers can't try it before purchasing).
• Buyers receive value through ownership.	• Buyers obtain value from experiences or events.
• Can be transported from manufacturer to seller and can pass through the hands of intermediaries.	• Are perishable (once performed, they are gone).
• Buyers can evaluate the quality of the items independently from the quality of the intermediaries.	• Provider must match supply to demand, since unused services cannot be saved until later.
• Can be standardized and mass-produced.	• In most cases, the buyers' satisfaction occurs over relatively brief periods, during which the services are performed.
• Buyers can depend on quality to be consistent with each repeat purchase.	• Most services cannot be transported or transferred through intermediaries.
	• Providers may have to interact directly with the buyers.
	• Cannot be standardized or mass-produced.
	• Quality can vary over time.

Market Structure Comparison

Considerations	Types of Market Structures			
	Pure Competition	Oligopoly		Monopoly
Uniqueness of each company's product	None	Hardly any		Unique
Number of competitors	Many	Few		None
Size of competitors to size of market	Small	Large		None
Control of price by company	None		Some (with care)	Complete

The Business Cycle

Expansion

Trough

Contraction

Peak

Expansion

Time

Economic Activity

Relating to Markets and Marketing

- A market is a group of sellers and a buying population with corresponding selling/buying behavior.

- A market is a group of sellers in search of buyers with money to spend and the willingness and the power to spend it.

- Marketing is a social and managerial process by which individuals and groups obtain what they need and want through creating and exchanging products and value with others.

- Marketing focuses on the needs of buyers rather than on selling whatever products the company wants to convert to cash.

- Marketing is the sophisticated strategy of assessing and producing what the consumer wants.

- Marketing involves the entire business, its organization and allocation of funds, and its strengths and weaknesses relative to its competition.

- Marketing is the umbrella under which all business efforts take place.

- Marketing determines the needs and wants of target markets, then blends together design, communications, pricing, and delivery of appropriate and competitively viable products and services.

- Marketing is the analysis, planning, implementation, and control of programs that create, build, and maintain beneficial exchanges with target buyers to achieve organizational objectives.

- Marketing requires knowledge of customer-desired goods, including raw materials, suppliers, resourcing, and manufacturing.

- Marketing is the first step in the conceptual design and styling of new products.

- Marketing is fully integrated with product development and manufacturing.

- Marketing controls the promotion and distribution of products by first analyzing the preferences and demands of consumers.

- Marketing involves follow-up studies of consumer reactions to marketing strategies in order to make proper adjustments before repeating the cycle.

- Marketing is dynamic—it is constantly adapting to change.

- Marketing is concerned with insights and research into consumer behavior to answer questions such as: Who are the customers? What do the customers want? Where do the customers live? How do the customers react to promotion, prices, fashion trends, product attributes, salespeople, etc.? Why are the customers interested in certain products (pleasure, status, etc.)?

A Free-Market Business

Name_____ **Date** _____ **Period** _____

Interview a business owner and fill out the following information.

1. Name of the business: _____

2. Is this business a proprietorship, partnership, or corporation?_____

3. Describe that form of ownership and why it is the best for this business. _____

   _____

   _____

   _____

4. Is the product of the company a good or a service? _____

   _____

   _____

5. Describe the product. _____

6. Describe the target market of the business. _____

   _____

   _____

   _____

7. How does supply and demand affect this business? _____

   _____

   _____

   _____

8. What companies compete with this business?_____

   _____

   _____

9. How does the competition affect the business? _____

   _____

   _____

10. What types of promotional activities are done by the company? _____

    _____

    _____

11. Other interesting information (pricing, distribution, marketing, etc.): _____

    _____

    _____

    _____

    _____

Basic Economic Concepts

Name_____

Date_____**Period**_____ **Score**_____

Chapter 3 Test

Matching: Match the following terms and identifying phrases.

_____ 1. People who buy and use finished products.

_____ 2. The process of finding or creating a profitable market for specific goods or services.

_____ 3. Intangible activities or benefits that are performed and have value.

_____ 4. Physical products that are made by manufacturers.

_____ 5. Money left over after expenses and taxes have been deducted from what was received from the company's sales.

_____ 6. Fluctuations in the level of economic activity that occur with some regularity over a period of time.

_____ 7. The block of consumers that a company wants as customers and toward whom it directs its marketing efforts.

_____ 8. Industrial materials and manufacturing capabilities.

_____ 9. Rivalry between two or more independent businesses to gain as much of the total market sales, or customer acceptance, as possible.

_____ 10. The process through which products are obtained (designed, developed, or presented for resale) and promoted to the point of sale, trying to match those products to established market requirements to make a profit.

A. business cycle

B. competition

C. consumers

D. goods

E. marketing

F. merchandising

G. profit

H. resources

I. services

J. target market

True/False: Circle T if the statement is true or F if the statement is false.

T   F   11. Fashion-related businesses are crucial to the U.S. economy through the materials and services they buy, produce, and sell, and the wages and taxes they pay.

T   F   12. Goods are either products or services.

T   F   13. In a free-market system, companies with products to sell can charge any price and sell to anyone willing to pay that price.

T   F   14. Supply refers to the types of products that consumers are willing to buy at a certain time at various prices.

(Continued)

Name_____

T F 15. An example of an apparel product with a market structure of an oligopoly is T-shirts.

T F 16. Economies of scale are cost increases as a result of low-volume production.

T F 17. A sole proprietorship is owned by just one person, although it may have many employees.

T F 18. A partnership is always owned by just two people, although it may have many employees.

T F 19. Private corporations exist to provide a social service rather than to make a profit.

T F 20. A marketing-oriented approach determines customer desires before manufacturing products.

Multiple Choice: Choose the best response. Write the letter in the space provided.

_____ 21. Retailers are companies that _____.
  A. make goods
  B. sell merchandise in small quantities to consumers
  C. offer products for sale to industrial businesses
  D. sell goods in bulk to limited numbers of customers

_____ 22. In a free-market system, _____.
  A. the government and individuals make key economic decisions equally
  B. people freely choose what to buy in the marketplace
  C. there is heavy government control of what is bought and sold
  D. None of the above.

_____ 23. When there is more competition, _____.
  A. the profits per item sold are lower for the businesses involved
  B. products tend to be of a higher quality and more innovative
  C. prices for similar products are lower for customers
  D. All of the above.

_____ 24. A standard of living indicates the _____.
  A. way people live, based on the kinds and quality of goods and services they can afford
  B. price levels for products that are in demand
  C. competitive nature of the marketplace
  D. number of owners involved with most businesses

_____ 25. Characteristics of markets that operate as oligopolies include _____.
  A. a few large rival firms producing competitive products
  B. firms that dominate the market for a product and usually react to one another's actions
  C. difficulty of entering and exiting the industry
  D. All of the above.

(Continued)

Name_____

_____ 26. A continuum is a _____.
  A. company with no competition that produces large volumes of a product
  B. sliding scale from one extreme to another with infinite different points along it
  C. continuous supply of goods being manufactured from constantly replenished resources
  D. basic form of business organization that will continue even if the owner dies

_____ 27. Unlimited personal liability for a business means _____.
  A. financial prosperity for the owner if bankruptcy is declared
  B. responsibility for the business's debts and obligations
  C. that mergers can be transacted with other businesses whenever feasible
  D. the business is in a competitive industry rather than being a monopoly

_____ 28. Partnerships _____.
  A. are not incorporated
  B. have higher profit potential than sole proprietorships because of pooled talents and responsibilities
  C. might have conflict and lack of clear-cut management responsibility
  D. All of the above.

_____ 29. Consumer confidence _____.
  A. is a feeling of certainty by consumers to spend their money
  B. is highest during recessions, because things are sure to get better in the future
  C. causes a drop in competition for most apparel retailers
  D. relates to extra supply and less demand

_____ 30. Merchandising always involves _____.
  A. dealing with profits and competition
  B. businesses that are incorporated
  C. varying degrees of planning, buying, and selling
  D. working with consumers to satisfy their whims

Essay Questions: Provide complete responses to the following questions or statements.

31. Describe the market structures of pure competition and monopoly.

32. List at least three advantages and three disadvantages of the corporate form of business ownership.

33. Briefly explain the four main elements of a marketing mix.

Substance of the Fashion Industry

Objectives

After studying this chapter, students will be able to

- describe the two ways of viewing the fashion industry's channel of distribution.
- define and recognize vertical integration.
- explain commodity/fashion/seasonal goods.
- list other industries that deal with textile products.
- identify trade associations and industry publications.
- name the geographic areas for each segment of the industry.

Teaching Materials

Text, pages 64–80
Fashion Terms
Fashion Review
Fashion in Action

Student Workbook
A. *Traveling the Pipeline*
B. *Non-Apparel Textile Marketing*
C. *Your Fashion Industry Quiz*
D. *Read and React*
E. *Differences Described*

Teacher's Resources
The Use of Textiles, reproducible master 4-1
The Scope of the U.S. Textile/Apparel Industry, transparency master 4-2
Soft Goods Chain, transparency master 4-3
Distribution Chain Concepts, transparency master 4-4
The Main Types of Apparel Goods, transparency master 4-5
Industrial Marketing Is Different from Consumer Marketing, transparency master 4-6
Chapter 4 Test

Introductory Activities

1. Use the following questions as starters for a discussion to involve students in the subject matter. Add other questions that are pertinent to the chapter and to this group of students for further introductory discussion.
   - What steps are involved from the beginning fibers until garments are bought by consumers?
   - Starting with a textile fiber, name the steps involved to produce a garment you are wearing.
   - What additional types of businesses help fashion producers design and sell their goods?
   - For what other types of goods (other than apparel) can you think of that textiles are used?
2. *The Use of Textiles*, reproducible master 4-1. Students are asked to list ways that textiles are used in homes, in the medical field, for military purposes, and in heavy construction. Expand the answers into a discussion that includes every possible way students think textiles are used.
3. *The Scope of the U.S. Textile/Apparel Industry*, transparency master 4-2. Use this transparency as a basis of discussion about the importance of the textile/apparel industry.

Teaching Strategies to Reteach, Reinforce, Enrich, and Extend Text Concepts

The Soft Goods Chain

4. **RF** Write the definition for *channel of distribution* on the board. Then, to clarify how channels of distribution work and that they do not apply only to fashion goods, have students tell (as best they can) what the channel of distribution is for a car, television set, framed oil painting, and other goods.

5. **RT** Have 10 students line up in front of the class. They should assemble in groups of four, three, two, and one—for the textile segment, apparel segment, retail segment, and end users, respectively. Starting with fiber production, have each student describe, in order, each product or function through the textile/apparel pipeline. Other class members should add to the commentaries by raising their hands to give their responses.

6. **RF** Have students discuss why "customers" are not necessarily end-use consumers. Also discuss why prices can be kept lower if there are fewer middle-people between the beginning and end of the channel of distribution of a product.

7. **RT** *Soft Goods Chain*, transparency master 4-3. Use this transparency master to graphically illustrate the chain of events textiles go through to reach consumers.

The Four-Groups Approach

8. **RF** Have four students line up in front of the class, with each holding up a sign representing the "primary group," "secondary group," "retail group," or "auxiliary group." Starting with the primary group student, have each one describe, in order, his or her product or function through the four-groups approach. Tell who sells to whom and how they depend on each other. Other class members should add to the commentaries by raising their hands and being called on.

9. **RT** Hold a discussion about the similarities and differences between the standard soft goods chain and the four-groups approach. Then end with the simple conclusion that they are really the same but are merely shown (presented) in different ways.

10. **EX** Make information about factoring available for the students. Factoring is an auxiliary service to all segments of the fashion industry and is provided by financial institutions. The factors buy the accounts receivable at a discounted rate, collect the face amount, but assume all losses resulting from uncollectible debts. Hold a discussion about how fashion businesses can decrease their collection risk this way, increase their working capital immediately, and eliminate their own credit and cash receivables operations. Over $50 billion is factored in the fashion industry each year.

11. **RF** Have students find and tear out or photocopy newspaper or magazine advertisements or articles that show auxiliary businesses to the fashion industry. Have them show these to the class, discuss the content, and mount them on a bulletin board for others to read.

Vertical Integration

12. **RF** *Traveling the Pipeline*, Activity A, WB. Students are asked to respond to questions and statements related to the textile/apparel pipeline.

13. **RF** Have students explain vertical integration forward and backward. Then hold a discussion about the pros and cons of apparel manufacturers opening stores. What are the pros and cons of retail stores expanding their private label lines while reducing the number of name brand lines they carry? Do apparel manufacturers have retailing expertise? Do retailers have design and manufacturing expertise? Is the rate of vertical integration accelerating these days? Are old business partners turning into competitors? Where might this fight for control of the pipeline end up in the long run?

14. **ER** Have students visit a factory outlet store and a major retail chain/department store. Have students assess the quality and styling of the goods in the factory outlet, and ask an employee if the items are the same as are sold to full-price retailers. In the chain/department store, have students also assess the quality and styling of the goods. Have students see if any of the same brands are sold there, as in the factory outlet, and how many private label lines are stocked.

15. **EX** *Distribution Chain Concepts*, transparency master 4-4. Use this to guide a class discussion about more advanced distribution chain concepts.

Commodity, Fashion, and Seasonal Goods

16. **EX** *The Main Types of Apparel Goods*, transparency master 4-5. Use this as an overhead or reproduce it for all the students to keep. Use it for class discussion to clarify descriptions and expand details of fashion merchandise, commodity merchandise, and seasonal merchandise.

17. **RF** Ask students to explain why correct decisions about fashion merchandise can result in large profits, and wrong decisions can cause huge financial losses or even force companies out of business. Relate this to style and timing risk for companies that deal with fashion goods. Then discuss the smaller style and timing risks for commodity and seasonal items.

18. **ER** Have students discuss the statement: "Since the strongest sales of certain seasonal items occur at a similar time each year, forecasting is straightforward."

19. **ER** Have students discuss why the differences in fashion, commodity, and seasonal merchandise affect businesses located at all points of the soft goods chain. Why is a different strategy and sales forecast needed for each separate category?

Other Textile End-Use Industries

20. **RF** *Non-Apparel Textile Marketing*, Activity B, WB. Students are asked to cut out pictures of non-apparel textiles and analyze the use of these textiles.
21. **RT** Hold a discussion about the pie chart in text illustration 4-14. Have students separately discuss each of the statements within the three categories of end-use markets of textile products.
22. **RT** Have the students comment about the demand for household textile items being related to the health of the economy, as well as to housing starts and interest rates. Also discuss how and where household textile products are sold and why furniture is not mass-produced like garments.
23. **ER** Arrange for a class trip to a furniture showroom that has an interactive video (in-store CAD) system. The computer will show students how different selected fabrics look on various furniture styles. Discuss how orders can be placed through computer linkages to the factory. Relate this technology to possible garment design/ordering of the future. Also have the students look at textiles used on furniture while there.
24. **RF** Hold a class discussion about why industrial textile marketing is done at a high level of management, why continuous research and development is needed for industrial textiles, and why transportation is the largest market for industrial textiles. Review 4-19 in the text. Then, have students add to the reproducible master 4-1, *The Use of Textiles*, which they filled out before reading the chapter.
25. **EX** Show students a video about consumer and industrial categories of goods and services. A video is available from D.E. Visuals.
26. **ER** Obtain information about Techtextil trade fairs for industrial textiles on the Internet at www.usa.messefrankfurt.com or www.techtextil. messefrankfurt.com.
27. **ER** *Industrial Marketing Is Different from Consumer Marketing*, transparency master 4-6. Use this as an overhead or reproduce this to pass out to the students. Going around the room, have each student read and explain the meaning of the next bullet item. Let other students add to the meaning after raising their hands and being called on.

28. **RT** Discuss the personal reasons people do home sewing as well as reasons home sewing has declined in the past few decades. Ask students their feelings about doing home sewing projects.

Fashion Industry Associations and Publications

29. **RT** Discuss the general objectives of all trade associations. Cite specific activities of certain trade organizations that illustrate how they accomplish the objectives. Apparel trade associations are described, and links are included on Web sites and various textile/apparel university sites. Your school or local library might also have the reference book *Encyclopedia of Associations* that describes most associations, including their purposes, activities, and publications. Encourage students to find out about the International Textile & Apparel Association, Inc.
30. **RF** Assemble a collection of as many textile/apparel trade publications as possible by requesting sample copies from the publishers. Include as many as possible from illustration 4-23 of the text, as well as others you may know of, especially related to your part of the country. Some addresses/phone numbers are listed in this guide's Resource List, and others can be obtained from library or Internet references. *Women's Wear Daily, DNR*, and many other trade publications are listed on the Web site www.fairchildpub.com/fairchild.htm. Allow time for students to look through all of them. Then hold a class discussion about what types of information each contains and how each satisfies the needs of its target market. Mention the fact that a "digest" (such as the *Textile Technology Digest*) includes condensed abstracts of articles from other sources. To delve deeper into the content, complete articles can be obtained from their original sources.
31. **ER** Obtain a copy of the latest Retail Calendar of *STORES* magazine from the National Retail Federation. It is a guide to the retail industry's key events, many of them being trade shows of apparel and retail-related organizations. Have the students read through the almost 100 event sponsors of trade shows during the year, which are listed in the front of the booklet. Then, for this month, notice all the various trade shows that are going on and where they are being held.
32. **RF** Assemble printed materials (trade advertisements and flyers) about specific soft goods-related trade shows. This can be done by calling major industry trade associations. Encourage students to look at the materials to see what is offered at these events.

Geographic Locations of Industry Segments

33. **ER** Divide the class into three groups. Have the groups study about the history and location of U.S. textile production, apparel production, and retailing, respectively. Have them also find out about today's areas of industry concentration. Then have each group give an organized and informative report to the rest of the class, including the use of visual aids.

34. **RF** *Your Fashion Industry Quiz*, Activity C, WB. Students are asked to write one true/false question for each of the chapter sections. They are then asked to exchange activity guide pages with another classmate to complete the quiz.

35. **RF** *Read and React*, Activity D, WB. Students are asked to think about statements related to fashion and write their reactions.

36. **RF** *Differences Described*, Activity E, WB. Students are asked to differentiate between various terms presented in the chapter.

Additional Enrichment Activities

Research

37. Have students research one or more fashion information (forecasting) services. In the library or on the Internet they might look for Nigel French or Design Intelligence (headquartered in London); The Doneger Group; Ellen Sideri Partnership, Inc. (ESP); Promostyl; or www.wgsn.com. Have students find out information such as what services are offered, what products and markets are covered, how many reports are prepared each year, who are the clients, how far ahead of the retail season the predictions are done, and what fees must be paid for the services.

38. Have students do research about household textile businesses. They might study the recent consolidation, modernization, and refocusing of domestics and home furnishings vertical mills and manufacturers. (Have students start by finding information about West Point Stevens, Fieldcrest Cannon, Springs Industries, Dundee Mills, Crown Crafts Inc., and/or Revman Industries.) They might research which retailers sell the most domestics and linens by dollar amounts or as a percentage of their sales (such as JCPenney, Wal-Mart, Kmart, Sears, Target, Spiegel, Domestications, and Bed, Bath & Beyond). Have students present their findings in an oral or written report.

39. Have students do in-depth research about a specific textile/apparel industry trade association or trade publication. Have them write a report about their findings, incorporating points of what was discussed in the chapter.

Projects

40. Invite a member of The Fashion Group International (FGI) from your city to speak to the class. Have the person explain the group's activities, how to become a member, and what members gain from membership in the group. A member of the American Society of Interior Designers or other trade association might be substituted if available.

41. Have students visit a local furniture store, department store, and "bed and bath" shop. Have them make a chart that compares the three types of retailers according to as many aspects as possible about how they market each category of their household textile products. An oral presentation to the class, explaining the findings shown on the chart, should also answer questions about the marketing of domestics, furniture items, and other household textiles.

42. Have students complete a simple home sewing project and bring it to class. As they show their items, have them describe if its completion gave them a certain degree of creative enjoyment, proper fit, individuality, money savings, or better quality of construction than similar store-bought items. Also, did the students feel that the project brought out any disadvantages of home sewing?

Answer Key

Text

Fashion Review, page 80

1. The original source is fibers from plants/animals or chemical companies. Middle-people are in yarn production, fabric manufacturing and finishing, apparel designing/manufacturing/sales, and retail buying and selling. The ultimate user is the consumer who wears the item.

2. Companies within the pipeline sell to other companies (who are their customers) rather than to end-use consumers.

3. The mills knit, weave, or otherwise join yarns into fabrics.

4. the wholesale segment—most fashion goods are sold and shipped directly from manufacturers to retailers at a wholesale price.

5. An additional amount is needed to cover the retailer's costs for heat, lights, taxes, sales help, other expenses, and profit.

6. The primary group depends on the secondary group to sell their products down through the chain. The secondary group depends on the primary group to provide the materials for them to make their products. Both primary and secondary groups gain information, expertise, assistance, and promotion from the auxiliary group.
7. (Student response.)
8. Commodity products are staple goods that hardly ever change in design and are in constant demand. Fashion products are always changing in design and it is hard to predict the demand. Seasonal products can be either commodity or fashion products and change in demand with the seasons of the year.
9. Industrial textile products are increasing and apparel fabrics are decreasing in relation to the total U.S. market.
10. Expected lifetime for apparel is approximately four years and household textiles is about 10 years.
11. bed linens, bathroom items, and table and kitchen linens
12. strength and durability, colorfastness, and stain resistance
13. Traditionally, gallery programs have displayed actual furniture pieces of company's lines. A new in-store computer design system uses interactive video catalogs that visualize different coverings for custom-covered furniture, print photo-like mock-ups of selections, and sometimes are linked to the factory to place the order.
14. (Give three examples. Student response.)
15. for a feeling of achievement, proper fit, creative individuality, to save money, and for quality of construction
16. improve industry business conditions; encourage the use of the industry's products; promote common interests of the members; serve as a source of market intelligence and business development; gain advantageous passage of legislation and government support; sponsor seminars, convention expositions, and trade shows; provide technical assistance and support; provide networking opportunities
17. (Student response.)
18. (Student response.)
19. good sources of power, lower-wage labor, proximity to raw materials, lower taxes, and plentiful, inexpensive land
20. They are becoming more automated and efficient.

Student Workbook

Traveling the Pipeline, Activity A

1. a. Fibers are produced either from naturally grown sources or from chemical mixtures.

b. Yarns are formed by spinning or twisting fibers together at yarn mills.
c. Textile mills weave, knit, or otherwise join yarns into fabrics.
d. bleaching, dyeing, printing, or applying special coatings to impart color, texture, pattern, ease of care, and other characteristics to fabrics
e. creating new versions of garments, accessories, or other items
f. mass production of the designed fashions in factories
g. selling the manufactured garments in large quantities to retail stores
h. Retailers buy finished goods in large amounts from manufacturers at wholesale prices.
i. Retailers sell one item at a time directly to many different consumers.

2. the combining of two or more steps of the pipeline within one company and under one management
3. assure a timely supply of goods into the stores (or can charge lower prices since a middle-person has been eliminated)
4. They compete with the retailers who are their own customers, who usually buy their products to sell in their stores, which causes bad feelings.
5. Retailers become their own suppliers and can assure themselves a certain level of quality, timely delivery, and lower price.

Differences Described, Activity E

1. Channel of distribution is the route that goods and services take from the original source, through all middle-people, to the ultimate user. The soft goods chain is the channel of distribution for apparel and home decorating textiles.
2. Fibers are very thin, hair-like strands that can be quite short or very long; the basic units in making textile products. Greige goods are yard goods in an unfinished state.
3. Yarns are continuous strands of textile fibers spun into a form suitable for processing into fabrics. Fabrics are long pieces of cloth (yard goods).
4. Wholesalers are middle-people who purchase large quantities of goods from manufacturers and sell small quantities to retailers. Resellers is another name for wholesalers.
5. The primary group of the four-groups approach includes the suppliers of raw materials (textiles, leathers, and furs) in the soft goods chain. The secondary group is the manufacturing segment of the chain that makes fabricated products.
6. Raw materials are fibers, fabrics, leathers, and furs from which fashion products are made. Fabricated products are sewn garments, accessories, and other manufactured items.

7. The retail group of the four-groups approach includes stores, catalogs, TV home shopping channels, Internet retail sales, and other retail enterprises that sell finished goods to those who want to buy and use them. The auxiliary group includes organizations that support or help businesses associated with the soft goods chain (such as market researchers, forecasters, fashion publications, advertising agencies, buying services, modeling agencies, and trade associations).

8. Forward integration is combining a business at one step of the distribution channel with another farther toward the end of the chain (closer to the end user). Backward integration is combining a business at one step of the distribution channel with another toward the beginning of the chain (closer to the raw materials).

9. Commodity products are staple goods that hardly ever change in design and are in constant demand. Fashion products are goods that are always changing, having style and timing risk.

10. Private label goods are produced only for a particular retailer and have the retailer's special trademark or brand name. Seasonal goods change in popularity or demand with the seasons of the year.

11. Domestics include bed, bath, and kitchen textiles. Home furnishings textiles include window treatments, furniture coverings, and miscellaneous items such as throw pillows and lamp shades.

12. Geotextiles are industrial textiles that relate to the earth's surface. Composites are textiles combined with other materials, such as for use in commercial hose, belting, car fenders, and boat hulls.

13. Trade associations are nonprofit, voluntary organizations made up of businesses that have common interests. Trade publications are magazines, newspapers, and books that deal specifically with a certain industry or segment of an industry.

14. Textile performance is how a fabric performs, measured by durability, colorfastness, stain resistance, and other attributes. Industrial textiles are technical fabrics sold to commercial business customers according to specifications and performance quality rather than a fashion look.

15. *Women's Wear Daily* is a trade newspaper that covers all aspects of the women's fashion industries. *DNR* is a weekly newsmagazine that reports the textile and menswear industries.

Teacher's Resources

Chapter 4 Test

1.	E	16.	T
2.	B	17.	F
3.	G	18.	F
4.	J	19.	T
5.	I	20.	F
6.	D	21.	C
7.	C	22.	B
8.	A	23.	A
9.	H	24.	D
10.	F	25.	D
11.	T	26.	A
12.	F	27.	D
13.	T	28.	D
14.	T	29.	B
15.	F	30.	A

31. (See 4-1 in the text.)
32. The primary group is made up of suppliers of raw materials, such as textiles, leathers, and furs. The secondary group is the manufacturing segment that makes garments, accessories, or other fabricated products. The retail group does the final selling/distribution to the end users (consumers). The auxiliary group is made up of organizations that support (help) the other businesses associated with the soft goods chain.
33. (Student response.)

The Use of Textiles

Name_____ **Date** _____ **Period** _____

1. List as many ways as you can that textiles are used in homes. _____

_____

_____

_____

_____

_____

2. List as many ways as you can that textiles are used in the medical field. _____

_____

_____

_____

_____

_____

3. List as many purposes as you can that textiles are used for the military._____

_____

_____

_____

_____

_____

4. List as many ways as you can that textiles are used in construction._____

_____

_____

_____

_____

_____

5. Other than for apparel and the categories mentioned above, in what other areas can you think of that textiles are used?_____

_____

_____

_____

_____

_____

The Scope of the U.S. Textile/Apparel Industry

The U.S. textile/apparel industry supplies a U.S. market that annually consumes:

- 1 billion pairs of trousers

- 2 billion shirts and blouses

- 600 million sweaters

- 480 million activewear items

- 39 billion square yards of textiles (13,000 square miles)

- 17 billion pounds of fabric (70 pounds per person)

- 20% of the world's textiles

Soft Goods Chain

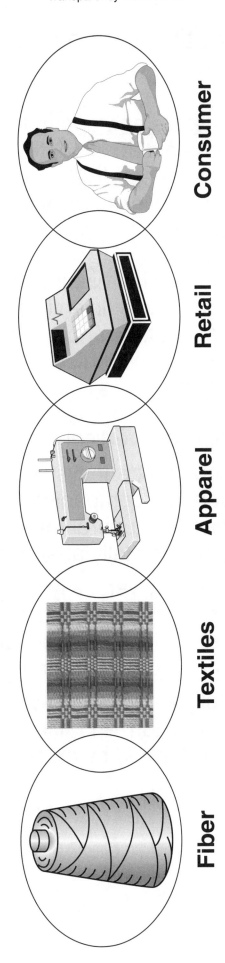

Consumer

Retail

Apparel

Textiles

Fiber

Source—Textile/Apparel Technology Corporation—[TC]^2

Distribution Chain Concepts

- Activities of the <u>textile and apparel segments</u> of the soft goods chain deal almost completely with the business-to-business (B2B) market. The <u>retail segment</u> stresses business activities for the consumer market (B2C).

- In an effective channel of distribution, <u>information</u> (as well as goods) flow efficiently among the parties—suppliers, retailers, and consumers—for style preferences, merchandise timing, quantities, qualities, pricing, etc.

- Distribution chains are vertical marketing systems.

    A. Some are "independent systems," with all parts being independent companies (The fiber firms, textile companies, apparel manufacturers, and retailers are not officially attached to each other.).

    B. Some are "partially vertically integrated systems," with a few of the steps owned by one company (such as fiber through finished fabrics, or apparel manufacturing through retailing).

    C. Some are "fully vertically integrated systems," with all supply production, and final distribution to consumers performed by one corporate entity.

The Main Types of Apparel Goods

Type of apparel goods	General description	Examples of apparel items	Percentage of apparel market	Length of selling time at retail	Considerations for fashion businesses
Fashion Merchandise	Goods with strong current customer appeal	The latest looks in dresses, suits, sportswear, etc.	About 35%	About 10 weeks (2½ months)	Limited lifespan; unpredictable; high risk; impulse buying
Commodity Merchandise	Staple items with long, steady demand	Underwear, sleepwear, men's dress shirts, luggage, etc.	About 20%	Sell all year	Predictable styles and sales volumes
Seasonal Merchandise	Wider appeal than fashion goods but change with the seasons	Swimsuits, shorts, sandals, skiwear, wool sweaters, coats, etc.	About 45%	About 20 weeks (5 months)	Take on attributes of fashion and/or commodity merchandise, depending on items

Industrial Marketing Is Different from Consumer Marketing

Industrial marketing addresses business (commercial) customers rather than individual customers.

- Industrial marketing is aimed at a small number of large size customers who make volume purchases.

- Industrial marketing is concentrated in certain regions of the country where markets are located.

- Industrial marketing is influenced by customer demand at various points down the chain.

- Industrial marketing depends on other parts of the total product being available.

- Products are often sold in unfinished form because they might branch off for different end uses.

- Salespeople have technical educations and backgrounds; besides selling, they are often problem solvers.

- Buyers are more technically oriented. They are interested in specifications, cost effectiveness, and the selling company's reputation (rather than buying because of emotion, impulse, or fashion reasons).

- Quality, delivery time, future service/assistance is often more important than price.

- Pricing might include trade discounts, quantity discounts, preferred customer treatment, or other special arrangements. (*List price* is the official published price; *net price* includes deductions.)

- Promotion is done at trade shows and in trade publications or catalogs stressing technical data rather than fashion.

Substance of the Fashion Industry

Name_____

Date_____ Period_____ Score_____

Chapter 4 Test

Matching: Match the following terms and identifying phrases.

_____ 1. The exchange of ideas, information, or services among an interconnected group of people.

_____ 2. A way of showing the flow of goods from fiber to retail that includes the primary, secondary, retail, and auxiliary groups.

_____ 3. The channel of distribution for apparel and home decorating textiles.

_____ 4. The combining of two or more steps of the pipeline within one company and under one management.

_____ 5. Magazines, newspapers, and books that deal specifically with a certain industry or segment of an industry.

_____ 6. Requiring many workers to make the products, rather than relying heavily on machines and technology.

_____ 7. Yard goods in an unfinished state.

_____ 8. The route that goods and services take from the original source through all middle-people to the ultimate user.

_____ 9. Nonprofit, voluntary organizations made up of businesses that have common interests.

_____ 10. Merchandise produced only for a particular retailer and with the retailer's special trademark or brand name.

A. channel of distribution

B. four-groups approach

C. greige goods

D. labor intensive

E. networking

F. private label goods

G. soft goods chain

H. trade associations

I. trade publications

J. vertical integration

True/False: Circle *T* if the statement is true or *F* if the statement is false.

T   F   11. The soft goods chain is also called the textile/apparel pipeline.

T   F   12. The textile segment of the soft goods chain starts with fabric manufacturing.

T   F   13. Fabrics are finished by bleaching, dyeing, printing, or applying special coatings to greige goods.

T   F   14. Resellers are often associated with wholesale sales of inexpensive accessories and small nonfashion goods.

T   F   15. Sewn garments, accessories, and other items are also called duplicated products.

T   F   16. Commodity products are staple goods that hardly ever change in design and are in constant demand.

(Continued)

Name_____

T   F   17. The percentage of apparel fabrics is increasing, and industrial textiles are decreasing, in relation to the total U.S. market.

T   F   18. Apparel textile products are expected to last longer than household textiles.

T   F   19. Household "domestics" include bed, bath, and kitchen textiles.

T   F   20. The transportation category has the smallest market for industrial textiles.

Multiple Choice: Choose the best response. Write the letter in the space provided.

_____ 21. For companies at the beginning and middle of the soft goods chain, "customers" are _____.
A. end-use consumers
B. the auxiliary businesses that support them
C. companies positioned at the next step of the overall chain
D. All of the above.

_____ 22. Yarns are _____.
A. very thin, hair-like strands from naturally grown sources or chemical mixtures
B. continuous strands of spun fibers in a form suitable for processing into fabrics
C. bleached or dyed greige goods
D. usually knitted rather than used in woven fashion

_____ 23. Designing is the process of _____.
A. creating new versions of garments, accessories, or other items
B. growing or making fibers from unknown chemical mixtures
C. vertically integrating chemistry with retail sales ideas
D. All of the above.

_____ 24. The retail selling price for goods covers the _____.
A. original cost of the goods, paid by the retailer, plus some profit for the retailer
B. retailer's expenses for heat, lights, and taxes
C. retailer's expenses for sales help and other wages/salaries
D. All of the above.

_____ 25. Fashion market researchers/forecasters _____.
A. provide information about colors and other trends that are occurring in the consumer marketplace
B. are consulting and reporting firms that analyze and interpret the trends
C. give advice for businesses to try to understand and satisfy upcoming consumer demand
D. All of the above.

_____ 26. An example of forward integration is when _____.
A. manufacturers open factory outlet stores
B. retailers directly compete with textile producers
C. retailers develop their own private label brands
D. apparel textiles are used for household textile purposes

(Continued)

Name_____

_____ 27. Seasonal products _____.
   A. do not include fashion or commodity merchandise
   B. include such items as basic underwear, men's business shirts, and luggage
   C. include the latest fads in dresses and jewelry
   D. include such items as swimsuits and skiwear

_____ 28. Industrial textiles _____.
   A. are technical rather than fashionable
   B. are sold to commercial business customers according to industrial specifications
   C. have specialized uses that require a great deal of continuous research and development
   D. All of the above.

_____ 29. Trade associations try to _____.
   A. separate the interests of their members
   B. gain advantageous passage of legislation and government support
   C. have their members attend the seminars, conventions/expositions, and trade shows of other industries
   D. All of the above.

_____ 30. Today, the U.S. textile industry is _____.
   A. comprised of fairly large companies mainly concentrated in North and South Carolina and Georgia
   B. located everywhere, with companies of all sizes producing different types of fabrics
   C. becoming less automated and efficient since most textiles are produced "offshore"
   D. located among lofts in New York City and plants in California

Essay Questions: Provide complete responses to the following questions or statements.

31. Draw and label the complete soft goods chain (textile/apparel pipeline).

32. Name and briefly describe the main groupings of the four-groups approach.

33. Name and briefly describe at least three of the main reasons people do home sewing.

CHAPTER 5

Satisfying the Fashion Market

Objectives

After studying this chapter, students will be able to

⊖ distinguish between market growth, share, and segmentation.

⊖ describe the importance and methods of market research.

⊖ summarize the concept of product development.

⊖ explain the latest fashion industry information technology.

⊖ explain the efforts that are being made for overall industry excellence.

⊖ describe how the industry is improving its image.

Teaching Materials

Text, pages 81–101
Fashion Terms
Fashion Review
Fashion in Action

Student Workbook
A. *Working with Market Share*
B. *Fashion Market Research*
C. *Interest in Technology*
D. *The Improving Textile/Apparel Industry*
E. *Fashion Market Flash Cards*

Teacher's Resources
Feelings About Soft Goods Marketing, reproducible master 5-1
The Total Market Potential, transparency master 5-2
Market Segmentation Categories, transparency master 5-3
Growth of "Megapolitan" Areas, transparency master 5-4
The What and Why of the Universal Product Code, transparency master 5-5

Radio Frequency Identification (RFID) Blips, transparency master 5-6
Electronic Data Interchange (EDI), transparency master 5-7
Quick Response Discussion, reproducible master 5-8
Push and Pull Comparison, transparency master 5-9
Chapter 5 Test

Introductory Activities

1. *Feelings About Soft Goods Marketing*, reproducible master 5-1. To encourage students to begin thinking about the subjects covered in this chapter, ask them to state their opinions as mini-essays about soft goods marketing sentences on the lines provided.

2. Assign one of each of the following terms to a section of the class:
   A. conspicuous consumption
   B. birth rate
   C. supply chain management
   D. empty nesters
   E. clustering techniques
   F. disposable income
   G. generic market
   H. discretionary income
   I. market development
   J. age distribution
   K. competitive advantage
   L. market penetration

   Have each group look up information about their term in business/economic sources, discuss the meaning within their group, and report their findings to the class. Then have students be alert during the study of the chapter to when they can say their term applies to the content being studied.

Market Growth and Share

3. **ER** *The Total Market Potential*, transparency master 5-2. Use this transparency to illustrate a market's "capacity to consume." Discuss each of the three main factors that make up the total market potential for a business. You may want to present the last box as the "ready, willing, and able" factor.

4. **RF** Hold a class discussion about the differences between market growth and market share. Discuss how changes in one or more of the three market potential factors might affect market growth for particular fashion products (or commodity, fashion, and seasonal categories). Also discuss what a business might do to "grow their market share" by better satisfying any of those factors.

5. **RT** Ask students to explain why companies try to increase their market share, what a larger market share does to their costs and selling prices, and what effect these have on their competitors.

6. **RF** *Working with Market Share*, Activity A, WB. Students are asked to evaluate questions about market size and market share, and then write their reactions to given statements.

Market Segmentation

7. **RF** Have students analyze the information in text illustration 5-3. Ask students to interpret the importance of the trends they notice for the apparel markets from the percentage change for the future (last column on the right), such as the aging population. This is also effective if the students make a line or bar graph of the data presented in the chart.

8. **ER** Discuss the following statements: "Target marketers believe the customer should be the focus of all business and marketing activity," "People with money make markets," and "When the wife earns, the family spends."

9. **RF** Discuss the current demographics in the neighborhoods around your school and any obvious changes that have taken place in those demographics over the past decade. Discuss how demand for particular types of clothing items differs by geographic location and urban or rural location.

10. **EX** Have various resources about market segmentation available for students to study. Examples might be *American Demographics* magazine (www.demographics.com) or one of many reports from Kalorama Information (www.MarketResearch.com), especially about apparel markets. Reports such as *World Marketing Forecasts* and *Regional Markets: Demographics of Growth & Decline* are on CD-ROM. Some of these are very expensive and might be available through a library.

11. **RT** Ask students to define *psychographics*. Have students explain the significance of recent psychographic changes to consumer fashion purchases. How does the increasing number of women who work outside the home affect the demand for such items as women's business suits, cooking aprons, or Girl Scout uniforms?

12. **ER** Obtain the latest demographic information available from federal, state, and local government agencies, as well as some trade associations. Specific business summaries and trend analyses are also available in the library or on the Internet. Share this information with the class.

13. **ER** Show a video about market segmentation to the class. One example is *Market Segmentation, Targeting, and Positioning: Developing a Focus* from D.E. Visuals.

14. **RF** In relation to market segmentation and target marketing, have the class discuss the statement "It is better to serve a group of consumers well all of the time than all consumers well none of the time." Also discuss the target rule for all businesses: "Know your customer" (total market potential, demographics, psychographics, desired level of service, feelings about prestige vs. price, and when they like to shop). A company's customer profile consists of the demographic and psychographic characteristics of the people who comprise the target market and the purchasing patterns they display.

15. **RF** *Market Segmentation Categories*, transparency master 5-3. Use this transparency to clarify the demographic and psychographic market segmentation categories discussed in the text. Then expand into other ways to segment markets by discussing geographic and behavioristic segmentation of markets.

16. **EX** *Growth of "Megapolitan" Areas,* transparency master 5-4. While going through this transparency with the class and simultaneously displaying a map of the United States, have students point out each listed megapolitan area. Ask students to give their definition of the word *megapolitan*. Also, discuss the fact that researchers predict these megapolitan areas to almost double by 2050.

17. **RF** Have students discuss why it is difficult for businesses to stay on top of changing consumer demographics and psychographics if the changes are gradual.

18. **RF** Ask the students how they would have marketed fashion goods to young adults of the no-rules "hippies" of the 1960s, the "yuppies" (young urban professionals) of the 1980s, or the "millennials" (generations X and Y) of the 2000s who tend to be confident, yet sheltered, team players, accepting of rules and authority, optimistic, and high achievers.

Market Research

19. **RT** Have students discuss the importance of trying to obtain quantitative as well as qualitative information when doing market research. Also, individually discuss each of the six main methods of market research summarized in the chapter. Tell students about lesser-used advisory panels, such as teen boards, college boards, or career women, comprised of groups of consumers consulted by retailers to give opinions and advice.
20. **ER** Show students a video or report about market research. Several *Marketing Research* videos are available from D.E. Visuals.
21. **RF** *Fashion Market Research*, Activity B, WB. Students are asked to conduct their own market research about a pictured fashion garment and answer additional questions.
22. **ER** As a class, design an effective questionnaire for a specific line of fashion products for use in surveys, consumer panels, or focus groups. Have students formulate comprehensive items such as "Rank in order the following factors in terms of their importance in your decision to purchase or not purchase this item" (quality, price, suitability, color, style, etc.), or "Check in the space provided how you feel about each statement" (strongly agree, agree, uncertain, disagree, or strongly disagree; or from not at all important to very important). Have students try to keep survey items short, limited to one idea, and use simple/clear language. The opening survey item might be an interest grabber, followed by general questions and leading up to more specific questions. Personal questions should be placed last.
23. **ER** For extra credit, ask students to read one of Paco Underhill's books, such as *Boom: Marketing to the Ultimate Power Consumer—The Baby Boomer Woman,* or *Why We Buy: The Science of Shopping,* or *Call of the Mall: The Geography of Shopping.* All are available at www.envirosell.com, www.amazon.com, or other booksellers. Market research done by recording customer activity on strategically placed video cameras, combined information obtained by researchers in the store who observe shopping activities and interview customers as they enter and exit is explained.

Product Development

24. **RT** In a class discussion, compare the definition of *product development* given in the text chapter with this one: "Product development is offering new or improved products for present markets."
25. **RF** Discuss with the class how market research and product development are tied together, using the statement "Identify the consumer, then change the product or design a new one."
26. **ER** Divide the class into three "retail product development" groups. For a hypothetical store or department, have the groups formulate a strategy (based on results of market research they make up) of
   A. stocking new, different styles or brands
   B. developing "me-too" products, like the styles their competitors sell
   C. updating recently successful lines into newer versions
   Have the students show how their market research results justify their decision about product development.
27. **ER** Show the class a video about product development. New Product Development is available from D.E. Visuals.
28. **ER** Lead a student discussion about how fashion businesses might obtain new product ideas from internal sources (product development employees), customers (market research results), competitors (products that others are successfully selling), suppliers (who know trends of the market and what other customers are requesting), and other sources (trade magazines, shows, government statistics, and forecasters).

Fashion Industry Information Technology

29. **RT** Discuss with the class how information systems are groups of computer components that can be combined and programmed to accomplish certain outcomes depending on business needs. Have students try to describe different fashion business tasks that are accomplished efficiently and effectively with current information systems.
30. **ER** *The What and Why of the Universal Product Code*, transparency master 5-5. Use this master as a basis of discussion about the updated universal product code. Also, gain more information on the Web site, www.1sync.org.
31. **RT** Hold a class discussion about the advantages and disadvantages of radio frequency identification (RFID) data communication, "miniaturized technologies," and other automatic identification technologies summarized in the book. Also discuss voice (speech) data entry so people can have their hands free to work. Ask any of the

students who might have had experience with combining pen input (signature capture) or finger print identification with bar code scanning at retail checkout to describe it.

32. **EX** *Radio Frequency Identification (RFID) Blips*, transparency master 5-6. Distribute this to students to read and think about the statements. Then have students discuss each statement with others or with the entire class.

33. **RT** *Electronic Data Interchange (EDI)*, transparency master 5-7. Use this master to help students visualize how information moves throughout the chain. Also describe the meaning of each of the "benefits" bulleted items. Mention that EDI procedures are now moving to XML communication via the Internet for every aspect of global trade management.

34. **EX** *Interest in Technology*, Activity C, WB. Students are asked to indicate their interest about statements that extend their learning about industry information technology. Then they are to write about their favorite statement.

Cooperation for Industry Excellence

35. **RT** Discuss book illustration 5-22. Follow various lines from textile mills to apparel producers to retailers to illustrate the Quick Response partnerships.

36. **RF** Hold a class discussion about how computer-collected point-of-sale (POS) data helps companies with their market research. Discuss how the "pull" system of Quick Response (rather than the old "push" system) directly correlates with the marketing approach to selling goods (versus the old manufacturing approach) studied in Chapter 3. Also, discuss how "the whole can be greater than the sum of its parts" with synergy. Ask students why they think QR was first used for commodity apparel items, but is now also being used for fashion goods. Finally, have the students explain how the information pipeline runs parallel with the product pipeline.

37. **ER** *Quick Response Discussion*, reproducible master 5-8. Students are asked to express their thoughts about problems the Quick Response program had to overcome for the industry to gain excellence. Follow up with a class discussion about each point.

38. **ER** *Push and Pull Comparison*, transparency master 5-9. Use this transparency to compare the production-driven and market-driven approaches for various business considerations.

39. **ER** Obtain a copy of the latest [TC]² Educational Services Course Catalog for students to look through. It gives background about [TC]², shows and tells about the teaching/training/coaching

staff, and describes the courses and other activities offered.

40. **RF** Have students explain why [TC]² says it is doing its work "through the power of the Teaching Factory." What impact does a percentage of government funding have on [TC]² if politicians change their minds about its value?

Improving the Industry's Image

41. **RF** Obtain trade journal articles about ethics and social responsibility as well as environmental efforts of textile/apparel companies. Make the articles available for students to study. Also have students bring to class any articles they can find in newspapers or magazines.

42. **RF** *The Improving Textile/Apparel Industry*, Activity D, WB. Students are asked to complete questions that pertain to chapter section content.

43. **ER** Show the class the video *Encouraging Environmental Excellence*. It is available from the American Textile Manufacturers Institute or online at www.atmi.org/search/index.asp as well as a list of E3 member companies.

44. **RT** *Fashion Market Flash Cards*, Activity E, WB. Students are asked to cut out flash cards that are provided and go through them with a classmate.

Additional Enrichment Activities

Research

45. Have students look up U.S. Census Bureau statistics about family spending for clothing at different income levels. They should be able to obtain annual dollar amounts and percentage of income at each level. Also have students obtain information about Metropolitan Statistical Areas (MSAs).

46. Have students research "compliance labeling" that has become mandatory for companies wanting to participate in Quick Response partnerships. Internet information is available about Voluntary Inter-Industry Communications Standards (www.vics.org), the Uniform Code Council (www.uc-council.org), the Association for Retail Technology Standards (ARTS) of the National Retail Federation (www.nrf-arts.org), and/or the organization for Automatic Identification Manufacturers (www.aimusa.org).

47. Have students research the strong trend toward consumer use of smart cards. Students should study what the technology includes, the extensive use of the cards in Europe, and how their use is now growing in popularity in the U.S.

48. Have students research B2B use of the Internet for EDI-type transmissions, as well as XML communication. Have them find out about the advantages, such as reliability of connections as well as encryption for security. Also, have students consider the disadvantages, such as new software needs, having all partners hooked to the Internet, and additional security concerns.

49. Have students research trade information about information technology and report their findings to the class. They might start by finding out about the RisCON Convention and Exhibition (held by the National Retail Federation), ID Expo (held by the computer technology identification industry), and SCAN-TECH (held by the Automatic Identification Manufacturers). Also have them obtain copies of ID Systems magazine and Retail Information Systems (RTS) magazine.

Projects

50. Invite a technology expert to class to talk about bar codes, scanners, open systems, EDI, RFID, the very small aperture terminal, and other information technology. Also have the speaker answer students' questions.

51. If your school is in the Southeastern U.S., invite a speaker from the National Textile Center (NTC) University Research Consortium. It includes Auburn University, Clemson University, Georgia Tech, and North Carolina State University. If your school is near the Chicago area, visit or invite a speaker from the CAD/CAM Training Center for Sewn Products. This joint effort of Chicago's Apparel Industry Board, the Chicago Manufacturing Center, and Gerber Garment Technology Inc., is located in space donated by the Chicago Apparel Center. If you are near Los Angeles or other locations that have technology centers, try to incorporate them into your program.

Answer Key

Text

Fashion Review, page 101

1. Market growth is an increase in the size of the entire market, while growth in market share is an increasing part of the total market controlled by a firm.
2. exclusive to the owner and secret from others
3. Qualitative implies what the customers want, and quantitative measures how strongly they want it.
4. because further immediate probing can be done in response to information being collected
5. because change is always occurring, so products cannot stay the same and continue to sell
6. Universal Product Code (UPC) plus UPC-A, which includes numbers as well as the original lines and spaces.
7. electronic (computerized) optical scanners
8. the placement of the label on the product or container, physical aspects of the labels, information content, type and symbol specification, label printing levels of quality, correct contents of shipments, and other identification of goods.
9. Electronic Product Code (EPC)
10. Video cameras read bar codes or recognize a product's "signature," such as size, shape, or color of package.
11. (Student response.)
12. Companies only need to replace a certain part rather than the entire computer system and can make incremental technology upgrades over time.
13. They hire an independent information technology consulting organization to oversee the system and coordinate their automation strategy.
14. It is the electronic computer linkage of companies to transmit communications automatically between them.
15. (List four:) reduces costs of clerical work, data entry, and printing; paperwork and postage costs are almost eliminated; accuracy increases; provides the ability to track goods as they move through the chain; improves efficiency; increases sales and lowers costs
16. instantaneous as it occurs
17. With a pull, the right merchandise is available for market demand. With a push, products are sent to the market that consumers may not want.
18. to strengthen the competitive position of the U.S. soft goods chain against imported goods
19. high school equivalency programs, continuing education courses, college tuition assistance, on-site child care centers, tutors for school-age children, counseling services, substance abuse rehabilitation programs, flexible work hours
20. They often lead local efforts on recycling, waste minimization, planting trees, etc.

Student Workbook

Working with Market Share, Activity A

1. all of North America
2. the local town
3. several counties within states in the Northwest
4. Susie's Dress Shoppe
5. JCPenney
6. The Northwest Bridal Outlet
7.–15. (Student response.)

The Improving Textile/Apparel Industry, Activity D

1. a. More foreign merchandise was sold in American stores than goods made in the U.S.
   b. Many U.S. companies had failed to modernize with new equipment and technology.
   c. Some unsound financial decisions had been made, resulting in low profits.
2. high costs, low quality, and lack of trust between companies
3. The industry and all of its parts would gain strength.
4. member firms, consumers, and the U.S. economy
5. partner manufacturers to produce those same items to replenish the store's stock
6. Computers prompt their partner textile firms to automatically send more of the required goods to the apparel manufacturers.
7. because merchandise decisions are automatically made based on demand information
8. They are identical.
9. Improved focus on consumer needs, accuracy of communications, higher quality standards, and more efficient purchasing, production, and distribution.
10. making the soft goods industry more competitive, productive, and cost-effective
11. AMTEX
12. A research consortium of four Southeastern universities that provides academic research to help the U.S. textile/apparel chain be strong and competitive.
13. Crafted With Pride in U.S.A. Council (CWP)
14. environmental groups within companies that lead local efforts on recycling, waste minimization, and planting trees
15. diapers, mops, plastic wood, home insulation

Teacher's Resources

Chapter 5 Test

1. D		16. T
2. A		17. T
3. E		18. F
4. I		19. F
5. F		20. T
6. J		21. C
7. G		22. D
8. C		23. B
9. H		24. A
10. B		25. A
11. F		26. C
12. T		27. C
13. F		28. C
14. T		29. C
15. F		30. D

31. Market growth is an increase in the size of the entire market, with more products sold and higher total dollars of sales. Market share is the part of the total market controlled by a firm, usually computed by sales and indicated as a percentage of the total industry.
32. (Describe two:) Surveys ask questions to consumers via mail, telephone, or mall intercepts. Consumer panels consist of participants who keep diaries. Focus groups consist of a dozen or so people in a room with a facilitator who asks questions, shows items, or leads a discussion as company representatives watch from behind a see-through mirror/window. Computer databases are electronically formulated from consumer actions and purchases. Electronic feedback tests use computers to receive qualitative as well as quantitative information with an indicator knob.
33. Computer hardware is electronic equipment consisting of keyboards, monitors, and printers. Computer software is electronic operating systems that tell the computer to do the required procedures.

Feelings About Soft Goods Marketing

Name_____ **Date** _____ **Period** _____

In the space provided, state your opinions in a mini-essay about each of these soft goods marketing sentences.

1. I think the total market for fashion goods is getting bigger (or smaller) because _____

_____

_____

_____

_____

_____

2. In my opinion, companies in the soft goods chain know (or don't know) their customers well because _____

_____

_____

_____

_____

_____

3. If I owned a business that wanted to find out about consumer tastes and changing trends, I would have the business do the following: _____

_____

_____

_____

_____

_____

4. The technology that I think the fashion industry uses includes _____

_____

_____

_____

_____

_____

5. I think the fashion industry can improve its image by _____

_____

_____

_____

_____

_____

The Total Market Potential

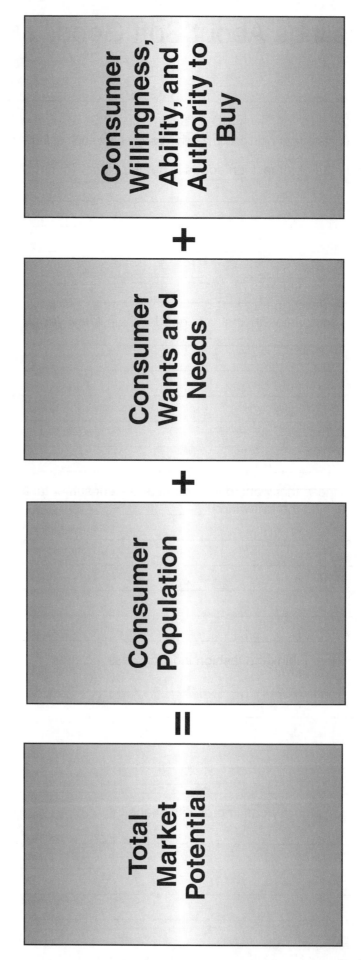

Consumer Willingness, Ability, and Authority to Buy

+

Consumer Wants and Needs

+

Consumer Population

=

Total Market Potential

Market Segmentation Categories

These are the most common types of market segmentation to identify groups of customers:

Category	Aspects	
Demographic (basic statistics)	Age Gender Race Buying power Family life cycle Nationality/Ethnicity	Education Religion Income Occupation
Psychographic (thinking patterns)	Values Lifestyle Self-concept	Attitudes Social class Personality
Geographic (physical location)	World region National region County Neighborhood Population/market density Terrain and climate	Nation State City
Behavioristic (relationship or response to products)	Brand loyalty Benefits sought Amount and type of usage	

Growth of "Megapolitan" Areas

These "megapolitan" areas have less than one-fifth of the land in the U.S.A. but contain more than two-thirds of the population. Their continued growth affects demographic and psychographic markets, especially for apparel.

Megapolitan Area	Approx. 2006 Population	Biggest City	Main Industry
Northeast (Richmond, VA up to Boston, MA)	52.5 million	New York	Finance
Midwest (Madison, WI southeast to Cincinnati, OH)	41.8 million	Chicago	Manufacturing
Southwest (Southern California east to Las Vegas)	23.3 million	Los Angeles	Entertainment
Piedmont (Birmingham, AL northeast to Raleigh, VA)	20.1 million	Atlanta	Banking and trade
I-35 Corridor (San Antonio, TX north to Kansas City, MO)	16 million	Dallas	High-tech
Mid-North California (San Francisco east to Sacramento, CA)	12.5 million	San Francisco	High-tech
Gulf Coast (Houston, TX east to Mobile, AL)	12.4 million	Houston	Energy
Peninsula (Miami north to Orlando, FL)	12.2 million	Miami	Tourism
Northwest (Eugene, OR up through Western Washington)	7.7 million	Seattle	Aerospace
Valley of the Sun (South-Central Arizona)	4.7 million	Phoenix	Home building

Based on studies done at Virginia Tech and other universities.

The What and Why of the Universal Product Code

The updated Universal Product Code (UPC-A):

- Is a 14-digit number that uniquely identifies items by vendor, style, color, and size.

- Is represented in a bar code that can be scanned quickly and easily.

- Uses versatile and practical symbology.

- Captures accurate data for computer merchandise information input.

- Can be integrated into all types of packaging and labeling.

- Is the proven marking system used throughout the soft goods chain.

- Is administered by 1SYNC, a not-for-profit company that oversees the Global Data Synchronization Network (GDSN).

- Reduces merchandise distribution and transaction time throughout the textile/apparel pipeline.

- Provides uniform merchandise information throughout the chain.

- Provides good customer service with automatic response.

- Reduces shipping, receiving, and sale transaction costs.

- Helps to keep retailers stocked with the right items in a timely manner.

Radio Frequency Identification (RFID) Blips

- RFID requires collaboration with other companies in the supply chain and the protection of privacy.

- Widespread use of RFID may take years, but it is inevitable.

- The price of RFID tags must come down to gain acceptance, and they must work reliably with RFID readers.

- RFID strategy must be implemented globally and become a "digital supply chain."

- RFID implementation must be assessed periodically, understanding that it is difficult to calculate or quantify the costs and benefits of RFID.

- EPCglobal Inc. is the standards organization that encourages the use of Electronic Product Code (EPC) technology.

- "Edgeware" or "middleware" is software that captures RFID data, interprets its content, and sends the information where it is needed. Computers are sensing and thinking.

- Item-level RFID tagging will help tremendously for product recalls, warranties, battling counterfeit products, and returns. (For instance, it identifies returned merchandise by date sold, store location, and whether or not it was stolen. It also alerts staff when shoplifting is occurring.)

- Item-level RFID tagging will allow retailers to do physical inventory in an hour or two per day and then replenish the shelves overnight.

- One privacy area is the responsibility of continuing to track garments with item-level tagging after they are sold to consumers and in use. Improvements, as well as consumer education will be needed to explain RFID's benefits and dispel misconceptions.

- In the future, item-level RFID will allow shoppers to simply walk past a scanning station with their filled cart, and all items will be automatically calculated without having to be removed. (This is already in use with toll highway transponders and gas station payments.)

- XML is the "language" of RFID data formats for structured documents and e-commerce transactions over the Internet. It is explained on www.xml.com for those who want to know more specifics about it.

Electronic Data Interchange (EDI)

What Is EDI?

Computer-to-computer transmission of business transactions between business partners

Benefits

- Cuts paperwork costs
- Improves cash flow
- Reduces inventory levels and carrying costs
- Eliminates errors from rekeying
- Decreases markdowns
- Just-in-time inventory
- Increases business volumes without increasing clerical staff

This is now moving toward Internet transmissions where registered users log onto Web sites to activate transactions with business partners.

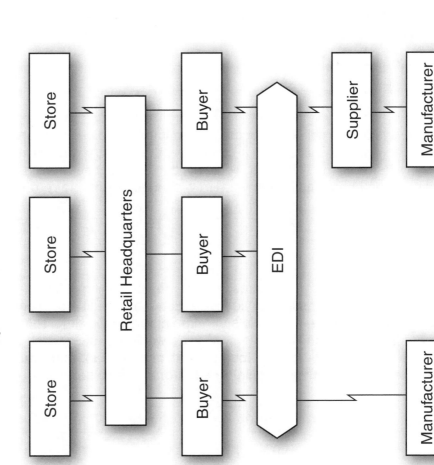

Adapted from IBM Information Services

Quick Response Discussion

Name_____ Date _____ Period _____

From its inception in the mid-1980s until it gained widespread use in the 1990s, there was slow acceptance of the Quick Response program by many firms in the textile/apparel pipeline. In the space provided, express your thoughts about **problems the Quick Response program had to overcome** in order for the industry to gain excellence. Then discuss each point as a class, knowing that QR is now a successful program.

1. For many decades, buyer/seller segments of the soft goods chain had been adversaries. Buyers at the next step in the chain had always tried to get the highest quality at the very lowest prices from companies in the previous segment. Sellers had tried to sell the lowest quality at the highest price to those in the next segment. Companies sought the products from whomever they could get the "best deal." However, **the success of Quick Response depends on trusting relationships between partners in the textile/apparel pipeline.** _____

_____

_____

2. Company sales figures, garment designs, and marketing plans had always been proprietary information, never to be revealed to outside individuals, and especially not to go into the information systems of other companies! This new Quick Response program was asking them to directly link their information systems with companies backward and forward in the soft goods chain so everyone would have access to certain information. **There was a great fear of loss of privacy.**

_____

_____

_____

3. It had always been a challenge for companies to get good prices when selling their products, cover their expenses, and end up with a profit. Now the industry was asking them to spend a lot more money with "the chance" that they would get that amount back in higher sales within several years. **It was a large initial capital investment with a questionable return.** _____

_____

_____

_____

4. Companies had always placed large orders at the beginning of the season to cover their estimated needs for the entire season—textile mills ordered a lot of fibers, apparel manufacturers order lots of fabrics, and retailers ordered lots of garments. With Quick Response, firms were supposed to only order a small amount to see how sales would go, after which items would be replenished automatically. **This presented a loss of control and a risk that future merchandise items and timing depends on others providing additional future supply.** _____

_____

_____

_____

(Continued)

Name_____

5. As computers had been slowly installed into companies during the beginnings of electronics, different companies had acquired very different systems to do their work. However, the success of Quick Response depends on company systems being able to communicate with each other automatically. **Standardization and integration of technologies was hard to put together from the fragmented structure of the industry.** _____

_____

_____

6. After doing business procedures a certain way for many years, Quick Response requires new computer transaction skills for employees at all levels. This also requires a different type of company management that supports an emphasis on technology. **A sudden need for high-tech personnel had to be satisfied.**_____

_____

_____

7. Previously, companies that did business together could drop each other and add others if the relationship was somehow unsatisfactory. Suppliers had to provide dependable quality, timely deliveries of goods, and satisfactory service. If they didn't, companies would buy from different suppliers next time. **With Quick Response, long-term trading partners have to be identified and agreements established.** _____

_____

_____

8. Previously, companies could choose their suppliers in a very open, competitive market. However, with long-term Quick Response partnerships being established, the goods of some suppliers became unavailable or at the lowest priority level (since automatic replenishment for partners is mandatory) to companies that were not yet a part of the new system. **Small companies outside the QR system might have a harder time getting their orders.** _____

_____

_____

9. If sufficient industry-wide cooperation for the new, "revolutionary" QR program did not evolve, it would not make any improvement to the competitiveness of the U.S. industry against imports from other countries. For a positive impact, **a committed "critical mass" is needed for QR through the commitment of companies industry-wide.** _____

_____

_____

10. Finally, **what if the system goes down?** _____

_____

_____

Push and Pull Comparison

Considerations	Push (production-driven approach)	Pull (market-driven approach)
Attitudes toward customers	They should be glad we are trying to make products for them.	Their needs determine company plans.
Products offered	The company sells what it can make.	The company makes what it can sell.
Role of market research	If used—to determine customer reaction	To determine customer wants/needs and how well the company is satisfying them
Interest in information	Only used for technology and cost-cutting	A critical objective in order to satisfy customer wants/needs
Focus of advertising	Concentrates on product features and quality	Shows how products satisfy wanted/needed benefits
Role of packaging	Used merely as protection for the product	Designed for customer convenience and a selling tool
Inventory levels	Set with production requirements in mind	Set with customer requirements and costs in mind
Transportation arrangements	Use cheapest way of storing and moving	Efficient for good customer service
Importance of profit	The residual left after costs are covered	A critical objective that accompanies pleasing the customer
Role of customer credit	Viewed as a necessary evil	Viewed as a customer service

Satisfying the Fashion Market

Name_____

Date_____**Period**_____ **Score**_____

Chapter 5 Test

Matching: Match the following terms and identifying phrases.

_____ 1. Groups of computer components that work together by combining collection, classification, storage, retrieval, and dissemination of data toward a certain outcome.

_____ 2. Product codes with dark bars and white spaces of varying widths, used on merchandise tags for electronic data collection.

_____ 3. Dividing the total market into smaller groups that contain similar characteristics.

_____ 4. Statistics that try to explain consumer behavior through such variables as lifestyle, values, attitudes, and self-concept.

_____ 5. The hiring of independent specialists to do particular work rather than using company employees.

_____ 6. An industry-wide program that ties together the entire textile/apparel pipeline using barcode data, EDI technology, and long-term customer-supplier partnerships.

_____ 7. Computer components from different suppliers that are compatible with one another to be mixed and matched.

_____ 8. The exchange of information and transactions through computer linkages between companies, using an understood digital format.

_____ 9. The process of carrying a product idea through stages from initial conceptualization to actual appearance in the market.

_____ 10. Vital statistics of human populations, broken down by such factors as age, gender, race, education, religion, income, and occupation.

A. bar codes

B. demographics

C. electronic data interchange (EDI)

D. information systems

E. market segmentation

F. outsourcing

G. open systems

H. product development

I. psychographics

J. Quick Response

True/False: Circle *T* if the statement is true or *F* if the statement is false.

T   F   11. The company with the largest market share usually has the highest per-item costs.

T   F   12. The most popular methods to segment markets are with demographics and psychographics.

T   F   13. Production-driven (push) manufacturing takes advantage of the information pipeline.

(Continued)

Name_____

T   F   14. "Green" products are produced in an environmentally friendly way.

T   F   15. Proprietary information is available to the public and usually in the reference section of libraries.

T   F   16. When a communication program or device is interactive, it reacts to people's responses.

T   F   17. The Universal Product Code (UPC), or standard bar code, has been updated to UPC-A that includes numbers as well as bars and spaces.

T   F   18. Bar codes are read electronically by bar code printers that feed information into the computer.

T   F   19. RFID means "reader for identification data."

T   F   20. Product code scanning has diminished the number of errors of previous incorrect human data entry.

Multiple Choice: Choose the best response. Write the letter in the space provided.

_____ 21. Target marketing is _____.
A. trying to serve all consumers in the market in the best possible ways
B. selling products to the broadest possible part of the market to make the most profit
C. defining the specialized niche of the market to whom the company wishes to make its greatest appeal
D. trying to target competition that beat them by using strategic tactics

_____ 22. Today's consumer market _____.
A. has more relaxed social patterns, requiring more casual apparel
B. wants easier care for their garments as well as quality and value
C. is aging, but remaining more active and living to an older age
D. All of the above.

_____ 23. Market research is the _____.
A. study of business practices and policies concerning markets
B. process of systematically gathering and analyzing information relating to particular markets
C. publishing of laboratory data about new fibers and fabrics
D. All of the above.

_____ 24. Qualitative information shows _____.
A. what products the customers want
B. how strongly the customers want certain products
C. why the customers want certain products
D. which customers want the most products

_____ 25. Findings from market research are used to _____.
A. correct current market problems and capture new market opportunities
B. establish outsourcing relationships
C. verify if partnerships have been established with too many suppliers
D. establish companies' market growth compared to competitors

(Continued)

Name_____

_____ 26. Product development for apparel manufacturers is _____.
   A. developing new fibers or fabric characteristics to meet specific needs in the market
   B. stocking specific up-to-date merchandise in stores and providing new customer services
   C. designing and producing garments that are predicted to be in demand when they "hit the stores"
   D. All of the above.

_____ 27. Product codes that companies use should be verified to meet industry "compliance" issues so _____.
   A. the data "captured" by checkout readers will match data on the receipt given to the customer
   B. apparel producers can be prepared for an aging market
   C. the bar codes are acceptable to other companies as the goods move through the soft goods chain
   D. market research can be able to segment the market into target categories

_____ 28. Magnetic stripes _____.
   A. allow computers to respond to human voices for data input and/or operating commands
   B. have a small microprocessor embedded in the plastic with data that can be read electronically
   C. are along the back edge of credit cards to be run through reading devices
   D. use video cameras to read bar codes or identify a product through its "signature"

_____ 29. Social responsibility is _____.
   A. cooperative interaction of parts for a total effect greater than its parts
   B. working together in an endeavor, collaborating to assist each other
   C. going beyond what is legal, to do what helps society
   D. All of the above.

_____ 30. The Textile/Clothing Technology Corporation, [TC]^2, _____.
   A. is a not-for-profit industry-wide organization
   B. is a coalition of textile, apparel, and retail firms, government, academia, and labor/trade organizations
   C. operates an apparel and related sewn-products production facility in Cary, NC
   D. All of the above.

Essay Questions: Provide complete responses to the following questions or statements.

31. Explain the difference between market growth and growth in market share.

32. Describe at least two methods of doing market research.

33. Briefly explain computer hardware and computer software.

Textile/Apparel
Building Blocks

CHAPTER **6**

Textile Fibers and Yarns

Objectives

After studying this chapter, students will be able to

- list the main characteristics of natural and manufactured fibers.
- explain how fibers are marketed.
- summarize the role of leather and fur as primary materials in fashion.
- describe new fiber innovations.
- explain how fibers are made into yarns.

Teaching Materials

Text, pages 104–125
  Fashion Terms
  Fashion Review
  Fashion in Action
Student Workbook
  A. *Fiber Information*
  B. *Associate with an Association*
  C. *Merchandising with Fibers*
  D. *Textile Fiber and Yarn Review Match*
Teacher's Resources
  What Are Textile Fibers and Yarns? reproducible master 6-1
  Wool Fibers, transparency master 6-2
  How Many Cashmere Goats Per Garment? transparency master 6-3
  Characteristics of Manufactured Fibers, reproducible master 6-4
  Why It Is Difficult for Companies to Enter the Manufactured Fibers Industry, transparency master 6-5
  Difficulties of Fiber Innovation, transparency master 6-6
  Life Cycle of EcoSpun®, transparency master 6-7

The EcoTherm™ Process, transparency master 6-8
Fibers and Yarns Under the Microscope, transparency master 6-9
Examples of Textured Yarns, transparency master 6-10
Chapter 6 Test

Introductory Activities

1. *What Are Textile Fibers and Yarns?* reproducible master 6-1. As a discussion starter, ask students to answer the provided questions as best they can. After students have worked on this independently, use it for discussion. As the discussion progresses, reinforce ideas that are correct. For incorrect responses, explain to the students that they will learn the facts in this chapter.
2. Discuss why the earliest planning of textile/apparel color and texture must take place at the primary level.
3. Discuss why fashion merchandisers should be familiar with the different fibers and their characteristics and properties.

Strategies to Reteach, Reinforce, Enrich, and Extend Text Concepts

Natural Fibers

4. **RT** Discuss the differences between cellulosic natural fibers and protein natural fibers. Have students give examples of each.

5. **RT** Discuss the differences between staple fibers and filament fibers.

6. **ER** Order or download some of the fact-filled educational booklets, charts, teaching kits, and audio visual aids from the National Cotton Council (www.cotton.org/pubs/cottoncounts/resources.cfm). Share them with the class. Also check materials on the "list of other cotton related educational sites" at the bottom of that Web page.

7. **EX** Show students a video about the growing and processing of cotton all the way to becoming finished denim. *Cotton Production* is available (as well as a Study Guide) from The Curriculum Center for Family and Consumer Sciences. *Field Trip: Cotton Production* is available from D.E. Visuals.

8. **ER** Obtain materials that tell about the history of the wool fiber, the various stages of wool production, and wool's characteristics. *Wool...A Natural*, the chart *Wool Fiber in the Making*, and the book *The Pendleton Story* are all available from Pendleton Woolen Mills. Packets, posters, samples, and videos can also be obtained from the American Wool Council (www.sheepusa.org and the "ASI materials").

9. **EX** *Wool Fibers*, transparency master 6-2. Use this transparency to show students the physical structure of the wool fiber, which allows it to have resiliency. Also explain the difference between long and short staple wool fibers for more expensive, smoother worsted fabrics and less expensive, fuzzier woolen fabrics.

10. **RT** Have the class discuss why silk is considered to be a specialty fiber. Have students define *sericin*, *weighted silk*, *tussah*, and other silk terms.

11. **EX** Ask students to investigate why silk is less expensive now than it was in the past. (Possible responses might be better and more mechanized production methods and quantity retailing through mail-order, which has made silk more accessible to consumers.)

12. **RF** Have students discuss the similarities and differences among the four main natural fibers. Stress the fiber advantages and disadvantages for particular types of fashion items.

13. **EX** *How Many Cashmere Goats Per Garment?* transparency master 6-3. While showing this transparency to the class, have students discuss why specialty hair fibers are usually expensive, especially considering that there are limited quantities of these animals. Have students do some research to find out when, how, and from where cashmere and camel hair are obtained.

14. **ER** Obtain the latest Annual Report from Cotton Incorporated (www.cottoninc.com). Pass it around the class for students to look at. Have them note all the organization's marketing efforts, programs, and research. Also, point out (at the back of the report) the many members of the board of directors, as well as a budget of about $75 million. Also try to obtain information about Cotton Incorporated's latest promotional campaigns.

15. **ER** Obtain materials from the Wool Bureau, Inc. (www.wool.com and then "sitemap") to show students the forecasting, marketing, and other information provided by this trade group. These types of materials are distributed regularly to those who produce and/or sell wool products.

16. **EX** Have materials sent from the Mohair Council of America, International Silk Association, and International Linen Promotion Commission. Thoroughly discuss them with the class.

17. **RF** Show the class a PowerPoint CD of 257 magnified images of natural fibers. Volume 1 of *Digital Textiles* is available from D.E. Visuals.

Leather and Fur

18. **EX** Have students read more about leather processing and leather apparel. The following books can be obtained from the Shoe Trades Publishing Company (or may be available from the library*): Complete Handbook of Leathercrafting; Leather Clothing, Its Manufacture and Maintenance; Theory and Practice of Leather Manufacture*; and *Physical Chemistry of Leather Making*.

19. **ER** Show students a video about leather production and how leather is used in fashion goods. *Leather: The Material That Combines Fashion and Function* is available from D.E. Visuals.

20. **EX** Discuss and debate the controversy surrounding use of leather and fur for fashion items.

21. **ER** Obtain information from the many Web sites that deal with leather and fur. A few are: www.leatherassociation.com, www.leatherdirectory.com, www.leather-fur.com, www.furs-.com, www.furtrade.org, and www.furcommission.com.

22. **RT** Explain the three segments of the fur industry: animal pelt producers, fur processors, and product manufacturers. Also discuss with the class how fur fashions are sold at the retail level.

Manufactured Fibers

23. **RT** Have students define *manufactured fibers*, including a description of cellulosic and noncellulosic types. Also have students describe the three main steps in producing manufactured fibers.

24. **RF** From a mixed list of generic groups and variant trade names, have students tell which are generics and which are variants. Also have students explain how they can tell which is which.

25. **RT** Discuss with the class the effects that fibers have on the characteristics of finished fabrics and end-use products.

26. **RF** *Characteristics of Manufactured Fibers*, reproducible master 6-4. Students are asked to mark the appropriate squares that show the properties of the manufactured fibers listed. This might be good as a homework assignment to make sure students are familiar with the information in text illustration 6-26.

27. **RF** Divide the students into two teams. Have the teams stand on opposite sides of the classroom. The team that starts should give the name of a manufactured fiber generic group. The other team (with members consulting with each other, but without looking in the text) should then name at least two variants in that generic group, two advantages of the fibers, two disadvantages, and two typical apparel uses. After giving the answers, that team will give the name of a different generic group for which the other team must provide the information. This should continue with alternating turns until all generic groups have been covered.

28. **ER** Hold a class discussion about how the six main characteristics of fabrics (texture, strength, shrinkage, warmth, absorbency, and durability) depend on each fabric's fiber content. Have the students look up and write down the definitions of the characteristics so they understand what is being discussed.

29. **EX** Obtain the latest version of the *Textile World Manmade Fiber Chart* from *Textile World Magazine*. Share its information with students and discuss the general meaning of the scientific data presented.

30. **ER** Show students a video about natural and manufactured fibers. *Textiles* is available from Cambridge Educational, D.E. Visuals, and Insight Media. *Clothing Fibers* is available from the Learning Seed, Insight Media, The Curriculum Center for Family and Consumer Sciences, VMS, Inc., and D.E. Visuals. *Fibers—Manufactured and Natural* is available from Meridian Education Corporation and D.E. Visuals.

31. **RT** Discuss with the class why branded specialty fibers are produced in smaller amounts and command a premium price, while commodity fibers are produced in large amounts for more common textile products.

32. **RF** Discuss with the class how petroleum prices impact apparel costs because polyester and nylon fibers and other petrochemical raw materials for apparel manufacturing are based on supplies and prices of crude oil.

33. **RF** *Fiber Information*, Activity A, WB. Students are to answer questions about natural and manufactured fibers. All the answers can be found in the content of the chapter.

34. **ER** *Why It Is Difficult for Companies to Enter the Manufactured Fibers Industry*, transparency master 6-5. While showing this to the class, discuss each point from the standpoint of a new firm trying to become a manufactured fiber company.

35. **ER** *Difficulties of Fiber Innovation*, transparency master 6-6. While showing this transparency to the class, have students discuss each bulleted item.

36. **ER** Obtain materials from the American Fiber Manufacturers Association to share with the class. Have students watch the video *Manufactured Fibers*. Have them check out AFMA's Web site, www.fibersource.com, as well as www.fabriclink.com, www.lycra.com, and others they might find on the Internet.

37. **RF** Show the class a PowerPoint CD of 242 images of manufactured fibers. Volume 2 of *Digital Textiles* is available from D.E. Visuals.

38. **RT** *Life Cycle of EcoSpun®*, transparency master 6-7. Use this transparency to illustrate how beverage containers can be transformed into polyester for garments.

39. **RT** *The EcoTherm™ Process*, transparency master 6-8. Use this transparency to reinforce the students' knowledge of how manufactured fibers are produced while showing the results of combining innovation with a concern for the environment.

40. **RT** Explain how fiber denier affects the final textile products. Conclude by discussing the attributes of microdeniers.

41. **RF** Discuss with students that almost all fibers (natural and manufactured) have trade associations that promote their fibers with logos. Bring examples of these to display in the classroom.

42. **RT** Have students find examples of cooperative advertising (within the textile/apparel pipeline if possible). Have them show their examples to the rest of the class and explain who the cooperating sponsors are.

43. **RF** *Merchandising with Fibers*, Activity C, WB. Students are asked to mount two pictures of apparel items made from different natural fibers and two from different manufactured fibers. Then they should write down the characteristics of each fiber that make it good for that use and compare their pictures with those of other class members.

Spinning Fibers into Yarns

44. **RT** *Fibers and Yarns Under the Microscope*, transparency master 6-9. Use this as an overhead or reproduce it to distribute to the students. Thoroughly discuss each of the four examples that are shown.

45. **ER** Have students make a bulletin board that shows and labels examples of natural fibers, manufactured fibers, and yarns.

46. **RF** *Examples of Textured Yarns*, transparency master 6-10. As you show this overhead, discuss how texturing adds bulk, stretch, softness, and wrinkle-resistance to yarns.

47. **RT** Have students use an interactive CD. *The Basics of Yarn Manufacturing* is available from Cotton Incorporated.

48. **ER** *Associate with an Association*, Activity B, WB. Students are asked to research a fiber or yarn trade association in the library or on the Internet. They are then to complete the provided information sheet and share the information in an oral report to the class.

49. **RF** Show the class a PowerPoint CD of 130 images of yarns. Volume 3 of *Digital Textiles* is available from D.E. Visuals.

50. **ER** Obtain materials from the American Yarn Spinners Association (AYSA, www.textileweb.com) to share with students.

51. **RF** *Textile Fiber and Yarn Review Match*, Activity D, WB. Students are asked to match fiber and yarn terms with their definitions.

Additional Enrichment Activities

Research

52. Have students do research on a manufactured fiber of their choice. They should prepare an oral or written report about the fiber's history, characteristics, production, uses, and how variants have been named.

53. Have students trace the history of textiles from their beginnings to the present day. Have students draw a "textiles time line" that shows events in textile history to the correct dates. Then discuss the very slow changes for past centuries and the accelerated changes of today. Besides using resources in the library or on the Internet, many textile companies offer promotional materials about the development of their fibers. Fiber trade associations also offer accounts of textile history. Find out about the American Textile History Museum in Massachusetts at Web site www.athm.org. Finally, the students may want to watch the video *Textiles: Birth of an American Industry*, available from Insight Media.

54. Have students conduct research in the library or on the Internet about one of the latest developments in textile technology. Examples might be the production of naturally colored cotton; the new wool that is washable, light-weight, and non-itchy; polyester made from recycled soda bottles; manufactured fibers made from genetically-engineered corn, soybeans, seaweed, etc.; and extrusion of manufactured fibers in various shapes for different characteristics. Have students report their findings to the class.

Projects

55. Have students visit a fabric store and compare prices of various fabrics made from the different natural and manufactured fibers.

56. If materials have not already been obtained, have students contact one of the many fiber or yarn trade associations to request their materials. While they wait for the materials to arrive, they should do library and/or Internet research about the association. After they have received and organized their materials into an interesting and informative format, have them share them with the class.

57. Invite a craftsperson to class who uses a spinning wheel to spin yarn from fibers. Have the person demonstrate how the fibers are twisted and pulled together as they are spun into a strong, continuous piece of yarn from which fabrics can be knitted or woven.

Text

Fashion Review, page 125

1. textiles (fibers, yarns, fabrics), leathers, and furs
2. to provide the right products for their target market
3. staple (name one:) cotton, wool, linen; filament: silk
4. It is comfortable to wear and easy to dye.
5. It is springy and returns to its original shape when stretched or wrinkled.
6. It is expensive to produce, has limited durability, and needs special care.
7. sample fabrics for the upcoming fashion season (that show new textile styling and color trends, and information about suppliers, cost, and new textile developments)
8. cotton: Cotton Incorporated (or the National Cotton Council); wool: Wool Bureau, Inc.; silk: International Silk Association, and flax: International Linen Promotion Commission
9. because their supply is limited and their processing is complicated
10. the demand for meat since the hides are a by-product of the meatpacking industry
11. animal pelt producers, fur processors, product manufacturers
12. because they are produced by chemical companies and essentially require only raw materials, power, and labor
13. It pulls body moisture to the surface of the fabric where it can evaporate.
14. between laboratory engineering and mass production
15. solution spinning
16. They are soft, luxurious, and drapable. They are also wrinkle-resistant, wind-resistant, and water-repellent, yet breathable.
17. spandex
18. more than one organization, such as a fiber company, an apparel manufacturer, and/or a retailer
19. Monofilament yarns are simply one filament, usually of a high denier; multifilament yarns are many filaments twisted together to make a thicker strand; spun yarns are made by mechanically spinning staple fibers into a continuous strand.
20. Blends are made when two or more fibers are put together before being spun into yarn; combination yarns contain two or more yarn plys, each of different fibers.

Student Workbook

Fiber Information, Activity A

1. a. cellulosic fibers from plants
   b. protein fibers from animals or insects
2. the type of plant or animal and the growing conditions
3. cleaning, straightening, grading, sorting, combing
4. cotton—from the boll of the cotton plant
   linen—from the stem of the flax plant
   wool—from the fleece of sheep
   silk—from the cocoon of silkworms
5. seed pods of cotton plants
6. because they tend to shrink and wrinkle
7. the breed and health of the sheep, climate where raised, and where on the sheep's body the fibers originate
8. Nothing—there is no difference.
9. none
10. flax (linen)
11. a cellulosic fiber from the stalks of a woody-leafed plant called China grass
12. (List five:) camel hair, angora, mohair, cashmere, llama, vicuña, alpaca
13. cellulosic—from regenerated plants; noncellulosic—from petrochemicals
14. a. Solid raw materials are melted with heat or dissolved by chemicals to form a thick, syrupy liquid.
    b. The liquid is extruded through a spinneret to form filament fibers.
    c. The filaments are stretched and hardened to become usable fibers.
15. only when a fiber is developed that is different in chemical composition from other fibers
16. to identify the fibers with that company
17. They can be heat-treated to set pleats, mold shape, or emboss fabric designs.
18. They feel clammy and build up static electricity that causes them to "spark" and cling to the wearer.
19. because it is environmentally friendly
20. because of promotional campaigns (advertising and publicity) by chemical companies that produce fibers
21. It is the farthest from the final selling to consumers and time must be allowed for many complicated production processes before the products are finished.
22. to get the best performance features of each

Textile Fiber and Yarn Review

Match, Activity D

1. G	8. D	15. L
2. O	9. F	16. E
3. J	10. A	17. R
4. N	11. P	18. H
5. T	12. K	19. S
6. B	13. M	20. Q
7. I	14. C	

1. RR	8. MM	15. LL
2. II	9. HH	16. EE
3. SS	10. DD	17. JJ
4. CC	11. TT	18. PP
5. GG	12. FF	19. BB
6. QQ	13. OO	20. NN
7. AA	14. KK	

Teacher's Resources

Characteristics of Manufactured Fibers, reproducible master 6-4

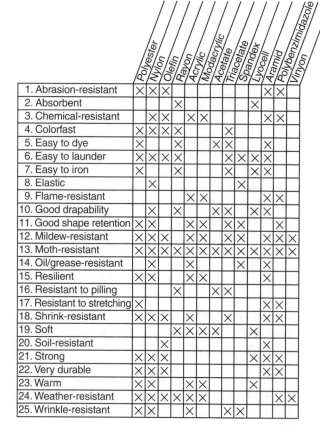

	Polyester	Nylon	Olefin	Rayon	Acrylic	Modacrylic	Acetate	Triacetate	Spandex	Lyocell	Aramid	Polybenzimidazole	Vinyon
1. Abrasion-resistant	X	X	X								X	X	
2. Absorbent				X					X				
3. Chemical-resistant		X	X		X	X					X	X	
4. Colorfast	X	X	X	X			X						
5. Easy to dye	X			X		X	X			X			
6. Easy to launder	X	X	X	X				X	X	X	X		
7. Easy to iron	X			X				X		X	X		
8. Elastic		X							X				
9. Flame-resistant					X	X					X	X	
10. Good drapability		X		X			X	X		X	X		
11. Good shape retention	X	X			X	X			X	X		X	
12. Mildew-resistant	X	X	X		X	X			X	X	X	X	X
13. Moth-resistant	X	X	X	X	X	X	X	X	X	X	X	X	X
14. Oil/grease-resistant		X		X					X		X		
15. Resilient	X	X			X	X					X		
16. Resistant to pilling				X			X	X					
17. Resistant to stretching	X										X	X	
18. Shrink-resistant	X	X	X		X		X				X	X	
19. Soft				X	X	X	X			X			
20. Soil-resistant			X							X			
21. Strong	X	X	X								X	X	X
22. Very durable	X	X	X								X	X	
23. Warm	X	X			X	X				X			
24. Weather-resistant	X	X	X	X	X	X						X	X
25. Wrinkle-resistant	X	X			X		X	X					

Chapter 6 Test

1. E		16. T	
2. A		17. F	
3. F		18. T	
4. B		19. T	
5. J		20. T	
6. C		21. B	
7. H		22. D	
8. D		23. B	
9. I		24. C	
10. G		25. A	
11. T		26. C	
12. F		27. C	
13. T		28. A	
14. T		29. A	
15. F		30. C	

31. Animal pelt producers breed and raise the animals on fur farms or ranches. Fur processors "dress" (clean, stretch, dye) the pelts to make them soft, flexible, and more suitable for use in consumer products. Product manufacturers make the pelts into finished coats, jackets, garment trimmings, and accessories.

32. (1) Solid raw materials are melted with heat or dissolved by chemicals to form a thick, syrupy liquid. (2) The liquid is extruded through a spinneret to form filament fiber. (3) The filaments are stretched and hardened to become usable fibers.

33. Denier describes fiber (usually filament) thickness or diameter. Higher numbers indicate thicker threads. Microdeniers are ultra-fine (about half the denier of fine silk) manufactured fibers. They are soft, luxurious, and drapable. Fabrics made from them are wrinkle-resistant, wind-resistant, and water-repellent, yet breathable. They are used primarily in rainwear and active sportswear.

What Are Textile Fibers and Yarns?

Name_____ **Date** _____ **Period** _____

Think about the following questions and give the most complete answer you can. You are not expected to know all the answers, but your thoughts combined in a discussion with others should result in ideas and discoveries that will be learned about in this chapter.

1. From where do you think textile fibers come? _____
   _____
   _____
   _____

2. List the names of at least three different fibers. _____
   _____
   _____
   _____

3. What fibers do you think are present in the clothes you are wearing? _____
   _____
   _____
   _____

4. What other materials (besides fibers) are used to make apparel? _____
   _____
   _____
   _____

5. How do you think research and development can improve the characteristics of fibers? _____
   _____
   _____
   _____

6. How are textile fibers made into yarns? _____
   _____
   _____
   _____

7. What types of marketing do you think is done for fibers and yarns? _____
   _____
   _____
   _____

8. Why are textile fibers and yarns referred to as textile/apparel building blocks? _____
   _____
   _____
   _____

Wool Fibers

**Physical structure
of the wool fiber:**

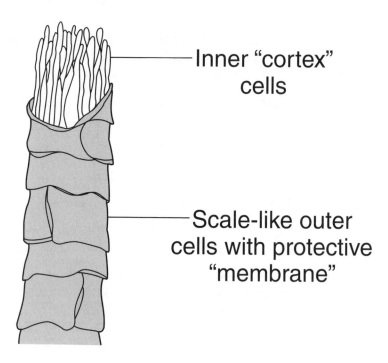

Inner "cortex"
cells

Scale-like outer
cells with protective
"membrane"

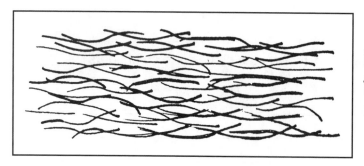

Long staple, combed wool
fibers for high-quality
worsted yarns and fabrics

Short staple, looser wool
fibers for less expensive
woolen fabrics

How Many Cashmere Goats Per Garment?

The following number of goats must be sheared for the fleece to go into these garments:

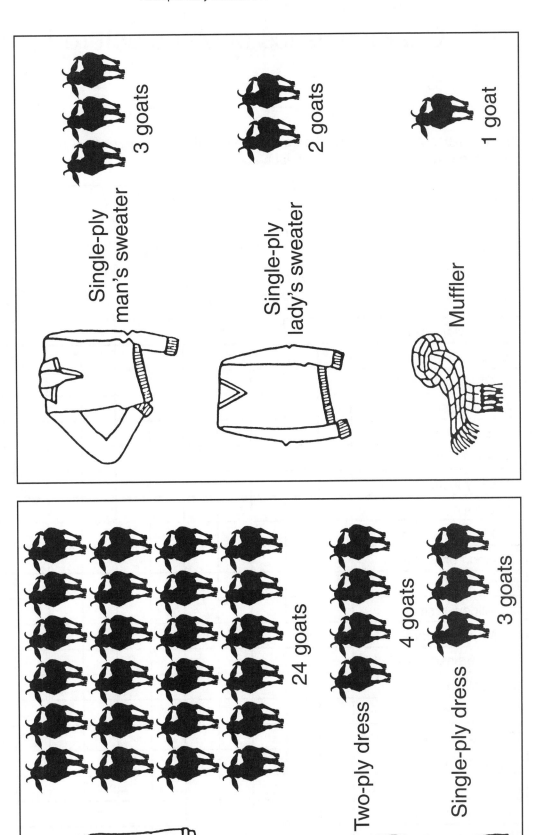

Single-ply man's sweater — 3 goats

Single-ply lady's sweater — 2 goats

Muffler — 1 goat

Coat — 24 goats

Two-ply dress — 4 goats

Single-ply dress — 3 goats

Characteristics of Manufactured Fibers

Name_____ Date _____ Period _____

Characteristics of manufactured fibers are listed in the following chart. Put an "X" in each appropriate box to show the typical properties of each fiber.

	Polyester	Nylon	Olefin	Rayon	Acrylic	Modacrylic	Acetate	Triacetate	Spandex	Lyocell	Aramid	Polybenzimidazole	Vinyon
1. Abrasion-resistant													
2. Absorbent													
3. Chemical-resistant													
4. Colorfast													
5. Easy to dye													
6. Easy to launder													
7. Easy to iron													
8. Elastic													
9. Flame-resistant													
10. Good drapability													
11. Good shape retention													
12. Mildew-resistant													
13. Moth-resistant													
14. Oil/grease-resistant													
15. Resilient													
16. Resistant to pilling													
17. Resistant to stretching													
18. Shrink-resistant													
19. Soft													
20. Soil-resistant													
21. Strong													
22. Very durable													
23. Warm													
24. Weather-resistant													
25. Wrinkle-resistant													

Why It Is Difficult for Companies to Enter the Manufactured Fibers Industry

- High financial investment is needed because it is a capital-intensive industry.

- A high level of technical knowledge is needed.

- The industry is very competitive, with lots of producers.

- There are low profit margins on basic products. Thus, either large production runs of commodities are needed or expertise to identify market niches plus the flexibility to satisfy them quickly.

- Fibers must be suited to end-uses because specific manufactured fibers are not designed for multiple uses.

- Companies must do multilevel marketing and assistance (industrial through consumer) since success of the final product depends on processors later in the chain.

- High research and development expenditures are needed to stay in the marketplace since innovations and technologies move so quickly.

Difficulties of Fiber Innovation

- The introduction of a new generic fiber is very expensive.

- Low profit margins give limited money to absorb costs of innovation.

- Polymer chemistry has limited variables.

- For success, improvements must be additive rather than at the expense of present fiber properties.

- It is hard to accurately assess the marketability of a new product.

- A new fiber may have a shorter life span and a smaller volume being used than the older fiber it replaced.

- A new fiber may quickly become obsolete and be replaced by an even newer fiber before it can establish itself in the market.

- Company reorganization may be needed to accommodate the new fiber.

- A new fiber could reduce the need for an industry segment and cause unemployment.

Life Cycle of EcoSpun®

Source: Wellman, Inc.

1. Plastic beverage bottles are recycled by consumers across the country.

2. The bottles are sorted by type and color, crushed, and chopped into flakes.

3. The tiny flakes are liquefied.

4. The liquid is extruded through a spinneret, creating fibers that are stretched for strength. They are crimped, cut, and baled.

5. Fabric is made by knitting or weaving, and then made into garments and home fashion products.

The EcoTherm™ Process

1. Consumer recycles plastic.

2. Recycled bottles are washed and chopped into flakes.

3. Flakes are converted to pellets

4. Schuller uses pellets to make Micro-Fiber™.

5. Fibers are converted into EcoTherm™ insulation blanket.

6. Apparel manufacturers insulate products with EcoTherm™.

7. Insulated apparel is shipped to retailer.

8. Consumer purchases new apparel insulated with EcoTherm™.

Source: Schuller International

Fibers and Yarns Under the Microscope

Continuous Monofilament

Multifilament Yarn

Staple Fibers

Staple Yarn

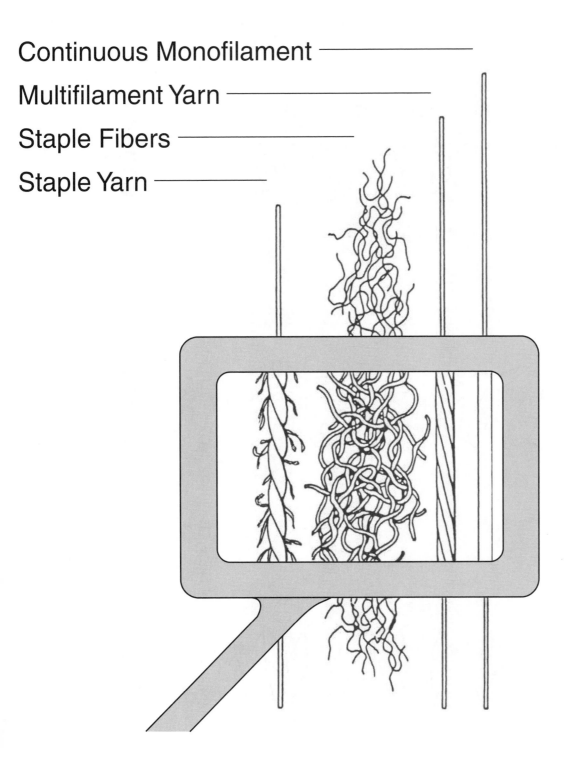

A yarn from staple fibers has fiber ends sticking out from it.
It is "fuzzier" than a yarn made from filament fibers.

Example of Textured Yarns

Looped

Coiled

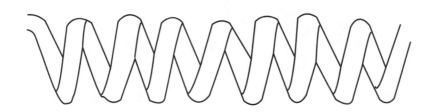

Crimped

Textile Fibers and Yarns

Name_____

Date_____ **Period**_____ **Score**_____

.

Chapter 6 Test

Matching: Match the following terms and identifying phrases.

_____ 1. Chain-like chemical structures of molecules from which many manufactured fibers are made.

_____ 2. Cotton, linen, rayon, acetate, and triacetate.

_____ 3. Wool, silk, and specialty hair fibers.

_____ 4. Long, fine, continuous threads found naturally as silk, or continuously extruded when manufactured.

_____ 5. Manufactured fibers modified slightly within their generic groups, resulting in changes in the properties of the fibers.

_____ 6. Identifications of families of manufactured fibers, categorized according to similar chemical compositions.

_____ 7. Short lengths of natural fibers or of filament fibers that have been cut.

_____ 8. Each strand of yarn in yarn with many strands.

_____ 9. Manufactured fibers or yarns processed with chemicals, heat, or special machinery to add visual surface characteristics (such as bulk or stretch).

_____ 10. The process of drawing, twisting, and winding individual fibers into long, cohesive strands of yarns.

A. cellulosic fibers

B. filament fibers

C. generic groups

D. ply

E. polymers

F. protein fibers

G. spinning

H. staple fibers

I. textured

J. variants

True/False: Circle *T* if the statement is true or *F* if the statement is false.

T F 11. The earliest planning of color and texture takes place at the primary level.

T F 12. The most popular fiber worldwide is spandex.

T F 13. Long staple wool fibers go into high quality worsted yarns and fabrics.

T F 14. When a fiber is resilient, it is springy and returns to its original shape when stretched or wrinkled.

T F 15. Wool is the only filament natural fiber.

T F 16. Fabric made from the flax fiber is called linen.

T F 17. The process that converts animal hides into finished, usable leather is called graining.

(Continued)

Name_____

T   F   18. Because manufactured fibers are made by chemical companies rather than by nature, there can be a constant supply of stable inventories of uniform size and quality.

T   F   19. Innovation is the creative, forward-thinking introduction of new ideas.

T   F   20. Missionary selling is convincing customers that they need a product before trying to sell it to them.

Multiple Choice: Choose the best response. Write the letter in the space provided.

_____ 21. Fibers can be divided into the two main groups of _____.
A. leathers and furs
B. natural and manufactured
C. expensive and cheap
D. spun and extruded

_____ 22. The quality of wool fibers depends on _____.
A. the breed and health of the sheep
B. the climate where the sheep are raised
C. where on the sheep's bodies the fibers originate
D. All of the above.

_____ 23. Down is _____.
A. a cellulosic fiber from the stalks of a woody-leafed plant called China grass
B. lightweight and an extremely effective insulator
C. one of the least expensive fibers on the world market
D. All of the above.

_____ 24. Fabric libraries of fiber trade associations _____.
A. offer consumers a chance to read about the developments of that particular fiber
B. offer bolts of fabric made from the trade association's fiber with yardages available to home sewers
C. contain sample fabrics of that fiber for the upcoming fashion season for fashion professionals to use as a resource
D. are used as locations for that association's trade conventions and exhibitions

_____ 25. The most dominant leather used in apparel (shoes, purses, and garments) is _____.
A. cattlehide because the supply of leather depends on the demand for meat
B. eelskin because it has fashion interest as well as durability
C. reptile skins (lizards, snakes, alligators) because other types of animals are protected by law
D. goat hide because overpopulated herds throughout the world must continually be thinned

(Continued)

Name_____

_____ 26. When a retailer accepts merchandise to sell in the store, but does not own it and receives a percentage of the sale price, the arrangement is called _____.
A. leased selling
B. "faux" selling
C. consignment selling
D. synthetic selling

_____ 27. Manufactured fibers sold by a generic group and not identified with any specific manufacturer are _____.
A. polyester variants
B. staple filaments
C. commodity fibers
D. All of the above.

_____ 28. The fiber advantage of wicking is _____.
A. the dispersing or spreading of moisture or liquid through a given area, such as pulling body moisture to the surface of a fabric where it can evaporate
B. having a low melting point that allows fibers to be heat-treated to set pleats, mold shape, or emboss fabric designs
C. the ability to resist static electricity buildup that causes fabrics to "spark" and cling to the wearer
D. the resistance to abrasion from surface wear and rubbing

_____ 29. Cooperative advertising _____.
A. is when costs are shared by more than one organization, such as a manufacturer and retailer
B. is often done by trade associations when natural and manufactured fibers are used together in blends
C. increases the advertising costs of the companies involved, since more ads are run
D. All of the above.

_____ 30. Mechanical spinning and solution spinning result in _____.
A. manufactured fiber monofilament yarns and multifilament yarns, respectively
B. blended ply yarns and combination yarns, respectively
C. staple fiber spun yarns and manufactured fiber multifilament yarns, respectively
D. dry finished yarns and wet finished yarns, respectively

Essay Questions: Provide complete responses to the following questions or statements.

31. Briefly describe the three main segments of the fur industry.

32. Briefly describe the three main steps used to produce manufactured fibers.

33. Define *denier* and briefly discuss microdenier attributes and apparel uses.

Textile Fabrics and Finishes

Objectives

After studying this chapter, students will be able to

- identify the most common fabric constructions.
- describe the main fabric finishing procedures.
- recognize the importance of quality and performance standards.
- summarize important aspects of the textile industry.
- explain how finished fabrics are sold down the chain.
- cite textile industry trade information.
- tell about future predictions for textiles.

Teaching Materials

Text, pages 126–147
  Fashion Terms
  Fashion Review
  Fashion in Action
Student Workbook
  A. *Basic Fabric Construction*
  B. *Other Fabric Constructions*
  C. *Fabrics and Finishes Match*
  D. *Inform the Customers*
  E. *Textile Fabrics and Finishes Review*
Teacher's Resources
  Selvage Under the Microscope, transparency
    master 7-1
  Basket Weave, transparency master 7-2
  Rib Weave, transparency master 7-3
  Leno Weave, transparency master 7-4
  Looped and Cut Pile, transparency master 7-5
  Helpful Hints for Grain Direction, transparency
    master 7-6
  Full-Fashioned Shaping, transparency master 7-7
  Fabric Lineup Game, reproducible master 7-8
  Selling Greige Goods, transparency master 7-9

  Selling Finished Fabrics, transparency
    master 7-10
  Read, Respond, and Discuss, reproducible
    master 7-11
  Chapter 7 Test

Introductory Activities

1. Ask students to name as many ways as they can think of to construct fabrics from yarns. After weaving and knitting have been briefly discussed, ask them how they think nonwovens, laces, braids, quilted, and bonded fabrics are constructed. Then tell them these interesting details await them in the chapter!
2. Have students describe as many ways as they can to color and finish fabrics. Ask if any of them have ever dyed textile products and what the method and outcome were. Have any of them ever sprayed a fabric protector onto furniture upholstery or a raincoat? Did the protective finish seem to work?
3. Have the class discuss what they think the relationship is between the technology, fashion, and the marketing of textiles.

Strategies to Reteach, Reinforce, Enrich, and Extend Text Concepts

Fabric Design and Construction

4. **RT** Explain the difference between structural design and applied design of fabrics. Then, with several different samples of fabrics or with the fabrics of the garments they are wearing, have students describe the structural and applied design features of each.

5. **RF** *Selvage Under the Microscope*, transparency master 7-1. Use this master as you discuss the warp yarns of the lengthwise grain and the weft yarns of the crosswise grain of fabrics. Show students how yarns turn back at the selvage of fabrics to go the other way without having raw edges that will ravel. Also, have students look at the selvages of some fabric swatches under a microscope.

6. **RF** *Basic Fabric Construction*, Activity A, WB. Students are asked to cut 80 pieces of yarn (2½ inches each) from a skein of knitting yarn. They are then asked to weave the yarns to create samples of the weaves named in the activity. Small looms can also be purchased from Nasco and hobby shops.

7. **RF** Show the class PowerPoint CDs about specific types of fabric construction. *Digital Textiles, Volume 4: Plain Weaves, Volume 5: Twills and Satins, Volume 6a; Fancy Weaves, Volume 7: Knits,* and *Volume 8: Other Fabrications* are available from D.E. Visuals. Interactive CDs from Cotton Incorporated include *The Art of Weaving* and *The Art of Knitting.*

8. **ER** Discuss why bias cut garments drape well and are more expensive than those cut on straight grain.

9. **RT** *Basket Weave*, transparency master 7-2. Use this transparency master to illustrate the basket weave. Explain to students that this is a variation of the plain weave and compare it to other weaves.

10. **RT** *Rib Weave*, transparency master 7-3. Use this transparency master to illustrate the rib weave. Explain to students that this is a variation of the plain weave and compare it to other weaves.

11. **RT** *Leno Weave*, transparency master 7-4. Use this transparency master to illustrate the leno weave. Explain to students that this is a variation of the plain weave and compare it to other weaves.

12. **RT** *Looped and Cut Pile*, transparency master 7-5. Have students discuss pile fabrics as they look at this transparency. If available, have them look at samples of several types of pile fabrics, possibly under a microscope or magnifying glass.

13. **RT** Explain to students the advantages and disadvantages of knits in various garments. Include flexibility, stretch and recovery, versatility, wrinkle-resistance, snags, runs, body-revealing shaping, and other attributes. Show samples of various types of knitted fabrics and garments.

14. **EX** *Helpful Hints for Grain Direction*, transparency master 7-6. Have the class discuss each of the bulleted points as you show this transparency. If possible, show samples of appropriate fabrics to illustrate the points being discussed.

15. **RF** *Full-Fashioned Shaping*, transparency master 7-7. As students look at this master, have them discuss hand knitting vs. knitting machines and full-fashioned shaping vs. cutting and sewing of garment parts to achieve fit. Have students try hand knitting, including full-fashioned shaping.

16. **RF** Show students a video that shows weaving, knitting, and other textile aspects. *Understanding Fabrics* is available from D.E. Visuals, VMS, Inc., Meridian Education Corporation, Nasco, and Learning Seed. *Eagleknit Makes Basics Right* is available from Insight Media.

17. **RF** *Other Fabric Constructions*, Activity B, WB. Students are asked to obtain four fabric samples of unique constructions, such as lace, brocade, artificial suede, double-knit, pile, or quilted fabrics. They are asked to unravel a corner of each sample if possible. They are then asked to indicate the type of construction, whether the fabric has been dyed or printed, any obvious finishes, and other details they notice about each one.

Fabric Finishing

18. **RF** *Fabrics and Finishes Match*, Activity C, WB. Students are asked to match fabrics and finishes with their definitions.

19. **RT** Explain the role that converters play in satisfying the needs of the fashion market.

20. **RT** Explain why dyeing textile products later in the soft goods chain does a better job of meeting market demand and reduces manufacturing and retail risks.

21. **RF** Have students find or draw examples of each of an overall print, directional print, border print, even (balanced) plaid, and uneven plaid. Have them show and explain their examples to the rest of the class.

22. **EX** Have students look up various types of applied designs in art books, including realistic, stylized, abstract, and geometric motifs. Have them find examples of directional and nondirectional prints. Discuss the characteristics of each type of motif, especially for use in apparel (such as matching), as the class looks at examples.

23. **RT** Have students explain the meaning of the following finishes: *permanent, durable, temporary,* and *renewable.* Also discuss terms that end in *proof, resistant,* or *repellent.* Show labels or hangtags to the class that contain some of these terms and describe the types of garments on which they might appear.

24. **RF** Show students a video about wool processing through finishing. *A Tour of a Woolen Mill: From Fiber to Fabric* is available from Nasco.

25. **RF** Have students work with finished fabric samples and workbooks. *Fabric Lab* is available from Learning Seed, Meridian Education Corporation,

and VMS, Inc. Fabric file cards and tripod magnifiers are available from Nasco. *New Fabrics, Then Fibers* has a video, sample, fabrics, and curriculum materials. It can be obtained from Teacher's Media Company, VMS, Inc., The Curriculum Center for Family and Consumer Sciences, Nasco, and Meridian Education Corporation.

26. **ER** Show the class a video about many fabrics, their advantages, and which ones are best for different types of garments. *Visiting a Fabric Store* is available from Insight Media, Meridian Education Corporation, and D.E. Visuals.

27. **RF** Show the class PowerPoint CDs about fabric finishing. D.E. Visuals offers *Digital Textiles, Volume 9: Dyes and Prints* and *Volume 10: Finishes,* as well as *Applications of Textiles* and *Textile Professor.* Cotton Incorporated offers *The Science of Dyeing & Finishing.* Nasco and The Curriculum Center for Family and Consumer Sciences offer *Applications of Textiles.*

28. **RF** Have students play "Fabric Grab Bag" with swatches of material. Provide enough fabric swatches so each student will be able to get one. Put the swatches into a paper bag. Have one student at a time stand, pick a fabric swatch from the bag, and describe it to the rest of the class. Students should try to identify the fiber, fabric construction, and finishing methods used. When each student has given as much information as possible about his or her swatch, others should add comments. This can also be done by having students describe the fabrics in the clothes they are wearing.

29. **RT** *Fabric Lineup Game,* reproducible master 7-8. Students are asked to pick terms, explain their meanings, and finish with a bingo-like game.

Quality and Performance Standards

30. **RT** Explain the difference between quality standards and performance standards. Discuss the importance of product quality and how the added expense of higher quality or textile testing can be cost-effective. Have students express their thoughts about paying more money for a better pair of jeans or a longer-lasting prom gown. Discuss how sometimes consumers understandably consider fashion or a low retail price to be more important than how sturdy a fabric is.

31. **RT** Have students discuss the statement, "Quality can't be inspected or tested into a product; it has to be manufactured into it."

32. **ER** Have the class discuss the advantages and disadvantages of quality standards versus increased use of fast machine technology. Advantages include such factors as reduced cost per unit of material produced, fewer machines required to produce and finish more material, and reduced labor costs due to automation and production gains. Disadvantages include such factors as less tolerance for error with higher speeds, machine downtime is more expensive with fewer machines and higher production rates, and constant quality monitoring is needed to quickly identify quality problems.

33. **ER** Have a class discussion about the synergy among quality organizations. The International Organization for Standardization (ISO), in Geneva, Switzerland, develops European and worldwide standards. The American Society for Quality (ASQ), in Milwaukee, Wisconsin, adopts and coordinates ISO standards with American National Standards for American companies. The ASQ also offers Six Sigma training and certification. More information is available on the Web sites of these organizations.

The Textile Industry

34. **RF** Show students a video that reviews materials from Chapter 6, while also showing the technology of fabric formation. Textile Research Center Field Trip and a Study Guide are available from The Curriculum Center for Family and Consumer Sciences.

35. **ER** Obtain forecasting projections from fiber companies or textile trade organizations. Hold a class discussion about the usefulness of this information to textile producers.

Selling the Finished Fabrics

36. **RF** *Selling Greige Goods,* transparency master 7-9. Use this master as a basis of discussion about the selling of greige goods.

37. **RF** *Selling Finished Fabrics,* transparency master 7-10. Use this master as a basis of discussion about the selling of finished fabrics and compare it to transparency master 7-9 in a discussion about the two different levels of the pipeline. Discuss who the customers are who buy the textiles in each case.

38. **ER** Obtain kits of file boxes with finished fabrics on cards. A glossary of fabric terms, tips on fabric uses, and other apparel-related information is included. *Nasco's General Fabric File Kit* and *Nasco's Knit Fabric File Kit* are both available from Nasco.

39. **EX** *Inform the Customers,* Activity D, WB. Students are asked to write four questions with answers that customers might ask an employee of a retail store that sells fashion goods. Then, with a partner, students are to role-play the parts of the customer and salesperson.

Trade Information

40. **ER** Obtain information from all or some of the following organizations to share with students: American Association of Textile Chemists & Colorists, Knitted Textile Association, Textile Distributors Association, National Knitwear & Sportswear Association, National Textiles & Apparel Association, Computer Integrated Textile Design Association (CITDA), National Textile Center (NTC), American Fiber Manufacturers Association Inc., and International Textile Manufacturers Federation (ITMF).

41. **RF** Show the class a video about the textile industry. *Textiles: Birth of an Industry* is available from Teacher's Media Company.

42. **ER** Obtain sample copies of textile trade journals, such as *Textile World* and *Textile News*, for students to review. If your students are Spanish speaking, obtain a copy of *Mundo Textil*, which is the Spanish version of Textile World. Also try to obtain information from the trade organizations and journals about industry trade shows and exhibitions. Some examples are International Fashion Fabric Exhibition, Interstoff Textile Fair (Germany), Ideacomo (Italy), Premiere Vision (France), and Canton Trade Fair (China).

The Future of Textiles

43. **ER** In a class discussion about innovation for fibers, fabrics, and finishes, have students try to predict various new ways that textiles might be used 50 years from now.

44. **RT** *Textile Fabrics and Finishes Review*, Activity E, WB. Students are asked to respond to review questions and statements.

45. **RF** *Read, Respond, and Discuss*, reproducible master 7-11. Have students write their thoughts about the provided statements. Then have them use what they have written as a basis for a class discussion.

Additional Enrichment Activities

Research

46. Have students do library and/or Internet research to gather historic and current information on bleaches and dyes, mercerization and permanent press chemical finishes, beetling, fabric scribing and sandblasting, microwave-based curing for wrinkle-resistant garments, different Tartan plaids, denim fabrics and finishing, boiled wool knits, simulated leathers, the latest digital printing developments, virtual drape for computer fabric simulation, or another related topic. Have students prepare an oral or written report about their findings.

47. Have students do library and/or Internet research about ISO 9000 (in general, relating to all industries). Students should prepare a report that describes the various parts of ISO 9000, what is involved in each, how to achieve certification, and the probable rewards for companies that achieve it. Check Web site www.iso.ch.

48. Have individual students or small groups research different major textile companies, such as the International Textile Group (ITG), Forstmann, Flen Raven Inc., Milliken, and Sarah Lee Knit Products. In oral or written reports, students should describe the types of products the companies make, whether the firms are vertically integrated, to what markets they sell, where their sales offices and production facilities are located, and any other pertinent information that can be gathered.

49. For an advanced class, or one with a more technical slant, have students research and summarize air-jet, projectile, water-jet, rigid rapier, and flexible rapier weaving machines. Other research subjects might be microencapsulation, solar fabrics for military tents (to power lights, computers, ventilation, etc. within them), smart fabrics that contain washable computer chips, antimicrobial-treated fabrics, or similar textile innovations.

Projects

50. If there are any textile mills in your area, contact them about hosting a tour of their operations for your students. Have the students do research about the company and its operations before going so they are well informed and can get the most out of the visit as possible.

51. Take a class trip to a fabric store. Have students read the labels on the fabric bolts as to fiber content and price. They should also notice how different fabrics are constructed and finished. What fabrics ravel easily? What different types of finishes are evident? Are several color combinations available of the same print? Also investigate www.fabric.com.

52. Prepare a display of fabrics dyed or finished by various methods. Label each sample, post on a bulletin board, and describe the method used for finishing.

53. Have students experiment with the colorfastness of fabrics by rubbing samples of new colored/printed fabrics over a dry white towel or handkerchief. Repeat the experiment with the same fabric using a wet white towel or handkerchief. Notice if any color has rubbed off and the differences in the colorfastness of the various fabric samples.

Text

Fashion Review, page 147

1. fiber content, type of yarn, fabric construction, finishing
2. Structural design is achieved by "building in" texture or interest to fabrics when they are manufactured. Applied design is accomplished by adding color, pattern, or other design features to the structural design after the fabric has been made.
3. Warp yarns go in the lengthwise direction and form the lengthwise grain; filling yarns go crosswise and form the crosswise grain.
4. plain, twill, satin
5. Pile fabrics have loops or clipped yarn ends projecting from the surface; the fiber ends form nap on the fabric's surface that appears different when viewed from various directions.
6. Gauge is the number of stitches, or loops, per inch; a higher gauge number indicates a closer and finer knit.
7. circular knitting machines and flat knitting machines
8. Weft knitting has one yarn strand that forms a horizontal row of interlocked loops; warp knitting forms long lengthwise rows in a zigzag pattern.
9. with a combination of heat, moisture, chemicals, and friction and/or pressure applied
10. the applying of colors, designs, or surface treatments that change the look, feel, or performance of fabrics
11. between textile mills and apparel manufacturers
12. because they do not own production equipment; they contract with others that have specialized machinery so they can quickly change their fabric styles to meet customer demands
13. Stock-dyeing is done to natural fibers and solution-dyeing is done by adding color to manufactured fiber solution before extrusion.
14. piece dyeing
15. It gives manufacturers flexibility late in the pipeline, after fashion demand has been calculated, resulting in a faster response to market demand.
16. (List four:) roller, screen, rotary screen, heat transfer, flocking, digital
17. Permanent finishes last the life of the garment; durable finishes last through several launderings or dry cleanings; temporary finishes last only until the fabric is washed or dry-cleaned; renewable finishes are temporary but can be replaced or reapplied.
18. Computer-aided design and computer-aided manufacturing; they have shortened product development cycles, enabled firms to calculate the production cost and figure the selling price of fabrics before they are knitted or woven, increased flexibility and the capacity to innovate, lowered costs, and allowed for tracking of all procedures through the production line.
19. They all sell finished fabrics. Textile jobbers buy (take ownership of) fabric at low prices from companies that can't use it and sell it to those that can use it; textile brokers act as a liaison between textile sellers and buyers to match their needs and never own the fabric; textile retailers are stores that sell fabric and sewing supplies to consumers over-the-counter.
20. Worldwide standards of living are going up.

Student Workbook

Fabrics and Finishes Match, Activity C

1. C	14. J
2. L	15. V
3. E	16. T
4. P	17. B
5. A	18. X
6. F	19. K
7. O	20. D
8. G	21. W
9. R	22. M
10. H	23. Y
11. S	24. N
12. I	25. Z
13. U	26. Q

Textile Fabrics and Finishes Review, Activity E

1. structural design and applied design
2. weaving and knitting
3. diagonally
4. large and intricate designs
5. the West Coast, especially California
6. They automatically increase or decrease the number of stitches to shape the finished garment.
7. They are very stretchy and usually loosely knitted, resembling hand-knitting.
8. warp knitting
9. tricot
10. They have no grainline, minimum stretch, do not ravel, and are relatively inexpensive.
11. openwork fabrics made by crossing, twisting, or looping yarns into designs
12. a method of permanently laminating together two layers of fabric that are already constructed
13. because those are produced as finished textiles or products
14. a fabric is made of two or more fibers that take dyes differently; it is then put into dye baths of different compositions of dyes which results in various predictable patterns

15. Even plaids are the same in both the lengthwise and crosswise directions; uneven plaids are different in one or both directions.
16. because it is accurate, fast, and efficient
17. because it prints small lots of fabric more cheaply, in finer detail, and with a wide range of colors
18. Proof means complete protection; resistant or repellent means the finish provides partial protection.
19. mechanical and chemical finishes
20. the degree of excellence of a product
21. new manufacturing machinery and procedures to match production with market demand for fabrics that have the desired characteristics
22. projections of colors, textures, weights, and finishes that will meet public fashion acceptance when the fabrics finally reach consumers
23. Many staple fabrics are imported from other countries; most novelty fabrics are made and finished in the U.S. or other countries that have fashion industries.
24. It is going from one that requires many workers to make the textiles to one that uses mainly machines and advanced technology.
25. polyester, novelty yarns, and knitting

31. The plain weave is the simplest and most common fabric weave in which each filling yarn passes successively over and under each warp yarn, alternating each row. The basket weave is a variation of the plain weave with two or more filling yarns passing over and under the same number of warp yarns.
32. Garment dyeing offers fast market response because it is done later in the pipeline than fiber, yarn, or piece dyeing. Garments manufactured of undyed yarns are dyed in requested colors only after specific orders are received.
33. A permanent finish lasts the life of the garment. A durable finish lasts through several launderings or dry cleanings, but loses its effectiveness over a period of time. A temporary finish lasts until washing or dry cleaning. A renewable finish is temporary but can be replaced or reapplied.

Teacher's Resources

Chapter 7 Test

1.	H	16.	T
2.	F	17.	F
3.	E	18.	T
4.	B	19.	T
5.	A	20.	F
6.	J	21.	D
7.	D	22.	A
8.	C	23.	C
9.	G	24.	B
10.	I	25.	C
11.	F	26.	B
12.	T	27.	D
13.	T	28.	D
14.	T	29.	B
15.	F	30.	C

Selvage Under the Microscope

(Yarns turn back and go the other way, forming a strong edge that does not ravel.)

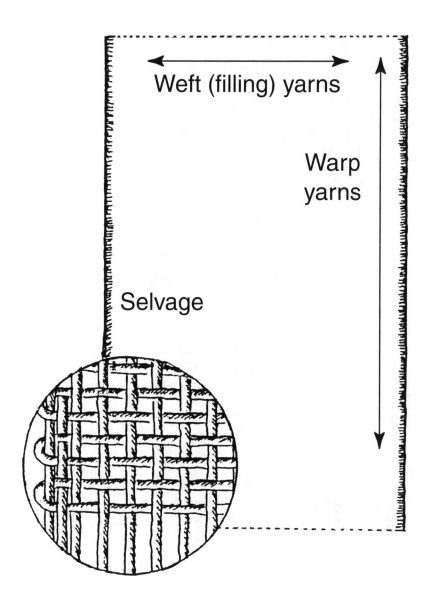

Weft (filling) yarns

Warp yarns

Selvage

Basket Weave

(Two or more warp and weft yarns pass over and under each other.)

Rib Weave

(Weaving very different sized warp and weft yarns gives a ribbed appearance.)

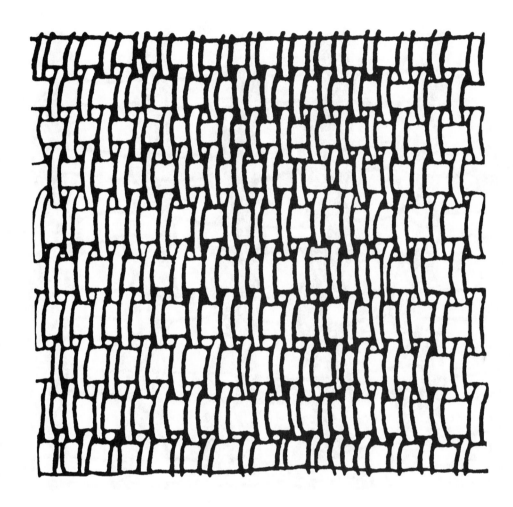

Leno Weave

(This weave has open spaces, but is a strong, stable construction.)

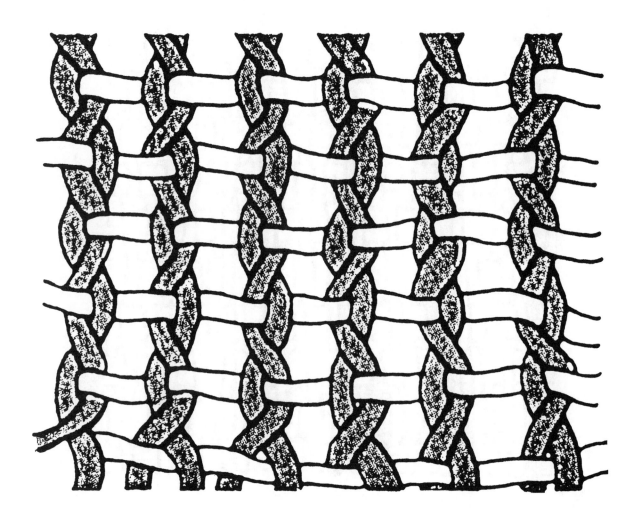

Looped and Cut Pile

(Pile is formed by extra weft yarns that extend above the fabric surface.)

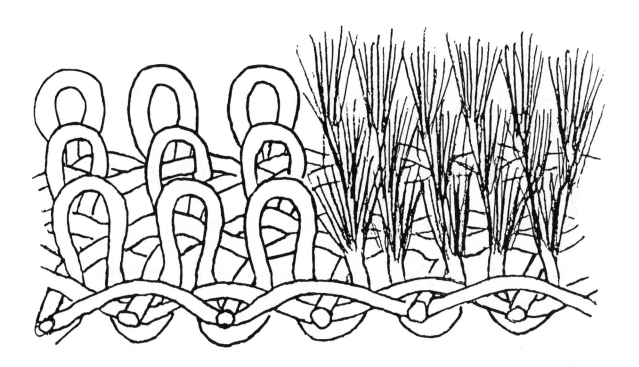

Helpful Hints for Grain Direction

- Lengthwise grain (warp) is always parallel to the selvage.

- There are usually more warp yarns per inch than weft yarns.

- Warp yarns are usually finer and stronger than weft yarns.

- Warp yarns usually have less stretch than weft yarns.

- Stripes usually run in the warp direction.

- Rows of cords are usually in the warp direction of corduroys.

- The longer dimension of checks is usually in the warp direction.

- Weft yarns always form the nap in napped fabrics.

- Lower grade, loose twist, and uneven yarns are usually weft.

Full-Fashioned Shaping

(Full-fashioned shaping is an indication of quality.)

Fabric Lineup Game

Name_____ **Date** _____ **Period** _____

As your name is called, pick one of the following terms and explain its meaning. When the term has been thoroughly explained, write it into any of the squares below and cross it off the printed list. This procedure should be repeated until all the terms have been defined and placed arbitrarily in the different squares. Your teacher (or a student) should act as the "caller" and write down the same terms on separate small pieces of paper. The pieces of paper with the terms should be placed into an opaque container. Then play a bingo-like game with the caller pulling out one at a time, reading the terms out loud, and setting them aside. Place buttons or pebbles on the squares containing the terms that are called. The first student to get a solid covered line of five squares going vertically, horizontally, or diagonally wins the game by calling out "Fabric!"

applied design	colorfast	forecasting services	grain	bleaching
staple fabrics	converters	mechanical finishes	hand	nonwovens
chemical finishes	knitting	performance standards	dyeing	overruns
quality standards	printing	structural design	selvage	true bias
novelty fabrics	weaving	warp yarns	gauge	weft yarns

Selling Greige Goods

(As opposed to finished goods)

- More technical knowledge is needed.

- Prices fluctuate based on supply and demand.

- Larger orders are placed.

- Minimum fashion influence is involved.

- There are lower prices and profit margins.

- There are fewer customers (mostly to converters).

- All inventory can be sold (It is unfinished.).

- Mill quality/reputation is important.

Selling Finished Fabrics

"Piece goods" salespeople need knowledge of

- fibers, fabric construction, and fashion

- relationships through the soft goods chain

- the importance of timing

- end-use trends

- customer price limits

- general sales techniques

- company products, policies, practices

- the importance of customer feedback to the firm

Read, Respond, and Discuss

Name_____ **Date** _____ **Period** _____

Write your thoughts about the following statements on the lines, and try to expand the topic further. Then share your thoughts with others by having a class discussion about each statement.

1. Weaving yarns closely together gives a strong, dense fabric. When yarns are woven loosely, the fabric is lighter and more porous. _____

_____

_____

2. A textured effect is achieved by weaving low-twist and high-twist yarns together. _____

_____

_____

3. "Stretch" woven fabrics are made with stretchable yarns. Knits have natural stretch because of the fabric construction. _____

_____

_____

4. Sometimes separately knitted shaped collars, cuffs, and trim pieces are sewn onto full-fashioned knit garments. _____

_____

_____

5. Hypercolor™ is a "thermochromatic" dyeing system that enables cotton fabric to change color with body temperature and environment. It is known as a "metamorphic color system" because it changes with circumstances. _____

_____

_____

6. With today's automation, a single operator might oversee 100 weaving or knitting machines in a textile plant. _____

_____

_____

7. Textile machinery has a long, useful life, and output can be increased by adding extra work shifts.

_____

_____

8. To construct open-effect leno weave fabrics, warp yarns are used in pairs and cross each other before weft yarns are inserted. This adds strength and prevents slippage of the yarns. _____

_____

_____

_____

(Continued)

Name_____

9. Leno weave fabrics are used in shirts, lined handbags, curtains, thermal blankets, and mosquito netting. They are also used for bags for laundry, fruits, and vegetables. _____

_____

_____

_____

10. Felt is a nonwoven fabric. If wool fibers are used, they "felt" naturally when heat, moisture, and pressure are applied. The scales of the wool fibers interlock and hold themselves matted together.

_____

_____

_____

11. Felt fabrics are thick and somewhat stiff. They are not as strong as woven or knitted fabrics. They can be molded into shapes, and are often used for hats and handicraft projects. _____

_____

_____

_____

12. Some nonwoven fabrics are "needle punched" to hold their fibers tangled together. A bed of needles is punched down through a web of fibers and then withdrawn, creating a mechanical interlocking of the fibers. Small holes, regularly placed, are evident in the fabric._____

_____

_____

_____

13. Bonded fabric layers may be similar or different, combining knitted and woven fabrics, or lace or other fabrics. Sometimes a layer of foam is included for warmth, or a stable fabric is bonded to a "flimsy" fabric for stability. Tricot knit is often used as a backing fabric since it is inexpensive and allows some stretch. _____

_____

_____

_____

14. A major consideration in textile finishing is color. The Color Association of the U.S. publishes its color charts (forecasting 2 years ahead) for those who subscribe to their service. The predictions are followed by all segments of the fashion industry to coordinate the same colors at the same time.

_____

_____

_____

15. Besides having meetings and exhibitions, textile trade groups develop "sourcing directories" that list industry firms alphabetically and by business category. For instance, separate listings of sources for specific fabrics, linings, and trims help suppliers sell those products and customers know where to get them._____

_____

_____

Textile Fabrics and Finishes

Name_____

Date_____ Period_____ Score_____

Chapter 7 Test

Matching: Match the following terms and identifying phrases.

_____ 1. Product ratings according to levels of defects.

_____ 2. Fashion fabrics that change with style trends.

_____ 3. Finishes that affect the size, appearance, and surface of fabrics.

_____ 4. Finishes that become part of fabrics through reactions with the fibers.

_____ 5. Surface design added onto a fabric.

_____ 6. "Built-in" texture or interest to fabrics when they are manufactured.

_____ 7. The way fabrics feel to the touch.

_____ 8. Businesses that convert greige goods to finished fabrics and distribute those fabrics.

_____ 9. Product ratings according to suitability for specific end uses.

_____ 10. Commodity textile products made continuously each year, with little or no change in construction or finish.

A. applied design

B. chemical finishes

C. converters

D. hand

E. mechanical finishes

F. novelty fabrics

G. performance standards

H. quality standards

I. staple fabrics

J. structural design

True/False: Circle *T* if the statement is true or *F* if the statement is false.

T F 11. Weaving is the procedure of laying two sets of yarns next to (parallel to) each other.

T F 12. Selvage is strong, will not ravel, and runs along both edges of woven fabrics.

T F 13. Bias grain is diagonal on the fabric.

T F 14. The satin weave produces a shiny fabric surface.

T F 15. The number of stitches, or loops, per inch in a knitted fabric is the nap.

T F 16. Full-fashion shaping is done by increasing or decreasing knit stitches to shape the finished garment.

T F 17. Plaiting is a method of permanently laminating together two layers of fabric.

T F 18. Dying is a method of giving color to textiles using coloring agents.

T F 19. When something is cost-effective, the benefits outweigh the expense.

T F 20. Mill overruns are when dye bath solutions spill onto adjoining bolts of fabric.

(Continued)

Name_____

Multiple Choice: Choose the best response. Write the letter in the space provided.

_____ 21. The appearance and performance of fabrics depend on their _____.
  A. fiber content and type of yarn
  B. fabric construction
  C. finishing
  D. All of the above.

_____ 22. Warp yarns _____.
  A. form the lengthwise grain of woven fabrics
  B. are also called filling yarns
  C. are carried back and forth by a "shuttle"
  D. All of the above.

_____ 23. For the twill weave, _____.
  A. the finished fabrics are always reversible
  B. tricot is one of the main examples
  C. a diagonal wale results from short "floats" that pass over two or more yarns at regular intervals
  D. All of the above.

_____ 24. Terry cloth in towels is a good example of a _____.
  A. looped corduroy fabric
  B. looped pile fabric
  C. weft knit fabric
  D. clipped pile fabric

_____ 25. Knitting is a fabric construction method of _____.
  A. weaving a continuous yarn in a looped pattern
  B. bonding yarns in a matted arrangement
  C. looping yarns together
  D. crossing yarns in the filling direction

_____ 26. The largest concentration of U.S. knitted fabric producers is _____.
  A. in the Southeastern United States, where most of the textile industry is located
  B. on the West Coast, especially in California
  C. in the Midwest, because the harsh winters require more clothes
  D. in New England, where most sheep are raised

_____ 27. Nonwovens are _____.
  A. made from a compact web of fibers, not yarns
  B. held together with a combination of moisture, heat, chemicals, friction, and/or pressure
  C. have no grainline, are relatively inexpensive, and are often used for disposable purposes
  D. All of the above.

(Continued)

Name_____

_____ 28. A chemical finishing process that removes any natural color from fibers or fabrics is
_____.
- A. mercerizing
- B. cross-dyeing
- C. calendering
- D. bleaching

_____ 29. Colorfast implies that _____.
- A. a fabric is able to be dyed quickly and completely
- B. the color in a fabric will not fade or change with normal expected use and care
- C. certain dyes will last more effectively with this fabric than others
- D. All of the above.

_____ 30. The general process for adding color, pattern, or design to the surface of fabrics is
known as _____.
- A. rolling
- B. painting
- C. printing
- D. heat transferring

Essay Questions: Provide complete responses to the following questions or statements.

31. Briefly discuss the plain weave, including the basket weave.

32. Explain the market timing significance of garment dyeing as opposed to fiber, yarn, or piece
dyeing.

33. Briefly describe the meaning of permanent, durable, temporary, and renewable finishes.

PART THREE

Designing and Producing Apparel

Using Design in Fashion

Objectives

After studying this chapter, students will be able to

- explain the importance of each element of design in relation to fashion.
- apply the principles of design to apparel.
- describe how harmony is achieved in garment designs.
- discuss how to use design to create illusions that enhance appearance.

Teaching Materials

Text, pages 150–168
Fashion Terms
Fashion Review
Fashion in Action

Student Workbook
- A. *Going Deeper with Color*
- B. *Define and Draw the Line*
- C. *Shape and Texture*
- D. *The Design Principles*
- E. *Relating to Design*

Teacher's Resources
Design Elements in Today's Fashions, reproducible master 8-1
Psychological Associations of Colors, transparency master 8-2
Color Value, transparency master 8-3
Line Types and Directions, transparency master 8-4
Effects of Line Placement, transparency master 8-5

Working with Today's Fashions, reproducible master 8-6
Chapter 8 Test

Introductory Activities

1. Ask students about what colors are their favorite to wear and why they think those colors make them look and feel good. Do the same for shapes, lines, and textures. This will help raise student awareness of these elements and encourage them to begin thinking about the content of the chapter.
2. *Design Elements in Today's Fashions*, reproducible master 8-1. Have students discuss the importance of colors, shapes, lines, and textures in everyday living, such as in architecture, paintings, cars, home interiors, and especially in apparel. Then have students complete the activity. Have students save this activity for use again after studying the chapter.
3. Have each student write a paper describing what clothes in their wardrobes they like best and which ones they like least. Students may want to include their favorite dress-up outfit and try to analyze why it is their favorite, such as how it makes them feel when they wear it.
4. Put up posters in the classroom to get students interested in the chapter and illustrate its content. Students can refer to the posters as they study the chapter. *Elements and Principles of Fashion Design* posters are available from VMS, Inc.

Using the Elements of Design

5. **RT** Have students look at text illustration 8-1. Point out to them how the elements and principles of design are used to achieve harmony in apparel. Have them discuss why it is important for fashion merchandising professionals to have an understanding of how the elements and principles of design are used in apparel.

6. **RT** Discuss why color is one of the most exciting design elements. Then ask students to describe the three dimensions (descriptive qualities) of color—hue, value, and intensity.

7. **ER** *Psychological Associations of Colors*, transparency master 8-2. While using this master, hold a class discussion about the symbolism and associations of each of the colors. Discuss which ones are dressy or casual and which ones are appropriate for fun parties or serious religious services.

8. **RF** *Color Value*, transparency master 8-3. Although this shows tints and shades of the hue red, also discuss tints and shades of blue, green, and other colors. Have students mix a tempera paint hue with white and with black to produce a color value chart of their own. Bring to students' attention that there are infinite degrees of value from one end to the other.

9. **RF** Show students one or more basic videos about color as it relates to people's lives and fashion. *Color in Everyday Life* is available from The Curriculum Center for Family and Consumer Sciences, Learning Seed, Insight Media, and D.E. Visuals. *Color Communicates* can be obtained from Insight Media and Meridian Education Corporation. *Understanding Color* is available from D.E. Visuals and Meridian Education Corporation. *Color Perceptions* is available from Insight Media. *The Power of Color* is available from Nasco and The Curriculum Center for Family and Consumer Sciences. *The Power of Color* is available from Nasco.

10. **RF** Have students cut out pictures from catalogs or magazines of outfits that illustrate at least four of the six major color schemes. Have them show their pictures to the rest of the class and describe the colors and color schemes.

11. **RT** Describe the effects of the use of color in apparel. Have students find examples of these in catalogs or magazines. Discuss these with the rest of the class. Mention that color contributes 60% to consumers' buying decisions. Encourage students to use proper color terminology, such as advancing and receding colors, warm and cool colors, bright and dull colors, and primary or secondary hues.

12. **EX** Have students use color guidebooks that show different color combinations for designers. *Color Harmony Workbook, Complete Color Harmony,* and others are available from ST Publications.

13. **ER** Obtain information from the Color Association of the U.S. (www.colorassocation.com) in New York City and the International Colour Authority (www.internationalcolourauthority.com) in London. Find out about their services, color trend information, educational programs, and influence on fashions worldwide. Share these with the class.

14. **RF** *Going Deeper with Color*, Activity A, WB. Students are asked to identify specific color schemes, name the colors used, give a fact or statement about the color scheme, and match descriptions with examples of color use.

15. **RT** Have students discuss how various silhouettes in clothing affect the appearance of the people wearing the clothes.

16. **RF** Have students cut out pictures of outfits from catalogs or magazines that clearly illustrate structural lines and decorative lines. Have students show their pictures to the rest of the class and describe the illusions created on the parts of the body that the lines cross.

17. **RT** *Line Types and Directions*, transparency master 8-4. As students look at this transparency, have them discuss where in apparel each type of line might be found and the effect it has on appearance.

18. **RF** *Define and Draw the Line*, Activity B, WB. Students are asked to define terms, briefly describe the effect each type of line has in apparel, and draw an example of each.

19. **RT** *Effects of Line Placement*, transparency master 8-5. Use this transparency to illustrate the effects of line in skirts.

20. **RF** *Shape and Texture*, Activity C, WB. Students are asked to find a picture of a fashionable outfit, describe the silhouette of the outfit, and explain if it would flatter various parts of the human body or not. Then students are to answer questions and find examples of different textures.

21. **RF** Have students cut out pictures from catalogs or magazines of outfits that clearly illustrate structural texture and added visual texture. Have them show their pictures to the rest of the class and describe the illusions created on the parts of the body where the texture is used. Ask students if they have ever bought garments because they liked the feel of the material.

22. **RT** Show students a video to reinforce what has been learned in this section of the chapter. *Design I: The Elements* is available from Nasco, The Curriculum Center for Family and Consumer Sciences, and Meridian Education Corporation. A CD-ROM, *Design Elements*, is available from Nasco.

Using the Principles of Design

23. **RT** Have students define *balance*, including *formal* and *informal balance*. Have students draw examples of balance on the board, with seesaw drawings that show formal and informal balance.

24. **RF** Have students describe the proportion of all parts of an outfit for a small person and a large person. Have them discuss the proportion of colors, shapes, lines, and textures that are good or bad for each person. Also include the sizes of accessories that are best for each person. Include magazine or catalog photos as examples for the discussion.

25. **RF** Have students find magazine or catalog photos that show emphasis in apparel. Ask students to explain the visual effect created by the specific emphasis shown in each case.

26. **RF** Have students find pictures or draw examples of clothing with repetition, gradation, and radiation. Ask them to show and explain to the class how rhythm moves through the outfit in each case.

27. **ER** Have students use computer programs to study the use of design elements in clothing. *Your Ideal Silhouette* and *Suit Yourself* are available from Meridian Education Corporation.

28. **RF** Have students discuss the following statement: "Elements are the building blocks of design. Principles are the guidelines for combining those building blocks."

29. **RT** Show students a video to reinforce what has been learned in this section of the chapter. *Design II: The Principles* is available from Nasco, Meridian Education Corporation, and The Curriculum Center for Family and Consumer Sciences. *Design: Applying the Elements* is available from Meridian Education Corporation.

30. **RT** Use a CD-ROM presentation about design with the class. *Visual Design Basics* is available from Learning Seed and The Curriculum Center for Family and Consumer Sciences.

Harmony

31. **RF** With the students looking at text illustration 8-27, have the class discuss how the elements of design are used according to the principles of design to create harmony in the outfit shown.

32. **RF** *The Design Principles*, Activity D, WB. Students are asked to work with balance, proportion, emphasis, and rhythm. They are to answer questions and draw examples with the final goal of achieving harmony.

33. **RF** *Working with Today's Fashions*, reproducible master 8-6. Have students complete this activity after reviewing their responses to reproducible master 8-1.

Illusions Created by Design

34. **RT** With the students looking at charts 8-28 and 8-29 in the text, discuss why each of the points listed achieves the particular effects of height, width, or attention.

35. **RF** Show students a video about using the elements and principles of design to advantage in clothing. *Your Clothes Lines Are Showing* is available from Social Studies School Service. *Elements and Principles of Design* is available from Insight Media, D.E. Visuals, Nasco, and The Curriculum Center for Family and Consumer Sciences. *Eye for Design* can be obtained from Learning Seed.

36. **RF** *Relating to Design*, Activity E, WB. Students are asked to identify phrases that do not fit with other descriptions of illusions created by design. Then they are to analyze mini-cases dealing with design illusions.

37. **RF** Have students discuss the following statement: "Poor design causes an unpleasant reaction, making things appear confusing, out-of-place, or ugly. Good design, with pleasing harmony, adds to people's happiness and enjoyment."

Additional Enrichment Activities

Research

38. Have students research and prepare a report about the seasonal approach to skin coloring. Have students find out about skin tones and how people's personal coloring should be considered when they are selecting apparel colors. Books that are good resources for this are *Fashion!* from Goodheart-Willcox Publisher, and *Color Me Beautiful* and *Color for Men* by Carole Jackson. They are available at bookstores or from Amazon.com. Color analysis swatch kits, videos, and workbooks are available from Nasco. Have students prepare a summary of how to recognize people within each of the four seasons. Also, have them tell what colors are the most attractive for people in each seasonal category. Finally, have students tear out and mount magazine or catalog pictures of outfits that have good colors for each of the seasonal categories.

39. Have students research what the seven most common body types or general shape categories are (answer: tall and thin, tall and heavy, short and thin, short and heavy, top-heavy, thick middle, and hip-heavy). Have students describe each and tell what apparel characteristics they would encourage for people who have those types of body shapes. A good source for this information is *Fashion!* from Goodheart-Willcox Publisher.

Projects

40. Invite a color analysis consultant to class to give a demonstration on how important color is in achieving the best look in clothing for specific people.

41. Have students select three articles of clothing from current magazines or catalogs. After mounting the pictures on paper, have students create different color schemes for each outfit.

42. Have students make booklets that contain collections of fashion photos or drawings from magazines or catalogs. On labeled pages, have students clearly show and explain examples of each of the elements of design as well as each of the principles of design. Most photos will show several elements and principles, but only one should be specified as an example for each photo.

Answer Key

Text

Fashion Review, page 168

1. by studying about, observing, and experimenting with design
2. color, shape, line, texture
3. balance, proportion, emphasis, rhythm
4. color
5. White reflects light, and black absorbs it.
6. red, yellow, blue; orange, green, violet (purple)
7. Warm colors are from red to yellow on the color wheel. They give a feeling of activity and cheerfulness and suggest an outgoing, lively mood. Cool colors are from green to violet on the color wheel. They give a restful, calm, quiet, relaxing feeling, suggesting a subdued mood.
8. the triad color scheme
9. Light, warm, and bright colors advance, and dark, cool, and dull colors recede.
10. green
11. Fluorescent lights make colors look bluer; incandescent lights give a yellow cast and pale the look of some colors.
12. vertical lines
13. because they reflect light and emphasize body contours
14. They emphasize the areas where they are used and increase the apparent size of the wearer.
15. formal balance and informal balance
16. scale
17. $\frac{3}{8}$ of the total figure is from the waist to the top of the head, and $\frac{5}{8}$ of the body is from the waist to the soles of the feet.
18. The design is cluttered and confusing.
19. how to enhance the appearance of particular body shapes
20. (Student response. See charts 8-28 and 8-29 in the text.)

Student Workbook

Going Deeper with Color, Activity A

1. complementary; red-orange and blue-green
2. triad; red-violet, yellow-orange, blue-green
3. monochromatic; different tints, shades, and intensities of blue
4. accented neutral; white, gray, violet
5. analogous; yellow and green

6. split-complementary; violet, yellow-green, yellow-orange
7. C
8. A
9. G
10. B
11. E
12. D
13. F
14. Warm colors seem to advance, making the body look larger. Cool colors seem to recede, making the body look smaller.
15. (Student response.)

Define and Draw the Line, Activity B

1. Horizontal lines go from side to side like the horizon. They carry the eye from side to side, giving the impression of less height and more width, making the body look shorter and wider.
2. Vertical lines go up and down. They give the impression of added height and slimness and make the body look taller and thinner.
3. Jagged lines change direction abruptly in zigzag patterns. They should be used sparingly because they are very noticeable and can create a jumpy, confused feeling.
4. Diagonal lines are on a slant. Shorter more horizontal diagonals create width, while longer more vertical diagonals create a leaner, taller effect.
5. Straight lines go straight. They are bold and severe, suggesting dignity, power, and formality. They can look stiff if overdone.
6. Curved lines are rounded and circular. They add interest and smoothness and appear to be soft, gentle, and youthful. They give a charming, graceful, and flowing feeling, but also increase the apparent size of the human shape.
7. Structural lines are formed when garments are constructed, such as at the seams, darts, pleats, tucks, and edges. They create visual interest in garments and are especially noticeable if the fabric is plain.
8. Decorative lines are applied lines, created by adding details to the surface of clothing. These lines from fabric design or trims add style and personality to garments, often accentuating structural lines.

Shape and Texture, Activity C

2. (Student response may include smooth, rough, dull, shiny, stiff, crisp, fuzzy, bulky, nubby, soft, shaggy, harsh, sheer, loopy, furry, scratchy, pebbly, sparkling, fine, lightweight, medium-weight, and heavyweight.)
3. because of the way light is reflected from the surface of the fabric

The Design Principles, Activity D

1. equilibrium or steadiness among the parts of a design
2. informal balance
3. formal balance
4. Their scale is related, with the top area smaller than the bottom, three pleats on each side of the blouse, and all matching the size of the body. The print and buttons are also in proportion.
5. The main emphasis is at the neckline. It draws the attention to the face and creates a taller feeling. A secondary emphasis is the cuffs of the sleeves, which keeps the view high on the body.
6. gradation—there is a progression of smaller and lighter areas to darker and larger areas in the skirt as the eye moves toward the bottom (hemline)
7. radiation—lines are emerging from a central point in the front like rays.
8. repetition—lines, shapes, colors, or textures are repeated in a garment through edges, trim, etc.
9. harmony

Relating to Design, Activity E

1. (Circled) horizontal lines. (Added) vertical lines (or other from left side of book chart 8-28).
2. (Circled) narrow silhouettes. (Added) wide silhouettes (or other from right side of chart 8-28).
3. (Circled) cool hues. (Added) warm hues (or other from right side of chart 8-29).
4. (Circled) light, bright colors. (Added) dark, dull colors (or other from left side of chart 8-29).
5. the thin belt and small fabric design—to be in proportion with her figure
6. Choose bulky sweaters, wide pleated pants, horizontal lines, and contrasting colors of the top and pants.
7. Use items from "taller, thinner looks" and "avoid attention" lists for blouses. Use items from "shorter, wider look" and "attract attention" lists for skirts and slacks.
8. Bad choices; she should look at smooth, flat sweaters in matching dark, dull, cool colors to simple, straight pants that are loose enough to skim the body easily.
9. He needs wide silhouettes, vertical lines, emphasis near the top, and medium textures and colors.
10. The blue dress because the cool hue, soft unpatterned fabric of flat texture, and minimal decoration will de-emphasize her body while the white collar will bring attention to her face. She should avoid the shiny fabric in a bright, warm hue with applied decoration away from her face.

Teacher's Resources

Chapter 8 Test

1. A
2. E
3. H
4. B
5. F
6. I
7. C
8. G
9. J
10. D
11. F
12. F
13. T
14. F
15. F
16. T
17. T
18. T
19. F
20. F
21. C
22. D
23. D
24. A
25. C
26. B
27. C
28. B
29. A
30. B

31. (See 8-1 in text.)
32. (See 8-5 in text.)
33. Formal balance is equilibrium created in a design with symmetrical parts, such as design details being the same on each side of a centerline. Informal balance is equilibrium in a design created with an asymmetrical arrangement in which design details are divided unequally from the center.

Design Elements in Today's Fashions

Name_____ **Date** _____ **Period** _____

Look at or collect pictures of current fashions in magazines and catalogs. Analyze the fashions to determine the newest fashion colors, shapes, lines, and textures. Then write responses to the following questions. Save this activity for use again at the end of the chapter.

1. What is the "color story" for this fashion season? Are the new colors modifications of colors used last year or are they new on the fashion scene? _____

   _____

   _____

   _____

2. What are some of the new "fashionable" names that are given to regular colors by the fashion industry? (Sometimes "hot pink" is "rose" or "magenta." Sometimes "lime green" is "chartreuse." How about "cobalt blue," "hunter green," and "raspberry"?)_____

   _____

   _____

   _____

3. What new descriptive names can you think up for the fashionable colors of this season? _____

   _____

   _____

   _____

4. What shapes (silhouettes) are shown in current fashions? Where are they loose, tight, etc.?

   _____

   _____

5. Where are the dominant lines placed in current fashions? Are there specific seamlines, garment edge shapes, etc.? _____

   _____

   _____

   _____

6. What textures are being shown in current fashions? Are they smooth, rough, shiny, dull, bulky, etc.?

   _____

   _____

   _____

Psychological Associations of Colors

Red:	Heat, danger, anger, passion, sentiment, excitement, vibrance, power, aggression, love, energy.
Orange:	Lively, cheerful, joyous, warm, energetic, hopeful, friendly, emotional.
Yellow:	Bright, sunny, cheerful, warm, prosperous, cowardly, deceitful.
Green:	Fresh, friendly, peaceful, balanced, lucky, envious, hopeful.
Blue:	Calm, restful, highly-esteemed, serene, tranquil, truthful, cool, formal, spacious, sad, depressed.
Purple:	Royal, dignified, powerful, rich, dominating, dramatic, mysterious, wise, passionate, spiritual.
White:	Innocent, youthful, faithful, pure, peaceful.
Black:	Mysterious, tragic, serious, somber, dignified, silent, sophisticated, mourning, strong, wise, evil.
Gray:	Modest, sad, old, gloomy.

Color Value

White	Light Pink	Pink	Dark Pink	Red	Deep Red	Burgundy	Dark Burgundy	Black

Tints (Getting lighter) — **Hue** — **Shades (Getting darker)**

Line Types and Directions

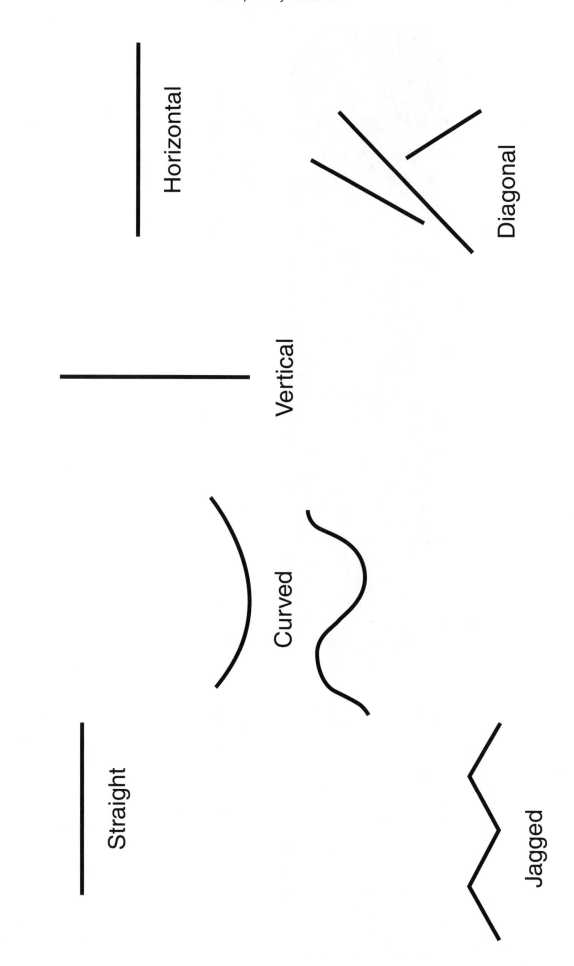

Horizontal

Diagonal

Vertical

Straight

Curved

Jagged

Effects of Line Placement

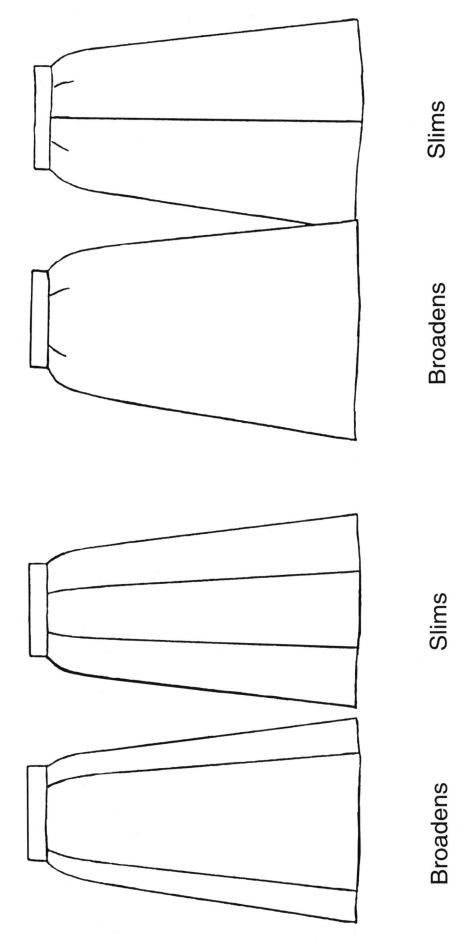

Slims

Broadens

Slims

Broadens

Working with Today's Fashions

Name_____ **Date** _____ **Period** _____

Review the work with current fashions that you did before studying this chapter (reproducible master titled *Design Elements in Today's Fashions*). Then write responses to these questions.

1. Summarize the colors, shapes, lines, and textures being used in current fashions. _____

   _____

   _____

   _____

   _____

2. What kinds of balance, proportion, emphasis, and rhythm are being used in this season's apparel?

   _____

   _____

   _____

   _____

3. What body build assets are flattered by today's trends? _____

   _____

   _____

   _____

   _____

   _____

   _____

4. What physical liabilities can be easily camouflaged with the latest trends? _____

   _____

   _____

   _____

   _____

5. What physical liabilities are hard to hide with the latest fashions? _____

   _____

   _____

   _____

   _____

6. Attach a current fashion photo to this page that shows a harmonious outfit. Explain how the elements of design have been used according to the principles of design to create harmony. _____

   _____

   _____

   _____

Using Design in Fashion

Name_____

Date_____**Period**_____ **Score**_____

Chapter 8 Test

Matching: Match the following terms and identifying phrases.

_____ 1. The principle of design that implies equilibrium or steadiness among the parts of a design.

_____ 2. The element of design that is a distinct, elongated mark as if drawn by a pen.

_____ 3. The principle of design concerned with the pleasing arrangement of the design elements to produce a feeling of continuity or easy movement of the observer's eye.

_____ 4. A circle with colors shown and used as a guide to study how to choose and combine colors.

_____ 5. Black, white, and gray colors rather than true hues.

_____ 6. The overall form or outline shape of an outfit or clothing style.

_____ 7. Principle of design that uses a concentration of interest in a particular part or area of a design.

_____ 8. A principle of design that concerns the spatial (size) relationship of all parts in a design to each other and to the whole.

_____ 9. An element of design concerned with the tactile quality of goods, or how the surface feels and looks.

_____ 10. Pleasing visual unity of a design created by a tasteful relationship among all parts within the whole.

A. balance

B. color wheel

C. emphasis

D. harmony

E. line

F. neutrals

G. proportion

H. rhythm

I. silhouette

J. texture

True/False: Circle *T* if the statement is true or *F* if the statement is false.

T F 11. Shape (silhouette) is the most exciting design element.

T F 12. A tint is darker than a pure hue, toward black.

T F 13. A monochromatic color scheme uses different tints, shades, and intensities of one color.

T F 14. An accented neutral color scheme combines tan and brown.

T F 15. A quiet, shy person is often more comfortable wearing bold, warm, bright colors and striking contrasts.

(Continued)

Name_____

T   F   16. Short, horizontal diagonal lines create the effect of width, while long, vertical diagonals create height.

T   F   17. Finishes and designs applied to the surface of fabrics are considered to be added visual texture.

T   F   18. Garments that bring out the natural proportions of the body are usually flattering and pleasing.

T   F   19. The shape of a female's body is called her physique.

T   F   20. Emphasis leading the eye up creates a shorter, wider look.

Multiple Choice: Choose the best response. Write the letter in the space provided.

_____ 21. Intensity is the _____.
A. name given to a color, such as blue, red, or green
B. lightness or darkness of a color, ranging on a gradation scale from almost white to almost black
C. brightness (clarity) or dullness (muddiness) of a color
D. All of the above.

_____ 22. Warm colors _____.
A. represent fire, sun, and brilliance
B. are from red to yellow on the color wheel
C. give a feeling of gaiety, activity, and cheerfulness
D. All of the above.

_____ 23. A complementary color scheme _____.
A. uses hues that are directly across from each other on the color wheel
B. creates the greatest contrast of colors when used side by side
C. rarely uses its colors together in full strength
D. All of the above.

_____ 24. Slimming colors include _____.
A. navy blue, dark blue-violet, and burgundy
B. black, white, and gray
C. red, orange, and brown
D. navy blue, true blue, and baby blue

_____ 25. Decorative lines _____.
A. include seams, darts, pleats, tucks, and garment edges
B. are especially noticeable if the fabric of the garment is printed or textured
C. are applied lines created by adding details to the surface of clothing
D. All of the above.

(Continued)

Name_____

_____ 26. Curved lines used in apparel _____.
  A. are bold and severe, suggesting dignity, power, and formality
  B. appear to be soft, gentle, and youthful, but may make the human shape look larger
  C. are very noticeable and can create a jumpy, confused feeling
  D. give the impression of added height and slimness, making the body look taller and thinner

_____ 27. The ideal body is said to be _____.
  A. six feet tall and somewhat rounded
  B. as slender as possible
  C. eight heads tall, with ⅞ of it below the head
  D. of "average" height, width, and weight

_____ 28. Repetition is accomplished with _____.
  A. a gradual increase or decrease of similar design elements, also called progression
  B. repeated lines, shapes, colors, or textures in a garment
  C. lines, patterns, or colors emerging from a central point like rays
  D. All of the above.

_____ 29. Body build is _____.
  A. the relationship among the different areas of the total human form
  B. what the shape of a male's body is called
  C. how a fashion figure is drawn—from legs to torso to head
  D. how the illusions of height or width are created through fashion design

_____ 30. To attract attention to areas with apparel, _____.
  A. use cool hues and soft fabrics
  B. put structural accents and applied decoration there
  C. use plain, unpatterned fabrics
  D. All of the above.

Essay Questions: Provide complete responses to the following questions or statements.

31. Name and show in chart form how the elements of design are used according to the principles of design to attractively create harmony.

32. Draw a color wheel and label the primary, secondary, and intermediate hues.

33. Describe formal and informal balance.

The Fashion Design Segment

Objectives

After studying this chapter, students will be able to

- explain the price market categories of apparel.
- define designer collection showings.
- describe how designers capitalize on their name recognition.
- summarize the designing process for fashions.
- identify the world's fashion centers and their specialties.
- recognize some influential fashion design names and labels.
- cite U.S. fashion associations and awards.

Teaching Materials

Text, pages 169–193
- *Fashion Terms*
- *Fashion Review*
- *Fashion in Action*

Student Workbook
- A. *Designer Myths or Truths*
- B. *Designer Trade Aspects*
- C. *What's the Difference?*
- D. *Fashion Design Segment Review*
- E. *Fashion Design Quiz*

Teacher's Resources
- *Fashionable Internet Research*, reproducible master 9-1
- *Examples of Designer Logos*, transparency master 9-2
- *Chambre Syndicale de la Couture Membership Requirements*, transparency master 9-3
- *Services Offered by Chambre Syndicale de la Couture*, transparency master 9-4
- *Fashion Reflections*, reproducible master 9-5
- *Fashion Design News Tidbits*, reproducible master 9-6
- Chapter 9 Test

Introductory Activities

1. Ask students to name fashion designers with whom they are familiar. Ask them to describe the designers' logos, their types of fashions, in what city they do their work, and if their names are on any other types of products, such as perfumes, household linens, or sunglasses.

2. Ask students what they know about the fashions and designers from countries other than the U.S. Have students discuss the fashions of France, Italy, Great Britain, Japan, Hong Kong, and other world locations.

3. *Designer Myths or Truths*, Activity A, WB. Students are asked to indicate if they think given statements are myths or truths. After students have worked on this independently, use it as a basis for a class discussion that introduces the chapter. (The correct answers are explained on the back of the page.)

4. Have books available in the classroom for students to consult while studying this chapter. Examples are *Dictionary of Fashion and Fashion Designers*, *20th Century Fashion*, *Couture*, *The Great Designers*, *Magic Names of Fashion*, *Who's Who in Fashion*, and many others.

Strategies to Reteach, Reinforce, Enrich, and Extend Text Concepts

Price Market Categories of Apparel

5. **RT** As the class looks at textbook Figure 9-2, have students discuss the price ranges, design levels, and target customers for the categories. Discuss how the quality, company or designer reputation, and customer expectation level goes up or down as the price goes up or down. Finally, discuss how the levels are less distinct now, blending together into one continuum.

6. **EX** Divide the class into five groups. Assign a different price market category to each group. Have students study about the designers, manufacturers, retailers, and consumers that are associated with that group. They might want to visit retail

stores and look in catalogs to find some of the information. Have the groups discuss if any of the designers or labels have several price lines so their fashions are in other categories. Have the groups report their findings to the rest of the class, also describing typical prices for a shirt, pair of slacks, sweater, and other garments in their category.

7. **RF** Ask students why they think designers are such vital employees to the success of manufacturing firms. Discuss how designers at lower price categories become "type cast" at that design level, which often causes them to have trouble moving up to a higher level.

8. **RF** Hold a class discussion about the recent feeling that budget consumers have not been offered fashion, quality, or fit in their garments in the past. Also, discuss the fact that there is a great opportunity for larger profits at that level of the market. Have the students try to think of ways of accomplishing this.

Collection Showings

9. **RF** Show students collection showings for the latest season. They are available from VIDCAT, shown on the cable TV Style Channel, and on Web sites such as www.infomat.com (which also has the calendar of fashion events).

10. **ER** Have students check the dates of specific collection showings on Internet sites. Examples are www.fashion-411.com, www.olympusfashionweek.com, and www.infomat.com.

11. **EX** *Fashionable Internet Research*, reproducible master 9-1. Have students use a computer search engine (such as www.google.com) to find specific answers to the questions. Then have a class discussion about the information found on the Internet Web sites.

12. **ER** Ask students to find articles from newspapers on file in the library or on Internet sites that tell about and show designer collection showings in the past year or two. Have each student discuss the information that he or she found. You may wish to keep a "teacher file" of clippings and pass out copies of them for students to use. Some Internet sites to try are www.firstview.com, www.STYLE.com, and Web sites of individual designers.

Capitalizing on Name Recognition

13. **RT** *Examples of Designer Logos*, transparency master 9-2. Use this transparency as a basis for a class discussion about the significance of logos to reinforce designers' distinctive images. Ask students if they can think of other designer logos that are not shown on the transparency.

14. **RF** Show students a video about how designers expand into multimillion-dollar businesses by marketing their names. *The Story of Fashion* is available from Insight Media. *When Fashion Is the Message: Marketing an Image* from D.E. Visuals and Meridian Education Corporation. *How Clothing Is Sold: Fashion Merchandising* from D.E. Visuals.

15. **ER** Have students look up information and read about designer secondary lines. Examples include Donna Karan's "DKNY," Calvin Klein's "CK," Ralph Lauren's "Lauren," Oscar de la Renta's "Oscar," and Emanuel Ungaro's "Emanuel." How successful are they? Who buys them? What are the general price ranges?

16. **RF** Have students look up the meaning of the word *diffusion*. Then hold a class discussion about why bridge/secondary lines are also called *diffusion lines*.

17. **RF** Ask students to describe designer licensing of other types of products (such as perfumes, sunglasses, and luggage). Have students describe the types of licensed icons they have seen on apparel lately such as cartoon figures, sports personalities, sports teams, or corporate products. Ask students what licensed apparel products they or their family members have purchased, such as shirts, fleecewear, jackets, caps, and sneakers.

18 **RT** Discuss designer franchising. Ask students to name and describe any franchise stores they have heard of or have seen. (Most students have probably never been in a designer franchise store.) Discuss the usual locations of designer franchise stores, their clientele, and their merchandise.

19 **EX** Obtain one or more sewing pattern catalogs. Have the students look at the designer patterns to assess the designs and desirability for home sewers.

The Designing Process

20. **RT** Have students look at textbook figure 9-14. Hold a class discussion about how long ahead of the retail selling of apparel the various activities take place. Also discuss how and why this timing is lengthened with overseas production and shortened with Quick Response linkages and manufacturing done within close geographic areas to the market.

21. **RF** Hold a class discussion about the stealing of designs. What do students think about knockoffs appearing on the market at the same time or before the original designs? (Previously, the cheaper version didn't appear until the next season, so the original firm had a full selling season first.) Should designers who have been copied just consider it an accepted hazard of doing business in this industry? Should designers who have been copied be flattered that others liked their design ideas, which gives the designers the reputation of being fashion leaders?

22. **ER** Have students try to come up with design ideas for fashions. What ideas can they think of from looking at fabrics? What newsworthy events and personalities give them ideas? Are there any social movements or new values or attitudes emerging? How about popular movies and TV shows that might have an impact? After discussing these and other sources of ideas, have each student draw one original design (possibly over a sketched pattern catalog figure) and explain to the class the inspiration for the design.

23. **RF** Show students a video about inspiration for design originality. *The Women's Wear Industry* and *The World of Fashion* can be obtained from D.E. Visuals. *The Trend: Where Fashion Begins* is available from D.E. Visuals and Meridian Education Corporation.

24. **RF** Have the class discuss the use of technology in fashion design. Although CAD was slow to enter the fashion design segment, explain the recent increase in CAD designing. (Now most fashion designers do their work with CAD systems.). A CD that might be used is *CAD Fundamentals* or *Apparel CAD* software, both from VMS, Inc.

World Fashion Design Centers

25. **RT** *Chambre Syndicale de la Couture Membership Requirements*, transparency master 9-3. As you show this transparency, ask students to discuss the importance of the points of membership to the Chambre Syndicale de la Couture of Paris.

26. **RT** *Services Offered by Chambre Syndicale de la Couture*, transparency master 9-4. As you show this transparency, ask students to discuss the services offered by the Chambre Syndicale de la Couture of Paris.

27. **RF** Show students a video about American sportswear from the Victorian period to the present. *All American: A Sportswear Tradition* is available from Fairchild Visuals.

28. **RF** *Fashion Reflections*, reproducible master 9-5. Students are asked to read and reflect on quotes from editors of popular fashion magazines and rewrite their understanding of the meaning of each quote.

29. **RT** Discuss why each country has some talented fashion designers. Ask students to explain why they think some countries have gained more fashion acclaim than other countries.

30. **RF** Show students a video about Italian designers. *Fashion: Italian Style* is available from D.E. Visuals and VMS, Inc. *The Craftsmanship of Fashion: The Italian Touch* is available from D.E. Visuals.

31. **EX** *Fashion Design News Tidbits*, reproducible master 9-6. As students read and discuss these true statements as a class, emphasize the changes that have occurred in the fashion design segment since the late 1990s. Stress that fashion has become global big business tied to media power. It has the illusion of being small artistic companies, but is really large commercial enterprises with big money tied tightly to worldwide customers. The key is the strength of the brand name (label).

Some Influential Fashion Designers

32. **RF** Show students a video about the history of fashion design that reviews events and designers through the years. *History of Apparel Design: 1930 to the 21st Century* is available from Nasco, VMS, Inc., The Curriculum Center for Family and Consumer Sciences, and Meridian Education Corporation. *Top 10 Fashion Designers* is available from Teacher's Media Company. Videos about specific designers are also available, and designer biographies are sometimes shown on the cable channel A&E.

33. **RF** Have students check out lists of designers on the Internet. They might "search" www.fashion.about.com, www.fashionwindows.com, www.fashion.net, and other Web sites.

U.S. Fashion Awards and Associations

34. **ER** Obtain materials from the Council of Fashion Designers of America (CFDA) and the International Association of Clothing Designers (IACD). Discuss the activities and importance of the trade organizations with the class. Also discuss their projects to help charitable causes such as those for AIDS patients, cancer research, and clothes for the homeless.

35. **RF** *Designer Trade Aspects*, Activity B, WB. Students are asked to read statements that give them new information, check their degree of interest in each statement, and write an explanation about the statement they feel is the most interesting.

36. **RT** *What's the Difference?* Activity C, WB. Students are asked to describe the difference between chapter terms that are presented in pairs.

37. **RT** *Fashion Design Segment Review*, Activity D, WB. Students are asked to answer questions after reviewing the chapter.

38. **RF** *Fashion Design Quiz*, Activity E, WB. Students are asked to write one true/false question for each of the chapter sections and exchange pages with a classmate to answer each other's questions correctly.

Additional Enrichment Activities

Research

39. Have students do research about a designer of their choice, possibly someone new on the scene who is not mentioned in the chapter. Have students prepare a profile about the designer including the designer's educational preparation and design background, business size and location, characteristic types of work, relative price range, and types of clients. Also, students should draw or show the designer's logo if they know it and attach pictures or illustrations of actual designs to their report.

40. Have students trace the history of French couture from its beginnings with the House of Worth in the 1850s to today. Who have been the most famous designers, for what types of creations are they remembered, and who have been their famous clients?

41. Have students do research about the high fashion industry consolidation of companies/labels. They might especially research LVMH Moet Hennessy Louis Vuitton, the Gucci Group NV, Pinault-Printemps-Redoute (PPR), or Industrie Zignago Santa Margherita S.p.A.

Projects

42. Have students design a bulletin board display about eight or ten top fashion designers of today. It can be titled *Some Designers of Today*. The display should include a picture of each designer, the designer's logo, where each designer does business, some pictures of each designer's creations, and any other concise but relevant facts about the designers.

43. Rent the movie *Prêt-á-Porter* or *The Devil Wears Prada*. Show the movie to the students. Follow with a discussion of the truthful nature of its humor and the portrayals of actual people involved with high fashion. Discuss the "shallow" implications of the movie contrasted with the actual business aspects of the fashion industry.

44. Divide the class into groups to read selected chapters of the content-packed book *The Fashion Conspiracy* by Nicholas Coleridge. Have each group of students present an oral "group book report" to the rest of the class about their assigned section of the book.

45. After having students study about a particular apparel franchise company (including corporate structure, location, decor, advertising, and merchandise), arrange a class trip to one of its franchise stores. Consult with the owner or manager ahead of time for permission to bring the class. Perhaps the owner or manager may be willing to speak to the class about being in the franchise business. Have the students look at the merchandise, the layout and decor of the store, and the advertising. When back at school, have the students discuss what they learned and write a thank-you note to the store proprietor.

Answer Key

Text

Fashion Review, page 193

1. quality of the materials, the type and amount of labor used, the complexity of the style and construction, and the reputation of the designer or manufacturer
2. designer: the designer's salon; bridge: fashionable dress shops or special designer sections of upscale department stores; better: selected specialty or department stores; moderate: department and chain stores and specialty apparel stores; budget: low-priced chain and discount stores
3. with the press releases using photographs and video footage of the showings
4. They stage the shows at one common site and accept corporate sponsor donations of money and products
5. so factory production can satisfy the multiple orders in time to ship the merchandise to stores
6. (Describe two:) Videotapes are sent; selected guests are invited to a breakfast, brunch, or lunch where there is modeling of the collection; 3-D view-masters are sent with slides of the collection.
7. that the items should be of fine quality and in good taste
8. Manufacturers gain the status of the name that gives an image of fashion quality and prestige. Retailers can stock name products that sell well to consumers who want to identify with particular designers. Designers get large financial royalties.
9. Celebrity licensing associates the name of movie stars, famous athletes, and other celebrities with products. Character licensing is tied to cartoon characters. Corporate licensing features logos or depictions of copyright commercial products.
10. Advantage: They can get their businesses off the ground quickly with instant name recognition. Disadvantage: They have no control of the parent firm's products or distribution reliability.
11. They can control the design and distribution of their products. They have limited liability. They need less capital to expand quickly into market areas (increased profits).

12. (List three:) There is no legal copyright protection against it. It saves money for manufacturers. It enables producers to get fast-selling styles out immediately. It enables similar styles to be available at several price levels.
13. (List four:) forecasting services; past fashion movement; art movements; new stage plays; popular movies and TV shows; news events; new living patterns; nature; prestigious people; foreign and American fashion magazines; fabrics from textile firms or other cultures; changing economic, social, and political conditions; inventive young people on the streets; trends in consumer attitudes and purchasing patterns; retail store owners and buyers
14. Electronic graphics interchange allows garment parts, colors, and prints to be changed with a computer command. 3-D imaging enables a designer to view a design from all sides.
15. New York, Paris, Milan, London, Tokyo, Hong Kong (and others)
16. (List three:) They must: be recognized as talented and successful; agree to abide by a set of rules against copying; do a minimum number of original outfits per collection; have a minimum number of staff models and production workers; and cooperate with showing dates.
17. (List two for each:) Italy—beautiful fabrics; sophisticated prints; sportswear; knitwear; menswear. Great Britain—high-quality RTW men's tailored apparel; fine rainwear; punk clothes; tweeds, woolens, lamb's wool, and cashmere. Germany—well-made, conservatively styled RTW for women and men; inspirational textiles. Scandinavia—knitted woolens; patterned ski sweaters; furs; leathers; innovative fabric designs; gold and silver jewelry with clean-cut designs. Spain—leather; suede; beading. Canada—outerwear; furs; decorative household linens.
18. Their strikingly unusual shapes and fabrics do not lend themselves to volume production; the exchange rate between the Japanese yen and other currencies makes Japanese goods very expensive in some countries.
19. Council of Fashion Designers of America (CFDA)
20. Licensees are the manufacturers of the products, and licensors are the designers or owners of the well-known labels.

Student Workbook

What's the Difference? Activity C

1. Couture is the custom-made designer segment of the fashion industry for the highest priced "class" market. Bridge lines are "secondary" or "diffusion" lines of well-known designers, priced between the designer and better categories.
2. The moderate category is made up of medium-priced merchandise with well-known brand names. Budget is the lowest-priced category of apparel, found on retail racks and shelves for the mass market.
3. Custom-made apparel is made-to-order with individual fit for the client and one-of-a-kind exclusiveness. Ready-to-wear (RTW) garments are produced in factories according to standard sizes, especially women's apparel.
4. An adaptation is a design that reflects the outstanding features of another design but is not an exact copy. A knock-off is a copy of another, usually high-priced, garment.
5. Margin is the profit per item. Perceived difference is the idea in customers' minds that items stand out from others, usually because of image and quality.
6. A collection is the total number of garments in a designer's or apparel manufacturer's seasonal presentation, especially for high-priced garments. A line is a group of styles and designs that are produced and sold as a set of new selections for a given season.
7. Licensing is an arrangement in which a manufacturer is given the exclusive right to produce and market goods that bear the famous name of someone who, in return, receives a percentage of wholesale sales. In franchising, a firm grants a retailer the right to use a famous or established name and trademarked merchandise in return for a certain amount of money.
8. The franchiser is the designer or well-known corporation whose name is on the products, but has no direct ownership of the franchise. The franchisee is the person or group that owns the retail business.
9. House boutiques are small retail shops owned by designers that sell items with the designer's label. Designer patterns are replicas of actual designer fashions offered to home sewers by commercial pattern companies.
10. Prophetic fashions are styles that are identified early as future best-sellers in many price ranges. Electronic graphics interchange allows garment parts, colors, and prints to be changed with computer commands, with design options built into software.
11. A design stylist is a person who creates knock-offs by simplifying garments that are popular in higher priced categories. A couturier is a high fashion designer.
12. A logo is a symbol that represents a person, firm, or organization. A caution is the admission or entrance fee required from commercial customers to attend French designer showings. It is intended to deter copying and is applied toward purchases.
13. Haute couture is the high fashion designer industry of France that creates original, individually-designed fashions. Alta moda is the high fashion design industry of Italy.
14. The Chambre Syndicale de la Couture is the trade association for top designers of the Paris couture.

The Council of Fashion Designers of America (CFDA) is a trade association of top U.S. designers.

15. Fashion piracy is the stealing of design ideas without the permission of the originator. Prêt-á-porter is the French designer ready-to-wear ("prêt") industry.

Fashion Design Segment Review, Activity D

1. They walk down the runway to cheers and applause from the invited guests.
2. fine fabrics and trimmings, custom construction, modeling fees, costs for hairdressers, make-up experts, lighting, music
3. Fall-winter collections are shown in late February to early April, and spring-summer collections are shown in September/October.
4. Scheduling for shows is arranged by industry organizations in each fashion city.
5. (List three:) too expensive, consumers have access to excellent quality mass-produced fashions, lifestyles and attitudes have changed (want more clothes), require fittings—take a long time to be made
6. Publicity from the showings keeps the designers' names famous and helps maintain demand for their other business dealings.
7. The famous name might be compromised with products that have an unacceptable level of design or quality.
8. They arrange licensing deals and check to be sure the products are worthy of the designers' labels.
9. They must satisfy their franchisees and consumers.
10. almost a year (seven to nine months)
11. best-selling items in a manufacturer's line that are recut for production the next season
12. The design is not made up in fabric until it is just right.
13. France
14. to determine qualifications for couture houses and requirements for their showings and to deal with their common problems and interests
15. (List three:) sponsors a school for apprentices of the couture industry, represents members in relations with the French government, arbitrates disputes, regulates working hours and uniform wage arrangements, coordinates the dates of showings, registers those who will attend showings
16. Trade buyers are essentially buying copying rights.
17. They have close proximity to the U.S. and cheaper sources of supply.
18. Hong Kong
19. the Council of Fashion Designers of America (CFDA)
20. the CFDA Lifetime Achievement Award

Teacher's Resources

Fashionable Internet Research, reproducible master 9-1

1. A. New York City
   B. Los Angeles
   C. Melbourne; sometimes Sydney
   D. Ngee Ann City, Singapore
   E. New Delhi, India
   F. Milan, Italy
   G. Moscow, Russia
2. It produces all of them.
3. Publisher of the Fashion Calendar that schedules shows and designer time slots.
4. Commemorative plaques are embedded along Seventh Avenue to pay tribute to top American fashion designers.
5. (Student response.)

Chapter 9 Test

1. F	11. T	21. D
2. A	12. F	22. C
3. G	13. F	23. A
4. B	14. F	24. B
5. J	15. T	25. C
6. C	16. T	26. A
7. H	17. T	27. D
8. D	18. F	28. B
9. I	19. T	29. D
10. E	20. T	30. A

31. (Name and describe three:) The designer category provides original high-priced fashions for the tiny "class" market. The bridge category offers secondary lines of well-known designers, with limited-edition garments of expensive fabrics and fine details produced in small quantities. The better category has high-quality garments at a more reasonable price, designed by talented experts who are unnamed on the label. The moderate category is made up of medium-priced merchandise with well-known brand names that are available to and worn by most people. The budget category is the lowest-priced category for the mass market with almost no original designing (down-scaled knockoffs).
32. (See text Chart 9-26.)
33. (List five:) forecasting services; past fashion movement; art movements; new stage plays; popular movies and TV shows; news events; new living patterns; nature; prestigious people; foreign and American fashion magazines; fabrics from textile firms or other cultures; changing economic, social, and political conditions; inventive young people on the streets; trends in consumer attitudes and purchasing patterns; retail store owners and buyers

Fashionable Internet Research

Name_____ **Date** _____ **Period** _____

Complete the following Internet research activity.

1. Do a quick Internet search of the following, and write down the dates and location of each, its sponsors, and a highlight that you find interesting:

   A. Olympus Fashion Week _____

   _____

   B. Mercedes-Benz Fashion Week_____

   _____

   C. Mercedes Australia Fashion Week _____

   _____

   D. Singapore Fashion Festival _____

   _____

   E. Lakme Fashion Week_____

   _____

   F. Milan Fashion Week _____

   _____

   G. Fashion Week in Moscow_____

   _____

2. What is the relationship of the company IMG Fashion to the above shows? _____

   _____

   _____

   _____

3. What part in the New York shows has Ruth Finley played for more than 50 years? _____

   _____

   _____

4. Describe New York City's Fashion Walk of Fame. _____

   _____

   _____

   _____

5. After searching the key words, "fashion designers," which resulting Web site is your favorite and why?

   _____

   _____

   _____

Examples of Designer Logos

 Pierre Cardin—Stylized use of both initials

 Oleg Cassini—Interlocking initials

 Liz Claiborne—Name in small embroidery

 Hubert De Givenchy—"G" used geometrically

 Fendi—F and inverted F placed together

 Guy Laroche—Stylized lines to form initials in a box

 Christian Dior—Capital initials inside a rectangle

 Ralph Lauren—Small embroidered polo player

 Oscar de la Renta—Initial of his first name

Chambre Syndicale de la Couture
Membership Requirements

- Couturier must submit a formal written request for membership.

- Fashion house must have Paris workroom(s) doing quality work.

- Collections must be designed by designer or staff member and custom-made to fit clients.

- Collections must be presented twice a year (fall/winter shown in July; spring/summer shown in January).

- Collections must include at least 50 ensembles of both day and evening designs.

- Collections must be presented to clientele in specifically arranged places.

- At least 20 sewing workers must be employed.

Services Offered by Chambre Syndicale de la Couture

Provides:

- collective representation with the French government

- arbitration of disputes

- regulation uniform wages and working hours

- sponsorship of a school for couture business education

- registration of copyrights for new designs of members

- coordination of dates/times of collection showings

- checking of press and buyer accreditation and issues admission cards for showings

Fashion Reflections

Name_____ **Date** _____ **Period** _____

Read and reflect on these quotes from editors of fashion magazines, fashion designers, and others in the industry. Rewrite your understanding of the meaning of each quote in your own words.

1. "After sitting through countless (European) shows, it's always a pleasure to return to (the U.S.). American designers never fail to provide a modern distillation of all the important trends."—Anna Wintour, Editor-In-Chief, Vogue _____

_____

_____

_____

_____

2. "The fashion designer does only half the job. It remains for each woman to know herself well enough to gravitate to the dress or costume that will do the most for her."—Molie Parnis, designer

_____

_____

_____

_____

3. "It's not just what's on the runway that influences us all. It's the audience, the models, the makeup, the music, the backstage chaos, the frenzy. Sure, you want to check yourself into a (mental institution at the end). But what wonderful insanity."—Linda Wells, Editor-In-Chief, *Allure* _____

_____

_____

_____

_____

4. "Today, a woman hates being bossed around, and she definitely refuses to be told how to get dressed. She's got that knocked: she gets her fashion inspiration everywhere—from top designers, from MTV, from her favorite movies."—Elizabeth Crow, Editor-In-Chief, *Mademoiselle*_____

_____

_____

_____

_____

5. "Life is complicated. Clothes should be simple."—The philosophy of the Tom & Linda Platt Collection

_____

_____

_____

_____

(Continued)

Name_____

6. "The influence of the American designer is felt all over the world. After the eclecticism of London, the elegance of Milan, and the exuberance of Paris (showings, the U.S.) always steps up to the plate with real-life fashion and stunning modern sportswear."—Liz Tilberis, Editor-In-Chief, *Harper's Bazaar* _____

_____

_____

_____

7. "Through research, increasing their exposures, enlarging their visions, stimulating their curiosities, exciting their imaginations, and gaining encouragement for innovation, designers put together things that are already there, differently and better."—Anonymous _____

_____

_____

_____

8. "The best designers have a sense of style that goes way beyond the way we dress. Today, fashion is about the way we live, whether it's expressed by the chic suit, the well-dressed bedroom, or the perfectly turned-out table."—Dominique Browning, Editor-In-Chief, *House and Garden* _____

_____

_____

_____

_____

9. "I always think the best way to dress is when the person notices you first and the dress after."—Oscar de la Renta in *Business Windsor*_____

_____

_____

_____

10. "I design clothes for women who want to buy them."—Oscar de la Renta in *Business Windsor*

_____

_____

_____

_____

_____

Fashion Design News Tidbits

Read and discuss the following true statements.

1. Perry Ellis International, Inc. is a Miami-based design house whose namesake designer is no longer living. However, the label still has original designs, imports, and many licenses for men's, women's, and children's products in the U.S. and more than 26 countries worldwide.

2. Textile and apparel companies spend thousands of dollars each year buying original artwork for design inspirations. However, these valuable assets often then get put into drawers, are sent out to customers, and are frequently lost or misplaced. Prototype fabrics and designs are also valuable assets, but finding these samples often relies on diligent searches by designers, sales staff, or administrative aides.

3. Stan Miller is a fashion designer as well as president of the Council of Fashion Designers of America (CFDA). The CFDA used to manage the New York Fashion Week collection showings, but that was taken over by IMG. Fern Mallis had been executive director of CFDA for many years, but she joined IMG when it became the fashion event organizer.

4. Singer Jennifer Lopez and Andy Hilfiger (brother of designer Tommy Hilfiger) joined forces to start an urban lifestyle collection called "Sweetface Fashions." Items are designed by Lopez's costume designer, Leiga Morris, in cooperation with Lopez and Hilfiger, and produced in China and Guatemala. The line includes girlswear, jeans, swimwear, footwear, accessories, sunglasses, and perfume. The project is handled by the New York-based holding company Music Entertainment Fashion, founded by Lopez and Hilfiger.

5. The U.S. design firm Donna Karan International Inc. and all Donna Karan's trademarks are now owned by the French luxury goods holding company LVMH Moet Hennessy Louis Vuitton. Designer Donna Karan and her husband, Stephan Weiss, who had managed her company, were paid hundreds of millions of dollars for the business and tradenames. Ms. Karan will continue as chief designer of the labels. Bernard Arnault, LVMH's chairman and owner, has built up a formidable portfolio of fashion brands through acquisition, including many other labels.

6. Gucci Group is another multinational fashion company with holdings of many fashion labels, including Yves Saint Laurent. This consolidation and globalization of the fashion world gives more importance to projecting a strong image through advertising, runway shows, and licensing. Small, less financially strong companies are finding it tougher to compete against these "deep-pocketed" conglomerates that present fashion collections like Las Vegas extravaganzas. With retail buyers and the press seeing hundreds of shows in their four-city semiannual marathon, a winning show that sticks in their minds is crucial.

7. Fashion Web sites are creating almost real-time coverage of collection showings to the entire world, with high-quality, unauthorized Internet images showing all details. Top fashion designers are fuming about their designs being stolen almost as soon as they are presented.

8. The British expression for "ready-to-wear" is "off-the-peg."

The Fashion Design Segment

Name_____

Date_____**Period**_____ **Score**_____

Chapter 9 Test

Matching: Match the following terms and identifying phrases.

_____ 1. Business arrangement in which a manufacturer is given the exclusive right to produce and market goods that bear the famous name of someone who, in return, receives a percentage of wholesale sales.

_____ 2. Secondary lines of well-known designers, priced between the designers and better categories.

_____ 3. Symbol that represents a person, firm, or organization.

_____ 4. The total number of garments in a designer's or apparel manufacturer's seasonal presentation, especially for high-priced garments.

_____ 5. Garments, especially women's apparel, produced in factories according to standard sizes.

_____ 6. The custom-made designer segment of the fashion industry for the highest priced "class" market.

_____ 7. The idea in customers' minds that items stand out from others, usually because of image and quality.

_____ 8. Business arrangement in which a firm grants a retailer the right to use a famous or established name and trademarked merchandise in return for a certain amount of money.

_____ 9. The French designer ready-to-wear ("prêt") industry.

_____ 10. Copy of another, usually higher-priced, garment.

A. bridge lines

B. collection

C. couture

D. franchising

E. knock-off

F. licensing

G. logo

H. perceived difference

I. prêt-á-porter

J. ready-to-wear (RTW)

True/False: Circle *T* if the statement is true or *F* if the statement is false.

T   F   11. Custom-made garments are made-to-order for individual clients of designers.

T   F   12. Design stylists work as couture assistants, creating new designs for collections.

T   F   13. Couture collections are very profitable; most of the line is sold soon after the showing.

T   F   14. Ready-to-wear collections are shown three months before retail selling to consumers takes place.

T   F   15. A franchisee is the person (or group) that owns a franchise business.

(Continued)

Name_____

T   F   16. Skilled home sewers can buy designer patterns to make their own designer clothes.

T   F   17. Electronic graphics interchange allows garment parts, colors, and prints to be changed with computer commands.

T   F   18. The top couture collections are the most important fashion events to sell to retail store buyers.

T   F   19. Haute couture is the name for the high fashion designer industry of France.

T   F   20. Alta moda is the name for the high fashion designer industry of Italy.

Multiple Choice: Choose the best response. Write the letter in the space provided.

_____ 21. In the fashion industry, a "line" _____.
A. is a group of styles/designs that are produced and sold as a set of new selections for a given season
B. is like a "collection," but usually of moderate and lower-priced garments
C. might contain from 60 to 200 garments
D. All of the above.

_____ 22. Designer ready-to-wear garments _____.
A. feature low-quality fabrics and construction
B. are mass-produced in large quantities in designer-owned manufacturing plants
C. are referred to as secondary lines
D. All of the above.

_____ 23. House boutiques of designers _____.
A. are small retail shops owned by the designers
B. are only located in or near the designer's headquarters
C. feature altered design samples from collection showings
D. All of the above.

_____ 24. The stealing of design ideas without the permission of the originator is known as _____.
A. style lending
B. fashion piracy
C. design borrowing
D. unauthorized apparel

_____ 25. Prophetic fashions are _____.
A. the newest designs that are the most creative and fashion-forward
B. designs from foreign fashion centers, which are included in U.S. fashion week showings
C. styles that are identified early as future best-sellers in many price ranges
D. designs from newly discovered design talents, who are financed by wealthy backers

_____ 26. The Chambre Syndicale de la Couture is the _____.
A. trade association for Paris couture designers
B. "chamber" (location) of the French apparel manufacturing industry office
C. collective syndicate of Italian high fashion designers
D. trade organization for all European high fashion designers

(Continued)

Name_____

_____ 27. Japanese fashion designers _____.
- A. often design, manufacture, and sell their clothing lines themselves all over the world
- B. can produce goods quickly and often provide merchandise ahead of other fashion centers
- C. are known for strikingly unusual shapes and fabrics that do not adapt well to volume production
- D. All of the above.

_____ 28. Hong Kong _____.
- A. is considered to be a "sleeping giant" for fashion, with a large land mass and huge population
- B. used to do cheap production of other country's designs and now produces its own fashions
- C. is expected to form its first organized fashion design association in the near future
- D. All of the above.

_____ 29. The most important fashion awards today are _____.
- A. known as the Coty Awards
- B. voted on by a national jury of newspaper and magazine fashion editors
- C. known as the Cutty Sark Awards
- D. presented by the Council of Fashion Designers of America (CFDA)

_____ 30. An advantage for franchisees in a franchise arrangement includes the fact that they _____.
- A. can get their business off the ground quickly with instant name recognition
- B. have a lot of control of product design and quality
- C. can be assured of reliable deliveries
- D. All of the above.

Essay Questions: Provide complete responses to the following questions or statements.

31. Name and describe any three of the five price market categories of apparel.

32. Name and briefly describe the work of three fashion designers or design firms mentioned in this chapter.

33. List at least five sources of inspiration that designers might use when creating new fashions.

Ready-to-Wear Manufacturing

Objectives

After studying this chapter, students will be able to

- summarize the business aspects of apparel manufacturing.
- explain inside and outside shops.
- describe preproduction procedures from costing and editing the line to cutting the garments.
- discuss the process and methods of apparel production.
- explain employee concerns of health and safety, as well as equitable pay.
- describe offshore production.

Teaching Materials

Text, pages 194–213
  Fashion Terms
  Fashion Review
  Fashion in Action
Student Workbook
  A. *Expanding Your Ready-to-Wear Knowledge*
  B. *Manufacturing Business Team*
  C. *Create a Fashion Apparel Line*
  D. *Manufacturing Crossword*
Teacher's Resources
  U.S. Apparel Industry, transparency master 10-1
  Costing Analysis, reproducible master 10-2
  Expectations of Empowerment Programs, reproducible master 10-3
  Seated Workstation Adjustments, transparency master 10-4
  Standing Workstation Adjustments, transparency master 10-5
  Manufacturing Competencies, transparency master 10-6
  Digest and Discuss, reproducible master 10-7
  Chapter 10 Test

Introductory Activities

1. Ask students to describe how they think factory production of apparel is done. Have them use brainstorming to try to think of several different ways. Then tell them that interesting details about factory production of apparel await them in this chapter.
2. Assign one of each of the following terms to a section of the class: production line balancing, croquis, batch oriented production, excess capacity, work flow analysis, retooling, cross-trained operators, empowerment, repetitive stress injury, cottage industry, wage parity, real income, flexible work groups, product hand-off. Have each group look up information about their term in the library, on the Internet, in trade journals, or in other sources as appropriate. Then ask students to discuss the meaning within their group and report their findings to the class. Ask them to be alert when reading the chapter and comment when their term applies to the content being studied.
3. Have the class discuss what they think the relationship is among technology, apparel manufacturing, and the costs and quality of finished fashions.

Strategies to Reteach, Reinforce, Enrich, and Extend Text Concepts

The Business of Apparel Manufacturing

4. **RT** As students look at text illustration 10-1, discuss with the class how apparel production is a conversion process that transforms input into

output. Have them relate the same process to other products, such as cars, buildings, and restaurant meals. In each example, discuss how each of the factors of production (text illustration 10-2) is used. Thoroughly discuss the factors of production in relation to apparel manufacturing.

5. **RT** *U.S. Apparel Industry*, transparency master 10-1. Use this master as you discuss where most apparel plants are located and the average number of employees at the plants.

6. **RF** Show students one or more videos about the apparel manufacturing industry. *The Women's Wear Industry*, *The Men's Wear Industry*, and *The Children's Wear Industry* are available from D.E. Visuals. *Clothing Design and Manufacture* plus *Apparel Manufacturing: An Overview* are available from Insight Media. *Factors Influencing the Apparel Industry* is available from D.E. Visuals.

7. **EX** Have students find out about garment districts and apparel manufacturing resources from Internet sites. They might start with www.dpoa.com (Los Angeles) and www.fashioncenter.com, (New York City) and then extend their search to other cities.

8. **RT** Discuss the relationship among automation, productivity, costs, and employment in apparel manufacturing. Discuss the statement, "Productivity improvement requires efficiency coupled with innovation."

9. **RF** Have students explain why successful apparel manufacturers are the ones that keep their costs low, their quality high, and their selling prices in line with their competitors. Also have students explain how apparel firms use profits.

10. **RF** Ask students to review textbook Figure 10-5. Then divide the class into three groups, one for each of the competitive approaches. Have each group research that approach and prepare a report with visuals outlining their points. With the low-cost approach, make sure that elastic demand (a percentage change in price produces a greater percentage change in the quantity sold) and inelastic demand (a percentage change in price produces a smaller percentage change in the quantity sold) are covered. Stress why U.S. companies usually cannot compete on cost, the risks involved in offering differentiated products, and satisfying a market niche in profitable ways.

11. **ER** Have students make a large calendar for the bulletin board that shows (with different colors for each fashion season) when manufactured apparel lines for the many seasons are shown to retail buyers and when they are delivered to the stores. Have them consult with trade calendars, manufacturers, and retailers to gather correct information. Then hold a class discussion about the display.

Inside and Outside Shops

12. **ER** Obtain materials from the American Apparel Contractors Association to share with the students.

13. **RF** Have students discuss the advantages and disadvantages of being an outside shop or apparel jobber. Ask the students about the company's control of design (maximum control done in-house) and quality of construction (minimum control done by contractors). Also discuss capital investments, the ability to specialize, and volume flexibility.

14. **ER** Ask students to gather information about apparel contractors (American and worldwide) by searching "sewing contractors" on the Web sites www.fashiondex.com, www.ThomasNet.com, www.sewing-contractors.com, www.apparelsearch.com, www.infomat.com, and others.

15. **EX** Pretend the class owns a contract sewing factory. Ask students to decide what types of work they would do, how they would market their services to get business from apparel companies, how they might obtain their equipment and find their workers, how they would stay competitive in today's global and technological marketplace, how they might maintain steady (rather than erratic) work loads, how they could offer fast response time, and other aspects of being a contractor. Discuss the fact that contractor's costs can be lower because they specialize in certain types of garments, and they have lower selling costs. Discuss how contractors are now expanding into design, development, and marketing (becoming like inside shop apparel companies, but often doing store private label brands). Discuss the fact that many contractors now have the latest automation and offer store-direct deliveries.

Preproduction Procedures

16. **RT** While students look at text illustration 10-11, discuss the general areas of preproduction, production, and postproduction, as an introduction to the activities within those areas. Mention that some outside shops do cutting and parts preparation in-house, sending cut parts to the contract factories they use. Other companies have the contractors do their cutting and parts preparation. Also discuss that the entire process takes almost one year (from beginning design ideas to distribution to retail stores) and then starts all over again.

17. **RF** With students looking at text illustration 10-13, discuss the facts that fixed costs must be covered no matter how many units (garments) are produced and variable costs increase with the number of units produced (a certain amount per unit).

18. **EX** *Costing Analysis*, reproducible master 10-2. Students are asked to fill out a worksheet about the costing of a garment from a mail-order catalog. They should work with percentages of costing categories, dollar amounts, a cost-price squeeze explanation, and how sales volume and profit might suffer if expected quality is compromised to the customers.

19. **RF** Hold a class discussion about why cost analyses should not be the only considerations in deciding on what materials to use in apparel designs to generate profits. Ask students what would happen if chosen materials would not be available for reorders, or if the quality or colors would not be true to the samples when the yard goods are delivered.

20. **ER** Show the class a video about ready-to-wear manufacturing. *Fashion 2000: Developing an Apparel Line* is available from Insight Media, D.E. Visuals, VMS, Inc., Meridian Education Corporation, and Nasco.

21. **RF** With the class divided into groups of about five students each, have each group edit a line of apparel. Have them start with at least 20 pictures of garments cut from different types and price levels of mail-order catalogs, and end up with 10 garments in a cohesive line. Students should decide on a market category for their line, suggest changes of details to offer garments of similar style and price levels, and decide on colors or textures that coordinate or complement each other. Have each group describe their line and the process they went through to the rest of the class.

Apparel Production

22. **ER** Obtain to keep in the classroom for reference the *Glossary of Garment Industry Terms*. It and other apparel industry reference books are available from Bobbin Miller Freeman.

23. **RF** Have students discuss all the different specific production processes they think take place for the sewing of a pair of jeans. Have them decide what different skill levels are needed for the different jobs and the types of specialized machines or attachments needed.

24. **ER** Divide the class into four groups and assign each one to a different apparel production method (traditional tailor system, progressive bundle system, unit production system, and modular manufacturing). Have the students study more about the methods assigned to them and give a thorough report to the class, with pictures or other visual aids if possible. In conclusion, ask the students to summarize the pros and cons of each system.

25. **EX** Show students a video about apparel production. *How Clothing Is Made: A Garment Industry Field Trip* is available from The Curriculum Center for Family and Consumer Sciences, Insight Media, Nasco, Learning Seed, VMS, Inc., and D.E. Visuals. *Fabric to 501s: Levi Strauss & Company* is available from Meridian Education Corporation, The Curriculum Center for Family and Consumer Sciences, and VMS, Inc. Four other videos from VMS, Inc., include *Introduction to Manufacturing Technology*, *Manufacturing Systems*, *Manufacturing Resources*, and *Manufacturing Processes*.

26. **RF** *Expectations of Empowerment Programs*, reproducible master 10-3. Students are asked to respond to given statements about empowerment and then discuss the statements as a class.

27. **RF** *Expanding Your Ready-to-Wear Knowledge*, Activity A, WB. Students are asked to answer questions, define new terms, and think about situations. Then students are asked to use each point for class discussion.

28. **EX** Hold a class debate about the use of prison labor to produce apparel for the federal government (mostly for the military). How are these huge, noncompetitive contracts (the government must use prison products, even if they are more expensive) between prisons and the government driving some U.S. apparel companies (which employ law-abiding taxpayers) out of business? How can the government balance the advantages of such prison work programs (prisoners keep busy, learn a trade, work off their debts, and make money for the prison system) against its responsibilities to citizens? How about the facts that prison manufacturing has almost no overhead expense, no benefits to pay, and no shareholders to evaluate their methods? Also, no taxes are paid on the profits. Have students represent both sides of this government funded program that directly competes with private business.

29. **RT** Assign students to review preproduction and production of apparel manufacturing for the rest of the class. Have them explain the following as completely as possible: apparel designing, pattern making, sample making, editing the line, buying the materials, pattern grading, marker making, fabric cutting, parts preparation, inside shop construction, outside shop contracting, and finishing.

Employer Concerns

30. **RF** Ask students to discuss the causes of increased cumulative trauma disorders in apparel production. Subjects might include today's greater focus on productivity, increased speed of output, an aging workforce, more highly repetitive (finely specialized) jobs in garment assembly, and automated tasks push manual jobs harder. Discuss how it is difficult to determine what caused an

injury that may have taken many months or years to develop. Also discuss why prevention is better than treatment. Note that it has been shown that having workers stand up to do operations and moving around between stations is better for the back, legs, and arms than sitting and doing one operation all day.

31. **RT** *Seated Workstation Adjustments*, transparency master 10-4. Use this transparency as a basis of a class discussion about the points made on the transparency.

32. **RT** *Standing Workstation Adjustments*, transparency master 10-5. Use this transparency as a basis of a class discussion about the points made on the transparency. Also, discuss the fact that many new factory sewing operations are done standing, moving, and doing several (or changing to) different operations during the day.

33. **RF** Hold a class discussion about how to pay apparel production workers fairly for their skills while motivating them to be as productive as possible, helping them to get enjoyment and pride from doing the work, and fostering cooperation with others for a team effort. Why is individual piecework pay considered to harm employee empowerment and teamwork? Why is operator training in technical and interpersonal skill areas so important? How hard do students think it might be for workers who have been receiving piecework pay to change to other types of pay? How can workers be more committed, with more job satisfaction and higher productivity?

Offshore Production

34. **EX** Form two debate teams of class members: one to argue in favor of offshore production and the other to argue in favor of domestic production. Have them do research to become well versed about the points they will make. Have them consider economic views of the U.S. and foreign countries, humanistic views of U.S. workers versus survival needs of workers in depressed nations, and political views of countries that trade with each other.

35. **RF** Have students discuss garment production at wage rates of $.35/hour in Haiti or $.70/hour in Honduras (even though foreign visits by U.S. management, packaging, and shipping are additional costs) versus production that takes the same amount of time to do in an Alabama factory at $7.00 an hour. Have students evaluate why apparel firms and retailers use foreign manufacturing sources.

Chapter Review

36. **ER** *Manufacturing Business Team*, Activity B, WB. Students are asked to form apparel manufacturing business teams, consider given questions, give their company a name, and explain their business in detail to the rest of the class.

37. **ER** *Create a Fashion Apparel Line*, Activity C, WB. Students are asked to pretend they are creating a fashion apparel line and answer the provided questions.

38. **RT** *Manufacturing Competencies*, transparency master 10-6. To expand on the points of this entire chapter, use this transparency as you discuss the points presented. Have the class discuss how manufacturing companies can be successful in the industry if they are proficient in all of these competencies.

39. **RT** Show the class a video that reviews the overall apparel industry. *Factors Influencing the Apparel Industry* is available from The Curriculum Center for Family and Consumer Sciences and D.E. Visuals. *Seventh Avenue: America's Premier Fashion Center* is available from D.E. Visuals.

40. **RT** *Manufacturing Crossword*, Activity D, WB. Students are asked to complete a crossword puzzle of terms from the chapter using the clues listed.

41. **ER** *Digest and Discuss*, reproducible master 10-7. Ask students to read the statements, digest their meanings, write their thoughts about them, and discuss them with others.

Additional Enrichment Activities

Research

42. Have students do library and/or Internet research to gather information about the history of the apparel industry to share with other students. Have those doing the research find out about the industrial revolution, division of labor, development of the tape measure, standardized sizes, sewing machines, factory production, locations and conditions of manufacturing plants, the idea of stocking inventories, and other historical milestones.

43. Have students research an apparel manufacturer whose goods are widely known (preferably a public corporation). They should find out the location of the company's headquarters and ask the company to send an annual report and other

available information. Business reference books in the library or listings on the Internet should be able to add to the information. Students should describe the price market category of the company's lines, the target customer, locations of manufacturing plants and sales offices, whether it is an inside or outside shop, size and make-up of the design staff, types and names of retailers the company sells to, and the company's sales volume.

44. Ask students to research the following in relation to apparel manufacturing and report their findings to the class.
    - manufacturing terms: *tolerances to specifications, Kanban, hand-off, bump back*
    - sourcebooks/directories to locate suppliers of fabrics, trims, notions, fashion forecasts, CAD services, other needs (including names, availability, costs, and how often published)
    - the content of the [TC]² CD-ROM program about time study rating skills

Projects

45. If there are any apparel manufacturing plants in your area, contact them about hosting a tour of their operations for your students. Have the students do research about the company and its operations before going so they are well informed and can get the most out of the visit as possible. After the tour, have students discuss the processes and technology involved in the production of clothing. Also have students write a thank-you note that mentions specifics about their visit.

Answer Key

Text

Fashion Review, page 213

1. design risks, economic conditions, and cyclical trends
2. Some companies have failed, and some have merged into larger companies because of the competitive nature of the industry and necessary costly automation.
3. They can sell stock to get capital.
4. for new equipment, market research, product development, bonuses for valued employees, pay for new employees, dividends to stockholders
5. being the low-cost source for products; offering differentiated products; satisfying a narrow market niche

6. because American companies have developed flexibility for shorter runs and faster style changes than the foreign long production runs of commodity items
7. spring and fall
8. Inside shops are firms that do all stages of production from design concept and fabric purchasing through all sewing procedures to the shipment of finished garments. Outside shops are firms that handle everything but the sewing and sometimes the cutting.
9. price, quality, timely delivery, and capabilities of providing product variety
10. with a plan that estimates demand for various colors, styles, sizes, quality, and price in the company's market
11. the company's basic pattern for particular body measurements, from which fashion patterns are created
12. to identify them for manufacturing, selling to retailers, and distribution
13. They change or revise it.
14. small quantities of garments that are made up and placed in retail stores to test the designs for consumer reaction
15. trusted quality, fair prices, on-time delivery, options for returns, and the ability to supply more goods later if needed
16. Water-jet cutters use a thin stream of very high-pressure water to cut a small stack of fabric layers; laser-beam cutters vaporize a single layer of fabric with an intense, powerful beam of light.
17. an overhead product carrier on a computerized conveyor system
18. because hardly any employees become sick or disabled, medical insurance costs go down, and disability compensation payments are reduced
19. All members of a group share in extra incentive rewards when the team exceeds work expectations.
20. Offshore production is done in overseas sewing shops. Domestic production involves manufacturing done in one's own country.

Student Workbook

Expanding Your Ready-to-Wear Knowledge, Activity A

1. Input (fabric, thread, buttons) is transformed (by sewing) into output (finished garments or accessories).
2. to see which employees have the highest productivity on that particular operation.

3. Variable costs are expenses that increase or decrease with the volume of sales. Fixed costs are overhead expenses that remain the same regardless of sales volume.
4. Materials and direct labor increase or decrease with the volume of items produced. Overhead costs stay the same no matter how many items are produced.
5. (Student response.)
6. It goes down.
7. "Approximate share of wholesale selling price"
8. Because the costing structure of every size firm has similar percentages, even if the actual numbers produced are extremely different.
9. Technology provides the ability to specialize, plus flexibility, lower costs, and faster deliveries of orders, just like contracting does.
10. (Student response.—This causes pressure to work faster, cumulative trauma disorders, etc.)
11. (Student response.)
12. (Student response.)

Manufacturing Crossword, Activity D

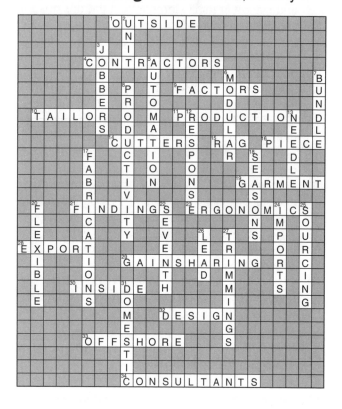

Teacher's Resources

Chapter 10 Test

1. G
2. E
3. I
4. D
5. H
6. C
7. J
8. B
9. F
10. A
11. T
12. T
13. F
14. F
15. T
16. F
17. T
18. F
19. T
20. T
21. C
22. B
23. A
24. C
25. D
26. A
27. B
28. C
29. C
30. C

31. Resources include land and materials. Labor is workers. Capital includes money and equipment. Business leadership gives ideas and organization.
32. striving to be the low-cost source as an advantage (imported commodity products); pursuing differentiation through fashion styling, quality, performance, etc. (designer brand names); focusing on a narrow market niche, catering to specific buyers' needs and tastes
33. specialization, flexibility, lower costs, and faster delivery of orders

U.S. Apparel Industry

15 States = 72% of all employees

Northeast 39

Southeast 93

California 29

Average U.S. Plant Employment: 46

Costing Analysis

Name_____ **Date** _____ **Period** _____

Cut out a picture of a garment from a catalog, answer the following questions, and attach the picture to this page when you are finished with the exercise.

Divide the retail selling price of your pictured garment in half (and rounded off to a whole dollar) as an estimate of the wholesale price. Fill out the following chart with the percentages listed in text illustration 10-13 and the correlating dollar amounts for your design. Then fill in "adjusted percentages" that show what would happen to the profit percentage if costs for materials, direct labor, and overhead were each to go up 2% and the wholesale price had to stay the same in order for the garment to sell. Finally, complete the activities at the bottom of the page.

Costing Category	Percentage of Wholesale Price	Dollar Amount	Adjusted Percentages
Materials: Fabric/Findings/Trimmings			
Direct Labor			
Overhead			
Profit			
Wholesale Price			

Describe a **cost-price squeeze**, which is usually caused by increased competition in inflationary times:

_____

_____

_____

What would happen to sales if the company decided to use less expensive fabric and trimmings and keep the same wholesale price in order to increase profits? Why? _____

_____

_____

_____

Computer **spreadsheets** are used for costing analyses, with calculations programmed into them to help with this type of work. Dollar amounts for specific yardages of materials, construction labor, and other costs can be put in, then manipulated and refined within the system. The system indicates where costs should be lowered and automatically shows the wholesale price for each style number. Sketch your impression of a spreadsheet page on another piece of paper (with a lot of columns for "scenarios") and share it during a discussion with the class.

Expectations of Empowerment Programs

Name_____**Date**_____**Period**_____

Write your reaction to each of the following statements. Then discuss the statements as a class.

1. Employees who are empowered should be able to (or trained to) set goals and strive to achieve them._____

_____

_____

_____

2. Empowered employees should be trusted to use their own workstyles (including schedules, activities, and deadlines) to achieve their goals. _____

_____

_____

_____

3. Empowered employees should be given specific, appropriate assignments._____

_____

_____

_____

4. Empowered employees should be given the amount of authority (permission to make decisions) that matches their responsibilities. _____

_____

_____

_____

5. Empowered employees should be held accountable for results and praised when the results are good._____

_____

_____

_____

6. Employers might start by empowering employees a small amount and follow successes with increased empowerment. _____

_____

_____

_____

(Continued)

Name_____

7. Employers must provide the necessary resources (such as supplies, equipment, and training) for empowered employees to succeed. _____

_____

_____

_____

8. Employers should resist the temptation to solve problems, and employees should be taught to treat problems as learning opportunities. _____

_____

_____

_____

9. Requirements for reports should be minimized, encouraging concise and quick communications between management and team members, possibly through occasional conferences, brief memos, or periodic statistical reports. _____

_____

_____

_____

10. Managers must be supportive and affirming of empowered employees and back their people up through mistakes as well as successes._____

_____

_____

_____

11. Explain why the process of empowering workers often takes a long time._____

_____

_____

_____

_____

_____

_____

Seated Workstation Adjustments

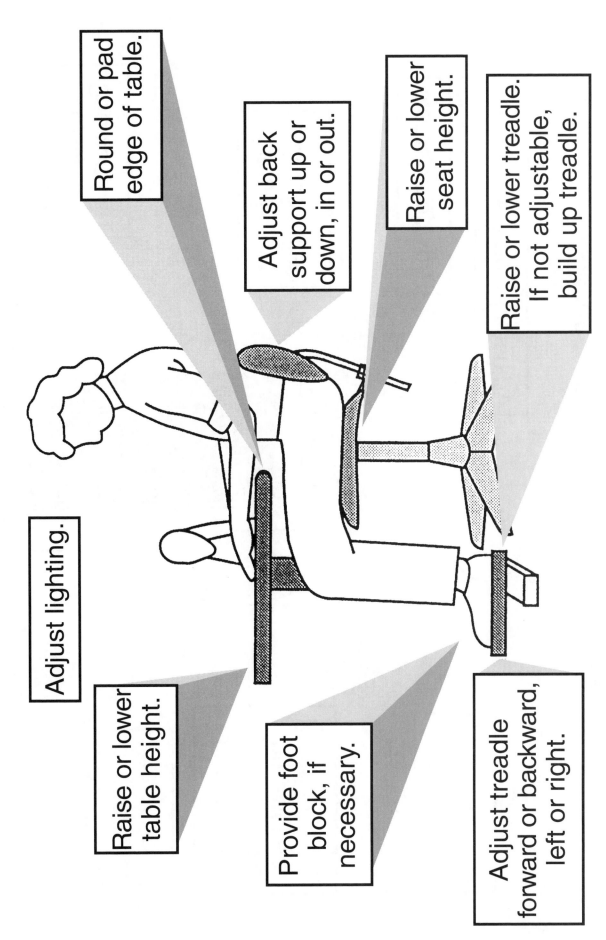

Round or pad edge of table.

Adjust back support up or down, in or out.

Raise or lower seat height.

Raise or lower treadle. If not adjustable, build up treadle.

Adjust lighting.

Raise or lower table height.

Provide foot block, if necessary.

Adjust treadle forward or backward, left or right.

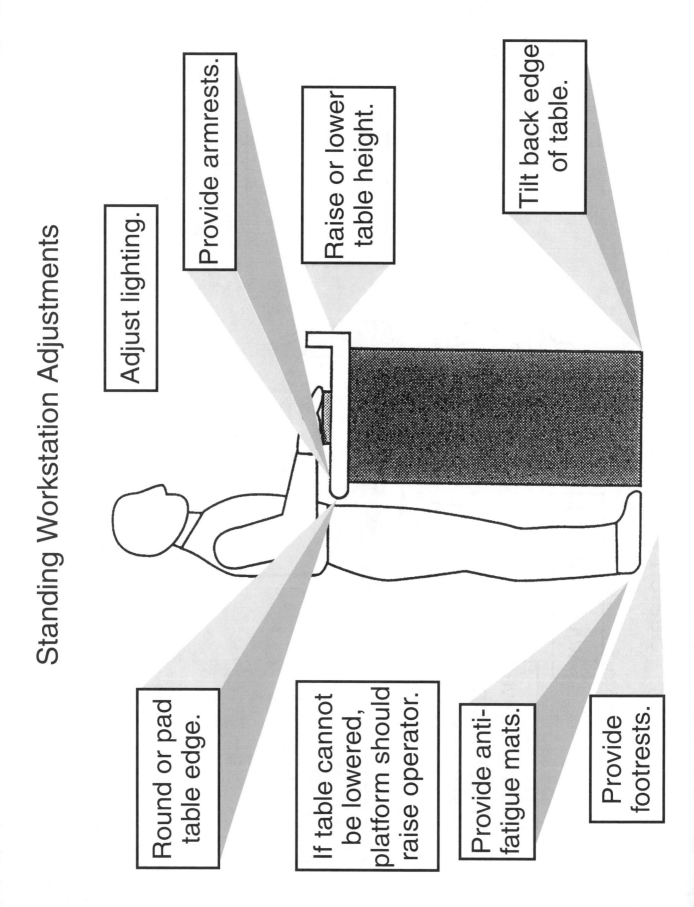

Standing Workstation Adjustments

Adjust lighting.

Provide armrests.

Raise or lower table height.

Tilt back edge of table.

Round or pad table edge.

If table cannot be lowered, platform should raise operator.

Provide anti-fatigue mats.

Provide footrests.

Manufacturing Competencies

- Develop competitive (low-price, high-quality) sources.

- Provide flexible production (with contractors or plant sites).

- Respond to in-season style (fashion) preferences.

- Respond to ongoing volume (quantity demand changes).

- Be conscious of employee, environmental, and industry concerns.

Digest and Discuss

Name_____ **Date** _____ **Period** _____

Read the following statements, digest their meanings, write your thoughts about them, and discuss them with other students or the entire class.

1. When a garment manufacturer is interested in a particular fabric, a fabric cut is ordered. This is 8 to 10 yards to make a sample garment and evaluate the design. If the manufacturer decides to purchase the fabric, negotiations begin concerning price, quantity, delivery, reorder availability, and if many other manufacturers will be using the same fabric. _____

   _____

   _____

   _____

2. Some manufacturers are now even outsourcing their preproduction procedures. Design and pattern making service bureaus offer computer-aided design systems and accept specifications electronically from distant customers. _____

   _____

   _____

   _____

3. Manufacturers use either open markers or closed markers. Open markers contain full pattern pieces that allow the cutting of whole garment parts while closed markers use half-pattern pieces and are used with folded fabric. _____

   _____

   _____

   _____

4. Inside shops that do not want to deplete cash reserves for equipment that may be obsolete in a few years are turning to leasing as a preferred method of staying up with equipment and technology needs. _____

   _____

   _____

   _____

5. Time studies are used to determine piecework pay rates for sewing machine operators. These help find easier, smarter methods and measure human output. However, new manufacturing systems are not using them because of product quality and employee health problems. _____

   _____

   _____

   _____

6. Wealth is created in only three ways: through agriculture (raising crops or livestock), extraction (mining and fishing), or manufacturing (making goods). Beyond those, all other economic activities transfer wealth but don't create it._____

   _____

   _____

   _____

Ready-to-Wear Manufacturing

Name_____

Date_____**Period**_____ **Score**_____

Chapter 10 Test

Matching: Match the following terms and identifying phrases.

_____ 1. Goods that come into the country from foreign sources.

_____ 2. Commercial products sent out of a country to other countries.

_____ 3. The seeking of vendors or producers of desired goods.

_____ 4. Human engineering that matches human performance to the tasks performed, the equipment used, and the environment.

_____ 5. A measure of how efficiently/effectively resources are used, calculated by dividing output by employee hours expended to achieve that output.

_____ 6. Procedure of calculating the estimated expenses of producing something.

_____ 7. The ergonomic matching of jobs and equipment to employees, the company's output requirements, compensation plans, and worker behaviors that are reinforced.

_____ 8. Independently-owned sewing factories that produce goods for apparel firms.

_____ 9. Area within a fashion city where most of the apparel companies are located.

_____ 10. The use of machinery to perform physical tasks that were previously performed by humans.

A. automation

B. contractors

C. costing

D. ergonomics

E. exports

F. garment district

G. imports

H. productivity

I. sourcing

J. work design

True/False: Circle *T* if the statement is true or *F* if the statement is false.

T   F   11. Production is the transformation of resources into a form that people need or want.

T   F   12. Since apparel manufacturing is labor-intensive, low-wage manufacturing locations have an advantage.

T   F   13. The apparel industry consists almost entirely of small privately owned firms.

T   F   14. Most apparel manufacturers have 10 or more production seasons, depending on the merchandise category.

T   F   15. The potential for apparel manufacturers to produce more than the market can absorb causes intense competition for manufacturers not to lose their retail accounts to others.

(Continued)

Name_____

T   F   16. Inside shops handle all apparel production tasks except the sewing and sometimes the cutting.

T   F   17. The company's basic pattern for particular body measurements, from which fashion patterns are created, is called the sloper.

T   F   18. When manufacturers "edit" a line, they make all of their designs into sample garments.

T   F   19. The process of making garment patterns into a complete range of larger and smaller sizes is grading.

T   F   20. Machines that move bolts of cloth back and forth on cutting tables are called spreaders.

Multiple Choice: Choose the best response. Write the letter in the space provided.

_____ 21. The possibility of high profits and/or devastating losses for apparel manufacturers results from _____.
A. the materials and services it uses
B. changing wages and tax rates
C. design risks, economic conditions, and cyclical trends
D. All of the above.

_____ 22. The functional parts of garments, such as zippers, hooks, snaps, thread, and labels are called _____.
A. fabrications
B. findings
C. trimmings
D. materials

_____ 23. Distinct retail selling periods are called _____.
A. fashion seasons
B. summer and winter
C. holiday events
D. All of the above.

_____ 24. The New York garment district is called _____.
A. the "Pushboy Area" because bins and racks of materials and garments move through the streets
B. the "Garment Loft Area" because so much production is still done within the buildings
C. "Seventh Avenue" because it is centered along both sides of that avenue
D. "Contractor Lane" because New York garment manufacturing is mostly done by contractors

_____ 25. Apparel manufacturing firms that never produce any of their own goods are referred to as _____.
A. sourcing consultants
B. inside shops
C. contractors
D. apparel jobbers

(Continued)

Name_____

_____ 26. Popular designs of the previous season that are used again with some changes are said to be _____.
    A. refabricated
    B. reused
    C. repeated
    D. recapitulated

_____ 27. Specific garment designs are identified for manufacturing, selling, and distribution with _____.
    A. selling specifications
    B. style numbers
    C. markers
    D. All of the above.

_____ 28. New items that are added to manufacturer's lines between design seasons are called _____.
    A. samples
    B. samplings
    C. sweeteners
    D. croquis

_____ 29. The combining of several manufacturing steps into one continuous computerized process is called _____.
    A. the tailor system
    B. section sewing
    C. data integration
    D. vertical construction

_____ 30. Manufacturing that assigns one specific task to each person along an assembly line is called _____.
    A. modular manufacturing
    B. gainsharing
    C. piecework
    D. flexible manufacturing

Essay Questions: Provide complete responses to the following questions or statements.

31. Name and briefly describe the four factors of production.

32. List and briefly describe the three main basic competitive approaches.

33. List the four main advantages for apparel firms to use contractors.

Wholesale Apparel Marketing and Distribution

Objectives

After studying this chapter, students will be able to

→ discuss inventory management of goods.

→ explain benchmarking and quality programs.

→ describe trademark protection.

→ identify technological advances in apparel manufacturing.

→ explain how and where apparel producers sell their finished goods.

→ describe the distribution of fashion items.

→ summarize apparel industry trade information.

Teaching Materials

Text, pages 214–232
  Fashion Terms
  Fashion Review
  Fashion in Action
Student Workbook
  A. *Wholesale Apparel Marketing Facts*
  B. *Apparel Sales and Distribution*
  C. *Apparel Business Responses*
  D. *Fashion Market Match*
  E. *Group Pick and Pursue*
Teacher's Resources
  Materials Handling Expenses, transparency master 11-1
  Right the First Time, transparency master 11-2
  Manufacturing-in Quality, reproducible master 11-3
  The Fight Against Counterfeiting, transparency master 11-4
  Technology in Apparel Manufacturing, reproducible master 11-5
  Balanced Flow Supply Chain, transparency master 11-6
  Improving the Weak Link, transparency master 11-7
  Chapter 11 Test

Introductory Activities

1. Ask students what they think *inventory* means and have them explain the importance of businesses having the right amount or type of inventory as often as possible. Also ask them for their thoughts on how apparel manufacturers sell and distribute their goods. This will indicate how knowledgeable the students already are and start them thinking about the content of the chapter.

2. Have students discuss the importance of quality in manufactured goods. Ask students if they can tell some ways of instilling pride in workers to achieve high quality all the time.

3. Have each student write a paper describing why fashion merchandisers in the retail segment should understand the processes prior to retail in the soft goods chain. Students should include why fashion professionals should have a knowledge of textiles as well as how apparel is produced, sold, and distributed. Then divide the class into groups to discuss their papers and to consolidate their separate ideas into one cohesive group paper to be read to the rest of the class and discussed.

Strategies to Reteach, Reinforce, Enrich, and Extend Text Concepts

Inventory Management

4. **RT** Have students discuss in depth the three main types of inventories described in the text.

5. **RT** *Materials Handling Expenses*, transparency master 11-1. Although apparel manufacturers try to find the cheapest labor to produce their goods, labor only totals about 11 percent of the final cost of making the items (fabrics, trimmings, and notions make up the largest cost). It has been estimated that 80 percent of the time between raw materials and delivery to the retailer is

nonvalue-added materials handling time, and 27 percent of the *expense* of the final product can be attributed to materials handling (as shown). Hold a class discussion about this, emphasizing how decreasing the amount of time allocated to materials handling would also lower the expense.

6. **RT** Have students look at text figure 11-2. Hold a class discussion about situations of having too little, too much, and the wrong inventories. Also discuss why the timeliness of fashion merchandise exaggerates the effects of incorrect inventories.

7. **RF** Have students discuss how electronic linkage partnerships help companies keep lean and timely inventories for market demand. Discuss why inventory control is one of the primary competitive advantages of U.S.-based manufacturers. Also discuss how opportunity cost (the benefit given up if resources are not used to best advantage) must be considered when weighing risks versus rewards to make inventory choices.

8. **RF** Ask students to find the latest information about ERP on the Internet by using a search engine to search for the exact phrase *enterprise resource planning*. Have students read the information they find and report to the class about how ERP completes the CAD-CAM package and ties the entire pipeline together for smooth inventory management.

9. **RF** For advanced classes, show a video about the business strategy of inventory, rather than just a recordkeeping function. *Inventory Control* is available from D.E. Visuals. *Materials Handling* is available from VMS, Inc.

Benchmarking for Quality Products

10. **RT** Discuss with the class how benchmarking results in change that brings about better processes.

11. **RF** Select four students (or ask for volunteers) to summarize quality control, quality circles, quality assurance, and total quality management (TQM) programs.

12. **ER** *Right the First Time*, transparency master 11-2. Use this transparency as you discuss with students how quality that is manufactured into products the first time can benefit in lower final costs and provide better customer satisfaction for continued purchases. Discuss a proactive approach to quality versus a reactive approach.

13. **RF** *Manufacturing-in Quality*, reproducible master 11-3. Students are asked to think about and respond to statements, and then discuss the statements as a class.

Trademark Protection

14. **RF** Have students research recent situations concerning counterfeit fashion goods in the library or through the Internet. Articles appear periodically in the *Wall Street Journal* and other publications.

15. **RF** Show the class a video about counterfeit goods. *Name Brand Counterfeiting: A Global Economic Crisis* is available from D.E. Visuals.

16. **EX** Have students look for registration and trademark symbols in fashion advertisements. Show them some examples that you have collected over time. Also ask them to look for such symbols on labels and hangtags attached to retail merchandise when they are shopping.

17. **RT** Hold a class discussion about the importance of protecting a company's trademark and the consequences to those who deal with counterfeit goods.

18. **ER** *The Fight Against Counterfeiting*, transparency master 11-4. Use this transparency as you discuss with students how apparel firms are combating counterfeiting.

Technological Advances in Apparel Manufacturing

19. **RT** With students looking at text figure 11-10, discuss how computer-integrated manufacturing (CIM) ties together all functions to try to achieve hands-off production. Then ask students to explain how this reduces manufacturing bottlenecks and data entry errors, and why CIM standards are needed.

20. **ER** Show the class a video about technological advances in apparel manufacturing. *Microdynamics: A Learning Tour* is available with study guide from The Curriculum Center for Family and Consumer Sciences. *Advanced Manufacturing* and *Computer Integrated Manufacturing* videos are available from VMS, Inc. and Cambridge Educational.

21. **RT** Hold a class discussion about demand flow manufacturing, flexible manufacturing with computer-changeable machines, totally computer-produced garments that are custom-ordered, stitchless electronic injection sewing, ultrasonically fused seams, tubular molded garments, and other ideas about future apparel manufacturing.

22. **ER** *Technology in Apparel Manufacturing*, reproducible master 11-5. Students are asked to read and respond to paragraphs and then discuss the subjects as a class.

23. **RF** *Wholesale Apparel Marketing Facts*, Activity A, WB. Students are asked to indicate whether statements are true or false. Then they are to write each false statement as a true statement with supporting information. The statements in the activity are from the first half of the text chapter.

Selling the Finished Apparel

24. **ER** Have students relate CAD and CAM technology as an advantage for selling the finished apparel. Discuss computer color printouts of designs to show retail customers, quick visualizations of color and style changes suggested by customers, hard copies of styles for customers to evaluate their purchases, enlarged printouts for sales presentations, status of when order manufacturing will be completed, etc.

25. **RT** Have students discuss in depth why manufacturers show merchandise at markets and how they accomplish their goals, by using chart 11-18 in the text. Discuss the importance of each of the points presented.

26. **EX** Show students a video about wholesale selling. *Seventh Avenue: America's Premier Fashion Center* and *Wholesale & Industrial Salesmanship* are available from D.E. Visuals.

27. **ER** Make reference materials about apparel industry contracts available for students to study. Have students research the Worth Street Textile Marketing Rules on www.atmi.org/Pubs/worth.asp including standard contract sections and a code of procedures. Although most contractual arrangements are satisfactory, arbitration is encouraged to settle disputes (rather than litigation) under the General Arbitration Council of the Textile & Apparel Industries. Have students find out about the provisions of awards (decisions) that contain directives to the disputing parties.

28. **RT** Have students discuss the advantages and disadvantages of trunk shows for both manufacturers and retailers. Discuss what price points (levels) are most common for trunk shows.

29. **EX** Have students experience wholesale apparel sales over the Internet by searching for "dress manufacturers," "Sportswear," or another key apparel term on one or several of the following Web sites:
www.apparelwebmart.com,
www.onlinemerchandisemart.com,
www.californiamart.com,
www.thefashionassociation.org/press.htm,
www.usawear.org, www.americasmart.com,
and the sites of specific manufacturers. Then discuss why retailers are angry if their suppliers sell to consumers via their Web sites rather than just to retailers (answer: they are in direct competition with their retail accounts). Also discuss requests by retailers that manufacturers ship directly to consumers who order over retail Web sites so retailers do not need to keep the goods in stock.

Distribution of the Finished Apparel

30. **RT** Explain to the class the distribution functions of order processing, shipping on time, providing customer service, and handling returns.

31. **RF** Have students discuss the following statement: "Over the long haul, an apparel company has a much greater chance of succeeding if it serves multiple distribution channels with a varied product mix."

32. **RF** *Balanced Flow Supply Chain*, transparency master 11-6. While showing this transparency to the class, discuss how the "continuous flow distribution system" minimizes costs and maximizes revenues. Also discuss that it is a more detailed version of the market-driven "pull" approach to the textile-apparel pipeline shown in illustration 5-23 of the text. It requires collaboration between trading partners and the use of technology.

33. **RT** Hold a class discussion about why apparel companies (and retailers) often outsource their distribution and logistics functions. Discuss the costs and specific expertise needed for "pick/pack" duties, trucking, and consolidation of deliveries (economies of scale). Also talk about distribution centers and widespread geographic locations. Discuss service and price considerations of a distribution network (including clearing imports through customs). Have students check the Web site www.shipsmo.com.

34. **EX** Define the new term *intermodal shipping* for the class (cargo packaged into large standardized containers for efficient handling among all types of transportation—ship, train, truck, etc.). Have a class discussion about how intermodal shipping is putting efficiency into the supply chain for large shipments, but is not as effective for small, more customized inventory flow.

35. **RF** Ask students to describe the main modes of transportation for goods (train, truck, ship, and airplane). Have them explain the pros and cons of each for various situations of apparel distribution. They should include relative cost, speed, number of locations served, door-to-door options, ability to handle all types of fashion goods, frequency of scheduled shipments, and dependability of meeting time demands.

36. **ER** Make materials about UCC-128 labeling, commonly referred to as compliance labeling, available for students to study. In business partnerships, vendors must have bar code labels at specific locations on their cartons. This coordinates with the advance ship notice and eliminates the need to open cartons and verify contents. After students have studied the materials, hold a class discussion about the positive effects

compliance labeling has on shipment accuracy, inventory control, company productivity, a competitive edge, and satisfied customers.

37. **RF** *Improving the Weak Link*, transparency master 11-7. While using this transparency, have students discuss each one of the links of the chain in relation to its size (strength) shown on the transparency. Moving from left to right, have students discuss the activities of each category and why it is probably as strong or as weak as it is. Then have them describe ways of strengthening the link, especially warehousing and delivery. Discuss how the customer service link would become stronger with improvements in previous links. This reviews the processes in the manufacturing segment as well as discussing distribution.

38. **RF** Show students a video that summarizes the logistics topics of transportation, warehousing, and materials handling. *Physical Distribution*, *Channels of Distribution*, *Managing the Chain of Distribution*, and *Wholesaling Fashion Merchandise* are all available from D.E. Visuals. A PowerPoint CD, *Systems of Distribution Channels* can also be obtained from D.E. Visuals.

39. **RF** *Apparel Sales and Distribution*, Activity B, WB. Students are asked to complete an activity about apparel sales and distribution. Students should review the text chapter as they complete this activity.

40. **EX** *Apparel Business Responses*, Activity C, WB. Students are asked to write their thoughts about given statements and then participate in a class discussion about each situation described. Many new industry concepts and terms are introduced in this activity.

Apparel Industry Trade Information

41. **ER** Obtain materials from apparel industry trade associations, such as the American Apparel and Footwear Association (AAFA); International Apparel Federation (IAF); and National Association of the Sewn Products Industry (SEAMS). Also gather materials about industry trade shows, such as MAGIC Marketplace, ASAP Global Sourcing Show, Material World, Chicago Men's Wear Collective, FAME, NAMSBY, STYLEMAX, and others. Also obtain distribution trade journals, such as *Consumer Goods Manufacturer*. Have students study the materials and discuss the purposes and duties of the various groups, shows, and trade journals.

42. **ER** Have students research the history of apparel industry trade unions. Have students find out about sweatshops, low wages, long hours, locked factory doors, unsanitary conditions, and child labor. Ask students to read about the homework system of clothing manufacture and the Triangle Shirtwaist Company fire. Have them discover the feelings of honest apparel manufacturers (who make up the majority of the industry), what is being done to shut down disreputable factories, and how the situation is monitored.

43. **RT** *Fashion Market Match*, Activity D, WB. Students are asked to match chapter terms and definitions.

44. **ER** *Group Pick and Pursue*, Activity E, WB. With other classmates, teams of students are asked to pick one of four choices to research. Then they are to prepare a group presentation to the class, including visual aids.

Additional Enrichment Activities

Research

45. Have students research total quality management (TQM). They should find out about the work done by Dr. W. Edward Deming, when and why TQM was first implemented in Japan rather than the U.S., and the results for companies that follow TQM thinking and procedures. Also ask students to research the quality improvement work of Dr. Joseph M. Juran. Have students report their findings to the rest of the class so other students can gain from the information.

46. Have students research the Malcolm Baldrige National Quality Award that recognizes quality achievements of U.S. companies and publicizes successful quality strategies. Have students report on the effects the award has had on textile/apparel companies, how companies are judged to win the annual award, and what companies have won the award.

47. Have students research and report on the protection of products and logos from counterfeiters. Have them explain ex parte seizure of the U.S. trademark and copyright laws, and the part played by U.S. marshals. What other legal avenues are open to those whose products are being illegally replicated?

48. Have small groups of students research the recent technological advances that are affecting apparel production and distribution and give a report to the class. Have students interview people who work in the industry, if possible. They should seek information about computerized programmable sewing machines, robotics, the use of artificial intelligence, speech recognition, ANSI X12 data formats for standardized EDI business transactions, CIM standards, the Serial Shipping

Container Code (SSCC), the National Cargo Security Council (NCSC), cross-docking for flow-through distribution centers, and global positioning systems (GPS) for tracking shipments.

Projects

49. In groups of several students, have groups study about specific indications of quality in apparel. Also have them select a standard garment, such as a shirt or a pair of jeans, to bring to class. Looking at the inside, outside, materials, seams, and details of the garment, have the students recognize and evaluate all indications of the level of quality of their chosen garment. Each group should make a chart of their findings to post on the bulletin board.

50. Invite a representative from the closest apparel mart near your school to speak to the class. Ask the speaker to bring materials from the mart, such as a list of vendors, map of the facilities, and calendar of market weeks for various apparel categories. Have the students study about the mart ahead of time and prepare a list of questions they would like to have answered.

Answer Key

Text

Fashion Review, page 232

1. preproduction fabrics, trimmings, and notions
2. product obsolescence and excessive carrying costs
3. a computerized system of planning production materials and levels of inventory
4. Proactive makes processes better to do everything right the first time; reactive fixes problems after they occur.
5. the costs of inspection, doing work over, or having items returned by unhappy customers
6. They can register them with the Patent and Trademark Office of the federal government.
7. because the programming is changed on software rather than having to manually alter the machinery
8. spreading, cutting, and movement through the sewing line
9. less downtime, better product quality, and lower expenditures for replacement machines
10. with liquid polymer thread or fused seams that might be heat-sealed with ultrasonic energy
11. a meeting place for buyers and sellers of goods, usually with many sellers in close proximity to each other

12. formal, well-prepared showings of a company's goods to potential customers
13. upward for strong sellers and downward for items less desired by retail buyers
14. actual sales are measured against the forecast figures
15. reorders
16. their own customers
17. dividing merchandise into smaller lots and moving it to individual stores from company distribution centers
18. It is fast for long distances, but is expensive.
19. apparel industry executives and decision makers
20. to keep as many jobs as possible in the U.S. (rather than the work going to offshore locations)

Student Workbook

Wholesale Apparel Marketing Facts, Activity A

1. F	10. F
2. T	11. T
3. T	12. F
4. F	13. T
5. T	14. T
6. T	15. T
7. F	16. T
8. T	17. F
9. T	18. T

Statement #1: The inventories of manufacturers include raw materials, work-in-process, and finished goods. Retail inventories are only finished goods. Both manufacturers and retailers also have inventories of business support goods.

Statement #4: Computerized production applications reduce materials handling time by balancing the work flow more efficiently and bypassing some human contact with the work. There is higher material utilization, productivity, and quality control.

Statement #7: The strength of MRP II is planning, while the strength of just-in-time is execution and quality improvement.

Statement #10: American business has discovered that improved quality is not an expense. Instead, it generates profits.

Statement #12: Because of technology and business conditions, staffs have been cut in many companies, making it even more critical that each employee's work be superior and valued.

Statement #17: The best application for robotics is in repetitive procedures, in which the same process is done constantly.

Apparel Sales and Distribution, Activity B

1. This direct-order system gives faster response and helps to keep prices as low as possible.
2. so buyers can see their lines at any time
3. They risk losing some of their retail accounts that become upset by this practice of bypassing the retailers.
4. They serve as customer service personnel to help their retail accounts maintain low and effective inventory levels that bring good profits. They also show retailers the new style numbers that are introduced mid-season.
5. Sales managers supervise the sales force and lead sales forecast planning. Independent sales reps sell collections of several different manufacturers' lines that are not in competition with one another but that are sold to similar target consumers.
6. One or several of: large photographs for store displays, counter cards, newspaper advertising mats, customer mailing pieces or bill enclosures, in-store programs that provide training talks to salespeople, personal appearances by the firm's designer, videotapes of collections, fashion shows, or trunk shows.
7. Customers can see and buy from the producer's entire line (ordering any style, color, or size for later delivery) and also enjoy meeting a designer or company representative. Retailers can sell more items without the risk of carrying them in their inventory. Both manufacturers and retailers can evaluate consumer feedback about the line and enhance their images by associating with each other.
8. to facilitate the identification and shipping of containers among vendors, distributors, and retailers, and to support the flow of merchandise through retailers' distribution centers
9. Merchandise is tracked at all times, and store managers know exactly when shipments will arrive so employees can stay busy with other tasks until a truck is arriving at the unloading dock.
10. Logistic specialists know the best methods and have the right equipment to be especially efficient in maximizing the flow of goods for faster deliveries at lower costs.
11. They will be totally automated with bar codes and advanced scanners to electronically identify, sort, route, and ship goods in an uninterrupted flow.
12. to maintain the economic well-being of the industry and its companies, in hopes that its members can offer high quality goods at competitive prices

Fashion Market Match, Activity D

1.	X	14.	F
2.	R	15.	E
3.	A	16.	K
4.	P	17.	W
5.	L	18.	B
6.	Z	19.	V
7.	I	20.	H
8.	N	21.	T
9.	S	22.	J
10.	D	23.	O
11.	M	24.	G
12.	Q	25.	Y
13.	C	26.	U

Teacher's Resources

Chapter 11 Test

1.	H	16.	T
2.	J	17.	T
3.	F	18.	T
4.	E	19.	T
5.	A	20.	F
6.	B	21.	D
7.	G	22.	D
8.	C	23.	B
9.	D	24.	D
10.	I	25.	B
11.	F	26.	D
12.	T	27.	B
13.	T	28.	A
14.	T	29.	C
15.	F	30.	A

31. *Raw materials*—preproduction fabrics, trimmings, and notions. *Work-in-process* (WIP)—garment parts and sections, and partially complete garments. *Finished goods*—completed items ready to be shipped to customers
32. (Explain two: Any of the bottom six segments of text illustration 11-18.)
33. truck (highway), plane (air), ship (ocean), and train (rail)

Materials Handling Expenses

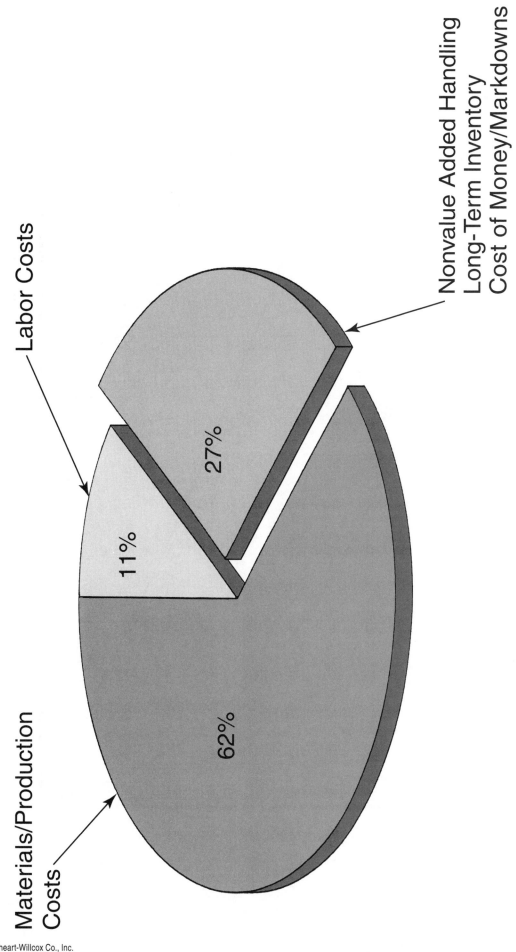

Labor Costs

Nonvalue Added Handling
Long-Term Inventory
Cost of Money/Markdowns

27%

11%

Materials/Production
Costs

62%

Source: Textile/Clothing Technology Corporation [TC][2]

Right the First Time

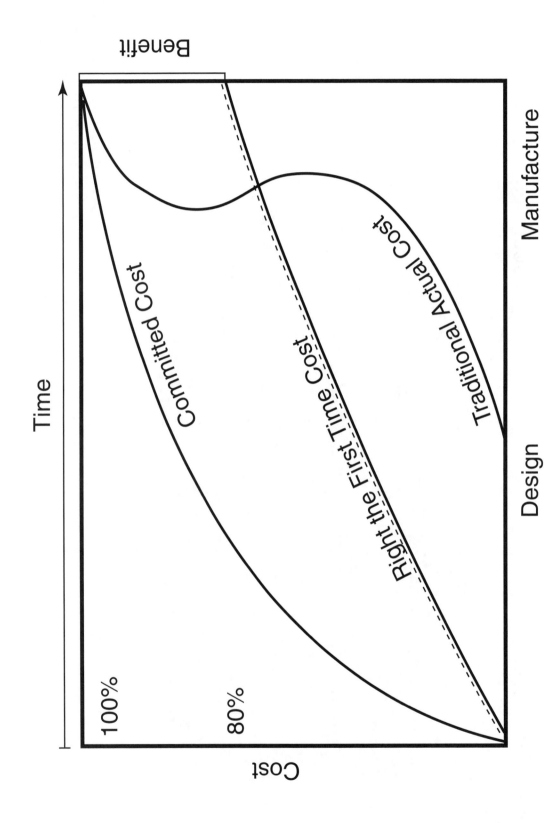

Source: General Sewing Data (GSD) Methods Workshop, Atlanta

Manufacturing-in Quality

Name_____ **Date** _____ **Period** _____

Think about and respond to the following statements. Then discuss the statements as a class.

1. What do you think is meant when companies say they manufacture-in quality? _____

_____

_____

_____

_____

2. Look up the word *intrinsic* in the dictionary. Then explain why the intrinsic quality of garments sets brands apart and results in customer loyalty. _____

_____

_____

_____

_____

3. More apparel manufacturers now have technical designers who work to interpret and keep quality standards in their companies' lines. _____

_____

_____

_____

_____

4. The use of a computerized specification package is a plus for communicating fit and quality standards to factories electronically, internationally, and in a similar language._____

_____

_____

_____

_____

5. With the possibility of many factories in different locations producing a company's line, consistency of quality, sizing, and styling is hard, but important, to achieve._____

_____

_____

_____

_____

The Fight Against Counterfeiting

- French luxury brands, Louis Vuitton, Chanel, and Lacoste, have demonstrated at Paris's de Gaulle Airport warning travelers visiting Italy not to bring back counterfeit goods. Hand-outs have warned of stiff fines and jail terms of up to three years for illegally importing fake goods.

- Abercrombie & Fitch Company has run an aggressive anti-counterfeiting campaign in the United Kingdom because of the appearance of fake Abercrombie and Hollister brand goods. The campaign has targeted both manufacturers and sellers, with both criminal and civil legal actions authorized by British law. These cheap fakes are damaging the A&F name.

- Customs agents in Europe and the U.S. are cooperating with major apparel firms to apprehend and punish smugglers of counterfeit goods. They work to inspect and intercept shipments headed to sellers of the products. Counterfeit merchandise is seized and destroyed.

- Contract sewing factories used by apparel firms sometimes manufacture extra garments, unauthorized by the brand. Then the factories sell the garments on the "grey market." Dishonest factory partners are dropped and sometimes are forced out of business.

- Trying to fight the tide of illegal merchandise, apparel companies are using high-tech elements in their labels, providing their contract factories with just enough to cover production. These include metallic strips or serial numbers woven into the labels, covert yarns that are visible under certain light wavelengths, washable holograms, specific RFID tags, etc. Normal counterfeiters won't bother to try to duplicate these elements.

Technology in Apparel Manufacturing

Name_____ **Date** _____ **Period** _____

Read and respond to the following paragraphs. Then discuss each subject as a class.

1. Interactive computing is used in some factories. When the worker inserts a plastic "bundle card" into a slot, the computer either talks to the operator through headphones or displays a message on a mini-screen such as: "Good morning, Linda. Yesterday you worked 8 hours and your productivity earned 8.4 hours of pay, making you 105% efficient. Today you'll be doing the same sewing task, which should make you even more efficient, probably earning 8.9 hours of pay. This bundle should take you 23 minutes. If you need any help, press the 'help' key. By the way, Linda, happy birthday!" _____

_____

_____

_____

_____

_____

2. Robotics include programmable machines that are "islands of automation" accomplishing certain tasks. CIM links those machines to do entire continuous operations and can be programmed with particular garment styles through the central computer. The affected sewing machines respond by adjusting sewing speeds, stitch lengths, and buttonhole placement. Pressing stations modify temperature and dwell time. Different runs of garments come off the end of the line without the machines having to be shut down and retooled to change the procedures. Some programmable machines can now read a bar code ticket on garment parts and automatically change for that style on-the-spot. _____

_____

_____

_____

_____

_____

3. Quick Response started with commodity items. However, QR then forced many fashion apparel manufacturers to be more sophisticated, making EDI exchanges of POS information, purchase orders, retail inventory counts, forecasts, and other information a daily part of business. These manufacturers are capable of receiving all the information they need to know and can tell exactly how much of each item should be delivered to individual stores today, tomorrow, or the next day.

_____

_____

_____

_____

_____

(Continued)

Name_____

4. Modular manufacturing is performed standing up to allow greater mobility of operators. However, most of the sewing machines use a foot pedal control, causing the operator's weight to shift to one leg. This can eventually result in ergonomic spine or hip problems or affect the operator's equilibrium. Electronic eyes can start and stop machines, but speech recognition can control speed variation as well (such as start, stop, slow, medium, fast, lift, and trim). It is also good for workers with lower body disabilities. The voice reference pattern of the trained operator is downloaded into a portable microphone control and connected to the host computer. Any language, dialect, or accent can be used. _____

_____

_____

_____

_____

_____

5. Small and midsized apparel manufacturers participate in technological progress without draining their wallets by making incremental investments. Incremental investments are acquisitions of additions or attachments for existing equipment, designed to technically upgrade the equipment while avoiding the costs of completely new machines. Since almost 80% of U.S. apparel manufacturers employ fewer than 50 people, their limited size makes it hard to make large-scale investments. However, they must stay competitive. By adding to their systems gradually but continually, they upgrade their equipment to a competitive technological level without making significant capital expenditures.

_____

_____

_____

_____

_____

_____

Balanced Flow Supply Chain

Goal: To minimize costs and maximize revenues.

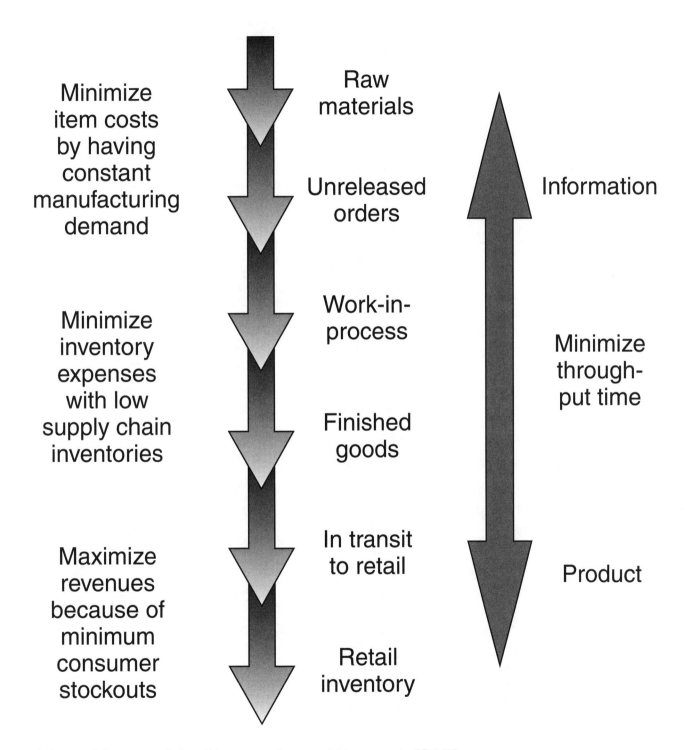

Minimize item costs by having constant manufacturing demand

Minimize inventory expenses with low supply chain inventories

Maximize revenues because of minimum consumer stockouts

Raw materials

Unreleased orders

Work-in-process

Finished goods

In transit to retail

Retail inventory

Information

Minimize through-put time

Product

Adapted from work by Clemson Apparel Research (CAR)

Improving the Weak Link

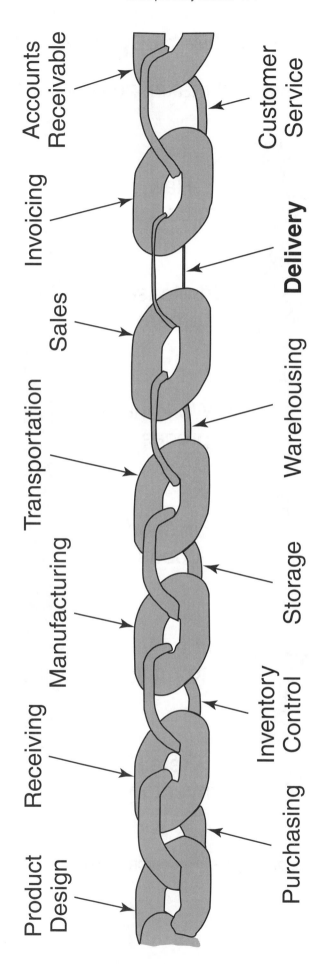

Accounts Receivable

Customer Service

Invoicing

Delivery

Sales

Transportation

Warehousing

Manufacturing

Storage

Receiving

Inventory Control

Product Design

Purchasing

Source: Ryder Dedicated Logistics, Inc.

Wholesale Apparel Marketing and Distribution

Name_____

Date_____ **Period**_____ **Score**_____

Chapter 11 Test

Matching: Match the following terms and identifying phrases.

_____ 1. All activities of goods not involved in actual production processes, such as moving, storing, packing, and transporting of the materials, semifinished parts, or final garments.

_____ 2. Company-owned sales areas where merchandise is displayed and selling staffs answer questions and take orders.

_____ 3. The process of maintaining inventories at a level that prevents stockouts and minimizes holding costs.

_____ 4. The selling of products in two steps of the channel of distribution, such as a manufacturer selling goods to regular retailers as well as operating company-owned retail outlets.

_____ 5. Buildings or complexes that house showrooms of apparel manufacturers.

_____ 6. The continuous process of measuring a company's products, services, and practices against companies that are world-class leaders.

_____ 7. The handling details of storing and physically moving merchandise to the proper locations.

_____ 8. A combination of many electronic steps of a production system, toward "hands-off" manufacturing.

_____ 9. Selling only to one retailer in a certain geographic trading area on an exclusive basis or only to a particular chain of retail stores nationally.

_____ 10. Mechanically accomplished tasks done by automated equipment.

A. apparel marts

B. benchmarking

C. computer-integrated manufacturing (CIM)

D. confined

E. dual distribution

F. inventory control

G. logistics

H. materials handling

I. robotics

J. showrooms

True/False: Circle *T* if the statement is true or *F* if the statement is false.

T   F   11. Goods held on hand for the production process or for sales to customers are called resources.

T   F   12. A warehouse is a holding facility for storing backup stocks of supplies or finished goods.

(Continued)

Name_____

T   F   13. A trademark is any word, name, logo, device, or combination of these used to identify and distinguish goods of one company from others.

T   F   14. CIM allows for maximum coordination and centralized control of production operations.

T   F   15. Technology transfer is getting slower because more sophisticated technology is being developed.

T   F   16. During market weeks, retail store buyers go to fashion market cities.

T   F   17. Sales forecasting predicts the quantity of each item that will be sold during a fiscal time period.

T   F   18. A contract is a written agreement between a buyer and seller, detailing all conditions of the sale.

T   F   19. Advance ship notices use EDI and standardized shipping container markings to detail the contents of shipments.

T   F   20. The letters AAFA stand for the Association of Apparel Factory Administrators.

Multiple Choice: Choose the best response. Write the letter in the space provided.

_____ 21. Having too much inventory causes _____.
A. extra handling of merchandise
B. product obsolescence
C. excessive carrying costs
D. All of the above.

_____ 22. Manufacturing resource planning (MRP II) is a _____.
A. merchandise ordering and shipping procedure for distribution between Quick Response partners
B. continuous process of inventory control that seeks to deliver a small quantity of materials precisely where and when they are needed
C. proactive quality program that seeks to create high-quality products the first time and every time
D. computerized method of planning production materials and levels of inventory

_____ 23. Benchmarking is a _____.
A. reactive approach that fixes problems after they occur
B. proactive approach to make processes better
C. hyperactive approach that tries to do too much too fast
D. superactive approach that tries to accomplish more than can be expected

_____ 24. The ongoing process of total quality management (TQM) _____.
A. focuses on internal requirements needed to deliver the right products in the very best way
B. is a long-term commitment for continuous improvement of service and satisfaction beyond customers' expectations
C. encompasses the concepts of empowerment of employees, work teams, and benchmarking
D. All of the above.

(Continued)

Name_____

_____ 25. Counterfeit fashions are _____.
    A. usually sold by upscale retail boutiques
    B. a threat to the reputation and sales of legitimately trademarked items
    C. made by legitimate factories that are illegally paid with counterfeit money
    D. All of the above.

_____ 26. In the future, demand flow manufacturing (DFM) will _____.
    A. quickly produce individual affordable garments on demand from consumers
    B. depend upon valid, timely data collection and communication
    C. capture computer order information remotely and use it to manufacture customized garments
    D. All of the above.

_____ 27. Sales presentations are _____.
    A. usually done to inform production workers how many garments must be manufactured
    B. formal, well-prepared showings of a company's goods to potential customers
    C. intended to solidify management's thinking about quantities of supplies needed for manufacturing
    D. All of the above.

_____ 28. A fiscal period is _____.
    A. a financial accounting period, usually one year
    B. never the same as the calendar year
    C. the length of time that new technology pays for itself through cost savings
    D. All of the above.

_____ 29. A trunk show involves _____.
    A. production overruns that are brought to exhibit halls in trunks and sold on the spot at low prices
    B. items that are unsuccessful "dogs" but are nicely accessorized to be shown, for sale, on models
    C. a collection of samples brought to a store by a producer for a limited amount of time to take orders
    D. samples of many producers sold by an independent sales representative ("rep")

_____ 30. UNITE _____.
    A. are the initials for the labor union of textile and apparel manufacturing workers
    B. is a method of consolidated shipping in which two or more shippers put together a truckload
    C. is the abbreviation for technology that sends electronic data between collaborating companies
    D. is a type of enterprise resource planning that orders production resources via Web sites on the Internet

Essay Questions: Provide complete responses to the following questions or statements.

31. Name and briefly describe the three main groups of inventory for manufacturers.

32. Briefly explain two reasons why manufacturers show merchandise at markets other than to sell their goods.

33. What are the four different modes of transportation used to ship garments?

PART FOUR

Retail
Business Fundamentals

CHAPTER 12

The Retail Segment

Objectives

After studying this chapter, students will be able to

- list the functional areas of retail firms.
- explain the main types of apparel retailers.
- describe store ownership groups.
- summarize retail trade information.

Teaching Materials

Text, pages 234–252
- *Fashion Terms*
- *Fashion Review*
- *Fashion in Action*

Student Workbook
- A. *Retail Segment Outline*
- B. *E-retailing RE-ality*
- C. *The Retail Life Cycle*
- D. *Retail Functions*
- E. *Retail Matching*

Teacher's Resources
- *Manufacturers vs. Retailers*, transparency master 12-1
- *Analyze the Comment*, reproducible master 12-2
- *Chain Stores*, transparency master 12-3
- *Compromise Strategy of Discount Department Stores*, transparency master 12-4
- *Review the Chapter*, reproducible master 12-5
- *Research a Retailer*, reproducible master 12-6
- Chapter 12 Test

Introductory Activities

1. *Manufacturers vs. Retailers*, transparency master 12-1. Use this transparency for a class discussion about the differences between wholesale and retail segments of the industry. This will provide a good transition from Chapter 11.
2. With students referring to illustration 12-1 in the text, introduce the five basic steps of retailing. Ask students to describe what they think is involved with each step. Their answers will indicate how much retailing knowledge they already have.
3. **RF** *Retail Segment Outline*, Activity A, WB. Have students page through the text to create a chapter outline by filling in the blanks with the correct chapter headings/subheadings and descriptions.

Strategies to Reteach, Reinforce, Enrich, and Extend Text Concepts

Functional Areas of Fashion Retail Firms

4. **ER** *Analyze the Comment*, reproducible master 12-2. Students are asked to write their reactions to several statements about retailing. Have students discuss the statements and their reactions.

5. **RT** Divide the class into five groups and assign a different retail functional area to each for further study. Have each group explain its functional area in detail to the class.

6. **ER** Show the class a video about the organization of retail companies. *The Retail Store* is available from Meridian Education Corporation, Cambridge Educational, and D.E. Visuals.

Main Types of Apparel Retailers

7. **RT** After clarifying the difference between general and specialized merchandisers, have students name specific examples of each category.

8. **RT** Review with students the many types of retailers listed in illustration 12-7 in the text. Discuss the examples within each category and their characteristics.

9. **RF** Ask students to name a retail company that has a flagship store. Where are branches located?

10. **RF** Show a video that examines the mass merchandising retail format. *The Mass Merchandising* video available from D.E. Visuals is an example.

11. **RF** Have students discuss the different types of stores in a nearby shopping mall. Ask students to name the anchor stores.

12. **RT** *Chain Stores*, transparency master 12-3. Use the transparency to review the key features of chain stores.

13. **ER** Show the class a biographical video about a pioneer in the retail field. Suggestions are biographies about *J.C. Penney, R.H. Macy, Neiman Marcus, Sam Walton,* and *The Woolworths* from Cambridge Educational and Meridian Education Corporation. Also make books available for students, such as *Sam Walton: Made in America, The Nordstrom Way, Call of the Mall, Clicks, Bricks and Brands,* and others.

14. **EX** Have students discuss specific retail companies that have gone through phases of the wheel of retailing. The "entry phase" is marked by low status, innovation, and low prices to gain customer acceptance. In the "trading-up phase," the retailer tries to differentiate itself by locating in nicer facilities, offering more services, and stocking better merchandise. Its prices rise. In the "vulnerability phase," new low-cost retailers slip into the slot where the retailer began and steal the customers. Also discuss why "better stores" sometimes diversify into discount and specialty stores. For example, Target discount stores, Mervyn's lower-priced clothing, B. Dalton books, and other chains.

15. **EX** *E-retailing RE-ality,* Activity B, WB. Students are asked to read statements about Internet retailing aloud in pairs, with one reading the "opinion" and the other the "reality."

16. **RF** Hold a class discussion about how large general merchandisers are now offering every type of goods under one roof, including apparel, housewares, groceries, pharmacy items, and gardening products. Services, such as banking and medical clinics are also available.

17. **RT** Ask individual students to name and describe one type of discount retailing until all types are reviewed for the class. For each type, have the class identify examples. Repeat the exercise for specialty stores and nonstore retailers. (With the discussion of discount stores, evaluate the power of "the big three," Wal-Mart, Kmart, and Target.)

18. **ER** *Compromise Strategy of Discount Department Stores*, transparency master 12-4. Use the transparency to review the distinct characteristics of both department and discount stores, and the compromise strategy of discount department stores. Ask students to name several chains that qualify as discount department stores.

19. **RF** Have students discuss the fact that most of the 1.5 million retail companies in the U.S. are small stores with annual sales below $1 million. Have students name the small retailers they know. Are any of them truly mom and pop stores?

20. **RF** Ask students to bring apparel mail-order catalogs to class. Have them discuss each mail-order business, focusing on the type, price, and quality of merchandise offered; methods used to get customers' attention; and other aspects of mail-order retailing. Pass catalogs around the room for all to see.

21. **RT** Discuss television and computer retailing with the class. Ask students to relate their opinions of and experiences with these forms of retailing. Discuss the issue of reverse logistics since television and computer retailing have more returned merchandise than stores where consumers can touch and try on the goods.

22. **RF** *The Retail Life Cycle,* Activity C, WB. Students are asked to provide examples of businesses at each stage of the business life cycle.

23. **RF** *Retail Functions,* Activity D, WB. Groups of students, each representing a main functional area, are asked to describe how to handle their respective responsibilities.

24. **ER** Show the class a video about retail trends. Suggestions are *Value Shopping in America: A Major Force in Retailing* from D.E. Visuals; and *Fashion 2000: Trends in Apparel Marketing* from VMS, Inc.

Store Ownership Groups

25. **RT** Discuss the impacts of horizontal integration and store ownership groups.
26. **ER** Have students conduct a search to learn the names of corporate owners of major local retail stores.
27. **EX** For an overview of store ownership groups and their various stores and brands, have students search corporate information on the following Web sites:
    www.saksincorporated.com, www.fds.com, www.limitedbrands.com, www.neimanmarcusgroup.com, www.searsholdings.com, www.gapinc.com, and www.charmingshoppes.com. Then have a class discussion about the consolidation of retailers into large corporations and the disappearance of many old retail company names.

Retail Trade Associations and Publications

28. **ER** Obtain copies of various retail trade magazines and share them with the class.
29. **RT** *Review the Chapter*, reproducible master 12-5. Use the master as a handout for students to answer review questions.
30. **RF** *Retail Matching*, Activity E, WB. Students are asked to match retailing terms with their definitions.
31. **EX** Ask students to find retail trade information on the Internet. Suggested Web sites are www.nrf.com, www.icsc.org, www.shop.org, www.retail-leaders.org, www.internetretailer.com, and the retail association of your state.

Additional Enrichment Activities

Research

32. *Research a Retailer*, reproducible master 12-6. Students are asked to research one of the subjects listed and write a report.
33. Have students research a category of retailing and present a report to the class using visual aids. Topics may include any category in illustration 12-7 of the text.

Projects

34. After studying this chapter, schedule a field trip to stores in the area that represent several different retail categories, or have students visit them independently. Ask students to write a report explaining their reactions to the different types of stores.
35. Have students contact the National Retail Federation (NRF) to obtain information on the organization's purpose, services, membership requirements, and trade shows. Also ask them to check the library and the Internet (www.nrf.com) for information on the association. Have them present their findings to the class.
36. Invite a retail store manager or department head to class to discuss his or her business, its strategy, and the effects of industry changes on the business in recent years.
37. Have several students work as a team to report to the class the contents of a comprehensive book on U.S. retailing. Individuals can focus on their respective chapter(s). An excellent reference is the book, *Land of Desire—Merchants, Power and the Rise of a New American Culture,* by William Leach.

Answer Key

Text

Fashion Review, page 252

1. It is a service business that exchanges merchandise for money or credit.
2. If the retailing effort isn't effective, products are not sold, companies do not make money, and everyone in the chain suffers.
3. merchandising
4. It is concerned with physically managing and maintaining the store—housekeeping, customer service, protection and security, delivery, and receiving and marking the merchandise.
5. It involves advertising, display, public relations, publicity, and special events.
6. Superstores sell large volumes so they can offer greater selections at low prices.
7. (Choose five:) credit, return or exchange privileges, pleasant restrooms, gift wrapping, service desks, home delivery, liberal payment plans, restaurants, bridal registries, wardrobe consultants, personal shopping assistants

8. They are smaller than conventional department stores and do not carry as wide a range of goods.
9. They may be either, depending on the store.
10. small stores in malls, located between the "destination" anchor stores
11. discount stores
12. selling large amounts of staple goods and mass-produced garments at lower prices
13. They sell brand-name or designer merchandise they buy at below-wholesale prices.
14. The manufacturer is assured an outlet for its products; the stores are assured of having merchandise to sell.
15. time-stressed consumers who want to do all of their shopping in one place
16. They have little time to shop; they can browse through catalogs during their spare moments; their free time is only when stores are closed; they are dissatisfied with crowded stores and malls, inadequate parking, and lack of service and personal safety in conventional retail locations.
17. postal rates for catalogs and merchandise shipping costs
18. Shoppers view merchandise on their computer monitors at home and order online.
19. expensive merchandise and products that require specialized knowledge or skills
20. (List three: Student response.)

Student Workbook

Retail Segment Outline, Activity A

I. Areas of Fashion Retail Firms
  A. Merchandising
  B. Financial control—Supervising the budget and overseeing the spending activities of the store or retail firm.
  C. Store operations—Physically managing and maintaining the store.
  D. —Deals with hiring, training, and rewarding employees with raises or bonuses; arranging for benefits; formulating human relations policies; and keeping employee records.
  E. Sales promotion—This involves advertising, display, public relations, publicity, and special events.

II. Types of Apparel Retailers
  A. —Large-scale general merchandisers that offer many varieties of merchandise grouped into separate departments.
    1. Branch stores
    2. Junior—Smaller than conventional department stores, and do not carry as wide a range of goods.
  B. Chain stores—A group of stores (usually 12 or more) that is owned, managed, merchandised, and controlled by a central office.
  C. Discount stores—Retail establishments that sell merchandise at lower than recognized market-level prices.
    1. Off-price discounters—Retailers that sell brand name or designer merchandise at lower than normal prices.
    2. Dollar stores—
    3. —Manufacturer-owned-and-operated discount stores that sell only the merchandise the manufacturer makes, at reduced prices.
    4. Wholesale warehouse clubs—Specialize in bulk sales of a limited selection of nationally branded staple merchandise at rock-bottom prices.
    5. Hypermarkets—Huge, warehouse-type "supercenters" that sell almost every type of merchandise and target time-stressed consumers.
  D. Specialty stores—large, limited.
    1. Specialty chains—Specialty stores that are part of a regional or national chain.
    2. —Small stand-alone shops or distinctive areas within larger stores that sell unusual, few-of-a-kind apparel, accessories, or decorative items.
    3. Licensed merchandise stores—"Concept shops" built around licensed merchandise.
    4. Airport retailers—
  E. —Retailers that sell without a conventional store facility.
    1. Mail-order retailing—Selling merchandise through catalogs that are distributed to consumers.
    2. Telecommunication retailing

3. Personal selling—Moving merchandise directly to customers through door-to-door sales or selling parties/showings in homes or work environments.
F. Fashion retailing
1. Variety stores—Small town "dime stores" that offer a few items in many classifications of lower-priced merchandise.
2. Kiosks and carts—
3. Catalog—Stores that display sample items of merchandise mainly sold through catalogs.
4. Leased departments—Areas within retail stores that are stocked and operated by someone else.
III. Ownership groups—Corporations formed by individual stores joining together into central ownership.
IV. Retail Trade Associations and Publications

The Retail Life Cycle, Activity C

Stage 1: computer retailing portals, supercenters and hypermarkets that combine food products and general merchandise

Stage 2: (Name four:) factory outlets, category killers, television retailing, licensed merchandise stores, spin-off stores, dollar chains

Stage 3: (Name four:) department stores, specialty department stores, chain stores, discount chains, off-price discounters, specialty chain stores, franchise stores, mail-order retailers

Stage 4: variety stores, junior department stores, catalog showrooms

Retail Matching, Activity E

1. E	9. F
2. N	10. J
3. L	11. B
4. A	12. I
5. D	13. P
6. G	14. M
7. C	15. O
8. K	16. H

Teacher's Resources

Review the Chapter, reproducible
master 12-5

1. finished, manufacturers, consumers
2. planning products (types, quantities, etc.) to sell, buying goods from suppliers, receiving the goods, arranging them in convenient locations, selling the goods
3. how to wear or combine articles of clothing and accessorize outfits, thus creating consumer demand
4. outside accountants and advertising agencies
5. It deals with supervising the budget, credit and collections (incoming money), spending activities (outgoing money), loans, and inventory control.
6. It deals with hiring, training, and rewarding employees. It is concerned with benefits, human relations policies, employee records, job performance evaluations, and "outplacement" of terminated employees.
7. because they must cover the costs of having more personnel and extra services
8. There is no main store. Instead, there is a central headquarters that is not attached to any of the stores.
9. Some are local or regional, and others are operated nationwide.
10. Large chains have such enormous buying power that manufacturers can afford to produce private label merchandise for them at lower prices.
11. It is an evolutionary process in which stores that feature low prices gradually upgrade themselves with more elaborate facilities and services to broaden their appeal, resulting in higher prices, different customers, and lower-priced competitors replacing their previous price slot.
12. They sell large quantities of merchandise and have lower expenses.
13. because they are competing against the same goods being sold by the manufacturer at much lower prices

14. They offer faster order processing and shipping, better inventory management, improved merchandise quality, customer help from telemarketing associates, and easier return procedures.
15. (List three:) fur departments, beauty salons, shoe repair centers, fine jewelry departments, restaurants, name designer goods
16. They can use centralized volume buying and effective merchandising techniques, and they can combine functions to operate with fewer levels of management.
17. the latest strategies, ideas, and technologies of the industry

Chapter 12 Test

1. I	16. T
2. D	17. T
3. F	18. T
4. C	19. T
5. G	20. F
6. B	21. D
7. H	22. B
8. A	23. C
9. E	24. A
10. J	25. D
11. T	26. B
12. T	27. C
13. T	28. D
14. T	29. A
15. F	30. D

31. (List three:) planning products (types, quantities, etc.) to sell, buying goods from suppliers, receiving the goods, arranging them in convenient stores or selling formats, selling the goods to consumers
32. (List three:) merchandising, financial control, store operations, personnel, promotion
33. (List three:) consistently low selling prices, bare facilities with low overhead, customer self-service, high sales volume (fast turnover rates), low (small) profit margins

Manufacturers vs. Retailers

Manufacturers (Wholesalers)	Retailers
• Sell directly to businesses.	• Sell directly to the general public.
• Interact with retail buyers. (Contacts go both ways between sales reps and retail buyers.)	• Interact with consumers who make the contact to buy.
• Sell large quantities in few transactions.	• Sell small quantities in numerous transactions.
• Negotiate variable price arrangements and use bulk pricing (lower per-unit costs for large purchases).	• Have a "set price" policy, which involves higher unit selling prices.
• Do not emphasize company location/ atmosphere.	• Emphasize company location/atmosphere.

Analyze the Comment

Name_____ **Date** _____ **Period** _____

Read the following comments, focusing on the bold terms. Then write your reaction to each in the space provided.

1. Retail sales are one-third of our economy. In other words, we have a **consumer-oriented economy**.

   _____

   _____

   _____

   _____

2. Retailers should be the **purchasing** agents for consumers, not the selling agents for manufacturers.

   _____

   _____

   _____

   _____

3. Each manufacturer produces a limited style of goods, but consumers want a wide selection. Consequently, retailers **gather and assort** merchandise from several sources for the many customers.

   _____

   _____

   _____

   _____

4. Since manufacturers want production economies of scale, retailers accomplish a **break-bulk** function by allocating smaller quantities to different areas of the market. _____

   _____

   _____

   _____

   _____

5. Retailers bridge the **space gap** between manufacturers' factories and consumers' homes by ordering and moving products to convenient, central store locations. _____

   _____

   _____

   _____

   _____

6. Merchandise is offered for sale by retailers well ahead of the wearing season as **insurance** against consumers changing their minds when the season arrives. Consumers now object to this timing, however, and prefer having items available during the season of wear._____

   _____

   _____

   _____

   _____

   _____

(Continued)

Name_____

7. Retailers have joined together to launch **www.Plussize.com**, an online shopping site for the 65 million plus-sized women in the U.S. (half of the country's females). Companies participating include Lands' End, Liz Claiborne, Spiegel, Nordstrom, and Coldwater Creek, and others. _____

_____

_____

_____

8. Shopping mall developers/owners like kiosks, referred to as **retail merchandising units (RMUs)**. Besides providing lease income, the RMUs offer shopping excitement, foster new types of retail businesses, and are possible permanent tenants for store sites in the future._____

_____

_____

_____

9. To survive, compete, and grow, retailers must have the **capital** needed to modernize their stores, introduce new concepts, and install new labor-saving technologies to service their customers better.

_____

_____

_____

10. The National Retail Federation (NRF) offers a **Small Store Survival handbook** that identifies strengths and weaknesses of independent retailers in the areas of merchandising, marketing, management, finance, and human resources. Besides the book's help and ideas for improvement, NRF members can call a toll-free number to have questions answered. _____

_____

_____

_____

11. "Cyberstores" must anticipate the **search words** that consumers will use on general search engines and e-retailing sites to find specific items. These many different names for goods must be set up in the system. _____

_____

_____

_____

12. When consumers shop online, they often search but do not buy. A challenge for e-retailers is to encourage **conversions** to purchases by shoppers rather than their abandoning the Web site.

_____

_____

_____

_____

Chain Stores

- Can be national, regional, or local

- Follow the policies and operations decided by a central headquarters office

- Have similar appearance and merchandise in all stores

- Offer merchandise purchased in volume by headquarters, resulting in market power

- Usually carry a percentage of private label goods

- Do not have a flagship store

- Have regional administrative structures (when large)

Compromise Strategy of Discount Department Stores

Discount Stores

- Low-rent location
- Bare facilities
- Customer self-service
- Low prices and quality
- Low profit margins
- High sales volume

Department Stores

- Downtown location
- Plush facilities
- High prices and quality
- High profit margins
- Low sales volume

Discount Department Stores

- Suburban locations
- Modest, pleasant facilities
- Limited services
- "Value" prices and quality
- Average profit margins
- Average sales volume

Review the Chapter

Name_____ **Date** _____ **Period** _____

Provide complete responses to the following questions or statements.

1. Fill in the blanks: Retailing is the link that moves _____ goods from _____ to_____.

2. Briefly describe the basic steps of retailing. _____

    _____

    _____

    _____

    _____

3. To encourage sales, what education to consumers must the presentation of items in retail stores accomplish? _____

    _____

    _____

4. If proprietors of small stores do not have the skills or interest in doing the financial books or advertising activities for their businesses, who can help them? _____

    _____

    _____

    _____

5. Briefly describe the retail functional area of financial control._____

    _____

    _____

    _____

6. Briefly describe the retail functional area of personnel. _____

    _____

    _____

    _____

7. Why do department stores have somewhat higher operating expenses than other stores? _____

    _____

    _____

    _____

8. What is the main store of a chain called? _____

    _____

    _____

    _____

(Continued)

Name_____

9. Are chain organizations usually local or national in scope? _____

_____

_____

_____

10. Why are prices in chain stores often lower than those in department stores? _____

_____

_____

_____

11. Describe the wheel of retailing theory. _____

_____

_____

_____

12. How can discounters earn good profits with only small markups? _____

_____

_____

_____

13. Why have some department stores refused to carry lines that are also sold through the producer's factory outlet stores? _____

_____

_____

_____

14. In what ways have direct-mail marketers improved their customer service recently? _____

_____

_____

_____

15. Give specific examples of at least three common types of leased departments. _____

_____

_____

_____

16. Why can stores within retail corporate ownership groups operate more efficiently than they can as independents? _____

_____

_____

_____

17. What do attendees learn at the NRF Annual Convention & Expo? _____

_____

_____

_____

Research a Retailer

Name_____ **Date** _____ **Period** _____

Research one of the following subjects or choose another that your teacher approves. Organize your thoughts below and write a complete report on separate sheets of paper.

- Changed image and strategy of JCPenney since the 1980s
- Continued success of Wal-Mart versus the demise of independent small-town merchants
- Federated-Macy's merger and the strategy to regain strength of its many store names
- Development, size, and business strategy of Bloomingdales, Dillard's, Saks Fifth Avenue, Nordstrom, Dayton Hudson (now Target), or Neiman Marcus
- History and emergence of The Limited (including all of its store divisions) to rival most other stores today
- History and franchise strategy of Benetton
- The Montgomery Ward chronology, from its founding in 1872 to its involvement in cable television to its disappearance into the Sears chain
- History of Lands' End and results of recent changes of top management and e-tailing
- Background and success of QVC Network
- Management and strategic ups and downs of Kmart
- European (Parisian) origins of Carrefour, its retailing philosophy, and its lack of success in the U.S.

  Other:

  _____

  _____

  _____

  _____

  _____

  _____

  _____

  _____

  _____

  _____

  _____

  _____

  _____

  _____

  _____

  _____

  _____

The Retail Segment

Name_____

Date_____ **Period**_____ **Score**_____

Chapter 12 Test

Matching: Match the following terms and identifying phrases.

_____ 1. Corporations formed by individual stores joining together into central ownership.

_____ 2. Large-scale, fashion-oriented retailers that offer many varieties of merchandise grouped into separate departments.

_____ 3. Original main stores that usually house the executive, merchandising, and promotional offices for retail companies.

_____ 4. Groups of stores (usually 12 or more) that are owned, managed, merchandised, and controlled by a central office.

_____ 5. Retailers that market all types of goods in multiple price ranges to satisfy many needs of a broad range of customers.

_____ 6. Additional stores, owned and operated by a parent store, and usually located in suburban or metropolitan shopping areas.

_____ 7. Retailers that offer limited lines of related products targeted to more defined customers.

_____ 8. Major "destination stores" that provide the attraction needed to draw customers to shopping centers or malls.

_____ 9. Retail establishments that sell merchandise at lower than recognized market-level prices.

_____ 10. Retailers that combine wholesaling and retailing on a "no frills," cash-and-carry basis.

A. anchor stores

B. branch stores

C. chain stores

D. department stores

E. discount stores

F. flagship stores

G. general merchandisers

H. specialized merchandisers

I. store ownership groups

J. wholesale warehouse clubs

True/False: Circle *T* if the statement is true or *F* if the statement is false.

T F 11. Retail businesses try to minimize operating expenses while maximizing sales and customer satisfaction.

T F 12. Junior department stores carry limited assortments of apparel, housewares, gifts, and household textiles.

T F 13. Off-price discounters sell brand name or designer merchandise at lower than normal prices.

(Continued)

Name_____

T   F   14. Hypermarkets have huge spartan facilities and function as combination grocery and discount stores.

T   F   15. Category killers carry small selections of almost all product categories at very low prices.

T   F   16. Boutiques are small shops with unique images that usually sell unusual items.

T   F   17. Nonstore retailing includes mail-order selling, telecommunication retailing, and personal selling, among others.

T   F   18. A leased department is a department within a store, operated by an outside firm.

T   F   19. The National Retail Federation (NRF) is the world's largest retail trade association.

T   F   20. STORES is a newspaper published by a well-informed retail consultant.

Multiple Choice: Choose the best response. Write the letter in the space provided.

_____ 21. "Mom and pop" stores _____.
A. are independent owner-operated stores located throughout America
B. are small stores run by a husband and wife or a proprietor and a few employees
C. offer consumers more convenience and personal service than retail giants
D. All of the above.

_____ 22. Smaller format discount stores that offer low-priced value, efficiency, and excitement for shoppers are called _____.
A. junior branches
B. dollar stores
C. university and airport shops
D. branch chains

_____ 23. The wheel of retailing _____.
A. is a way for retailers to gain more success and higher profits
B. shows the continual processes of planning, buying, and selling that recycles indefinitely
C. is an evolutionary process in which stores that feature low prices gradually upgrade themselves
D. results from stores being continually sold to new ownership groups

_____ 24. Mass merchandisers offer large amounts of predominantly _____.
A. staple goods and mass-produced garments
B. U.S.-manufactured merchandise
C. upscale, brand-name items
D. All of the above.

_____ 25. Factory outlets _____.
A. are manufacturer-owned-and-operated discount stores that sell only merchandise of the manufacturer
B. operate as a vertical distribution system that eliminates the cost of a middle person
C. assure manufacturers with stores for their products and assure the stores will have merchandise
D. All of the above.

(Continued)

Name_____

_____ 26. Almost all specialty stores _____.
   A. have higher volume and lower prices than discounters
   B. carry good selections of limited classifications of merchandise
   C. are aimed at most levels of consumer demographics and psychographics
   D. are "mom and pop" stores

_____ 27. Licensed merchandise stores are _____.
   A. general merchandisers that sell specialized goods
   B. franchises that make and sell licensed goods
   C. "concept shops" that sell licensed goods
   D. factory-outlet boutiques of licensed goods

_____ 28. Direct-mail marketing _____.
   A. appeals to busy people who have little regular time to shop
   B. is another name for mail-order retailing
   C. uses computerized mailing lists for target audiences
   D. All of the above.

_____ 29. Telecommunication retailing _____.
   A. includes television retailing and computer (electronic) retailing
   B. is mainly done with catalogs, but also displays sample items in stores where items are picked up
   C. is a result of small-town variety stores upgrading with new technology
   D. was one of the first new retail formats to go into use in the 21st Century

_____ 30. Horizontal integration _____.
   A. is a category into which factory outlet stores and private label products fall
   B. has been proven to be the best method for selling general merchandise
   C. is one of the main areas that personnel departments deal with
   D. combines, under common ownership, companies at the same location on the channel of distribution.

Essay Questions: Provide complete responses to the following questions or statements.

31. Name at least three of the basic steps of retailing.

32. Name at least three of the retail functional areas of responsibility.

33. Name at least three characteristics of the basic discount retailing strategy.

Retail Positioning

CHAPTER 13

Objectives

After studying this chapter, students will be able to

- explain how to target a specific retail market.
- analyze consumer buying motives.
- describe how stores differentiate themselves from competitors.
- summarize merchandise and service product strategies.
- interpret various pricing strategies.
- explain place strategies of site location and facility design.
- summarize promotion strategies.
- identify changing trends in retail positioning.

Teaching Materials

Text, pages 253–273
  Fashion Terms
  Fashion Review
  Fashion in Action
Student Workbook
  A. *Retailing Myth or Truth*
  B. *Retail Advertising*
  C. *Retail Positioning Puzzle*
  D. *Retail Positioning Tree*
  E. *Retail Positioning Facts*
Teacher's Resources
  Consumer Purchasing Behavior, transparency
    master 13-1
  Assortment Breadth and Depth, transparency
    master 13-2
  Pros and Cons of Everyday Low Pricing,
    transparency master 13-3
  Revitalizing Central Business Districts,
    transparency master 13-4
  Retail Market Considerations, transparency
    master 13-5

Aspects of Retail Facilities, transparency
    master 13-6
Link the New Terms, reproducible master 13-7
Retail Positioning Questions, reproducible
    master 13-8
Positioning a Retailer, reproducible master 13-9
Chapter 13 Test

Introductory Activities

1. Referring to illustration 13-1 in the text, introduce the class to the concept of retail positioning strategy and its key components.
2. Have students discuss the image of various retail stores that are familiar to them. Ask them to explain how the products, prices, promotional efforts, and location(s) reinforce each store's image.

Strategies to Reteach, Reinforce, Enrich, and Extend Text Concepts

Targeting a Specific Market

3. **RT** Have students review the use of computer databases to profile customers through examination of their credit card purchases, discussed in the text. Ask students to explain how retailers can use data-driven relationship marketing to develop "customer intimacy."
4. **RF** Discuss the specific "size" markets that are targeted by apparel stores, such as Lane Bryant (women's large sizes), Petite Sophisticate (women's small sizes), and Big & Tall Shoppes (men's large sizes). Ask students to identify other types of target markets, such as bridal, maternity, and skiwear.

231

5. **ER** Have students discuss the following consumer segmentation terms that are sometimes used to define apparel target markets: *bargain*, *mainstream*, *moderate*, *traditional*, *upscale*, *advanced-fashion*, or *better*. Can students think of any other descriptive terms to define markets for retailers?

6. **RF** With students referring to illustration 13-5 in the text, have volunteers tell the class where their decision-making process usually falls on the buying-motive continuum. Ask each volunteer if his or her position on the continuum falls in the same spot for every purchase or in different spots depending on the situation. (A leading study found that 26 percent of buyers are influenced by reason, 34 percent by emotion, and 42 percent by both.) Also have students discuss whether product or patronage motives affect their shopping.

7. **RF** *Consumer Purchasing Behavior*, transparency master 13-1. Use the transparency to have students explain each element of purchasing behavior. Have them discuss why knowledge of buying behavior is important to retailers.

Differentiating from Competitors

8. **RT** Discuss with the class the four main types of competition in retailing. Have students give specific examples that illustrate each type in relation to apparel sales.

9. **RT** Ask students to explain the importance of the factors that can differentiate retailers, listed in illustration 13-10 of the text. Can they name other important factors not listed in the chart?

10. **ER** Have students respond to the following statements: "Keeping other stores out of a market is not possible, so retailers must differentiate their stores in ways that reduce or eliminate comparisons with other retailers." "Some stores try to prevent having a well-defined image because they want to appeal to a wide market." Do the statements reflect good retail positioning strategies?

11. **RF** Show students a video about differentiating from competitors. An example is *Taking Customers Seriously*, available from D.E. Visuals.

12. **RF** Have students discuss the specific ambiance of several different retail stores. In each case, ask them to explain how the ambiance relates to the store image, or "retail personality," for the desired target market.

Product Strategy

13. **RT** On the board write: "assortment breadth = VARIETY; assortment depth = QUANTITY." Ask students to name specific examples of stores that follow the three different product strategies shown in illustration 13-15 of the text, describing different assortments of styles, colors, and sizes of merchandise in stores.

14. **ER** Show the class a video about product strategy. Possible choices are *Managing Merchandise Assortments* and *A Retailing Strategy: The Store Is the Brand* from D.E. Visuals; *How Clothing Is Sold: Fashion Merchandising* from Learning Seed, Nasco, and VMS, Inc.; and *Merchandising: The Store as Persuasion* from Learning Seed.

15. **ER** *Assortment Breadth and Depth*, transparency master 13-2. Use the transparency for a class discussion about the assortment strategy of different types of retailers. Have students notice that many of the larger stores offer narrow and deep assortments, while smaller stores usually have broad and shallow assortments.

16. **RF** Ask students to explain why stores that specialize in certain merchandise must always have a deep enough assortment to never be out of staple items of their specialty. Also discuss the fact that offering shoppers a larger variety of choice does not necessarily lead to more sales.

17. **RT** Have students discuss why service selection is included with merchandise selection in the product strategy of retail stores.

Price Strategy

18. **RT** Have students explain why the "right price" for a certain product is the amount that retailers are willing to accept and that consumers find satisfactory to pay.

19. **EX** *Pros and Cons of Everyday Low Pricing*, transparency master 13-3. Use the transparency for a class discussion on the advantages and disadvantages of the everyday low pricing (EDLP) policy. Have students explain why they believe each point is an advantage or a disadvantage.

20. **ER** Show the class a video about price strategy. *Fundamentals of Price*, *Pricing Products*, *Pricing Goods & Services*, and *Pricing: Relating Objective to Revenues and Costs* are all available from D.E. Visuals.

21. **RF** Have students discuss the following statements: "To get the best price, 10-15 percent of consumers will go to any length, even sacrificing time and convenience." "EDLP appeals to about 35 percent of consumers because they feel they get good value and are busy with work and children." "Most consumers are happy with a 'satisfactory price' along with good selection, quality, and fast/easy checkout." "Many retailers put an inflated retail price on goods so they can put the goods 'on sale' and still make a good profit."

Place Strategy

22. **RF** Have students consider the stores they, their families, and their friends frequent because of location. Ask students to explain the importance of a store's location to its success. Have them provide examples to support their conclusions.

23. **RF** Have the class discuss how national and regional chains identify where to place new stores as they expand. Ask students to identify good site locations in the local area for a discount chain store, an upscale specialty store (possibly in a lifestyle center), and other types of retail establishments.

24. **RF** Ask students to identify specific types of store clusters in the local area. Have them name the characteristics of each type of cluster.

25. **ER** *Revitalizing Central Business Districts*, transparency master 13-4. Use the transparency for a class discussion on business revitalization methods that have been used or considered in your area. Ask students to describe shopping areas they have seen that successfully used one or more of these efforts to increase business.

26. **EX** *Retail Market Considerations*, transparency master 13-5. Use the transparency for a class discussion about the many points to consider when a retailer chooses a good location for a new store.

27. **RF** Have students discuss why stores that sell upscale designer fashions are located in exclusive shopping areas, while budget mass merchandisers are located along highways near highly-populated areas.

28. **RT** *Aspects of Retail Facilities*, transparency master 13-6. Use the transparency for a class discussion about the factors to consider when planning a retail facility.

29. **RF** Show students a video that discusses retail sites and interior arrangements. *Retail Site Selection* is available from D.E. Visuals. *Secrets of Selling: How Stores Turn Shoppers into Buyers* is available from Insight Media.

30. **RF** Show students reference books and magazines about store facilities, available from ST Publications and Retail Reporting Corp. Examples are *Storefronts & Facades* and *Stores of the Year* by Martin M. Pegler, which contain many photos, and VM+SD (Visual Merchandising and Store Design magazine). Also, *The Budget Guide to Retail Store Planning & Design* is a small book with informative text written by Jeff Grant.

31. **RF** *Retail Positioning Puzzle*, Activity C, WB. Students are asked to define the chapter's title and fill in the blanks of a chart with the chapter terms defined on the worksheet.

32. **EX** Have students try to name the many types of "sales support" activities that take place in just 20 to 25 percent of store space. These include customer service areas (dressing rooms, complaint desk, catalog desk, public restrooms, and returned-goods area), merchandise service areas (goods receiving, checking and marking area, stockrooms, and alterations room), and staff areas (offices, lounges, conference rooms, and locker rooms). Also discuss how sales support areas are usually sandwiched on one floor of a multilevel store, placed as a "central core" surrounded by selling areas, placed at the periphery of the selling area, or added as an annex appendage to the store.

33. **RT** Ask students to describe the interior decor of area stores that have different price strategies.

Promotion Strategy

34. **EX** Hold a class discussion about the various types of promotion used by specific retailers in your area. Ask students to bring to class store advertisements and announcements about retail special events. Ask students if they see any strategies that would benefit area retailers.

35. **RF** *Retail Advertising*, Activity B, WB. Students are asked to choose three distinctly different retailers, analyze each according to several factors, and attach samples of their advertising to the worksheet.

36. **RT** *Retail Positioning Tree*, Activity D, WB. Students are asked to fill in the blanks of a chart by identifying the chapter terms defined on the worksheet.

37. **EX** *Link the New Terms*, reproducible master 13-7. Students are asked to read unfamiliar terms defined on the worksheet and describe how each term relates to specific chapter content of the text.

Recent Trends in Retail Positioning

38. **RF** Have students discuss the importance of stores offering efficiency for busy shoppers. Ask students to describe specific retailers that provide good, convenient, fast service to shoppers.

39. **RF** *Retailing Myth or Truth*, Activity A, WB. Students are asked to indicate if statements are myth or truth. Have students fill out the worksheet independently, keeping them flat on their desks. (Answers are on the back of the page.) Then use the activity for a class discussion.

40. **RF** Have students discuss entertainment as a destination activity combined with a shopping area. Ask students to name specific examples of areas that offer this combination. Have information about the Mall of America (Minnesota), the West Edmonton Mall (Canada), or other entertainment/

shopping destination areas available for students to review.

41. **RT** *Retailing Positioning Facts*, Activity E, WB. Students are directed to answer questions as a chapter review.

42. **RT** *Retail Positioning Questions*, reproducible master 13-8. Use the master as a handout for additional review of the chapter or for earning extra credit.

Additional Enrichment Activities

Research

43. Have students do library and/or Internet research to gather information about the annual Macy's Thanksgiving Day Parade. Televised nationally, the parade features balloons in the shapes of characters as high as five stories. Ask students to report how long this tradition has been sponsored, the image-building power of this promotional event, its relationship to the success of the Macy's Company, and other interesting facts.

44. Have students research the economics of retail leases in malls or shopping centers. Ask them to investigate leases with a base rent that have a percentage-rent clause above a certain level of sales, and "pass-through charges," such as common area maintenance costs (CAM charges). They might start on Web sites www.firstmartin.com or www.about.com. Have students answer the following questions: Do some small stores have the right to break their leases if a major anchor tenant closes? Why do some stores decide to "dress up" (remodel) their current locations instead of paying higher rents at big shopping centers? What happens to rents and retailers' power to negotiate when too much retail space has been built for the market, creating a retail space glut?

45. Ask different students to research the store layout philosophy of Kohls and the merchandise sizing and pricing philosophy of Chicos. Have the students explain to the class how the philosophies are different from traditional retailers, if they are successful, and why.

Projects

46. Have students read a book that relates to retail positioning and prepare an oral or written book report. Suggested books are *Like No Other Store* by Marvin Traub, *Why We Buy* by Paco Underhill, *The Experience Economy* by James Filmore and B. Joseph Pine II, and *Retail Entertainment or*

Lifestyle Stores by Martin Pegler, *Why People Buy Things They Don't Need* by Pam Danzinger, *Retail Selling Ain't Brain Surgery, It's Twice as Hard* by James Dion, *Winning at Retail* by William Ander and Neil Stern, *Clicks, Bricks, and Brands* by Martin Lindstrom, *The Nordstrom Way* by Robert Spector and Patrick McCarthy, *On Target: How the World's Hottest Retailer Hit a Bull's Eye* by Laura Rowley, and others.

47. *Positioning a Retailer*, reproducible master 13-9. Use the master as a handout for students to do a comprehensive study of a retailer of their choice. Students can work on the assignment individually or in groups.

48. Have students visit a mall to observe the different types of stores located there, the images they present, and the overall design of the mall. Then have students work individually or in groups to design their idea of a "perfect" mall. Ask them to draw a floor plan, label the different areas, identify the flooring material for the mall, and determine a color scheme. Ask students to identify the locations in the mall that are most desirable for retailers.

49. Invite the manager of a mall or the facility manager of a large store to speak to the class about retail "place strategy." Have students prepare appropriate questions ahead of time, especially about technology for scientific site selection modeling.

Answer Key

Text

Fashion Review, page 273

1. They can either change their target market or redesign their marketing mix to once again satisfy the original target market.
2. the company's ideal target market consumer
3. It is a response to conscious reasoning, based on logical thinking and decision making.
4. because the rate of population growth has slowed and people are spending less money on material goods
5. the emphasis on presenting goods in the early or later stages of the fashion cycle
6. to adjust to changing demographics, the desire to attract additional customers, or to differentiate itself from increased competition
7. its entire selection of goods and services
8. Stocking a broad assortment may limit the depth that can be carried, and stocking a deep assortment may limit the breadth.
9. It is a price that brings about the sale, generates a profit, satisfies customer expectations, and meets competitive situations.

10. a very good location, a high level of service, and a merchandise assortment of exclusive brand names
11. (List five:) They are in an inconvenient location; are a self-service organization; concentrate on high-volume sales; stock private-label merchandise; lower their costs with innovative technology; forego expensive promotional efforts.
12. with parking garages, security patrols, and closing streets to make mall-like settings
13. regional shopping centers located in tall buildings in large cities
14. Too many stores are competing for too few sales dollars.
15. how concentrated a presence the retailer has in a specific area
16. minimizing operating expenses while maximizing sales and customer satisfaction
17. advertising, publicity, visual merchandising, and special events
18. In the past, shopping was done for more pleasure and psychological satisfaction. Today people are in a hurry and want to accomplish shopping tasks efficiently, or they want to be entertained as they shop.
19. (Name three:) convenient parking, faster checkout, ease of finding products, desired products in stock, leaving the customer alone to make shopping decisions, an organized atmosphere with no surprises
20. They promote themselves together to draw consumers to the site, who then take advantage of both the entertainment and shopping segments.

Student Workbook

Retail Positioning Puzzle, Activity C

1. where a store situates itself in the consumer market, which guides how it satisfies its target customers while differentiating itself from competitors
2. OPERATIONAL
3. BREADTH
4. SELECTIVE
5. EVERYDAY LOW
6. BUYING
7. VALUE
8. DEPTH
9. PRODUCT
10. EXCLUSIVE
11. DIRECT
12. LIFESTYLE
13. MERCHANDISING
14. PATRONAGE
15. INDIRECT
16. VERTICAL
17. INTENSIVE
18. PRESTIGE

Retail Positioning Tree, Activity D

1. image
2. tenant
3. central
4. regional
5. community
6. assortment
7. product mix
8. neighborhood
9. super-regional
10. price promoting
11. rational behavior
12. emotional behavior
13. purchasing behavior
14. signage
15. ambiance
16. price war
17. strip malls
18. market coverage
19. sales promotion

Retailing Positioning Facts, Activity E

1. They end up satisfying no market at all.
2. (List three:) working directly on the selling floor, listening to customer feedback from the company's staff, working with a focus group, doing customer surveys
3. rapidly changing retail patterns, external economic conditions, and the buying motives of target customers
4. emotional buying motives, which fashion marketers appeal to in fashion advertising, visual merchandising, and sales training
5. a combination of both
6. lifestyle competition
7. (Name six:) credit privileges, generous return policies, telephone ordering, home delivery, well-appointed restrooms, gift wrapping, in-store restaurants, free parking, alterations, jewelry repair
8. upscale = luxurious surroundings; mid-priced = pleasing surroundings; low-priced = no particular ambiance
9. They should be courteous, knowledgeable, helpful, and dressed at a similar fashion level to the merchandise for sale in the store.
10. Shoppers would leave without any purchases and would probably never return.
11. by changing the merchandise assortments, services, ambiance, and promotion over time
12. small amounts of many different styles; upscale, prestige retailers with customers who are selective about style, size, and color exclusivity
13. department and specialty stores that cater to midrange fashion and quality
14. the amount consumers are willing to pay and retailers are willing to accept; also, the price that is satisfactory to the customer both before and after the sale

15. Retailers that sell low volumes usually have high unit markups, and those with high sales volumes have low markups.
16. the pricing of merchandise at a limited number of predetermined price points
17. site location and physical site design
18. those who live in the city, downtown workers at lunch time, and tourists or business visitors to the city
19. open-air shopping sites with upscale, well-known apparel and home fashion specialty stores, as well as trendy restaurants
20. because customers will travel farther for their goods
21. if it is visible to vehicle and/or pedestrian traffic, compatible with its surroundings, and convenient for consumers
22. It is too time-consuming.
23. mass merchandisers, dollar stores, and Internet sites
24. They compete for consumer time and money, but not for sales of merchandise.

Teacher's Resources

Retail Positioning Questions,
reproducible master 13-8

1. credit data and customer purchase information
2. relatively few styles, but a lot of them in many sizes and colors; mass merchandisers, who stock the latest fast-selling items in large quantities, and have high inventory turnover rates
3. (Name four:) materials, construction, style, fit, guarantees
4. They house many stores in one location, with duplication of merchandise in close proximity.
5. items with a designer's name, styles in the introductory phase of the fashion cycle
6. (List three:) more credible pricing, reduced advertising and other costs, a steadier flow of sales, better partnerships with vendors
7. regional shopping centers
8. easy movement of customers and sales personnel, maximum merchandise exposure and selling areas
9. (List five:) dressing rooms, restrooms, checkout counters, back room receiving and stock areas, staff offices, employee training areas
10. shoppertainment

Chapter 13 Test

1.	I	16.	T
2.	G	17.	F
3.	H	18.	F
4.	F	19.	T
5.	A	20.	T
6.	B	21.	D
7.	C	22.	C
8.	D	23.	B
9.	E	24.	D
10.	J	25.	A
11.	T	26.	B
12.	T	27.	B
13.	T	28.	C
14.	F	29.	B
15.	F	30.	B

31. Both are specific guidelines established by management. Merchandising policies keep inventory choices on track. Operational policies make the retail site appealing for the target market, through physical appearance and customer services.
32. Direct competition is rivalry between two or more companies using the same type of business format. Indirect competition is rivalry between two or more companies using different types of business formats to sell the same type of merchandise.
33. Rational buying behavior is a response of conscious reasoning. Emotional behavior is a response based on feelings.

Consumer Purchasing Behavior

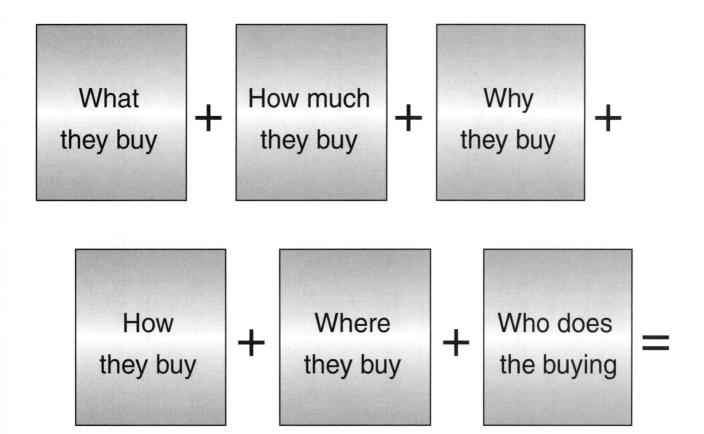

| What they buy | + | How much they buy | + | Why they buy | + |
| How they buy | + | Where they buy | + | Who does the buying | = |

Purchasing behavior

Assortment Breadth and Depth

Chain Stores	• Department store chains—narrow, deep range of proven styles • Upscale specialty chains—broad and shallow newer fashions • Discount chains—broad and shallow range of commodity items
Mass Merchandisers	• Narrow and deep assortments of currently popular styles
Off-Price Discounters	• Broad and shallow inventories of available goods
Mail-Order Retailers	• Narrow and deep range of proven styles
Independent Department Stores	• Broad and shallow at start of new selling seasons • Narrower and deeper as customer preferences become known
Independent Specialty Stores	• Usually broad and shallow of certain categories only

Pros and Cons of Everyday Low Pricing

Pros of EDLP	Cons of EDLP
• Restores credibility of retail pricing to the consumer	• Erodes consumer loyalty when prices seem too high
• Reduces costs of advertising, markups, and markdowns	• Limits ability to create excitement and build traffic with special sales
• Offers customers fair prices when they want to shop	• Increases need for other types of in-store promotions
• Lessens selling peaks and valleys	• Can reduce total demand
• Increases partnerships with vendors since the price of their goods will not be reduced	• May be dependent on vendors
• Lowers the cost of goods from manufacturers since they can match production with demand	• Reduces opportunistic buys that would increase margins

Revitalizing Central Business Districts

- Convert some streets to pedestrian malls

- Modernize physical facilities

- Reduce traffic congestion with one-way streets and modern traffic control devices

- Construct new upscale residential areas

- Organize existing businesses to develop and promote the downtown area

- Provide safe and convenient modes of transportation and parking

Retail Market Considerations

Market Potential

- Population—total number of people, density, and demographic characteristics (age, sex, income, occupation, etc.)

- Buyer behavior—store loyalty, the benefits sought, purchase situations, usage rates, and psychographics (values, attitudes, lifestyle, and interests)

- Physical environment—forms of recreation, choices of clothing, goods/services preferences

Retail Considerations

- Competitors—type, number, size, and strategy

- Distribution—delivery ease, availability of suppliers, costs for shipping or storing, etc.

- Advertising/promotion—media availability, coverage to target audience, costs, etc.

- Government/legal factors—zoning restriction, licenses needed, building codes, taxes, signing requirements, etc.

Aspects of Retail Facilities

Site Compatibility	Store Visibility	Consumer Convenience
• Compatible type of facility with surrounding area • Compatible size of facility with overall site	• Correct height to be seen • Proper setback from roads • Good angle for consumers to notice	• Ease of vehicle entry to and exit from site • Ample parking • Safe/convenient pedestrian access to facility

Link the New Terms

Name_____ **Date** _____ **Period** _____

Read the following new terms and definitions. Then tell how each term relates to specific chapter content of the text.

1. **Cohort** is a group of individuals statistically having common factors in a demographic study.

   _____
   _____
   _____
   _____

2. **Atmospherics** are environmental factors intended to create/suggest particular moods or emotions, such as to enhance shoppers' likelihood of buying merchandise. _____

   _____
   _____
   _____

3. **Salon selling**, used only in high-end retailing, keeps merchandise other than that used for display purposes out of sight, with salespeople choosing and bringing items from the stockroom for individual customers to see and try on. _____

   _____
   _____
   _____

4. **Gross adequacy** is the total amount of business available to all competing retailers within a trading area. _____

   _____
   _____
   _____

5. **Net adequacy** is the amount of business available to a single retailer within a trading area.

   _____
   _____
   _____

6. **Drawing power** is the strength a retailer has in getting customers/sales from a certain trading area.

   _____
   _____
   _____

Retail Positioning Questions

Name_____ **Date** _____ **Period** _____

Provide complete responses to the following questions or statements.

1. What information contained in retailers' computer systems can help companies quickly analyze and segment their customer base? _____
_____

2. Describe a narrow, but deep, merchandise assortment and the type of store that would stock it.
_____
_____
_____

3. Name four specific examples of product qualities that instill loyalty in customers for certain fashion trade names._____
_____
_____
_____

4. How do malls enable consumers to comparison shop? _____
_____

5. What types of items of relatively low quality might be highly priced? _____
_____
_____

6. Name three advantages for stores that use everyday low pricing (EDLP). _____
_____
_____
_____

7. Into what category of shopping centers do most enclosed malls fall? _____
_____

8. Name two operational considerations for efficient retail architectural design. _____
_____
_____

9. Name five examples of specific store interior sales support areas. _____
_____
_____
_____
_____

10. What word expresses the combination of shopping and entertainment?_____
_____

Positioning a Retailer

Name _____ **Date** _____ **Period** _____

Visit a specific store to check the points listed here and prepare a comprehensive report with your findings.

Store name: _____

Type of store: _____

Image and fashion level: _____

_____

_____

Target market: _____

_____

Competition: _____

_____

_____

Store location: _____

Analysis of location: _____

_____

_____

Type of store cluster: _____

Exterior store appearance

Compatibility of type and size of facility with site and surroundings: _____

_____

_____

_____

Store visibility to customers (height, setback, and angle): _____

_____

_____

_____

Convenience of vehicle entry/exit, ample parking, and safe, convenient pedestrian access: _____

_____

_____

_____

Analysis of signage: _____

_____

_____

_____

Store interior

Colors: _____

_____

_____

(Continued)

Name_____

Flooring: _____

_____

Wall and ceiling treatments: _____

_____

_____

Cleanliness and organization: _____

_____

_____

Traffic flow and sight lines: _____

_____

_____

Types and locations of sales support areas: _____

_____

_____

Types of promotion: _____

_____

_____

Breadth and depth of merchandise assortments: _____

_____

_____

Pricing level: _____

_____

_____

Merchandise quality/pricing relationship: _____

_____

_____

Service selection: _____

_____

_____

Other observations (furnishings, music, etc.): _____

_____

_____

Retail Positioning

Name_____

Date_____**Period**_____ **Score**_____

Chapter 13 Test

Matching: Match the following terms and identifying phrases.

_____ 1. Having enough locations to adequately cover selected target markets.

_____ 2. A policy of setting high prices on items to attract customers who want quality goods or the status of owning expensive and exclusive merchandise.

_____ 3. Advertising special price reductions of goods to bring in shoppers who will then buy other items as well.

_____ 4. Blanket coverage to serve all customers of a market.

_____ 5. Atmosphere that has great influence on retail fashion image.

_____ 6. The number of different categories or classifications of merchandise offered.

_____ 7. The quantity of each item offered in the assortment categories or classifications carried.

_____ 8. The reasons people buy what they buy.

_____ 9. Using one retail location to serve either an entire market area or some major segment of that market.

_____ 10. The selling of items below the price suggested by vendors of the goods.

A. ambiance

B. assortment breadth

C. assortment depth

D. buying motives

E. exclusive market coverage

F. intensive market coverage

G. prestige pricing

H. price promoting

I. selective market coverage

J. value pricing

True/False: Circle *T* if the statement is true or *F* if the statement is false.

T F 11. If retailers do *not* define their target markets and positions clearly, they usually end up satisfying no market at all.

T F 12. When retail managers talk about their customer, they mean the store's ideal target market consumer.

T F 13. Restaurants and retail stores vying for consumers' time and dollars is an example of lifestyle competition.

T F 14. A retailer's product mix is how it combines its upscale and discount branch stores in a community.

T F 15. A store's assortment is its total number of stores and their locations.

(Continued)

Name_____

T   F   16. Market constraints on pricing usually control how much consumers are willing to pay for specific goods.

T   F   17. A tenant mix is how stores, parking, and receiving areas are placed within a geographical market area.

T   F   18. Central business districts compete well with suburban areas because they are so well planned.

T   F   19. The best store location offers good visibility to consumers, compatibility with its surroundings, and convenience for customers.

T   F   20. The interior space of stores is divided into selling areas and sales-support areas.

Multiple Choice: Choose the best response. Write the letter in the space provided.

_____ 21. Retail positioning relates to _____.
A. where a store situates itself in the consumer market
B. how a store satisfies its target customers while differentiating itself from competitors
C. how a store blends the marketing mix variables
D. All of the above.

_____ 22. Product motives involve _____.
A. customers' consistent buying from certain retailers or favoring particular stores
B. advertising messages that influence the reasons consumers buy products
C. consumer purchases based on qualities or images of certain products
D. All of the above.

_____ 23. Vertical competition _____.
A. involves a fight for consumers' pastimes
B. is between businesses at different levels of the supply chain
C. is a problem throughout the soft goods chain, but has been helped by Quick Response
D. is between businesses at the same level of the supply chain

_____ 24. A store's unique fashion image is formed by a combination of its _____.
A. merchandise fashion level and services offered
B. physical exterior and interior environments
C. employees and promotion
D. All of the above.

_____ 25. A price war is when _____.
A. competitors drastically lower their prices to try to undersell each other
B. the cost of merchandise from supplier partners becomes too expensive
C. too many discount stores locate in a trading area
D. All of the above.

_____ 26. Everyday low pricing (EDLP) _____.
A. encourages consumers to shop when there are special sales
B. tries to instill a sense of trust and consistency toward pricing
C. tends to increase advertising and other costs of merchandise marking and promotion
D. All of the above.

(Continued)

Name_____

_____ 27. Place strategy relates to _____.
  A. the location of vendors from whom stores buy their inventories
  B. retail site location and physical store design
  C. research done to identify specific target markets
  D. the price/quality relationship of goods for the target market area

_____ 28. "Power centers" or "mega malls" that draw customers from 20 miles or more are categorized as _____.
  A. regional shopping centers
  B. neighborhood shopping centers
  C. super-regional centers
  D. community shopping centers

_____ 29. A strip mall is _____.
  A. an old mall that is refurbished by stripping off the old facade and replacing it with a new look
  B. an unenclosed line of stores connected by a walkway in front of the stores
  C. a large mall that takes most shoppers away from other shopping centers
  D. a new mall format that combines entertainment with shopping

_____ 30. A store's signage _____.
  A. consists of the fixtures, lighting, color, and materials used in the interior layout
  B. is the total of all the signs that attract consumers' attention and identify the store and its offerings
  C. involves all activities that encourage consumer interest in purchasing goods or services
  D. is the strategy that combines retail efficiency with "shoppertainment"

Essay Questions: Provide complete responses to the following questions or statements.

31. Differentiate between merchandising and operational policies.

32. Differentiate between direct and indirect competition.

33. Differentiate between the buying motive responses of rational and emotional behavior.

Retail Merchandise

Objectives

After studying this chapter, students will be able to

- explain how women's apparel is sized and classified.
- describe the production and sizing of men's apparel.
- explain how infants' and children's apparel is promoted and sized.
- name various accessory groups.
- describe fashion-related cosmetics industry products.

Teaching Materials

Text, pages 274–294
- *Fashion Terms*
- *Fashion Review*
- *Fashion in Action*

Student Workbook
- A. *Apparel Merchandise Categories*
- B. *Accessories*
- C. *Retail Terms Differences*
- D. *Retail Merchandise Questions*

Teacher's Resources
- *Women's Apparel Sizes*, reproducible master 14-1
- *How to Measure Men's Sizes*, transparency master 14-2
- *Men's Apparel Sizes*, reproducible master 14-3
- *Clothing Sizes for Infants to Preschoolers*, reproducible master 14-4
- *The Perishability of Apparel*, transparency master 14-5
- *Thoughts About Merchandise*, reproducible master 14-6
- *A Final Review*, reproducible master 14-7
- Chapter 14 Test

Introductory Activities

1. Hold a class discussion about hardlines and softlines. Explain that some hardlines are considered "durable goods," which are items lasting more than three years. Examples of big-ticket durable goods are cars, computers, and major appliances. Have students look at illustration 14-1 in the text to discover the merchandise categories within softlines groups. Also show students all the specialty apparel catalogs available from JC Penney (www.JCPenney.com/jcp/ProductList) and other retailers.

2. Ask students if they can explain how women's, men's, children's, and infants' apparel is sized. Have them name some classifications of women's and men's apparel. Their answers will indicate how much retail merchandise knowledge they already have.

3. Have students work individually or in teams to list as many accessory categories as possible. Ask volunteers to name one category from their list until all nine categories—footwear, hosiery, handbags and small leather goods, belts, jewelry, headwear, scarves, neckties, and handwear—are identified.

Strategies to Reteach, Reinforce, Enrich, and Extend Text Concepts

Women's Apparel

4. **RT** Report to the class that womenswear is the largest, most important segment of retail merchandise. Ask students to explain why.

5. **RF** Make available for students, or have each student bring to class, a mail-order catalog from a chain retailer or women's apparel company. As students go through the catalog, have them find examples of the merchandise classifications listed in illustration 14-5 of the text.

6. **RF** *Women's Apparel Sizes*, reproducible master 14-1. Use the master as a handout for students to study women's size charts and answer related questions.

7. **RF** Ask students to name specific shops that specialize in certain women's size categories. Have students discuss experiences with different fit of same-size clothing from different manufacturers. Discuss "vanity sizing" (downsizing) by some brands to woo consumers with smaller sizes. Ask if any of the students have worn a smaller size in a more expensive brand of garment.

Men's Apparel

8. **RT** Discuss with the class how men's apparel has become more casual, both for work and nonwork activities. Ask students to use magazine and newspaper pictures to provide examples. Include active sportswear in the discussion.

9. **RF** Make available for students, or have each student bring to class, a mail-order catalog from a chain retailer, such as JCPenney, or a men's apparel company. As students go through the catalog, have them find examples of the merchandise classifications listed in illustration 14-15 of the text.

10. **ER** Have students work individually or in teams to find four photos of menswear suit separates from advertisements or catalogs. Ask students to show the class how the separates might be mixed and matched together or with other garments. Have students explain why this information would be important for retail employees in menswear departments to know.

11. **ER** *How to Measure Men's Sizes*, transparency master 14-2. Use the master for a class discussion about measuring men's sizes correctly. Ask for two male volunteers to demonstrate correct measuring procedures. (A tape measure will be needed for the demonstration.)

12. **ER** Hold a class discussion about the problems with fit for apparel manufacturers, retailers, and consumers with returned merchandise, lost sales, brand dissatisfaction, and time wasted in fitting rooms. Studies show that 50 percent of women and 62 percent of men say they can't find a good fit in apparel, and 50 percent of catalog returns are because of fit problems.

13. **RF** *Men's Apparel Sizes*, reproducible master 14-3. Use the master as a handout for students to study men's size charts and answer related questions.

14. **ER** Show the class a video about retail merchandise. *The World of Fashion* and *The Men's Wear Industry* are available from D.E. Visuals.

Infants' and Children's Apparel

15. **RF** Have students study the "Boys" and "Girls" size charts in a JCPenney catalog, located in the middle section of the book. Hold a class discussion about the "Regular," "Slim," "Husky" (boys) or "Plus" (girls), and "Student" size categories.

16. **RF** *Clothing Sizes for Infants to Preschoolers*, reproducible master 14-4. Use the master as a handout for students to study infants to preschoolers' size charts and answer related questions.

17. **RF** *Apparel Merchandise Categories*, Activity A, WB. Students are asked to mount pictures of garments for women, men, infants, and children onto the worksheet and write responses to related questions.

18. **RF** Show the class a video about this section of the chapter. *The Children's Wear Industry* is available from D.E. Visuals.

Accessories

19. **RT** Have individual students report as much academic information as they can about a single accessory category, including how it is marketed, until all nine categories are covered. Let other students add to the information.

20. **EX** Have students check size categories and measurements for hats, gloves, rings, and other accessories. Mail-order catalogs of these items can provide the information.

21. **RF** Show the class a video about this section of the chapter. *Accessories* is available from Cambridge Educational and Meridian Education Corporation.

22. **ER** Make background books about accessories available for students. *Fashion Accessories: The Complete 20th Century Sourcebook* and *20th Century Jewelry: The Complete Sourcebook* are available from VMS, Inc. *Heavenly Soles* by Mary Tasko is available from the Shoe Trades Publishing Company. Dictionaries of footwear and shoe terms are also available. Have students report interesting facts to the class.

23. **EX** *The Perishability of Apparel*, transparency master 14-5. Have students find the definition of perishable. Use the master as a transparency for a class discussion. Ask students to explain why each of these categories is important for apparel and accessory retailers to keep in mind.

24. **RF** *Accessories*, Activity B, WB. Students are asked questions about accessories and are directed to attach pictures showing accessory

use and provide explanations on how they enhance the garments.

25. **EX** Have students discuss items of clothing that are worn by both sexes of all ages and seem to defy fashion obsolescence, such as jeans and fleecewear. Discuss "athleisure" footwear, or stylish sneakers that offer high performance. Ask students to evaluate apparel items that seem to be universal favorites.

Cosmetics Industry Products

26. **RF** Have students explain the cosmetics industry's three main segments: cosmetics, toiletries, and fragrances. Ask them to compare prestige lines with mass market cosmetics lines. Provide information to them about The Cosmetic, Toiletry, and Fragrance Association (www.ctfa.org).

27. **RT** *Retail Terms Differences*, Activity C, WB. Students are asked to define chapter terms.

28. **EX** *Thoughts About Merchandise*, reproducible master 14-6. Use the master as a handout for students to react to comments about apparel merchandise. Have students share their reactions in a class discussion.

29. **RF** *Retail Merchandise Questions*, Activity D, WB. Students are asked to write thought-provoking multiple choice questions about retail merchandise, then exchange their papers with a classmate and answer the questions correctly.

30. **RT** *A Final Review*, reproducible master 14-7. Use the master as a handout for students to review the chapter or earn extra credit.

Additional Enrichment Activities

Research

31. Have students research the standardization of women's apparel sizes. Have them find out how the WAVES (of World War II, 1942) were measured to become the basis of sizes that are still used today. Ask students to research how times have changed (for example, no girdles!) and how the population has changed (such as aging and ethnic composition). Have students research recent attempts to restudy the measurements of women in the U.K. and the U.S. (www.size.org and www.sizeusa.com), the sponsor of the research ([TC]^2), and reasons manufacturers and retailers like the current system. Also have students check on Intellifit booths in many Levi's and other stores (www.intellifit.com), and a software engine to recommend well-fitting apparel to specific online and catalog apparel shoppers (www.therightsize.com).

32. Have students research the dramatic changes in the intimate apparel industry of the past few decades. Have them identify the major companies of 20 years ago, 10 years ago, and today, as well as changes in the products and in the market's perceptions of modesty and feminine beauty.

33. Have students research the recent availability of fashionable apparel for "Plus Size" women, which is almost 25 percent of total annual women's apparel retail sales. Have students consider the acceptance of larger models, specialized stores just for this market segment, and stylish merchandise offered at all price levels.

34. Have students check library and Internet sources on Nike, Inc., a company that grew quickly because of the success of sport shoes. Several reference books, *Just Do It* by Phil Knight, the founder of Nike, and *Swoosh* by J.B. Strasser and L. Becklund, are available from the Shoe Trades Publishing Company. How is Nike, Inc. doing today? Ask students why.

35. Have students research a particular producer of womenswear, menswear, or childrenswear. They can get ideas for companies by looking at labels of merchandise in retail stores or checking on Web sites that list apparel manufacturers, such as www.iacde.com, www.gidc.com, www.fashioncenter.com, www.apparel.net, and www.usawear.org. Have students contact the company for information, search library business reference books, check indexes for periodical articles, and get information from the Internet. Ask students to investigate the types and sizes of garments produced by the company, how their lines are retailed, where the headquarters and showrooms are located, where production is done, recent financial results, and any restructuring of the firm (such as mergers or acquisitions) that has occurred in the last 10 years.

Projects

36. Have students study the history of men's fashions for the past 150 years and write a comprehensive report about the changes that have taken place. Ask them to include photocopied illustrations to reinforce their key points.

37. Take a class trip to a department store or mall. Have students observe the various women's, men's, infants', and children's apparel sizes and classifications. With a measuring tape, measure and record the bust, waist, and hip widths of a similar dress in low-, medium-, and high-priced stores or departments to see if upscale labels have downsized their items. Also have students observe the presentation and coordination of various accessories in the store(s).

38. Invite a local expert on women's apparel, men's apparel, infants' and children's apparel or accessories to speak to the class. Have students prepare a list of questions in advance.

Answer Key

Text

Fashion Review, page 294

1. yard goods, apparel, household textiles, and miscellaneous soft goods
2. Each company limits its production to only one or a few related size categories, price ranges, and merchandise classifications.
3. the popular larger sizes of female apparel
4. because each company has a different idea about the proportions of its target customer and develops its designs to fit that particular customer
5. Garments with expensive labels have a smaller size marked on them, thus having a larger fit. (A garment that is a size 10 or 12 from a budget manufacturer is a size 8 in a more expensive label.)
6. because the jackets and pants are bought individually as separate tops and bottoms
7. Sewing of jackets/coats is tedious and complicated, requiring highly skilled operators. Sizing is complex, and working with tweeds, checks, plaids, and pinstripes requires precise sewing skills. For sportswear, style and design features are emphasized rather than exact fit and meticulous workmanship.
8. the production of a limited number of units of a particular item, fewer than an average production run
9. slacks: waist measurement and inseam length; shirts: neck measurement and sleeve length
10. the big and tall market
11. spring/summer, fall, and holiday
12. (1) numerical sizes in increments of 3 months, from 3 to 24 months; (2) newborn, small, medium, large, and extra large
13. They have built-in stretch that "grows" with the infant. They also provide warmth and ventilation.
14. flammability of materials, especially for sleepwear; securely fastened buttons, snaps, and trims so they cannot be pulled off and swallowed or poked into a nose or an ear
15. Preteen is more sophisticated.

16. (Describe three:) large armholes, well-marked backs and fronts, easy-to-fasten front closings, elastic waistlines
17. impulse purchases
18. the width, which swings between narrow and wide
19. Prestige lines are sold by department and specialty stores; mass market cosmetics lines are sold by discount and variety stores, supermarkets, and drugstores.
20. because of minimum packaging and lack of promotion

Student Workbook

Accessories, Activity B

1. articles added to complete or enhance outfits; the secondary items that dress up or set off garments for a complete fashion look
2. by pulling different garments together, updating old garments, and dressing outfits up or down to look dressy or casual
3. (Name three:) simple chains, loop earrings, pearl necklaces, circle bracelets
4. (Student response.)

Retail Terms Differences, Activity C

1. Hardlines, also called hard goods, are nontextile items such as major appliances, tools, etc. Softlines, or soft goods, are made from textiles, sometimes called dry goods.
2. The women's apparel size category is for females with larger proportions. The petite apparel size category is for shorter females, (usually under 5'4"), with shorter torsos, arms, and legs.
3. Double-ticket is not a size category but is the marking of apparel with two combined sizes. Half-sizes are garments for heavier, short-waisted women.
4. Active sportswear includes garments for sports participation that are also worn during leisure time. Suit separates are jackets and trousers (or skirts) that mix and match into many different outfits.
5. Infants are babies from birth to when they start to walk at about one year. Toddlers are young children who are actively moving around and walking.
6. Self-help features are attributes of garments that enable children, as well as people with disabilities and the elderly, to dress themselves. Growth features are attributes of garments that allow them to be "expanded" as children grow.

7. Impulse purchases are made without much planning. Substitutable goods are items that can be used in place of each other.

8. Fine jewelry is expensive jewelry, usually very high quality, of genuine metals and gemstones, and is retailed by jewelry stores. Bridge jewelry is good-quality jewelry, made to look like fine jewelry but less expensive.

9. Extenders are "multipliers" that can be mixed and matched within a wardrobe for more outfits. Costume jewelry is "fashion jewelry" that is inexpensive, often of plated metals and artificial stones.

10. Cosmetics are products to be applied to the face, skin, or hair to improve appearance. Toiletries are personal care products used in grooming.

11. Fragrances are products that add a pleasant scent. Brand-line representatives are trained cosmetics salespeople who advise customers on the proper use of the cosmetics lines being sold.

12. To down-size is to use smaller size numbers for equal body measurements in more expensive fashions. Dual sizing is the combining of two size dimensions, such as neck plus sleeve length combinations for men's shirts or waist plus inseam combinations for men's slacks.

13. Footwear is an accessory category that includes dress shoes, casual shoes, boots, slippers, and athletic shoes. Hosiery is stockings, including panty hose, tights, knee highs, leg warmers, and all other socks.

14. Prestige cosmetic lines are cosmetic products with high-quality, exclusive images sold by department and specialty stores. Mass market cosmetics lines are inexpensive and are sold by discount and other lower-price retailers.

Teacher's Resources

Women's Apparel Sizes, reproducible master 14-1

1. fully developed women of average height, weight, and proportions
2. for shorter females within the misses category
3. for taller females within the misses category
4. XS = extra small; S = small; M = medium; L = large; XL = extra large; XXL = extra extra large.
5. females with larger proportions
6. heavier, short-waisted women
7. fully developed, small-boned and short-waisted females
8. Junior sizes are odd numbers while the others are even.

Men's Apparel Sizes, reproducible master 14-3

1. a combination of two size dimensions, such as neck plus sleeve length (men's shirts), waist plus inseam (men's slacks), etc.
2. chest size
3. waist measurement and inseam (inside leg) length
4. neck measurement and sleeve length
5. 3XLT
6. Many stores discount merchandise and others charge for alterations.

Clothing Sizes for Infants to Preschoolers, reproducible master 14-4

1. for babies, from birth to when they start to walk (at about one year)
2. height and weight
3. children who are actively moving around and walking
4. Preschoolers are taller and more slender than toddlers, and starting to have a defined waistline.

A Final Review, reproducible master 14-7

1. Goods are a store's articles of merchandise, and lines are groups of related products.
2. womenswear, menswear, and infants' and children's apparel
3. about 10 weeks
4. height to weight and bone structure, which also coordinates with the relationship among the chest, waist, and hip measurements
5. 9/10, 11/12, or others
6. They wear a smaller apparent size.
7. because high-priced apparel is made with expensive fabrics from upscale fabric lines and low-priced apparel is made of inexpensive fabrics
8. sportswear
9. They sell bulk quantities of their lines to retailers at wholesale prices, as well as selling directly to consumers through their own retail stores.
10. Land and labor are less expensive.
11. Quality control is more necessary for the complex tailoring.
12. fabric weight and fiber content
13. comfort and practicality
14. They should be wide and crisscross in the back, or inserted through shirt shoulder tabs.
15. one inch smaller to one inch larger than shown in the size chart
16. Fragrance sales decrease because scents are a luxury item bought with discretionary income.

Chapter 14 Test

1. I
2. J
3. F
4. A
5. D
6. G
7. C
8. B
9. H
10. E
11. T
12. F
13. T
14. F
15. T
16. T
17. T
18. T
19. T
20. T
21. C
22. B
23. B
24. A
25. D
26. A
27. A
28. C
29. B
30. B

31. Hardlines, also called hard goods, are nontextile items such as major appliances, tools, etc. Softlines, sometimes called dry goods, are made from textiles.
32. extra small, small, medium, large, extra large, extra extra large
33. (Name three: Student response. See illustration 14-5 in the text.)

Women's Apparel Sizes

Name_____ **Date** _____ **Period** _____

Review the charts on the next page, then answer the questions below.

1. Describe the general body shape of the misses size category. _____
   _____
   _____
   _____

2. Describe what is meant by *misses petite* sizes. _____
   _____
   _____
   _____

3. Describe what is meant by *misses tall* sizes. _____
   _____
   _____
   _____

4. What is the meaning of each of the capital letters at the top of the chart for misses sizes (each of which combines two numbered sizes)? _____
   _____
   _____
   _____

5. Describe the general body shape of the *women's* size category._____
   _____
   _____
   _____

6. Describe the general body shape of *half-sizes.* _____
   _____
   _____
   _____

7. Describe the general body shape of the *junior* size category. _____
   _____
   _____

8. When comparing junior sizes (3, 5, 7, etc.) to misses and women's sizes, what is the most obvious difference? _____
   _____
   _____
   _____

(Continued)

Name_____

Misses Sizes

Petites, Misses, Talls Sizes	Petites: 4′11″–5′3″		Misses: 5′3½″–5′7½″						Talls: 5′8″–5′11″		
	XS		S		M		L		XL		XXL
	0	2	4	6	8	10	12	14	16	18	20
Bust (in inches)	30½-31	31½-32	32½-33	33½-34	34½-35	35½-36	36½-37½	38-39	39½-40½	41-42½	43-44½
Waist (in inches)	22½-23	23½-24	24½-25	25½-26	26½-27	27½-28	28½-29½	30-31	31½-32½	33-34½	35-36½
Hips (in inches)	33-33½	34-34½	35-35½	36-36½	37-37½	38-38½	39-40	40½-41½	42-43	43½-45	45½-47

Women's Sizes

	Women's Petites: 4′11″–5′3″					Women's: 5′3″–5′7″				
Women's Petite Sizes	14WP	16WP	18WP	20WP	22WP	24WP	26WP	28WP	30WP	32WP
Women's Sizes	—	16W	18W	20W	22W	24W	26W	28W	30W	32W
Bust (in inches)	38-39½	40-41½	42-43½	44-45½	46-47½	48-49½	50-51½	52-53½	54-55½	56-57½
Waist (in inches)	30-31½	32-33½	34-35½	36-37½	38-40	40½-42½	43-45	45½-47½	48-50	50½-52½
Hips (in inches)	40½-42	42½-44	44½-46	46½-48	48½-50	50½-52	52½-54	54½-56	56½-58	58½-60

Junior Sizes

Sizes	Petite Juniors: 4′11″–5′3″		Juniors: 5′3½″–5′7″		Tall Juniors: 5′8″–5′11″		
	S		M		L		XL
	3	5	7	9	11	13	15
Bust (in inches)	32-32½	33-33½	34-34½	35-35½	36-37	37½-38½	39-40
Waist (in inches)	24-24½	25-25½	26-26½	27-27½	28-29	29-30½	31-32
Hips (in inches)	34½-35	35½-36	36½-37	37½-38	38½-39½	40-41	41½-42½

How to Measure Men's Sizes

(If a measurement falls between two sizes, men should order the next larger size.)

- Keep the measure tape snug, but not tight.

- For the **chest**, measure around the fullest part. With arms hanging relaxed at the sides, hold the tape up under the arms and across the shoulder blades.

- For the **waist**, measure around the waist, over the shirt (but not over slacks or a belt) where pants are normally worn.

- For the **inseam**, measure a pair of slacks of the right length, from crotch to hem bottom.

- For the **shirt collar**, measure around the base of the neck.

- For the **sleeve length**, measure from the center of the back neck, around the raised and bent elbow, to the wrist bone.

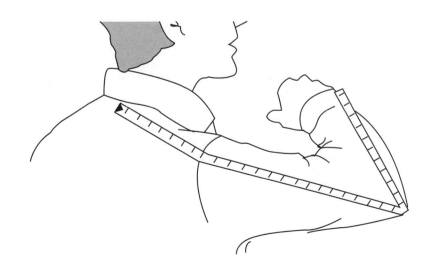

Men's Apparel Sizes

Name_____ **Date** _____ **Period** _____

Review the charts on this and the next page, then answer the questions below.

1. Describe *dual sizing*. _____

_____

_____

_____

2. Within figure type categories, what measurement is essential for determining sizes of men's suits
and sportcoats? _____

_____

Men's Sportcoat Sizes

Height and Build		Chest (in inches)
Regular Sizes	Short Length (5′4″-5′7½″)	40-44
	Regular Sizes (5′8″-5′11½″)	38-46
	Long Length (6′-6′3½″)	40-46
Extra-Tall Sizes	(6′4″-6′7″)	44-48
Big Sizes	Reg. Length (5′8″-5′11½″)	48-56
	Long Length (6′-6′3½″)	48-56

3. What are the two measurements needed to determine the sizes of men's slacks? _____

_____

Men's Slack Sizes

Height and Build	Waist (in inches)	Inseam (in inches)
Regular Sizes (5′8″-6′3½″)	32-44	30-34
Extra-Tall Sizes (6′4″-6′7″)	38-42	36
Big Sizes (5′8″-6′3½″)	46-54	30-34

4. What are the two measurements needed to determine the sizes of men's long-sleeved shirts?

_____

(Continued)

Name_____

5. Since height is very important in determining correct fit, what size shirt should a 6-foot man with a 19-inch neck order? _____

_____

Men's Shirt Sizes

Regular (5′8″ to 5′11½″)					
Sizes (in inches)	**S**	**M**	**L**	**XL**	**XXL**
Neck	14-14½	15-15½	16-16½	17-17½	18-18½
Chest	34-36	38-40	42-44	46-48	50-52
Waist	28-30	32-34	36-38	40-42	44-46
Sleeve	32½-33	33½-34	34½-35	35-35½	35½-36

Tall (6′ to 6′3½″)					Extra-Tall (6′4″ to 6′7″)				
Sizes (in inches)	**MT**	**LT**	**XLT**	**XXLT**	**Sizes (in inches)**	**MXT**	**LXT**	**XLXT**	**2XLXT**
Neck	15-15½	16-16½	17-17½	18-18½	**Neck**	15-15½	16-16½	17-17½	18-18½
Chest	38-40	42-44	46-48	50-52	**Chest**	38-40	42-44	46-48	50-52
Waist	32-34	36-38	40-42	44-46	**Waist**	32-34	36-38	40-42	44-46
Sleeve	34½-35	35½-36	36-36½	37-37½	**Sleeve**	35½-36	36½-37	37-37½	38-38½

Big Regular (5′8″ to 5′11½″)						Big Tall (6′ to 6′3½″)					
Size (in inches)	**1XL**	**2XL**	**3XL**	**4XL**	**5XL**	**Size (in inches)**	**1XLT**	**2XLT**	**3XLT**	**4XLT**	**5XLT**
Neck	17½	18-18½	19-19½	20-20½	21-21½	**Neck**	17½	18-18½	19-19½	20-20½	21-21½
Chest	48	50-52	54-56	58-60	62-64	**Chest**	48	50-52	54-56	58-60	62-64
Waist	42-44	46-48	50-52	54-56	58-60	**Waist**	42-44	46-48	50-52	54-56	58-60
Sleeve	35-35½	35½-36	36-36½	36½-37	36½-37	**Sleeve**	37	37-37½	37½-38	38-38½	38-38½

6. Why are fewer trousers being custom-hemmed by retailers these days? _____

_____

_____

Clothing Sizes for Infants to Preschoolers

Name_____ **Date** _____ **Period** _____

Review the charts on this and the next page, then answer the questions below.

1. Define *infant sizing*. _____

_____

_____

_____

2. What two measurements are used for infant sizes? _____

_____

Age-Related Clothing Sizes for Infants

Size	Height (in inches)	Weight (in pounds)
3 Months	up to 24	up to 13
6 Months	24½-26½	13½-18
12 Months	27-29	18½-22
18 Months	29½-31½	22½-26
24 Months	32-34	26½-29
36 Months	34½-36½	29½-32
48 Months	37-40	32½-36

General Clothing Sizes for Infants

Size	Height (in inches)	Weight (in pounds)
NB (Newborn)	up to 24	up to 14
S (Small)	24½-28	14-19
M (Medium)	28½-32	20-25
L (Large)	32½-36	26-31
XL (Extra Large)	36½-38	32-36

(Continued)

Name_____

3. Define *toddlers*. _____

_____

4. How is preschool sizing different from toddler sizing? _____

_____

_____

Toddler Apparel Sizes

Toddler Size	Height (in inches)	Chest (in inches)	Waist (in inches)	Weight (in pounds)
1 T	29½-32	19-19½	19½	21-25
2 T	32½-35	20-20½	20	25-29
3T	35½-38	21-21½	20½	29-33
4T	38½-41	22-22½	21	34-38

Preschool Apparel Sizes

Slim Sizes	Height (in inches)	Chest (in inches)	Waist (in inches)	Weight (in pounds)
3	36-38½	20½-21	18½-19	24½-28
4	39-41½	21½-22	19-19½	28½-33
5	42-44½	22½-23	19½-20	33½-38
6	45-46½	23½-24	20-20½	38½-43
6X or 7	47-48½	24½-25	20½-21	43½-50

Regular Sizes	Height (in inches)	Chest (in inches)	Waist (in inches)	Weight (in pounds)
3	36-38½	21½-22	20½-21	28½-32
4	39-41½	22½-23	21-21½	32½-37
5	42-44½	23½-24	21½-22	37½-42
6	45-46½	24½-25	22-22½	42½-47
6X or 7	47-48½	25½-26	22½-23	47½-54

The Perishability of Apparel

Physical Perishability	• Loss of marketability due to physical damage (rips, stains, fading, lost buttons, broken zippers, etc.)
Style Perishability	• Loss of marketability due to fashion changes that cause obsolescence
Seasonal Perishability	• Loss of marketability due to items going out of season
Competitive Perishability	• Loss of marketability because competitors are selling more aggressively (due to enhanced promotions, better prices, etc.)

Thoughts About Merchandise

Name_____**Date** _____ **Period** _____

Consider the following statements and write your thoughts about each in the space provided.

1. Baby outfits are so cute that sometimes people buy a lot of them even though they may be worn only a few times before the baby outgrows them._____

_____

_____

_____

2. As people age, their body proportions may change so much that standardized ready-to-wear clothing fits them differently from the way it did before. _____

_____

_____

_____

3. Increasing numbers of women in the workforce have created a greater demand for maternity fashions with a professional look._____

_____

_____

_____

_____

4. Many women prefer to buy separates rather than one-piece dresses because a better fit can be achieved with tops and bottoms of different sizes. _____

_____

_____

_____

5. Millions of choices of accessory products are displayed and sold in wholesale quantities to retailers at the Fashion Accessories Expo (FAE) held quarterly in New York City. _____

_____

_____

_____

6. Consumers' feet are important to the fashion industry since footwear is the largest accessory industry and hosiery is the second largest. _____

_____

_____

_____

(Continued)

Name_____

7. Unisex and combined sizes make production less expensive, which saves money for the industry and consumers and increases business profits._____

_____

_____

_____

8. When "big" looks are fashionable, accessories generally become bolder and larger in scale. Light, slender fashion silhouettes call for smaller-scale accessories. _____

_____

_____

_____

9. Jewelry should be suited to a person's age and personality, such as dignified, striking, bold, or youthful. It should be scaled to the size of the wearer and its texture and weight should complement the garment.

_____

_____

_____

10. Cosmetics companies and retailers often agree to *rubber-banding*, which allows the store to return merchandise to the manufacturer that does not sell within a specified time period. The merchandise is replaced with current products. _____

_____

_____

_____

11. A by-product obtained from wool processing is *lanolin*, a natural oil that is refined and used in cosmetic products. _____

_____

_____

_____

12. In the cosmetics industry, the term *doors* denotes the number of stores (retail outlets) in which the company's products are offered for sale. _____

_____

_____

_____

13. Recently, high-tech improvements have created lipstick that is long-lasting and nonsmearing. However, it dries the lips and is often used with a lip moisturizer. This doubles the products purchased—and profits made—and creates happy customers! _____

_____

_____

_____

_____

A Final Review

Name_____ **Date** _____ **Period** _____

Provide complete responses to the following questions or statements.

1. What are *goods* and *lines* in fashion retailing?_____

_____

_____

_____

_____

2. Name the main merchandise categories of apparel. _____

_____

_____

_____

3. How long do seasonal womenswear lines remain in retail stores before they are replaced with new merchandise? _____

_____

_____

4. Women's apparel sizes group women according to what relationships? _____

_____

_____

_____

5. Give an example of a double-ticketed size. _____

_____

_____

6. Why does downsizing cause customers of expensive womenswear lines to feel more fashionably slender? _____

_____

_____

_____

7. Why don't women's apparel producers usually make both expensive and low-priced lines?_____

_____

_____

_____

_____

8. What has been the fastest-growing segment of the menswear industry? _____

_____

_____

_____

(Continued)

Name_____

9. Describe the dual distribution of many menswear companies._____

_____

_____

_____

_____

10. Why is production of men's tailored suits and coats moving south from the New York, New Jersey, Pennsylvania area? _____

_____

_____

_____

11. Why has less contract manufacturing been used for menswear than for women's apparel production?

_____

_____

_____

12. What is the primary difference between seasons for tailored menswear?_____

_____

_____

_____

13. Instead of fashion trends, what is the usual basis for infant apparel purchases?_____

_____

_____

_____

14. How can the shoulder straps of toddler clothing be kept from slipping down?_____

_____

_____

_____

_____

15. Approximately how much fit variance do elastic waistlines provide? _____

_____

_____

_____

16. What usually happens to fragrance sales volumes when income levels go down? Why? _____

_____

_____

_____

_____

Retail Merchandise

Name_____

Date_____ **Period**_____ **Score**_____

Chapter 14 Test

Matching: Match the following terms and identifying phrases.

_____ 1. Attributes of garments that enable children, as well as people with disabilities or older people, to dress themselves.

_____ 2. Personal care products used in grooming.

_____ 3. Expensive jewelry, usually of very high quality, of genuine metals and gemstones, and retailed by jewelry stores.

_____ 4. Good quality jewelry made to look like fine jewelry but less expensive.

_____ 5. Marked with two combined but similar size numbers in different categories.

_____ 6. Products that add a pleasant scent.

_____ 7. "Fashion jewelry" that is inexpensive, often of plated metals and artificial stones.

_____ 8. Products to be applied to the face, skin, or hair to improve appearance.

_____ 9. Attributes of garments that allow them to be "expanded" as children grow.

_____ 10. A combination of two size dimensions, such as neck plus sleeve length combinations (men's shirts), or waist plus inseam combinations (men's slacks).

A. bridge jewelry

B. cosmetics

C. costume jewelry

D. double-ticket sizing

E. dual sizing

F. fine jewelry

G. fragrances

H. growth features

I. self-help features

J. toiletries

True/False: Circle *T* if the statement is true or *F* if the statement is false.

T   F   11. Women's apparel is divided into several general size categories by figure types.

T   F   12. Women's half-sizes are for women who have smaller proportions than average.

T   F   13. The women's "plus size" business deals in larger sizes of female apparel.

T   F   14. Menswear is the largest, most important segment of retail merchandise, with about 60 percent of apparel sales.

T   F   15. For men's tailored jackets, fashion emphasis is more on fabric design than on new styling.

T   F   16. A short run is the production of a limited number of units of a particular item—fewer than average.

(Continued)

Name_____

T   F   17. Toddler sizing is between infantswear and children's apparel.

T   F   18. Preteen sizes offer more sophisticated apparel styling than girls' sizes.

T   F   19. The larger sizes of boys apparel are often manufactured by menswear companies.

T   F   20. Accessories can be extenders to multiply wardrobe options and update garments.

Multiple Choice: Choose the best response. Write the letter in the space provided.

_____ 21. The misses size category is for fully developed females _____.
    A. with larger proportions than average
    B. that are small boned and short-waisted
    C. of average height, weight, and proportions
    D. between the ages of 14 and 24

_____ 22. The same women's apparel sizes from different manufacturers fit consumers differently because _____.
    A. sizing is standardized within the industry, but computer pattern making sometimes distorts it
    B. manufacturers intentionally make their designs to fit a particular target customer
    C. most producers change their slopers (basic patterns) when styles change
    D. All of the above.

_____ 23. Since most manufacturers of expensive fashions downsize their lines, they _____.
    A. can cut more garments out of a bolt of their pricey fabrics
    B. mark their garments with smaller sizes than less expensive lines made for the same measurements
    C. cause their customers to feel healthier since they are wearing a larger apparent size
    D. are encouraging all other manufacturers to standardize sizes in the entire industry

_____ 24. Garments used for sports participation and also worn during leisure time are referred to as _____.
    A. active sportswear
    B. exercise/dress wear
    C. athletic home wear
    D. corporate casual Friday wear

_____ 25. Suit separates _____.
    A. allow for more accurate fit with separate tops and bottoms
    B. extend men's wardrobes for business and casual occasions
    C. mix and match various jackets with different pants, which extends men's wardrobes
    D. All of the above.

_____ 26. Classifications of menswear include _____.
    A. tailored clothing, furnishings, and work clothing
    B. neckwear, underwear, and sleepwear
    C. hats, socks, caps, and robes
    D. All of the above.

(Continued)

Name_____

_____ 27. The sizing of infantswear relates to _____.
    A. heights and weights of infants
    B. what size diaper different infants wear
    C. whether or not an infant is walking
    D. comfort and practicality rather than fashion trends

_____ 28. Accessories are often impulse purchases because _____.
    A. they are expensive and beautiful, catching the eyes of shoppers
    B. even though they are placed near the rear of stores, they are needed to complete outfits
    C. consumers buy them on the spur of the moment without much planning
    D. All of the above.

_____ 29. Small leather goods, also called flatgoods, _____.
    A. are made to coordinate with millinery items
    B. include wallets, billfolds, coin purses, and small cases for business cards
    C. include belts, shoes, and handbags, but not luggage or briefcases
    D. All of the above.

_____ 30. Brand-line representatives _____.
    A. stock department store counters and racks with mass market cosmetics lines
    B. sell prestige lines of cosmetics
    C. replenish health and beauty aids in discount and drug stores
    D. All of the above.

Essay Questions: Provide complete responses to the following questions or statements.

31. Distinguish between hardlines and softlines.

32. Explain what the following size designations mean: XS, S, M, L, XL, and XXL.

33. Name and briefly describe at least three women's apparel merchandise classifications.

Planning to Buy

Objectives

After studying this chapter, students will be able to

- describe the merchandise planning function.
- outline internal and external sources of planning information.
- explain factors to be considered in preparing financial and merchandise assortment buying plans.
- describe ongoing inventory management planning.
- explain the variables in selecting merchandise sources.

Teaching Materials

Text, pages 295–316
  Fashion Terms
  Fashion Review
  Fashion in Action

Student Workbook
  A. *Planning Sales and Stock Turnover*
  B. *Working with Stock-to-Sales Ratio and OTB*
  C. *Merchandise Planning Review*
  D. *Sourcing Merchandise Outline*
  E. *Planning to Buy Fill-in-the-Blanks*

Teacher's Resources
  Merchandising—The Planning Process, transparency master 15-1
  Gathering Planning Information, transparency master 15-2
  Considerations for Preparing Buying Plans, transparency master 15-3
  Open-to-Buy Facts, transparency master 15-4
  Some Planning Thoughts, reproducible master 15-5
  Vendor Selection Process, transparency master 15-6
  Popular Private Labels, transparency master 15-7
  Review the Information, reproducible master 15-8
  Chapter 15 Test

Introductory Activities

1. Have students refer to illustration 15-1 in the text while discussing the merchandising cycle. Emphasize that this chapter deals with the planning phase of the cycle. Ask them why merchandising is best illustrated by a circle instead of a straight line, which has a beginning and an end.

2. Have students imagine they are responsible for planning the merchandise a store will sell. Ask them how they would decide what items to stock and where to buy them. Would they stock brand name goods, private label items, or a combination of both? Would their merchandise be made in the U.S. or offshore? Have students discuss the different approaches they think they might take and the reasons why.

3. Have students describe the merchandise selections at specific stores in the area. Ask them to estimate the number of different manufacturers that are used to provide the assortment of goods for each.

Strategies to Reteach, Reinforce, Enrich, and Extend Text Concepts

The Merchandise Planning Function

4. **RF** *Merchandising—The Planning Process*, transparency master 15-1. Use the transparency for a class discussion of the considerations involved in merchandise planning.

5. **EX** Hold a class discussion on the complexity of the merchandise planning procedure. Discuss how merchandisers must analyze fashion trends and timing, maintain a specific image for a target market, estimate future demand for certain goods, follow store policies about stock breadth and depth, stay within a spending budget, offer goods within the correct price range, and try to make the highest possible profit. Have students

explain how handling these responsibilities involve decisions about specific merchandise styles, colors, sizes, quality, and costs.

6. **RT** Distinguish between "departmental" and "classification" buying. Have students tell why classification buying has become the most-used method. Also ask students why departmental buying is more responsive to customers (because it is done specifically for that store's department) and why computer POS statistics are needed for classification buying (because the customers are not personally known).

Gathering Planning Information

7. **RF** *Gathering Planning Information*, transparency master 15-2. Use this transparency to show students the flow and many sources of information that enable retail decision makers to plan retail merchandise needs.

8. **RF** Show students a video about merchandise planning information. *Planning the Purchase: Retail Buying* is available from D.E. Visuals and Insight Media.

9. **RT** Discuss why each of the sources of internal and external information is relevant to merchandise planning. Also discuss the probable accuracy of information from each source.

10. **EX** Obtain government or industry figures on the monthly percentage volume of apparel sales throughout an average year. Have students explain why December is traditionally the highest month and January is the lowest. Also have students discuss why knowing the percent of yearly inventory for each month helps with planning calculations.

Preparing Buying Plans

11. **RF** *Considerations for Preparing Buying Plans*, transparency master 15-3. Use the transparency to discuss the importance of balancing inventory cost, variety, quantity, and timing when preparing buying plans.

12. **EX** *Planning Sales and Stock Turnover*, Activity A, WB. The worksheet gives a deeper explanation of planning considerations and presents problems and questions about sales planning for students to solve.

13. **RF** Discuss the significance of the following average turnover figures for certain types of goods: misses dresses, 3.5; men's apparel, 2.4; children's footwear, 2.2. Average turnover figures for classifications of goods are available annually from the National Retail Federation (MOR Report).

14. **RF** Since stock turnover represents the degree of balance between sales and stocks, ask students to explain why it is alarming if there is a drop in stock turnover. Reasons may include the following: the assortment may not be as good as

before, or more working capital is needed for the same volume of sales.

15. **ER** Create retail math problems (or have students create them) to compute stock turnover using cost of merchandise sold divided by average inventory at cost, or sales in units divided by average inventory in units. Calculations should parallel those shown in 15-9 of the text, but use different figures. Write the equations on the board to emphasize their similarities.

16. **RT** Discuss with the class why inventory levels might be decreased when the cost of working capital is high. Also discuss why inventory levels might be increased when vendors offer special quantity discounts.

17. **RF** Write *4*, *5*, and *6* on the board and have the class discuss the significance of having an inventory that is four, five, or six times the amount that will be sold in a month. Explain that a lower ratio is more advantageous if a high number of lost sales do not result because of lack of items. Also discuss that, since these are annual averages, actual figures calculated for each month can move significantly above or below these.

18. **RF** Show students a video about buying plans. *Stock Turnover* and *Stock-Sales Ratio* and *Planned Purchases and Open-to-Buy* are available from D.E. Visuals.

19. **RF** *Open-to-Buy Facts*, transparency master 15-4. Use the transparency to explain the concept of open-to-buy and its importance to good planning.

20. **EX** *Working with Stock-to-Sales Ratio and OTB*, Activity B, WB. The worksheet gives a deeper explanation of stock-to-sales ratios and OTB, and includes six related problems to solve.

21. **RF** Discuss with the class how classification buying speeds inventory turns, lowers stock investments in slower selling classifications, and lowers potential markdowns (since complete collections are not ordered).

22. **RT** Hold a class discussion about basic stock lists that show minimum and maximum quantities to carry to more easily determine reorder amounts. Also discuss model stock lists, which are more general to allow for retail fashion buying decisions.

Additional Planning Considerations

23. **RT** Ask students to describe the differences between substitute products and complementary products.

24. **RT** Have students explain the different types of buying: specification, consignment, memorandum, regular price-line, advance, and promotion buying. Also have students explain job lot, irregulars, seconds, and closeout goods. Tell the class that other promotion items might be end lots (last year's

fashions), miscellaneous sizes, and off colors/patterns that did not sell to buyers at full price.

25. **ER** *Some Planning Thoughts*, reproducible master 15-5. Students are asked to consider statements about the merchandise planning function, write their reaction to each, and discuss them with classmates.

Ongoing Inventory Management Planning

26. **RF** Show students a video about managing merchandise according to demand and time in the selling season. *Managing Merchandise Assortments* is available from D.E. Visuals.
27. **RT** Have students differentiate between stub-ticket control, card-control, and computerized inventory management systems.
28. **RF** *Merchandise Planning Review*, Activity C, WB. Students are directed to answer questions on the chapter material covered thus far.
29. **RF** Show students a video that explains how technology linkages between stores and distribution centers allow for good inventory management. *Inventory Management Systems* is available from D.E. Visuals.
30. **RF** Hold a class discussion about automatic replenishment of stock by vendors and about vendor-managed inventory (VMI). Discuss the fact that large vendors partner with their large retail accounts and no longer take manual orders. This eliminates small retailers from carrying the goods of those vendors. Also, discuss that for some brands of merchandise, small retailers cannot find salespeople from which to buy because the vendors have replaced salespeople with customer service teams who work with their regular, large accounts.

Selecting Merchandise Resources

31. **RF** *Vendor Selection Process*, transparency master 15-6. Use the transparency to discuss the steps involved in selecting vendors from whom to acquire merchandise.
32. **ER** Have the class discuss how vendor preticketing has evolved into floor-ready merchandise. Also discuss why the Voluntary Interindustry Communications Standards (VICS) committee has established standards for hangers, labels, packaging, cartons, delivery bar codes, and all other aspects of coordinating (standardizing) goods between vendors and retail sales floors.
33. **ER** Order the report *A System's View of Vendor-Managed Inventories* from the American Apparel and Footwear Association for students to study.
34. **RF** Discuss with the class why—with Quick Response EDI linkages between retailers and vendors—retailers are placing larger orders with fewer vendors.

35. **RT** *Sourcing Merchandise Outline*, Activity D, WB. Students are asked to outline the chapter section, writing titles, definitions, or concise explanations where needed. Have students compare their responses with other students and discuss the importance of the planning process.
36. **RF** Show students a video about branded goods. *Brand Marketing: Why We Eat, Drink & Wear Brand Names* and *Brand Management: Building an Image* are available from D.E. Visuals and Insight Media. *A Retailing Strategy: The Store Is the Brand* is available from D.E. Visuals.
37. **RT** With the class referring to illustration 15-25 in the text, discuss the advantages of buying from a single supplier versus dispersing the buying among several suppliers.
38. **RT** With the class referring to illustration 15-28 in the text, discuss each of the advantages and disadvantages of private label programs.
39. **RF** *Popular Private Labels*, transparency master 15-7. Use the transparency to discuss private labels, and ask students to comment about their knowledge of each. Mention that many of the designer's names are fictitious. Discuss the fact that more private label goods are now sold at retail than name brands.
40. **RF** Discuss with the class the "product velocity advantage": U.S.-produced goods may cost more than those from offshore, but faster, more responsive QR replenishment increases sales and creates happy customers with in-stock positions.
41. **ER** Show the class a video about global sourcing. *Merchandise Sourcing in the Global Marketplace* is available from D.E. Visuals.
42. **RF** Referring to illustration 15-30 in the text, have the class discuss each of the advantages and disadvantages of buying from foreign sources.
43. **RT** *Planning to Buy Fill-in-the-Blanks*, Activity E, WB. Students are asked to fill in the blanks with vocabulary words from the chapter.
44. **RT** *Review the Information*, reproducible master 15-8. Use the master as a handout for students to review the chapter or earn extra credit.

Additional Enrichment Activities

Research

45. Have students research computer merchandise forecasting programs that prepare buying plans based on customer demand rather than management initiatives. (Two popular apparel retail systems are the Merchandise Planning System and the Unit Management System.) Have students

report on how computer systems do the following: project inventory levels and pricing six to ten months into the future; sort information by classification for each store a buyer oversees; analyze profitability of styles, colors, and sizes; make quantitative recommendations for reorders, transfers, and markdowns; and customize responses for all vendor sources.

46. Have students research letters of credit (LCs) that are used to finance merchandise orders placed with overseas manufacturers. Ask students to explain what the procedure of payment is, why money is tied up for long periods of time, why the process is used for offshore orders, and other pertinent information.

47. Have students research consumer acceptance of brand name merchandise versus private label goods in various merchandise categories. Statistics are reported by the National Retail Federation, published in *STORES* and *Apparel* magazines, and available through library reference indexes.

48. Ask students to research Internet merchandise sourcing sites, how they can be located, and what is available on them. Have them use search engines to learn about the Private Label Brand Apparel Workshop of the National Retail Federation, The Directory of Brand Name Apparel Manufacturers, Retail Works Resource Directory, Stores Retail Buying Guide, and Virtual Garment Center.

Projects

49. Have students visit a mall that has anchor department stores and various types of small stores. Have students compare the selections of manufacturer brand merchandise and private label goods. Also ask them to notice the variety and amounts of items offered in the inventories of the stores. If possible (and if done as a class field trip), arrange ahead of time to have a store buyer or manager talk to the class about planning merchandise buying. When students return to the classroom, have them compare their observations.

50. Have students cut out two pictures of private label garments and two pictures of manufacturer brands of merchandise from catalogs or advertisements. Have students mount the pictures on pages that contain a description of the types of stores that own or stock the labels. Also have students judge the price/quality value of each and add other information that is appropriate.

51. Have groups of students plan the merchandise buying for a particular type of store and a specific fashion season. As they select merchandise and accessories appropriate for the store, ask them to cut out typical examples from various fashion magazines and mail-order catalogs. Have students mount the pictures, make charts of their buying plans, and present an oral report to the rest of the class.

Answer Key

Text

Fashion Review, page 315

1. New merchandise replenishes the retailer with styles that reflect the trends that have occurred since the last merchandise was bought.
2. because a small shop buyer usually does the selling as well
3. what stock could have been sold if it had been available
4. They can identify potential new products, preferred product assortments, current stock deficiencies, and changing customer wants.
5. because of their extensive exposure to the marketplace and interaction with other retailers
6. Products of higher-priced retailers usually tell what is coming and should be ordered by lower-priced retailers; merchandise stocked by lowest-priced retailers shows what might be dropped.
7. increasing the turnover rate for a better return on the investment (to maximize profits)
8. economic conditions, market strength, new styles, company policy changes, promotional plans, and events that might affect future selling
9. Stock turnover indicates an average figure for a certain time span, such as six months or one year. The stock-to-sales ratio is a figure for a specific point in time. They are both guides to help estimate the amount of stock required in relation to sales.
10. an ideal stock situation with sufficient items to meet demand, breadth, and depth to satisfy all customers, and a reasonably low investment in inventory
11. Basic stock plan items are staple goods with consistent demand and dependable sales, while model stock plan items are fashions that rise to and then fall out of favor.
12. They plan a broad but shallow assortment for early in the season, a broad and deep assortment during the peak selling time, and a narrower assortment of the most popular items late in the season.
13. The producer has the opportunity to control the terms of the sale and overcome retail resistance to new products; the retailer can test goods without risking investment.
14. The retailer usually pays a lower price. The manufacturer benefits from business during slack periods.
15. Because retailing has become so competitive and consumer credit so available, assortments of goods must provide customers with instant gratification.
16. The goods are usually the latest styles; prices are lower; goods can be made to the retailer's specifications; merchandising support is usually available.
17. (List three: Student response.)
18. through the trade press, consumer magazine articles and advertisements, fashion buying

consultants, market directories, networking with other fashion professionals, and looking at other stores' merchandise

19. (State two advantages and two disadvantages. Student response.)
20. striving for more efficient production and faster response time, more accurate fashion timing, and flexibility for reordering

Student Workbook

Planning Sales and Stock Turnover, Activity A

1. seasonal planned sales = $450,000 + [$450,000 × 5% increase projection] = $450,000 + [$450,000 × .05] = $450,000 + $22,500 = $472,500
2. seasonal planned sales = $300,000 − [$300,000 × 2% decrease projection] = $300,000 − [$300,000 × .02] = $300,000 − $6,000 = $294,000
3. $140,000
4. by adding together the monthly sales figures in the "Sales" column
5. $140,000 × 2 = $280,000 annual planned sales
6. $22,000; the same as the BOM stock figure for January 1
7. $280,000 ÷ 7 = $40,000 (The $280,000 figure is the total of all numbers in the retail inventory column divided by seven since there are seven retail inventory amounts.)
8. Seasonal stock turnover = $140,000 ÷ $40,000 = 3.5
9. Annual stock turnover = 3.5 × 2 = 7

Working with Stock-to-Sales Ratio and OTB, Activity B

1. BOM stock for December = $180,000 × 6.3 = $1,134,000
2. Fewer goods are offered, from which customers can make selections. They must choose from the goods available, but many of those items sell because of the low prices. Also, not many goods are sold immediately after the holidays.
3. BOM stock for November = $36,000 × 4.1 = $147,600 (the same as the EOM for October)
4. June OTB balance = $1,680,000 − $940,000 − $690,000 = $50,000
5. none, buying is already over budget by $2,600
6. September OTB balance = $52,000 − $8,000 − $10,000 − $900 − $1,100 − $400 − $12,000 = $19,600 to spend mostly on dresses

Merchandise Planning Review, Activity C

1. estimating, as correctly as possible, consumer demand and how it can best be satisfied
2. consumers
3. a small shop
4. because that is when the planning and buying takes place
5. They should register their observations about customers so buyers can act on that feedback.
6. by using surveys, panels, customer counts, and sample products to determine preferences
7. It is biased toward the vendor's goods.
8. They have market news and trends, industry statistics, and vendor advertisements.
9. what products are being sold and what merchandising tactics are being used to sell them
10. Items that sell quickly may not be available for reorder. The retailer then loses the opportunity of additional sales and creates unhappy customers who are not able to find what they want.
11. The retailer is well stocked while an item is in high demand and low in inventory when the demand drops off.
12. February through July, and August through January
13. an analysis of last year's plan and results
14. to maintain the proper mix and level of goods
15. They only take sales away from existing products because of customers switching brands.
16. an arrangement in which the retailer takes title to the goods when they are received, but unsold goods may be returned to the vendor after a specified time
17. items with imperfections, such as slight mistakes in manufacturing
18. They do not provide information fast enough.

Sourcing Merchandise Outline, Activity D

A. 1. Manufacturers—Buyers visit vendor showrooms, or manufacturers' sales representatives visit buyers at their stores.
   2. Wholesalers
   3. Web sites and catalogs—These are usually for basic items, and contain photos or drawings and sometimes fabric swatches.
   4. Importers—Imported goods are sourced through showrooms in American market centers or U.S. agents of foreign producers.
B. 1. Merchandise offerings—The goods must be suited to the retailers' customer group, price, quality, fit, and fashion level. There should also be new products and good pricing.
   2. Practices and policies
   3. Vendor services—These include markdown insurance, return privileges, sales training, promotional assistance, vendor preticketing, and floor-ready merchandise.
   4. Past performance—Considerations of past performance include such things as the vendor's fairness, sending the right count of items ordered, delivery timing, reliability with product quality, and turnaround time.

C. — Key resources are developed for each category of goods to be purchased, and classification resources are used for only certain items. Enough vendors are selected for reliable supply, but not so many as to be confusing. (Student response.)

D. — Selecting merchandise sources for retailers involves evaluations and decisions about emphasizing designer names, national brands, their own private label goods, or some combination of these. (Student response.)

E. — Retail buyers source goods globally, seeking the best deals from each of many countries. They seek higher markups for bigger profits, unusual styling, and other advantages. However, some disadvantages must also be considered. (Student response.)

Planning to Buy Fill-in-the-Blanks, Activity E

1. planning
2. buying
3. indirect
4. direct
5. merchandising cycle
6. retail buyers
7. departmental
8. classification
9. want
10. comparison
11. stock turnover
12. buying plans
13. dollar merchandise plan
14. stock-to-sales ratio
15. open-to-buy
16. assortment plan
17. stock-keeping unit
18. basic stock plan
19. model stock plan
20. never-out
21. complementary products
22. specification buying
23. consignment
24. regular price-line
25. advance
26. promotion
27. stub-ticket control
28. card-control
29. inventory-management
30. electronic point-of-sale
31. vendor-managed inventory
32. floor-ready merchandise
33. turnaround
34. offshore sourcing
35. exchange rate

Teacher's Resources

Review the Information, reproducible master 15-8

1. Indirect selling is nonpersonal promotion aimed at a large general audience. Direct selling is the exchange of merchandise to individual consumers in return for money or credit.
2. They report what merchandise has been sold, indicate what goods are unwanted (returned or marked down), and relate sales results to advertising, promotional events, media used, publicity received, and/or weather conditions.
3. because few buyers spend much time on the sales floor
4. Profits are lower because goods left over must be sold at reduced prices.
5. actual inventory and sales results
6. The retailer has control in setting the selling price and may have the right to pay for the goods as they are sold, which allows for better cash flow and does not affect open-to-buy dollars.
7. from manufacturers
8. necessities that consumers purchase regularly, with a minimum of shopping, from the most accessible retail outlets
9. mass merchandisers
10. because they want to sell as much as possible through as many outlets as possible
11. the manufacturer's procedure of attaching labels and price tags to merchandise, as specified by the retailer
12. fairness, sending the right count of items ordered, delivery timing, reliability with product quality
13. a medium number of suppliers; to spread commitments on the basis of profit opportunity and/or to broaden stock assortments
14. specialists in given classifications that retail buyers use as resources for certain items that are especially good
15. They are priced lower, have higher markups, and give better profits than manufacturer brands.
16. buying goods from overseas producers or contracting with foreign manufacturing plants for private label goods

Chapter 15 Test

1. F
2. G
3. I
4. J
5. C
6. E
7. A
8. D
9. B
10. H
11. F
12. F
13. T
14. T
15. F
16. F
17. T
18. F
19. T
20. T
21. D
22. A
23. D
24. B
25. B
26. B
27. A
28. D
29. A
30. C

31. (See illustration 15-1 in the text.)
32. (Name three:) merchandise offerings, practices and policies, services, past performance
33. (Name two advantages and two disadvantages. See illustration 15-30 in the text.)

Merchandising—The Planning Process

- Market considerations

- Product considerations

- Brand/image considerations

- Financial considerations

- Fair and dependable supply considerations

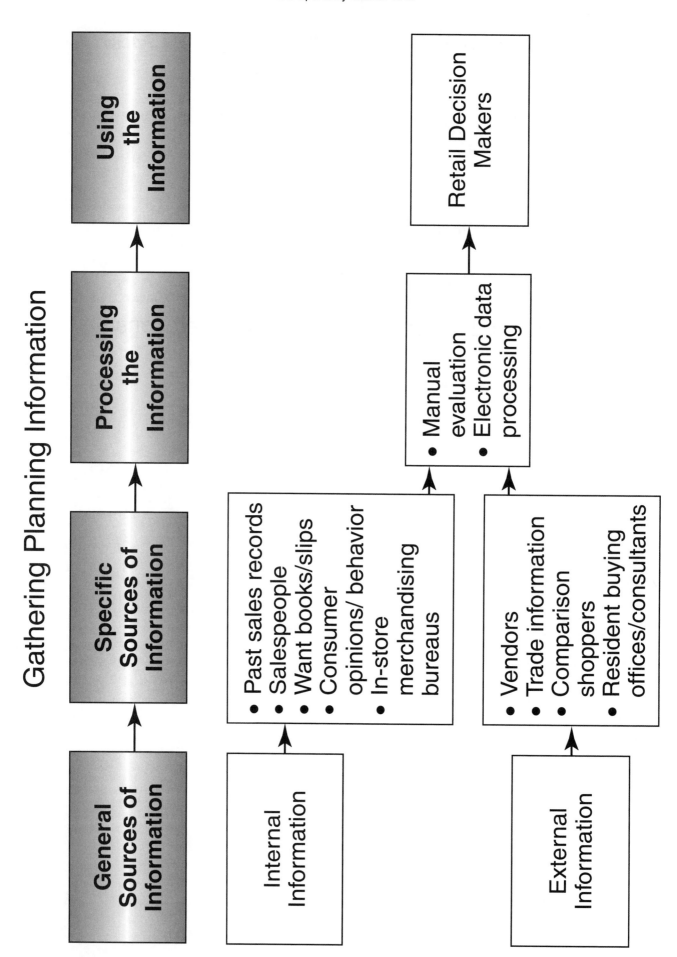

Gathering Planning Information

General Sources of Information → **Specific Sources of Information** → **Processing the Information** → **Using the Information**

Internal Information →
- Past sales records
- Salespeople
- Want books/slips
- Consumer opinions/ behavior
- In-store merchandising bureaus

External Information →
- Vendors
- Trade information
- Comparison shoppers
- Resident buying offices/consultants

→
- Manual evaluation
- Electronic data processing

→ **Retail Decision Makers**

Considerations for Preparing Buying Plans

Inventory Cost:	• The total dollar amount the company can spend on goods to achieve its financial objectives.
Inventory Variety:	• The breadth of goods (different types of items) the retailer should stock to satisfy target consumers.
Inventory Quantity:	• The depth (how many of each item) the retailer should stock to meet expected sales.
Inventory Timing:	• When the goods should be offered for sale to satisfy market demand.

Open-to-Buy Facts

- OTB is the total dollar amount budgeted minus the value of goods yet to be delivered in a specified period (usually one month).

- OTB for each buyer is broken down for each category or classification of merchandise.

- An OTB report (usually prepared weekly) summarizes the relationship between inventory and sales.

- The OTB report indicates
  - amount of merchandise on hand at the beginning of the period
  - amount of merchandise already received for the period
  - amount of merchandise already sold for the period
  - current inventory
  - merchandise on order
  - markdowns

Some Planning Thoughts

Name_____ **Date** _____ **Period** _____

Consider the following statements and write your reaction to each. Then discuss the statements with classmates.

1. Retail merchandise planners must not forget that, besides style, consumers want quality, fit, and value. _____

_____

_____

2. Brand name merchandise offers familiarity, reliability, and quality to a store's customers. _____

_____

_____

3. Retailers that sell private label goods say that "customers buy from the store, not from the manufacturer."_____

_____

_____

4. The **Private Label Expo** is a trade show that promotes contractors that retailers can hire to make their own lines of apparel._____

_____

_____

5. Consumer back-to-school purchases and adult fall purchases indicate the relative level of sales for the holiday season (percentage higher or lower than normal)._____

_____

_____

6. As a general rule, merchandise in lower price ranges has a higher stock turnover than higher-priced goods. _____

_____

_____

7. **Stock turnover** signifies the number of times that goods have been turned into money, and subsequently, money turned back into goods. _____

_____

_____

8. Accurate sales forecasting for each merchandise category should result in accurate buying as long as adjustments are made as conditions change. _____

_____

_____

9. **Customer demand rigidity** is an assessment of customer willingness to accept substitutes. ____

_____

_____

(Continued)

Name_____

10. The **stock-to-sales ratio** indicates the velocity at which stock will sell, usually ranging from 4.5 to 5.0 for women's clothing stores. _____

_____

_____

11. Stock-to-sales ratios improve with Quick Response replenishment of inventory that arrives only when needed. Consequently, the same amount of sales is made with less stock kept on the premises.

_____

_____

12. As a general rule, customers are more rigid (less willing to accept substitutes) early in the selling season. _____

_____

_____

13. **Regular price-line buying** involves buying first-quality goods currently in demand, usually at established prices. _____

_____

_____

14. Sometimes **promotional goods** have been specifically produced by the manufacturer to offer at a lower-than-normal promotional price. _____

_____

_____

15. A balanced assortment is sometimes known as the **merchandise pyramid**. Buyers plan the most important items with the best sales and profit for the bottom, then work their way up to the "fluff" at the very top that rounds out the assortment. _____

_____

_____

16. The most popular sizes in a merchandise classification are the **core sizes**. They are the mid-range sizes that make up most of the order. _____

_____

_____

17. **Forecasting software systems** are now available to make sure retailers plan the optimum color and size mix of merchandise to order for individual stores. _____

_____

_____

18. **Maximum inventory** is the number of SKUs needed to cover expected sales during the re-order and delivery periods, plus a **safety stock** for unexpected sales or problems in getting ordered merchandise.

_____

_____

Vendor Selection Process

- *Identify* many sources of supply for the store's merchandise categories.

- *Contact* sources of supply that seem good for the store's merchandise classifications.

- *Evaluate* specific sources for desired style, quality, price, timing, reliability, technology compatibility, ability to reorder, etc.

- *Coordinate* these vendor evaluations with the separate merchandise inventory planning.

- *Negotiate* with sources for particular merchandise items and buying arrangements (in next chapter).

Popular Private Labels

Retail Store	Some Private Labels
JCPenney	Arizona Jean Co. Worthington Stafford St. John's Bay
Kmart	Attention Athletech Basic Editions Jaclyn Smith Joe Boxer Route 66
Lord & Taylor	Kate Hill
Macy's	Alfani Charter Club INC International
Nordstrom	Classiques Entier Evergreen Norsport Preview International Tesori
Target	Cherokee Isaac Mizrahi Mossimo
Wal-Mart	Faded Glory George

Review the Information

Name _____ **Date** _____ **Period** _____

Provide complete responses to the following questions or statements.

1. Name and briefly describe the two different types of selling that merchandising involves. _____

   _____

   _____

   _____

   _____

2. In what ways do past sales records help a buyer plan purchases? _____

   _____

   _____

   _____

3. Why do buyers have little or no direct contact with customers? _____

   _____

   _____

   _____

   _____

4. What might result if a retail buyer orders more merchandise than is needed?_____

   _____

   _____

   _____

   _____

5. Retail planning must include provisions for constant adjustment based on what two factors? ____

   _____

   _____

6. Describe the retail advantages of memorandum buying. _____

   _____

   _____

   _____

7. From what type of merchandise source do retailers usually order quantities of fashion goods? __

   _____

8. What are convenience goods? _____

   _____

   _____

   _____

   _____

(Continued)

Name_____

9. What category of retailer buys a great deal of foreign goods? _____

_____

_____

10. Why do vendors not like to confine goods so one retailer has exclusivity in a trading area? _____

_____

_____

_____

11. What is vendor preticketing? _____

_____

_____

_____

12. List four types of past performance of vendors that retail buyers might evaluate. _____

_____

_____

_____

_____

13. How many suppliers should be used? Why? _____

_____

_____

_____

_____

14. What are classification resources?_____

_____

_____

_____

_____

15. What type of pricing, markups, and profits do private label goods usually have, compared to manufacturer brands?_____

_____

_____

_____

_____

16. What is offshore sourcing? _____

_____

_____

Planning to Buy

Name_____

Date_____Period_____ Score_____

Chapter 15 Test

Matching: Match the following terms and identifying phrases.

_____ 1. The dollar or merchandise unit amount that buyers are permitted to order for their store, department, or apparel category or classification for a specified time period.

_____ 2. When a retailer submits definite specifications to a manufacturer rather than looking for goods already produced.

_____ 3. A calculated number that shows dollar sales volume in relation to the dollar value of average inventory.

_____ 4. The number of times the average inventory is sold and replaced in a given period.

_____ 5. Items that supplement or accessorize other basic products.

_____ 6. A financial buying budget for planned stock, sales, and profit of a department or store for a six-month period.

_____ 7. A buying plan that projects the variety and quantity of SKUs to be carried by a store or department to meet customer demand.

_____ 8. An activity of department store buyers who purchase merchandise for only their own departments.

_____ 9. The activity of purchasing only one classification of merchandise, often done by chain store buyers.

_____ 10. The smallest unit for which sales and stock records are kept.

A. assortment plan

B. classification buying

C. complementary products

D. departmental buying

E. dollar merchandise plan

F. open-to-buy (OTB)

G. specification buying

H. stock-keeping unit (SKU)

I. stock-to-sales ratio

J. stock turnover

True/False: Circle *T* if the statement is true or *F* if the statement is false.

T   F   11. External resources of merchandising information include salespeople, vendors, and merchandising bureaus.

T   F   12. Want books and/or slips are used to record merchandise items that salespeople want to sell in their departments.

T   F   13. Comparison shoppers check (and report back to their companies) merchandise, prices, ambiance, and services of competing and noncompeting retailers.

(Continued)

Name_____

T F 14. Retailers should ideally be well-stocked while an item is in high demand and try to be low in inventory when demand drops off.

T F 15. When the cost of working capital is high, it is prudent to increase inventory levels.

T F 16. While stock-to-sales ratios indicate average figures for certain time spans, stock turnover figures are for a specific point in time.

T F 17. A balanced assortment has sufficient items to meet demand and satisfy customers, while maintaining a reasonably low investment in inventory.

T F 18. A never-out list is made up of goods that customers will ask for, so these items do not need to be displayed out in store merchandise areas.

T F 19. With vendor-managed inventory (VMI), sales and stock turnover rates have increased, and carrying costs and markdowns have decreased.

T F 20. Floor-ready merchandise (FRM) has all the tags, labels, and hangtags attached and is in packages or on hangers when arriving at retail stores.

Multiple Choice: Choose the best response. Write the letter in the space provided.

_____ 21. When gathering merchandising information, past sales records _____.
A. show what goods are unwanted because they have been returned or marked down
B. detect both sudden and gradual changes in consumer preferences
C. indicate the results of advertising and promotional events
D. All of the above.

_____ 22. If retail buyers order less merchandise than needed, _____.
A. items may not be available for reorder, which causes lost opportunities for additional sales
B. sale prices of goods will have to be reduced, which lowers margins and profits
C. the inventory has to "work harder" with an increased turnover rate
D. All of the above.

_____ 23. Retail buying plans _____.
A. are written for a specific time period and for a set amount of money
B. include both financial estimates and merchandise item estimates
C. describe the types and quantities of retail merchandise to purchase
D. All of the above.

_____ 24. The two main methods for developing merchandise assortments are _____.
A. stock turnover planning and stock-to-sales ratio planning
B. the basic stock plan and the model stock plan
C. open-to-buy (OTB) and stock-keeping unit (SKU) planning
D. financial planning and control, and assortment planning

_____ 25. An arrangement whereby a retailer takes title to goods when they are received but unsold goods may be returned to the vendor after a specified time is referred to as _____.
A. consignment buying
B. memorandum buying
C. stock-out buying
D. specification buying

Name_____

_____ 26. The systematic writing of purchase orders and normal reorders with vendors is known as _____.
A. specification buying
B. regular price-line buying
C. promotion buying
D. advance buying

_____ 27. Selected, discontinued goods, usually of various sizes and colors, sold at a low price are known as _____.
A. closeout goods
B. irregulars
C. seconds
D. All of the above.

_____ 28. Consumers these days want instant gratification, which _____.
A. makes accurate retail inventory management more important, to fulfill their immediate wants
B. means they will buy items at other stores if the original store does not have them
C. is the unwillingness to defer fulfillment of their wants to some future time
D. All of the above.

_____ 29. Convenience goods are _____.
A. necessities that consumers purchase regularly from the most accessible retail outlets
B. items that retailers order from wholesalers at reduced prices
C. seasonal goods that are ordered through sales catalogs
D. stock items that must be recorded by EPOS equipment for convenient reordering

_____ 30. Preferred vendors with which retailers consistently place large orders are known as _____.
A. primary source vendors
B. classification resources
C. key resources
D. brand name suppliers

Essay Questions: Provide complete responses to the following questions or statements.

31. Draw the merchandising cycle with proper labels included.

32. Name three vendor attributes that retailers analyze when evaluating resources of goods.

33. Name two advantages and two disadvantages of retail buyers buying from foreign sources.

Merchandise Buying

Objectives

After studying this chapter, students will be able to

→ summarize the activities of market weeks and trade shows.

→ list domestic fashion market centers and apparel marts.

→ state factors involved in buying foreign goods.

→ describe the market resources available to buyers.

→ summarize strategies of market trips and merchandise selection.

→ explain the process of writing orders.

Teaching Materials

Text, pages 317–337
 Fashion Terms
 Fashion Review
 Fashion in Action
Student Workbook
 A. *The When and Where of Merchandise Buying*
 B. *A Buying Team*
 C. *Buying Term Matching*
 D. *Purchase Order Considerations*
Teacher's Resources
 Retail Buyers at Market Weeks, transparency master 16-1
 New York's Fashion Center, transparency/reproducible masters 16-2A and 16-2B
 Dallas Apparel Mart, transparency master 16-3
 Buying Foreign Goods, transparency master 16-4
 Orders Placed Through RBOs, transparency master 16-5
 Read and Discuss, reproducible master 16-6
 Merchandise Buying/Replenishment Comparison, transparency master 16-7
 A Buying Frenzy! reproducible master 16-8
 Chapter 16 Test

Introductory Activities

1. Refer the class to illustration 15-1 in the text. Note that the planning phase of the merchandising cycle was studied in the previous chapter, while the buying phase will be studied in this chapter. Tell students that future chapters will explain the two different functions of the selling phase.
2. Ask students to look through this chapter and write an outline of its contents by using the section headings and subheads. Then have students read each line of the outline aloud.
3. Hold a class discussion about the continuous task of procuring fashion merchandise, involving merchandise selection, ordering, and receiving. Point out that this chapter will cover the merchandise selection and ordering functions of procurement.

Strategies to Reteach, Reinforce, Enrich, and Extend Text Concepts

Market Weeks

4. **RT** Hold a class discussion about the types of activities that occur in market centers during market weeks.
5. **RF** *Retail Buyers at Market Weeks*, transparency master 16-1. Use the transparency for a class discussion on the many reasons for buyers attending market weeks.
6. **RT** Have students review illustration 11-18 in the text to review the advantages of market weeks for vendors.

Trade Shows

7. **RT** Have students review the advantages and disadvantages of retail buying at trade shows.

Apparel Marts

8. **RF** Obtain materials for students to study from the apparel mart(s) nearest your location. Internet addresses and other contact information for the AmericasMart-Atlanta, California Market Center (CMC), Chicago Apparel Center, Dallas International Apparel Mart, and Miami International Merchandise Mart appear in the *Using Other Resources* section of the Introduction to these *Teacher's Resources*.

9. **RF** Hold a class discussion about illustration 16-13 of the text. Have students individually go through the advantages and disadvantages, especially for smaller stores, of buying at regional marts instead of taking buying trips to New York City.

Domestic Fashion Markets

10. **RF** Have students make charts that list the advantages and disadvantages of retail buying in New York City. Follow with a discussion of all the points made on the students' charts.

11. **ER** *New York's Fashion Center*, transparency/reproducible masters 16-2A and 16-2B. Use the masters to make handouts for students to follow while showing transparencies of New York's famous garment district. Use master 16-2A to show students the general location of the Fashion Center and its proximity to well-known destinations, such as the Empire State Building, Times Square, and Central Park. Use master 16-2B to show students that similar apparel and accessory categories tend to cluster together in the garment district. Point out the location of Bryant Park, where designer collections are shown twice a year. Also mention that Macy's department store is located in an entire block at the south side of the Fashion Center, and 5th Avenue is directly to the east, where many upscale retail stores are located.

12. **RF** *Dallas Apparel Mart*, transparency master 16-3. Use the transparency to discuss the groupings of apparel types on each floor. Ask students to describe the convenience of conducting retail buying in this type of environment.

13. **RT** *The When and Where of Merchandise Buying*, Activity A, WB. Students are asked to review the first half of the chapter by responding to questions and statements.

Buying Foreign Goods

14. **ER** Have students find magazine, newspaper, or Internet articles about market weeks or trade fairs in European, Asian, or other locations.

15. **EX** Show the class a video about foreign sourcing. *The Fashion Fair: Buyers and Sellers Under One Roof* is available from D.E. Visuals and Meridian Education Corporation.

16. **EX** *Buying Foreign Goods*, transparency master 16-4. Use this transparency to expand the information about buying foreign goods provided in the text. Have students explain the subtle differences among the categories.

Helpful Buying Resources

17. **RT** Have students refer to illustration 16-21 in the text as they discuss the types of resident buying offices used by retail buyers. Also have them refer to illustration 16-23 in the text to discuss the services provided by resident buying offices.

18. **EX** *Orders Placed Through RBOs*, transparency master 16-5. Use the transparency to have a class discussion on the different types of orders that can be placed through resident buying offices.

19. **RF** Discuss with the class how buying offices are able to pool the purchasing power of several client stores together to negotiate purchases at prices that individual stores could not obtain on their own.

20. **RT** Discuss with the class how merchandise brokers and reporting/consulting services are used by retail buyers.

Market Trip Strategies

21. **RF** Show students one or more videos about the fashion buying process: *An Introduction to Fashion Merchandising* from Nasco, Insight Media, and Cambridge Educational; *Buyers, Markets, and Marts* from D.E. Visuals; and *Judging Clothing Workmanship* from Meridian Education Corporation.

22. **EX** Have students imagine being buyers at market, trying to deal with the massive number of fashions they view and information they receive. Ask how students might rate merchandise items by using a method such as letters, numbers, stars, or checks. How completely would they take notes? How would they edit the line? How fast would they leave paper? What terms of sale would they negotiate?

23. **RF** *A Buying Team*, Activity B, WB. Students are asked to form retail buying teams with classmates and develop plans for a fictitious buying trip. Have students explain their decisions to the class.

Writing the Orders

24. **RT** Hold a class discussion about purchase orders, completion dates, and specific terms of POs. Discuss the pros and cons of negotiating for the best price, terms of sale, shipping and delivery, and added services (such as markdown money, discounts, packaging for resale, and returns) in relation to maintaining good supply partnerships.

25. **RT** *Buying Term Matching*, Activity C, WB. Students are asked to match chapter terms and definitions.
26. **RF** Show students a video about trade discounts and writing orders. *Trade/Quantity Discounts, Cash Discount/Dating/Freight Charges, The Buyer Visits the Market to Make the Purchase*, and *What You Buy Does Make a Difference* are available from D.E. Visuals.
27. **EX** *Read and Discuss*, reproducible master 16-6. Use the master as a handout for students to read thought-provoking statements about merchandise buying and discuss them as a class.
28. **RF** *Merchandise Buying/Replenishment Comparison*, transparency master 16-7. Use the transparency to review and compare the traditional merchandise ordering system with the Quick Response replenishment system. Discuss how companies that use QR have made major gains in logistics with synchronized movement of information and goods.
29. **EX** *Purchase Order Considerations*, Activity D, WB. The worksheet presents new information on negotiating with vendors and asks students, working in groups as "buying teams," to fill in the purchase order.
30. **RT** *A Buying Frenzy!* reproducible master 16-8. Use the master as a handout for students to review the chapter or earn extra credit.

Additional Enrichment Activities

Research

31. Have students research the Robinson-Patman Act. Have them learn when the law was enacted and how it limits price discrimination to keep competition fair for small businesses. Ask students to present their findings to the class.
32. Have students research and report on resident buying offices, their development, and their reduced numbers today. Ask students to gather information about: mergers and acquisitions among RBOs; their track record at satisfying the needs of retailers; and the effects of fewer independent retailers, the growth of regional marts, and Quick Response partnerships.
33. Have students research and report information about Associated Merchandising Corporation (AMC), The Doneger Group, Global Purchasing Companies, and other apparel industry sourcing services that maintain buying offices in major markets throughout the world. Have them report details about the firms' buying for department, specialty, and discount store chains as well as

providing these retail clients with private label merchandise. To supplement general information about the buying offices, have students check trade journals or the Internet for the latest facts.
34. Have students research the Worth Street Textile Market Rules that provide standard clauses for apparel industry contracts, including arbitration instead of litigation (lawsuits) to settle disputes over merchandise orders.
35. Have students do Internet research about apparel markets/marts and dates of market weeks. They might visit www.americasmart.com, www.dallas-marketcenter.com, www.dpoa.com, www.californiamart.com, and www.fashioncenter.com.

Projects

36. If your school is located in or near a city with a fashion mart or market center, plan a field trip to visit various parts of it. Have students help you plan a trip that is specific to your geographic area. For New York City, call 212-764-9600, and for an organized fashion tour of Los Angeles, phone 213-734-0400.
37. Have students investigate reference materials that are available to apparel manufacturers and retail buyers to connect with each other. They might start by searching "retail buying directories" on www.worldcatlibraries.org, finding *Sheldon's Retail Directory of the United States and Canada* and *Phelon's Resident Buyers and Merchandise Brokers* and other references that explain the types of stores serviced, categories of merchandise bought, buyers names, and other listings.
38. Invite a retail buyer to speak with the class. Have the buyer explain the merchandise planning, selecting, and ordering procedures for his or her store. Ask the buyer about buying trips and market-week experiences. Ask about the use of buying resources, market trip strategies, and negotiating and writing the orders.

Answer Key

Text

Fashion Review, page 337

1. so they know what quantities to produce and have enough time to make and ship the garments
2. because of the competition of many suppliers located in close proximity to one another
3. (Name three:) cooperative advertising in newspapers or magazines; sample ads to run with the store's name added; point-of-sale selling aids; in-store training assistance through brochures, videos, or company reps visiting the store

4. (List two:) They cover areas of fashion that might be lost at major market weeks; they display the work of unusual or small designers who can't afford to exhibit at major marts; they present unique merchandise.
5. small, independent retailers who may be located far from New York City
6. only authorized manufacturers and buyers
7. New York City
8. (List two advantages and two disadvantages. Student response. See illustration 16-15 in the text.)
9. Dallas market weeks are known to be representative of the whole U.S. and if fashions are successful there, they will probably be popular throughout most of the country.
10. to buy from a U.S.-based import agent
11. service businesses in main fashion market centers that employ buyers who scout fashion markets to provide client retailers with advance market information and buying help
12. lower prices through quantity discounts, more clout in the marketplace, and more reliable deliveries
13. large chain buyers
14. by phone, fax, or EDI connections
15. by attending preliminary seminars, clinics, and fashion shows at resident buying offices; reading market area retail advertisements; visiting local stores
16. It results in minimal garment samples and more design originality.
17. items that are not needed, are the wrong price, or are otherwise incorrect for the retailers target customers
18. (List three:) discounts, payment period, transportation and delivery schedules, services to be included, point of transfer of title, allocation of transportation costs
19. for specification goods, foreign goods, long production goods, and promotional goods
20. Retailers can end up with different goods than expected, and manufacturers can lose favor and be pressured to take return goods.

Student Workbook

The When and Where of Merchandise Buying, Activity A

1. three to six months
2. about three months ahead of the selling season
3. by visiting market centers during market weeks, or other exhibition/trade shows
4. so buyers will spend more time in that vendor's showroom

5. (List three:) accessorized and professionally modeled in their showrooms; mannequin displays and hanging on racks in showrooms; videos; fashion shows
6. current availability of goods, prices, delivery schedules, and terms of sale
7. because of large quantity orders, buying broken sizes or imperfects, end-of-season items from the previous line, ability to negotiate, and advantageous payment schedule or good discount terms
8. observing how other retailers shop the market, meeting the buyers of competing and noncompeting retailers, sharing ideas and experiences, phone calls between stores during mid-season
9. in vendors' showrooms and in market-area stores
10. small
11. (Name four:) Los Angeles, Dallas, Chicago, Miami, Atlanta
12. after hours, when mart selling is no longer formally taking place
13. a calendar of scheduled events and tickets to attend certain events
14. reasonably priced childrenswear and "sunshine sportswear"
15. Seattle, Washington
16. (Student response.)

Buying Term Matching, Activity C

1. E		11. Q
2. M		12. I
3. K		13. B
4. A		14. H
5. P		15. O
6. D		16. L
7. G		17. N
8. T		18. R
9. J		19. S
10. F		20. C

Teacher's Resources

A Buying Frenzy! reproducible master 16-8

1. from less than a week to about two weeks in some major markets
2. The smaller number of exhibitors make major buying harder to do; they are temporary events, without the ongoing service of year-round marts.
3. major fashion areas in the United States
4. Dallas
5. cruise fashions, swimsuits, lightweight activewear
6. They locate available textiles, find the right factories, try to ensure the best deals, and follow-up on orders to check quality and delivery dates.

7. so the RBOs will bring their merchandise to the attention of buyers

8. because they have in-store resources of sales records, plans, current merchandise, and store personnel to use

9. because market conditions or unexpected trends may require changes when actual items are seen

10. They are the most reliable and provide the most profitable goods for the store.

11. a list of style numbers and often sketches of the items

12. There they can check store sales records, merchandise on hand, committed orders, and get signatures from higher management, if required.

13. when they are completed with the terms and conditions of the transactions and signed by both parties

14. the manufacturer promises to ship orders when they are completed, rather than by an exact date

15. because retailers can end up with different goods than expected and manufacturers can lose favor and be pressured to take returned goods

16. to satisfy individual customers or to meet the requirements for window displays, fashion shows, or other special events

Chapter 16 Test

1.	F	16.	F
2.	C	17.	F
3.	H	18.	T
4.	E	19.	F
5.	B	20.	F
6.	I	21.	C
7.	J	22.	D
8.	A	23.	D
9.	D	24.	A
10.	G	25.	D
11.	F	26.	B
12.	T	27.	C
13.	F	28.	A
14.	T	29.	B
15.	T	30.	D

31. (Name two advantages and one disadvantage. See illustration 16-13 in the text.)

32. (Name three:) Los Angeles, Dallas, Chicago, Miami, Atlanta (Students may justify other responses.)

33. (List three: See illustration 16-23 in the text.)

Retail Buyers at Market Weeks

- Buy goods for their stores.

- Gain a sense of the market.

- See entire lines of vendor's latest merchandise.

- Discover new sources.

- Meet and consult with manufacturing managers.

- Get special terms and purchases.

- Gain promotion or selling help from manufacturers.

- Network with other buyers.

- Get ideas about new merchandise display techniques.

- Attend educational seminars, meetings, and other events.

New York's Fashion Center

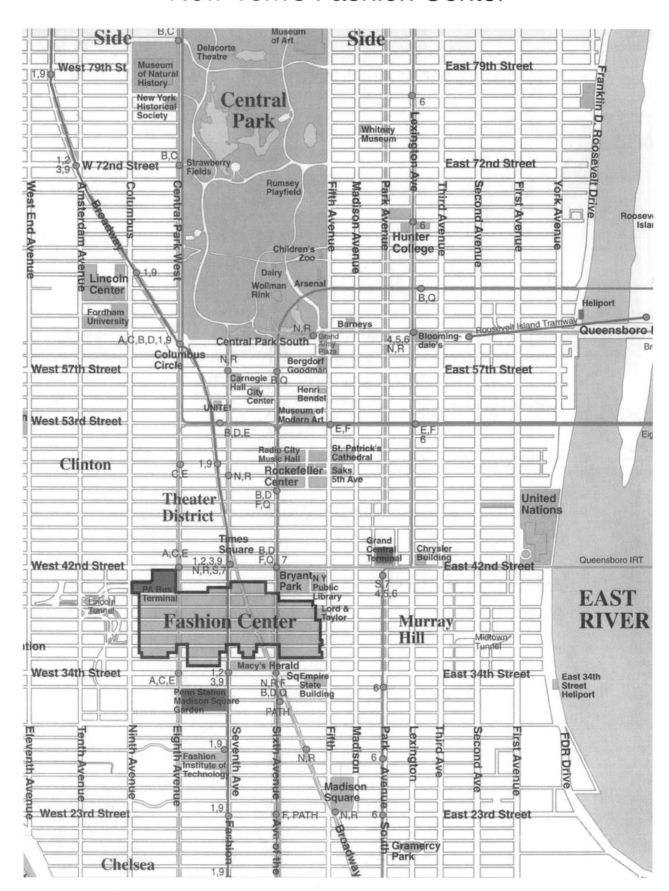

New York's Fashion Center

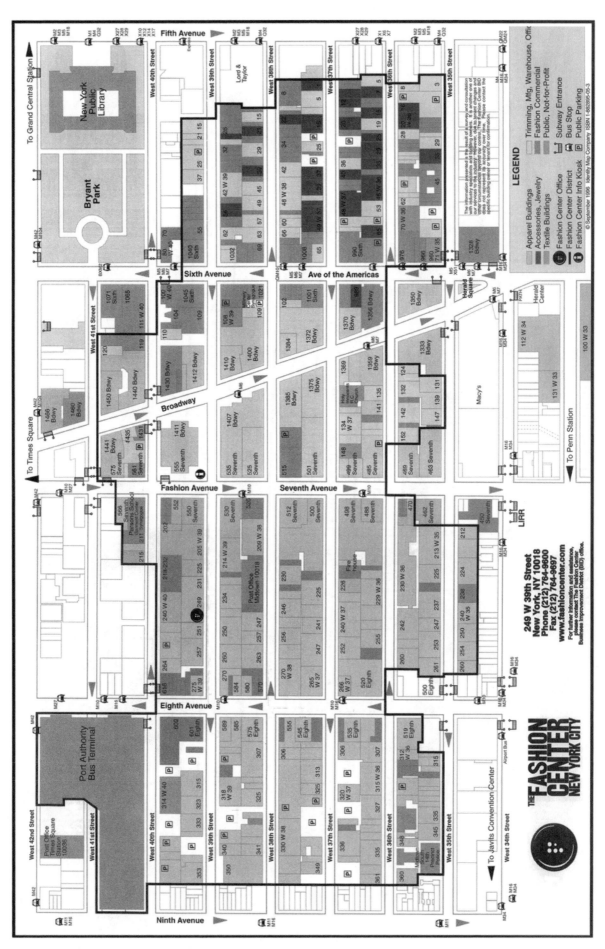

Dallas Apparel Market

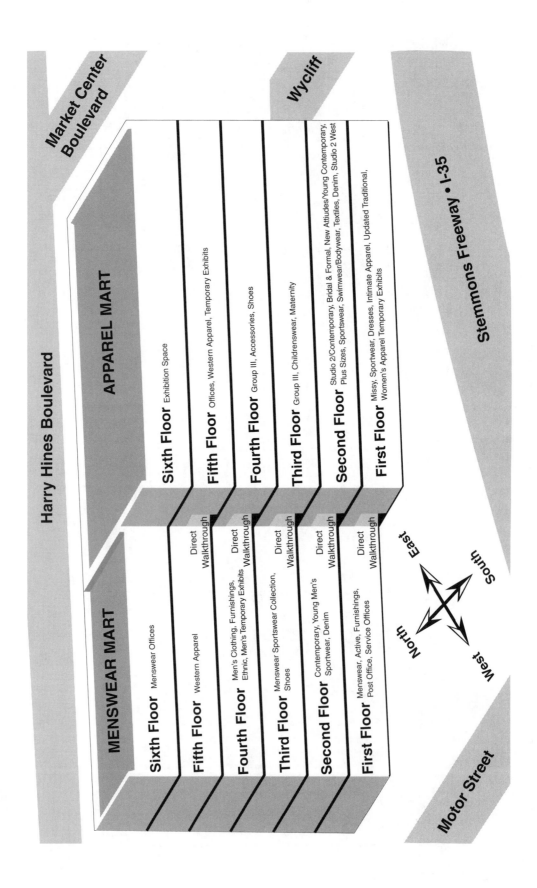

APPAREL MART

Sixth Floor Exhibition Space

Fifth Floor Offices, Western Apparel, Temporary Exhibits

Fourth Floor Group III, Accessories, Shoes

Third Floor Group III, Childrenswear, Maternity

Second Floor Studio 2/Contemporary, Bridal & Formal, New Attitudes/Young Contemporary, Plus Sizes, Sportswear, Swimwear/Bodywear, Textiles, Denim, Studio 2 West

First Floor Missy, Sportwear, Dresses, Intimate Apparel, Updated Traditional, Women's Apparel Temporary Exhibits

MENSWEAR MART

Sixth Floor Menswear Offices

Fifth Floor Western Apparel

Fourth Floor Men's Clothing, Furnishings, Ethnic, Men's Temporary Exhibits

Third Floor Menswear Sportswear Collection, Shoes

Second Floor Contemporary, Young Men's Sportwear, Denim

First Floor Menswear, Active, Furnishings, Post Office, Service Offices

Direct Walkthrough

Market Center Boulevard

Harry Hines Boulevard

Wycliff

Stemmons Freeway • I-35

Motor Street

North • East • South • West

Buying Foreign Goods

Method	Explanation
Travel to foreign market weeks.	U.S. retailers observe foreign design trends firsthand and buy merchandise for their stores.
Attend fashion fairs of foreign goods.	U.S. retailers attend fairs held in the U.S. or abroad, featuring goods from specific countries.
Source merchandise from a U.S.-based import agent.	These agents represent retailers in the buying process or source their own goods to sell wholesale.
Use commissionaires.	Independent buying agents in foreign locations find goods and put together sourcing deals.
Use international programmed sourcing.	International buying organizations of foreign suppliers contract to source goods for retailers.
Have foreign corporate buying offices.	International buying organizations owned by large firms source goods for their companies.

Orders Placed Through RBOs

Type	Explanation
Open Orders	Only basic details are provided, such as how many of a type of garment, the general retail price, and "good" colors.
Specific Orders	Specific details are provided, such as manufacturers' names, styles, size, colors, and date when needed.
Distribution Orders	New styles are sent by RBO reps to selected stores, which are not committed to take them.
Confirmation Orders	RBO reps place firm orders with the manufacturers if the stores like and desire more of the new styles that arrived with the distribution orders.
Sample Orders	Trusted RBO reps are given limited-order discretion to obtain new items in modest-size orders without specific approval (as long as open-to-buy is available).

Read and Discuss

Name_____ Date _____ Period _____

Read the following statements, consider their meanings, and discuss them as a class.

1. Going to market is exciting, exhilarating, and glamorous. It also is hectic, exhausting, and sometimes overwhelming. Buyers compare hundreds of items within a short time span. They also talk with sales representatives and executives, attend meetings, network with other buyers, and visit market center stores. Not a minute can be wasted. A possible quick snack and some phone calls are all that can be squeezed between appointments.

2. Progressive apparel vendors have online Web sites. A great deal of retail buying can now be done by "going to market" on the Internet. It is cheaper and less exhausting to visit these "cyber showrooms," but personal interaction, networking, and the exhilarating excitement of the market is missed.

3. Some new styles are introduced by manufacturers in mid-season, long after market weeks are finished. Highly accepted styles may be made in a wider assortment of fabrics or colors than originally shown. New fads may come into demand and be produced. Large manufacturers are increasingly offering new items throughout the season.

4. Apparel manufacturers and retail buyers try to arrange deliveries to be timed to arrive at stores in a continuous flow of merchandise for consumers. Today's retail customers like to see new fashions each time they visit a store. Both customers and salespeople require the stimulation of new and exciting merchandise.

5. New technology has shortened the vendors' response time. With Internet communications, robotic manufacturing, and overnight deliveries, previous six-month manufacturing processes are now accomplished in six weeks or six days. With new apparel designs created year-round, fewer retailers place an entire season's orders "up front" so more open-to-buy is available to spend during the season and for reorders.

6. Retailers no longer want merchandise delivered from vendors before it is needed. Orders used to be dated to arrive a month or two early. Now, if a store needs items for April selling, the retail buyer may write the order as "start-ship 3/15, complete 3/30."

7. At some marts, buyers can even purchase new display racks, mannequins, and visual merchandising supplies for their stores. That is one-stop shopping for retailers, the very people who try to provide one-stop shopping for consumers!

8. Experienced buyers take photographs of individual items when they "work a line" at market. Digital cameras connect directly to a computer for image downloading, e-mailing to coworkers, storage for future reference, and printing. The photos help when writing purchase orders and for reorders and returns.

9. Industry trade shows, with about 200 apparel lines, are attracting a growing number of retail buyers and fashion editors. The clothes generally are what "real people" will wear instead of bizarre, far-out creations that designer showings often feature.

10. Buyers for stores near market centers usually shop more often, but for a shorter period of time. Buyers who must travel a long distance go to market less often, but for longer visits.

(Continued)

Name_____

11. A market trip spending advance—for meals, taxis, and other incidental expenses—is usually given to the buyer by the store. Buyers should keep complete, accurate expense records during the market visits, with receipts obtained whenever possible.

12. The independent resident buying office fee paid by retailers is usually one-half to one percent of the past year's sales. Thus, large retail firms pay higher total fees than small firms, but they also buy proportionally more goods through the RBO's services.

13. Many retail buyers evaluate goods according to three factors: *suitability* for their customers' and store's image; *availability* of ordering the goods in various quantities, sizes, and styles; and *adaptability* of the supplier to make product changes for the needs of the retailer and its customers.

14. Since manufacturers edit their lines after getting "a sense of the market," retail buyers who order early may be notified later that they will not get some of their style picks. Manufacturers have minimum order requirements, known as **cutting tickets**, that go into effect before production begins.

15. With merchandise now available all 12 months and orders being filled faster, buyers worry less about having too few goods. Retailers are buying much "closer to need" and allowing as little time between selection and delivery as possible.

16. Buyers often go ***cherry picking***. This means they select from each vendor only a few items that represent the best of these lines.

17. ***Factoring*** is a way of financing business dealings that uses outside financial sources (factors) to provide operating capital and serve as the company's credit and collection department. For instance, a retailer might sell its ***accounts receivable*** (money owed by customers who have bought goods) to a factor, for which the retailer gets money to buy new goods from vendors. The factor assumes the responsibility and risks of collecting the money owed the retailer and charges a "factoring commission" fee for the service.

18. Several hundred menswear firms have their offices in one New York building at 1290 Avenue of the Americas with others nearby.

19. The FOB (free on board) point is the origin where title to merchandise passes to the buyer. If apparel goods are bought ***FOB factory***, the title passes to the store at the factory and the store must pay transportation and insurance costs. Retailers try to negotiate delivery terms of ***FOB store*** so the seller pays delivery costs.

20. With B2B linkages, retailers can check the status of orders online through factory information systems. Now inventory is even sometimes held at the supplier and delivered directly from supplier to consumer, bypassing the retailer's distribution center and inventory.

21. To motivate retailers to pay their bills early (within a predetermined time), some vendors offer an extra **anticipation discount** of 1 to 2 percent. These vendors often have cash flow problems, needing the money fast to pay manufacturing costs.

22. Since large retailers buy tremendous dollar amounts of merchandise, they are powerful in the marketplace and are said to write with a "big pencil!" However, they often dictate rock-bottom prices that minimize profits of manufacturers signing the contracts because these suppliers need the business.

Merchandise Buying/Replenishment Comparison

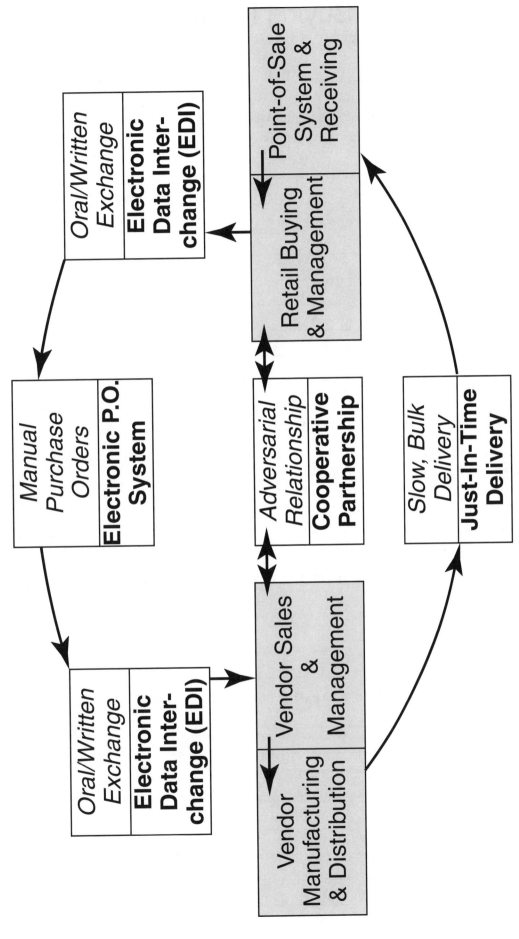

Oral/Written Exchange	**Electronic Data Inter-change (EDI)**

Manual Purchase Orders	**Electronic P.O. System**

Oral/Written Exchange	**Electronic Data Inter-change (EDI)**

Point-of-Sale System & Receiving
Retail Buying & Management

Adversarial Relationship	**Cooperative Partnership**

Slow, Bulk Delivery	**Just-In-Time Delivery**

Vendor Sales & Management
Vendor Manufacturing & Distribution

Bold Lettering = Quick Response replenishment

Italic Lettering = Old, traditional system

A Buying Frenzy!

Name_____ **Date** _____ **Period** _____

As you review the chapter, answer the following questions.

1. How long do market weeks last? _____

_____

_____

2. Name two disadvantages of trade shows. _____

_____

_____

_____

_____

3. What are domestic market centers? _____

_____

_____

4. What market center is the largest wholesale complex in the world? _____

_____

5. What specific types of apparel are considered "sunshine sportswear"? _____

_____

_____

_____

6. What services do commissionaires provide for private label goods that are bought on the basis of specifications? _____

_____

_____

_____

7. Why do manufacturers cater to the desires and needs of buying offices? _____

_____

_____

_____

8. Why can buyers make more informed decisions when buying from traveling sales representatives?

_____

_____

_____

_____

(Continued)

Name_____

9. Why must buying plans prepared for market weeks contain flexibility? _____

_____

_____

_____

_____

10. Why are most major purchases ordered from key resources? _____

_____

_____

_____

_____

11. What appears on the order pads that vendors provide to buyers?_____

_____

_____

_____

_____

12. Why do buyers often wait to get back to their retail offices to write merchandise orders? _____

_____

_____

_____

_____

13. When do purchase orders become legally binding contracts?_____

_____

_____

_____

_____

14. What does *as ready* mean? _____

_____

_____

_____

_____

15. Why might the placing of open orders with manufacturers be a dangerous practice? _____

_____

_____

_____

_____

16. Why might buyers place special orders for goods? _____

_____

_____

_____

_____

Merchandise Buying

Name_____

Date_____ Period_____ Score_____

Chapter 16 Test

Matching: Match the following terms and identifying phrases.

_____ 1. A written contract authorizing the delivery of certain goods at specific prices and times.

_____ 2. Merchandise orders that have not been filled within the time specified and have not been canceled by the buyer.

_____ 3. Additional orders of the same merchandise as ordered previously.

_____ 4. Orders placed with a resident buyer or vendor, without any restrictions as to style, color, price, or delivery.

_____ 5. An arrangement in which merchandise is shipped to the retailer for inspection before the final purchase decision is made.

_____ 6. Orders for merchandise to satisfy individual customers rather than for regular stock.

_____ 7. The conditions governing a sale, as set forth by the seller.

_____ 8. Merchandise orders with a longer lead time before the delivery date.

_____ 9. Promises to buy from favored vendors over a period of time, with no detail of colors, sizes, or shipment until later.

_____ 10. Stock orders for line merchandise.

A. advance orders

B. approval buying

C. back orders

D. blanket orders

E. open orders

F. purchase order

G. regular orders

H. reorders

I. special orders

J. terms of sale

True/False: Circle *T* if the statement is true or *F* if the statement is false.

T   F   11. Procurement is the physical delivery of goods by producers to retailers.

T   F   12. Only those style numbers that have enough retail orders to make production profitable are made.

T   F   13. Trade shows are held for consumers to express their opinions about new fashion trends.

T   F   14. Apparel marts enable manufacturers and retail buyers to come together in one convenient location.

T   F   15. Only authorized manufacturers and buyers are admitted to marts for market weeks.

(Continued)

Name_____

T   F   16. Domestic market centers are geographical areas that sell household linens.

T   F   17. New York City has one of the largest permanent apparel mart buildings in the world.

T   F   18. Although the majority of retail buying takes place during market weeks, buyers may visit most markets at any time.

T   F   19. Frequent buying trips must be taken to keep staple goods in retail inventories.

T   F   20. When buyers edit the line, they write descriptions of the merchandise they have been shown.

Multiple Choice: Choose the best response. Write the letter in the space provided.

_____   21. Market centers are _____.
A. suburban locations where malls are located
B. where the central streets and avenues of fashion cities cross
C. concentrated areas where goods are created, produced, and sold at wholesale prices
D. office locations of regional department stores

_____   22. Market weeks are scheduled periods of time _____.
A. during which retail buyers shop the various lines of vendors
B. during which producers officially introduce their new lines of merchandise
C. that last from less than a week to about two weeks in some major markets
D. All of the above.

_____   23. When and how often buyers visit markets are determined by the _____.
A. size and price range of the department or store
B. speed with which the market is developing new styles
C. distance of the store from the market
D. All of the above.

_____   24. A mart showroom guidebook, given to retail buyers when they register for each market week _____.
A. is called a market directory
B. has drawings of the styles of each vendors' lines
C. indicates sample orders for specialty shops, chain stores, and other types of retailers
D. All of the above.

_____   25. The simplest method to source internationally (such as for small stores) is to _____.
A. attend market weeks in foreign fashion cities
B. contract with foreign factories to produce private label goods
C. attend merchandise fairs in foreign lands
D. buy from a U.S.-based import agent

_____   26. Independent buying agents who live in other countries and know their laws and resources are _____.
A. valuable contacts, but usually dishonest
B. called commissionaires
C. paid a salary whether they source a small number or large number of items
D. All of the above.

(Continued)

Name_____

_____ 27. First cost is the _____.
A. price of foreign goods as they enter the U.S., without considering management travel expenses
B. original price of fabrications, notions, and trimmings before private label goods are produced
C. wholesale price for goods in a foreign country of origin, exclusive of shipping costs and duties
D. the price that was originally quoted, which usually goes up as inflation raises costs worldwide

_____ 28. Resident buying offices (RBOs) _____.
A. are service businesses that provide market information and retail help in major fashion market centers
B. are paid by the hour when retail buyers come into the market center and hire them
C. have staff buyers that travel to market centers as market weeks are presented in different locations
D. All of the above.

_____ 29. Retail buying visits to vendors are organized _____.
A. with the least important resources visited early in the week and key resources saved to visit last
B. according to merchandise classifications and price lines
C. to occur after lunch each day, following trend research in the mornings
D. All of the above.

_____ 30. The term leave paper refers to _____.
A. all the notes and item descriptions written about goods that are eliminated during purchase decisions
B. business cards given by retail buyers to vendors, requesting store visits from sales representatives
C. notes and information that are lost during the course of confusing market days and must be remembered
D. writing completed orders with vendors, usually during market week

Essay Questions: Provide complete responses to the following questions or statements.

31. Name at least two advantages and one disadvantage of buying at regional marts.

32. Name at least three cities where major apparel marts are located.

33. List at least three specific services provided by resident buying offices.

PART FIVE

Strategies for
Retail Success

CHAPTER 17

Communicating Information

Objectives

After studying this chapter, students will be able to

→ discuss internal business communicating.

→ describe how the communication process works.

→ explain nonverbal communication.

→ summarize how human verbal communication skills are used in business.

→ list basic communication aids and technologies for business.

→ lead a discussion about communication technology advancement in the world of fashion marketing.

Teaching Materials

Text, pages 340–359
   Fashion Terms
   Fashion Review
   Fashion in Action
Student Workbook
   A. *Getting the Message*
   B. *Group Communication*
   C. *Added Communications*
   D. *Communication Technology Quiz*
   E. *Communication Match*
Teacher's Resources
   Obstacles to Effective Communication,
      reproducible master 17-1

Business Letter Identification, reproducible
   master 17-2
Communicate About Communication,
   reproducible master 17-3
Parts of a Computer, transparency master 17-4
Steps in Using Information, transparency
   master 17-5
*Relating Business Communications and
   Technology*, transparency master 17-6
Communication Truths, reproducible master 17-7
Communication Review, reproducible master 17-8
Chapter 17 Test

Introductory Activities

1. Divide the class into six groups and assign a different chapter objective to each. Have each group read its objective in unison and imagine aloud the related topics the text should cover to accomplish the objective. This will focus students onto the content of the chapter.

2. Have one or more small books available about basic communication. Have students look at them to create interest in the subject. One example is *Effective Communication Skills* available from VMS, Inc.

3. *Obstacles to Effective Communication*, reproducible master 17-1. Use the master as a handout for students to explain how certain factors serve as obstacles to an exchange of information, thus blocking effective communication from taking place.

Internal Business Communicating

4. **RF** Discuss with the class the organizational transformations and changes in communication that companies go through as they become larger and more complex. Have students add their comments.

5. **RT** With students referring to illustration 17-4 in the text, discuss the lines of formal communication. Have students comment on why the display manager should not take problems directly to the president of the company. Have students notice that the degree of specialization increases with positions lower down the chart. Also discuss the delegation of authority throughout organizations.

The Communication Process

6. **RT** Have students refer to illustration 17-6 in the text as they discuss how the communication process takes place.

7. **ER** Show the class a video about the communication process. *How to Develop Effective Communication Skills*, *Solving Your Communications Crisis*, and *Integrated Marketing Communications* are all available from D.E. Visuals.

8. **RF** *Getting the Message*, Activity A, WB. Students are directed to answer two questions and rate themselves on how well they send and receive messages.

9. **ER** *Group Communication*, Activity B, WB. Working in small groups, students are asked to complete one of three communication tasks and present their supporting materials to the class.

Nonverbal Communication

10. **ER** Show students a video on nonverbal communication. Choices include *Nonverbal Communication* from D.E. Visuals and The School Company, *Body Language* and *Reading People* from Learning Seed, *It's Not What You Say: Mastering Basic Communication* from The Curriculum Center for Family and Consumer Sciences, *Positive Body Language* from The School Company, and *Mechanics of Communication* from Cambridge Educational.

11. **RF** Assign one of the following nonverbal communication projects for homework: watch people from a distance and try to decipher what they are saying through their body language; watch TV with the volume turned down, paying attention to the movements, gestures, and expressions of the actors; or watch people at a crowded city corner or mall intersection to observe what nonverbal messages are sent by how people dress, walk, and stand. Have students report their research findings to the rest of the class the next day.

Verbal Communication Skills

12. **RF** Have students form pairs to practice their listening and speaking skills with fashion business topics. When one student speaks, the other must listen. Neither student may respond to the other without first summarizing what was just said. Incorrect summaries must be clarified before the conversation is allowed to continue.

13. **ER** Show students one of the many videos about how to communicate well: *Communicating with Confidence to Get the Job Done*, *Communicating for Results: How to Be Clear, Concise & Credible*, and *Listening: The Key to Productivity* and *Communication Skills: What Everyone Needs to Know* are available from D.E. Visuals. *Everyday Telephone Manners* is available from Learning Seed; *Are You Listening?* is from The Curriculum Center for Family and Consumer Sciences. *The Art of Effective Communication* is available from VMS, Inc. and Learning Seed. *Verbal Communication* and "Basic Communication" videos about *Listening, Speaking, Writing,* and *Reading* are available from Cambridge Educational. Several videos about telephone skills are also available from Cambridge Educational, The School Company, and D.E. Visuals.

14. **ER** Have students "read with a purpose" an article in a fashion magazine or trade journal. Have them tell the class how their reading method was different from previous reading they have done. Also have them give a complete summary of the content of the article they read.

15. **RF** Have students demonstrate how to correctly answer a telephone at a business, take a telephone message, place a specific retail buying order, and leave a complete and concise voice mail message.

16. **RF** Have students use a computer program about communications. DOS software is available for *Communicate! Skills for School, Business, and Everyday Life* and *On-the-Job Telephone Skills* from Cambridge Educational.

17. **RT** *Business Letter Identification*, reproducible master 17-2. Have the students use their handouts to identify the standard parts of a business letter. Have them explain why business letters should be brief, thorough, and similar in format.

18. **EX** *Communicate About Communication*, reproducible master 17-3. Students are asked to read and discuss statements presenting new terms and information.

19. **RF** *Parts of a Computer*, transparency master 17-4. Show this transparency for a class discussion on how the parts of a computer work together to accomplish the output the user desires.

Technology for Information Management

20. **RF** *Added Communications*, Activity C, WB. The worksheet directs students to judge whether given statements express interesting aspects of fashion business communications. Students are asked to explain their reactions to the statement they find most interesting.

21. **RF** *Steps in Using Information*, transparency master 17-5. Use this transparency to discuss the steps that are followed in information management to reach useful end results.

22. **RF** Show students a video about information technology. *Communication Technology and Desktop Publishing*, and *Video Basics of Word Processing* are available from Cambridge Educational. *Interpreting Technical Information* is available from The School Company. *Communicate/Collaborate/Cooperate* and *High-Tech/High Return Marketing* are available from D.E. Visuals.

23. **ER** Have students learn more about using the Internet and other information systems. D.E. Visuals offers the videos *Roadmap to the Internet*; *More Time, More Money: Getting It All Done*; and *Advertising and Marketing on the Internet*. Cambridge Educational has the videos *Networking on the WWW and Beyond*. The School Company offers *Interpreting Technical Information*.

24. **EX** *Communication Technology Quiz*, Activity D, WB. Students are asked to write true/false questions, then form pairs to exchange their work. Have students take their classmate's quiz, check their answers, and correct any errors.

25. **EX** Obtain a copy of the trade magazine *Retail Info Systems News (RIS)* from Edgell Communications to show and discuss with the class. Also gather information from the National Retail Federation (NRF) about their Association for Retail Technology Standards (ARTS).

Communication Technology Advancement

26. **EX** *Relating Business Communications and Technology*, transparency master 17-6. Show the transparency and provide students with handouts for a class discussion on the types of communications and technology existing at different business employment levels. Start at the bottom of the chart and work upward. Discuss how communication technology permits higher-level decisions because of flexible systems that combine internal data already in the system with thought processes for strategic direction.

27. **RT** *Communication Truths*, reproducible master 17-7. Use this as a handout for students to answer true/false questions as they review business communications.

28. **RF** *Communication Match*, Activity E, WB. Students are asked to match chapter terms and definitions.

29. **RF** *Communication Review*, reproducible master 17-8. Use the master as a handout for students to review the chapter or earn extra credit.

30. **ER** Have students write a professional e-mail message requesting information from one of the sources listed in the Introduction of these resources.

Additional Enrichment Activities

Research

31. Have students research how to give a speech. Then have them organize their information, follow their own advice, and give a speech to the class about how to give a speech. Encourage the students to organize their information, speak clearly, use proper grammar, try to be calm, show confidence and enthusiasm, vary their tone of voice, speak loudly and slowly enough to be understood, keep good eye contact, and maintain good posture and body language.

32. Have students research and prepare a report to the class about how to conduct business meetings. Have them make visual aids, including one about correct parliamentary procedure. You may want to follow their research report with a video, such as *Conducting a Productive Meeting* from D.E. Visuals.

33. Have students research the Federal Communications Commission (FCC) deregulation rules on telephone service and the implementation of the Telecommunications Act of 1996. Have students relate how these rules offer benefits for retailers through lower costs and better electronic commerce.

Projects

34. Have students cluster into the same groups that were formed in Item 1. Have them address their chapter objectives again, this time presenting concise reports to the class on the topics in the text that relate to their respective objectives.

35. Invite an apparel or retail employee to class. Ask the guest to discuss the types of communication he or she uses on the job and the abilities needed, such as reading, listening, speaking, writing, and using computer and telephone skills.

36. Have each student write a set of circumstances for a fashion business scenario that requires a written business communication. Examples include a manufacturer with rising sales that is considering renting mart space in several locations, a retailer that is looking for a vendor of a specific type of merchandise, and a retailer that has received a complaint from a customer. Then have students pair off, exchange their scenarios, and reply to their partner's scenario by writing a business letter, memo, fax, or whatever is needed to respond to the given situation.

Answer Key

Text

Fashion Review, page 359

1. Workers have less contact with top managers; more rules and policies are written down; communication becomes more standardized and formal.
2. a company's official structure, indicating lines of authority
3. Data consists of numbers, statistics, facts, and figures that may be meaningless without interpretation. When data is processed, the result is information that is relevant, accurate, timely, and complete.
4. Response includes the reactions of the receiver to the message, and feedback is the part of the receiver's response communicated back to the sender.
5. communication through body movement
6. Read the first paragraph, main headings, and last paragraph.
7. (Student response.)
8. (List three:) making sales presentations to buyers, giving media interviews, conducting training sessions for retail sales staffs, moderating fashion shows (Students may justify other responses.)
9. Make an outline of the ideas, facts, or order of events you want to communicate, then write about the most important topic first and the least important last.
10. research results, new ideas, information about situations, or problems that need action
11. friendliness, sincerity, and interest
12. Costs of computer systems have come down, the systems are easier to use, and more people are now computer literate.
13. (List six:) suppliers, the financial community, customers, competitors, government, labor, the local community, stockholders
14. management information systems, e-commerce, strategic technology directions for firms
15. They are automatically adjusted according to the mathematical formula established in the system.
16. forecasts, purchase orders, production schedules, shipping information, POS data
17. They can put their merchandise online, as a form of direct marketing, so consumers can use their home computers to comparison shop and make purchases.
18. It saves the time and expense of traveling to other locations, increases the number of people who can participate in decision making for more complete information and agreement on decisions, and improves turnaround time for design decisions, thus satisfying customer needs.
19. More people are involved in the decision-making process because they can readily access the information and add their input.
20. (List five:) target marketing, credit applications, recognizing credit card fraud, sales forecasting, predicting results from specific promotional activities, determining the optimum SKU mix for stores, calculating markdowns that enable a certain amount of inventory to be sold by a particular date

Student Workbook

Getting the Message, Activity A
exchanging information for results
the sender and the receiver
(Student response.)

Communication Match, Activity E

1. E	14. H
2. D	15. G
3. B	16. F
4. A	17. V
5. Q	18. T
6. O	19. S
7. N	20. R
8. K	21. U
9. M	22. P
10. Z	23. C
11. X	24. I
12. W	25. L
13. J	26. Y

Teacher's Resources

Business Letter Identification, reproducible master 17-2

1. letterhead
2. date
3. inside address
4. salutation
5. body content
6. complimentary close
7. signature, typed name, title
8. reference initials
9. so they will be read and understood
10. so their content is clear

Communication Truths, reproducible master 17-7

1. F	9. T
2. T	10. T
3. F	11. T
4. T	12. F
5. T	13. F
6. F	14. T
7. T	15. F
8. F	16. T

Communication Review, reproducible master 17-8

1. The sender is the source or the party sending the message; the receiver is the destination of the message.
2. Encoding is the process of the sender putting thoughts into symbolic form to be meaningful for the receiver. Decoding is the process by which the receiver assigns meaning to the symbols encoded by the sender.
3. the unplanned static, distortion, or interference during the communication process that might result in the receiver getting a different message from the one that was sent

4. knowing why you are reading something so you can focus on the information you really need
5. because the mind interprets them to be unimportant
6. To get feedback, ask for the receivers' thoughts about what you have said.
7. the company logo and name, address, and phone and fax numbers
8. a detailed explanation of your needs, timing of the needs, and statement of appreciation for the help
9. because they are usually short, deal with only one subject, and are often on a company form with areas to fill in
10. date and time of the call, who the message is for, who the message is from, the caller's telephone number and extension, and the content of the message
11. working out of a home via a computer network
12. more powerful computers, lower cost systems, automated capture of SKUs, and customer-tracking programs
13. to communicate the subtleties of designs and new trends
14. It is an interactive electronic system in which data and graphics are transmitted from the database of a computer network over telephone lines and displayed on a subscriber's computer screen.
15. video conferencing
16. Expert systems must be set up by an industry expert to go through specific processes. Neural systems learn internally from their previous activities.

Chapter 17 Test

1. I	16. T
2. D	17. T
3. A	18. F
4. J	19. T
5. F	20. T
6. B	21. C
7. E	22. D
8. G	23. B
9. C	24. A
10. H	25. D
11. T	26. D
12. F	27. B
13. T	28. B
14. F	29. B
15. F	30. C

31. (See illustration 17-6 in the text.)
32. (List five:) return address or printed letterhead, date, inside address, salutation, body content, complimentary close, signature followed by typed name and title, reference initials
33. (Student response.)

Obstacles to Effective Communication

Name_____ **Date** _____ **Period** _____

Think about this statement: "Business communication is the exchange of information for results." Then describe how the following factors could serve as obstacles to an exchange of information, thus blocking effective business communication. Finally, try to think of two other factors that might also block business communication and describe how.

1. Language barriers: _____

_____

_____

_____

_____

_____

2. Culture: _____

_____

_____

_____

_____

3. Terminology: _____

_____

_____

_____

_____

4. Fear of change:_____

_____

_____

_____

_____

5. Unrelated noise: _____

_____

_____

_____

_____

(Continued)

Name_____

6. Reading skills: _____

_____

_____

_____

_____

7. Listening skills: _____

_____

_____

_____

_____

8. Writing skills:_____

_____

_____

_____

_____

9. Additional factor:_____

_____

_____

_____

_____

10. Additional factor:_____

_____

_____

_____

_____

Business Letter Identification

Name_____ **Date** _____ **Period** _____

Identify the standard parts of the following business letter. Then answer the questions below on another piece of paper.

1. _____

2. _____

3. _____
   _____

4. _____

5. _____
   _____

6. _____

7. _____
   _____
   _____

8. _____

> *Fashion Services Group*
> *906 Santee Street*
> *Los Angeles, CA 90136*
> *Phone: 213-555-9060   Fax: 213-555-9160*
>
> October 20, _____
>
> Mr. Adam Forchetti, Sales Manager
> California Sportswear Company
> 3448 Hill Avenue
> San Francisco, CA 92468
>
> Dear Mr. Forchetti:
>
> As a resident buying office in the Los Angeles market, we would like to evaluate your fashion offerings for possible future purchases.
>
> Please send us information about your new spring line as soon as possible. We would like drawings/photos, fabric swatches, and any other information you care to provide to us. However, please do not have a salesperson call our office.
>
> If your apparel lines are within the price, quality, and fashion level ranges of our clients, we will be in touch with you shortly to discuss the matter further.
>
> Thank you for your prompt response to this request.
>
> Sincerely,
>
> *Martha J. Esposito*
>
> Martha J. Esposito
> Sportswear Market Representative
>
> MJE/ssh

9. Why should business letters be brief and thorough? _____

10. Why do all business letters follow a similar format? _____

Communicate About Communication

Name_____ Date _____ Period _____

Read the following statements and discuss them as a class.

1. Another example of internal business communication is periodic **performance reviews**, which are discussions of employees' job performance with their supervisors. Written and oral evaluations summarize employees' accomplishments, strengths, and weaknesses. Employees and supervisors also discuss future goals, aspirations, and resulting changes in compensation and job levels.

2. **Grapevines** are unofficial lines of communication in organizations that bypass formal chains of command. They often contain personal gossip about coworkers or management. Also, grapevines can sometimes provide factual tips to managers that aid decision making and give feedback on employee attitudes. The challenge is to discern which grapevine information is accurate and useful and which is misleading and damaging.

3. The information source strongly affects the **validity** of business communications. For instance, a statement from a company's president almost always has more attention paid to it than the same message from a junior salesperson.

4. When reading business communications, the words must be read carefully. Additionally, to minimize misunderstandings, sometimes more important information is gained by **reading between the lines** for more subtle meanings.

5. **Telephone tag** is when people alternately return phone calls to others who are out or unavailable. However, with voice mail, business messages can be transmitted quite accurately without actually speaking with the other person.

6. **Photocopying** is a common office technology. It allows business people to distribute fashion sketches, photographs, or written business messages to everyone who needs them. Most photocopying machines can enlarge or reduce images by specific percentages, and some can also duplicate images in correct color.

7. **Micrographics** are used for storage and retrieval of miniaturized versions of documents, often on microfilm or microfiche filmstrips. Much less storage space is used this way compared to paper documents. Special magnifying equipment is needed to view the contents, and a hard copy of the desired information can be produced in full size.

8. Desktop publishing software programs often promote the fact that users can take advantage of their **WYSIWYG ("wissywig")** factor. The initials stand for "what you see is what you get." This means that every page layout shown on the monitor screen will have the same appearance on paper.

9. On Web sites, there are often **links** that, when clicked on, take the user farther into a direction of the information subject of the site.

10. Traditional EDI transmissions (intranets) are being replaced by private Internet messages (Web-based **extranets**) that contain electronic forms and appropriate information between business partners. These are reshaping information movement in the supply chain.

11. A **firewall** is a built-in computer barrier that guards the entrance of a private network, keeping out unauthorized or unwanted traffic. This creates a secure site.

Parts of a Computer

- The input device, such as a keyboard or scanner, sends information to the central processing unit (CPU).

- The CPU processes information and holds it in memory.

- The software program is the set of directions that tells the computer how to process the information.

- The monitor is a screen showing what is being accomplished.

- The printer outputs a hard copy of the information.

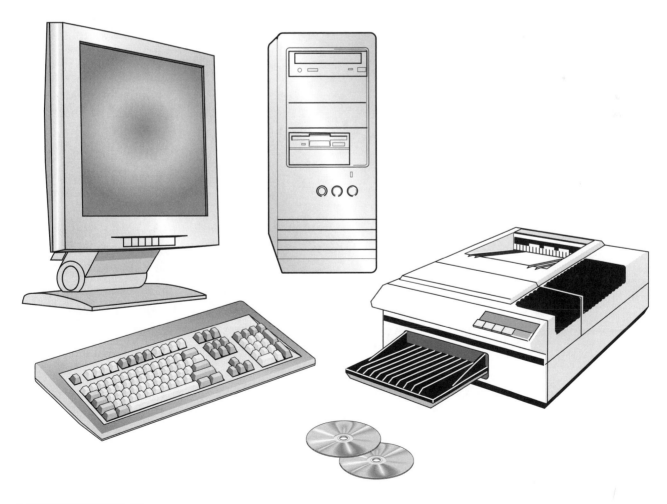

Steps in Using Information

1. *Locate information* from external and internal sources.

2. *Gather information* from research, business intelligence, records, surveys, etc.

3. *Process information* manually, electronically, or using a combination of both.

4. *Utilize information* by making decisions as a result of the acquired and processed facts.

Relating Business Communications and Technology

Employment Level	Information Structure	Technology Needs
Strategic—Top executives (chief executive officer, vice presidents, etc.)	*Unstructured and flexible,* relating to external and internal situations	*Decision making* about corporate strategy, positioning, mission, profits, and cash flow
Managerial—Middle managers of production, sales, planning	*Somewhat structured* to coordinate corporate strategy with operations	*Monitoring* inventory levels, sales, accounts receivable and payable, and administration
Operational—Front-line managers, supervisors, salespeople	*Very structured* to accomplish production, sales, and other jobs	*Tracking* specific inventory, work accomplished, day-to-day functions
Transactional—Task-oriented workers	*Highly structured and* related to repetitious, internal matters only	*Data entry* of orders, invoices, receipts, forms, etc.

Communication Truths

Name_____**Date**_____**Period**_____

Read the following statements and decide which are true. Circle *T* if the statement is true or *F* is the statement is false.

T   F   1. Automated conferencing is a computer holding file that can be accessed only with the proper code.

T   F   2. Business communication is the exchange of information for results.

T   F   3. Decoding is the use of recording devices to accept phone messages from callers when the recipient is not available.

T   F   4. Desktop publishing is computer creation, editing, and production of documents that are of a similar quality to that produced by typesetters.

T   F   5. Electronic calendaring is computer networking that allows the storage, retrieval, and input to employees' appointment calendars.

T   F   6. An electronic mailbox is the simultaneous communication by audio, video, or computer between geographically dispersed people.

T   F   7. Encoding is the message sender's process of putting thought into symbolic form to be meaningful for the receiver.

T   F   8. Voicemail is the message receiver's process of translating the meaning of the thought sent by the message sender.

T   F   9. A formal business report is a written business communication with a cover, title page, table of contents, executive summary, and a complete analysis of a complex issue.

T   F   10. Informal business reports are shorter, less-rigid business papers, such as those prepared about sales, work progress, market research, or business calls.

T   F   11. Information management includes the activities that generate an orderly and timely flow of relevant information to support business activities.

T   F   12. In the communication process, "noise" is the practice of working out of one's home using a computer.

T   F   13. In the communication process, the receiver is the source of a communication message.

T   F   14. In the communication process, the response is the reaction of the receiver of a communication after being exposed to the message.

T   F   15. Telecommuting is static, distortion, or interference during the communication of a message.

T   F   16. In the communication process, feedback is a message response communicated back to the sender or source.

Communication Review

Name_____ **Date** _____ **Period** _____

As you review the chapter, answer the following questions.

1. Describe a message *sender* and *receiver*. _____

_____

_____

_____

2. Describe both *encoding* and *decoding* in the communication process. _____

_____

_____

_____

3. In the communication process, what is *noise*?_____

_____

_____

_____

4. What is meant by *reading with a purpose*? _____

_____

_____

_____

5. Why do we "tune out" or not remember many of the sounds we hear? _____

_____

_____

_____

6. When speaking, what can you do to check whether your messages are being received accurately?

_____

_____

_____

7. What information does the printed letterhead on business stationery display? _____

_____

_____

_____

8. What should be included in a business letter that requests information?_____

_____

_____

_____

(Continued)

Name_____

9. Why are business memos easier to write than letters? _____

_____

_____

_____

10. What should be included in telephone messages that are written for someone else?_____

_____

_____

_____

11. What is the meaning of *telecommuting*? _____

_____

_____

_____

12. What are the main reasons for the abundance of fashion merchandising data today? _____

_____

_____

_____

13. Why are visual aids especially important to the fashion industry? _____

_____

_____

_____

14. What is an online service? _____

_____

_____

_____

15. What version of automated conferencing most resembles face-to-face communications? _____

_____

_____

16. In the overall category of artificial intelligence, how are *expert systems* and *neural systems* different?

_____

_____

_____

_____

Communicating Information

Name_____

Date_____ **Period**_____ **Score**_____

Chapter 17 Test

Matching: Match the following terms and identifying phrases.

_____ 1. Communication instructional display items that appeal mainly to people's vision.

_____ 2. The sending, storing, and receiving of messages via computers to electronic mailboxes.

_____ 3. The process of asking open-ended questions, paying careful attention to the replies, and then asking further questions to probe more deeply and clarify confusing points.

_____ 4. The activity of entering, editing, storing, and printing words with a computer.

_____ 5. The sending and receiving of messages without using words.

_____ 6. Computer systems displaying behavior that would be regarded as intelligent if it were observed in humans.

_____ 7. The use of special equipment to electronically transmit visual images.

_____ 8. Questions that require multiple-word answers rather than merely a yes or no.

_____ 9. The use of a computer to make charts, drawings, or other visuals.

_____ 10. Sending messages with the use of words.

A. active listening

B. artificial intelligence

C. computer graphics

D. electronic mail

E. facsimile transmission

F. nonverbal communication

G. open-ended questions

H. verbal communication

I. visual aids

J. word processing

True/False: Circle *T* if the statement is true or *F* if the statement is false.

T F 11. Business communication can be defined as exchanging information for results.

T F 12. Every company has an informal organization that has nothing to do with how the organization accomplishes its goals.

T F 13. The communication process involves transmitting meaningful messages between parties that are clearly understood.

T F 14. Body language is the "signing" that is done to benefit people with hearing impairments.

T F 15. A memorandum is a formal business letter, and a memo is an informal business note.

(Continued)

Name_____

T   F   16. Examples of informal business reports are sales reports and work progress reports.

T   F   17. Information management activities generate orderly and timely flows of relevant information to support business activities.

T   F   18. E-mail uses voice-recording devices to accept telephone messages from callers.

T   F   19. The Internet is a global network connecting millions of computers that all work together to share information and enable the World Wide Web (WWW) to exist.

T   F   20. Neural computing involves perception, learning, automatic programming, and problem solving.

Multiple Choice: Choose the best response. Write the letter in the space provided.

_____ 21. A company's organization chart shows the _____.
   A. goals that specific activity groups should strive to achieve
   B. extra organizations that workers can join, such as ball teams and card-playing groups
   C. company's official structure and lines of authority
   D. development of the company from its founding to now

_____ 22. As companies become larger and more complex, _____.
   A. fewer decisions are made at the top, with empowerment moving downward
   B. titles gain in importance and jobs become more defined and specialized
   C. more rules and policies are established and written down
   D. All of the above.

_____ 23. Data consists of _____.
   A. relevant, accurate, timely, and complete information
   B. numbers, statistics, facts, and figures that need interpretation
   C. understandable knowledge of target markets and niche merchandising
   D. All of the above.

_____ 24. When people "read with a purpose," they _____.
   A. know why they are reading the material and focus on the needed information
   B. always read the material slowly and usually read it a second or third time
   C. highlight all headings, important sentences, and unfamiliar words
   D. All of the above.

_____ 25. Speaking skills _____.
   A. help individuals express their thoughts and ideas to others
   B. have a large influence on people's personal and professional lives
   C. are improved during presentations with good visual aids
   D. All of the above.

(Continued)

Name_____

_____ 26. Formal business reports _____.
   A. contain an executive summary page at the beginning that is written after the report is finished
   B. are usually long and analyze complex issues
   C. have a cover, title page, table of contents, body, and situation analysis with recommendations
   D. All of the above.

_____ 27. Firms have computers for most employees now because _____.
   A. prewritten computer forms offer the most convenient method of taking telephone messages
   B. computer systems are more affordable and easier to use
   C. computers have built-in job objectives that make work easier to accomplish
   D. management can always check what job each employee is working on

_____ 28. Telecommuting is _____.
   A. the transfer of information using communicating signals and computers
   B. working from home with a computer that can communicate with the company computer system on another network
   C. interconnecting computing equipment to others in an electronic community network
   D. using a cellular phone to make business calls during driving time in the car

_____ 29. Desktop publishing uses computers to _____.
   A. set up appointments on peoples' calendars
   B. create, edit, and produce documents that are of a similar quality to those produced by typesetters
   C. calculate numbers that are placed in rows and columns according to preset equations
   D. All of the above.

_____ 30. When communication technologies expand the industry's "information loop," _____.
   A. artificial intelligence can run most functions of businesses
   B. the financial costs of the technology go up in proportion to information in the loop
   C. more people are involved in the decision-making process
   D. All of the above.

Essay Questions: Provide complete responses to the following questions or statements.

31. Illustrate the communication process as a drawing within a background of "noise."

32. List at least five of the eight main parts of business letters.

33. Discuss proper telephone use in business.

Concepts for Successful Selling

Objectives

After studying this chapter, students will be able to

⊖ describe all aspects of the direct selling function.

⊖ explain how to create a selling environment with stock preparation and merchandise knowledge.

⊖ demonstrate the selling steps.

⊖ explain how to perform various types of merchandise sales transactions.

Teaching Materials

Text, pages 360–378
Fashion Terms
Fashion Review
Fashion in Action

Student Workbook
A. *Working with Garment Labels*
B. *Discussing Selling Skills*
C. *Role-Playing to Make Sales*
D. *Techniques for Closing the Sale*
E. *Selling Terms Fill-in-the-Blanks*

Teacher's Resources
Steps in the Consumer Buying Process, transparency master 18-1
Professional Sales Associate Key Duties and Tasks, transparency master 18-2
Performing Stockkeeping Duties, transparency master 18-3
Guidelines on Communicating with Customers, transparency master 18-4
Analyze the Selling Mistakes, reproducible master 18-5
Expand Your Knowledge, reproducible master 18-6
Selling Calculations, reproducible master 18-7
Selling Questions, reproducible master 18-8
Chapter 18 Test

Introductory Activities

1. With students looking at illustration 18-1 in the text, hold a general discussion about the functions of merchandising. Discuss how this illustration is just a different way of showing the parts of the merchandising cycle. This repetition will help students remember the main parts of merchandising, as well as relate what they have previously learned to the content of this chapter. Also discuss the differences between indirect and direct selling.

2. *Steps in the Consumer Buying Process*, transparency master 18-1. Go through all the individual steps consumers take, usually subconsciously, when making retail purchases. Ask students to remember these steps to coordinate with the retail selling steps that will be studied in this chapter.

3. Have a class discussion about how important the selling function is to the success of retail stores. Also discuss the importance of a professional appearance for salespeople in the field of fashion retailing.

Strategies to Reteach, Reinforce, Enrich, and Extend Text Concepts

The Direct Selling Function

4. **RT** Hold a class discussion about why salespeople <u>are</u> the retail store to consumers. Discuss the roles salespeople play in representing the store to customers as well as providing valuable customer feedback to store management. Also discuss the value of good selection, training, supervision, and motivation of salespeople.

5. **RT** Discuss the "costs" of retailers having too few salespeople, too many salespeople, or the wrong kind of salespeople.

6. **ER** *Professional Sales Associate Key Duties and Tasks*, transparency master 18-2. Use this as an overhead to discuss the six main areas of work done by retail sales associates. These key duties and tasks have been established by the National Retail Federation in developing the retail industry's skill standards in order to enable retailers to evaluate the competencies of sales associates.

7. **EX** Show students a video that illustrates the importance of sales to both consumers and companies. *Everybody Starts in Sales* is available from Meridian Education Corporation and D.E. Visuals.

8. **RF** Hold a class discussion about compensation for salespeople, including sales quotas, incentives, and commission pay. Also discuss the evaluation of salespeople according to their units-per-transaction (UPT) numbers and their average dollar amount per sale.

9. **ER** Discuss the following definition: "Salesmanship is the art of convincing someone to exchange money for goods, resulting in a mutual profit or benefit to both buyer and seller." Also discuss the fact that most customers don't really have "needs," but are happy to satisfy their "wants" if the knowledge, image, and enthusiasm of a salesperson sells them goods rather than just shows them.

Creating a Selling Environment

10. **RF** *Performing Stockkeeping Duties*, transparency master 18-3. Use the transparency to discuss each of the bulleted items. Ask students to explain all the activities they think must be accomplished for each of the stockkeeping duties.

11. **RT** Hold a class discussion about keeping the selling floor of a retail store in order. Include the amount of merchandise, presentation of goods, and straightening and restocking store fixtures.

12. **EX** Show students a video that extends their knowledge of merchandise labeling. *Understanding Hangtags and Labels* is available from Meridian Education Corporation and *Branding, Packaging & Labeling* is available from D.E. Visuals.

13. **RT** With all students referring to illustration 18-14 in the text, discuss the information that is required on garment labels. Also discuss the optional marketing information that is often included on garment hangtags.

14. **ER** Have students gain more knowledge about RN labels by searching "registered number" on the Federal Trade Commission Web site www.ftc.gov. General knowledge can be found on the "Frequently Asked Questions" section, and information about specific suppliers can be found by entering their RN numbers into the "Search" database. Also have students check www.textileaffairs.com for a guide to label requirements and apparel care symbols.

15. **ER** *Working with Garment Labels*, Activity A, WB. Students are asked to study the permanent labels on two different garments, record their findings, and answer related questions.

Using the Selling Steps Effectively

16. **ER** Show students one or more videos available about selling skills: *Selling Skills* from

Cambridge Educational; *Secrets of Selling* from D.E. Visuals and Insight Media; *Communicating with Customers* from Learning Seed and D.E. Visuals; and *Winning Over Even the Most Difficult Customer, 7 Things Never to Say to Your Customers!,* and many others from D.E. Visuals.

17. **EX** *Discussing Selling Skills*, Activity B, WB. In small groups or as a whole class, students are to discuss statements that contain new information.

18. **RF** Ask students to discuss the following statement: "Good salespeople are consultants for customers rather than sellers for retail stores."

19. **RT** With students looking at Illustration 18-17 in the text, review the main points of each of the selling steps.

20. **RF** *Guidelines on Communicating with Customers*, transparency master 18-4. Show this transparency while discussing each of the bulleted points with the class. Have students individually describe what each point means.

21. **RT** Discuss suggestion selling, add-ons, trading up, more than one selling, and special offers with the class.

22. **ER** *Analyze the Selling Mistakes*, reproducible master 18-5. Use the handout to have students comment on several factors representing common mistakes salespeople make. Have students discuss the mistakes with classmates. (If you choose to have a class discussion, suggested answers are provided in these *Teacher's Resources*.)

23. **RT** With students referring to Illustration 18-21 in the text, discuss each point from the perspective of satisfying the customer as well as the business/company. Have students explain why compromise actions are often required.

24. **RF** *Role-Playing to Make Sales*, Activity C, WB. Pairs of students acting as "customer" and "salesperson" are asked to pick one of seven selling situations to demonstrate to the class. Feedback from the class is requested.

25. **EX** *Techniques for Closing the Sale*, Activity D, WB. The worksheet explains seven types of sales closing techniques and gives examples. Students are asked to create their own example for each and answer related questions.

26. **ER** *Expand Your Knowledge*, reproducible master 18-6. Students are asked to respond to different sales scenarios. Have them discuss their ideas with classmates.

Merchandise Sales Transactions

27. **RT** After having a class discussion about cashiers, checkout counters (check stands), checkout terminals (cash registers), and sales slips, have students compute different percentage sales taxes on variously priced items. Then discuss the importance of the price look-up feature in today's computerized POS systems.

28. **RF** Discuss with the students the methods of payment at retail stores, such as paying by check, credit card mechanisms, paperless signature capture, debit cards, and smart cards. Discuss the added costs to retailers for collecting state sales taxes, such as remitting money and correctly filling out government forms (estimated at $3.48 for every $100 of sales tax collected). Also discuss rain checks, layaway purchases, and C.O.D. send arrangements.

29. **ER** Show students a basic video about calculating merchandise sales transactions. *Department Store Math* is available from Nasco. *Point of Sale* is available from D.E. Visuals.

30. **RF** *Selling Calculations*, reproducible master 18-7. Students are asked to calculate different inventory values, pay scales, sales taxes, and correct change owed to customers from sales transactions. While reviewing the "Total Amount of Pay Earned" chart, emphasize that federal requirements for minimum wage do not apply to the retailing industry when combined with a commission-based pay structure.

31. **RT** *Selling Terms Fill-in-the-Blanks*, Activity E, WB. Students are to place correct chapter vocabulary terms into descriptive sentences.

32. **RT** *Selling Questions*, reproducible master 18-8. Use this handout for a chapter review or as an opportunity for students to earn extra credit.

Additional Enrichment Activities

Research

33. Have students research the history of retail selling. They might research the four principles of Aristide Boucicaut (founder of the Bon Marche in Paris), on which the early department store selling methods were based. American retailers, such as John Wanamaker, used those principles in their own ways to establish selling methods that continue today.

34. Have students research product and labeling laws that are designed to protect consumers. Ask students to find out their enactment and amendment dates as well as their purposes and provisions. Have the students include the Wool Products Labeling Act, Fur Products Labeling Act, Flammable Fabrics Act, Textile Fiber Identification Act, Fair Packaging and Labeling Act, and Care Labeling of Textile Wearing Apparel Ruling.

35. Have students research the many payment options for Internet purchases, mainly by credit card, check, or virtual debit. Have students compare the security features that each contains to protect customer privacy of information. Some options to

start with might include PayPal, e-Check, Secure-eBill, Beyond Credit Push, Bill Me Later, Verisign, CyberCash, CheckFree, and others.

Projects

36. Have students visit different market levels of retail stores (better, moderate, discount). Have them compare their observations of salespeople, stockkeeping, merchandise knowledge, use of the selling steps, and other aspects of salesmanship.

37. Obtain a copy of *Raising Retail Standards* from the National Retail Federation. Ask students to study why the program was developed, who is involved, how skill standards are helping the retail industry, what served as the framework of the standards, how/where they are taught, and other facts that are also found in trade publications. Have students make a bulletin board display that outlines the specifics of the six basic modules. Discuss the program with the class.

38. Invite to class a retail store salesperson. Have the salesperson explain all parts of his or her job and answer questions from students to clarify all other details of the work.

39. Obtain a copy of the Textile Fiber Products Identification Act and the *Writing a Care Label* booklet for students to study. These materials are available from regional offices of the Federal Trade Commission (FTC) or its headquarters: FTC, Bureau of Consumer Protection, Division of Textiles and Furs, Washington, DC 20580 (Phone: 202-326-2222).

40. Have a group of students review a comprehensive book about selling skills by dividing the chapters among themselves. Then have the students present an oral report with appropriate visual aids on their respective chapters. Some books to consider are *Fundamentals of Selling* by Len Berry, *How to Win Friends and Influence People* by Dale Carnegie, *When Customers Talk...Turn What They Tell You Into Sales* by T. Scott Gross and BIGresearch, *Hug Your Customers: The Proven Way to Personalize Sales and Achieve Astounding Results* by Jack Mitchell, and many others.

Answer Key

Text

Fashion Review, page 378

1. They lead to higher sales and greater profits for the retailer and to better service for customers.
2. They return for future purchases and spread the word to others about the retailer and its products.
3. Sales clerks are generally employed by stores with lower-priced merchandise and usually only

facilitate routine sales transactions (order takers). Sales associates are employed by high-service retailers and use more formal or creative selling skills (order getters).

4. The sales-oriented approach pushes products on customers in a slick, high-pressure way. The customer-oriented approach involves making customers feel important, identifying their needs, and finding the best solutions.

5. credibility, honesty, problem-solving capabilities, and product knowledge

6. to help prepare workers for sales floor success, reduce turnover, and trim training costs

7. (Name three:) prizes, merchandise, cash bonuses, days off, profit-sharing opportunities, commission-based pay, hourly pay based on previous sales productivity, recognition at sales meetings

8. because of errors in filling the order, unacceptable substitutions, late delivery, defective merchandise, or other breaches of the contract

9. putting out goods to maintain stock levels; sorting and arranging by color, size and/or classification; using appropriate hangers or shelf arrangements; straightening merchandise during hours of low traffic, setting up and cleaning selling fixtures

10. removable "signs" that are attached to the outside of garments with strings, plastic bands, pins, staples, or adhesives

11. that the customer may look lost or bewildered (The opening remark should be a question or statement related to the situation, especially about merchandise.)

12. to get the customer to agree to see and hear more about the merchandise

13. Ask open-ended questions and use active listening.

14. (Student response. Answers may include any of the following:) Slow down the pace; use a positive approach; ask for clarification; turn objections into reasons for buying; be tactful and clear

15. getting a commitment from the customer to buy the merchandise

16. (List three:) add-ons, trading up, more than one, special offers (definitions in text glossary)

17. the process of salespeople doing everything possible to strengthen relationships with customers

18. (List four:) compute sales tax; tabulate sales by department; update inventory records; identify low-cost conditions; provide information about the existence of merchandise at other stores; do price look-ups

19. that the card has not been reported stolen, the account is not overdue, and the amount of the purchase does not take the account above the approved credit limit

20. so additional items are not stolen and placed into the bags later

Student Workbook

Selling Terms Fill-in-the-Blank, Activity E

1. incentives
2. compensation
3. indirect selling
4. trial confirmation
5. rain check
6. client books
7. rack jobbers
8. organizational climate
9. responsive selling
10. C.O.D. send
11. price look-up
12. add-ons
13. benefits
14. sales quotas
15. direct selling
16. layaway
17. trading up
18. commission
19. prospect
20. stockkeeping
21. labels
22. returns to vendors
23. suggestion selling
24. sales tax
25. receiving
26. solutions
27. hangtags
28. packaging

Teacher's Resources

Analyze the Selling Mistakes, reproducible master 18-5

1. To customers, there is a fine line between confidence and arrogance. Confident salespeople make sales, but arrogant salespeople lose sales.

2. People would rather buy from someone they know and like. Salespeople are most successful if they find a link between themselves and customers.

3. If salespeople think the price is too high, they either make excuses or try too hard to sell. Salespeople may benefit from making a list of reasons that prices are fair. Then they should sell value, service, and themselves.

4. It does no good to tell customers anything about what the store or department has to offer without knowing whether the salesperson's services are needed. Salespeople should learn to draw out customers' specific needs before making presentations.

5. Salespeople must listen well to sell. They should ask questions at least half the time, and draw out responses that keep the customer dominating the conversation.

6. It makes salespeople look bad when they "knock" the competition. They should sell their own company, and substitute the words "industry standard" for competition, if needed. Salespeople should never say anything bad about anyone else.

7. Salespeople should ask questions that make customers evaluate new information and qualify needs and finances. They should ask questions that separate their company from the competition.

8. Salespeople should make it clear how they can help, sometimes telling stories about how they have helped other customers. They should give as much help and service as possible—the sale will follow naturally.

Selling Calculations, reproducible master 18-7

1. $92.64, $138.96, $61.76, $36.78, $137.28, $203.20, $90.44, $424.80, $415.80, $110.16, $308.00, $206.00, $226.00, $194.32, Total = $2,646.14

2.

SKU #	Description	Quantity	Unit Price	Total Price
211G	One-size-fits-all Velour bathrobe: green	1	$15.44	$15.44
211B	One-size-fits-all Velour bathrobe: blue	3	15.44	46.32
211V	One-size-fits-all Velour bathrobe: violet	1	15.44	15.44
426M	White blouse with draped neckline: size medium	3	12.48	37.44
426L	White blouse with draped neckline: size large	4	12.70	50.80
7354	Elastic waistline slacks: black/white tweed	6	19.80	118.80
8668	Large print scarves: wool, fringed	2	9.18	18.36
92-460	Wool suit jacket: 1 size 12, 1 size 14	2	38.50	77.00
92-461	Silk suit blouse: 1 size 12, 1 size 14	2	25.75	51.50
92-463	Wool suit skirt: 1 size 12, 1 size 14	2	28.25	56.50
9888	Heather cardigan sweater: 1 size M, 2 size L, 1 size XL	4	13.88	55.52
			Total:	$543.12

3.

Total Amount of Pay Earned= (hourly wage × # hours worked) + (value of merchandise sold × % commission)	Average Pay per Hour= total amount of pay ÷ number of hours worked
($4.75 × 7) + ($375 × .10) = $33.25 + $37.50 = **$70.75**	$70.75 ÷ 7 = **$10.11**
($3.25 × 6) + ($325 × .15) = $19.50 + 48.75 = **$68.25**	$68.25 ÷ 6 = **$11.38**
($2.42 × 8) + ($425 × .17) = $19.36 + $72.25 = **$91.61**	$91.61 ÷ 8 = **$11.45**
Zero hourly pay +($425 x .24) = 0 + $102.00 = **$102.00**	$102.00 ÷ 7.5 = **$13.60**

4. because the more sales they make for the store, the higher pay they receive

5.

$ Tax Amount	$ Total Selling Price
$.90	$30.88
1.35	31.33
1.25	26.21
3.09	50.59
.90	40.89
.74	19.24
1.11	19.61
1.60	29.35

6. $1.84, 2 pennies, $2.00, $17.50, $6.77, $1.77, $11.25, $4.00, 23 cents, $40.06

Selling Questions, reproducible
master 18-8

1. general promotion to the public, such as advertising, publicity, and special events
2. They have reduced their number of sales employees and cut back on formal sales training for employees.
3. that their needs provide sales opportunities, they appreciate helpful suggestions, and they will be loyal to salespeople and stores that have their interests at heart
4. self-confidence, leadership, and stress tolerance
5. the feeling that salespeople have about their opportunities, value, and rewards for good performance
6. the actual physical exchange of goods between the vendor's transporting agent and the retailer
7. Rack jobbers are paid only for goods sold, with a percentage going to the retailer.
8. small pieces of ribbon or cloth that are permanently attached to garments and contain printed information
9. the covering, wrapper, or container in which some merchandise is placed
10. approach and greeting
11. fear of rejection
12. when an additional item can be obtained as a result of purchasing an item
13. They start the selling steps over again in a never-ending cycle.
14. a cash register receipt that shows the money amounts for items, tax, and the sales total of transactions

Chapter 18 Test

1. F	16. F
2. G	17. F
3. J	18. T
4. H	19. T
5. E	20. T
6. C	21. B
7. I	22. C
8. B	23. D
9. D	24. A
10. A	25. A
11. T	26. B
12. T	27. B
13. F	28. C
14. F	29. B
15. T	30. D

31. Direct selling is the exchange of merchandise to individual consumers in return for money or credit (personal selling). Indirect selling is nonpersonal promotion aimed at the public or a large general audience.
32. (Name three:) fiber content (generic names), percentages of fibers (listed in order by weight from most to least), identity of responsible party (registered number of producer or distributor), country of origin (where item was assembled)
33. (List five in correct order:) approach and greeting, classifying customers, presentation of merchandise, overcoming objections, closing the sale, supplementary suggestions, maintaining relationships

Steps in the Consumer Buying Process

The buying consumer

1. recognizes a want or need (desires a new suit).

2. identifies product parameters (style, color, etc.).

3. gathers information (availability, price, etc.).

4. searches for solutions among the information (best fashion value, location of store, etc.).

5. makes a purchase decision (buys the item).

6. evaluates the purchase (positive feelings or buyer's remorse).

Professional Sales Associate Key Duties and Tasks

Provide personalized customer service	Sell and promote products	Monitor inventory	Maintain appearance of department or store	Protect company assets	Work as part of a department or store team
• Initiate customer contact. • Build customer relations.	• Determine customer needs. • Build the sale.	• Take inventory. • Transfer inventory.	• Maintain stock, selling, & customer service areas. • Maintain product presentation & displays.	• Identify and prevent loss. • Follow safety procedures.	• Support coworkers. • Create a competitive advantage.

Source: National Retail Federation

Performing Stockkeeping Duties

- Verifying incoming stock and packing slips

- Working with stock control records and systems

- Sorting by classification, color, size, etc.

- Checking appropriate hangers, packaging, and presentation

- Cleaning merchandise fixtures

- Restocking/rehanging merchandise

Guidelines on Communicating with Customers

- Relax and establish eye contact for a comfortable conversation.

- Start with broad, open-ended questions and move toward narrower, specific questions.

- Do not assume you know or understand the customer's needs before they are explained.

- Keep questions simple, focused on one idea at a time, and easy to answer.

- "Listen" to all the customer's words, ideas, body language, opinions, etc.

- Show interest in what customers have to say and respect their intelligence.

- Be quiet when customers want to talk.

- Do not be distracted by a customer's appearance or speech.

- Use clarifying questions or statements to test your understanding of messages.

Analyze the Selling Mistakes

Name_____ **Date** _____ **Period** _____

Explain in the space provided why the following are common mistakes that salespeople make. Then discuss these selling mistakes with your classmates.

1. Knowing everything: _____

_____

_____

_____

2. Not making friends first: _____

_____

_____

_____

3. Thinking your store's price is too high: _____

_____

_____

_____

4. Selling before wants have been established: _____

_____

_____

_____

5. Talking too much: _____

_____

_____

_____

6. "Putting down" the competition: _____

_____

_____

_____

7. Not asking the right questions: _____

_____

_____

_____

8. Not selling in terms of yourself as well as the customer: _____

_____

_____

_____

Expand Your Knowledge

Name_____ **Date** _____ **Period** _____

Consider the new information presented here and respond to each question or statement in the space provided. Then discuss the information and your responses with classmates.

1. To *identify customers*, salespeople in bridal departments follow engagement announcements in the local newspaper and invite these women to the store. Men's clothiers use lists of recent college graduates, who often are likely customers for business attire. Where might other types of stores get useful information to identify customers? _____

   _____

   _____

   _____

2. Some stores *classify customers* in different ways. For instance, the "mainstream customer" is primarily looking for function and price, while the "classic customer" is looking for quality combined with special sales. The primary motivation of the "updated customer" is to obtain the latest fashion trends. What other classifications of customers (not mentioned in the text) can you describe?

   _____

   _____

   _____

3. One type of customer is the *arguer*. Arguers distrust salespeople, thinking they try to misrepresent the facts. Salespeople should avoid arguing and just show the merchandise as factually as possible. Then arguers can judge items for themselves. Write a fictional dialogue between an arguer and a salesperson. _____

   _____

   _____

   _____

4. Salespeople must listen carefully to "hear" customers' needs. Then they should sell benefits that lead to *solutions* rather than selling the product. For instance, a woman might visit a dress store to find the right look for an upcoming event (solution) rather than to specifically buy a dress. Describe another solution to a situation that would result in a garment sale. _____

   _____

   _____

   _____

5. Taking a *physical inventory*, usually once a year, is a sales staff's duty. This "inventory audit" involves an actual counting and recording of stock in the department or store at that time. It verifies the retail dollar value of merchandise on hand and shows SKU counts and total quantities. Why isn't a physical inventory needed more often? _____

   _____

   _____

   _____

(Continued)

Name_____

6. ***Suggestion selling*** is not merely asking a customer at checkout, "Is that all?" Customers who buy McDonald's hamburgers are always asked if they want fries with their orders, resulting in thousands of additional sales of fries each day. Salespeople should always ask a man buying a new suit if he needs any shirts, ties, or socks. This helps the customer, rather than leaving him to discover later that he still doesn't have everything he needs to complete the outfit. Describe another situation in which suggestion selling might help a customer as well as store sales. _____

_____

_____

_____

7. ***Reinforcing the purchase*** decision makes customers happy with their purchase as well as with the store and the salesperson. It also motivates them to want to return to that store in the future. One example of reinforcing a purchase decision is saying, "Ms. Jones, this is a beautiful dress you have purchased. I know you will receive many compliments from others and enjoy wearing it." Write another scenario about reinforcing a purchase decision. _____

_____

_____

_____

8. Retail managers should make sure that salespeople put ***customers first***. Sometimes salespeople put stock duties first because the condition of stock on the retail selling floor is easier to monitor than the level of customer service. Explain another way in which salespeople might not put customers first. _____

_____

_____

_____

9. ***Traffic*** refers to the number of customers who visit the store and how often they visit. Usually, higher traffic means higher store sales. How do traffic figures help stores match peak and slow times to the number of sales associates and managers scheduled to work?_____

_____

_____

_____

10. With the increase in ***consumer identity fraud***, new ID devices are being developed to ensure the customer using a credit card or check to buy merchandise is the right account owner. Can you think of other methods to combat identity fraud besides photo verification, fingerprinting, and eye scanning? _____

_____

_____

_____

Selling Calculations

Name_____ **Date** _____ **Period** _____

Compute answers for the following. A calculator may be used.

1. *Brenda's Dress Shoppe* received the following merchandise today from one of its suppliers. Since Brenda is busy doing other chores, please help her by computing the total (extended) wholesale price of each SKU received and of the entire shipment that was delivered.

SKU #	Description	Quantity	Unit Price	Total Price
211G	One-size-fits-all Velour bathrobe: green	6	$15.44	
211B	One-size-fits-all Velour bathrobe: blue	9	15.44	
211V	One-size-fits-all Velour bathrobe: violet	4	15.44	
426S	White blouse with draped neckline: size small	3	12.26	
426M	White blouse with draped neckline: size medium	11	12.48	
426L	White blouse with draped neckline: size large	16	12.70	
426XL	White blouse with draped neckline: size extra large	7	12.92	
7187	Wrap dress, long sleeves: 3 size S, 4 size M, 6 size L, 5 size XL	18	23.60	
7354	Elastic waistline slacks: black/white tweed	21	19.80	
8668	Large print scarves: wool, fringed	12	9.18	
92-460	Wool suit jacket: 1 size 12, 1 size 14	8	38.50	
92-461	Silk suit blouse: 1 size 12, 1 size 14	8	25.75	
92-463	Wool suit skirt: 1 size 12, 1 size 14	8	28.25	
9888	Heather cardigan sweater: 1 size M, 2 size L, 1 size XL	14	13.88	
Total:				

2. Brenda's other shop across town needs the following items to be sent over as soon as possible: 1—211G; 3—211B; 1—211V; 3—426M; 4—426L; 6—7354; 2—8668; one each of sizes 12 and 14 of 92-460, 92-461, and 92-463; and 4-9888 (1 size M, 2 size L, 1 size XL). Make an inventory record like the one above that shows the items and the value of the inventory that will be transferred to the other store.

3. Calculate the amount of pay earned by the salespersons in the following situations:

Base Hourly Wage	Number of Hours Worked	%Commission Earned on Sales	$ Value of Merchandise Sold	Total Amount of Pay Earned	Average Pay per Hour
$4.75	7	10%	$375		
$3.25	6	15%	$325		
$2.42	8	17%	$425		
None	7½	24%	$425		

Name_____

4. Think about why good salespeople (and those in upscale stores) like to work for a higher commission and lower base hourly wage. Also think about why less aggressive salespeople (and those in stores with lower-priced goods) like to have a higher hourly base wage. Why does commission serve as an incentive to encourage salespeople to work harder? _____

_____

_____

5. Calculate the sales tax amount and total selling price for each of the following items. (Although different tax rates are shown here for practice, the tax rate is usually constant for apparel sold in the same state on the same sales slip.)

Item Description	Price	Tax Rate	$ Tax Amount	Total Selling Price
211G—Bathrobe	$29.98	3%		
211V—Bathrobe	$29.98	4½%		
426M—Blouse	$24.96	5%		
7187—Wrap dress	$47.50	6½%		
7354—Tweed slacks	$39.99	2¼%		
8668—Wool scarf	$18.50	4%		
8668—Wool scarf	$18.50	6%		
9888—Cardigan sweater	$27.75	5¾%		

6. Calculate the change that a customer should be given in each of the following purchase situations.

$ Total of Purchase	Money Given by Customer	Change Given Back to Customer
$18.16	$20.00	
$34.98	$35.00	
$3.14	$5.14	
$22.50	Two $20 bills	
$23.23	Three $10 bills	
$43.23	Two $20 bills and one $5 bill	
$88.75	$100.00	
$56.28	$60.28	
$21.77	Four $5 bills and two $1 bills	
$109.94	Three $50 travelers checks	

Discuss with classmates how retailers might have their employees count aloud the change they give to customers.

Selling Questions

Name_____ **Date** _____ **Period** _____

As you review the chapter, answer the following.

1. Describe indirect selling._____

_____

_____

_____

_____

2. What have some retail companies done to try to lower their operating costs (which has deteriorated their direct selling)? _____

_____

_____

_____

_____

3. What three customer assumptions are considered important in customer-oriented selling? _____

_____

_____

_____

_____

_____

4. What positive selling attributes do stores like their employees to display?_____

_____

_____

_____

_____

5. What does a company's organizational climate describe? _____

_____

_____

_____

6. In stockkeeping duties, what is receiving? _____

_____

_____

_____

_____

(Continued)

Name_____

7. For rack jobbers, how are their companies and their retail outlets paid? _____

_____

_____

_____

8. Define *labels*. _____

_____

_____

_____

9. Define *packaging*._____

_____

_____

_____

10. What is the first retail selling step? _____

_____

_____

_____

_____

11. Why do some salespeople dislike or omit trying to close the sale? _____

_____

_____

_____

12. What is a special offer? _____

_____

_____

_____

_____

13. Why are follow-up contacts after sales called preselling? _____

_____

_____

_____

14. What is a sales slip? _____

_____

_____

_____

Concepts for Successful Selling

Name_____

Date_____**Period**_____ **Score**_____

Chapter 18 Test

Matching: Match the following terms and identifying phrases.

_____ 1. Physical characteristics of items.

_____ 2. Responding to the customer's presence rather than going out to find customers.

_____ 3. A salesperson's questions to a customer to get an indication of what needs to be done to close the sale.

_____ 4. Increasing sales by encouraging more items to be bought in addition to the customers' original purchases.

_____ 5. A deferred purchase arrangement of setting aside a customer's merchandise until the customer has fully paid for it.

_____ 6. Payment and benefits for work accomplished.

_____ 7. Obtaining larger sales by selling higher-priced, better-quality merchandise to customers.

_____ 8. A salesperson's book of customers' names, addresses, phone numbers, sizes, and important dates.

_____ 9. Deciding how many salespeople are needed at various times to meet work demand.

_____ 10. Additional merchandise items, such as related items to create complete outfits.

A. add-ons

B. client book

C. compensation

D. employee scheduling

E. layaway

F. product features

G. responsive selling

H. suggestion selling

I. trading up

J. trial confirmation

True/False: Circle *T* if the statement is true or *F* if the statement is false.

T F 11. The costs for direct salespeople comprise one of retailers' largest operating expenses.

T F 12. Stores like their employees to display self-confidence, leadership, and stress tolerance.

T F 13. A company's organizational climate shows the job descriptions of all employees.

T F 14. Sales quotas are limits of how much each salesperson is allowed to sell in a given time period.

T F 15. Incentives are used to stimulate salespeople to achieve higher results.

T F 16. Rack jobbers sell specialty garments to upscale retailers that feature the items in fashion shows.

T F 17. Labels are detachable "signs" that are affixed to the outside of garments.

(Continued)

Name_____

T   F   18. Benefits are favorable outcomes received, and solutions are answers to problems.

T   F   19. The process of salespeople doing everything possible to strengthen relationships with customers is referred to as bonding.

T   F   20. A sales slip is a printed receipt that shows prices paid for items, tax, and the sales total of the transaction.

Multiple Choice: Choose the best response. Write the letter in the space provided.

_____ 21. If a retail firm has too few salespeople, _____.
A. it is usually located in the suburbs
B. some important direct selling tasks may not be done properly or at all
C. money is wasted
D. All of the above.

_____ 22. Salesclerks (rather than sales associates) _____.
A. are said to be "order getters"
B. are generally employed by stores with higher-priced merchandise
C. usually only facilitate routine sales transactions
D. All of the above.

_____ 23. The customer-oriented (rather than sales-oriented) sales approach _____.
A. involves making customers feel important, identifying the needs of customers, and finding the best solutions for the needs
B. assumes customer needs provide sales opportunities and customers appreciate helpful suggestions
C. assumes customers will be loyal to salespeople and stores that have their interests at heart
D. All of the above.

_____ 24. Stockkeeping activities include _____.
A. receiving, preparing, and protecting merchandise before it is sold
B. dusting and sweeping the selling floor
C. studying the information on hangtags, labeling, and packaging
D. selling goods to customers

_____ 25. Goods are returned to vendors by retail stores because of _____.
A. vendor errors in filling the order or breaches of the contract
B. dislike by more than half of the retail sales associates
C. inefficient retail receiving methods
D. retail errors in preparing the merchandise for the selling floor

_____ 26. The information on hangtags _____.
A. is required by law to be visible to consumers when items are purchased
B. is not required by law and can be removed before garments are worn
C. takes up most of the informational space on merchandise packaging
D. is considered to be a method of personal selling

(Continued)

Name_____

_____ 27. Retail customers who are interested in hearing pertinent information from salespeople are considered to be_____.
    A. casual lookers
    B. undecided customers
    C. decided customers
    D. arguers

_____ 28. "More than one" selling is _____.
    A. selling the same item to a customer as the previous customer bought
    B. when the customer can get an additional free item as a result of purchasing an item
    C. selling more than one of the same or similar item
    D. attaching or packaging two or more items together before placing them for sale

_____ 29. The rate of employees quitting and being replaced is known as_____.
    A. staffing irregularities
    B. employee turnover
    C. cash/wrap deficiencies
    D. job circulation

_____ 30. A feature of most electronic POS is that when prices are changed in the master computer, scanned purchases at checkout are priced accordingly. This is called _____.
    A. paperless signature capture
    B. certified rain check
    C. deferred purchase layaway
    D. price look-up

Essay Questions: Provide complete responses to the following questions or statements.

31. Explain direct selling and indirect selling.

32. Name three of the four types of garment label information required by the Textile Fiber Products Identification Act (not permanent care requirements).

33. Name at least five of the seven selling steps in order.

Calculating for Best Results

Objectives

After studying this chapter, students will be able to

- identify various business financial records of firms.
- describe the parts of an operating statement.
- summarize comparative analysis of operating ratios and other performance indicators.
- evaluate pricing considerations and strategies.
- complete various merchandise pricing calculations.

Teaching Materials

Text, pages 379–394
- *Fashion Terms*
- *Fashion Review*
- *Fashion in Action*

Student Workbook
- A. *Working with the Operating Statement*
- B. *Doing Comparative Analysis*
- C. *Calculating Differences*
- D. *Discussing Retail Finances*
- E. *Merchandise Pricing*

Teacher's Resource
- *Operating Statement Formula*, transparency master 19-1
- *Strategies of Pricing Levels*, transparency master 19-2
- *Typical Flowchart of Returns*, transparency master 19-3
- *When to Take Markdowns*, transparency master 19-4
- *Reasons for Markdowns*, transparency master 19-5
- *Practice Makes Perfect*, reproducible master 19-6
- *Learning Even More*, reproducible master 19-7
- *Calculations Review*, reproducible master 19-8
- Chapter 19 Test

Introductory Activities

1. Have students look through some annual reports to see the general types of financial reporting and analyses that are done by companies. Annual reports can be obtained by contacting the executive offices of public companies such as: fiber and fabric companies (BASF, Burlington Industries, Dan River, DuPont, Forstmann); apparel manufacturers (Liz Claiborne, Hartmarx, Kellwood); and retailers (GAP, Kmart, JCPenney, QVC, Sears Roebuck). Most can be ordered from the company's Web site.
2. Discuss with the class why it is important for fashion merchandisers to understand the financial aspects of business. Also discuss the importance of merchandise pricing to the overall profitability of companies.
3. Ask students to describe stores that seem to price their goods higher or lower than the competition. Do some stores always seem to have their merchandise on sale? How do students feel about these stores?

Strategies to Reteach, Reinforce, Enrich, and Extend Text Concepts

Financial Records

4. **RT** Discuss ledger accounts with the class, including cash receipts, cash disbursements, sales, purchases, payroll, equipment, inventory, accounts receivable, and accounts payable.
5. **RF** Show the class a video about inventory related to financial calculating. *The Story of Inventory* is available from D.E. Visuals.

The Operating Statement

6. **RT** *Operating Statement Formula*, transparency master 19-1. As you show this transparency to the class, discuss the multiple formula of the main parts of every company's operating statement. Explain the calculations of each of the three components separately, having students discuss why each calculation makes sense. Ask students why the operating statement is also sometimes called the income statement. Why is it important to watch trends of sales, expenses, and profit/loss over time?

7. **ER** Show students a video that explains how all aspects of the business world are dependent on the bottom line of profit and loss. *Business Education* is available from The School Company.

8. **RF** Discuss that the term *gross* means before deductions (original larger number) and the term *net* means after deductions (smaller final number). Then illustrate those points by going through the calculations for gross and net sales and gross and net profit. Discuss with students the differences between net sales and net profit.

9. **RT** Have students discuss the separate expense groups of selling, administrative, and general expenses.

10. **RT** Have the class refer to illustration 19-1 in the text. Going around the room, have individual students summarize each line of the statement from the top to the bottom. Also have students explain the importance of each line and the reason for its particular placement order.

11. **RF** *Working with the Operating Statement*, Activity A, WB. Students are asked to consider a business case study and prepare an operating statement for it.

12. **RF** Share a PowerPoint CD with the students about business finances. *Financial Aspects of Business* is available from D.E. Visuals.

Comparative Analysis

13. **RT** Ask students to explain what comparative analysis shows and why it is so important. Have students explain why companies should evaluate net sales in relation to the following: the percentages of cost of goods sold, gross margin, operating expenses, and net profit. Discuss why the net sales figure is so important and is used as the denominator for these "operating ratios" of selected operating statement items.

14. **ER** Obtain from *Apparel* magazine (usually in the July issue) the most recent annual listings of apparel businesses ranked according to profit margins, sales, and net income. Also obtain similar tables from *STORES* magazine (National Retail Federation) that ranks retail companies. Share these with the class.

15. **RT** Ask students to explain why sales per square foot is such an important performance objective and indicator in most types of retailing. Discuss why different types of stores have such different sales per square foot numbers. Discuss profitability range, same-store sales growth, comparable-store sales, average sales per hour, average items per transaction, and average dollars per transaction (the entity after the "per" is the denominator). Mention that most retailers have an industry standard against which they measure themselves, such as National Retail Federation statistics or their Buying Group median.

16. **RF** *Doing Comparative Analysis*, Activity B, WB. Students are asked to review information in the book chapter section. Then they are to work problems about a case, answer questions, and write word problems for a classmate to calculate.

17. **RT** Discuss expense management issues with the class, such as fixed and variable costs and controllable and uncontrollable expenses.

Pricing Considerations

18. **RF** With the class, discuss how the "right pricing" facilitates the exchange process, generates both sales and profits, and is consistent with customer expectations.

19. **RT** Have students explain each of the main objectives of companies' pricing strategies (overall profitability, sales volume, deterrence of competition, and image). Then have students discuss odd-figure pricing, loss leaders, and the consequences of overbuying.

20. **ER** *Strategies of Pricing Levels*, transparency master 19-2. Use this transparency for a class discussion on the three basic pricing strategies to gain the best profits from the market and the factors associated with each.

21. **RF** *Typical Flowchart of Returns*, transparency master 19-3. While showing this transparency, have students follow routes taken by returned merchandise until all items are sold or disposed of in some way.

Pricing Calculations

22. **EX** Show students a video about pricing in relation to market pressures. *What Is a Price?* is available from Learning Seed. *Markup, Markdown, Pricing Strategy: Defining Value,* and *Fundamentals of Pricing* are available from D.E. Visuals. The latter is not directly related to the fashion industry but does present the concepts well for advanced classes.

23. **RT** Ask students to explain the relationship of product quality to markups. Discuss that markups and markdowns are calculated both in dollar amounts and in percentages. Also ask why the

same markup percent is usually not used for all items in the store.

24. **RT** Ask students to explain the relationship of stock turnover (studied in Chapter 15) to markdowns. Also discuss why markdowns are a retailing fact of life, needing careful management and planning.

25. **ER** *When to Take Markdowns*, transparency master 19-4. While the class views this transparency, have students discuss the timing, explanation, and benefits listed for the two timing options.

26. **ER** *Reasons for Markdowns*, transparency master 19-5. Use the transparency for a class discussion of the buying factors, selling factors, and other reasons retailers mark down merchandise.

27. **RF** Share a PowerPoint CD about pricing with students. *Pricing Strategies & Concepts* is available from D.E. Visuals.

28. **RF** *Practice Makes Perfect*, reproducible master 19-6. Students are asked to solve math problems involving dollar markup, markup percent of cost, markup percent of selling price, keystone markup retail price, percentage markdown, and markdown percent of ticketed retail price.

29. **RT** Ask students to explain why the maintained markup percent is the most important indicator of retail pricing success.

30. **RT** *Calculating Differences*, Activity C, WB. Students are asked to describe the difference between given pairs of chapter terms.

31. **EX** *Learning Even More*, reproducible master 19-7. Students are introduced to new material and asked to write their reaction to it before discussing it with classmates.

32. **EX** *Discussing Retail Finances*, Activity D, WB. Students are to discuss given statements in small groups or as a whole class.

33. **RT** *Calculations Review*, reproducible master 19-8. Use this master as a handout for students to review the chapter or earn extra credit.

34. **RF** *Merchandise Pricing*, Activity E, WB. Students are asked to solve merchandise pricing problems and answer related questions.

Additional Enrichment Activities

Research

35. Have students do research on "factoring," a financing method especially used within the textile/apparel pipeline. Have students report their findings to the class, explaining how factors provide operating capital to companies by buying their accounts receivable. Factors also serve as companies' credit and collection departments. Have students draw an illustration (with arrows) as a visual aid to explain the process to the class. Also have students tell the benefits and risks of this financing method for both the factors and the textile/apparel/retail companies.

36. Have students research what retailers do with excess closeout merchandise that does not sell, even after large markdowns. Have them search "surplus merchandise," "surplus goods," or "merchandise liquidation" on the Internet. Have them log onto www.TheReturnExchange.com. Students should share the information gathered with the entire class, possibly also discussing the disposal of excess goods on eBay.

Projects

37. Have students examine some annual reports to calculate different types of operating ratios. Have students make a large poster for a bulletin board that shows the ratios for the last three to five years for a specific company. Also have students point out the up-and-down trends of income, expenses, and profit/loss.

38. Have students obtain a firm's sales productivity information for the last five years from the manager or other executive of a nearby retail company. (Publicly held companies will share this information more readily than privately held companies.) Have students turn in a report analyzing as many of the following as possible: sales per square foot, stock turnover, stock-to-sales ratio, same-store sales, comparable-store sales, average sales per hour, average items sold per transaction, and average dollars per transaction.

39. Invite a business accountant to speak to the class after the chapter has been studied. Have the accountant speak about operating statements, comparative analysis, and product pricing strategy.

Answer Key

Text

Fashion Review, page 394

1. Cash receipts are money received from cash sales; cash disbursements are money that has been paid out.
2. Merchandise price × volume sold = sales – cost of goods sold = gross margin – operating expenses = net profit (or loss) before taxes
3. to determine the net profit (or loss) figure
4. The number is placed in parentheses.
5. Returns are when customers are given a full refund or credit for items they bring back to the store. Allowances are price reductions on items that may be slightly damaged, but that customers decide to purchase at a lower price.

6. dollar amount of inventory at the beginning of the year, plus money spent on new inventory, minus inventory left at the end of the year
7. selling expenses, administrative expenses, and general expenses (Examples are student response.)
8. by dividing net sales into the various operating statement items that are listed below it in the statement
9. by comparing the same ratios over time as well as with competitors' and industry averages
10. They increase profits.
11. average sales per hour, average items per transaction, and average dollars per transaction
12. Controllable expenses are those over which companies have direct control, and uncontrollable expenses are those over which companies have no control. (Student response for example of each.)
13. state laws that attempt to preserve competition by restricting lower-than-usual pricing
14. (List one of each:) advantages—offers a good choice of merchandise to customers, allows for ordered merchandise that is not received, increases the chance of sales; disadvantages—increased costs, unsold goods that must be disposed of
15. It seems smaller to consumers, encourages retailers to think in terms of retail prices and their resulting profits, and is easier to compare with other stores and with published trade numbers that are usually reported by percentage of net sales.
16. because of style changes, damaged items, lower prices at competing stores, or an original price that is too high to provide consumer value
17. because the total number also includes many items that were not marked down, but sold at full price
18. past experience, trade averages, and competitors' prices
19. a charge to a vendor from a retailer to help compensate for losses from reduced selling prices of that vendor's goods
20. It is a combination of both markups and markdowns and shows what the retailer actually receives when products sell.

Student Workbook

Working with the Operating Statement, Activity A

1. Sum of all merchandise prices × volume sold = sales

$87 × 100	=	$ 8,700
$75 × 150	=	11,250
$60 × 300	=	18,000
$45 × 450	=	20,250
$38 × 600	=	22,800
$25 × 800	=	20,000
$10 × 700	=	7,000
Annual sales	=	$108,000

2. $58,000 (given in case explanation)
3. Sales – cost of goods sold = gross margin
   $108,000 – $58,000 = $50,000 gross margin
4. $12,000 rent + $1,800 utilities + $1,200 miscellaneous = $15,000 operating expenses
5. Gross margin – operating expenses = net profit (or loss) before taxes
   $50,000 – $15,000 = $35,000 net profit
6. Then the company would have had a net loss, and Sam would have had no salary and might have owed some money.
7.

Boutique of Gifts
Operating Statement
For the Year Ending _____

Gross sales.........................	$108,000	
Less: Returns and allowances........	$400	
Net sales............................		$107,600
Cost of goods sold:		
Beginning inventory, at cost..........	$ 5,000	
Purchases	$ 58,000	
Cost of goods available for sale......	$ 63,000	
Less: Ending inventory at cost........	$ 5,000	
Cost of goods sold		$ 58,000
Gross margin.........................		$ 49,600
Less: Operating expenses:		
Administrative expenses ($3,000 × 12).	$ 36,000	
General expenses	$ 15,000	
Total Expenses		$ 51,000
Net profit (or loss)		($ 1,400)

8. $400 of returns and allowances plus $1,000 more in salary

Doing Comparative Analysis, Activity B

1. COGS ratio = $\dfrac{\text{COGS}}{\text{net sales}}$

   Last year = $\dfrac{\$48,000,000}{\$75,000,000}$ = .64 = 64%

   This year = $\dfrac{\$52,000,000}{\$80,000,000}$ = .65 = 65%

2. Expense ratio = $\dfrac{\text{operating expenses}}{\text{net sales}}$

   Last year = $\dfrac{\$20,000,000}{\$75,000,000}$ = .27 = 27%

   This year = $\dfrac{\$20,000,000}{\$80,000,000}$ = .25 = 25%

3.

	Last year figures	Last year ratios	This year figures	This year ratios
Net sales	$75,000,000	100%	$80,000,000	100%
Cost of goods sold	48,000,000	64%	52,000,000	65%
Gross margin	$27,000,000	36%	$28,000,000	35%
Expenses	20,000,000	27%	20,000,000	25%
Net profit	$ 7,000,000	9%	$ 8,000,000	10%

4. Gross margin ratio = $\dfrac{\text{gross margin}}{\text{net sales}}$

Last year = $\dfrac{\$27,000,000}{\$75,000,000}$ = .36 = 36%

This year = $\dfrac{\$28,000,000}{\$80,000,000}$ = .35 = 35%

5. Profit margin = $\dfrac{\text{net profit}}{\text{net sales}}$

Last year = $\dfrac{\$ 7,000,000}{\$75,000,000}$ = .09 = 9%

This year = $\dfrac{\$ 8,000,000}{\$80,000,000}$ = .1 = 10%

6. Annual sales per square foot = $\dfrac{\text{annual net sales}}{\text{square footage of selling space}}$ = $\dfrac{\$5,500,000}{20,000}$ = $275 sales per square foot

7. 50′ wide × 90′ deep = 4,500 square feet of selling space per store
   4,500 square feet × $300 per square foot = $1,350,000 estimated annual sales per store
   $1,350,000 sales per store × 16 stores = $21,600,000 estimated total annual sales

8. GMROS = $\dfrac{\text{gross margin}}{\text{selling space}}$ = $\dfrac{\$94,500}{4,500}$ = $21 gross margin per foot of selling space

Calculating Differences, Activity C

1. An operating statement is a summary of the financial results of a firm's operations over a specified period of time. It is the same as (and also called) an income statement.

2. Gross sales are the total dollar amount received from sales (gross revenues). Net sales are the actual dollars earned and kept from sales during an accounting period (gross sales minus returns and allowances).

3. Cost of goods sold is an accounting of what has been spent on goods that have been sold to customers during the period. Expense management is the process of planning and controlling operating costs.

4. Gross margin is the sum of money available to cover expenses and generate a profit (gross profit). Profit margin, also known as return on sales (ROS), is a ratio that measures profit as a percentage of net sales.

5. Comparative analysis is the periodic examination and comparison of financial data to try to measure the effectiveness of the company's overall strategy. Operating ratios are mathematical relationships of income and expense figures that measure firms' effectiveness in generating sales and managing expenses.

6. Net profit is a resulting positive number after expenses have been deducted from the gross margin figure. Profitability range is the difference between the most profitable and the least profitable lines of merchandise, based on profit per square foot of selling space.

7. Sales per square foot is a retail comparison figure to determine success versus previous years or against other companies, calculated by dividing total sales by total square feet. Sales productivity is retail effectiveness and efficiency shown through such results as average sales per hour, average items sold per transaction, and average dollars per transaction.

8. Same-store sales growth is a barometer for success that compares the results of each succeeding year against previous years, usually shown in a percentage increase or decrease. Comparable-store sales is an analysis of a retailer's sales in relation to close competitors that have similar corporate or store sizes, expense structures, merchandise lines, departmental structures, and ways of operating.

9. Fixed costs are overhead expenses that remain the same regardless of sales volume. Variable costs are expenses that increase or decrease with the volume of sales.

10. Odd-figure pricing is the retail pricing of merchandise a few cents less than a dollar denomination. Loss leaders are low-priced articles on which stores make little or no profit because of lowering the price for promotional reasons.
11. Markup is the amount added to the cost of merchandise to determine the selling price, sometimes called *markon*. A keystone markup is doubling the cost price to arrive at the retail price.
12. The initial markup is the difference between merchandise cost and the selling price originally placed on merchandise. A maintained markup is the difference between the total cost of the merchandise and its final selling price, or how much profit the company was able to achieve over the cost of the goods for a time period.

Merchandise Pricing, Activity E

1. Price changes on goods that are in stock: it increases if the replacement cost of items from vendors has gone up, and decreases for special sales and to move slow-selling goods.

2. Markup % of cost = $\dfrac{\text{dollar markup}}{\text{cost}} = \dfrac{\$114.56 - \$64}{\$64} = \dfrac{\$50.56}{\$64} = .79 = 79\%$

   Markup % of selling price = $\dfrac{\text{dollar markup}}{\text{selling price}} = \dfrac{\$50.56}{\$114.56} = .44 = 44\%$

3. 75% of cost + cost = $48 + $64 = $112 *or* 1.75 × cost = 1.75 × $64 = $112
   (This problem can be calculated in two ways.)

4. Shirt selling price = $\dfrac{\text{cost}}{1 - \text{markup \%}} = \dfrac{\$15}{1 - .40} = \dfrac{\$15}{.6} = \$25$

   Trouser selling price = $\dfrac{\$24}{.6} = \$40$

5. Gown selling price = $\dfrac{\text{cost}}{1 - \text{markup \%}} = \dfrac{\$152}{1 - .62} = \dfrac{\$152}{.38} = \$400$

   Suit selling price = $\dfrac{\$190}{.38} = \$500$

6. $48 cost + $48 markup = $96 retail price *or* $48 cost × 2 = $96 retail price
7. estimating a percentage of sales for markdowns, discounts, and stock that is damaged or stolen.
8. $68.95 ticketed price × .25 = $17.24 markdown dollar amount; $68.95 − $17.24 = $51.71
   or $68.95 ticketed price × (1−.25) = $68.95 × .75 = $51.71 selling price
   (This problem can be calculated in two ways.)
9. Markdown % of ticketed price = $\dfrac{\text{markdown \$ amount}}{\text{original ticketed price}} = \dfrac{\$55.50 - \$44.95}{\$55.50} = \dfrac{\$10.55}{\$55.50} = .19 = 19\%$

10. Markdown % = $\dfrac{\text{total \$ markdowns}}{\text{total net sales}} = \dfrac{\$15,300}{\$102,000} = 0.15 = 15\%$

11. because it is a combination of both markups and markdowns
12. Maintained markup % = original markup % − ([100% − original markup %] × markdown %)
    = 48% − ([100% − 48%] × 12%) = 48% − (52% × 12%) = 48% − 6.24% = 41.76%

Teacher's Resources

Practice Makes Perfect, reproducible master 19-6

1. Retail price minus wholesale cost = dollar markup
   A. $39.95 − $22.00 = $17.95
   B. $32.99 − $17.25 = $15.74
   C. $41.50 − $23.50 = $18.00
   D. $24.98 − $14.00 = $10.98
   E. $15.75 − $8.80 = $6.95

2. $\dfrac{\text{dollar markup}}{\text{cost}}$ = markup percent of cost
   A. $\dfrac{\$17.95}{\$22.00} = .816 = 81.6\%$
   B. $\dfrac{\$15.74}{\$17.25} = .912 = 91.2\%$
   C. $\dfrac{\$18.00}{\$23.50} = .766 = 76.6\%$
   D. $\dfrac{\$10.98}{\$14.00} = .784 = 78.4\%$
   E. $\dfrac{\$6.95}{\$8.80} = .7898 \text{ (or .79)} = 79\%$

3. $\dfrac{\text{dollar markup}}{\text{selling price}}$ = markup percent of selling price

   A. $\dfrac{\$17.95}{\$39.95} = .449 = 44.9\%$

   B. $\dfrac{\$15.74}{\$32.99} = .477 = 47.7\%$

   C. $\dfrac{\$18.00}{\$41.50} = .434 = 43.4\%$

   D. $\dfrac{\$10.98}{\$24.98} = .4396$ (or .44) $= 44\%$

   E. $\dfrac{\$\,6.95}{\$15.75} = .441 = 44.1\%$

4. Wholesale cost $\times$ 2 = retail price
   A. $\$22.00 \times 2 = \$44.00$
   B. $\$17.25 \times 2 = \$34.50$
   C. $\$23.50 \times 2 = \$47.00$
   D. $\$14.00 \times 2 = \$28.00$
   E. $\$8.80 \times 2 = \$17.60$

5. Ticketed retail price $\times (1 - .25)$ = dollar selling price
   A. $\$39.95 \times .75 = \$29.96$
   B. $\$32.99 \times .75 = \$24.74$
   C. $\$41.50 \times .75 = \$31.13$
   D. $\$24.98 \times .75 = \$18.74$
   E. $\$15.75 \times .75 = \$11.81$

6. Ticketed retail price − markdown price = dollar markdown;
$\dfrac{\text{dollar markdown}}{\text{ticketed retail price}}$ = markdown percent of ticketed retail price

   A. $\$39.95 - \$32.98 = \$6.97$; $\dfrac{\$\,6.97}{\$39.95} = .174 = 17.4\%$

   B. $\$32.99 - \$25.99 = \$7.00$; $\dfrac{\$\,7.00}{\$32.99} = .212 = 21.2\%$

   C. $\$41.50 - \$32.50 = \$9.00$; $\dfrac{\$\,9.00}{\$41.50} = .217 = 21.7\%$

   D. $\$24.98 - \$19.95 = \$5.03$; $\dfrac{\$\,5.03}{\$24.98} = .201 = 20.1\%$

   E. $\$15.75 - \$12.00 = \$3.75$; $\dfrac{\$\,3.75}{\$15.75} = .238 = 23.8\%$

7. yes (hopefully!)

Calculations Review, reproducible master 19-8

1. ongoing records of company debits and credits, as a result of business activities, maintained in a book or computer program
2. employee wages and deductions, such as social security and income taxes
3. sales (revenues), costs (expenses), and profit or loss
4. It is written at the top of the statement.
5. the total dollar amount received from sales, determined by multiplying the individual prices of all items sold by how many of each were sold
6. if their expenses are larger than their sales
7. the actual dollars earned and kept from sales during the accounting period
8. to determine the exact inventory for the new year's start and the previous year's end so the cost of goods sold (COGS) can be calculated
9. by "perpetual inventory" records, such as POS statistics
10. net profit (or loss)
11. because companies of different sizes can be compared on an equal basis with percentages
12. because they stock large amounts of small items with fast sell-through and with prices that are not regularly reduced, rather than fewer items that are very large in size and frequently offered at special reduced prices

13. fewer markdowns and lower inventory expenses
14. fixed and variable costs
15. They borrow less money.
16. Price is the amount of money charged for a product or service. Price also is the amount of financial outlay that consumers are willing to exchange for the benefit of having or using products or services and that retailers are willing to accept.
17. the type of merchandise, the price of the items, and the time of the selling season or fashion cycle
18. demand

Chapter 19 Test

1. E	7. B	13. T	19. T	25. D
2. H	8. D	14. T	20. T	26. D
3. J	9. G	15. F	21. A	27. D
4. C	10. F	16. T	22. B	28. C
5. A	11. F	17. F	23. B	29. D
6. I	12. T	18. T	24. A	30. A

31. volume sold; cost of goods sold; operating expenses

32. Gross margin ratio = $\dfrac{\text{gross margin}}{\text{net sales}}$ = $\dfrac{\$216,000}{\$480,000}$ = 0.45 = 45%

   Profit margin = $\dfrac{\text{net profit}}{\text{net sales}}$ = $\dfrac{\$52,800}{\$480,000}$ = 0.11 = 11%

33. Average number of items per transaction = $\dfrac{\text{total items sold}}{\text{total \# transactions}}$ = $\dfrac{320}{128}$ = 2.5

   Average dollars per transaction = $\dfrac{\text{total dollars of sales}}{\text{total \# transactions}}$ = $\dfrac{\$2,176}{128}$ = $17

Operating Statement Formula

Merchandise price × Volume sold = Sales

Sales – Cost of goods sold = Gross margin

Gross margin – Operating expenses = Net profit (or loss) before taxes

Strategies of Pricing Levels

Pricing *higher than* competition	Pricing *the same as* the competition	Pricing *lower than* the competition
• Reaps higher profit per unit sold • Results in lower turnover rates • Must offer additional consumer benefits	• De-emphasizes pricing • Promotes the store, products, location, and service	• Earns lower profit per unit sold • Promotes faster turnover • Results in higher total volume

Typical Flowchart of Returns

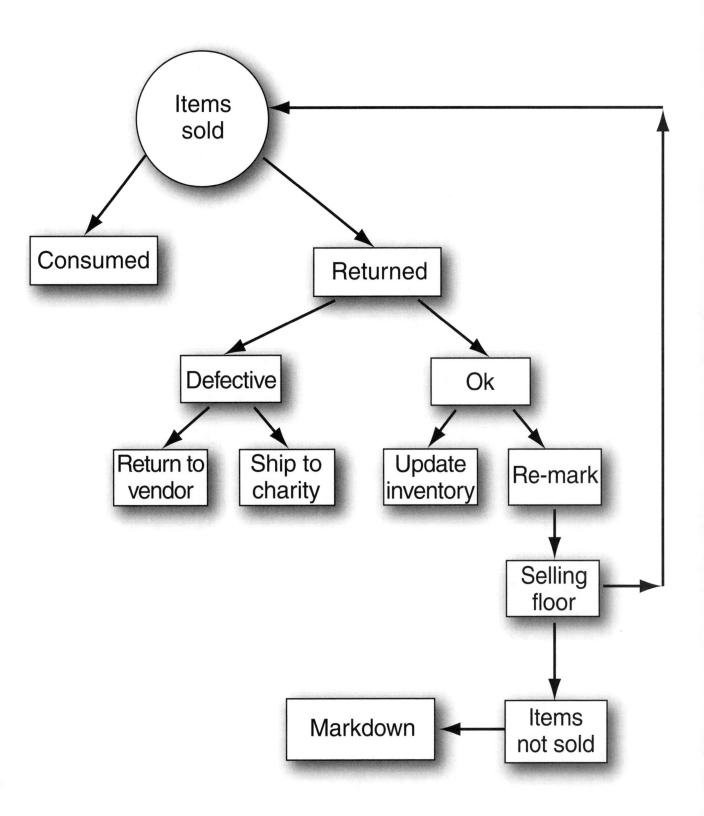

Source: Monarch Marking Systems

When to Take Markdowns

Timing	Explanation	Benefits
Early Markdowns	Reducing the price of slow-selling items early in the season	• Encourages customer traffic • Results in smaller markdowns • Encourages fresher stock • Lowers expenses • Reduces risks • Shows good market response
Late Markdowns	Maintaining the original price until a major clearance sale is held late in the season	• Creates an "event" • Encourages immediate purchases • Preserves store's exclusive image • Allows for "creative selling"

Reasons for Markdowns

Related to Buying:	• assortment errors • weak colors, sizes, fit • poor timing • wrong quality • supplier errors
Related to Selling:	• pricing errors • no competitive differences • lack of sales stimulation
Other Causes:	• market/economy changes • unexpected fashion changes • unseasonal weather • damaged merchandise

Practice Makes Perfect

Name_____ **Date** _____ **Period** _____

As you review the textbook chapter, answer the following and show your work. You may use a calculator after writing out the appropriate equation. Round decimals to the closest tenth.

1. Find the dollar markup on the following merchandise:
   A. Dresses: wholesale cost = $22.00; retail price = $39.95
   B. Sweaters: wholesale cost = $17.25; retail price = $32.99
   C. Shoes: wholesale cost = $23.50; retail price = $41.50
   D. Shirts: wholesale cost = $14.00; retail price = $24.98
   E. Neckties: wholesale cost = $8.80; retail price = $15.75

2. Figure the markup percentage of cost of the items listed above.
   A.
   B.
   C.
   D.
   E.

3. Figure the markup percentage of selling price of the items listed above.
   A.
   B.
   C.
   D.
   E.

4. What is the retail price of each of the items if a keystone markup is used by the retailer?
   A.
   B.
   C.
   D.
   E.

5. Using the retail prices given in Question 1, what should the selling prices be with a 25% markdown?
   A.
   B.
   C.
   D.
   E.

6. What is the markdown percent of the ticketed retail price if the reduced retail price is marked as follows in each case?
   A. $32.98
   B. $25.99
   C. $32.50
   D. $19.95
   E. $12.00

7. Have you noticed that the markup or markdown **_dollar amount_** is always the numerator, with the cost, selling price, or original ticketed price as the denominator? _____

Learning Even More

Name_____ **Date** _____ **Period** _____

Think about the following statements and write your reaction to each. Then discuss what you have learned with classmates.

1. If considered separately from the operating statement, such as for an individual department within a store or one store in a chain organization, **gross margin** is the difference between the total final selling price of goods (net sales) and the total amount that was paid for the goods (cost). _____
   _____
   _____

2. A firm's **net worth**, shown on the **balance sheet**, is the total assets (what is owned) minus total liabilities (what is owed). It represents owner (or shareholder) equity in the business. _____
   _____
   _____

3. **Return on investment (ROI)** is profit earned as a certain percentage of a business's invested capital. It shows efficiency of management and viability of product lines. An ROI target is usually set, to which internal comparisons are made over time, or external comparisons with competitors.
   _____
   _____

4. **Gross margin return on investment (GMROI)**, calculated by dividing gross margin by average inventory, is considered to be the highest standard of performance measurement for department stores. _____
   _____
   _____

5. Companies that pay their bills on time have eager suppliers available when they want new goods.
   _____
   _____

6. **Suggested retail pricing** is putting a price on retail merchandise that is recommended by the manufacturer to the retailer. However, when this is printed on a permanent tag with a lower price shown by the store, consumers often consider the suggested retail price to be an inflated, false price. _____
   _____
   _____

7. Some retailers seem to worry too much about the pricing of their **blow-outs** (best sellers) and **turkeys** (worst sellers), and ignore the remaining 80% of their merchandise. _____
   _____
   _____

8. Most retailers use the accounting method of **first-in, first-out (FIFO)**, which assumes that merchandise items are sold in the order in which they are obtained. In other words, older stock is sold before newer stock. _____
   _____
   _____

(Continued)

Name_____

9. Some aggressive merchandisers, such as off-price retailers, follow **automatic markdown schedules**. For instance, all merchandise not sold within 14 days (2 weeks) is marked down by 25%; after 21 days there is a 50% reduction; after 28 days (4 weeks) there is a 75% reduction; and after 35 days the remaining merchandise is given to charity._____

_____

_____

10. Companies are eager to stock their stores with lines that have almost constant **sell through**. In other words, the lines need few markdowns since they usually sell at full price._____

_____

_____

11. **Going rate pricing** is a system that focuses on the competition and the prices people are willing to pay rather than on costs. It is used particularly in businesses where costs are hard to determine, so markups cannot be used effectively in price setting._____

_____

_____

12. **Flexible markup pricing** considers many variables. Full costs are computed to set a minimum price at which the goods may be sold. The retailer works from this point with flexible markups, which are adjusted to meet changes in consumer demand, actions of competition, and general economic factors._____

_____

_____

13. To easily convert from cost to selling price, depending on the desired markup, some retailers use **markup conversion tables**. _____

_____

_____

14. Some retailers seem to offer **misleading "sale" prices** by lowering retail prices that were originally set too high—at levels that were never expected to sell. Also, it seems that stores have their merchandise "on sale" all the time._____

_____

_____

15. According to the Better Business Bureau's (BBB's) pricing policy ethics, merchandise should be offered at the price marked as the **original retail price** for 30 days to really qualify as the _retail price_. The BBB also feels that merchandise should be marked back to the original retail price after stores have _special sales_. _____

_____

_____

Calculations Review

Name _____ **Date** _____ **Period** _____

As you review the chapter, answer the following questions.

1. What are ledger accounts? _____

   _____

   _____

   _____

2. What does a payroll ledger account show? _____

   _____

   _____

3. What are the three basic components of an operating statement? _____

   _____

   _____

4. How do people know what time period is covered by a specific operating statement? _____

   _____

   _____

5. What is gross sales, and how is it determined? _____

   _____

   _____

   _____

6. How could a firm with large net sales end up with a loss? _____

   _____

   _____

7. What is net sales? _____

   _____

   _____

8. Why is a physical count of goods taken at the start of the fiscal year? _____

   _____

   _____

9. During weeks and months of the year when no physical inventory count is taken, how are these figures usually established? _____

   _____

   _____

   _____

10. On what figure is a company's income tax based? _____

    _____

    _____

(Continued)

Name_____

11. Why is it easier to compare companies with percentages than dollar figures? _____

_____

_____

_____

12. Why do card stores generally have higher sales per square foot than appliance stores? _____

_____

_____

_____

_____

13. Besides higher sales levels, what are two advantages of high turnover and low stock ratios? ____

_____

_____

_____

_____

14. What two costs constitute total costs? _____

_____

_____

_____

15. What is meant when it is said that, in general, department stores have lower debt levels than
discount and specialty stores? _____

_____

_____

_____

16. Define *price* in two ways. _____

_____

_____

_____

_____

17. What three considerations should retailers take into account when determining the size of price
reductions? _____

_____

_____

_____

18. To what one factor should the optimal timing and amount of markdowns relate? _____

_____

Calculating for Best Results

Name_____

Date_____ Period_____ Score_____

Chapter 19 Test

Matching: Match the following terms and identifying phrases.

_____ 1. A resulting positive number after expenses have been deducted from the gross margin figure.

_____ 2. A retail comparison figure to determine success versus previous years or against other companies, calculated by dividing total sales by total square feet.

_____ 3. Expenses that increase or decrease with the volume of sales.

_____ 4. Overhead expenses that remain the same regardless of sales volume.

_____ 5. An analysis of a retailer's sales in relation to close competitors that have similar corporate or store sizes, expense structures, merchandise lines, departmental structures, and ways of operating.

_____ 6. A barometer for success that compares the results of each succeeding year against previous years, usually shown in a percentage increase or decrease.

_____ 7. The periodic examination of financial data to try to measure the effectiveness of the company's strategy and operations.

_____ 8. The sum of money available to cover expenses and generate a profit.

_____ 9. Ratio that measures profit as a percentage of net sales.

_____ 10. A summary of the financial results of a firm's operations over a specified period of time.

A. comparable-store sales

B. comparative analysis

C. fixed costs

D. gross margin

E. net profit

F. operating statement

G. profit margin

H. sales per square foot

I. same-store sales growth

J. variable costs

True/False: Circle *T* if the statement is true or *F* if the statement is false.

T   F   11. Accounts receivable shows the balances the company owes to others.

T   F   12. Net sales is gross sales minus returns and allowances.

T   F   13. Operating ratios are mathematical relationships of income and expense figures that measure firms' effectiveness in generating sales and managing expenses.

T   F   14. The profitability range of product lines is based on the lines' profit per square foot of selling space.

(Continued)

Name_____

T   F   15. Lower debt levels increase companies' expenses and reduce profits.

T   F   16. "Price point" is a merchandising expression for the dollar amount at which an item is offered for sale.

T   F   17. $33.33 is an example of odd-figure pricing.

T   F   18. Loss leaders are low-priced articles on which stores make little or no profit.

T   F   19. Repricing includes both price increases and decreases on goods that are in stock.

T   F   20. The initial markup refers to the difference between merchandise cost and the selling price originally placed on merchandise.

Multiple Choice: Choose the best response. Write the letter in the space provided.

_____ 21. Ledger accounts are ongoing records of _____.
    A. company debits and credits as a result of business activities
    B. the people who have charge cards with the store
    C. ratios that analyze how the business is doing
    D. All of the above.

_____ 22. A fiscal year is _____.
    A. from January 1 through December 31
    B. an accounting period of one year
    C. the time period for all operating statements
    D. All of the above.

_____ 23. A physical count of inventory is done _____.
    A. when stock is high, so all items can be recorded
    B. at the start of the fiscal year, also giving the inventory for the end of the previous year
    C. using all the computer programs of the company
    D. All of the above.

_____ 24. The expense ratio is calculated by _____.
    A. dividing total operating expenses by net sales
    B. multiplying gross expenses times gross sales
    C. dividing inventory expenses by total sales
    D. multiplying inventory costs times net sales

_____ 25. Markdown money is_____.
    A. payment given to consultants to compute markdowns for retailers
    B. cash given to customers in place of offering lower sale prices
    C. a charge from the vendor when stores mark down their goods because of poor promotion or sales expertise
    D. a charge to a vendor from a retailer to help compensate for losses from reduced selling prices of that vendor's goods

_____ 26. Retail sales productivity is shown by calculating _____.
    A. average sales per hour
    B. average items per transaction
    C. average dollars per transaction
    D. All of the above.

(Continued)

Name_____

_____ 27. The main objectives of companies' pricing strategies include _____.
   A. overall profitability
   B. sales volume
   C. deterrence of competition and maintaining an image
   D. All of the above.

_____ 28. Overbuying by retail stores results in _____.
   A. improved final profits because more merchandise is available to sell
   B. better markups and fewer markdowns
   C. good choices for customers and an allowance for ordered merchandise that is not received
   D. All of the above.

_____ 29. The markup percent of cost of an item with a purchase cost of $24 and a retail price of $42 is _____.
   A. 18%
   B. 42.9%
   C. 57.1%
   D. 75%

_____ 30. An item originally priced by a retailer at $42 that is reduced to a selling price of $35 has a markdown off the original ticket price of _____.
   A. 16.7%
   B. 20%
   C. 75%
   D. 83.3%

Essay Questions: Provide complete responses to the following questions or statements.

31. Fill in the missing parts of the basic operating statement formula:

   Merchandise price × _____ = sales

   Sales − _____ = gross margin

   Gross margin − _____ = net profit (or loss) before taxes

32. Calculate the gross margin ratio and profit margin for a company with $480,000 net sales, $216,000 gross margin, and $52,800 net profit. Show your work. (You may use a calculator.)

33. What are the average number of items and dollars per transaction if 320 items are sold for a total of $2,176 in 128 transactions? Show your work. (You may use a calculator.)

CHAPTER 20

Service, Safety, and Security

Objectives

After studying this chapter, students will be able to

→ summarize customer service, including service levels, quality, and features.

→ explain aspects of consumer credit and payment processing.

→ describe how safety relates to both customers and employees.

→ tell about store security measures that deal with external and internal theft.

Teaching Materials

Text, pages 395–414
  Fashion Terms
  Fashion Review
  Fashion in Action
Student Workbook
  A. *Customer Service Cases*
  B. *Questioning Credit Services*
  C. *Group Safety and Security*
  D. *Service, Safety, and Security Crossword*
  E. *Safe and Secure Statements*
Teacher's Resources
  What Is Involved in Retail Safety and Security? reproducible master 20-1
  Delivering Retail Customer Service, transparency master 20-2
  Common Causes of Complaints, transparency master 20-3
  Systems for Handling Retail Complaints, transparency master 20-4
  Fun with Customer Service, reproducible master 20-5
  Assessing Consumer Credit Worthiness, transparency master 20-6
  Check Acceptance Checklist, transparency master 20-7
  Reducing Customer Theft, transparency master 20-8

Be Smart During a Robbery, transparency master 20-9
One More Review, reproducible master 20-10
Service, Safety, and Security Research, reproducible master 20-11
Chapter 20 Test

Introductory Activities

1. Have students discuss their viewpoints of retail customer service. Ask students what customer services they think are important for various types of stores. What services would they offer if they owned a retail store? Also have them consider the extra expenses of providing certain services. This will start them thinking about the content of the chapter and make them more observant of the customer services where they shop.

2. Discuss with the class the different payment methods that stores offer to consumers making retail purchases. How much do students know about making credit purchases with national credit cards and store-owned credit cards? How do credit card processing and check verification help ensure that stores receive the money due them? Ask the students if they have seen or used debit cards or smart cards. This will give you an idea of how much the students already know about the chapter content.

3. *What Is Involved in Retail Safety and Security?* reproducible master 20-1. Ask students to complete this activity to the best of their ability before studying the chapter. Then discuss the questions as a class. Tell students they will know all the answers to these questions, plus a lot more, after completing the chapter.

4. Discuss the importance of the content of this chapter by stressing that a combination of excellent service, safety, and security are vital to a retail company's strategy to maximize profits.

Customer Service

5. **RF** Have students discuss the differences between manufacturing and service businesses. Have them relate the fact that retailing is a service business to the importance of the customer service functions of stores. Ask students why retailing is considered a "people" business as well as a merchandise business.

6. **RT** With the class referring to illustration 20-3 in the text, discuss the characteristics and store types associated with the three main retail service levels. Relate the service levels to retail pricing and image. Also discuss these facts: most consumers prefer to shop at stores where salespeople are helpful but not pushy, and having more salespeople is not helpful unless they are knowledgeable.

7. **RF** *Delivering Retail Customer Service*, transparency master 20-2. Show the transparency while discussing the process of establishing a retail customer service program. Have students explain how each part of the process could be achieved.

8. **RT** Explain the concepts of service quality and service features with the class. Go through each of the service features emphasized in the textbook, with students discussing the aspects and importance of each.

9. **ER** Show students a video about customer service. D.E. Visuals offers *The Business of Customers, Commitment to Service and Quality, Relationship Marketing, Customer Service Excellence: It's in the Details, Winning Customer Loyalty: Eliminate Customer Turnoffs, Winning Customer Loyalty: Exceed Customer Expectations*, and *Listen & Win: How to Keep Customers Coming Back*. MindPerk offers *Customer Service, How to Give Exceptional Customer Service, Customer Service DVD Seminar*, and many other videos and CDs.

10. **RF** With the class referring to illustration 20-6 in the text, go from one student to the next as each explains a separate retail service. Have students comment on any personal experiences they have had with the service they are explaining. What human services are being replaced in some stores by technology (such as bridal registries and customer price scanning)? How do "blue laws" restrict store hours (prohibit Sunday operation)?

11. **ER** *Common Causes of Complaints*, transparency master 20-3. Use the transparency to discuss why each of the points listed is a common reason for consumers to complain to retailers.

12. **EX** *Systems for Handling Retail Complaints*, transparency master 20-4. Use the transparency for a class discussion on the three main complaint-handling systems used by retailers. Have students mention some retailers that use the various methods described.

13. **EX** *Fun with Customer Service*, reproducible master 20-5. Use the handout for students to express their opinions on a variety of customer service ideas. They are also asked to develop two ideas of their own. (These may include: having doormen at downtown stores hailing cabs for customers; free use of phones near cash registers for local calls; salespeople keeping swatches of customer's major apparel purchases to compare with new items customers are considering; offering coffee, tea, or wine; and shining men's shoes while they are removed to try on trousers.) Finally, hold a "retail service contest" by having each student submit his or her best customer service idea. Then have the class vote to determine the winner. (It must be a service that really is workable.)

14. **RT** *Customer Service Cases*, Activity A, WB. Students are asked to circle words or phrases that do not belong to a set and add words or phrases that do fit. Students are then asked to recommend good customer service for given situations.

15. **ER** Divide the class into small groups to develop a complete definition of *customer satisfaction* as it relates to retail sales. Have students assess why customer satisfaction can only occur with exceptional customer service. Assign different groups to discuss the customer service strategies of "under-promise, over-deliver," "hire and train the right people," "the customer service light switch makes a positive connection to get energy flowing between retailer and customer," and "proactively communicate."

Credit and Other Payment Services

16. **RT** Discuss with the class the three main types of credit plans offered to consumers by retailers.

17. **RF** Ask individual students to explain proprietary credit cards, private label credit cards, third-party credit cards, and secured credit cards.

18. **ER** Discuss with students the customer service features that retailers can build into their credit cards. For instance, Sears offers extra savings on purchases paid with the Sears card, sends out advance notices of sales, extends grace periods on selected purchases, allows refund credit without receipts if items were purchased with the card, allows customers to pick their payment-due date, has lower monthly minimum payments, and gives personal payment assistance to customers who are unemployed or seriously ill.

19. **EX** *Assessing Consumer Credit Worthiness*, transparency master 20-6. Show the transparency to discuss each of the "Three Cs" that are used to assess the likelihood of consumers paying their credit card bills.

20. **RF** Ask individual students to explain credit processing, check verification, check guarantees, and debit processing. Have the class offer reasons for the recent surge in the use of debit cards (such as overextended credit, consumers being declined credit, availability of technology, more people's knowledge of debit cards, and limit on shoppers to spend only what they have).

21. **EX** *Check Acceptance Checklist*, transparency master 20-7. While showing this as an overhead, instruct students what to look for when accepting personal checks from consumers for retail purchases. Discuss the telltale signs of a bad or suspicious check that salespeople should consider.

22. **EX** Discuss with students the fact that debit card issuers charge retailers the same fee as is charged for credit card transactions, even though debit cards take money directly from consumers' bank accounts and pose no danger of nonpayment. Essentially the card companies are charging a "risk fee" for what essentially is a risk-free transaction. (A retail class action lawsuit is in progress concerning this matter.)

23. **RT** *Questioning Credit Services*, Activity B, WB. Students are to answer questions about credit services.

24. **ER** Ask students to comment on these statements: "82% of consumers believe retailers that operate loyalty programs are more 'in touch' with their customers" and "organizing the business around the customer is emerging as a pivotal strategy for 21st-Century success."

Safety

25. **RF** Ask students to define safety (the prevention of bodily hurt or injury). Discuss the pros and cons of some consumers carrying personal protection devices with them when they shop, such as pepper spray or mace. Discuss how to protect retail consumers in the event of a fire, flood, bomb scare, protest, tornado, hurricane, earthquake, power outage, or other situations. Have information available about the Code Adam program, with six steps retailers should take if a child is reported missing in a store or mall.

26. **ER** Show students a video that explains the obligations and responsibilities concerning safety for both employers and employees. *Safety at the Workplace* is available from The School Company.

27. **EX** Discuss the use of security patrols on horseback or bicycles that are used outside of urban stores and in mall parking lots. Ask students to explain the advantages of horse or bicycle patrols compared to police patrols in cars or on foot. Also discuss why retailers are at risk for safety problems (such as easy public access, exchange of money, employees working alone or in small numbers, and late night shifts).

28. **EX** Order sample copies of booklets that are used in business for students to study. *Safety in the Store*, *Looking Out for Safety*, and others are available from Business & Legal Reports, Inc.

29. **RF** Divide the class into three groups. Assign one of the following bulletin board display topics to each—retail safety problems and prevention associated with: A.) criminal attacks on customers; B.) accidental injuries to customers; or C.) employee safety. When completed, have representatives from each group explain their displays.

Security and Loss Prevention

30. **RT** Discuss the different types of external and internal theft that affect retailers. Have the class refer to illustration 20-20 in the text and discuss various causes of shrinkage. Also discuss the fact that consumers bear the burden of paying higher prices to recover the losses of shrinkage from theft.

31. **EX** Show students a video that deals with security for loss prevention. *Shrinkage* is available from D.E. Visuals and VMS, Inc.

32. **RF** Discuss with the class how increased pre-employment "integrity screening" of retail job applicants has become a major loss prevention tool. This screening includes criminal conviction checks, credit history checks, past employment verification, drug screening, paper-and-pencil honesty tests, multiple interviews, and a review of worker's compensation claims. Also, retailers are pooling their knowledge through associations that keep records of people who have had retail ethical or criminal problems.

33. **EX** Obtain information from the National Retail Federation (NRF) about its Loss Prevention Conference and Exhibition, often held in June. Share the materials with the class, discussing the show's highlights and subjects covered. Also, the NRF Web site has a category of information under "Loss Prevention" that explains its committees, workshops, and printed information to combat retail problems of safety, security, and loss.

34. **ER** *Reducing Customer Theft*, transparency master 20-8. Use the transparency to have students explain and discuss the leading ways to reduce retail theft caused by customers.

35. **RF** *Group Safety and Security*, Activity C, WB. In small groups, students are asked to pick among given topics and prepare four scenarios. Students are then to present their material to the class for responses.

36. **EX** Ask students to check loss prevention information on the Internet, such as on Web sites www.losspreventiononline.com, www.retailspy.com, www.lptoday.com, and www.rlpx.com.

37. **ER** *Be Smart During a Robbery*, transparency master 20-9. While stressing that robberies rarely occur, use the transparency to have students discuss how to behave in case of a robbery. Ask students to give reasons for each direction listed.

38. **RT** *Service, Safety, and Security Crossword*, Activity D, WB. Have students review chapter vocabulary words by completing a crossword puzzle according to given clues.

39. **EX** *Safe and Secure Statements*, Activity E, WB. Students are asked to write their thoughts about given statements, try to expand each topic further, and share their thoughts with others in a class discussion.

40. **RT** *One More Review*, reproducible master 20-10. Use the master as a handout for students to review the chapter or earn extra credit.

Additional Enrichment Activities

Research

41. *Service, Safety, and Security Research*, reproducible master 20-11. Students are asked to research a retailer of their choice and write a comprehensive report, incorporating the answers to the questions on the handout. (This can be an individual or group assignment.)

42. Have students research the increased incidents of consumers using bad checks and/or filing for personal bankruptcy. Also have students consider the changing public perceptions of these situations and recent attitudes about repaying debts.

43. Have students research consumer fraud involving the return of items to retailers that have been worn (especially expensive outfits "borrowed" to wear to a party); false or stolen credit card applications; or illegal credit card transactions. Have students discover what steps retailers are taking or considering to combat these problems. How could better employee training help?

44. Have students research the use of "bioidentification" for cardless electronic POS transactions. An example of biometric technology is using an inkless thumb- or fingerprint for credit card verification. (Card readers in stores are being outfitted with pads to scan customers' fingertips and compare them with data stored on the credit card.)

45. Have students research the controversy of credit-transaction databases versus consumer privacy issues. Credit databases are being used to target customers for certain product and store promotions. Mailing lists that contain complete profiles of consumers are being sold as a way for credit card companies (and retailers) to make money. After researching the issue, can students recommend ways to keep the databases useful for customer relationship management without invading the privacy of consumers?

46. Have students research the Worker Protection Act, which is part of the Occupational Safety and Health Act (OSHA). Have students report their findings to the class.

47. Have students research the increased shoplifting threat of organized retail crime (ORT). These international "booster gangs" are highly skilled theft rings that target mall-based specialty apparel and department stores. Also have students find out what the retail industry and law enforcement are doing to combat these professional shoplifting rings (such as deterring this by alternating clothing hanger directions, locking valuable items to fixtures or in cases, having a store door-locking or air-fogging system, and use of other techniques).

Projects

48. As a homework assignment, have every student write a fictitious letter of complaint about one of the following: a defective merchandise purchase, mistreatment by a store employee, lack of parking, slow checkout lines, or some other retail customer service problem. After collecting the letters, distribute them so everyone receives someone else's letter. As a homework assignment, have students write replies to the complaint letters by responding as a retail store would. The response letter must try to appease the angry customer and solve the problem. If time permits during the following class period, have students read their sets of complaint and response letters.

49. Have students read a book about customer service. Suggestions are: *On Great Service: A Framework for Action* by Dr. Leonard Berry, *The Nordstrom Way: The Inside Story of America's #1 Customer Service Company* by Robert Spector, *Lessons from the Nordstrom Way: How Companies are Emulating the #1 Customer Service Company* by Robert Spector, *Best Practices in Customer Service* edited by R. Zemke and J. A. Woods, *Customer Service for Dummies* by Karen Leland, *Delivering Knock Your Socks Off Service* by Kristin Anderson, *Super Service: Seven Keys to Delivering Great Customer Service* by Jeff and Val Gee, *Customer Service Training 101: Quick and Easy Techniques That Get Great Results* by Renee Evenson, *The Big Book of Customer Service Training Games* by P. Carlaw and V. Deming, and many others. Have students report on the content of the book they read.

50. Have students read a book about security and loss prevention. Suggestions are: *Retail Security: 150 Things You Should Know* by Tyska and Fennelly, *Loss Prevention Guide for Retail Businesses* by Rudolph Kimiecik, *Absolutely Complete Retail Loss Prevention Guide* (4-volume set) by Bill Copeland, *Loss Prevention and Security Procedures* by Robert Fischer, *Effective Security Management* by Chuck Sennewald, *Shoplifters vs. Retailers: The Rights of Both* by Chuck Sennewald, *Loss Prevention Threats and Strategies* by Thomas Monson, and other related books.

Answer Key

Text

Fashion Review, page 414

1. Proactive customer service is listening to, understanding, and acting upon customer desires. Reactive customer service is after-the-fact handling of complaints.
2. self-service retailing, medium-service retailing, and full-service retailing
3. medium-service retailing
4. They pass them along to customers through higher prices.
5. Determine the most important service requirements of the company's specific target market.
6. how the company handles the complaint
7. facilitates the handling of purchases, especially with multiple products; protects the merchandise from inclement weather; preserves the privacy of customer purchases
8. abandon their merchandise selections and leave
9. They consolidate their deliveries for efficiency, have collect-on-delivery services, make callbacks, and assume liability for damaged or lost packages.
10. It stabilizes the timing of retail sales throughout the month, and customers tend to buy more goods and at higher prices, which increases sales volumes.
11. from customers' credit applications and recorded purchases that create a target marketing database
12. if the consumer is using a card that has been discontinued, is over its credit limit, or has been reported stolen
13. They recognize that pooled information is the most efficient and cost-effective way to stop bad checks from being accepted.
14. The store does not have to turn down sales or have high staffing expenses and financial losses.
15. customer safety, product safety, and employee safety
16. falls
17. (Name four:) Train employees in shoplifting prevention, control exits, post signs about cameras and prosecution, require receipts for all returns, close unattended checkout areas, and place monitors in secluded areas of the store. (Students may list other methods.)
18. a shoplifting prevention system that uses specially designed tags with small circuits that emit radio signals and can be sensed by detection pedestals or other devices placed at exits
19. at warehouses, loading docks, and stock rooms
20. (List five:) use of electronic article surveillance, employee screening and training, exception reporting software, closed circuit television surveillance, raised viewing platforms, inventory RFID tags, mirrors, point-of-sale monitoring (Students may justify other responses.)

Student Workbook

Customer Service Cases, Activity A

1. (circled:) fashion and specialty items; (added:) staple goods, convenience items, or others from the left side of Chart 20-3 in the text
2. (circled:) optional services; (added:) expected services or others from the center column of Chart 20-3 in the text
3. (circled:) convenience items; (added:) optional services or others from the right side of Chart 20-3 in the text
4. Call other branches of the store while Kendra is there—for that dress in red, in her size—and try to rush it to the store or Kendra's home.
5. She might renovate her store to be as elegant as practical and offer gift boxes with fancy bows on them. Then she might send a mailing out to personally announce the upgrades and invite customers to stop in for light refreshments, a chat, and shopping.
6. It won't do any good to add these amenities if the employees are grumpy and not trained to treat customers well. Make the employees feel good and train them how to make customers feel good. Then customers will enjoy the added features and sales will increase.
7. Carefully prepare simple but complete customer comment cards and instruct employees how to nicely request customers to complete them. Invite new members of the community to a special sale and try to obtain feedback then.
8. He should validate customer's parking tickets for the garage and put a nice secondary entrance (with a sign and fancy door) into the shop from the alley.
9. Add more checkout cashiers and/or hire someone to field the telephone calls, even if prices must be increased slightly.

Questioning Credit Services, Activity B

1. a 30-day charge account, or "regular charge," that is to be paid in full within a specific time period (usually 30 days) and has no finance charge or interest
2. This requires a small down payment and additional equal payments spread over several months or years.
3. a regular 30-day charge account that may be paid in full by a certain date with no finance charge or paid in monthly installments with interest charged on the unpaid balance
4. through special mailings and bill inserts
5. More office space, personnel, equipment, and communications are needed; fees and commissions must be paid to recover unpaid balances; some bad debts are never collected.
6. Retailers must pay financial institutions a service fee of a percentage of the amount of money charged. Customer relationships are depersonalized and buying habits can't be tracked.
7. because they are issued to consumers who are high credit risks
8. consumers who cannot qualify for unsecured credit
9. because they will probably be more loyal than average and might move toward regular, unsecured credit cardholders
10. They can charge cardholders located anywhere the maximum interest rate permitted in the state where the credit card bank is located.
11. because thousands of retailers are electronically dialing into the system for authorizations
12. one each to the customer, the retailer, and the credit card bank

Service, Safety, and Security Crossword, Activity D

Teacher's Resources

One More Review, reproducible
master 20-10

1. They establish a good relationship with customers.
2. to save money
3. services that are basic and necessary to the exchange process
4. specialty stores and upscale department stores
5. Other stores copy it and customers expect it as a normal occurrence.
6. costs of labor and utilities, personnel problems, and security risks
7. the settlement of customers' dissatisfactions with the store through mutual agreement on how to solve specific problems
8. added more or newer check-out terminals
9. encourage the sale of goods and/or be an income-producing service
10. because more pooled information is the most efficient and cost-effective way to stop bad checks from being accepted
11. because payment is made immediately, rather than at a later time
12. the prevention of bodily hurt or injury
13. falls
14. intended promises of product performance that are not expressed in written or oral form
15. credit card fraud, check fraud, robbery, shoplifting, and computer fraud
16. burglary, which is violent or after-hours theft
17. overhead cameras and other surveillance devices, tougher hiring procedures, and better employee training
18. with increased markups on merchandise

Chapter 20 Test

1. F	11. T	21. D
2. G	12. F	22. C
3. B	13. T	23. B
4. D	14. T	24. D
5. J	15. F	25. A
6. A	16. T	26. A
7. H	17. T	27. D
8. C	18. F	28. A
9. I	19. F	29. D
10. E	20. T	30. D

31. price positioning = self-service retailing; value positioning = medium-service; service positioning = full-service
32. customers and employees
33. CRM merges database information technology with customer service to analyze customers, respond individually to their needs, and build and maintain lasting relationships.

What Is Involved in Retail Safety and Security?

Name_____ **Date** _____ **Period** _____

Think about the following questions and give the most complete answers you can. You are not expected to know all the answers, but your thoughts combined in a discussion with classmates should result in ideas and discoveries that you will explore more fully in this chapter.

1. How would you define *safety*? _____
   _____
   _____

2. What are some ways that stores can provide customer safety?_____
   _____
   _____
   _____

3. What are some ways that stores can provide employee safety? _____
   _____
   _____
   _____

4. How would you define *security*? _____
   _____
   _____

5. What types of retail theft are committed by people in communities? _____
   _____
   _____
   _____

6. What types of retail theft do you think are committed by people who work for stores? _____
   _____
   _____
   _____

7. What are some ways that stores can prevent theft from people outside and inside the business?
   _____
   _____

8. Why do you think stores should be involved in safety and security issues?_____
   _____

Delivering Retail Customer Service

- Research customer expectations and desires.

- Develop the needed service features and actions.

- Implement the program by training and motivating employees.

- Communicate the appropriate promises and offers to consumers.

- Continually evaluate the program and execute improvements.

- Support the program with necessary resources and management availability.

Common Causes of Complaints

Goods-related:

- Wrong goods offered by store
- Small or poor selection
- Low quality for price
- Damaged goods

Service-related:

- Too few salespeople
- Rude/inattentive/unknowledgeable personnel
- Long/slow checkout
- Lack of alterations, delivery, and other services
- Poor handling of credit/payment accounts

Customer-related:

- Bought wrong product
- Changed mind about purchase
- Constant complainer

Systems for Handling Retail Complaints

Decentralized:	Handled by each separate department
Centralized:	Handled by a central complaint desk/office
Combination:	Handled first by the department, then if not resolved satisfactorily, sent to the central complaint desk/office

Fun with Customer Service

Name_____ **Date** _____ **Period** _____

Customer service of full-service retailers is most effective if it is uncommon and unexpected. With that in mind, give your opinions (both pro and con) of the following ideas.* Then, on another piece of paper, list some customer service ideas of your own. Finally, submit one of your ideas to a class "retail service contest" to select the customer service idea that is most likely to be effective.

1. A lingerie store prices its most expensive gowns to include extravagant gift wrap, black-tie messenger, and limousine delivery. _____

   _____

   _____

2. A salesclerk (working on commission) bakes a cake every time a "good" customer has a birthday. The store arranges for delivery. _____

   _____

   _____

3. A men's store sews numbered tags into every garment. When customers are in doubt about what matches what, they check the tags. _____

   _____

   _____

4. A children's store has a storyteller once a month and babysits the customers' children while parents go to a movie or a quiet dinner. _____

   _____

   _____

5. A gift store tracks important customer "gift" days and suggests appropriate purchases in time for delivery. _____

   _____

   _____

6. A children's shoe store tracks youngsters' ages and birthdays and sends cards directly to them.

   _____

   _____

7. A women's store acknowledges customer referrals with a basket of soaps and lotions. _____

   _____

   _____

8. Describe at least two of your customer service ideas on another piece of paper. _____

   _____

   _____

*Based on work by Bill Pearson, Retail Analysis & Planning, Pasadena, CA.

Assessing Consumer Credit Worthiness

Character:	Good personal attributes are needed to honor obligations.
Capacity:	High enough earning power is needed for the ability to pay.
Capital:	The more tangible assets (belongings) that are owned, the more likely the person is to pay.

Check Acceptance Checklist

- Is the check perforated? (Authentic personal account checks will be perforated on at least one side.)

- What is the check number? (Statistically, more checks with low numbers of new accounts bounce than high numbers of old accounts.)

- Is the check completely filled in?

- Was the check written on the day it is being presented?

- Did the customer write the check in the clerk's presence? (If not, he or she should be asked to re-sign it.)

- Do the signature and address on a photo ID match that on the check? (Checks with just a post office box address should not be accepted.)

- Has the retail staff had assertiveness training to ensure they are never intimidated into accepting or cashing a suspicious check?

Source: Check Center

Reducing Customer Theft

Detection Devices:

- Electronic tags on merchandise
- Convex mirrors placed high for viewing
- Closed-circuit TV/video monitoring
- Observation decks
- See-through (one-way) mirrors
- Floor-walking security personnel

Employee Efforts:

- Be alert at all times.
- Be aware of everything that is happening.
- Be visible and available in the store.
- Be organized in your job.

Observations:

- Watch customers' eyes, hands, and bodies.
- Watch customers' clothing.
- Watch for extra bags or false gift boxes.
- Watch loiterers or groups.
- Watch for mechanical devices.

Be Smart During a Robbery

- Stay as calm and quiet as possible.

- Do not make any sudden moves.

- Reassure the robber of your full cooperation.

- Do not try to apprehend the robber.

- Cooperate with the robber's wants.

- Notice the robber's clothing and physical appearance.

- Call police and store management only *after* the robber has left.

- Talk only to police and store management about the robbery.

One More Review

Name_____ **Date** _____ **Period** _____

As you review the textbook chapter, answer these questions.

1. How do retail customer services facilitate the buying process? _____
   _____
   _____

2. Why are some consumers willing to shop at self-service retailers? _____
   _____
   _____

3. What are essential services? _____
   _____
   _____

4. What types of stores use full-service retailing? _____
   _____
   _____

5. What are the usual results of a retailer starting a particular service?_____
   _____
   _____

6. What increases occur when store hours are extended?_____
   _____
   _____

7. What is complaint resolution?_____
   _____
   _____

8. For checkout flexibility and to counteract long waiting periods during busy times, what have some
   stores done?_____
   _____
   _____

9. In what two ways might an alteration service benefit retailers? _____
   _____
   _____

10. Why does the value of a check-verification database increase as the number of participants grows?
    _____
    _____

(Continued)

Name_____

11. Why is debit processing not a credit transaction? _____

_____

_____

12. What is meant by the term *safety*? _____

_____

_____

13. What type of personal accidents are the leading public liability claim? _____

_____

_____

14. What are implied warranties? _____

_____

_____

15. For retailers, what does external theft include? _____

_____

_____

16. What is robbery? _____

_____

_____

17. What measures are companies using to prevent internal theft?_____

_____

_____

18. How are loss prevention costs covered? _____

_____

_____

Service, Safety, and Security Research

Name_____ Date _____ Period _____

Research library and Internet sources about a local retailer of your choice. Then visit one or more stores of that retailer to answer the following questions. Detail your findings in a written report, organized according to the order that best suits your content.

- At what service level and with what price/service positioning does the retailer operate?

- What is the service quality of the retailer?

- What service features does the retailer provide? Are they consistent with the store's image?

- What are the store hours?

- What is the specific return policy of the store?

- How does the retailer handle complaints?

- What types of payment are accepted for merchandise?

- What credit and other payment services does the retailer provide?

- How does the store handle credit processing and check verification?

- What recommendations would you have for the store in terms of customer service?

- What customer safety measures are evident?

- How is employee safety provided and encouraged?

- What would you recommend to improve the store's safety?

- What methods are used for store security against external and internal theft?

- What would you recommend to improve the store's security?

- How would you rate this retailer for service, safety, and security?

Service, Safety, and Security

Name_____

Date_____ **Period**_____ **Score**_____

Chapter 20 Test

Matching: Match the following terms and identifying phrases.

_____ 1. Store-issued charge cards that are owned, operated, and managed by the company (in-house credit cards).

_____ 2. Charge cards linked to a savings account containing enough money to back up most or all of the credit line.

_____ 3. Electronic authorization of the probable risk of accepting individual personal checks from customers.

_____ 4. The money for each purchase is taken directly out of the consumer's bank account and electronically put into the merchant's bank account.

_____ 5. General purpose credit cards issued by outside institutions.

_____ 6. Personal check acceptance programs in which the risk falls on the bank/firm that authorizes the transaction.

_____ 7. How well services are performed to approach, meet, or exceed customer expectations.

_____ 8. The use of credit cards or other purchase charges that allow consumers to have merchandise immediately and pay for it later.

_____ 9. The difference between book inventory and actual physical inventory.

_____ 10. Charge cards with the store's name and logo, but issued and managed by a bank.

A. check guarantees

B. check verification

C. consumer credit

D. debit processing

E. private label credit cards

F. propriety credit cards

G. secured credit cards

H. service quality

I. shrinkage

J. third-party credit cards

True/False: Circle *T* if the statement is true or *F* if the statement is false.

T F 11. Customer service is the total of all enhancements offered to customers.

T F 12. Retailers should evaluate their customer service features about every five years.

T F 13. Longer store hours increase retail personnel problems and security risks.

T F 14. Long, slow checkout procedures are a customer service problem.

T F 15. A revolving charge account is a "regular charge" that is expected to be paid in full within a specific time period and has no finance charge or interest.

(Continued)

Name_____

T   F   16. A safe retail environment is needed to attract and keep customers and provide a safe workplace for store employees.

T   F   17. Store security involves loss prevention of merchandise, money, and other company possessions.

T   F   18. EAS (Easy And Safe) is a set of rules that store employees should learn and follow.

T   F   19. Source tagging is a label sewn into each garment that identifies the manufacturer in case there are customer complaints.

T   F   20. Pilferage is internal stealing of a company's inventory or cash in small, petty amounts.

Multiple Choice: Choose the best response. Write the letter in the space provided.

_____ 21. Customer service offerings include _____.
A. credit, convenient parking, and return privileges
B. gift wrapping, garment alterations, and layaway privileges
C. thank-you notes after purchases, bridal consultants, and free package delivery
D. All of the above.

_____ 22. The practice of a retail store marking the parking lot/garage stub as "paid" is called _____ parking.
A. accessible
B. convenient
C. validated
D. metered

_____ 23. The settlement of customers' dissatisfactions with a store through mutual agreement on how to solve specific problems is called _____.
A. returns and adjustments
B. complaint resolution
C. apologizing
D. customer negotiation

_____ 24. The retail service category of wrapping is _____.
A. bagging merchandise into a sack
B. putting customer's purchases into store wrap
C. gift wrapping with decorative paper plus a ribbon or bow
D. All of the above.

_____ 25. Statements by companies expressing their general responsibility for the quality and performance of the goods they make or sell are known as _____.
A. product guarantees/warranties
B. quality/performance viewpoints
C. qualitative/quantitative statements
D. All of the above.

(Continued)

Name_____

_____ 26. Installment credit _____.
   A. requires a small down payment and equal additional payments spread over time
   B. allows customers to pay what they can, whenever they can, to reduce their ongoing debt
   C. uses an implied agreement that the consumer will eventually pay the entire amount of debt
   D. is sometimes called an open account

_____ 27. Credit processing involves _____.
   A. an initial credit check and approval when someone originally applies for a credit card
   B. ongoing credit authorization when credit transactions are made
   C. a dial-out terminal to access the credit card database
   D. All of the above.

_____ 28. Shoplifting _____.
   A. is the stealing of merchandise from a retail store by a person posing as a customer
   B. has decreased in the last decade because of new technological devices
   C. is a misdemeanor, usually punishable with community service to make others aware of the problem
   D. All of the above.

_____ 29. Sweethearting is _____.
   A. a shoplifting method of distraction and theft done together by a man and a woman
   B. external theft done by delivery people who leave most of the orders but steal one or two items
   C. "front end" theft that can be defined as shoplifting by employees
   D. cashier employees providing discounts, uncharged items, or fraudulent returns to theft partners

_____ 30. Retail loss prevention strategies _____.
   A. are instituted by companies to prevent, recognize, and monitor security problems
   B. are aimed at reducing shrinkage from both external and internal theft
   C. often involve a combination of several types of surveillance, mirrors, and point-of-sale monitoring
   D. All of the above.

Essay Questions: Provide complete responses to the following questions or statements.

31. Name the service levels for price positioning, value positioning, and service positioning retail strategies.

32. For what two general groups is retail safety important?

33. Describe customer relationship management (CRM).

PART SIX

Fashion
Promotion

C H A P T E R **21**

Fashion Promotion Through Advertising and the **Press**

Objectives

After studying this chapter, students will be able to

⊖ explain the purposes for, and levels of, fashion promotion.

⊖ describe fashion promotion planning, follow-through, budgeting, and ethics.

⊖ summarize the purposes for, and types of, fashion advertising.

⊖ describe advertising agencies and freelancers.

⊖ summarize advertising strategy and media.

⊖ explain how to develop effective print advertisements.

⊖ identify parts of print advertisements.

⊖ define public relations and publicity.

⊖ give examples of the fashion press.

Teaching Materials

Text, pages 416–437
Fashion Terms
Fashion Review
Fashion in Action
Student Workbook
  A. *Multiple Fashion Promotion Choices*
  B. *Advertising Questions*
  C. *Analyzing a Fashion Ad*
  D. *Promotion Terms Matching*
  E. *Group Promotion Activities*
Teacher's Resources
Fashion Promotion Unit, transparency
    master 21-1

Appeals of Promotion Messages, transparency
    master 21-2
Effects of Retail Advertising, transparency
    master 21-3
Advertising Messages, transparency master 21-4
Promotion in the Capital System, reproducible
    master 21-5
Various Advertising Approaches, transparency
    master 21-6
Approximate Allocation of Advertising Dollars,
    transparency master 21-7
Planned and Unplanned Publicity, transparency
    master 21-8
Chapter 21 Test

Introductory Activities

1. *Fashion Promotion Unit*, transparency master 21-1. Use this transparency to introduce students to the content of the unit. Have students notice all the types of activities that are included in fashion promotion. Especially discuss the topics that will be covered in this chapter that send messages with words and pictures.
2. Review with the class the fact that promotion is indirect, nonpersonal selling to the general public to increase buying response. Also have students respond to the statement "Promotion is communicating with potential customers."
3. Ask students to describe the promotion of various retailers where they shop. Especially have students describe the types and amounts of advertising done by the retailers.

Strategies to Reteach, Reinforce, Enrich, and Extend Text Concepts

Fashion Promotion

4. **RF** With the class looking at text illustration 21-1, have students discuss how the emphasis of promotion should be changed for each stage of the fashion cycle. Have students discuss why promotion should emphasize different approaches in each stage. This will also help students review the fashion cycle.

5. **EX** Show students a video or CD about promotion strategy. *Promotion: Solving the Puzzle, Promoting Products, Sales Promotion: It's a Team Effort,* and *Sales Promotions* are all available from D.E. Visuals.

6. **RT** Have the class look at text illustration 21-3. Discuss how companies all along the soft goods chain promote to the final consumers. Discuss with students how consumer promotion from textile companies and apparel producers reinforces the retail promotion done toward consumers. Show the class (or have students find) some examples of consumer promotion done by companies in the textile or apparel segments of the pipeline. Also show examples of trade promotion if you can find any (located in trade publications).

7. **RF** Discuss with the class why sales promotion is more important lately (because of competition and similar merchandise). Discuss why overall retail promotion planning is usually done twice a year. Also discuss which retail employees are responsible for putting the promotion program into action.

8. **EX** *Appeals of Promotion Messages,* transparency master 21-2. Show the class this transparency and have students discuss each of the three basic promotion appeals. Also have students discuss which appeal is best for particular stores and situations.

9. **ER** After discussing how companies calculate their total promotion expenses, divide the class into three groups. Assign one of the following promotion budget allocation methods to each group: top-down approach, bottom-up approach, or affordability approach. Have students meet within the groups to discuss their subject, do further study to learn more, and prepare a report to present to the class.

10. **EX** Have students look at several different types of promotion from the same retailer. Ask students if they can identify any theme marketing efforts, in which the entire promotional campaign tries to send a cohesive message. Examples from the recent past include Benetton's United Colors and Bloomingdale's urban chic.

11. **RT** Ask students to explain the meaning of *ethics*. Have a class discussion about deceptive price promotion, deceptive product promotion, and deceptive sales practices. Include bait and switch and corrective advertising in the discussion.

12. **RT** *Multiple Fashion Promotion Choices,* Activity A, WB. Students are asked to write thought-provoking multiple choice questions about this section of the chapter. Then students are to exchange workbook pages with a classmate to try to answer each other's questions correctly.

Advertising

13. **ER** *Effects of Retail Advertising,* transparency master 21-3. Use this transparency as you discuss with the class how advertising can help retailers create awareness, knowledge, and feelings and attitudes.

14. **EX** *Advertising Messages,* transparency master 21-4. While viewing this transparency, have students discuss the two different types of action that advertising encourages. Have students explain how these relate to the two purposes of retail advertising mentioned in the text (getting customers into the site and contributing to the retailer's image). Also have students discuss the types of retailers that encourage each of the two types of action. Have students find and cut out advertisements that illustrate both.

15. **RF** Ask students to describe product advertising, institutional advertising, advocacy advertising, national advertising, regional advertising, local advertising, and cooperative advertising. If possible, have students bring in examples of each. Discuss the fact that most fashion ads are a combination of product and institutional advertising. Also, go through the advantages and disadvantages of cooperative advertising shown in text illustration 21-12.

16. **EX** Show students a video about advertising persuasion from both business and consumer viewpoints. *Advertising Tricks Without Gimmicks* is available from The School Company and Cambridge Educational. *Psycho-Sell: Advertising Persuasion* is available from D.E. Visuals and Insight Media. *Advertising Tactics* is available from Teacher's Media Company. *A Closer Look at Advertising* is available from Insight Media. *Why Ads Work: The Power of Self-Deception* is available from Learning Seed and D.E. Visuals. Additionally, *Psychology of Advertising, Advertising Agency,* and other advertising videos are available from D.E. Visuals.

17. **RF** Ask students to analyze fashion advertisements in current newspapers and fashion magazines. Have students notice that ads with many small pictures and featuring price savings give a store a bargain image. Ads with fewer, larger pictures and designer names project a prestige image. Then students should cut out photos and create an advertising layout for certain fashion goods. They should indicate in what publication(s) they would place the ad and why. Also ask students to explain why the particular fashion goods were selected to be featured in the ads.

18. **RT** Ask students to describe the advantages and disadvantages of fashion or retail advertising in different media, including newspapers, magazines, outdoor ads, direct mail, merchandise packaging, television, video, Internet Web sites, and telephone and business directories. Use text Illustration 21-13 for reference. Discuss the fact that advertisements should be scheduled with the appropriate media before they are prepared because space must be reserved in advance. Mention that for local retailers, a combination of print ads and direct mail advertising is most effective. Discuss the fact that some upscale apparel producers provide mailers aimed at their target market, but that do not include order forms. Customers must purchase items from the retailer that sent out the mailer. Also discuss the fact that advertising is one of the best ways marketers can take advantage of the World Wide Web.

19. **ER** Show the class a video about different advertising media. *The Advertising Media, Print Media, Broadcast Media, Newspaper Advertising,* and other videos are available from D.E. Visuals.

20. **EX** Ask students to discuss "word-of-mouth" advertising, as well as "Web-vertising" on Internet Web sites. If possible, ask students to check some apparel, retail, and trade association "Web-vertisements" on the computer.

21. **ER** *Promotion in the Capital System,* reproducible master 21-5. Students are asked to write their ideas in a response to a thought-provoking paragraph. Then they are to discuss their viewpoints with the class. Students should not be graded on their points of view.

22. **RT** With the class looking at text Illustration 21-19, discuss each of the functions of the fashion press.

23. **ER** *Various Advertising Approaches,* transparency master 21-6. While showing this transparency, have students go through each approach and explanation. Also have students give examples of each type of advertising, such as the fantasy/lifestyle of Ralph Lauren ads, sensuality of Calvin Klein jeans ads, testimonial of Kmart's Jaclyn Smith apparel, and slice of life situations of Cotton Incorporated.

24. **RT** *Advertising Questions,* Activity B, WB. Students are asked to write answers to given questions.

25. **EX** *Approximate Allocation of Advertising Dollars,* transparency master 21-7. While showing this transparency, have students discuss the approximate percentages of all (not just fashion) advertising purchased in various media. Have students notice which categories are the largest and the smallest, and discuss why. Also have students discuss that a small store in a large city is at a disadvantage with newspaper advertising costs because newspaper advertising space becomes more costly with a newspaper's larger circulation.

26. **ER** *Analyzing a Fashion Ad,* Activity C, WB. Students are asked to study print advertising in fashion publications, cut out a fashion ad, and analyze it according to given questions.

27. **EX** Obtain a free sample copy of *Retail Ad World* magazine via the Web site www.retailreporting.com or www.vizzbiz.com. Have students look at what it offers and discuss it in class.

Public Relations

28. **RT** Have students explain the similarities and differences between advertising and publicity. Have students discuss how if a firm has a really new or exciting message, publicity may be more effective than advertising. Also ask students to explain the use of press releases.

29. **ER** *Planned and Unplanned Publicity,* transparency master 21-8. While showing this transparency to the class, ask students to discuss the two main areas of publicity. Also discuss the proactive approach of distributing planned press releases for "damage control" in unfortunate business times instead of letting unplanned publicity do even more damage.

30. **RF** Discuss the possibilities of outsourcing public relations work to two different types of firms: publicity firms that write press releases and try to get free use of media time or space because of newsworthiness, and public relations firms that devise programs that project companies' public images through a planned program of activities. Also discuss that these are auxiliary firms (in the four-groups approach to the soft goods chain). Large fashion companies would not use these because they have their own public relations officer or staff. Discuss how good customer service by employees ties in with public relations.

31. **EX** Discuss with the class that publicity stories should appeal to broad cross sections of the public, as well as be truthful, dramatic, emotional, and unusual. Ask students to think of and describe specific types of stories they think would attract

media attention. Discuss "news blips" that depict new and unusual events, store innovations, improvements in working conditions, new store openings, and things currently important to the public.

32. **EX** Show students a video about public relations. *Public Relations* and *Everyone's Public Relations Role* are available from D.E. Visuals. To summarize the chapter thus far, *Advertising, Sales Promotion, and Public Relations* is available from Insight Media.

33. **RF** Have students cut out publicity from the newspaper to share with the class. Also have them tell about public relations efforts they have noticed on the radio or television.

The Fashion Press

34. **RF** Assemble a collection of fashion magazines, fashion trade journals, and fashion news articles from consumer magazines and newspapers. Have students look at all of them and discuss their content and format. Also have them notice instances of editorial credit.

35. **ER** Have students watch and report on shows that the fashion press presents on television, such as on the Fashion Television Channel, VH1, the Style Network, E!, and others. These often air on cable channels during weekend, afternoon, or evening hours.

36. **RT** *Promotion Terms Matching*, Activity D, WB. As a review, students are asked to match given terms from the chapter with their definitions.

37. **RF** *Group Promotion Activities*, Activity E, WB. Small groups of students are to pick and complete one of four given activities. Then they are to present their material to the rest of the class and let classmates ask questions or give constructive criticism.

Additional Enrichment Activities

Research

38. Have students do research about newer creative ways of reaching today's consumers. Have them discover "narrowcast" rather than "broadcast" methods that use unconventional media or use conventional media in unconventional ways so advertisers can "de-mass" their markets. Have students report their findings to the class.

39. Have students do research about media buying methods and strategies. Have them explain to the class the standardized ratio of cost per thousand, as well as evaluating reach, frequency, and continuity.

40. Have students research the history of fashion magazines. They should include in their research *Godey's Lady's Book*, *Burton's Gentlemen's Magazine*, *Metropolitan Monthly*, and *Delineator*. Have students find out how and when *Harper's Bazaar*, *Vogue*, *In Style*, *Elle*, and others were established. Ask students to report their findings to the class.

Projects

41. Have students read a book about fashion promotion, advertising, public relations, or the fashion press. *Retail Fashion Promotion and Advertising* by Mary Drake, *What Works in Fashion Advertising* by Peggy Winters, *Public Relations Kit for Dummies* by Eric Yaverbaum, and *The Wizard of Ads* by Roy Williams are a few examples of the many books available.

42. Have students do research on the Retail Advertising & Marketing Association (RAMA) which is a division of the National Retail Federation (www.rama-nrf.org). Have students understand the RAMA mission statement and find out about aspects of the organization such as awards, sponsorships, and education. Ask students to also find out about RAMA's Retail Advertising Conference (RAC) held every February, including the types of educational sessions held during the conference.

43. Have groups of students do sales promotion financial (not calendar) planning for specific retailers. Have each group plan the media forms of promotion for a particular retailer. Then, with a certain estimated promotion budget (such as $50,000), have them make a pie graph that shows the percentages of the budget that will go toward each promotion category (such as newspaper, radio, and direct mail advertising; fashion shows; displays; and publicity). Students should consider the most effective use of promotion dollars to reach the retailer's target market. Have each group explain their work to the rest of the class and mount their graph on the bulletin board. After all groups have given their reports, compare and discuss the similarities and differences of the graphs.

44. Have students analyze three fashion articles from current newspapers or magazines for form and content. Then, after gathering background information, the students should write a newsworthy fashion article about a current design or trend that could appear in that publication.
45. Have students study about the psychology of advertising and prepare an oral or written report. Have them include the psychology of Internet advertising as well as traditional ads.
46. After students have finished studying the chapter, have them do additional study about advertising agencies, fashion or retail advertising, and/or fashion journalism. Invite an employee of an advertising agency or fashion publication to speak to the class to reinforce and add credibility to what the students have learned.

Answer Key

Text

Fashion Review, page 437

1. inform, persuade, remind
2. to gain brand-name recognition and eventual shopping preference from the public
3. because of increased competition and the similar merchandise offered by many manufacturers and retailers
4. goals and objectives; message or theme; activities; timing; media mix; assignments of responsibility; budget; evaluation methods
5. so the appropriate items and trends are promoted properly
6. It assumes that the competitors' calculations are correct, and it is often hard to obtain accurate information on competitors' promotion budgets.
7. top-down approach, bottom-up approach, affordability approach
8. pricing practices, products, and sales practices
9. the Federal Trade Commission (FTC)
10. promotional messages to correct previous false or unethical claims
11. to get customers to the retail site and to contribute to the retailer's image
12. from client companies and commissions from the media into which they place ads
13. sales targets, brand names, and/or recall
14. sell advertising space and time, as well as arrange to have company advertisements produced
15. location
16. companies' names, logos, and slogans on shopping bags, gift boxes, and wrapping paper
17. Web sites
18. gain consumer attention and then guide them through all the parts of the ad to absorb the message and meaning
19. The company has little control over how the content of the message is presented or the timing of its presentation.
20. Actors and hosts wear the latest fashions, short segments on fashion are presented on news and talk shows, and fashion features air on many cable channels on a regular basis.

Student Workbook

Advertising Questions, Activity B

1. discount stores
2. address public issues or influence public opinion
3. companies that sell products on a nationwide basis and local merchants
4. Ads should be timed to be run when the merchandise is available.
5. the one, or combination, that most effectively and efficiently reaches the largest portion of the company's target audience
6. (List three for print:) newspapers, magazines, outdoor, direct mail, or merchandise packaging (List two for broadcast:) radio, television, video presentations
7. newspapers
8. with quantity buying, usually on a yearly basis
9. advertising circulars that are preprinted in full color for distribution with newspapers, especially the Sunday editions of metropolitan papers
10. weekly suburban and community papers
11. (Name three:) billboards, public transit ads, benches, free-standing signs
12. catalogs, mailers, bill enclosures
13. small, specialty retailers
14. because specific items of merchandise cannot be seen by the audience
15. repetition
16. because mass audiences can be shown the actual products in color and motion
17. a condensed summary of the advertising message
18. It puts together all the elements of the ad.

Promotion Terms Matching, Activity D

1. E
2. M
3. K
4. A
5. P
6. D
7. G
8. T
9. J
10. F
11. Q
12. I
13. B
14. H
15. O
16. L
17. N
18. R
19. S
20. C

31. to inform, persuade, and remind
32. With the top-down approach, senior managers who are familiar with the organization's overall financial picture develop the promotion budget allocations. With the bottom-up approach, the types and amounts of promotion are decided by the employees involved with carrying them out and "living with" the results. Budget estimates are then calculated.
33. (Correct answers are listed in text Illustration 21-12.)

Teacher's Resources

Chapter 21 Test

1. F
2. D
3. E
4. A
5. H
6. J
7. I
8. C
9. B
10. G
11. F
12. F
13. T
14. F
15. F
16. F
17. T
18. F
19. T
20. T
21. C
22. D
23. D
24. B
25. D
26. A
27. B
28. A
29. A
30. C

Fashion Promotion Unit

Chapter 21:

Advertising

Public Relations

The Fashion Press

Chapter 22:

Visual Merchandising (store interior layout, décor, merchandise presentation, displays)

Chapter 23:

Fashion Shows

Appeals of Promotion Messages

Depending on the target market, retailers make a:

- <u>patronage appeal</u> that emphasizes the rightness of the retailer, location, hours.

- <u>product appeal</u> that emphasizes the rightness of its merchandise.

- <u>price appeal</u> that emphasizes the right pricing for its customers.

Effects of Retail Advertising

Advertising helps retail companies create:

- consumer <u>awareness</u> of the retailer and its products.

- consumer <u>knowledge</u> of the retailer's image.

- consumer <u>feelings and attitudes</u> toward patronizing the retailer.

Advertising Messages

Advertising messages can encourage:

- <u>direct action</u>, which urges consumers to shop with the retailer now, to take advantage of a sale or other incentive. This results in immediate sales but not regular patronage.

- <u>indirect action</u>, which tries to influence consumers' views about the retailer's image as the place for them. This takes considerable time and money to develop, but encourages regular patronage.

Promotion in the Capital System

Name_____ **Date** _____ **Period** _____

Think about the following paragraph and write your ideas in a response to the points presented. Then discuss your viewpoints with the class.

"Some people feel that promotion is unethical because companies try to convince people to buy unnecessary products. Others argue that advertising encourages materialism at the expense of more worthwhile values, that it exploits stereotypes, and that it manipulates consumers subconsciously. Still others argue that money spent on promotion could be better used inventing new products or improving the quality of existing items. However, in our free society, promotion is part of the capital system. It provides a great amount of information to consumers and wages to promotional employees."

Student response:

_____

_____

_____

_____

_____

_____

_____

_____

_____

_____

_____

_____

_____

_____

_____

_____

_____

_____

_____

_____

_____

_____

_____

_____

_____

Various Advertising Approaches

Approach	Explanation
Fantasy or Lifestyle:	A beautiful model or people who are yachting or at a mansion are shown wearing items, hoping consumers will identify and buy.
Sensuality:	Erotic images are emphasized.
Testimonials:	A famous person endorses or puts his or her name on products.
Slice of Life:	Consumers are shown feeling good about using products.
Humor:	Entertaining ads encourage people to notice and remember them.
Comparison:	Products are compared to competing brands and come out ahead.
Reasons Why:	Benefits of products or store are emphasized, such as low price.
Causes:	Associated with public service to help social causes such as fighting cancer, AIDS, etc.

Approximate Allocation of Advertising Dollars

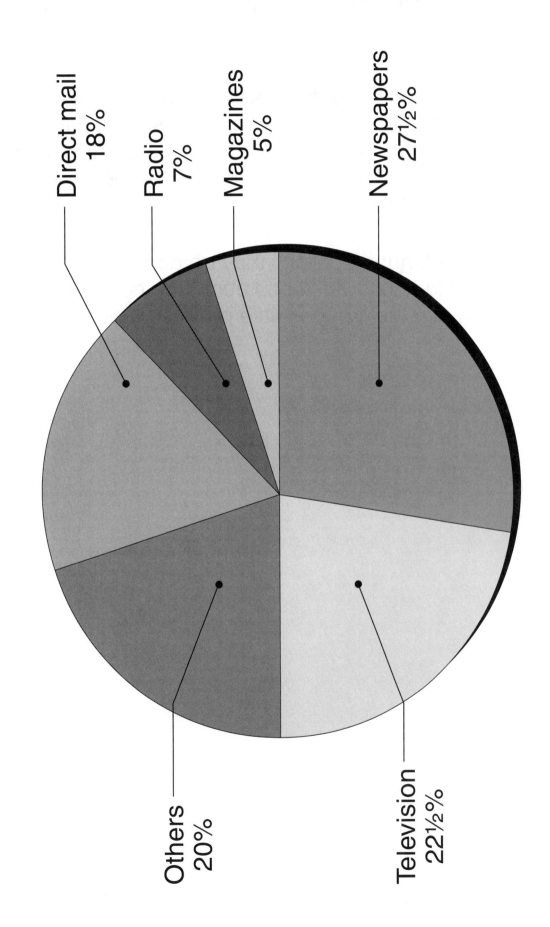

Direct mail
18%

Radio
7%

Magazines
5%

Newspapers
27½%

Others
20%

Television
22½%

Planned and Unplanned Publicity

- <u>Planned publicity</u> contains controlled news item released to the media. It is done with press kits, news releases, press conferences, letters to the editor, notices about newsworthy special events, etc.

- <u>Unplanned publicity</u> may be good or bad. It includes news stories about the company over which the firm has little or no control.

Fashion Promotion Through Advertising and the Press

Name_____

Date_____ Period_____ Score_____

Chapter 21 Test

Matching: Match the following terms and identifying phrases.

_____ 1. A promotional collection of materials presented as a portfolio with press releases and photographs and/or illustrations.

_____ 2. Acting or dealing in good morally evaluated ways.

_____ 3. Image or corporate advertising designed to sell public awareness and the reputation of an organization rather than selling specific products.

_____ 4. A plan that defines the target audience and summarizes the benefits and features of the product that will please that audience for an ad campaign.

_____ 5. Advertising designed to sell specific, identifiable merchandise items or lines or certain services and aimed at getting an immediate response.

_____ 6. Activities that try to build good relations with the various publics of an organization or product line.

_____ 7. Unpaid media coverage of news about an organization, or its products and activities, presented at the discretion of the media.

_____ 8. Mention in a publication of a manufacturer's tradename or specific retail sources for merchandise featured by the publication.

_____ 9. Promotional messages used to correct previous false or unethical claims.

_____ 10. A written "news" story sent as publicity to newspapers and magazines.

A. advertising platform

B. corrective advertising

C. editorial credit

D. ethics

E. institutional advertising

F. press kit

G. press release

H. product advertising

I. publicity

J. public relations

True/False: Circle *T* if the statement is true or *F* if the statement is false.

T   F   11. Promotion is personal selling to increase buying response.

T   F   12. Consumer promotion is aimed within the industry to the next segment of the distribution chain.

(Continued)

Name_____

T　F　13. A written promotion program details all of a company's promotion efforts for a certain period of time.

T　F　14. The person responsible for retail promotion planning and follow-through is called the promoter.

T　F　15. Advertising is a mass-communication message by an unidentified sponsor.

T　F　16. Mom-and-pop stores do the most advertising of all retailers.

T　F　17. Advocacy advertising is intended to address public issues or influence public opinion.

T　F　18. Media forms are the particular newspaper, magazine, and TV station used for an advertising campaign.

T　F　19. The fashion press includes the print and broadcast media that present and interpret fashion and industry news.

T　F　20. One of the functions of the fashion press is to shop worldwide markets for newsworthy styles to feature.

Multiple Choice: Choose the best response. Write the letter in the space provided.

_____ 21. The combination of all types of persuasive communication used by an organization to market itself and influence sales is known as the _____ mix.
A. marketing
B. advertising
C. promotion
D. press communications

_____ 22. Promotion of goods at the peak of the fashion cycle is most effective if aimed toward _____.
A. motivating customers and heightening their desire for merchandise
B. gaining customers' loyalty with reduced prices and reinforcing their choices
C. emphasizing price advantages with large markdowns
D. persuading consumers that the firm's version of the item is best and why

_____ 23. Retail promotion _____.
A. tries to create demand for the firm's products among the target market
B. is promotion by a store to its customers
C. is essentially local consumer promotion
D. All of the above.

_____ 24. Promotion goals and objectives _____.
A. should specify payment options for personalized sales messages
B. are usually based on past programs and should be well defined
C. include the types and quantities of advertisements, how often to run them, and over what length of time
D. All of the above.

(Continued)

Name_____

_____ 25. The promotion budget of fashion manufacturers and retailers is often based on _____.
   A. the firm's anticipated annual sales dollars
   B. the previous year's promotion expenditures
   C. what competitors spend on promotion
   D. All of the above.

_____ 26. Deceptive price promotion occurs when retailers _____.
   A. put higher original ticketed prices on items so they can mark them down to "sale" prices that are not really bargains
   B. make false or misleading claims about products they sell
   C. use bait-and-switch sales practices
   D. All of the above.

_____ 27. Service firms that provide advertising expertise are _____.
   A. layout freelancers
   B. advertising agencies
   C. promotion marketers
   D. advertising advocates

_____ 28. The primary medium used for local retail ads is _____.
   A. newspapers
   B. direct mail
   C. radio
   D. merchandise packaging

_____ 29. Parts of print ads include _____.
   A. headline, copy, and illustration
   B. salutation, complimentary close, and white space
   C. logo and/or slogan, reference initials, and signature
   D. All of the above.

_____ 30. Magazines aimed at consumers, with a fashion emphasis through articles, illustrations, and ads, are _____.
   A. consumer news magazines
   B. fashion trade journals
   C. fashion magazines
   D. fashion editorial journals

Essay Questions: Provide complete responses to the following questions or statements.

31. For what three purposes should fashion promotion be designed to accomplish?

32. Briefly explain the top-down and bottom-up approaches of allocating promotion budgets.

33. Give two advantages and two disadvantages of cooperative advertising.

Visual Merchandising

Objectives

After studying this chapter, students will be able to

- explain the importance of visual merchandising.
- describe the two main areas of store layout.
- summarize the aspects of merchandise presentation.
- describe the components of in-store displays.
- list the advantages, disadvantages, and types of window displays.
- describe nonstore visual merchandising.

Teaching Materials

Text, pages 438–459
  Fashion Terms
  Fashion Review
  Fashion in Action
Student Workbook
  A. *Visual Merchandising Outline*
  B. *Visual Merchandising Match*
  C. *Visual Merchandising Truths and Myths*
  D. *Visual Merchandising Facts*
  E. *Becoming Visual Merchandisers*
Teacher's Resources
  Interior Spaces of Stores, transparency
      master 22-1
  The Value of Interior Spaces, reproducible
      master 22-2
  Merchandise Location Decisions, transparency
      master 22-3
  Common Types of Interior Displays,
      transparency master 22-4
  Steps for Installing Window Displays,
      transparency master 22-5
  Visual Merchandising Review, reproducible
      master 22-6
  Catch These Points, reproducible master 22-7
  Chapter 22 Test

Introductory Activities

1. *Visual Merchandising Outline*, Activity A, WB. Students are asked to outline the text chapter by writing section titles on the form provided. They are to read each accompanying definition or explanation. Then they are to explain which section of the chapter they think will be most interesting to them and why. Finally, they are to keep their papers to review after studying the chapter.
2. In class, discuss examples of visual merchandising that students have noticed while shopping at retail stores. Ask students to describe various store interiors, merchandise presentations, interior displays, and window displays. Also, tell students they will learn all about these things in this chapter.
3. Ask students to describe what they believe are the main differences between visual merchandising and advertising. At the end of the discussion, have students read and discuss the first paragraph of the chapter.

Strategies to Reteach, Reinforce, Enrich, and Extend Text Concepts

The Importance of Visual Merchandising

4. **RT** Discuss with the class how visual images are a common language among the people of all communities and countries. Also, summarize the parts of visual merchandising as store layout and décor, merchandise presentation, and displays.
5. **RF** Have students relate visual merchandising to "the store as a theater."

6. **ER** Divide the class into small groups. Have each group meet to prepare a display calendar for a specific type of retailer for the year. The student groups should identify an appropriate variety of seasonal themes, store events, and/or community activities to feature. The display ideas should also reinforce the store's image and reputation.

The Store Interior

7. **RF** *Interior Spaces of Stores*, transparency master 22-1. Show this transparency to the class as students discuss the contents and use of store interior selling areas and sales support areas.

8. **RT** Have students explain grid and maze floor plan layouts. How do these affect sight lines for customers? Have students draw planogram examples of each on the board.

9. **ER** Obtain a book of retail shop planograms to share with the students. Discuss how a retailer can make dozens of photocopies of basic spaces drawn to a specific scale (often ⅛″ or ¼″ equals 1 foot) to use in planning different merchandise areas as seasons and conditions change. Also discuss how the grouping of merchandise helps improve merchandise planning, control, and the shopping atmosphere and lets customers find, compare, and select needed items.

10. **EX** Order sample copies of the magazine *Visual Merchandising and Store Design (VM+SD)* from ST Publications to share with the students. A subscription to *VM+SD* includes an annual Buyer's Guide that lists suppliers, products/equipment, store designers' associations, and the event calendar for the year. Check the Web site www.stpubs.com to see their other publications about store design, retail displays, sign design, and fashion merchandise presentation that can be used as reference materials for students. Also check www.ddimagazine.com for *Display & Design Ideas* magazine and www.retailreporting.com for *Store Planning & Design* Review.

11. **RF** Explain to the students that theme stores use décor intended to be interesting, distinctive, and remembered. For instance, a swimsuit shop might use bamboo and thatching over the dressing rooms and play the sounds of waves hitting the beach. Ask students to come up with original ideas of interior décor and audio atmospheres for different types of apparel stores. Also discuss the excitement and feeling of luxury created by chandeliers, mirrors, and other "special décor."

12. **EX** *The Value of Interior Spaces*, reproducible master 22-2. After emphasizing that math skills are necessary for most aspects of fashion merchandising, have students complete this activity. A calculator may be used. After

students have finished the assignment, have them discuss the value of retail interior spaces and the types of merchandise that would be placed in various locations within stores. Also discuss that rent allocations are higher along or at intersections of primary aisles than along secondary aisles.

13. **ER** *Merchandise Location Decisions*, transparency master 22-3. Show this to the class as an overhead and have students discuss each of the items about where to locate various merchandise in the interior of the store.

Merchandise Presentation

14. **RT** Ask students to describe shoulder-out and face-forward merchandise presentation, as well as capacity fixtures, feature fixtures, waterfalls, and wall standards. Discuss how wall sections are usually merchandised as one unit. Also discuss that selling floors look best if all fixture heights are of uniform height throughout a store or department.

15. **EX** Show students a video about merchandise presentation. *Visual Merchandising* is available from Cambridge Educational, Meridian Education Corporation, and D.E. Visuals. *Visual Merchandising: Look, Linger & Buy* is available from Insight Media and D.E. Visuals. *Merchandising: The Store as Persuasion* is available from D.E. Visuals, and *Visual Merchandising: The Art of Creating Unique Environments* is available from VMS, Inc.

16. **RF** Discuss with the class why color is one of the most important elements of merchandise presentation. Discuss the fact that once the store or department has customers' interest, the next goal is to draw them through the entire area to the back wall. Ask students how this can be done by having them give examples that they have noticed while shopping or working in stores (such as with various focal points).

17. **EX** Obtain information about the National Association of Store Fixture Manufacturers (NASFM) from www.nasfm.org, the NASFM Magazine, and the Globalshop Trade Show (an exhibition and conference for retail design professionals and visual merchandisers) (www.globalshop.org). It features specialized materials, products, and services, as well as interactive and point-of-purchase marketing ideas. Also obtain information about the National Association of Display Industries, Inc. from www.nadi-global.com and its STOREXPO exhibition (www.storexpo.info). Share the information with the class or have students explore the Internet sites themselves for more thorough learning.

Interior Displays

18. **RT** Discuss with students what displays are intended to do besides showing and selling merchandise.

19. **ER** *Common Types of Interior Displays*, transparency master 22-4. Use this transparency as a basis of a discussion about various types of interior displays.

20. **RF** Divide the class into four groups. Assign each group a different type of merchandise grouping (one-category, related, theme, or variety) to illustrate with several examples and describe it to the class.

21. **RT** Discuss functional props, decorative props, and structural props with the class. Discuss realistic and other types of mannequins, including other materials used to imitate human form in displays. Also discuss use, placement, wording, and readability of signage.

22. **EX** Show students a video about how to create fashion displays. *Fashion Display Skills* and *Pinning and Flying in Fashion Display* are available from Insight Media and D.E. Visuals. Additionally, *Display Lighting* is available from D.E. Visuals.

23. **ER** If AutoCAD equipment is available, obtain and use *Display Shop: The Store Layout and Design Library* from VMS, Inc. Students will be able to design their own store interior layouts and specific display fixture types and placements as they work with the software.

Window Displays

24. **RT** Have students discuss the advantages and disadvantages of window displays. Then have students describe the main types of display windows (enclosed, semi-enclosed, open, and island windows). Have students tell about stores where they have seen the windows and describe the displays in them. Have them discuss the statement "Window displays are to make the passers buy!"

25. **ER** *Steps for Installing Window Displays*, transparency master 22-5. While showing this transparency to the class, have students read through (in order) the main steps for dressing a window.

Nonstore Visual Merchandising

26. **RT** *Visual Merchandising Match*, Activity B, WB. Students are asked to complete a vocabulary word matching exercise.

27. **EX** *Visual Merchandising Truths and Myths*, Activity C, WB. Students are asked to read given statements, indicate if they think the statement is a myth or a truth, and check their answers on the back of the page. Then students are to discuss the statements as a class.

28. **RT** *Visual Merchandising Facts*, Activity D, WB. Students are asked to respond to questions about visual merchandising.

29. **RT** Discuss with the class how the elements and principles of design are used in visual merchandising. With students looking at illustration 8-1 of the text, go through each element and principle with students describing specific ways they could be used in displays.

30. **RT** *Visual Merchandising Review*, reproducible master 22-6. Use these additional chapter review questions as homework or as an optional extra credit assignment.

31. **RT** Have students review Activity A, WB (*Visual Merchandising Outline*), which they completed before studying the chapter. Ask students if the section of the chapter they thought would be the most interesting to them actually was the most interesting, and why or why not.

32. **EX** *Catch These Points*, reproducible master 22-7. Students are asked to think about given statements and write their reactions to each. Then students are to discuss what they have learned with classmates.

Additional Enrichment Activities

Research

33. Have students do research about the various lighting options for store interiors, merchandise presentation, and for interior and window displays. Have students prepare a report for the class that discusses the pros and cons of various types of lighting, both for store interiors and displays, such as purchase cost, cost of use, and effects achieved for fluorescent lights, incandescent high hats, track lighting, ambient or task lighting, Frensel lights, LED lighting, and other options. Ask students to include examples and illustrations as visual aids.

34. Have students do research on the materials and tools used for building retail displays. Have students relate the information to stores' images, sizes, merchandising philosophies, service policies, display staffs, and display budgets. When reporting to the rest of the class, have students present their information with visual aids and examples.

35. Have students research the requirements of the Americans with Disabilities Act (ADA) to which

retailers must adhere. Have students report to the rest of the class about the types of door openers that should be used, special restroom features, levels of counters, space between merchandise fixtures, Braille signage, and other aspects.

36. Have students conduct research in books and in retail stores about the many different types of merchandise presentation fixtures and mix-and-match systems. Students should include necktie displayers, rotating stands that hold earring cards, rope displayers for necklaces and bracelets, circular scarf wheels, tiered bins, valet fixtures for menswear, gondola units with adjustable shelves and storage space below, and as many as possible of the retail fixtures mentioned in text illustration 22-11. With pictures and/or drawings plus explanations, have students report their findings to the class.

Projects

37. *Becoming Visual Merchandisers*, Activity E, WB. Groups of students are asked to pick and complete one of two given activities. They are to present their material to the rest of the class and allow classmates to ask questions or give additional ideas and comments.

38. Arrange a field trip to a prominent retail store to visit the display department. Have students learn about the equipment needed; storage space and arrangement; procedures used for planning, constructing, and evaluating displays; how long it takes to develop each display; and what store personnel are involved in planning, executing, and evaluating displays. Also have the class walk around the store to look at current displays.

39. Invite a display worker from a local store to demonstrate how to fold merchandise for shelf presentation, pin a wall display, and dress a fixture. If possible, have that display worker show a collection of slides or photographs of the interior and window displays that have been featured by the store recently.

Answer Key

Text

Fashion Review, page 459

1. It is three-dimensional and real.
2. Retailers can meet their special requirements and minimize the limitations of their spaces before constructing the layout and stocking the store with merchandise; estimate the amount of materials needed, and plan all parts in correct proportion to each other.

3. their relationship with other departments and to traffic aisles
4. near the entrance, because it is the space most exposed to customers
5. at entrances, aisles, and focal points on walls
6. at the front of small stores, along aisles of mid-sized stores, and as a lead-in to each department of a large store
7. to encourage complete outfits to be purchased
8. merchandise, lighting, props, and signs
9. when a single manufacturer or brand name is featured
10. from fashion magazines, upscale competitors, manufacturers of the items, and by observing what fashion leaders are wearing
11. It maximizes the range of area that is covered and gives more distance between the hot, fading light source and items being displayed.
12. to physically support or hold merchandise
13. to establish a mood or attractive setting for the merchandise being featured
14. a confusing appearance and none of them standing out with a clear message
15. the type of merchandise to be displayed, display materials, props available, and display space
16. People are too busy to window-shop for leisure or curiosity, and there are fewer street-facing windows used for displays.
17. they can help distinctive retailers establish and maintain a unique image; they can stimulate and arouse shoppers' curiosity to the point of having them enter the store and wander through it
18. (Name three:) They reduce glare and reflection from window displays, enhance the store exterior, can be changed for special seasons or promotions, give added comfort to customers entering the store, and protect merchandise from ultraviolet ray damage.
19. This concentrates the viewers' sight line toward the center, hides the side lights that are used, and gives a feeling of depth perception to the presentation.
20. four-sided display windows that stand alone, often in lobbies

Student Workbook

Visual Merchandising Outline, Activity A

I. The Importance
II. Store Interior
    A. Selling area layout
    B. Store décor and atmospherics
III. Merchandise Presentation
    A. Merchandise fixtures
    B. Merchandise arrangements on walls

IV. Interior Displays
  A. Components of displays
    1. Merchandise
    2. Lighting
    3. Props
    4. Signage
  B. Planning interior displays
V. Window Displays
  A. Advantages and disadvantages of window displays
  B. Types of display windows
    1. Enclosed windows
    2. Semi-enclosed windows
    3. Open windows
    4. Island windows
VI. Nonstore Visual Merchandising

Visual Merchandising Match, Activity B

1.	M	14.	N
2.	L	15.	Q
3.	G	16.	P
4.	J	17.	Y
5.	O	18.	W
6.	H	19.	C
7.	K	20.	U
8.	F	21.	E
9.	X	22.	D
10.	T	23.	V
11.	R	24.	B
12.	I	25.	A
13.	S		

Visual Merchandising Facts, Activity D

1. (Name three:) educate consumers about a new item or trend or show how it can be worn or accessorized, provide pertinent information (such as price or special features), get attention for the store, introduce the store to prospective shoppers, build goodwill
2. the store's merchandise style, inventory level, and budget
3. (Any four from 22-11 in the text.)
4. (List four:) stimulate product interest, provide information, facilitate sales transactions, generate traffic flow, remind customers of planned purchases, create additional sales of impulse items
5. (Any three from 22-21 in the text.)
6. (Any four from 22-23 in the text.)
7. one-category groupings, related groupings, theme groupings, variety (assortment) groupings (Descriptions are student response.)
8. floodlighting, spotlighting, pinpointing (Descriptions are student response.)
9. functional props, decorative props, structural props (Descriptions are student response.)
10. ramped windows, elevated windows, shadowbox windows (Descriptions are student response.)

Teachers Resources

The Value of Interior Spaces, reproducible master 22-2

1. 148,500 × .20 = 29,700 square feet of sales support area.
2. 21,000 × .78 = 16,380 square feet of selling area; 21,000 × .22 = 4,620 square feet of sales support area; 16,380 + 4,620 = 21,000 total square feet of space.
3. Back quarter: $450,000 × .10 = $45,000; 3rd quarter: $450,000 × .20 = $90,000; 2nd quarter: $450,000 × .30 = $135,000; total: $45,000 + $90,000 + $135,000 + $180,000 = $450,000.
4. Main floor: $3,400,000 × .40 = $1,360,000; 2nd floor: $3,400,000 × .30 = $1,020,000; 3rd floor: $3,400,000 ×.15 = $510,000; basement: $3,400,000 × .15 = $510,000; total: $1,360,000 + $1,020,000 + $510,000 + $510,000 = $3,400,000.

Visual Merchandising Review, reproducible master 22-6

1. Visual merchandising reaches customers when they are at the store, resulting in immediate purchases.
2. merchandise and display changes
3. to place merchandise that is in greatest customer demand in prime selling spaces
4. fullness of stock and price value through quantity
5. 24 (one per inch)
6. straight arms, waterfalls, garment hangrods, and shelves
7. about five inches, or there is an understocked look and items may become out of reach
8. because they are economical
9. advertised, best-selling, high-margin, high-fashion merchandise
10. because pastel colors reflect light and dark colors absorb light
11. (Name four:) mannequins, stands, pedestals, panels, screens, steel tube forms, flat foam forms, small chairs or tables
12. to support functional and decorative props, and change the physical makeup of displays
13. (Name four:) counter signs, posters, hanging signs, banners and flags, elevator cards, easels
14. (Name three:) buyers, department heads, the merchandise manager, the display manager, display staff people
15. They use store space, require props and materials, and take time to plan, set up, and maintain
16. (Name two:) They are expensive to design, set up, and maintain. They create wear and tear on merchandise. There is bright glare off the glass.

Chapter 22 Test

1.	D	16.	T
2.	H	17.	T
3.	A	18.	F
4.	G	19.	F
5.	E	20.	T
6.	C	21.	C
7.	I	22.	D
8.	J	23.	A
9.	B	24.	B
10.	F	25.	B
11.	T	26.	A
12.	T	27.	D
13.	F	28.	D
14.	F	29.	B
15.	T	30.	C

31. (Name two:) one-category groupings, related groupings, theme groupings, variety (assortment) groupings (Descriptions are student response.)

32. Decorative props: display objects used to establish a mood or an attractive setting for merchandise being featured. Examples: mirrors, plants, artificial flowers, arches, pennants, bicycles, seashells, surfboards, packing peanuts, mobiles, books, furniture pieces, etc.

33. (Describe one of each:) Advantage: Help retailer establish and maintain a unique image; stimulate and arouse shoppers' curiosity to enter the store. Disadvantage: Expensive to design, set up, and maintain; create wear and tear on merchandise; glare of the glass for reduced display visibility.

Interior Spaces of Stores

Selling Areas:	• 75 to 80% of total space; contains merchandise for sale
	• For interaction between customers and store personnel
Sales Support Areas:	• Customer service areas—dressing rooms, cash/wrap area, complaint desk, restrooms, returns, payments
	• Merchandise service areas—goods receiving, checking and marking areas, stockrooms, alterations shop
	• Management/staff areas—clerical areas, management offices, lounges, locker rooms, conference rooms, training areas

The Value of Interior Spaces

Name_____ **Date** _____ **Period** _____

Complete the following and show your work. After finishing, discuss the value of retail interior spaces as a class. Also discuss the types of merchandise that would be placed in various locations within stores.

1. If a department store building has 148,500 square feet of space, and 80 percent of that space is devoted to selling areas, the department store has 118,800 (148,500 × .80) square feet of selling space. If the remaining 20 percent (100 percent – 80 percent) of building space is in sales support areas, how many square feet of support area are there?

   _____ square feet of sales support area

2. You are starting a new business venture, opening a specialty apparel franchise store. The franchiser recommends that 78 percent of your space be selling area. You are going to locate your store in a new mall with a space of 21,000 square feet that you can divide into selling and sales support areas. How many square feet will be in each of the areas? Also, check your work by adding the square footage of both sections together, which should equal the total square footage of the space.

   _____ square feet of selling area

   _____ square feet of sales support area

   _____ total square feet of space

3. Different locations in retail stores have different values or rent allocations. For instance, the decline in value of store selling space from front to back in a one-story shop is expressed in the "4-3-2-1 rule." In other words, 40 percent of a store's rental cost is allocated to the front quarter of the store by the entrance, 30 percent to the next quarter in from the front, 20 percent to the third quarter, and 10 percent to the back quarter. It is also expected that each quarter of the store will contribute that same percentage of sales revenue. If you expect your new franchise store to generate $450,000 in sales this year, the front quarter of the store should bring in $180,000 ($450,000 × .40) of sales. Fill in the amounts of the other spaces on the floor plan on the right.

Back of Store
- - - - - - - - - - - - - - - - - -
- - - - - - - - - - - - - - - - - -
- - - - - - - - - - - - - - - - - -
40% of sales = $180,000
——— Entrance ———

4. Different rent allocations are also assigned to locations within multilevel stores, such as department stores. For instance, a 3-story location with a basement would allocate 40 percent to the main floor, 30 percent to the second floor, and 15 percent to both the third floor and the basement. If the department store expects to have sales of $3,400,000 this year, what amounts of annual sales should be expected from each floor?

Third floor:	
Second floor:	
First floor:	
Basement:	

Merchandise Location Decisions

Merchandise location decisions depend on:

- Sales productivity ratio (rent-paying ability)

- Merchandise compatibility

- Space requirements

- Buying behavior of target customers

- Seasonality of demand

- Display requirements

Common Types of Interior Displays

Display Type	Explanation
Open display:	Merchandise is placed where customers can see, touch, and handle it.
Closed display:	Merchandise is visible, but can't be touched or handled, often for fragile or expensive items.
Wall display:	Merchandise is displayed along interior store walls, sometimes placed high for distance viewing.
Platform display:	Merchandise is shown on a built-up area or device.
Ledge display:	Merchandise is shown on ledges or other parts of the building structure.
End display:	Items are shown on an area at one end of a merchandise island or aisle.
Island display:	An open arrangement that can be viewed from all sides.
Shadowbox display:	Merchandise (usually small and expensive) is shown in a small, enclosed, box-like area with depth and a glass front.
Point-of-purchase (POP) display:	Merchandise is shown in a display provided by the manufacturer to help promote and sell its products.

Steps for Installing Window Displays

1. If possible, close window from view of passersby.

2. Remove all old merchandise, props, and fixtures.

3. Thoroughly clean the display space and replace burned-out bulbs.

4. Put new fixtures and forms into the display space.

5. Bring display merchandise into the window.

6. Place accessory merchandise and decorative props into window.

7. Place display signage appropriately.

8. Check the window to see that all details are complete.

9. Get feedback from others and approval from supervisor if needed.

Visual Merchandising Review

Name_____**Date** _____ **Period** _____

As you review the chapter, answer the following questions.

1. How is visual merchandising different from advertising? _____

    _____

    _____

    _____

2. Effective space planning for store interiors allows maximum flexibility for what?_____

    _____

    _____

3. Why do specialty stores often rotate the areas in which certain types of stock are located?_____

    _____

    _____

    _____

4. What impression is given to shoppers by an abundance of merchandise that is hung on shoulder-out hangbars?_____

    _____

    _____

    _____

5. On average, how many garments can be hung on a 24-inch-long hangbar?_____

    _____

6. What are the four most commonly used merchandise presentation fixtures in wall sections?_____

    _____

    _____

    _____

7. What is the maximum amount of space that should exist between garments hanging on wall fixtures and why? _____

    _____

    _____

    _____

8. Why are fluorescent lights used for general lighting in most retail stores?_____

    _____

9. What type of merchandise should be used for special in-store and window displays? _____

    _____

    _____

    _____

    _____

(Continued)

Name_____

10. Why is less lighting needed for displays that contain pastel colors than for those with dark colors?

_____

_____

_____

_____

11. Name at least four types of functional props for fashion displays. _____

_____

_____

_____

_____

12. What is the purpose of structural props in displays? _____

_____

_____

_____

13. Name at least four different types of signs that are used in retail stores. _____

_____

_____

_____

_____

14. For display work in large stores, name at least three types of employees that might be involved.

_____

_____

_____

_____

15. What factors make displays expensive?_____

_____

_____

_____

_____

16. Describe at least two disadvantages of window displays. _____

_____

_____

_____

Catch These Points

Name_____ **Date** _____ **Period** _____

Think about the following statements and write your reaction to each. Then discuss what you have learned in class.

1. To satisfy customer needs and retailer operations, sales support areas are placed in one of four locations: a) at the back or side edges of a store, b) in the center core, c) on one floor of a multi-level store, d) in an annex or appendage at the back of the store. _____
   _____
   _____
   _____

2. Merchandise should be grouped on the sales floor according to compatibility (what goes together). For the highest profits, lines with the highest sales productivity ratios should be located in the most valuable selling floor space. (See Chapter 19.) _____
   _____
   _____
   _____

3. Impulse goods should be placed in high exposure areas, such as along major aisles, at checkout terminals, etc. Items that shoppers will exert considerable effort to find can be placed in more remote areas. _____
   _____
   _____
   _____

4. Shoppers usually turn right when entering a store or getting off an escalator. Thus, selling space is more valuable just inside the entrance and at the top of the escalator, as well as to the right of those areas. _____
   _____
   _____
   _____

5. Complete mix-and-match merchandise fixture systems can be obtained from fixture distributors, mail-order fixture catalogs, and used fixture dealers. These systems can be fit together in many ways to offer flexibility for different merchandise and occasions._____
   _____
   _____
   _____

6. Types of display settings include realistic (actual room), semi-realistic ("vignette" setting), environmental (merchandise in use), fantasy (novel/surrealistic/whimsical), or abstract (nonrepresentative shapes, panels, arcs, etc.) settings. _____
   _____
   _____
   _____

(Continued)

Name_____

7. Sometimes display employees pose as passing customers and listen to consumers comment on their displays. Salespeople and other store employees may also be asked to critique interior and window displays._____

_____

_____

_____

8. Window display spaces should be well-ventilated to prevent the buildup of heat generated by lights and by the sun shining through the glass. Also, lights should be carefully placed for safety-never near flammable items. _____

_____

_____

_____

9. Someday, retailing might be all display without any stock. When customers see what they like, they will order to their measurements by computer the desired style number, fabric, colors, delivery, etc. Display work may become the most important part of retail sales. _____

_____

_____

_____

10. Sometimes remote displays are located away from a store, such as in an airport, hotel lobby, or convention center, to encourage visitors to the area to come to the store to shop. _____

_____

_____

_____

11. A rubber mallet (soft-surface hammer) is used to set up chrome fixtures and adjust their positions because the mallet does not nick or scratch the chrome._____

_____

_____

_____

12. Enclosed showcase displays should be well-lit, which gives the displayed merchandise an expensive image while increasing its visibility. _____

_____

_____

_____

Visual Merchandising

Name_____

Date_____ Period_____ Score_____

Chapter 22 Test

Matching: Match the following terms and identifying phrases.

_____ 1. A retail floor plan that has one or more primary aisles with secondary aisles intersecting them at right angles.

_____ 2. Store layout areas where merchandise is displayed and customers interact with sales personnel.

_____ 3. Merchandise presentation fixtures that stock large amounts of merchandise.

_____ 4. Store spaces that are devoted to customer services, merchandise receiving and distribution, management offices, and staff activities.

_____ 5. A free-flowing floor plan arrangement with informal balance.

_____ 6. Merchandise presentation fixtures that stock small amounts of merchandise that face outward toward shoppers.

_____ 7. The interior arrangement of retail facilities.

_____ 8. The physical presentation of goods in the most attractive and understandable ways in order to increase sales.

_____ 9. The style and appearance of interior furnishings.

_____ 10. The ways that goods are hung, placed on shelves, or otherwise made available for sale in retail stores.

A. capacity fixtures

B. décor

C. feature fixtures

D. grid layout

E. maze layout

F. merchandise presentation

G. sales support areas

H. selling areas

I. store layout

J. visual merchandising

True/False: Circle *T* if the statement is true or *F* if the statement is false.

T   F   11. Visual merchandising is three-dimensional and real, which is more effective than flat drawings or photos.

T   F   12. Selling floor layouts influence in-store traffic patterns, shopping atmosphere, and operational efficiency.

T   F   13. Merchandise in greatest customer demand is placed in the back since retail customers will search for it.

T   F   14. With a series of shelves or bins, large sizes are placed at the top going down to small sizes on the bottom.

T   F   15. Apparel manufacturers often supply free fixtures to stores for use with their lines.

(Continued)

Name_____

T   F   16. Displays are individual and notable physical presentations of merchandise.

T   F   17. Display employees reinforce images with the types of mannequins they show and by the manner in which the mannequins are dressed, positioned, and lit.

T   F   18. Wall washers are spotlights that focus narrow beams of light onto areas of walls.

T   F   19. Mannequins are structural props.

T   F   20. Signage is the total of all the signs of a store or location, including individual letters and complete signs.

Multiple Choice: Choose the best response. Write the letter in the space provided.

_____ 21. When designing the store layout, a planogram is drawn up to .
  A. enable ordering of the right types of merchandise
  B. spend the proper amounts on merchandise and displays
  C. show the arrangement of all selling and sales support areas
  D. All of the above.

_____ 22. Examples of retail merchandise fixtures are _____.
  A. shelves, tables, and bins
  B. rods, stands, and carousels
  C. forms, gondolas, and racks
  D. All of the above.

_____ 23. The most valuable selling area of every store is _____.
  A. near the entrance
  B. directly to the left of the entrance
  C. directly to the left of the top of the escalator
  D. halfway through the store on the center (primary) aisle

_____ 24. Shoulder-out merchandise presentation has _____.
  A. the front of hanging garments fully facing the viewer
  B. only one side of hanging garments showing from shoulder to bottom
  C. mannequins that are facing sideways in window displays
  D. folded shirts and sweaters that are overlapped flat on shelves to show only the shoulder area

_____ 25. "Slant arm" fixtures intended to hold one item per knob are called _____.
  A. A-frames
  B. waterfalls
  C. build-ups
  D. pedestal units

_____ 26. Wall standards are _____.
  A. vertical strips with holes into which various types of brackets and fixtures can be inserted
  B. uniformly sized sections of retail interior walls that are good for displays
  C. uniformly sized sections of retail interior walls that are good for merchandise presentation
  D. uniformly sized store spaces with walls dividing selling areas from sales support areas

(Continued)

Name_____

_____ 27. Lighting from beneath a display is called _____.
      A. overlighting
      B. beamspreading
      C. track lighting
      D. underlighting

_____ 28. Display work in small apparel stores _____.
      A. has the flexibility to change displays more often than large stores
      B. has a smaller amount of merchandise to choose from for displays
      C. involves fewer people
      D. All of the above.

_____ 29. One very long "run-on" window _____.
      A. should always be divided into smaller, cohesive display areas
      B. allows for more display flexibility and control than many smaller windows
      C. is not desirable for displays because it takes away too much merchandise from the selling floor
      D. is requested by most discount stores

_____ 30. The two main types of display windows are _____.
      A. ramped windows and shadowbox windows
      B. elevated windows and semi-enclosed windows
      C. enclosed windows and open windows
      D. island windows and closed windows

Essay Questions: Provide complete responses to the following questions or statements.

31. Name and briefly describe two types of merchandise display groupings.

32. Describe and give two examples of decorative props for retail displays.

33. Describe one major advantage and one major disadvantage of retail window displays.

CHAPTER 23

Special Event Fashion Shows

Objectives

After studying this chapter, students will be able to

- explain the many purposes of fashion shows.
- list the main types of fashion shows.
- identify the different aspects of planning for fashion shows.
- discuss the coordination of merchandise and models for the final lineup of fashion shows.
- summarize the coordination of the physical layout, music, choreography, and commentary of fashion shows.
- explain the aspects of promoting and presenting a smooth fashion show performance.
- describe the follow-up and evaluation procedures for fashion shows.

Teaching Materials

Text, pages 460–484
   Fashion Terms
   Fashion Review
   Fashion in Action
Student Workbook
   A. *Fashion Show Planning*
   B. *Fashion Event Fill-in-the-Blanks*
   C. *Setting the Groundwork*
   D. *Produce a Fashion Show*
Teacher's Resources
   Fashion Show Tasks, reproducible master 23-1
   *Benefits of Student/Retailer Cooperative
      Fashion Shows*, transparency master 23-2
   Gaining Retailer Understanding, reproducible
      master 23-3
   *Possible Configurations for Fashion Show
      Runways*, transparency master 23-4
   Promoting a Fashion Show, reproducible
      master 23-5
   Fashion Show Review, reproducible master 23-6
   More Fashion Show Thinking, reproducible
      master 23-7
   Chapter 23 Test

Introductory Activities

1. Have students discuss the general category of special events, especially in relation to fashion merchandising. Ask students to describe as many retail special events as they can think of other than fashion shows (such as designer or celebrity visits, flower shows, art exhibits, product demonstrations, contests, entertainment, and charity sale days). Also have students describe how they think the events build image and enhance sales in stores.
2. Show students a video about retail special events. *Promotion: How Retailers Use Special Events to Improve Market Share* is available from D.E. Visuals.
3. Ask students if they have ever attended a live fashion show. Ask those who have attended to describe their experiences. Also have students describe fashion shows they have seen on television, such as designer collection showings.
4. *Fashion Show Tasks*, reproducible master 23-1. Small groups of students are asked to discuss fashion show productions and fill out a chart with as many specific tasks as they can think of for given fashion show committees. Then they are to save the paper for discussion later in the chapter.

Strategies to Reteach, Reinforce, Enrich, and Extend Text Concepts

Fashion Shows Serve Many Purposes

5. **RT** Discuss consumer fashion shows presented by retailers. Have students describe why the selling of fashions that are modeled on live figures is more effective than visual merchandising or advertisements.

6. **RF** Discuss why the dynamic mixture of entertainment and fashion in fashion shows is still favored by designers as the best way to introduce buyers, trade media, and others to their latest collections.

7. **ER** Discuss the different types of cooperative fashion shows. Add another type of cooperative fashion show to the list—that of students and several retailers putting one on together. This is often the type of fashion show presented by fashion classes in schools.

8. **EX** *Benefits of Student/Retailer Cooperative Fashion Shows*, transparency master 23-2. While showing this transparency to the class, have students discuss each of the points presented. Also have students discuss the advantages of working with only one to three retailers for a show rather than many.

Types of Fashion Shows

9. **RT** Discuss the main types of fashion shows with the class, including production shows, formal runway shows, informal shows, and tearoom modeling.

10. **RF** Ask students to discuss the availability of televised and Internet fashion shows that enable most people to view new fashions. Also discuss charity shows (benefits) that are held to raise money for not-for-profit organizations such as hospitals and charitable foundations.

11. **RT** Ask students to explain how choreography and commentary can enhance fashion shows.

Planning Fashion Shows

12. **RF** Discuss the fact that putting on fashion shows takes lots of detail planning, arrangements, and hard work. Also discuss that good shows look like they are "easy to produce" to the audience. Have students relate the amount of preparation work to the smoothest-looking shows.

13. **RT** Discuss the duties performed by the fashion show coordinator. Discuss the responsibility and pressure on this person for an effective, flawless show.

14. **RT** Have students form into the same small groups as they were in when they filled out reproducible master 23-1, *Fashion Show Tasks*, before studying the chapter. Have all groups compare their chart with text illustration 23-7 to add, subtract, and discuss the jobs that fall under each fashion show committee.

15. **RT** Ask students to describe the difference between a guaranteed audience and a created audience for fashion shows.

16. **ER** Write the 12 months of the year on the board. Then have the class come up with appropriate themes for fashion shows given in each of the months. More than one theme may be given for each month.

17. **RT** Discuss the timing and location of fashion shows with the class.

18. **RT** Ask students to discuss safety and security considerations for fashion shows.

19. **RT** With students looking at text illustration 23-10, go through each individual item listed. Have students discuss fashion show costs and their importance to the show.

20. **RT** *Fashion Show Planning*, Activity A, WB. Students are asked to answer given questions about planning fashion shows.

21. **ER** *Gaining Retailer Understanding*, reproducible master 23-3. After doing the preliminary planning for a student/retailer fashion show, reproduce this for students. Ask students to use this as a guide for communicating with apparel retailers who are approached to participate in a cooperative fashion show. Students should take notes on other sheets of paper (each with the name of the retailer at the top) as they have discussions with personnel from different stores. If a fashion show will be held using student-made fashions, this may not be relevant.

Coordinating Merchandise and Models

22. **RT** Discuss fashion show merchandise selection, including why items should be chosen that match the age, sex, lifestyle, and spending habits of the audience.

23. **RT** Ask students to describe an ideal chart and why it is important in fashion show merchandise planning. Also discuss the merchandise pull for a fashion show while students look at the merchandise loan record in text illustration 23-14.

24. **RF** Call on individual students to describe each of the following: model list, model order, lineup, and fittings. Ask students to expand on the explanations in each case. Then discuss fitting sheets with the class looking at text illustration 23-17 and individual model lineup sheets with the class looking at text illustration 23-21.

Coordinating Physical Layout, Music, Choreography, and Commentary

25. **RT** Discuss the importance of the relationship between the layout of the site facilities to a smooth fashion show performance.

26. **EX** *Possible Configurations for Fashion Show Runways*, transparency master 23-4. Explain to students that most fashion show runways project into the audience area in a straight line. Then show them this transparency, discussing the runway options shown, especially for particular sites, events, and choreography. Discuss the importance of audience visibility of the runway in relation to the size and shape of the auditorium, retail store, restaurant, manufacturer's showroom, or hotel ballroom. Have students come up with other ideas for runway configurations.

27. **RF** Have students draw floorplan diagrams of an open ballroom that is set up with theater seating and table seating. Also have students draw the stage and runway, as well as the location of the dressing area.

28. **RF** Ask students to describe the types of music they would include in the music mix for different types of fashion shows. Also have them tell in what order the music would be arranged.

29. **RT** Discuss full commentaries, partial commentaries, and ad-lib commentaries. Discuss the importance of flexibility in using commentary cards.

30. **ER** Have students write descriptive words and phrases on the board about the latest fashions. Additional terms might be obtained from current fashion magazines. Discuss with the class how such a list can be helpful when writing a fashion show commentary. Any extra information might be included on filler cards, including how long a trend has been around and the variations that have occurred from season to season.

Promoting and Presenting the Show

31. **RT** Discuss with the class public service announcements, press shows, pasteups, and tear sheets. Also discuss the planning and coordination of invitations, tickets, and programs.

32. **RF** *Promoting a Fashion Show*, reproducible master 23-5. If no fashion show will be presented by the class, divide the class into five groups and use this as an activity that reinforces the content of the chapter. If the class will be presenting a fashion show, give this form to the Promotion Coordinator to divide duties among promotion committee members.

33. **ER** If planning a newsworthy fashion show, try to encourage representatives from the local press to attend. This can result in favorable publicity.

Rehearsals and Show Time!

34. **RT** Discuss fashion show rehearsals with the class. Also discuss the functions of dressers and starters.

35. **ER** Show students a video about giving fashion shows. *Behind the Scenes: The Fashion Show* is available from D.E. Visuals.

Follow-Up and Evaluation

36. **RT** Have students discuss the importance of follow-up and evaluation of fashion shows. Also discuss after-show cleanup such as striking the stage, stacking and storing the chairs, disposing of trash, sweeping the floor, and returning props and equipment.

37. **RT** *Fashion Event Fill-in-the-Blanks*, Activity B, WB. Students are to place correct chapter terms into given sentences. All terms asked for are in bold print or italics in the text chapter.

38. **ER** *Setting the Groundwork*, Activity C, WB. With the class divided into six groups, each group is to develop a specific form that was not shown in the text. The different types of forms are listed in this activity and described in the text. If required, students are to do further research. (It is not necessary to fill the forms out with any specific details.)

39. **ER** *Produce a Fashion Show*, Activity D, WB. The entire class is to be involved in producing a fashion show. The class is to assign jobs to students, prepare all forms, and accomplish all tasks of putting on a real show.

40. **RT** *Fashion Show Review*, reproducible master 23-6. Use these additional chapter review questions as homework or as an optional extra credit assignment.

41. **EX** *More Fashion Show Thinking*, reproducible master 23-7. Students are asked to think about given statements and write their reactions to each. Then students are to discuss what they have learned with classmates.

Additional Enrichment Activities

Research

42. Have students research the history of fashion shows, starting with the stationary doll exhibits of previous centuries that spread fashion news.

Have students present their findings in a report to the class. Visual aids should be included if possible.

43. Have students do library or Internet research about the fashion shows held at the most recent fashion week in Paris, Milan, London, New York, Los Angeles, Dallas, or other market center. Ask students to report on their findings.

Projects

44. Have students decide on a theme for a fashion show, including three main categories within the show. Then have students cut at least 21 pictures from fashion magazines, mail order catalogs, and/or home sewing pattern books. By sequencing the fashions and thinking about descriptions, a lineup can be established. Have students mount their lineups on the bulletin board with headings that describe the theme and main categories of the show. If you want to enlarge this project, also have students write commentaries about the fashions. They can read the commentaries as they show their bulletin board display to the rest of the class, as if it is a real fashion show.

45. Have a small group of students study about and practice how to model. Then have them run a modeling "clinic" to teach the rest of the class what they have learned about modeling. The clinic might also include group modeling with several models responding to the lead model according to choreography. Additionally, if possible, invite a model, modeling instructor, or modeling agency employee to class to speak to and work with the students.

46. Have students interview the person in charge of producing fashion shows at a local department or specialty store. Ask the person to describe the duties accomplished by all people who help plan and present fashion shows. Ask questions such as how they protect show merchandise and who they use for models. Write a complete report about the interview, relating the information to the content of this chapter.

Answer Key

Text

Fashion Review, pages 484

1. (Name five:) fashion shows, visits by designers or celebrities, art exhibits, product demonstrations, contests, entertainment, flower shows, charity sale days

2. couture designer collections shown to elite customers and the press; apparel manufacturers' lines shown to retail buyers; retail merchandise shown to consumers

3. production show; formal runway show; informal fashion show

4. An older audience wants softer music and a more explicit, detailed commentary. A younger audience needs louder, faster music with more entertaining action and less commentary.

5. 45 minutes, because it fits the attention span of most audiences

6. A large room can be set up for a formal show. Informal modeling can take place on the floor of the store. A runway may be set up near where the merchandise is located.

7. ticket sales, money from cooperative sponsors, or allocations from the company's total promotion budget

8. items the audience will buy and wear

9. In the first and last categories, to capture the attention of the audience and to leave a feeling of excitement and urgency to try on and buy some of the garments.

10. both the retailer and the fashion show merchandise committee

11. (Name three:) retail store employees; members of the sponsoring civic organization; modeling schools; students in fashion, acting, or dancing schools

12. (Name four:) walking, timing, posing, turning, and facial expressions

13. to give models the maximum time to change their outfits between appearances and to recognize who they follow in the lineup

14. for gathering accessories, organizing alterations, and writing the commentary

15. To plan the best design, dimensions, lighting, and building materials needed. Also, to help in planning models' entrances, exits, choreography, and timing for the show.

16. It is convenient, less expensive, and can provide a variety of sound.

17. stop, turn, pause, and pose

18. the show narrator

19. because the audience already has printed buying guides that contain information about each item

20. physically disassembling the set and returning props and equipment

Student Workbook

Fashion Show Planning, Activity A

1. the owner of the shop

2. merchandise coordinator, model coordinator, stage manager, promotion coordinator, commentator
3. a reminder list of details to be completed, follow-up dates for various tasks, and future needs for the show; after the show it is a helpful resource for planning future shows
4. with mailings to lists of store customers or general publicity and advertising to the public
5. The courtesy promotes the cooperative sponsor, can attract a larger audience if the name is well known, and can help the image of both the vendor and the store.
6. It should not conflict with other events, and it should take into account travel time to and from the show for models, show workers, and the audience.
7. where the audience is and the purpose, type, and size of the show
8. adequate seating arrangements, food service, and provisions for sound, lighting, staging, and dressing areas
9. what the site management will provide as far as room set-up, food and beverages, public address system, clean-up
10. policies about human safety and signed agreements about merchandise and equipment security
11. (Name three:) by preventing loose electrical cords from crossing the floor, meeting all fire code requirements, clearly marking emergency exits, spacing aisles for easy access
12. from higher sales after the show
13. the season, day of the week, and time of the day

Fashion Event Fill-in-the Blanks, Activity B

1. commentary
2. fittings
3. pasteup
4. special events
5. fashion shows
6. dressers
7. created
8. runways
9. choreography
10. lineup
11. pivots
12. striking the stage
13. theater seating
14. production show
15. cooperative
16. music mix
17. press show

18. tearoom
19. table seating
20. formal runway show
21. starters
22. merchandise pull
23. informal
24. guaranteed
25. rehearsals
26. coordinator
27. tear sheet
28. ideal chart
29. consumer
30. model list

Teacher's Resources

Fashion Show Review, reproducible master 23-6

1. by showing different brands, features of private label items, or special merchandise offerings
2. so they can show their creations and learn how to produce shows (model, plan, present, and evaluate fashion productions)
3. It is established before the show is organized and will attend regardless of the show.
4. because the amount of money going out must not exceed money available to use
5. the site and a caterer
6. choosing the best garments, shoes, and accessories for the show
7. 45 to 90
8. by color, styling details, design sophistication
9. people who wear garments and accessories to promote them
10. (Name three:) attractive and well-groomed; good hair and skin; well proportioned figure that fits a standard clothing size; a fashion sense; a cooperative, professional attitude
11. (Name two:) training, experience, representation by agencies
12. all model's names, telephone numbers, and apparel sizes
13. a brief garment description, category, model's name, and lineup number
14. (Name four:) tables, chairs, mirrors, clothing racks, sheet on the floor, full-length mirror at the exit
15. to add interest
16. model entrances, cues, runway routines, and exits
17. They list the major details of garments in outline form or short sections of script.
18. to make the next show even better

Chapter 23 Test

1.	A	11.	F	21.	B
2.	C	12.	T	22.	D
3.	E	13.	F	23.	C
4.	B	14.	T	24.	D
5.	G	15.	F	25.	B
6.	I	16.	T	26.	A
7.	J	17.	T	27.	D
8.	H	18.	F	28.	D
9.	D	19.	T	29.	D
10.	F	20.	F	30.	C

31. (List four:) set/runway construction, props, music, backstage work, sound, lighting, safety/security
32. full commentaries, partial commentaries, ad-lib commentaries
33. A pasteup is a draft of a print advertisement (to see how it will look in print). A tear sheet is an advertisement torn directly from the newspaper in which it ran (after it has been in print).

Fashion Show Tasks

Name _____ **Date** _____ **Period** _____

Working in small groups, discuss fashion show productions and fill out this chart with as many specific tasks as you can think of that would need to be done by each of the following fashion show committees. Save this activity for discussion later in the chapter.

Committee:	Tasks to Be Performed
Merchandise:	
Model:	
Promotion:	
Staging:	
Commentary:	
Hospitality:	

Benefits of Student/ Retailer Cooperative Fashion Shows*

Student Benefits	Retailer Benefits
Knowledge of retail operations	Promotes store name and image
Valuable industry contacts	Promotes lines carried
Show production planning skills	Adds creative merchandising ideas
Show production presentation skills	Solicits potential customers
Group teamwork cooperation	Increases confidence and respect
Personal responsibility	Adds to community goodwill
Outlet for creative expression	
Increased self-confidence	

*Partially based on work done by Dr. Renee D. Howerton, Louisiana State University

Gaining Retailer Understanding

Name_____ Date _____ Period _____

When producing a student/retailer cooperative fashion show, communication between the parties involved is of primary importance. To counteract misunderstandings and problems, use the following questions as a foundation for this communication*. Add other questions as needed for specific circumstances.

1. What expectations do retailers have for their business as a result of participating in a student fashion show? What criteria will these retailers use to measure success of the show against their expectations?

2. Are cooperating retailers aware of the capabilities of the students involved? Are the retailers aware of the limitations of the students?

3. Are the retailers willing to provide some funding for the production as well as merchandise? How much money will be available and how will it be distributed? Could retailers provide a location, audio system, runway platform, chairs, or any other service or equipment for the production?

4. Are the retailers willing to provide direction to help the students? In what way (such as guidance with lighting, sound, and seating arrangements) and by whom?

5. With whom at each retailer will the students be working? Are there specific times of the day or evening that are best for meetings and fittings?

6. How far ahead of the show will students be allowed to select the fashion show garments and have model fittings?

7. Are the retailers willing to actively solicit community support for the production? What promotion might retailers do for the fashion show?

8. Will the retailers do the handling, delivery, and return of fashion show garments or must students arrange to do that?

9. What are the retailer's policies concerning merchandise or equipment damaged as a result of the fashion show?

10. Does the retailer have any specific forms that must be signed by students or the school? If so, can they be evaluated before the cooperative effort is undertaken?

11. Other subjects to discuss for good communications and cooperation: _____

_____

_____

_____

_____

*Partially based on work done by Dr. Renee D. Howerton, Louisiana State University.

Possible Configurations for Fashion Show Runways

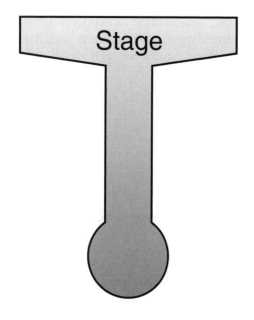

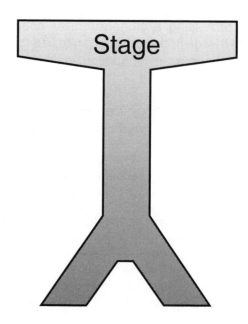

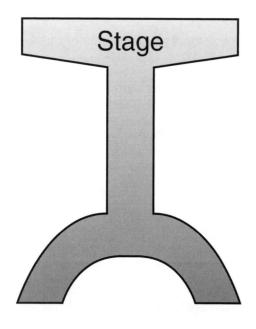

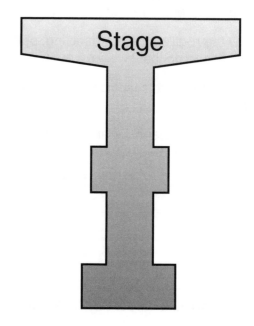

Promoting a Fashion Show

Name_____ **Date** _____ **Period** _____

Divide into five groups. Each group is responsible for accomplishing one of the tasks listed below. When finished, each group should present its work to the rest of the class. (This can also be used as a planning form for the promotion committee if a full fashion show is being presented, such as with Workbook Activity D.)

1. Find publicity or advertisements for fashion shows and other retail special events. Mount and label all the different examples and discuss the merits of each for different situations.

2. Plan press releases for specific mediums (newspaper, radio, etc.) as publicity for a fashion show. Write news articles and record the radio or TV releases as news stories.

3. Develop a newspaper advertisement and a radio commercial for a fashion show. Make an actual pasteup of the newspaper ad and record 30-second and 60-second versions of the radio ad.

4. Design the ticket for a fashion show, possibly to include names and addresses of attendees for a mailing list and/or to plan to give out door prizes. Also design the program to coordinate with the tickets. Include credit for contributors (especially if stores loan clothes), paid ads to help defray costs, a guide to the merchandise presented in the show, and names of committee members.

5. Design posters to promote a fashion show. Decide where the posters would be placed. Also design invitations to the show. Decide how and to whom the invitations would be distributed.

I am doing activity #_____ in the above list.

Names of others in my group are:

_____

_____

Background material in the text is on page: _____

I am specifically responsible to accomplish:

_____

_____

_____

_____

_____

_____

_____

_____

_____

_____

_____

_____

Fashion Show Review

Name_____**Date**_____ **Period**_____

As you review the text chapter, respond to the following.

1. How can fashion shows indicate the depth and breadth of merchandise carried by retailers? ____

_____

_____

_____

2. Why are fashion shows produced by fashion students?_____

_____

_____

_____

3. Describe a guaranteed audience._____

_____

_____

_____

4. Why is fashion show financial planning based on estimated revenues? _____

_____

_____

_____

5. An advance deposit is required for reserving what two services for a fashion show? _____

_____

_____

6. What does fashion show merchandise selection involve? _____

_____

_____

_____

7. How many outfits would typically be shown in a 45-minute fashion show? _____

_____

8. Within the merchandise categories of a fashion show, how might garments be organized? _____

_____

_____

9. Define *fashion models.*_____

_____

_____

(Continued)

Name_____

10. Name three attributes that fashion show models should have. _____
_____
_____
_____

11. Name two attributes that professional models have and amateur models do not have._____
_____
_____

12. What does a model list include?_____
_____
_____
_____

13. What information should fashion show garment tags include?_____
_____
_____
_____

14. Name at least four items that are in model dressing areas. _____
_____
_____
_____

15. Why should lighting change on cue as the show progresses?_____
_____
_____
_____

16. What specific actions does the show choreographer plan? _____
_____
_____
_____

17. Describe partial commentaries. _____
_____
_____
_____

18. Why is an evaluation of a fashion show helpful? _____
_____
_____
_____

More Fashion Show Thinking

Name_____ **Date** _____ **Period** _____

Think about the following statements and write your reaction to each. Then discuss what you have learned with the class.

1. Depending on the experience, knowledge, and budget of fashion show presenters, putting on an informal show might be preferable to a production show. It is wiser to do an excellent job with a small show than a poor job with a large show. _____

_____

_____

2. A more fashion-forward or younger audience can view merchandise at a faster pace than less-fashionable or older people. _____

_____

_____

3. For fashion show commentaries, index cards are often considered better than sheets of paper that rustle over the loud speaker._____

_____

_____

4. The use of colored lights on a fashion show background can set scenes without props. Use yellow for sports and swimwear, violet for formal wear, pink or red for lingerie/intimate apparel, and cool blue for outerwear. _____

_____

_____

5. An effective way to show the final lineup for a fashion show is with Polaroid or digital pictures of each outfit, taken at fittings or the rehearsal. Printouts of these are then arranged in order on a large poster with comments added. _____

_____

_____

6. Fashion show models often have only two minutes to change outfits, yet when modeling out on the runway they are supposed to look calm, composed, and perfectly "put together."_____

_____

_____

7. To develop a mailing list from a fashion show, part of the ticket can be filled out with each attendee's name and address. When the ticket is ripped at the door, one section is kept by the attendee and the section with the name/address is retained for the company's list. A number can also be put on both ends of the ticket for a door prize drawing._____

_____

_____

(Continued)

Name_____

8. Lighting changes in fashion shows may consist of changing the direction of the lights and filters to change the degree of brightness. Prolonged exposure to the same, even lighting can cause viewers to be insensitive to what is going on. _____

_____

_____

9. Fashion show commentaries are somewhat less emphasized lately, with audiences more stimulated by seeing details visually than from hearing descriptions. _____

_____

_____

10. Before a fashion show starts, models have more time to leisurely get into their first outfit. However, once dressed, they must not sit, smoke, eat, or drink at all. Merchandise must look fresh on the runway and be able to go back into stock for sale after the show. _____

_____

_____

11. Rather than having models run down a hallway to a dressing room, an empty corner backstage may be adapted as the models' dressing area. All equipment, garments, and mirrors are placed behind screens. However, everyone must be quiet or the audience will hear them! _____

_____

_____

12. Fashion shows often feature school clothes in August for back-to-school, evening gowns in December for New Year's Eve, spring suits in March for Easter, and swimwear in June. _____

_____

_____

13. When a fashion show is divided into several different segments, each garment is placed into one particular segment where it fits the best. This is called *slotting*. Then the lineup is decided._____

_____

_____

14. For the various segments of a fashion show, "scenes" can be set with roll-up (and down) blinds— bamboo blinds for beach/resort wear, Austrian blinds for formals/bridals, and Roman shades for daytime dresses and suits. Add some potted plants and the stage is set!_____

_____

_____

15. Stairs, ramps, platforms, risers, and turntables always work in fashion shows. However, they should never be too steep for model safety and walking ease. Archways, doorways, beaded curtains, and the opening of curtains work when the models make their entrances._____

_____

_____

16. The order of the garment designs in a collection showing is called the *run of show* in industry lingo.

_____

_____

Special Event Fashion Shows

Name_____

Date_____ **Period**_____ **Score**_____

Chapter 23 Test

Matching: Match the following terms and identifying phrases.

_____ 1. The planned arrangement of movement, such as with specific dance steps or gestured moves in a fashion show.

_____ 2. A fashion show audience that is established after the show is planned as a result of publicity and advertising.

_____ 3. The trying on of merchandise by models ahead of a fashion show to see how each garment looks and fits.

_____ 4. A spoken explanation of what is going on in a fashion show, especially pointing out specific features of each outfit being modeled.

_____ 5. A fashion show planning device that names all merchandise categories to be presented and the number of garments to be selected per category.

_____ 6. The removing of fashion show items from the retail sales floor to a show storage area.

_____ 7. People who cue fashion show models onto the stage in the correct order and at the right time, guided by the lineup and commentary script.

_____ 8. The order in which outfits will appear in a fashion show.

_____ 9. People who help fashion show models change and care for the clothes.

_____ 10. A fashion show audience that is established before the show is organized and will attend regardless of the show.

A. choreography

B. commentary

C. created audience

D. dressers

E. fittings

F. guaranteed audience

G. ideal chart

H. lineup

I. merchandise pull

J. starters

True/False: Circle *T* if the statement is true or *F* if the statement is false.

T   F   11. Special events are theatrical presentations of apparel and accessories on live models.

T   F   12. The person in charge of the entire fashion show presentation is the fashion show coordinator.

T   F   13. People will travel farther to see smaller, more casual fashion shows.

T   F   14. Fashion show merchandise selection involves choosing the best garments and accessories for the show.

(Continued)

Name_____

T F 15. A merchandise loan record gives details about where the items are kept after they are borrowed.

T F 16. Fashion models are the people who wear garments and accessories to promote them.

T F 17. Individual model lineup sheets help models clarify their order of appearance and outfits.

T F 18. The stage is an elevated walkway for the models that usually projects out into the audience seating area.

T F 19. The music mix is the combination of different music selections to create specific moods.

T F 20. Pivots are circular spins that models do just before leaving the view of the audience for one last look.

Multiple Choice: Choose the best response. Write the letter in the space provided.

_____ 21. Consumer fashion shows are presented by _____.
A. retailers to their salespeople to inform them about trends for consumers
B. retailers to consumers to promote themselves and their merchandise
C. consumers as entertainment at hospitals and nursing homes
D. All of the above.

_____ 22. An example of a cooperative fashion show that promotes both businesses is a show cosponsored by a _____.
A. designer/manufacturer with a retailer that sells the designer's/manufacturer's merchandise
B. fashion magazine with a retailer that carries the trends or lines featured in the magazine
C. home sewing pattern company with a fabric store that sells the patterns and fabrics that have been made into garments from the patterns
D. All of the above.

_____ 23. Models walking through the manufacturer's showroom or the sales floor of a retail store is a(n) _____ show.
A. production fashion
B. formal runway
C. informal fashion
D. tearoom modeling

_____ 24. The fashion show committee that oversees the site reservation and room/table decorations is the _____ committee.
A. merchandise
B. promotion
C. model/commentary
D. hospitality

(Continued)

Name_____

_____ 25. The first step in planning a fashion show budget is to _____.
  A. figure out expected expenditures by adding the estimates from all committees
  B. forecast expected revenues for the show
  C. analyze the budget from the previously presented fashion show and increase it slightly
  D. analyze the budget from the previously presented fashion show and cut costs slightly

_____ 26. Merchandise categories in a fashion show _____.
  A. should have the strongest fashion statements in the first and last categories
  B. usually progress from the most dramatic and formal to the most casual
  C. should be flexible for last minute changes of categories
  D. All of the above.

_____ 27. Fitting sheets are used for _____.
  A. preparing the lineup
  B. gathering accessories and writing the commentary
  C. organizing alterations that are done to make garments fit properly
  D. All of the above.

_____ 28. A fashion show commentator _____.
  A. is the show narrator
  B. describes the clothes being modeled
  C. interprets fashion trends for the audience
  D. All of the above.

_____ 29. Commentary cards _____.
  A. may be prepared during the fittings and used for the narration of the show
  B. include a description of the garment, accessories, and special selling features of each outfit
  C. include the model's name, show category, and lineup number
  D. All of the above.

_____ 30. Striking the stage refers to _____.
  A. drawing the configuration of the stage for the set design crew
  B. persons involved with the production evaluating the show after it is finished
  C. physically disassembling the set and returning props and equipment
  D. refusing to build the stage until the rehearsal schedule has been finalized

Essay Questions: Provide complete responses to the following questions or statements.

31. List at least four areas of responsibility that fall within the staging committee.

32. Name the three main types of commentaries that are used for fashion shows.

33. What is the difference between a print advertisement pasteup and tear sheet?

PART SEVEN

Fashion Business in Today's World

A Global Perspective

Objectives

After studying this chapter, students will be able to

→ cite U.S. and world trade trends and policy.

→ explain the relationship of textiles and apparel to developing nations.

→ identify the world's major trading blocs.

→ describe international sourcing for U.S. fashion importing.

→ point out international market opportunities for U.S. fashion exporting.

→ explain how to discover offshore sources and opportunities.

Teaching Materials

Text, pages 486–504
  Fashion Terms
  Fashion Review
  Fashion in Action
Student Workbook
  A. *Global Review*
  B. *Global Differences*
  C. *Analyzing a Fashion Trade Article*
  D. *Discussing Global Trade*
  E. *Researching Global Fashion*
Teacher's Resources
  Possible Ways to Evaluate Soft Goods Imports, transparency master 24-1
  Measuring Industry Data, transparency master 24-2

Results of the Elimination of Quotas, transparency master 24-3
Market Share for Countries of U.S. Imports, transparency master 24-4
Major Apparel-Producing Countries in Asia, transparency master 24-5
Approximate Textile/Apparel Labor Costs, transparency master 24-6
Free Trade/Protectionism Differences, transparency master 24-7
Business/Economic Effects of Imports on U.S. Textile/Apparel Manufacturing, transparency master 24-8
Advantages/Appeal of Imports, transparency master 24-9A
Disadvantages/Problems with Imports, transparency master 24-9B
Global Business Considerations, reproducible master 24-10
Global Business Discussion Topics, reproducible master 24-11
Chapter 24 Test

Introductory Activities

1. Ask students to come to class with a list of at least 10 foreign-produced apparel items they own and note the country from which each item came. Have students compare their lists with those of classmates. Ask students if they think they are typical apparel consumers. Also have the students give their thoughts about imports in relation to the strength of the U.S. economy and its textile/apparel businesses.

2. From annual reports that have been gathered in previous chapters, have students analyze what companies do importing, exporting, or have operations in other countries. Include the results of these investigations in a discussion of global business practices.

3. Discuss with the class how communication capabilities and transportation have made it easier for global fashion companies to have customers, competitors, suppliers, facilities, and investors throughout the world. Also discuss how international trade has recently grown faster for fashion goods than for other commodities.

Strategies to Reteach, Reinforce, Enrich, and Extend Text Concepts

Trade Trends and Policy

4. **EX** *Possible Ways to Evaluate Soft Goods Imports,* transparency master 24-1. Show this transparency as a basis of a discussion about why square meter equivalents are the best method of evaluating textile/apparel imports.

5. **EX** *Measuring Industry Data,* transparency master 24-2. After going through the information on this transparency, have students discuss why it is helpful to categorize types of apparel by NAICS number, as well as to calculate SMEs when analyzing import issues.

6. **RT** Have the students differentiate between free trade and protectionism.

7. **RF** With the class looking at text Chart 24-3, have students individually discuss each of the barriers to free trade.

8. **RF** *Results of the Elimination of Quotas,* transparency master 24-3. After discussing the definition of "quotas" with the class, from text Chart 24-3, use this transparency to evaluate the good and bad effects of the elimination of quotas and company strategy needed to succeed with the situation.

9. **RT** With the class looking at text Chart 24-4, have students individually discuss each of the arguments for and against protectionism. This can be used as a review activity if the issue of free trade has been debated in the class, as suggested at the end of the chapter in Fashion in Action #2.

10. **RF** *Market Share of Countries of U.S. Imports,* transparency master 24-4. Have students define *market disruption* and relate the effect of increasing import penetration to market disruption. Ask students to describe international diplomacy, transshipping, and dumping. Also have students go through the reasons companies dump products, shown in text Illustration 24-5.

11. **RT** Describe to the class how the World Trade Organization is reducing trade barriers around the world. Bring newspaper, Internet, and magazine articles about the WTO to class for students to read and discuss.

12. **ER** Discuss with the class the fact that the American Apparel and Footwear Association now admits non-U.S.-based companies as members. Emphasize how this reflects the current global nature of the U.S. apparel and footwear industry.

The Relationship of Textiles/ Apparel to Developing Nations

13. **ER** Lead a class discussion about textile and apparel manufacturing continually evolving from country to country as nations emerge. Ask students why wages in emerging countries eventually go up, or why cheap labor in emerging countries may only be a temporary condition. Relate the discussion to standards of living, costs of doing business, infrastructure, trade, foreign currency exchange, and bartering.

14. **RT** Ask students to describe structural adjustment and comparative advantage.

15. **RF** Have the class discuss information that should be obtained before trading with developing nations. Ask students to describe aspects of political stability, economic climate, infrastructure, and culture that are important for doing business with foreign countries.

The World's Major Trade Regions

16. **RT** Have students define the term *trading bloc*. Then have students review the world's main trading blocs by discussing text Illustration 24-8.

17. **RF** Have students review text Illustration 24-9 and then discuss marketing strategies of Japan.

18. **EX** Ask students to discuss the fact that Japan accomplished in 10 years what the U.S. did in 50 years and Great Britain did in 100 years.

19. **ER** *Major Apparel-Producing Countries in Asia,* transparency master 24-5. Use this transparency as a basis of discussion about the apparel manufacturing done in Asian countries, mostly to export to Western countries. Especially note the large numbers across the chart for China, compared to other countries.

20. **EX** Have a small group of students study further and report to the class on the European Union (EU). Have another small group of students study further and report to the class on the North American Free Trade Agreement (NAFTA). Then have the rest of the class evaluate the parallels

between the two as related to fashion marketing, including importing and exporting.

21. **RF** Have students discuss the Caribbean Basin Trade Partnership Act (CPTPA), the Dominican Republic-Central America Free Trade Agreement (DR-CAFTA), value added, and twin plant programs. Discuss why the more value countries can add to products, the higher their standard of living can become. After defining *parity*, ask students their opinions about granting parity to Caribbean and Latin American countries. Discuss why helping our neighbors might help or hurt our economy. Also discuss the advantage of close proximity to the U.S. market and lower costs than importing goods from Asia.

International Sourcing for U.S. Fashion Importing

22. **EX** *Approximate Textile/Apparel Labor Costs*, transparency master 24-6. Use this transparency as a basis of discussion about labor costs. Have students notice the countries that have higher and lower textile/apparel manufacturing labor rates than the U.S. To relate the information to NAFTA, have students find where the wages of Canada and Mexico fall in relation to the U.S. Discuss the opportunity for products made in this hemisphere to replace imports from the Far East. Tell students that since the passage of NAFTA, apparel industry employment has decreased in the U.S. and Canada and increased in Mexico. Also have students discuss labor rates of the other major trading blocs of the world.

23. **RF** *Free Trade/Protectionism Differences*, transparency master 24-7. Show this transparency and have students discuss how manufacturers, retailers, and consumers feel toward free trade and protectionism, and the reasons why.

24. **EX** Obtain international sourcing information for students to analyze. Suggestions are *The International Dictionary of Fashion Apparel Terminology*, *The Clothesource Handbook of Apparel Sourcing* (both on www.Amazon.com), and materials about The Apparel Sourcing Show (www.apparelexpo.com) or The Apparel Conference of the Americas: One Region…One Market…One Source (www.aapnetwork.net). Show these to the class and ask students to discuss their content.

25. **ER** *Business/Economic Effects of Imports on U.S. Textile/Apparel Manufacturing*, transparency master 24-8. Use this transparency as a basis of discussion about the weakening effects that imports have had on U.S. textile and apparel manufacturing as well as the country as a whole. Ask students to thoroughly discuss each of the points summarized on the transparency.

26. **RT** Ask students to describe the specific methods of offshore sourcing such as purchasing through domestic wholesale importers, buying directly from foreign sources, using foreign contractors, licensing agreements, franchising, joint ventures, and company-owned foreign facilities. During the discussion, make sure the meanings of *import merchants*, *resident sales agents*, *import commission houses*, *export merchants*, *export sales representatives*, and *wholly-owned subsidiaries* are understood.

27. **RT** *Advantages/Appeal of Imports and Disadvantages/Problems with Imports*, transparency masters 24-9A and 24-9B. Choose two small groups of students. Have the first group show transparency 24-9A with students clarifying each of the points in detail. Have the next group show transparency 24-9B with students clarifying each of those points in detail. Then hold a general class debate about the advantages and disadvantages of importing fashion apparel. Ask the class for ideas on how to balance needs in the U.S. with those of other countries and how to promote economic development abroad without disrupting the U.S. economy.

International Market Opportunities for U.S. Fashion Exporting

28. **RT** Have the class discuss text Illustrations 24-16 and 24-17 as they think about exporting possibilities for the U.S.

29. **ER** *Global Business Considerations*, reproducible master 24-10. In this activity, students are to analyze given business considerations for companies that plan to expand internationally. After writing their thoughts about each point in relation to textile/apparel companies, the class should discuss each of the points presented.

30. **RT** *Global Review*, Activity A, WB. Students are asked to answer questions about global trade.

31. **RF** Hold a class discussion about how America has been defensive about imports rather than offensive about exporting. Relate the information to the possible need for U.S. companies to be more aggressive risk-takers. Ask students to describe how the U.S. may not be able to compete against countries that are low-cost leaders, but may be successful at focusing on market niches by offering higher-priced differentiated products based on quality, service, and fashion timing.

32. **RF** Share with the class a PowerPoint CD that describes the impact of international business on the U.S. economy. *U.S. & International Trade* is available from D.E. Visuals and The Curriculum Center for Family and Consumer Sciences. Also,

the video *International Trade* is available from D.E. Visuals.

33. **RT** Have students discuss as many aspects of international retailing as possible. Also have them describe multinational corporations and satisfying market differences.

Discovering Offshore Sources and Opportunities

34. **EX** Show students a video about international business. *Retailing in Europe, Going Global, Merchandise Sourcing in the Global Marketplace, International Marketing: Competing in a Global Marketplace, Nonverbal Communication in a Global Marketplace*, and others are available from D.E. Visuals.

35. **RF** Have students discuss why the key to successful global business dealings is information. Ask students how fashion companies can try to identify the strategies of competitor nations, evaluate who the major players are in each segment and why, and try to predict future moves of the companies and countries.

36. **RT** *Global Differences*, Activity B, WB. Students are asked to tell the difference between given pairs of terms.

37. **ER** *Analyzing a Fashion Trade Article*, Activity C, WB. Students are asked to find a news article in a current publication that deals with a topic of this chapter. Then students are to mount it on the page and analyze it according to given questions.

38. **EX** *Discussing Global Trade*, Activity D, WB. Students are asked to discuss new information either in small groups or as a whole class.

39. **RT** *Global Business Discussion Topics*, reproducible master 24-11. Students are asked to respond to statements in written form and then to discuss the statements in class.

Additional Enrichment Activities

Research

40. *Researching Global Fashion*, Activity E, WB. Small groups of students are asked to pick and complete one of five research activities. Then students are to present their material to the rest of the class.

41. Have students research the availability of information about international apparel markets. You may want them to pick a certain country or part of the world to which they will pretend to export certain fashion items. They should check government and business references in the library and on the Internet, as on www.marketresearch.com, to see what reports, books, and other resources are available to them if they were really in business.

42. Have students research a global textile, apparel, or retail company. Examples are Levi, Fruit of the Loom, or Benetton. Have them report their findings to the class.

43. Have students study the fashion industry of a particular foreign location, such as Tokyo, London, Hong Kong, or Milan. Have students discover types of products, business operations, marketing strategy, and sales volume and report their findings to the class.

44. Have students research the Chief Textile Negotiator for the U.S. Trade Representative (USTR), representing U.S. textile/apparel issues with the World Trade Organization. Have students find out and report to the class who currently fills that position, the issues that have been debated, and the problems that have been resolved by that negotiator.

45. Have students research and report to the class about the many organizations that have joined together to address international textile/apparel trade. Web sites that will help with the research include www.apparelandfootwear.org, www.aapnetwork.net, www.otexa.ita.gov, www.buyusa.gov, www.usawear.org, www.tc2.com, www.customs.treas.gov, www.exim.gov, www.c-caa.org, www.spesa.org, and www.dataweb.usitc.gov.

Projects

46. Have students order reports (some are free) from the American Apparel and Footwear Association that deal with international apparel business issues. Subjects might include NAFTA, DR-CAFTA, the International Trade Administration (ITA) of the Department of Commerce, export declarations, transportation regulations, trends in the U.S. balance of trade, trade policies of the World Trade Organization (WTO), or other issues mentioned in this chapter. After students have studied the contents of separate reports, have them explain the information to the class.

47. Have students study about foreign currency exchange rates. Assign different students to countries in Asia and Europe. Also assign one or two students to study letters of credit. Then have students organize an "international financial seminar" with an agenda of what will be covered and all students taking part.

48. Have four students write and act-out a conversation about a fictitious but realistic import situation of the U.S. fashion industry. The four students should separately represent a consumer advocate, the CEO of a major U.S. apparel manufacturer, the CEO of a large U.S. retail company, and an apparel representative of UNITE (labor union). All actors should be prepared to explain and defend their viewpoints on imports from the perspective of the person they are representing.
49. Invite an international business person to speak to the class, especially if the person is employed by a textiles, apparel, or retail company. Encourage students to ask informed questions after the speaker has finished his or her presentation.

Answer Key

Text

Fashion Review, pages 504

1. the U.S.
2. more than 60 percent
3. sweaters and jackets/coats
4. to evaluate fabric quantity when figuring the penetration of textile/apparel imports
5. It lowers the price of U.S. exports and makes imports more expensive.
6. negotiating between nations, while balancing political and economic issues
7. U.S. government income is less because of reduced tariffs.
8. because cut fabric garment parts are hard to handle by automation
9. because production in developing countries has increased, while consumption of the products in the markets of developed countries has decreased
10. their consumers' purchasing power and standards of living; relative costs of doing business there
11. Countries with high wage rates supply apparel designs and textiles to garment producers in nearby lower-wage countries for sewing, after which finished goods are returned and sold at retail.
12. because they have a small land mass and limited natural resources
13. their rising labor costs, a shortage of labor, and access into the American market
14. because they are using overseas plants and labor to produce their goods instead of competing against them
15. a separate firm that is owned by the parent company

16. less than five percent of the world's population and about one-quarter of the world's buying power
17. by differentiated premium products for which they can charge a higher price
18. (Name three:) joint venture, licensing, franchises, and wholly-owned foreign retail operations
19. They must understand the cultural attitudes and practices of the people of that country. They must adapt their marketing and ways of doing business to each country, while preserving the coherence and style of their goods and services.
20. information

Student Workbook

Global Review, Activity A

1. China
2. Imports, exports, and exchanges of money.
3. It could bring trade retaliation.
4. the Committee for the Implementation of Textile Agreements (CITA)
5. Africa and Central Asia
6. Developed countries import more goods, and developing countries export more goods.
7. the European Union (EU)
8. cut, make, and trim—total production
9. They have increased.
10. large, young, and with low education levels
11. so they can stock their stores with what will sell for the highest profit, no matter where it comes from
12. Los Angeles and Miami
13. a business that buys and imports particular classifications or categories of goods
14. a separate firm that is owned by the parent company
15. the weaker dollar against other currencies and rising costs of foreign labor
16. Competition already exists there.
17. retail operations that serve customers in multiple countries

Global Differences, Activity B

1. Import penetration is the percentage of imports in a country's total market consumption, which measures foreign against domestic goods. Balance of trade is the relationship between the values of a country's imports and exports, described as a deficit or a surplus.
2. A trade deficit is the amount by which the value of imports exceeds exports. A trade surplus is the amount by which the value of exports exceed imports.

3. Free trade is a government's policy of allowing goods to flow freely in and out of its economy without interference. Protectionism is the opposite of free trade, which includes many government-imposed trade restraints.
4. Market disruption is a situation, usually caused by too many imports, that threatens a particular industry with products that are in direct competition with that industry. Comparative advantage is the ability of one nation to produce certain goods or services better than other nations because of specific circumstances.
5. Transshipping is the rerouting of goods to evade quota limits. Dumping is the selling of goods at lower prices in foreign markets than in the home market.
6. Parity is equal monetary value or treatment by the law. Value added is the increase in worth of products as a result of a particular work activity.
7. Structural adjustment is the process of industries and economies adapting to long-term shifts in competitiveness. Infrastructure is a country's existence and condition of roads, transportation systems, electricity, telephones, mail delivery, etc.
8. Political stability is the degree to which a country's laws and regulations are subject to change and are enforced. Economic climate is a country's purchasing power, standard of living, and relative costs of doing business.
9. The WTO is an international trade accord that reduces tariffs, quotas, and other trade barriers around the world. NAFTA is a trading bloc that includes the United States with Canada and Mexico.
10. Full package production supplies design-through-distribution services by vendors. A joint venture is an agreement that brings necessary skills or products of two companies together for added strength.
11. Globalization is the rapid growth of international commerce and communications that makes national boundaries less important, especially in economic matters. MNCs are companies that operate globally, with direct investment in several different countries.

12. Export merchants are foreign wholesalers who specialize in efficiently exporting goods from their countries. Export sales representatives are foreign natives who represent selected manufacturers but do not maintain a wholesale inventory.

Teacher's Resources

Chapter 24 Test

1.	G	16.	T
2.	I	17.	T
3.	C	18.	T
4.	B	19.	F
5.	A	20.	F
6.	F	21.	B
7.	E	22.	C
8.	D	23.	B
9.	J	24.	A
10.	H	25.	D
11.	T	26.	A
12.	T	27.	D
13.	T	28.	D
14.	T	29.	B
15.	F	30.	C

31. Free trade is a government's policy of allowing goods to flow freely in and out of its economy without interference. Protectionism is the opposite of free trade, which includes many government-imposed trade restraints.
32. (Describe two:) tariffs, quotas, tariff-rate quotas, voluntary export restraints, standards, subsidies, etc.—all described in text Chart 24-3.
33. A family of 25 European countries united for economic stability and with common policies of free trade among the members.

Possible Ways to Evaluate Soft Goods Imports

By weight: (No)	Evaluation in pounds causes distortions because of bottom weights, top weights, carpets, etc.
Monetary value: (No)	Evaluation in dollars gives lower estimates because imports usually have less wholesale value than the same domestic goods.
Physical quantity: (Yes!)	Square meter equivalents are a standardized unit of measurement, with conversion factors assigned to various items and specified in international agreements.

Measuring Industry Data

—All industry production, employment, and trade (such as imports and exports) are tracked by the North American Industry Classification System (NAICS).

—NAICS was developed jointly by the U.S., Canada, and Mexico to allow comparisons of business statistics across North America.

—NAICS Groupings for Apparel are identified in the following ways:

- The first two digits tell the industry sector (Sector **31** is manufacturing).

- The third digit tells the sub-sector (31**5** is apparel manufacturing).

- The fourth digit tells the industry group (315**1** = apparel knitted in textile mills; 315**2** = cut-and-sew garments; 315**9**=apparel accessories).

- The fifth digit further specifies the market (3152**2** = men's and boy's cut-and-sew apparel; 3152**3** = women's and girl's cut-and-sew apparel).

- The sixth digit is left to the discretion of the Canadian, Mexican, or U.S. industries to further designate information as they desire.

  —Further explanations are available by searching "North American Industry Classification System (NAICS)" on the Web site www.census.gov.

Results of the Elimination of Quotas

Good effects:
- Costs of quota brokers and traders are eliminated.
- Quota fraud is eliminated.
- Savings are passed on to consumers.
- Infrastructures and equipment improve in developing countries.
- Global economic welfare is improved (Producing countries export goods, but also consume goods of U.S. and other countries to gain higher standards of living.).
- Production occurs internationally according to expertise and competitiveness, rather than on quota allowances.
- Infrastructures and equipment improve in developing countries.

Bad effects:
- U.S. corporate sourcing strategies are in disarray.
- There is pressure for production in the lowest-cost countries.
- Infrastructures of roads, ports, and vessels cannot handle the increased demands.
- Some good, but high-wage, factories have closed; low-wage factories are stressed—losing quality and reliability.
- Since European quotas are also gone, countries close to that lucrative market choose to sell there, not the U.S.

Bottom line: Companies must have a clear strategy that
- Is unemotional and well thought out.
- Considers the company's products and vendor mix.
- Considers the political and economic situations of sourcing countries.
- Evaluates how each of these factors affect the others.

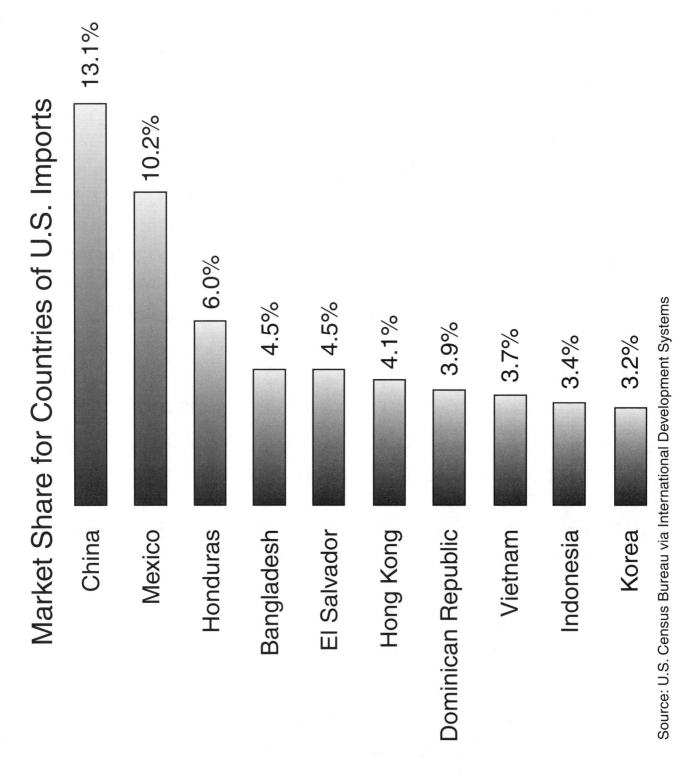

Market Share for Countries of U.S. Imports

China 13.1%
Mexico 10.2%
Honduras 6.0%
Bangladesh 4.5%
El Salvador 4.5%
Hong Kong 4.1%
Dominican Republic 3.9%
Vietnam 3.7%
Indonesia 3.4%
Korea 3.2%

Source: U.S. Census Bureau via International Development Systems

Major Apparel-Producing Countries in Asia

Country	Population	Number of Apparel Factories (Estimate)	Total Employed in Apparel Industry (Estimate)	Total Exports 2004/2005 U.S. $ billions	Total Apparel Exports U.S. $ billions	Apparel Sector's Share of Total Exports %	Imports by U.S. 2005 Jan/Oct U.S. $ millions	Imports by EU U.S. $ millions
Bangladesh	143 million	4,000	1.9 million	7.6	5.7	75	1,991	4,622
China	1.3 billion	38,970	4.6 million	593.0	61.0	10	13,469	16,062
India	1.1 billion	60,000*	4.0 million	79.7	6.0	8	2,523	3,496
Indonesia	220 million	2,368	377,000	69.7	4.3	6	2,427	1,717
Pakistan	151 million	5,000	700,000	12.3	2.7	22	1,054	1,389
Sri Lanka	19 million	830	350,000	5.7	2.6	46	1,392	1,071
Thailand	62 million	2,672	850,000	76.0	3.4	5	1,519	1,297
Vietnam	82 million	1,050	2.0 million	26.5	4.3 (Includes Textiles)	13	2,290	813

*small factories

Approximate Textile/Apparel Labor Costs
(In Relative U.S. Dollars)

Japan, Switzerland, Belgium, Denmark: $ 22.50

Holland, Austria, Norway: $ 20.00

Germany: $ 19.00

Sweden, France, Italy: $ 17.00

Canada, Finland: $ 13.40

United States: $ 11.75

Australia, England, Ireland: $ 10.20

Spain, Israel, Greece: $ 7.60

Taiwan, Turkey, Hong Kong, South Korea, Singapore: $ 4.50

Uruguay, Tunisia, Mexico, Argentina: $ 3.00

Venezuela, Colombia, Hungary, South Africa: $ 1.92

Morocco, Brazil, Czech Republic, Peru: $ 1.50

Slovakia, Malaysia, Syria, Thailand, Philippines: $ 1.10

Egypt, India, Zimbabwe, Pakistan, Indonesia, Nigeria: $ .52

Sri Lanka, Vietnam, Mainland China, Zambia, Kenya: $ .36

Bangladesh, Tanzania: $ .24

Free Trade/Protectionism Differences

Textile/Apparel Manufacturers	usually favor *protectionism*	since U.S. manufacturing can't compete against production in low-wage countries. However, many U.S. companies are now moving their own manufacturing offshore.
Retailers	favor *free trade*	so they can sell the widest selection of merchandise, at reasonable prices, with the highest possible markups.
Consumers	favor *free trade*	to be able to buy the best products for the money, regardless of where items are made. Patriotism and consumerism don't mix!

Business/Economic Effects of Imports on U.S. Textile/Apparel Manufacturing

Imports have:

- seriously reduced domestic company profits

- reduced job opportunities and wages of workers

- reduced company investments in new plants and equipment

- made it hard to attract new employees to the industry

- caused talented people to leave the industry for other opportunities

- reduced R&D, limiting future new products

- shrunk the U.S. manufacturing base, weakening the country

Advantages/Appeal of Imports

Lower costs:	Give higher values and higher retail markups/profits.
Product uniqueness:	Offers styling trends and labor-intensive finishes.
Not made in U.S.:	Some goods are only available if imported.
Different quality:	Lower for discounters and higher for upscale goods.
Smaller orders:	Offshore plants accept small quantity jobs.
Design reputation:	Foreign designers offer prestige/snob appeal.
Private label goods:	Exclusively manufactured to retailer's specs.
Helps poor nations:	Provides jobs for human survival.

Disadvantages/Problems with Imports

Bad timing and flexibility:	Long lead/ response times cause early buying.
Weak supplier loyalties:	Will take better offers and not produce yours.
Legal/financial problems:	Ties up money; currencies fluctuate; can't sue.
Misunderstandings:	Language and cultural differences.
Less control of product:	Quality/size can be wrong if not supervised.
Hidden costs:	Travel, communications, freight, lost sales.
Frequent buying mistakes:	Unsuitable or overbuying in foreign setting.
Hurts our economy:	Takes jobs away from our workers.

Global Business Considerations

Name_____ **Date** _____ **Period** _____

Since global business strategy must be well thought out, the points given below should be considered before companies expand internationally. Think about and write your thoughts concerning each point in relation to textile/apparel companies going global. Then discuss the points as a class.

1. Visit and study a new market to determine that it offers enough customers and high enough spending levels for profitability. _____

_____

_____

_____

2. Be obsessed with checking and completing all details about the infrastructure, culture, economy, industry, and competitors._____

_____

_____

_____

3. Tailor product assortments to meet the tastes/demands of the host country. _____

_____

_____

_____

4. Determine how to accomplish customer service and reliability. _____

_____

_____

_____

5. Make sure that data processing, distribution systems, and advertising are available. _____

_____

_____

_____

6. Determine that the company can comply with local regulations and attract local managers to run the business. _____

_____

_____

7. Commit sufficient but low investment at first to keep risk low. _____

_____

_____

_____

(Continued)

Name_____

8. Take a long-term view since a significant return on investment takes time. _____

_____

_____

_____

9. Set a strategy but be prepared to deviate from it._____

_____

_____

_____

10. Move rapidly forward if the country proves successful. _____

_____

_____

_____

11. Capitalize on worldwide sourcing. _____

_____

_____

_____

12. Determine your company's competencies and stick to them._____

_____

_____

_____

13. Position company technology so it can reduce costs and be used anywhere._____

_____

_____

_____

14. Form joint ventures, where appropriate, with partners that are chosen carefully._____

_____

_____

_____

15. Decentralize operations, where appropriate, and delegate authority._____

_____

_____

_____

16. Be willing to regress operationally when older methods are used in less-developed countries. __

_____

_____

_____

Global Business Discussion Topics

Name_____ **Date** _____ **Period** _____

Think about the following statements and write your ideas in a response to the points presented. Then discuss the statements with the class.

1. The number of U.S. residents represent only 5% of the world's population. That leaves large markets in other parts of the world. _____

   _____

   _____

2. A **ripple effect** is the spreading influence of an occurrence that diffuses throughout a community. For instance, apparel plant shutdowns in small U.S. towns affect restaurants, gas stations, movie theaters, and retail stores because unemployed workers don't have money to spend. _____

   _____

   _____

3. Plant shutdowns also cause higher taxes for those with jobs to support government benefits to those without jobs. Besides welfare, sometimes programs to retrain and relocate displaced workers are unsuccessful because workers are too old or lack motivation or abilities. _____

   _____

   _____

4. A simple description of **transshipment** is: merchandise is produced in country "A," labeled as if it was made in country "B," and then shipped through country "B" to country "C" (such as the U.S.).

   _____

   _____

5. The term **landed cost** refers to the total cost of imported goods. For apparel items, it would include the cost of garments, plus transportation, plus loading/unloading, plus duties or tariffs. _____

   _____

   _____

6. **Industrial targeting** is the intentional flooding of another country's market with particular goods to damage that industry. After the industry is weakened, foreign goods can take over. _____

   _____

   _____

7. A new word in international business is **glocal**—to think and run a business globally and act locally in each country. Retailers are trying to use "glocalisation" as they expand their operations internationally but remain sensitive to local market requirements. _____

   _____

   _____

(Continued)

Name_____

8. U.S. companies seek ***international capital*** to diversify their sources of financing. Some large retailers sell yen-based shares on the Japanese stock market to raise money. Others deal in the stock and bond markets of Hong Kong, Singapore, London, and other worldwide locations. _____

_____

_____

9. Many overseas apparel contractors are small and not highly automated. Electronic information transfer may not be feasible with foreign plants unless the U.S. company supplies and maintains hardware, software, and training. _____

_____

_____

10. The natural location for U.S. foreign-based operations has been in Canada because of its close proximity to the U.S. and lack of language barriers. _____

_____

_____

11. Japanese consumers desire American goods. They will pay high prices for a slice of "***idealized Americana***" through U.S. brand names and logos, especially jeans and leather jackets. U.S. mail order businesses have also been very successful there. _____

_____

_____

12. U.S. companies are considered throughout the world to be innovative, well-run firms that have good management and manufacture high-quality products. _____

_____

_____

13. To be profitable, foreign markets must have good income as well as a lot of people. For instance, of our NAFTA partners, Canada's population is about one-third that of Mexico, but Canada's consuming power is about four times greater than Mexico. _____

_____

_____

14. With ***downstream dumping***, components are dumped in one country and used to make a product that is then exported to another country. _____

_____

_____

15. With trade barriers falling and business dealings transacted over the Internet, we are moving to a ***single world economy***. Time zones have become insignificant, language differences are less of a barrier, and cultural differences are being eradicated._____

_____

_____

A Global Perspective

Name_____

Date_____**Period**_____ **Score**_____

Chapter 24 Test

Matching: Match the following terms and identifying phrases.

_____ 1. The process of industries and economies adapting to long-term shifts in competitiveness.

_____ 2. The amount by which the value of exports exceeds imports.

_____ 3. The selling of goods at lower prices in foreign markets than in the home market.

_____ 4. The ability of one nation to produce certain goods or services better than other nations because of specific circumstances.

_____ 5. The relationship between the values of a country's imports and exports, described as being a deficit or a surplus.

_____ 6. Equal monetary value or equal treatment by the law.

_____ 7. A situation, usually from too many imports, that threatens an industry with products that are in direct competition with that industry.

_____ 8. The percentage of imports in a country's total market consumption, which measures foreign against domestic goods.

_____ 9. The rerouting of goods to evade quota limits.

_____ 10. The amount by which the value of imports exceeds exports.

A. balance of trade

B. comparative advantage

C. dumping

D. import penetration

E. market disruption

F. parity

G. structural adjustment

H. trade deficit

I. trade surplus

J. transshipping

True/False: Circle *T* if the statement is true or *F* if the statement is false.

T   F   11. China is the largest exporter of manufactured textiles and apparel in the world.

T   F   12. Trade has been opening up throughout the world recently, referred to as "managed trade."

T   F   13. International diplomacy tries to balance negotiations between nations with political and economic issues.

T   F   14. The World Trade Organization is an international trade accord that reduces tariffs, quotas, and other trade barriers around the world, tries to liberalize trade, and serves as an international trade court.

(Continued)

Name_____

T   F   15. In general, developing countries import more goods and developed countries export more goods.

T   F   16. A country's infrastructure involves the existence and condition of roads, transportation systems, electricity, telephones, and mail delivery.

T   F   17. The North American Free Trade Agreement includes the U.S., Canada, and Mexico.

T   F   18. Twin plant programs use two manufacturing sites, with one in the U.S. and the other in a nearby low-wage country.

T   F   19. In general, retailers have always favored protectionism.

T   F   20. U.S. retailers have been much more successful than U.S. manufacturers in entering foreign markets.

Multiple Choice: Choose the best response. Write the letter in the space provided.

_____ 21. The greatest consuming market of soft goods in the world where countries want to send their goods is _____.
A. China
B. the U.S.
C. Europe
D. Asia

_____ 22. The amount of textile/apparel imports is now determined by fabric quantity _____.
A. in square yard equivalents plus type of fabric or garment
B. in linear yards of categorized textiles used for manufacture
C. in square meter equivalents organized by numbered fiber and garment categories
D. combined with product weight and monetary value

_____ 23. The initials "CITA" stand for the U.S. Government's _____.
A. Conference for International Textiles and Apparel
B. Committee for the Implementation of Textile Agreements
C. Consumer Initiative for Textiles and Apparel
D. Committee for Inactive Trade Applications

_____ 24. A country's political stability is _____.
A. the degree to which the country's laws and regulations are subject to change and are enforced
B. a country's purchasing power, standard of living, and relative costs of doing business
C. a country's set of social norms or values
D. All of the above.

_____ 25. The world's trading blocs _____.
A. are regional trade alliances that eliminate economic boundaries between the countries within them
B. are united by treaty or agreement for mutual support or joint action
C. negotiate trade alliances outside the auspices of the World Trade Organization
D. All of the above.

(Continued)

Name_____

_____ 26. Value added is the _____.
   A. increase in worth of products as a result of a particular work activity, such as sewing
   B. exporting of cut components followed by the reimporting of sewn garments
   C. worth of imports after they enter the U.S. and ownership transfers to retailers
   D. main provision of NAFTA and DR-CAFTA

_____ 27. Full package production focuses on supplying _____.
   A. design and sample work
   B. fabrics/findings/trims and all parts of construction
   C. packing and transportation arrangements
   D. All of the above.

_____ 28. Problems of sourcing goods from outside the home country include _____.
   A. hidden sales, distribution, and management costs
   B. added transportation and insurance costs and import fees
   C. shipping and customs delays and quality and fit variations
   D. All of the above.

_____ 29. The Los Angeles area is the "gateway" for textile and apparel imports from _____.
   A. the Caribbean
   B. the Pacific Rim
   C. Paris and Milan
   D. All of the above.

_____ 30. A joint venture is _____.
   A. a licensing agreement that also includes franchising
   B. an import merchant joining forces with an import commission house
   C. an agreement that brings necessary skills or products of two companies together for added strength
   D. a separate firm that is owned by a parent company

Essay Questions: Provide complete responses to the following questions or statements.

31. Describe free trade and protectionism.

32. Describe at least two barriers to free trade.

33. Describe the European Union.

CHAPTER 25

The Latest Fashion Business Trends

Objectives

After studying this chapter, students will be able to

- discuss the changing consumer market.
- explain niche specialization marketing.
- describe trends in retail formats.
- discuss the popularity and types of nonstore retailing.
- explain the current survival business strategies.
- summarize how technology is leading to customized goods.

Teaching Materials

Text, pages 505–529
Fashion Terms
Fashion Review
Fashion in Action

Student Workbook
- A. *Business Trends Quiz*
- B. *Strategy and Technology Review*
- C. *Fashion Business Trends Fill-in-the-Blanks*
- D. *Business Trends Know-How*
- E. *Alphabet Soup*

Teacher's Resources
Tomorrow's Consumers, transparency master 25-1
Best Small Store Qualities, transparency master 25-2
Personnel Training, transparency master 25-3
Business Trends Review, reproducible master 25-4
Merchandising Functions of Retail Computer Systems, transparency master 25-5
Business Functions of Retail Computer Systems, transparency master 25-6
Future Retail Structures, transparency master 25-7
Discuss Retail Business Trends, reproducible master 25-8
Chapter 25 Test

Introductory Activities

1. To stimulate interest in the chapter, have students discuss each of the following statements in relation to fashion business strategy:
   - The pace of change is accelerating.
   - It is productive to look at change as an opportunity rather than a threat.
   - Managing change is becoming harder because the nature of change is changing.
   - Change is becoming unpredictable, uncontrollable, and complex.
   - Retailers can respond to change either by ignoring it, reacting to it, or making other changes.
   - Understanding the forces of change is basic to identifying successful strategies for the future.
2. Show students a video that introduces the general subject of change in business. *Coping with Change in the Workplace* is available from Meridian Education Corporation.
3. Ask students to describe any fashion business changes that they have noticed over the past few years. Ask them if they have noticed more niche marketing, discount retailing, nonstore retailing, horizontal or vertical restructuring, or increased use of other retail formats.

Strategies to Reteach, Reinforce, Enrich, and Extend Text Concepts

Satisfying a Changing Consumer Market

4. **RT** Have students discuss the various points about today's consumers in Chart 25-1. Also discuss why the term *sale* has lost its meaning and how shoppers no longer have much customer loyalty to retailers.

5. **RT** Discuss the effects on retailers of consumers being time-poor, doing cross-shopping, and expressing their individual style rather than following the dictates of fashion and fads. Also discuss how retailers are trying to offer services (eateries, pharmacies, banking, medical clinics, etc.) to attract shoppers.

6. **ER** *Tomorrow's Consumers*, transparency master 25-1. While showing this transparency to the class, have students discuss each of the points presented.

7. **RT** Have a class discussion about marketing ideas aimed at specific demographic and psychographic groups, such as children, teens, ethnic populations, and single parents.

8. **RF** With students looking at text illustration 25-5, have students discuss each of the desires of the mature consumer market. Ask students to explain why it is important for fashion marketers to understand these desires.

9. **RT** Have students discuss cocooning, the latest lifestyle trends, and how consumers have been desensitized to entertaining stimulation. Discuss how retailers are trying to provide efficiency and fantasy to meet the needs of consumers.

Niche Marketing

10. **RF** With students looking at text illustration 25-9, clarify how broad mass markets can be divided into narrower market segments that can then be divided into extremely narrow segment niches. Have the class discuss specific stores with which students are familiar and into what types of markets, market segments, and segment niches the stores fit.

11. **RT** Have the class discuss micro-segmentation and niche manufacturing.

12. **RF** As students look at text illustration 25-10, go through each of the requirements for niche manufacturing. Have the class brainstorm about the types of niche manufacturing that might be done by textile and apparel manufacturers.

13. **EX** *Best Small Store Qualities*, transparency master 25-2. While showing this transparency to the class, have students discuss each of the points presented. Ask students to discuss how these qualities can counteract the similar assortments and lack of service of big stores that try to sell everything to everyone. Also discuss how these factors can instill customer loyalty.

14. **RF** Show the class a video about niche marketing. One suggestion is *Data Base Marketing: Critical to Success in Today's Environment*, available from D.E. Visuals.

15. **ER** Have the class discuss the concept of niche retailing. Ask students to distinguish between the terms *database marketing*, *data warehouse*,

and *data mining*. Then show students various specialty niche mail-order catalogs available from Spiegel, JCPenney, and independent direct marketers. Examples are catalogs of tall sizes, maternity wear, infant goods, children's apparel, female business attire, and fashion catalogs for minority groups.

Trends in Retail Formats

16. **RT** While students are looking at text illustration 25-13, have them discuss the characteristics of upscale retailers and the two main types of discount retailers. Have them relate this information to retailers in your area.

17. **RF** Ask students to explain how discount stores that previously offered inferior merchandise at low prices in the past have now moved into "value retailing" with brand-name goods. Ask students if they can tell about any regional discount merchandisers that have gone out of business as well as any national discounters that are thriving.

18. **RT** Have the class discuss the buying clout of large retailers, charge-backs against vendors, and the use of a category management strategy.

19. **ER** Ask students to explain the meaning of *overstoring* and then describe the overstoring (retail saturation) that is apparent in your area. Relating to retail saturation, have students discuss that in order to grow their businesses, retailers must either take market share from their competitors or increase the average transaction size of sales.

20. **ER** Show the class a video about trends in retail formats. Suggestions are *Trends in Apparel Marketing*, available from Meridian Education Corporation, VMS, Inc., and D.E. Visuals; *Retailing Trends in the New Millennium* and *Value Shopping in America: A Major Force in Retailing*, both available from D.E. Visuals.

21. **RF** Have the class turn to text illustration 25-17. Ask different students to read and expand on each of the points given. Ask students if they can think of any other reasons consumers like to shop from home. Also ask students to describe their experiences with home shopping. Then, from the business side, have students read and further explain the points listed in text illustration 25-18.

22. **EX** Ask students to describe their personal experiences with direct mail marketing, TV home shopping, and online commerce. Then have them try to describe the business side of each as if they were running a business in one of those areas. If you have Internet access, go to the Web site www.compucloz.com to show students a system that is licensed to retailers, department stores, and catalogs for online apparel sizing and "trying-on." Then go to www.fitme.com or www.landsend.com and search "Virtual Model"

to see how e-retailers provide this type of technology for computer shoppers.

23. **RT** *Business Trends Quiz*, Activity A, WB. Students are asked to write one true/false question for each of the sections from the beginning of the chapter through this section. Students are to write the correct answers on another piece of paper, writing false questions in corrected form. Then students are to exchange workbook pages with a classmate to answer each other's quiz.

24. **ER** Obtain a sample copy of *Internet Retailer* magazine from www.internetretailer.com or 1-800-535-8403 to show to the class. Get information on www.shop.org about a trade association that focuses on Internet retailing. Check www.shopzilla.com, www.shopping.com, or another "bot" to see an online comparison shopping service. Check on launching an e-retail Web site on www.interactiveapparel.com. Discuss how an entirely new method of retailing has become widely used within the past decade. Also discuss why multichannel retailing makes sense for most retail companies.

25. **RF** Have students discuss that one of the most important components of any Web retailing organization, after getting shoppers to their site, is the online customer service department—to handle questions and complaints over the phone or with an instant electronic response. Good order fulfillment and merchandise delivery (plus return) services are also of great importance.

26. **ER** Show the class a video about online and multichannel retailing. Suggestions are *Driving Traffic to Your Web Site, An Introduction to Web Site Design, Multichannel Retailing,* and *Interactive and Multichannel Marketing,* all available from D.E. Visuals.

27. **EX** Obtain materials from Multichannel Merchant Magazine (www.multichannelmerchant.com) to show students. These also include special reports, "Webinars," conferences, supplements, and a Web site featuring specialized subjects.

Survival Business Strategies

28. **ER** Have students explain the meanings of *strategy, consolidation, acquisition, divestiture, takeover, merger,* and *downsizing.* During the discussion of each term, ask students to give any business examples of these terms, especially related to the fashion industry. At the end of the entire exercise, discuss the concept of the overall "reengineering process" of businesses to continually improve to meet future challenges.

29. **RT** With the class looking at text illustration 25-25, have students individually go through each of the reasons companies merge. Have the class discuss the meaning of each with further explanations.

30. **RF** Have students discuss Chapter 11 bankruptcy (to reorganize and settle obligations) and Chapter 7 bankruptcy (liquidation).

31. **RT** Have students discuss the necessity of information technology with synchronized data in a standardized format to enable collaboration between supply chain partners.

32. **RT** Have students discuss the concepts of organizational performance and employee turnover. Then hold a class discussion about how the continuous training and development of the industry's most valuable assets (its workers) results in far greater returns than the dollars invested.

33. **EX** *Personnel Training,* transparency master 25-3. Use this transparency master as you discuss effective and ineffective personnel training.

34. **EX** *Business Trends Know-How,* Activity D, WB. Students are asked to write their thoughts about given statements, trying to expand the topic further. Then students are to share their thoughts with others by conducting a class discussion about each statement.

35. **EX** Show students materials from the www.wgsn.com Web site, or have students access the site. WGSN is the world's leading business-to-business news and information service for the fashion and style industries.

36. **ER** *Alphabet Soup,* Activity E, WB. Students are asked to match terms with descriptions. Then students are to write responses to cases, explaining changes that will help the companies improve their businesses for the 21st century.

37. **RT** *Business Trends Review,* reproducible master 25-4. Use these additional chapter review questions as homework or as an optional extra credit assignment.

Customization Through Technology

38. **ER** *Merchandising Functions of Retail Computer Systems,* transparency master 25-5. While showing this transparency to the class, have students discuss each of the merchandising functions that are available with today's retail computer systems.

39. **ER** *Business Functions of Retail Computer Systems,* transparency master 25-6. Have students discuss each of the business functions available with computer systems.

40. **RF** Hold a class discussion about agile manufacturing, with students discussing how each of the components listed in the text chapter contributes to the outcome. Then have students discuss mass customization.

41. **EX** Have students weigh the pros and cons of EDI on the Internet rather than through linked computer networks (such as speed, flexibility/versatility, privacy/security, reliability, meshing of

computer systems, verification of receipt of data, cost and accessibility, amount of data transmitted and stored, and geographical span). Discuss that the World Wide Web may be better for business-to-business transactions, even though it has some problems, than business-to-consumer transaction.

42. **ER** *Future Retail Structures*, transparency master 25-7. While showing this transparency to the class, go through the store-based and nonstore-based functions of future retail structures.

43. **RT** *Strategy and Technology Review*, Activity B, WB. Students are asked to write answers to review questions that deal with this and the previous sections of the chapter.

44. **RT** *Fashion Business Trends Fill-in-the-Blanks*, Activity C, WB. Students are asked to complete a fill-in-the-blank activity using chapter terms.

45. **RF** Have students discuss the fact that today's vendor-managed Quick Response will evolve into tomorrow's consumer-managed soft goods chain, also referred to as "apparel on demand."

46. **RT** Have the class look at text illustration 25-33. Going around the room, with students each taking the next line that compares the 20th and 21st centuries, conduct a discussion about the obvious and subtle differences. To stay focused on the current line being discussed, students might want to hold the edge of a piece of paper across the page as a marker.

47. **EX** *Discuss Retail Business Trends*, reproducible master 25-8. Students are asked to read given statements one at a time and discuss them as a class.

Additional Enrichment Activities

Research

48. Have students do research to find statistics about apparel businesses, such as the number of U.S. fashion-related companies, size and sales of the companies, private versus public ownership, where the headquarters and showrooms are located, the dollar amounts of materials and services they buy, the wages and taxes they pay, where the production of goods is done (domestic or where offshore), and recent mergers and acquisitions. Have the students report their findings to the class.

49. Have students do research about how databases are compiled for niche marketing. Have students find out how credit card purchases are used to pinpoint consumers' tastes, spending levels, and other information. Then have students further research how this information is being used for database marketing. In a report to the class, have them give both sides of the issue: retailers must have as much information about customers as possible to provide them with the best merchandise and service versus the growing complaints about consumer privacy.

50. Have students research the mergers of the Dayton Department Stores of Minneapolis and the Hudson Department Stores of Detroit into the Dayton Hudson Company (before the merger, the two original companies serviced similar target markets in separate, nearby locations), and then its redirection into Target; the combining of Sears, Lands' End, and Kmart; and the merger of Federated and May Department Stores with many old retail company names changing to Macy's. Have students assigned to do this research prepare a bulletin board display summarizing the merger. A different retail merger or buyout may be used if desired.

Projects

51. Have students study the damage that excessive charge-backs and markdown allowances imposed by powerful retailers have caused to vendors who sell goods to them. Timely articles occur about this in the *Wall Street Journal*, *Apparel*, and other apparel trade journals. Have other students study the view of retailers, who are the customers of the vendors and expect the promised floor ready merchandise (FRM) to be delivered on time and at the proper places. This viewpoint is often expressed in *STORES* magazine or other retail periodicals. Have the students hold a debate in front of the rest of the class that argues the two viewpoints.

52. Have students read a book about the content of this chapter. Suggestions include *Treasure Hunt: Inside the Mind of the New Consumer* by Michael J. Silverstein, *Just Ask a Woman: Cracking the Code of What Women Want and How They Buy* by Mary Lou Quinlan, *Don't Think Pink: What Really Makes Women Buy—And How to Increase Your Share of this Crucial Market* by Lisa Johnson and Andrea Learned, *Marketing to Women: How to Understand, Reach, and Increase Your Share of the World's Largest Market Segment* by Martha Barletta, *What's Cool About Retail from Warhol to Wal-Mart* by Tim Manners, *Dominating Market with Value: Advances in Customer Value Management* by R. Reid Reidenbach, *Think Big, Act Small* by Jason Jennings, *I Quit But I Forgot to Tell You* by Terri Kabachnick, *Mass Customization: The New Frontier in Business Competition* by B. Joseph Pine, *Markets of One: Creating Customer-Unique*

Value Through Mass Customization by James H. Gilmore, *Transformational Change: How to Transform Mass Production Thinking to Meet the Challenge of Mass Customization* by Thomas K. Wentz, *Pathways to Agility: Mass Customization in Action* by John D. Oleson, *Data Warehousing: The Route to Mass Customization* by Sean Kelly, *Agile Product Development for Mass Customization* by David M. Anderson, and *The Experience Economy* by James H. Gilmore and B. Joseph Pine II, *A Stitch in Time* by Frederick H. Abernathy, et. al. Then have students present a book report.

53. Try to obtain one or more of the latest apparel retailing reports from Kalorama Information (www.marketresearch.com). They are very expensive to buy, but might be available through a library. They include retail and apparel years in review, retail industry almanacs, retailer profile reports, and such reports as *Next Generation Home Shopping* and *Trends in Online Apparel Retailing*. Have students study the reports and summarize their findings to the class.

Answer Key

Text

Fashion Review, page 528

1. They learn to use it as an opportunity rather than a threat.
2. by being open long hours, having merchandise in stock, having help available, and providing fast/easy checkout
3. Baby boomers are moving into it and people are living longer.
4. the activities, thinking, and product style preferences of a company's niche market
5. issue rewards for shoppers who are frequent users or big spenders with a store's credit card
6. unique merchandise, product expertise, and strong customer service
7. They are often undercapitalized, with too much debt and no room for operational errors.
8. to fill new retail shelf space rather than to replenish consumer offtake
9. taken away their entrepreneurial flavor
10. Consumers cannot actually see, touch, and try on the merchandise before buying it.
11. stock outages
12. the vendor (supplier) who gets unsold goods back instead of being paid for them
13. It consists of graphic and written presentations of merchandise shown on the screen. The merchandise can then be ordered by touchtone telephone, computer modem, or a set-top box.

14. (List three:) Consumers are becoming more comfortable with the user-friendly technology. Prices are lower for PC equipment. More homes have computers as time passes. Security systems are being developed to confidentially place orders.
15. for gathering information—to do product research, check availability and pricing, and find special offers online
16. closing their least profitable branches, minimizing the size of their inventory holdings, and dropping unprofitable merchandise categories
17. because fashion items have higher margins per square foot and faster turnover than large, bulky items
18. renegotiated payment schedules, restructured debt, reorganized management, and trimmed-down operations
19. A middle layer has been eliminated.
20. the electronic collection of individual sizing information

Student Workbook

Strategy and Technology Review, Activity B

1. an oversupply of goods and retailers, and the fact that consumers are not spending
2. with acquisitions, takeovers, and mergers
3. buying another retail company
4. a company that is sold or sells part of its organization
5. a change in the controlling interest of a corporation
6. because of the expensive legal efforts required
7. through remodeling facilities and empowering employees (as well as decreasing energy and interest costs, and increasing theft prevention devices)
8. an orderly and fair settlement of obligations
9. 50 percent
10. fewer, more powerful companies that have huge buying power
11. National brands and designer merchandise are now in discount stores.
12. companies throughout the textile/apparel pipeline are working together
13. white fabric
14. Retail companies may be order-facilitators, with items not taken home from there.
15. Long lead times will be eliminated, with deliveries made in days rather than months.

Fashion Business Trends Fill-in-the-Blanks, Activity C

1. acquisition
2. strategy

3. retailing
4. clout
5. collaborative planning, forecasting, and replenishment
6. data mining
7. fast fashion
8. category
9. organizational
10. centers
11. direct
12. interactive
13. Internet
14. microsegmentation
15. retailing
16. multichannel
17. scanning
18. bankruptcy
19. customization
20. cocooning
21. charge
22. consolidation
23. overstoring
24. cross
25. liquidates
26. manufacturing
27. agile
28. cyber
29. merger
30. storefronts
31. downsizing
32. infomercial
33. restructuring
34. business-to-consumer

Alphabet Soup, Activity E

1. C
2. F
3. B
4. G
5. E
6. A
7. D

8. It should have flexible manufacturing that focuses on customers' needs. It should respond to the market pull of products it manufactures. It should encourage its R&D lab to use its innovation for different product ideas rather than just improving existing products.

9. It should consider change as an opportunity rather than a threat and seek out ways to be better. After evaluating its layered management hierarchy, a leaner, flatter company structure should be developed. This will also lead to empowerment of employees, possibly with team ideas and controls.

10. RST might consider changing its product mix to respond to the market. It might want to operate globally instead of nationally and give prime emphasis to foreign markets rather than just unloading unwanted goods offshore.

Teacher's Resources

Business Trends Review, reproducible master 25-4

1. They are demanding more and spending less.
2. lower-priced lines of basic goods and fashion-forward designer bridge collections
3. young children and the mature market
4. It is desensitizing them to traditional forms of shopping entertainment.
5. They need to complement big stores rather than compete against them by being highly focused, flexible, and creative to fill observed gaps between what consumers want and what mass retailing provides.
6. purchases are tracked with charge cards
7. general mass merchandisers and niche specialist category killers
8. training on how to use the new information systems for strategic decision-making
9. because regular mall space is so expensive
10. radio frequency identification and electronic product codes
11. Manufacturers and retail warehouses will ship orders directly to consumers.
12. for paper, postage, and delivery
13. They are prepared and produced ahead of being broadcast and the sponsors must pay to put them on the air.
14. via the World Wide Web (www) with home computers
15. Paper catalogs use large photographs and a small amount of written description; online catalogs have small, light photos and more text.
16. They go out of business through liquidation.

Chapter 25 Test

1. B	11. F	21. D
2. I	12. T	22. B
3. E	13. F	23. C
4. G	14. T	24. B
5. F	15. F	25. D
6. D	16. T	26. D
7. H	17. T	27. B
8. C	18. F	28. A
9. J	19. T	29. C
10. A	20. T	30. D

31. upscale retailers and low-price discounters
32. (Any four reasons from text illustration 25-17.)
33. Under Chapter 11 protection, companies stay in business while they try to settle obligations through renegotiated payment schedules, restructured debt, reorganized managements, and trimmed-down operations. Chapter 7 bankruptcy means going out of business and liquidating all assets, using the proceeds to pay outstanding debts on a percentage basis.

Tomorrow's Consumers

<u>Individualism</u>: will only buy fashions/goods that they like

<u>Immediacy</u>: will not have any patience to wait for merchandise they want *now*

<u>Value</u>: will expect the best quality and styling for the lowest price

<u>Convenience</u>: will expect clearly understood store arrangements and efficient check-out

<u>Access</u>: will go to easy locations or shop from home

<u>Entertainment</u>: will want a pleasurable experience when buying

Best Small Store Qualities

<u>Narrow focus</u>: a specific niche that has demand

<u>Passion for change</u>: lack of corporate rules or permanent vendor partnerships allow for flexibility to change with the market

<u>Essential technology</u>: keeping up with "the latest" for marketing, buying, and selling

<u>Necessary markup</u>: offering value with a fair profit

<u>Objective relationships</u>: choose vendors according to good result, communicate effectively, treat reliable suppliers well

<u>Confident buying</u>: know customers' wants ahead of demand and recognize the store's needs

<u>Aggressive merchandise management</u>: keep track of open-to-buy, do classification merchandising, avoid big store brands, and take appropriate markdowns

<u>Consistent advertising</u>: follow an advertising strategy that contacts customers regularly

<u>Exceptional staffing</u>: have well-paid salespeople, ongoing training, employee goal-setting, incentives, and low turnover

<u>Exemplary service</u>: uncommon customer service by all

<u>Uncompromising standards</u>: responsibility for all aspects of merchandising

Based on work by Bill Pearson, Retail Analysis & Planning, Pasadena, CA

Personnel Training

Personnel training is effective when it:

- boosts sales.

- cuts shrinkage.

- reduces employee turnover.

- improves customer service.

- increases profits.

Personnel training is *not* effective if the company:

- has poor hiring practices.

- lacks employee rewards or incentives.

- allows peer pressure against good performance.

- assigns more work as "punishment" for good work.

- "rewards" poor work with more attention.

Business Trends Review

Name_____**Date** _____ **Period** _____

As you review the chapter, answer the following questions.

1. What do we mean when we say consumers are "value-driven"? _____

   _____

   _____

   _____

2. What two types of goods are department stores expected to carry as a result of the cross-shopping trend? _____

   _____

   _____

3. What two age groups have been shown to have strong spending power these days? _____

   _____

4. What is the effect on shopping created by the intense visual stimulation that people receive from movies, TV shows, and news reports about crime and violence? _____

   _____

   _____

   _____

5. Since small retailers can't sell everything to everyone or compete evenly against large, powerful retailers, what should they do? _____

   _____

   _____

   _____

6. How do retail clienteling databases provide a transaction history of customers? _____

   _____

   _____

   _____

7. Into what two main categories are large discounters split? _____

   _____

   _____

8. What kind of training is especially required for previous buyers to do category manager tasks?

   _____

   _____

   _____

(Continued)

Name_____

9. Why are discount retailers usually in strip malls rather than regular malls? _____

_____

_____

_____

10. What do the letters RFID-EPC represent? _____

_____

11. If the increase of nonstore retailing lowers the inventory requirements of stores in the future, how will consumers get their goods? _____

_____

_____

_____

12. For what have direct-mail marketers experienced higher costs? _____

_____

_____

13. In what two ways are infomercials different from TV home shopping broadcasts? _____

_____

_____

14. How are Internet sales made? _____

_____

_____

_____

15. How does the appearance of merchandise differ between the mediums of mail-order and online catalogs? _____

_____

_____

_____

16. What happens to companies that declare Chapter 7 bankruptcy? _____

_____

_____

_____

Merchandising Functions of Retail Computer Systems

<u>Purchase order management</u>: includes all PO information (dates, reorders, cancellations, etc.)

<u>Receiving and distribution</u>: shows what is where, with barcoded shipping container marking (SCM)

<u>Point-of-sale (POS)</u>: scanning/payment transactions; automatic inventory adjustments; timely sales totals

<u>Price look-up (PLU)</u>: updated central system gives correct price and other data to all locations when items are scanned

<u>Inventory look-up</u>: availability of items at all sites

<u>Transfer and reorder recommendations</u>: responds to quantities relative to established recommended levels

<u>Electronic data interchange(EDI)</u>: linked ordering and other transactions can automatically take place between partners

<u>Vendor managed inventory (VMI)</u>: computer replenishment is automatically done by suppliers

Business Functions of Retail Computer Systems

<u>Ticket printing</u>: individualized options for ticketing different goods

<u>Sales and inventory analysis</u>: generates summary and trend reports

<u>Vendor performance</u>: can compute sell-throughs by style or by vendor

<u>Electronic physical inventory</u>: workers scan bar codes on items rather than writing down information

<u>Customer profiling</u>: tracks retail site visits, purchases, birthdays, preferences, names of family members

<u>Customized marketing</u>: information to build relationships, establish frequent buyer programs, enhance service

<u>Inter-company e-mail</u>: complete communication services within retail sites and/or entire corporations

<u>Accounting</u>: integrated financial packages

Future Retail Structures

Store based:

- Heavily entertainment driven

- Offer fashion excitement

- Social experience for consumers

Nonstore based:

- For replenishment of basics

- Offer customized products

- Enable consumer time savings

Discuss Retail Business Trends

Name_____ **Date** _____ **Period** _____

Read the following statements one at a time and discuss their meaning and importance as a class.

1. The retail industry will experience more change in the next decade than it did over the last 50 years.

2. Companies will increasingly focus on their core business and outsource everything else reducing unnecessary support personnel, cutting costs, and excelling at what they do best.

3. Consumers want more quality, selection, convenience, service, information, innovation, customization, and enjoyment for less money, time, effort, and risk.

4. Retailers are using private labels to micromarket with exclusive merchandise aimed at the lifestyles and demographics of their customers.

5. Successful retailers of the future will restructure and reorganize around a consumer-driven supply chain that will integrate merchandise and information flow.

6. Seamless data capture through partnered companies has moved fashion forecasting and market research to the retail end of the pipeline.

7. Businesses must run their operations to balance the needs of their four stakeholders: customers, suppliers, investors, and employees.

8. Constant merchandise flow is de-emphasizing design seasons, with decisions being made closer to market selling.

9. To succeed, retailers will have to juggle these former contradictions: optimize their in-stock position but own less inventory; provide more service but lower their payroll; raise quality but lower prices.

10. The technology for cyber shopping via virtual reality exists, but consumers' psychology and absorption of it must catch up to the concept.

11. Retailers and suppliers will do more joint planning, product development, and demand forecasting, and work will be carried out by the partnered business that can do it better at lower cost.

12. When things are changing fast, business-as-usual is a recipe for failure. Innovation becomes a critical survival skill.

13. Retailers are doing business with fewer suppliers, strategically investing and changing to benefit the partnership, but thus having a hard time exiting the partnerships or working with others.

14. It is very possible that the return from good employee training is 20 times the investment put into it.

15. With a new generation of "techno-literates" and older retrained "techno-competents," as well as cheaper and easier home technology, electronic shopping will increase dramatically as more options come online.

16. For credit card transactions, Internet retailers need "e-security" that includes a firewall, anti-virus software, no default passwords, encrypted cardholder-data transmissions, and restricted employee access to cardholder data.

17. With the Internet, the global distribution system is virtually limitless.

(Continued)

Name_____

18. All sectors are going to rely on technology: suppliers will substitute information for inventory in the pipeline, reducing costs and improving productivity; retailers will link with consumers through electronic retailing and customer relationship marketing.

19. Retailers must not only respect the cultural/racial diversity of their employees, but also train the employees to respect the diversity of the consuming public.

20. CPFR has been defined as "a business process for value chain partners to coordinate plans in order to reduce the variance between supply and demand"—the buying and selling companies have a collaborative agreement with specific business goals.

21. With cross-shopping, the same customer may buy a jacket from an exclusive shop, dress and jewelry from a department store, hosiery at the grocery store, and underwear at a discount store.

22. With escalated violence, security will be important to where and how consumers shop, encouraging electronic shopping and home delivery.

23. Lines are blurring between manufacturers and retailers, imports and exports, store and nonstore retailers, and distinct design seasons.

24. Micromerchandising and micromarketing will be facilitated by new technologies that enable mass customization, localized category assortments, and promotions to individual customers.

25. E-retailers use search engines and e-mail marketing to get traffic to their retail sites. However, once shoppers are on the home page, only effective merchandising will motivate them to browse and buy.

26. Periods of mergers and consolidations are an indication of an industry in turmoil, and usually result in stronger, more competitive companies.

27. Rather than the old retail evaluation system of what goods were bought from suppliers at low prices, companies are now gauging success on fast cycle time, high inventory turnover, and high gross margin return on inventory investment.

28. Mass customization causes a shift for fashion-related businesses since ever-changing trends, the growing need for individuality, and increasing product variety all present new challenges that require new technologies and innovative strategies.

29. With a saturation of retail space trying to lure consumer spending that is not growing, retailers must either take market share from their competitors or increase the average size of sales transactions.

30. Companies must try to control their costs because high-cost companies are either bought out or forced to declare bankruptcy.

31. The Worth Global Style Network (www.wgsn.com) offers up-to-the-minute industry news, trade show dates, trend information, and supplier lists to any member who logs on.

32. Retailers are upset when their suppliers sell goods directly to consumers via the Internet at low prices, thus competing against their retail accounts—like opening factory outlet stores.

33. Many Internet shoppers who abandon their shopping carts by clicking off are deterred from completing their purchasing because of high shipping and handling charges.

34. Companies must have both good technology and good employees—equipment and systems are only as good as the people who operate them.

35. Future garments might be self-cleaning, able to monitor peoples' vital signs (heart, lungs, etc.), call emergency help, pinpoint the wearer's exact location, record sound and pictures of the day's meetings, end obesity and cellulite, dispense vitamins into the skin, and duplicate what is being worn onscreen when ordered by a click during a TV performance.

The Latest Fashion Business Trends

Name_____

Date_____**Period**_____ **Score**_____

Chapter 25 Test

Matching: Match the following terms and identifying phrases.

_____ 1. Power in the marketplace that enables companies who have it to get promotions, rebates, and additional discounts from suppliers.

_____ 2. The existence of too many stores and shopping centers in a retail trading area, all vying for limited consumer dollars.

_____ 3. Analysis of computer database information from retail sales, using software to discover patterns and derive actionable responses.

_____ 4. Offering individually made items to everyone.

_____ 5. The reduction of the size of a business to reduce costs and become more efficient.

_____ 6. The consumer trend of combining purchases from both ends of the price scale.

_____ 7. The joining of two companies to form a new one.

_____ 8. Penalties or claims against vendors for not following the many different rules set by each retailer.

_____ 9. Large-scale, long-range planning for achieving an organization's objectives.

_____ 10. The purchase of another company, with the buying company gaining the controlling interest.

A. acquisition

B. buying clout

C. charge-backs

D. cross-shopping

E. data mining

F. downsizing

G. mass customization

H. merger

I. overstoring

J. strategy

True/False: Circle *T* if the statement is true or *F* if the statement is false.

T F 11. Successful, innovative companies use change as a threat rather than an opportunity.

T F 12. Successful retailers have merchandise in stock, help available, and fast/easy checkout.

T F 13. Supply chain collaboration is being replaced by RFID-EPC.

T F 14. Age groups with strong spending power today include children and the mature market.

T F 15. Cocooning is the preference of going out to buy a new "layer" of clothes.

T F 16. Regional discount merchandisers are often undercapitalized compared to national discount companies.

(Continued)

Name_____

T F 17. Category management involves managing product groups as business units and customizing them on a store-by-store basis to better satisfy customer needs.

T F 18. The rate of consumer purchases has grown faster than the expansion of retail space.

T F 19. Consumer-direct retailing is nonstore selling to consumers who shop from home.

T F 20. Online retailing is the selling of merchandise to consumers through personal computers.

Multiple Choice: Choose the best response. Write the letter in the space provided.

_____ 21. Almost all of today's consumers _____.
A. are more discriminating and have less time to shop than ever before
B. want products to be instantly available
C. are price-conscious and value-driven, demanding more and spending less
D. All of the above.

_____ 22. Desires of the mature consumer market include _____.
A. inexpensive items of the latest fads
B. convenient parking, clear signage, and easy-to-read garment tags
C. fashions that are advertised on slender supermodels
D. All of the above.

_____ 23. Microsegmentation is _____.
A. the production of specific lines of goods for special customers
B. a retail viewpoint that targets general fashion tastes
C. the dividing of an industry's total market into extremely narrow target markets
D. a demographic and psychographic analysis of the global economy

_____ 24. A system of data (usually stored electronically) that is gathered through market research, constantly updated, and used for company marketing activities is known as _____.
A. niche marketing
B. database marketing
C. market segmentation
D. fashion forecasting

_____ 25. About three-quarters of all discount retailing is controlled by _____.
A. Wal-Mart
B. Costco
C. Target
D. a combination of all three of these stores

(Continued)

Name_____

_____ 26. Fast fashion _____.
   A. is small, with lots of new designs brought to market quickly
   B. manufacturing is done in close proximity to the market
   C. goods are usually sold at full price because their limited supply is only available for a short time
   D. All of the above.

_____ 27. _____ retailing is when retailers use a combination of several ways of selling, such as stores, catalogs, and Web sites.
   A. Pure-play
   B. Multichannel
   C. Restructured
   D. Outlet

_____ 28. Electronic storefronts _____.
   A. let consumers scroll through the departments of a store that have been simulated electronically
   B. are the latest versions of previous wireless satellite ordering services
   C. are known as computer macromalls
   D. All of the above.

_____ 29. Business restructuring done through consolidation is _____.
   A. the change in the controlling interest of a corporation
   B. the inability to pay debts
   C. the uniting of two or more parts, such as jobs, departments, and divisions, into one
   D. known as vertical integration

_____ 30. Agile manufacturing _____.
   A. is a "seamless" data capture system of information, production, and delivery
   B. combines supply chain collaboration partnerships, Web-based EDI systems, and RF transmission of POS information
   C. combines single ply cutting, flexible assembly, and direct shipment of finished goods to consumers
   D. All of the above.

Essay Questions: Provide complete responses to the following questions or statements.

31. Into what types of retailers is the retail market polarized?

32. Name at least four reasons for the growth of home shopping.

33. Briefly describe Chapter 11 protection and Chapter 7 bankruptcy.

PART EIGHT

Your Future in the Fashion Industry

Is a Fashion Career in Your Future?

Objectives

After studying this chapter, students will be able to

⊖ assess popular views about fashion careers.

⊖ describe how to select a career path.

⊖ list educational requirements for fashion careers.

⊖ describe how to gain preliminary work experience.

⊖ explain what compensation can be expected in fashion careers.

⊖ describe ethical and legal issues of employment.

⊖ summarize the probable future for employment within the industry.

Teaching Materials

Text, pages 532–549
  Fashion Terms
  Fashion Review
  Fashion in Action
Student Workbook
  A. *Fashion Career Planning Maze*
  B. *A Career Self-Evaluation*
  C. *Fashion Careers Terms Match*
  D. *Research and Report*
Teacher's Resources
  Contents of Job Descriptions, transparency master 26-1
  Benefits of Job Descriptions, transparency master 26-2

Employment Levels, transparency master 26-3
My Career Goals, reproducible master 26-4
Implementing Values and Ethics Within Companies, transparency master 26-5
The Penney Idea, transparency master 26-6
Thoughts About Careers, reproducible master, 26-7
Fashion Employee Research, reproducible master 26-8
Chapter 26 Test

Introductory Activities

1. Have students try to think of all the different fashion-related employment within five or ten miles of your school. Then ask students to brainstorm as many fashion-related careers as possible, located anywhere. Expand this into a discussion about fashion jobs being located throughout the United States and the world.

2. Bring to class help wanted ads and job sections from newspapers and fashion trade publications. Ask students to do likewise. Focus on fashion-related employment. Have students analyze the ads to determine the types of jobs available and the qualifications needed.

3. Hold a fun class discussion on students' fantasies about their future careers in fashion. Have students imagine they have no limits or boundaries. What education or preparation would they get, what career would they have, where would they live, and with whom would they work? Let the students' dreams pique their interest in this chapter.

4. For colorful interest on a bulletin board, put up posters that apply to this chapter. Several are available from The School Company, including *Character Motivation: Hard Work Poster Set, Motivation for Career Success Poster Set,* and *School to Career Poster Set.*

An Overview of the Field of Fashion

5. **RF** Discuss with the class how some fashion careers are fascinating, challenging, and exciting. Also discuss the fact that success in these careers demands preparation, dedication, and hard work.

6. **RT** Ask individual students to define the terms *job, job description, career, career path,* and *career planning.* Have other students define *entry-level jobs, management positions, administration, middle management, upper management,* and *top management.*

7. **EX** *Contents of Job Descriptions,* transparency master 26-1. Use the transparency to explain that job descriptions describe a job, not the person who is performing the job. Discuss the fact that better performance and motivation are achieved when employees understand their jobs within the framework of the total company operation and its goals.

8. **EX** *Benefits of Job Descriptions,* transparency master 26-2. Use the transparency to discuss how written job descriptions benefit employees, their supervisors/managers, and the company.

9. **ER** *Employment Levels,* transparency master 26-3. Use the transparency to review each of the general levels of employment from the top to the bottom. Stress that there are very few people employed at the top levels and many people employed at the bottom levels. Also stress that all levels of work are important and can provide rewarding accomplishments and enjoyment when workers have a positive attitude.

10. **EX** Show students a video about using criticism as a constructive opportunity for professional growth and development in their careers. *The Arts of Criticism: Giving and Taking* is available from D.E. Visuals.

Selecting a Career Path

11. **RT** Have students describe what aspects of their adult life will be affected by their career choice and how. Discuss with the class that preparation for a career includes realistic and careful planning and study.

12. **EX** Show students one or more videos about selecting the right careers. Many are available from Sunburst Communications, The School Company, The Curriculum Center for Family and Consumer Sciences, JIST Publishing, Learning Seed, D.E. Visuals, and Meridian Education Corporation.

13. **ER** Have students use a multimedia program to help them match their interests with the characteristics of occupations. *Cambridge Career Center* is available from Cambridge Educational, and *Aptitude Skills Inventory* is available from The School Company.

14. **RT** Have students refer to Illustration 26-7 in the text as you hold a class discussion about the steps involved in career planning.

15. **ER** *Fashion Career Planning Maze,* Activity A, WB. Students are asked to use a continuous line to connect "Start" with "Great Career" in the maze. Then students are asked to create a list of successful career planning steps by writing the 10 phrases, in order, that are crossed by the line. Finally, students are asked to list 10 of the 11 wrong ways to plan a fashion career (phrases not crossed by the line).

16. **RF** Have a class discussion on the importance of interests, aptitudes, and skills in relation to career planning. Have students identify the interests, aptitudes, and skills that are best suited for various fashion careers, such as a textile scientist, fashion designer, retail buyer, or model.

17. **ER** *My Career Goals,* reproducible master 26-4. To help students start to set realistic career goals, have them think seriously about what type of work they may want to be doing in 5, 10, and 25 years. For each question, students will probably have different answers for the different times in their lives. Remind students that no particular answers are right or wrong. Students should evaluate their true feelings. You may also ask students to write a thorough analysis of their career goals in a report to turn in.

Strive Toward the Needed Training and Experience

18. **RT** Have students discuss the future job-related skills learned from extracurricular activities in school. Then hold a class discussion about career programs, certificate courses, associate's degrees, bachelor's degrees, master's degrees, doctorate degrees, and reciprocal agreements. Continue the discussion by explaining work-study programs, cooperative programs, internships, apprenticeships, and management

(executive) training programs. Relate these degrees and programs to preparation for various fashion-related careers. Also discuss the admissions requirements for schools beyond high school (such as high school diploma, SAT or ACT standardized test scores, written essays, interviews, personal recommendations, and art portfolios).

19. **EX** Have students use a multimedia program to learn job search tactics. Some are available from Cambridge Educational and The School Company.

20. **EX** Show the class a video about career planning, preparation, and job search strategies. Many are available from Cambridge Educational, D. E. Visuals, Learning Seed, The Curriculum Center for Family and Consumer Sciences, Meridian Education Corporation, and The School Company.

21. **ER** *A Career Self-Evaluation*, Activity B, WB. The worksheet asks students to answer questions exploring their career interests and abilities. Then students are asked to identify three industry tasks from Illustration 26-8 in the text that interest them and relate these to their abilities and interests.

22. **RF** Have students respond to the statement "The road to success is always under construction." Ask students to explain how this concept might apply to their future careers.

23. **ER** Show the class a video about gaining education and experience. Examples include *Distance Learning* from Meridian Education Corporation and *Apprenticeship* from Cambridge Educational.

24. **EX** Have interested students check into available scholarships and internships for those planning to enter apparel and retail industry jobs. Some places to start are the American Apparel Education Foundation Inc., National Retail Federation, and Textile/Clothing Technology Corporation.

What Compensation Can You Expect?

25. **RT** Have individual students define the terms *compensation*, *compensation package*, *seniority*, *hourly wage*, *overtime*, *minimum wage*, *salary*, *deductions*, *fringe benefits*, *prerequisite*, *bonus*, *incentive bonus*, and *year-end bonus*. Discuss each term in relation to fashion industry employment.

26. **ER** Show the class a video about work compensation. For instance, *How People Are Paid* is available from Learning Seed.

Ethical and Legal Issues of Employment

27. **RT** Ask the class to discuss business ethics, codes of ethics, and value statements. Also have students discuss workplace diversity and employment discrimination.

28. **EX** Show students a video about diversity. *Valuing Diversity* is available from Learning Seed and D.E. Visuals.

29. **ER** Show the class one or more of the following videos about ethics and/or sexual harassment in business: *Business Ethics* from Meridian Education Corporation and D.E. Visuals; *Sexual Harassment* and *Is It Sexual Harassment?* from Cambridge Educational and D.E. Visuals; *What Is Sexual Harassment?* from Learning Seed; *Harassment at Work: Saying No to Being a Victim* from The School Company; and *Doing Right* from D.E. Visuals.

30. **EX** Order sample copies of booklets about ethical and legal issues of employment from Business & Legal Reports, Inc. Examples of pamphlets that are available for companies to buy in quantity to distribute to their employees include *Sexual Harassment in the Workplace*, *About OSHA*, *Drug Testing and You*, and *The ADA & You*.

31. **RF** *Implementing Values and Ethics Within Companies*, transparency master 26-5. Use the transparency for a class discussion on what companies do to maintain high ethical standards. Have students discuss the importance of each item listed.

32. **ER** Have students use a multimedia program about sexual harassment. *Confronting Sexual Harassment: An Interactive Guide* and *Objectionable Actions?: An Interactive Look at Sexual Harassment Situations* are available from Cambridge Educational.

33. **EX** *The Penney Idea*, transparency master 26-6. Use the transparency to acquaint students with the value statement expressed by JCPenney in the early 20th century. Hold a class discussion about how viable these principles are today for the behavior of those who work for the JCPenney Company. Discuss the fact that legal and ethical business practices make good business sense. Discuss how the energetic spirit of Penney's efficient honesty has kept the company strong for the long-term welfare of everyone involved.

Fashion Industry Future for Employment

34. **RT** Discuss with the class the fashion industry's future for employment.

35. **RT** *Fashion Careers Terms Match*, Activity C, WB. Students are asked to match terms from the chapter with their definitions.

36. **EX** *Thoughts About Careers*, reproducible master 26-7. Ask students to read the statements presented, think about each one, and comment on them in a class discussion.

Additional Enrichment Activities

Research

37. Have students research fashion careers on the Internet. They may want to visit the Web sites www.fashion.about.com/cs/cooljobs, www.vault.com, www.jobsinfashion.com, www.allretailjobs.com, www.careerthreads.com, and www.fashioncareercenter.com. The site www.fashion-careers.com sells a book about fashion that students may want to read or you may want to have in the classroom for student research.

38. *Research and Report*, Activity D, WB. Students are asked to work in groups as they research one of four topics, present their material to the class, and respond to follow-up questions or comments from classmates.

39. *Fashion Employee Research*, reproducible master 26-8. Students are asked to interview an employee of a fashion business and report their findings to the class.

40. Ask students to research the code of ethics of the American Marketing Association. Have students report to the class their findings regarding: the responsibilities of marketers, the explanation of honesty and fairness, the rights and duties of parties in the marketing exchange process (in the areas of product development, management, promotions, distribution, pricing, and marketing research), and organizational relationships.

Projects

41. Have a copy of a recent *Occupational Outlook Handbook* (compiled by the U.S. Department of Labor) in your classroom for students to study. It is available, as well as workbooks, from VMS, Inc. Also request similar materials from your school career counselor or librarian.

42. Order the free catalog of occupational reference books and other career resources from JIST Publishing. Have students peruse the many materials that are available to help with career choice decisions, getting a job, and keeping a job. If your course budget allows, order one item that students select each semester. Soon you will have a valuable library of resources for the students to use.

43. Divide the class into groups of students to conduct surveys of several local companies to learn what benefits each provides. Have students ask about child care, parental leaves, flexible work schedules, and reimbursement for further education. Also have students ask about company codes of ethics or value statements, obtaining copies if possible. Have each group report their findings to the rest of the class.

44. Hold a debate on a controversial issue, such as requiring periodic drug testing for continued employment or defining sexual harassment in the workplace. Then have each side of the issue presented to the class by one or more students. Stress that answers to problems are not usually one-sided. This activity shows that problems often have to be faced by both employers and employees.

45. Invite a human resource (personnel department) director, preferably from a fashion-related company, to speak to the class. Have your guest speak about hiring policies; education requirements; job levels; pay, benefits, and bonuses at each level; job descriptions; and opportunities for advancement. Ask the speaker if the company has an executive trainee program for college graduates and/or training for employees without advanced education. Encourage students to ask other pertinent questions about the company or careers available. If this cannot be arranged, ask the school guidance counselor to speak to the class about college programs, occupational training, and careers.

46. Have students read a book about some aspect of this chapter. Then have students present a book report to the class to share its contents.

Text

Fashion Review, pages 549

1. because often retailers must be staffed when other businesses are closed
2. a written statement of what the employee holding a specific job is expected to do
3. Some change companies frequently, and others move up within the same company by proving themselves at each job level.
4. (Name four:) salesperson, assistant buyer, assistant manager, clerical assistant to a buyer, head of stock, executive trainee
5. devoted employees who prove themselves as strategic thinkers and hard workers
6. for 40 years or more
7. (Name three:) design, display, advertising, photography, illustration work
8. from school counselors, library materials, the Internet, trade associations, and people who work in the industry
9. because an unanticipated career direction could open up anywhere along the apparel pipeline if your eyes are open to the potential of it
10. because activities, especially those with leadership roles, can prepare students to deal with challenges in work situations
11. curriculums completed in trade schools
12. payment of at least part of a student's college tuition and/or book costs, or special learning experiences
13. training for an occupation by working under the direction and guidance of a skilled worker
14. an hourly wage or salary, paid vacation time, and other benefits
15. more than the usual 40-hour work week
16. a reward for high sales or productivity during a certain period of time
17. good hiring standards, training, and employee compensation and motivation programs
18. true
19. (Name three:) basic human rights, environmental concerns, product safety, destructive hostile takeovers, slanted government lobbying, inflated pricing
20. by publicizing the new successes, technology, and excitement taking place in the industry

Student Workbook

Fashion Career Planning Maze, Activity A

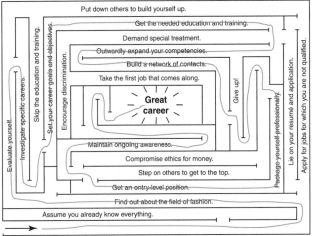

Successful fashion career planning:
1. Find out about the field of fashion.
2. Evaluate yourself.
3. Investigate specific careers.
4. Set your career goals and objectives.
5. Get the needed education and training.
6. Outwardly expand your competencies.
7. Build a network of contacts.
8. Package yourself professionally.
9. Get an entry-level position.
10. Maintain ongoing awareness.

Poor fashion career planning: (List in any order.)
1. Assume you already know everything.
2. Put others down to build yourself up.
3. Demand special treatment.
4. Skip the education and training.
5. Take the first job that comes along.
6. Lie on your résumé and application.
7. Apply for jobs for which you are not qualified.
8. Step on others to get to the top.
9. Encourage discrimination.
10. Compromise ethics for money.
11. Give up.

Fashion Careers Terms Match, Activity C

1. E		13. W	
2. F		14. T	
3. U		15. R	
4. C		16. V	
5. J		17. Q	
6. O		18. S	
7. X		19. A	
8. P		20. G	
9. D		21. H	
10. L		22. B	
11. M		23. N	
12. I		24. K	

(second group:)

1. EE		11. II	
2. KK		12. QQ	
3. MM		13. BB	
4. AA		14. HH	
5. PP		15. OO	
6. GG		16. LL	
7. DD		17. RR	
8. TT		18. NN	
9. JJ		19. CC	
10. FF		20. SS	

Teacher's Resources

Chapter 26 Test

1. F		11. T		21. D	
2. C		12. T		22. D	
3. H		13. T		23. D	
4. I		14. T		24. D	
5. A		15. F		25. C	
6. J		16. F		26. A	
7. G		17. T		27. B	
8. B		18. T		28. C	
9. D		19. T		29. A	
10. E		20. T		30. D	

31. A job is a specific work assignment or position within an industry with certain duties, roles, or functions. A career is a lifelong field of employment, or vocation, through which people progress.

32. Interests are what people like to do. Aptitudes are people's talents that they are naturally good at doing. Skills are people's abilities of doing specific tasks, usually developed with education and training.

33. An associate's degree is usually earned in two years at a community college. A bachelor's degree is usually earned in 4 years at a college or university.

Contents of Job Descriptions

- Summary—definition of job area

- Source of authority—to whom the job area is responsible

- Scope of authority—how far the job's influence extends

- Scope of job—detailed description of responsibilities in outline form according to functions

- Required personal and business abilities, skills, education, experience to hold the job

Based on work by Gene Levine Associates

Benefits of Job Descriptions

- **Introduces new employees to their jobs** in relation to duties, organizational connections, reporting procedures, etc.

- **Aligns functions and responsibilities** to minimize duplications of efforts with other jobs while striving to meet company goals

- **Establishes channels of communications** for expected exchange of information through the organization

- **Assists management in evaluating employee performance**

Based on work by Gene Levine Associates

Employment Levels

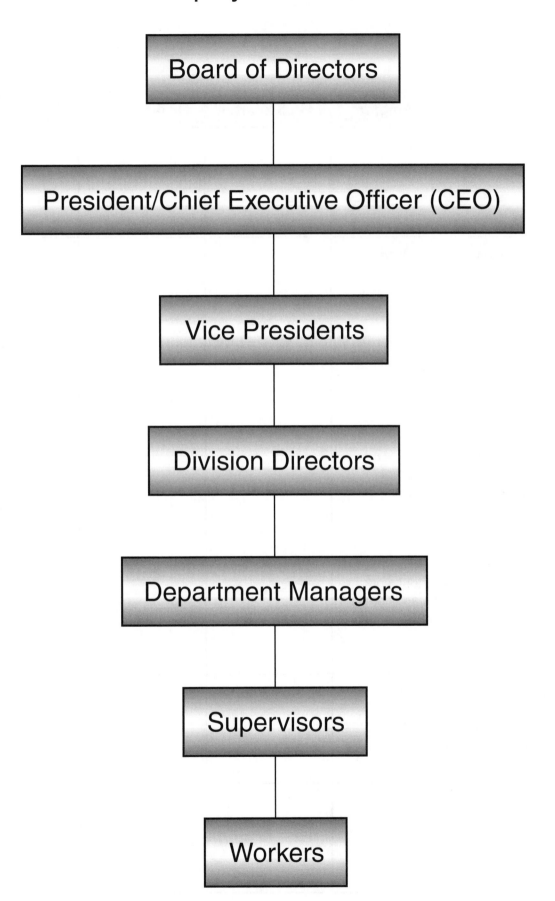

Board of Directors

President/Chief Executive Officer (CEO)

Vice Presidents

Division Directors

Department Managers

Supervisors

Workers

My Career Goals

Name_____ **Date** _____ **Period** _____

Career Questions to Answer	In 5 Years	In 10 Years	In 25 Years
What type of job would I like to have?			
Will I want to travel or stay close to home?			
Will I want to work in a city or a small town?			
Will I want to move to a different location or remain in the same geographic area?			
Will I prefer a regular 40-hour work week or one that requires additional hours and/or evening and weekend work?			
Will I want to receive high pay for handling nonstop pressure and responsibility, or receive low to medium pay for a job with manageable levels of pressure and responsibility?			
Will I want to work for someone else (large vs. a small company) or be self-employed?			

Implementing Values and Ethics Within Companies

- Stress them when recruiting and hiring to screen out incompatible job candidates.

- Incorporate them into employee training and education.

- Regularly explain compliance procedures to all employees.

- Show involvement and oversight from top management down through chains of command.

The Penney Idea

(Seven Principles Value Statement Expressed by JCPenney in 1913)

1. To serve the public, as nearly as we can, to its complete satisfaction.

2. To expect for the service we render, a fair remuneration and not all the profit the traffic will bear.

3. To do all in our power to pack the customer's dollar full of value, quality, and satisfaction.

4. To continue to train ourselves and our associates so that the service we give will be more and more intelligently performed.

5. To improve constantly the human factor in our business.

6. To reward men and women in our organization through participation in what the business produces.

7. To test our every policy, method, and act in this wise: "Does it square with what is right and just?"

Thoughts About Careers

Name_____ Date _____ Period _____

Read these statements, think about each one, and comment on them in a class discussion.

1. The four Ps of finding the right job are **planning**, **perseverance**, **passion**, and **patience**. In other words, job seekers must think carefully about what they want, have persistence in their efforts, feel a strong and focused direction from within, and practice discipline to wait for the right opportunity.

2. **Diversity** is not about one group "winning out" over another. It is about recognizing that everyone brings a unique and valuable perspective to the workplace. Ten different ideas and opinions are better than ten identical ones.

3. Many retailers are using **pre-employment screening services**. High-tech, automated programs are custom-tailored to specific situations. Some are Web-based to allow more candidates to apply. Retailers can be more selective in hiring, especially for the multitude of seasonal employees needed.

4. Periodic **performance appraisals** rate an employee's competence in a job, which is evaluated by a person of authority. Employees must be able to take constructive criticism with an open mind and a good attitude, then try to build on suggestions and correct weaknesses.

5. Information about **expected pay** for specific jobs in certain parts of the country can be obtained from the Bureau of Labor Statistics (an annual survey of jobs and their pay) and www.salary.com.

6. In a **tight labor market**, retail pay rates go higher to try to lure employees to work in stores. Also, retailers sometimes try to entice workers from nearby offices into working at the store in the evenings, or store customers into becoming sales associates (with referral bonuses paid to current employees).

7. Policies relating to sexual harassment and other employment issues need stringent education and training of employees. This **proactive stance** shows a company's commitment to increased awareness and prevention of problems rather than reacting to them.

8. Studies have found that **older workers** are dependable, reliable, and loyal. Also, they have a lot of knowledge, experience, and maturity. Retailers especially like seniors for part-time work, and the employees get extra cash, store discounts, and independence to enjoy life after retirement from a different career.

9. The Internet has emerged as a major vehicle for **recruiting mid-level retail employees**. Web sites offer data on salaries, available types of jobs, skills being sought, and ways to apply. Industry search-service sites recruit candidates and place them in jobs that match their qualifications.

10. Only **top management** positions receive six-figure pay (meaning over $100,000 per year). A seven-figure salary (over one million dollars per year) is rare in the fashion industry except for the very few most successful designers and heads of companies.

Fashion Employee Research

Name_____ **Date** _____ **Period** _____

Interview an employee of a fashion business and record his or her answers below. Report your findings to the class. (This may be done as an individual or group activity.)

1. For what company do you work? _____

2. What is the title of your position? _____

3. What are your duties?_____

   _____

   _____

4. How many hours do you work each day and each week? _____

5. Do you work regular weekday hours or weekends, holidays, or evenings? _____

   _____

6. What special skills are needed for your job? _____

   _____

   _____

7. What dress regulations are you required to follow? _____

   _____

8. What safety and security precautions are you required to follow? _____

   _____

   _____

9. What education prepared you for your job/career? _____

   _____

10. What company training did you receive to perform your job?_____

   _____

11. What other jobs have you held before this? _____

   _____

   _____

12. What additional skills and knowledge have you gained since taking this job? _____

   _____

   _____

(Continued)

Name_____

13. What are the most enjoyable aspects of your job?_____

_____

_____

_____

14. What do you like least about your job?_____

_____

_____

15. Is there other education that would have prepared you more completely? _____

_____

_____

16. What interesting or challenging experiences have you had with your supervisors and coworkers?

_____

_____

17. What are your career goals? _____

_____

_____

18. What are your overall feelings about your current job or future career?_____

_____

19. What other information would be helpful for students who may want to go into your type of work?

_____

_____

_____

_____

_____

Is a Fashion Career in Your Future?

Name_____

Date_____ **Period**_____ **Score**_____

Chapter 26 Test

Matching: Match the following terms and identifying phrases.

_____ 1. A certain predetermined pay rate per hour spent doing a job.

_____ 2. The use of good moral values in business dealings.

_____ 3. A fixed amount of pay, usually received once or twice a month, for doing all that is required for a particular job.

_____ 4. The length of time an employee has been in a job compared to others who do the same job.

_____ 5. Employment rewards in addition to wages, salary, or bonus.

_____ 6. The blending of different races, cultures, genders, ages, socioeconomic backgrounds, personality types, and intelligence levels into a productive employment team.

_____ 7. The lowest hourly pay rate established by law.

_____ 8. Extra monetary payment in addition to regular pay.

_____ 9. The process by which managers and employees lay out employees' futures with the firm, based on the firm's needs and each employee's strengths and weaknesses.

_____ 10. The treating of people differently related to prejudice rather than work performance.

A. fringe benefits

B. bonus

C. business ethics

D. career planning

E. employment discrimination

F. hourly wage

G. minimum wage

H. salary

I. seniority

J. workplace diversity

True/False: Circle *T* if the statement is true or *F* if the statement is false.

T   F   11. The seasonality of fashion work can result in hectic times followed by slow, dull periods.

T   F   12. A career path is the order of jobs worked in a person's life, often spanning 40 years or more.

T   F   13. People who want to be employed in fashion jobs should be computer literate.

T   F   14. Higher education and more training enables employees to have faster job advancement and higher pay.

T   F   15. Middle management positions are only achieved by devoted employees who prove themselves as strategic thinkers and hard workers.

T   F   16. When setting career goals, it is wise to be very specific.

(Continued)

Name_____

T   F   17. Extracurricular activities with leadership roles can prepare students to deal with challenges in work situations.

T   F   18. Certificate courses are curriculums completed in trade schools.

T   F   19. An apprenticeship is training for an occupation by working under the guidance of a skilled worker.

T   F   20. Compensation is payment for work done.

Multiple Choice: Choose the best response. Write the letter in the space provided.

_____ 21. A job description _____.
- A. is a written statement of what the employee holding a specific job is expected to do
- B. tells what authority the employee has
- C. outlines the expectations of accomplishments for that job
- D. All of the above.

_____ 22. People can move up the ladder to career success by _____.
- A. changing companies frequently, taking a higher job at each firm
- B. moving up in one company, proving themselves at each job level
- C. strengthening their skills and showing their talents
- D. All of the above.

_____ 23. Management positions deal with _____.
- A. planning and organizing the program of the organization
- B. controlling and implementing the program of the organization
- C. monitoring and running the program of the organization
- D. All of the above.

_____ 24. Jobs with the abbreviations of *CEO*, *COO*, and *CFO* are at the level of _____.
- A. lower management
- B. middle management
- C. upper management
- D. top management

_____ 25. An entry-level job is _____.
- A. performed on the first (ground) floor of office buildings or manufacturing plants
- B. a part-time work position held until a full-time position opens up
- C. a person's beginning job in a career
- D. the first job a person has, either part-time or full-time, often during high school years

_____ 26. To choose the right career path, you must _____.
- A. get to know yourself and learn about various careers
- B. buy (or make) a more professional wardrobe
- C. study hard at a top-notch college or university
- D. All of the above.

(Continued)

Name_____

_____ 27. A specific field of study in college is called the student's _____.
   A. master's degree
   B. major
   C. minor
   D. doctorate degree

_____ 28. Exchange programs with schools or colleges elsewhere are known as _____.
   A. career programs
   B. MBA arrangements
   C. reciprocal agreements
   D. credit substitution programs

_____ 29. Work-study programs _____.
   A. team schools with employers for students to get on-the-job career training
   B. are known as internships at high school and trade school levels
   C. are known as cooperative programs at college levels
   D. All of the above.

_____ 30. Executive trainee programs _____.
   A. are general orientations offered by most large companies for new employees with college degrees
   B. are also called management training programs
   C. usually include both classroom and on-the-job training
   D. All of the above.

Essay Questions: Provide complete responses to the following questions or statements.

31. What is the difference between a job and a career?

32. In self-evaluation, what is the meaning of interests, aptitudes, and skills?

33. What is the difference between an associate's degree and a bachelor's degree?

CHAPTER 27

Textile and Apparel Careers

Objectives

After studying this chapter, students will be able to

→ describe careers in textile research and development, design, and production.

→ summarize employment opportunities in apparel design and manufacturing.

→ explain sales and distribution opportunities in textiles and apparel.

Teaching Materials

Text, pages 550–570
Fashion Terms
Fashion Review
Fashion in Action

Student Workbook
A. *Categorizing Jobs*
B. *Textile/Apparel Employment Review*
C. *Careers Fill-in-the-Blanks*
D. *Developing a Textile or Apparel Line*
E. *Match the Qualifications*

Teacher's Resources
Going Further with Textile Employment, reproducible master 27-1
Types of Fashion Designers, transparency master 27-2
Become a Fashion Designer, reproducible master 27-3
Old and New Cutting Room Skills, transparency master 27-4
Expressing Apparel Design and Manufacturing Interest, reproducible master 27-5
Define "Team," transparency master 27-6
Marketing Plan for a New Product, reproducible master 27-7
Chapter 27 Test

Introductory Activities

1. Gather reference books to help you teach this and following chapters. Suggestions are *Textile and Apparel Production, Management, and Services* (Reference Book, Curriculum Guide, Student Activity Book, Answer Key, and Competency Profile Folder) and *Textile and Apparel Design Teacher's Instructional Guide*, both from The Curriculum Center for Family and Consumer Sciences. Cambridge Educational offers *Opportunities in Fashion*.

2. Show a PowerPoint CD to the class about careers in clothing services, clothing production and management, textile and clothing design, and merchandising and retailing. *Careers in Apparel & Textiles* is available from D.E. Visuals.

3. Ask students to explain why the success of textile and apparel manufacturing companies is so dependent on the fabric and garment designs created and the skill of the designers. Also discuss the fact that it takes both technical and artistic skills to produce a fabric and a fashion garment.

4. Discuss with the class that textile and apparel manufacturing jobs have always been very labor-intensive, requiring a high percentage of unskilled labor at low wages. Then discuss how the industry is now becoming more capital-intensive with automation and computer technology, requiring higher skill levels and paying better wages. Stress the fact that the best career opportunities arise for people with solid educational backgrounds and continually updated skills.

Strategies to Reteach, Reinforce, Enrich, and Extend Text Concepts

A Career in the Textile Industry

5. **RT** Ask students to discuss the field of textile research and development, including the jobs of textile research scientists, textile laboratory technicians, and textile testers. Ask students to describe the type of work, personal requirements, education needed, and salary level for each of the jobs discussed.

6. **EX** Show students a video about textile research. *Textile Research Center* is available from Nasco and The Curriculum Center for Family and Consumer Sciences.

7. **ER** *Going Further with Textile Employment*, reproducible master 27-1. Students are asked to consider statements containing new information, record their responses, and discuss the statements with the class.

8. **RF** Have individual students explain the jobs of fabric structural designer, fabric surface designer, print/repeat artist, colorist, strike-off artist, fabric stylist, fashion director (merchandiser), department manager, fabric librarian, and market analyst to the rest of the class. Ask students to describe the type of work, personal requirements, education needed, and salary level of each of the jobs. Then have students refer to Illustration 27-13 in the text to review how these and other jobs fit into a company's organization.

9. **RT** Ask students to discuss the field of textile production, including the jobs of textile production workers (operators), production supervisors, quality control inspectors, plant engineers, and industrial engineers.

A Career in the Apparel Industry

10. **RF** Have individual students explain the jobs and qualifications of fashion designers, design stylists, and sketchers. Clarify the fact that a fabric stylist is in charge of coordinating all business aspects of an entire line for a textile company, while a design stylist for an apparel company does only copying of garment ideas. Students may also want to discuss designers of accessories, jewelry, or furs, or others who must coordinate their designs with fashion garments.

11. **ER** *Types of Fashion Designers*, transparency master 27-2. Use this transparency to discuss the various types of fashion designers. Relate this information to the price market categories of apparel that were studied in Chapter 9 of the text. Also discuss the opportunities in fashion design because of the several levels of work, especially if CAD technology is learned.

12. **EX** Have students use a computer program to become instant fashion designers by combining given garment parts into entire new fashions. *ApparelCAD* software is available from VMS, Inc. Also, templates for drawing fashion designs, called *Fashion Studio Kits*, are available from HearthSong at www.hearthsong.com.

13. **ER** Record from TV, to show to the class, or encourage students to watch the reality show *Project Runway*. Aspiring fashion designers compete to be the best designer and must stay within specified costs, materials, or other parameters. Students will see how difficult it is to design and make outstanding fashions.

14. **RF** *Become a Fashion Designer*, reproducible master 27-3. Use the handout to have students pretend to be fashion designers. Students are asked to draw original creations on a female and a male figure and explain why they included the specific features in each design.

15. **RT** Ask students to discuss the jobs of sample cutter, sample maker, pattern maker, pattern grader, marker, spreader, cutter, and assorter. Discuss how some of these jobs will become obsolete as the use of computer technology becomes more widespread in all aspects of apparel manufacturing. Also discuss why knowing how to make or grade patterns and make markers by hand must first be understood in order to do an effective job with CAD equipment.

16. **EX** Inform the class about some job titles that are not discussed in the chapter. Examples are
   - technical designer—achieves the required quality level in a cost-efficient way
   - quality control specialist—guides manufacturing to meet production specifications and quality standards
   - training supervisor—trains workers on new tasks and specialized machines
   - machine technician—maintains factory equipment, diagnoses problems, and corrects malfunctions
   - offshore sourcing manager—determines where and how to have items manufactured worldwide

   Have students add others they have learned from reading trade journals or talking to employees in the industry. (New jobs evolve with circumstances.)

17. **RF** Have the class look back to Illustration 10-11 in the text to review the flowchart of apparel manufacturing in relation to the jobs described in this chapter.

18. **EX** Show students a video about apparel industry careers. Suggestions are *Careers in Fashion* from Nasco, Meridian Education Corporation, Insight Media, and VMS, Inc.; *Apparel and Textile Careers* from Insight Media and The Curriculum Center for Family and Consumer Sciences; *Fashion Careers* from Meridian Education Corporation; *Mastering Fashion Design: Studying with Vivienne Westwood* from Meridian Education Corporation and D.E. Visuals; and *Manufacturing* from Cambridge Educational.

19. **RT** Have students describe the apparel production jobs of sewing machine operator, finisher, inspector/trimmer, alteration hand, and presser. Have other students describe the production management positions of product manager, marketing manager, plant manager, production supervisor, piece goods buyer, and costing engineer. Ask students to explain the qualifications needed for management jobs, as well as for the positions of management trainee, production assistant, and costing clerk.

20. **ER** *Old and New Cutting Room Skills*, transparency master 27-4. Use the transparency to discuss each set of old and new procedures for apparel cutting. Stress that old methods had supervisors advising each employee of work assignments and efficiency levels, which are now available to operators from computer systems. Also stress that computer skills (including the abilities to read, use keyboards, and calculate numbers) are now essential for apparel industry employment.

21. **RF** *Expressing Apparel Design and Manufacturing Interest*, reproducible master 27-5. Use the handout to have students check their interest in becoming a fashion designer or going into apparel manufacturing work.

22. **EX** Show students one of the following videos about the value of teamwork in apparel production: *Getting Cooperation: Team Building That Works, Building Cooperation: How Everyone Can Win*, and *The Team Approach* from D.E. Visuals; *Attitude Towards Teamwork* from The School Company; and *Teamwork on the Job* and *All for One: Team Building in Action* from Cambridge Educational.

23. **RF** *Define "Team,"* transparency master 27-6. Use the transparency to have students analyze and discuss several meanings of the word team. Then have the class write their own definition on the board. Finally, ask students to explain why teamwork is so important in apparel manufacturing as well as in most other types of jobs. Stress that teamwork enables employees to take control of their jobs and do what needs to be done without constant direction.

Textile and Apparel Sales and Distribution

24. **RT** Discuss with the class the jobs of selling fibers, greige goods, finished fabrics, notions, and apparel lines. Have students describe the duties of and qualifications for these jobs. Also discuss how these jobs serve as the link between a company and its customers.

25. **EX** Show students one of the following videos about the path of fashion merchandise after production: *Transportation, Distribution, & Logistics* is available from Cambridge Educational; and *Wholesaling and Making Effective Sales Calls* from D.E. Visuals.

26. **RT** Ask students to explain the jobs of showroom salesperson, sales trainee, merchandise coordinator, showroom manager, traveling sales representative, account executive, and sales manager. Tell the class about merchandise control specialists who watch the rate of merchandise flow to determine how well items are selling in various localities, and who suggest that salespeople stress certain items or colors in particular parts of the country. Also have the class discuss the importance of salespeople reporting to their companies about market trends and buyer feedback.

27. **RF** *Categorizing Jobs*, Activity A, WB. The worksheet directs students to match various job titles with basic career categories in the textile and apparel segments of the fashion industry. Then students are asked to explain which job most appeals to them.

28. **ER** Have students prepare and give a sales presentation about a textile or apparel line to the rest of the class. Students should assume the identity of a showroom salesperson or a traveling sales rep. They should describe a fictitious line (possibly with pictures, actual fabrics or garments, or other visual aids) in a way they think would gain the highest possible number of sales. Students should point out the newest styling features, fiber content, and colors, including suggestions for apparel manufacturers to use the textiles or retailers to present and display the apparel. Also ask students to be ready to handle objections and close the sale.

29. **RT** *Textile/Apparel Employment Review*, Activity B, WB. Students are asked to answer questions as a review of the chapter.

30. **EX** Ask the class to discuss the changes in job duties for textile and apparel sales as a result of long-term Quick Response partnerships. Discuss the activities of salespeople in managing inventories and forming "customer service teams" to help customers meet their goals.

31. **RT** *Careers Fill-in-the-Blanks*, Activity C, WB. Students are asked to complete sentences by filling in the correct chapter term (shown in bold print or italics in the text).

32. **RT** Have students define *distribution*, which was studied in Chapters 3 and 11 of the text. Also have them discuss distribution centers and the job of traffic manager.

33. **EX** *Developing a Textile or Apparel Line*, Activity D, WB. Students are asked to imagine they are fashion industry employees handling real-life jobs. Divide the class into two groups of "employees," assigning one group to textile company employment and the other to apparel company employment. Give each student one (or more) specific job titles and have them learn all they can about the responsibilities of their respective jobs. Then ask students to perform their jobs while working on a team to develop a sample line. Finally, have both groups present their information and product lines to the rest of the class.

34. **ER** *Match the Qualifications*, Activity E, WB. Students are asked to read the qualifications of various individuals and match the job title most suited to each.

Additional Enrichment Activities

Research

35. Have students research the development and marketing of Tencel lyocell, Lycra spandex, or another textile product. The story of DuPont's Qiana® nylon in the 1970s is interesting, even though the product is no longer sold.

36. Have students research the historical development of textile dyeing and finishing in the United States. Have students discover why this work started near Paterson, New Jersey; how the jobs of dyers (commission, company, and master dyers) developed; and the current status and location of the dyeing industry.

37. Have students research the capabilities of the latest CAD design programs for textile design and production or fashion design and production. Ask students to report their findings to the class and initiate a discussion of the advantages and disadvantages of the new technology.

38. Have students research the latest specialized and computerized industrial sewing machines. Have students report to the class about the speed and flexibility of programmable machines and automated workstations. Also have students discuss the effects these developments have had on employee training, productivity, and fatigue, as well as machine maintenance.

Projects

39. *Marketing Plan for a New Product*, reproducible master 27-7. This can be used as a project for the entire class or for groups of students to do separately. Students are to study the steps of the master marketing plan and then think of a new type of textile product to bring to market by following the steps. Some ideas are: a warm but wickable knit fabric for use in winter sports underwear, a luxurious silk-like fabric that is stretchy and machine washable, a double-layer fabric that gives warmth but separates for coolness, and a swimsuit fabric that has the buoyancy of a life preserver.

40. Invite to class someone who works in textile or apparel design, sales, or distribution. Ask the person to tell students as many aspects of his or her job and company as possible, especially opportunities for employment. Then have students ask informed questions of the speaker. If this is not possible, try to have students interview, either by phone or in person, someone who works in one of the jobs mentioned. Have students prepare their questions ahead of time and, after the interview, present a report to the class.

41. Take a class trip to a nearby textile or apparel manufacturing firm. Have students quietly observe the jobs being done and ask the guide from the company about specific qualifications needed, wage rates, and fringe benefits.

42. Contact (or have students contact) trade organizations connected with the textile and apparel industries. Examples from the resource list included in the *Teacher's Resources* introduction are: the American Apparel Contractors Association, American Apparel and Footwear Association, American Apparel Producers' Network, American Association of Textile Chemists and Colorists, American Fiber Manufacturers Association, American Yarn Spinners Association, Canadian Apparel Federation, Canadian Textile Institute, Council of Fashion Designers of America, Custom Tailors and Designers Association of America, The Fashion Group International, International Apparel Federation, International Association of Clothing Designers and Executives, International Textiles and Apparel Association Inc., International Textile Manufacturers Federation, Knitted Textile Association, National Association of the Sewn Products Industry, National Knitwear and Sportswear Association, and National Textile Association. Ask students to study the information and find out what jobs are located where plus the preparation needed to hold them. Then have students report what they have learned to the class.

Answer Key

Text

Fashion Review, pages 570

1. a balanced representation of your best abilities; each piece should be mounted neatly and have your name on it
2. because it often takes months or years to invent a product or solve a technical problem
3. polymer chemistry, textile science, chemical engineering, or physics
4. textile mills or independent testing labs
5. works with the fabric mills that use the company's fibers to develop the correct types of yard goods for the market
6. manufactured fiber companies, natural fiber trade associations, and home sewing pattern companies
7. training in textiles, business, marketing, economics, psychology, and statistics
8. translate the company's color choices and applied print looks onto fabrics
9. textile production
10. (Name three:) forecasts amounts of raw materials needed, computes how much of each type of fiber or fabric to produce, does statistical analysis for quality control, does automatic weaving and knitting from CAD instructions
11. They adapt higher-priced fashion designs to the price ranges of their customers.
12. so they can stay within the production capabilities and marketing plans of their firms
13. by sketching on paper, draping fabric onto a dressmaker's form, or using CAD equipment
14. because of imports, the use of higher technology, and lower retail sales
15. because of the rapid pace and pressure for high performance
16. detail work and record keeping for plant managers
17. time and motion studies of industrial engineers
18. by reporting market trends that become apparent and feedback from buyers of their company's goods
19. a certain geographic selling area
20. quantitative methods, finance, accounting, and marketing

Student Workbook

Categorizing Jobs, Activity A

1. D	6. S	11. D	16. P
2. R	7. P	12. P	17. D
3. D	8. P	13. S	18. P
4. P	9. R	14. R	19. S
5. P	10. D	15. S	20. P

Textile/Apparel Employment Review, Activity B

1. They learn professional methods and gain experience while earning advanced degrees.
2. set up equipment, write down computations, and categorize experiment results
3. because apparel designers and manufacturers are guided by fabric offerings
4. by doing calculated drawings on graph paper
5. (Name four:) fabric mills, textile converters, garment producers that make their own fabrics, fabric design studios, forecasting services, retail private label product development offices, interior decorating fabric companies, computer graphics design firms
6. The former is a lower, more clerical job; the latter is a middle management position that helps compile lines, prepare story boards, do forecasting, and give design assignments and plant directions.
7. merchandiser
8. to apparel designers, manufacturers, buying offices, fashion magazines, and retail companies
9. Fabric swatches are clipped to cards on which detailed descriptions and sources of supply are recorded.
10. operate the machines that do the manufacturing procedures
11. make sure all environmental systems are operating properly
12. mass-produced, low-priced items
13. in ready-to-wear manufacturing firms (also with home sewing pattern companies)
14. because design specifications may have several revisions
15. sews sample garment designs together, following the designer's pattern, sketch, and specifications
16. producers of better-quality, higher-priced lines
17. plans and directs all marketing endeavors of the company
18. Fiber salespeople sell to yarn producers or fabric manufacturers; greige goods producers sell to converters.
19. a base salary plus a commission on the amount sold
20. "in-house" sales employees at the firm's sales offices, who present the line of goods to visiting buyers

Careers Fill-in-the-Blanks, Activity C

1. sketchers
2. sales managers
3. fashion director
4. print/repeat artist
5. motif
6. traffic managers
7. sample makers

8. portfolio
9. fabric librarian
10. product managers
11. industrial engineers
12. plant engineers
13. fabric structural designers
14. production supervisors
15. fashion designers
16. alteration hands
17. strike-off artist
18. market analysts
19. quality control inspectors
20. colorist
21. piece goods buyers
22. design stylists
23. fabric stylists
24. plant manager
25. department manager
26. costing engineer
27. textile testers
28. fabric surface designers
29. pattern graders
30. textile laboratory technicians

Match the Qualifications, Activity E

1. O
2. I
3. P
4. B
5. E
6. J
7. R
8. G
9. L
10. F
11. A
12. Q
13. M
14. C
15. N
16. K
17. H
18. D

Teacher's Resources

Chapter 27 Test

1. G
2. F
3. E
4. H
5. C
6. B
7. A
8. I
9. J
10. D
11. F
12. F
13. F
14. F
15. T
16. T
17. T
18. F
19. T
20. T
21. C
22. D
23. A
24. C
25. B
26. D
27. B
28. D
29. C
30. C

31. A fabric stylist is a textile company employee (executive) who serves as a bridge between the creative and business aspects of the company, coordinating fabric design, production, and sales. An apparel design stylist (copyist) is an apparel company employee who redesigns existing garments rather than creating new fashion designs.

32. A textile production worker operates the machines that do the manufacturing procedures to produce textiles. A sewing machine operator (sometimes called a sewing technician) has the same job in the apparel industry—an apparel production worker.

33. A plant manager is the executive in charge of all operations and employees at a manufacturing plant. A sales manager supervises several sales representatives in an established district of the country or a division of the company.

Going Further with Textile Employment

Name_____ **Date** _____ **Period** _____

Think about the following statements and write your thoughts about each in the space provided. Then discuss the statements with the class.

1. **Research and development employees** usually work in modern, well-equipped laboratories and belong to professional societies. The fees for the seminars and conferences these employees sometimes attend are paid by the companies that employ them._____

_____

_____

2. **Textile technicians and testers** should be organized, efficient, and like to work alone with equipment and chemicals. They must be able to follow precise instructions, do detailed work, and accurately record their test results._____

_____

_____

3. **Fabric designers** work months in advance of apparel manufacturing and retail sales to consumers. They must be good at anticipating trends in fabric construction, color, texture, and other qualities.

_____

_____

_____

4. A **woven fabric designer** creates original designs on a CAD system and may execute ideas on a hand loom. This person also sends out mill specifications and does quality control, research, and resource work. _____

_____

_____

5. A **knit designer** designs at a computer, executes knit swatches, and sets up knitting machines. Knitting skills and an understanding of textile and apparel production processes are necessary.

_____

_____

_____

6. A **lace and embroidery designer** does detailed technical drawings of intricate interlocking designs for lace and embroidery. This job usually does not deal with color. _____

_____

_____

7. A **screen print artist** executes the designer's ideas through screen printing. An understanding of color is necessary. Screen printing is used for limited custom fabrics or exclusive yardages in small amounts._____

_____

_____

(Continued)

Name_____

8. A *painted woven designer* executes painted woven designs by adding colorations with a CAD system or with an outlining pen and airbrush. _____

_____

_____

9. *Market analysts* research consumers' habits, needs, and wants. They spend time with forecasters to predict what products and colors will sell in the future and why. Then they help product managers develop the best textile products to meet the demand. _____

_____

_____

10. At textile dye plants, *hand dips* are often done first to perfect the color and see how it looks in a certain weave or knit. This establishes color accuracy before large dye lots are done. _____

_____

_____

_____

11. A candidate for the job of *fashion director* may be someone who has acquired fashion expertise at a smaller firm and wants more responsibility and higher pay, or a company employee who has demonstrated the ability to do the job. _____

_____

_____

_____

12. *Textile salespeople* may additionally sell to retail fabric stores and household goods producers. They may also help their companies participate in textile trend shows, possibly with garment samples, a video, slides, and/or commentary. _____

_____

_____

13. *Textile plant operations* include opening bales of fibers, cleaning and straightening the fibers, spinning the fibers into yarns, weaving or knitting fabrics, and chemically or mechanically finishing the fabrics. However, textile mills sometimes handle just one part of production: spinning, weaving, knitting, or finishing. _____

_____

_____

14. Each textile manufacturing step needs specialized machinery and skilled workers. Many companies have plants in more than one location, so employees are subject to transfer if their expertise is needed elsewhere. However, in general, *textile production workers* rarely travel. _____

_____

_____

_____

_____

Types of Fashion Designers

- **Custom**—do made-to-order fashions for individual clients

- **Designer/Bridge**—create upscale seasonal collections with top-quality materials and workmanship

- **Mass Production**—design ready-to-wear lines made in standard sizes for retail selling to consumers

- **Stylist**—do knock-off copies for mass production by adapting popular styles to lower quality and price levels

- **Freelance**—work on a private basis for several manufacturers or sell sketches of designs to manufacturers for their lines

Become a Fashion Designer

Name_____ **Date** _____ **Period** _____

Assume the identity of a designer of ladies' sportswear, women's evening gowns, men's sportswear, boys' beachwear, or another category of your choice. Draw an original creation on the two figures here. Then explain why you included the particular features in your designs.

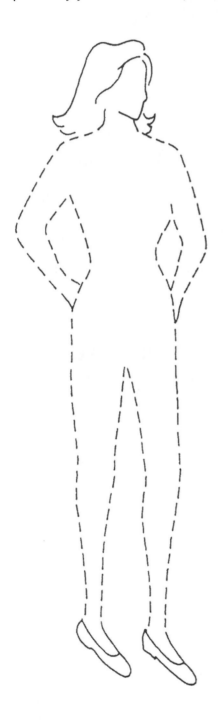

1.

_____

(Continued)

Name_____

2.

_____
_____
_____
_____
_____
_____
_____
_____
_____
_____
_____
_____
_____
_____
_____
_____
_____
_____
_____
_____
_____
_____
_____
_____

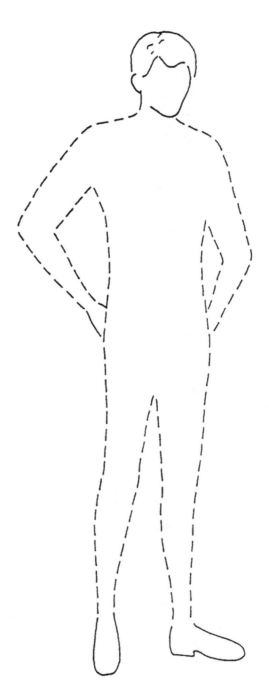

Old and New Cutting Room Skills

Old—manual spreading, knife cutting, and assembly of parts	New—automated, computerized cutting machines
Do work as directed by a supervisor.	Read and carry out computer-generated order plans.
Lift rolls of cloth to a spreading machine and "lay up" to be cut.	Thread ends of cloth into automated cutters.
Lay markers on cloth and cut with saw-type knife.	Input control data to auto-cutting equipment and begin processing.
Manually count, bundle, and stack component parts.	Move cut, precounted stacks of component parts into production.
Advise supervisor of quantity handled.	Read data on equipment and complete order plan documents.

Based on work of the Continuing Education Subcommittee, American Apparel and Footwear Association

Expressing Apparel Design and Manufacturing Interest

Name_____ **Date** _____ **Period** _____

For each statement in this and the next chart, place a check in the column that best represents your level of interest. Add your scores for each page according to the directions. (You will not be graded on your score.) Then answer the questions that follow.

Statements	Interested (3 points)	Unsure (1 point)	Not Interested (0 points)
Attending fashion shows to see new ideas.			
Creating original clothes for yourself or others.			
Researching new fashion ideas, trends, and colors.			
Combining different garments that can be worn together.			
Shopping for fabrics that can be used for new garments.			
Observing people's clothing and analyzing their style.			
Designing the costumes for a beauty contest.			
Learning how to develop a garment pattern by hand.			
Pinning fabric to a dressmakers' form to create garment ideas.			
Designing uniforms for a particular company.			
Embellishing an evening dress with sequins, beads, lace, etc.			
Being responsible for the new ideas for an entire clothing line.			
Checking the fit of clothes on models.			
Taking a class in fashion sketching.			
Making a pattern, to be used for production, on CAD equipment.			
Subtotals =			

Total score _____

If your total score is between 31 and 45, you have high interest in becoming a **fashion designer**. If your total score is between 15 and 30, you are interested in fashion design for yourself but not as a career. If your score is less than 15, you are probably not suited for a fashion design career.

How does your score correspond with your previous thoughts about being a fashion designer?_____

_____

_____

(Continued)

Name_____

Statements	Interested (3 points)	Unsure (1 point)	Not Interested (0 points)
Evaluating and hiring fashion designers for an apparel firm.			
Analyzing fashion designs to decide which ones will sell.			
Researching prices of fabrications, notions, and trims.			
Ordering large quantities of materials for a new apparel line.			
Negotiating with suppliers for the best prices and service.			
Traveling to Mexico to contact apparel production plants.			
Figuring out ways to cut apparel costs.			
Working with mass production apparel sewing techniques.			
Supervising garment workers to ensure that deadlines are met.			
Evaluating procedures/systems to improve production efficiency.			
Verifying that garments are shipped from the factory on time.			
Solving production problems to maintain quality standards.			
Investing money to produce next season's sportswear line.			
Working with financiers to enable a line to be produced.			
Learning to use the latest apparel manufacturing technology.			
Subtotals =			

Total score _____

If your total score is between 31 and 45, you have high interest in **apparel manufacturing management**. If your total score is between 15 and 30, you have interest in knowing about apparel manufacturing, but are probably not interested enough to enjoy it as a career. If your score is less than 15, you are probably not suited for apparel manufacturing as a career.

How does your score correspond with your previous thoughts about going into apparel manufacturing management? _____

_____

_____

If your combined score from both pages is over 75, you might be president of an apparel company someday!

Define "Team"

Source	Definition—A team is:
Webster's Collegiate Dictionary	A number of persons associated together in work or activity.
William Dyer (author)	A group of people who work together to accomplish individual goals effectively and efficiently while accomplishing the goals of the organization.
Technicomp (business firm)	An organized group of individuals working together in a cooperative manner to accomplish a common purpose.
Harvard Business School Press	A small number of people with complementary skills who are committed to a common purpose, set of performance goals, and approach for which they hold themselves mutually accountable.

Marketing Plan for a New Product

Name_____ **Date** _____ **Period** _____

With a group of classmates, follow the steps of this master marketing plan as your group brings an imaginary new type of textile product to market. Explain your marketing plan in the space provided. Do the extra work indicated in each step to the extent directed by your teacher. (You may not be able to do the later steps since you have no actual product to launch.)

1. **State your objective**. (State rationale for development, relationship with other company products, company's long- and short-range goals, and compatibility with pipeline firms that will further process the product.) _____

_____

_____

_____

_____

2. **Do market research**. (Determine demand and general market segment. Define accounts, competition, and market share.) _____

_____

_____

_____

_____

3. **Do product development work**. (Design, cost, test, and evaluate ongoing prototypes and all their uses. Use secret and/or public technology.)_____

_____

_____

_____

_____

4. **Conduct product testing**. (Define the target market, forecast sales volume, anticipate problems and servicing, indicate policies with accounts, and show promotional needs.) _____

_____

_____

_____

_____

5. **Identify the distribution path**. (Determine resources, dealers or further processors, shipping methods, and timing.) _____

_____

_____

_____

_____

(Continued)

Name_____

6. **Start production**. (Set ideal volume, raw material sources, inventory control, quality level, and personnel needs.)_____

_____

_____

_____

_____

7. **Do promotion**. (Determine brand name/trademark, packaging and labeling, warranties, advertising, endorsements, customer and public relations, and consumer education.)_____

_____

_____

_____

_____

8. **Launch the product**. (Handle market introduction, sales, and distribution. Educate retail POS personnel.) _____

_____

_____

_____

_____

9. **Evaluate and plan for the future**. (Assess market and product performance. Do continuous customer and consumer research to see trend changes, movements of competition, indications for product changes, improvements, and new markets.) _____

_____

_____

_____

_____

10. **Continue throughout the process:**

    ● Legal activities (patents, business laws, contracts) _____

    _____

    ● Financial activities (profit and overhead forecasts, overall costing, pricing, credit control and management, capital investment) _____

    _____

    ● International activities (Contract production overseas to import. Use domestic production and export the products. Open overseas plants. Participate in overseas shows. Have overseas representatives or sales offices.) _____

    _____

    ● Miscellaneous (Coordinate activities, seasonal timetables, communications) _____

    _____

Textile and Apparel Careers

Name_____

Date_____ **Period**_____ **Score**_____

Chapter 27 Test

Matching: Match the following terms and identifying phrases.

_____ 1. A manufacturing employee who makes sure all environmental systems are operating properly.

_____ 2. A purchasing agent who researches and buys the fabrics, trims, and notions for apparel manufacturing.

_____ 3. An employee who conducts market research to try to discover future market needs.

_____ 4. A fabric designer who does original textile surface designs of motifs, color combinations, and repeats.

_____ 5. An executive who determines the fashion direction the business will take and communicates that information throughout the organization.

_____ 6. Employee of a fiber company or trade association who is in charge of the fabric library.

_____ 7. A manufacturing employee who determines the overall price of producing each item.

_____ 8. A manufacturing executive who is in charge of every aspect of one of the company's lines or a specific category of items within a line.

_____ 9. An employee who manages a distribution center, trying to get products quickly from manufacturing to customers.

_____ 10. A cost and efficiency expert who saves companies' time and money.

A. costing engineer

B. fabric librarian

C. fashion director

D. industrial engineer

E. market analyst

F. piece goods buyer

G. plant engineer

H. print/repeat artist

I. product manager

J. traffic manager

True/False: Circle *T* if the statement is true or *F* if the statement is false.

T   F   11. In general, small companies have more specialized jobs and large companies have more combined jobs.

T   F   12. Textile and apparel manufacturing have traditionally been capital-intensive rather than labor-intensive.

T   F   13. Textile research scientists usually have a high school diploma and a trade school certificate.

(Continued)

Name_____

T   F   14. Fiber and fabric companies work closer to the retail selling season than others in the soft goods chain.

T   F   15. A motif is a design idea or theme.

T   F   16. Assistant to the stylist is an entry-level job with fabric companies.

T   F   17. The job of fashion designer is to create new ideas that combine function and beauty into new garments.

T   F   18. Sketchers cut out parts for sample garments and baste them together.

T   F   19. Spreaders lay out apparel manufacturing fabric for cutting.

T   F   20. Sales work is very competitive in the textile and apparel segments and is not for everyone.

Multiple Choice: Choose the best response. Write the letter in the space provided.

_____ 21. A case of loose, unfolded art or design papers showing a person's creative work is a(n) _____.
A. manila folder
B. art collection
C. portfolio
D. creative journal

_____ 22. Research and development _____.
A. leads to the development of new products and the improvement of old products
B. is done for fiber manufacturers, textile mills, and private testing laboratories
C. is done in government agencies and universities
D. All of the above.

_____ 23. Fabric structural designers _____.
A. work with textile weaving and knitting patterns
B. translate the company's color choices onto fabrics
C. translate the company's applied prints onto fabrics
D. All of the above.

_____ 24. The person responsible for an entire fabric type or market category for a textile firm has the job of _____.
A. colorist
B. converter
C. department manager
D. strike-off artist

_____ 25. People who oversee various manufacturing operations to maintain the highest worker productivity and product quality have the job of _____.
A. quality control inspector
B. production supervisor
C. vice president of merchandising
D. copyist

(Continued)

Name_____

_____ 26. Fashion designers must _____.
   A. have technical knowledge of fabrics, trimmings, and fit
   B. have expertise in pattern making, draping, and sewing
   C. understand manufacturing processes and costing
   D. All of the above.

_____ 27. People who reduce or enlarge patterns into all the different sizes produced by a manufacturer are pattern _____.
   A. makers
   B. graders
   C. markers
   D. assorters

_____ 28. People who oversee the workers in the factory have the job of _____.
   A. factory clerks
   B. production assistants
   C. production inspectors
   D. production supervisors

_____ 29. "In-house" sales employees at the firm's sales offices who present goods to visiting buyers are _____.
   A. sales trainees
   B. traveling sales representatives
   C. showroom salespeople
   D. account executives

_____ 30. Apparel company merchandise coordinators _____.
   A. are in charge of merchandise presentations to buyers in their company's showroom
   B. make sure the colors and pricing of coordinated garments are appropriate
   C. make sure their companies' merchandise is presented as effectively as possible in retail stores
   D. All of the above.

Essay Questions: Provide complete responses to the following questions or statements.

31. Describe the jobs of fabric stylist and apparel design stylist.

32. Describe the jobs of textile production worker and sewing machine operator.

33. Describe the jobs of plant manager and sales manager.

CHAPTER 28

Retail Careers

Objectives

After studying this chapter, students will be able to

⊖ explain retail career generalities.

⊖ describe retail sales positions.

⊖ summarize the merchandise management career track.

⊖ explain the store management career track.

⊖ describe the jobs of other retail employees.

Teaching Materials

Text, pages 571–587
  Fashion Terms
  Fashion Review
  Fashion in Action
Student Workbook
  A. *Retail Employment Differences*
  B. *Check It Out: Retail Job Availability*
  C. *A Closer Look*
  D. *Check It Out: Fashion Curriculums*
  E. *Retail Career Presentations*
Teacher's Resource
  Pros and Cons of Retail Jobs, transparency master 28-1
  Expressing Retail Career Interest, reproducible master 28-2
  Skills Needed by Retail Employees, transparency master 28-3
  Creating Superior Retail Staffs, transparency master 28-4
  Tasks of Store Merchandising Personnel, transparency master 28-5
  Buyers' Knowledge Needs, transparency master 28-6
  How Buyers Are Evaluated, transparency master 28-7

Tasks of Store Operations Personnel, transparency master 28-8
Retail Careers Review, reproducible master 28-9
Extra Thoughts About Retail Careers, reproducible master 28-10
Successful Retail Personalities, reproducible master 28-11
Chapter 28 Test

Introductory Activities

1. Plan an activity that informs students about the diverse career opportunities available in retailing. *The Retail Store* (also mentioned in Chapter 13) is a video available from Cambridge Educational, Meridian Education Corporation, D.E. Visuals, and Nasco. *You're the Boss* is a game about running a retail business. It is available from Sunburst. The "Opportunities in?" book entitled *Retailing* is available from Cambridge Educational.

2. Since about 40 percent of America's young people do retail work for their first job (16 percent of all retail employees are teenagers), ask the students in the class who have worked in retailing to tell about their jobs. Have these students explain what they liked most and least about the job. Since beginning jobs in retailing are usually the least satisfying, young people are sometimes discouraged from going into retailing as a profession. Ask the students to tell about jobs they saw higher-level employees doing that looked interesting to them. Tell the class they will learn about all types and levels of retail employment in this chapter.

3. Use a CD-based program and worksheets for vocabulary development so students can converse with the proper terms when considering retail careers. *Shoptalk—Clothing* is available from VMS, Inc.

Is a Retail Career in Your Future?

4. **RT** Discuss with the class how fashion merchandising will always be necessary since all consumers need to buy apparel.

5. **RF** *Pros and Cons of Retail Jobs*, transparency master 28-1. Use the transparency to discuss the advantages and disadvantages of retail jobs. Ask students to think of other advantages or disadvantages, such as being transferred to other store locations. (This might be an advantage to some and a disadvantage to others.)

6. **RT** Use illustration 28-4 in the text to discuss the two main functions of retailing (which will also become the two main career tracks described later in the chapter) and the addition of a financial manager for the three-functional organization.

7. **RF** Use illustration 28-5 in the text to discuss the organization of a large retail store. Then have students review text illustration 17-4. Point out how the same main five functional areas can have different titles in different large retail companies, but the careers are centered within the five major areas of merchandise, operations, finance, promotion, and human resources.

8. **EX** Show students a video about retail careers. *Fashion Merchandising: Concepts and Careers* is available from Meridian Education Corporation, Insight Media, and D.E. Visuals. *An Introduction to Fashion Merchandising* (also mentioned in Chapter 16) is available from Insight Media and Cambridge Educational. *Retailing: A Career for the 21st Century* is available from D.E. Visuals. *Mass Merchandising* is available from D.E. Visuals.

9. **RT** Use Figure 28-7 in the text to discuss steps in the two main career tracks of retailing. Ask students to further explain each of the jobs listed. Draw a pyramid on the board and write *vice president* at the top. List other jobs the appropriate number of times at their level under *vice president* to fill in the pyramid. This will illustrate how there are many buyers and department managers, but only one vice president of merchandising and one vice president of operations. Also ask students to analyze which career path they might like to follow.

10. **ER** *Expressing Retail Career Interest*, reproducible master 28-2. Have students complete the survey to help determine their interest in pursuing a retail career.

11. **EX** Discuss with the class the job desires of those in retail careers. Surveys report that retail employees want to look forward to coming to work at a fun place, employee discounts, and to know exactly what is expected of them in their role. Many would like flexible hours and want a company with a great brand image. About a third of retail employees are not satisfied with how the organization communicates with them, does not recognize their work performance, or does not give feedback on how their work contributes to the success of the organization.

Retail Sales Positions

12. **RT** Ask students to explain why retail salespeople are such valuable employees. Have students explain the job responsibilities and personal attributes that retail salespeople should have. Also ask students to explain the job of checkout cashier. Tell students that about 80 percent of current retail sales jobs are part-time. In the future, education and salary levels may go up, but the percentage of part-time employees may go down. Overall, retail salesperson jobs are expected to increase. Also, modern technology and psychological screening systems are now being used to identify job applicants who have a tendency to steal.

13. **EX** Show students a video that explores selling as an occupation. Many videos about selling careers and selling skills are available from Cambridge Educational, D.E. Visuals, Insight Media, Meridian Education Corporation, Nasco, and The School Company.

14. **ER** *Skills Needed by Retail Employees*, transparency master 28-3. Use the transparency to discuss the importance of skills necessary to retail employees. Mention that the National Retail Federation has established skill standards for retail sales associates.

15. **EX** *Creating Superior Retail Staffs*, transparency master 28-4. Use the transparency to discuss how a company can create a superior retail staff. Have students explain the meanings of each point more fully.

16. **ER** Obtain materials from the National Retail Federation (NRF) about its National Professional Certification in Customer Service based on its retail skill standards. Show and discuss them with the class. In preparation for the next section of the chapter, do the same with the NRF's Professional Certification in Management.

The Merchandise Management Career Track

17. **RT** Have students discuss the jobs of departmental buyer, classification (central) buyer, and category manager. Have the class study illustration 28-10

in the text to help them understand departmental buying. Ask students to describe different classifications that central buyers might oversee. Then have students describe product development or specification buying and sourcing. Have a class discussion about the qualifications needed by all types of retail buyers. Also mention how the role of buyers is changing to "production expert" because of electronic linkages and private label manufacturing.

18. **RF** *Tasks of Store Merchandising Personnel*, transparency master 28-5. Use the transparency to bring together all the tasks of store merchandising employees that have been studied in previous chapters. Ask students to discuss how these tasks combine into merchandising jobs.

19. **RF** *Buyers' Knowledge Needs*, transparency master 28-6. Discuss with students the importance of each knowledge need of retail buyers.

20. **EX** *How Buyers Are Evaluated*, transparency master 28-7. Use the transparency to discuss how retail buyers are evaluated for success in their jobs. Have students estimate how much pressure they think there is in the job of buyer.

21. **RT** Hold a class discussion about the duties of and qualifications for merchandise manager, divisional merchandise manager, general merchandise manager, and vice president of merchandising. Also have students explain the jobs of fashion director and assistant fashion director.

The Operations Management Career Track

22. **RT** Ask different students to explain the jobs of assistant department manager, department manager, assistant store manager, store manager, branch coordinator, district manager, regional manager, and vice president of stores. Encourage other students to add information when appropriate. Also discuss the intricacies of sales staff scheduling.

23. **ER** *Tasks of Store Operations Personnel*, transparency master 28-8. Use the transparency to discuss each of the tasks listed for store operations personnel.

Other Retail Employees

24. **RT** Review the tasks of stockkeeping employees. Also emphasize the main responsibilities of receiving merchandise, protecting it, and controlling its movements.

25. **RT** Select five students to form a panel with each student role-playing one of the following "experts:" stock clerk, head of stock, distribution planner, distribution center manager, and director of distribution planning. Ask all panel members to explain their jobs. Then have other students ask the panel members questions about their jobs.

26. **EX** Ask students to think about new occurrences in retailing and consider what new occupations might result in the future, even if they sound "far out" now. One example, evolving in recent times, is the company's CSO (Corporate Security Officer).

27. **RT** Ask students to describe the jobs of training supervisor, human resources director, customer service manager, alterations expert, garment fitter, comparison shopper, personal shopper (fashion consultant), and quality assurance tester.

28. **ER** Obtain and share with the class the *Mystery Shopper Tips Booklet* with CD from www.merchandiseconcepts.com/store.html. Have a class discussion about why some shoppers are hired or not hired, how to start your own comparison shopper business, and other aspects of that job. Mention that about 40,000 of the one million secret shoppers in North America are certified by the Mystery Shopping Providers Association.

29. **RT** *Retail Employment Differences*, Activity A, WB. Students are asked to explain the difference between given terms.

30. **ER** *Check It Out: Retail Job Availability*, Activity B, WB. Students are to research local retail job availability and answer given questions.

31. **RF** *A Closer Look*, Activity C, WB. Students are asked to analyze and compare four retail careers described in the chapter by filling out a given form. Then they are to find other classmates who chose the same careers and compare answers. Finally, the groups of students are to discuss each career for the class.

32. **EX** *Check It Out: Fashion Curriculums*, Activity D, WB. Students are asked to research fashion merchandising or retail curriculums offered at trade schools, junior colleges, and universities. They are to then answer given questions based on their findings.

33. **RF** *Retail Career Presentations*, Activity E, WB. Divide the class into groups. The groups are to choose from six given projects. After reviewing the chapter section concerned with their assignment and doing additional research, students should make presentations to the class.

34. **RT** *Retail Careers Review*, reproducible master 28-9. Students are asked to answer questions as they review the chapter. The activity can be used as a practice exercise for students who need review or as an extra credit assignment for those who wish to raise their grades.

35. **RF** *Extra Thoughts About Retail Careers*, reproducible master 28-10. Students are asked to read statements and comment on them during a class discussion.

Additional Enrichment Activities

Research

36. *Successful Retail Personalities*, reproducible master 28-11. Students are asked to choose one from a given list of previous or present heads of successful retail companies. Students are to research the person's background and career and give current details about the retail business with which the person is associated. Students should write a report based on their findings.

37. Ask students to research the duties of a manager of a small apparel store. Then have the students role-play being a manager and write a report on how they would prepare the merchandise plan, buy goods for the store, determine selling prices, and evaluate how well merchandise is selling. Students should use correct retailing terminology.

38. Have students research the Mazur Plan of retailing, which was published in 1929 and remains the standard four-functional organization plan for small- to medium-sized retailers today. Have students report their findings to the class.

39. Have students do Internet research of retail companies and careers with them. They might log onto www.allretailjobs.com, www.retailjobmart.com, www.retailmanager.net, www.jobsinfashion.com, www.fashioncareercenter.com, www.nrf.com/retailcareers, www.questmerchandiser.com, or ask a search engine for other sites about retail careers. Sites of retailers, such as www.federated-fds.com, www.walmart.com, www.gapinc.com, www.target.com, www.dillards.com, www.neimanmarcus.com, www.nordstrom.com, www.limitedbrands.com, and others have menus to click (often at the bottom of the home page) for information about careers with that company. You may want to ask students to list job titles they see on particular sites, salaries (if provided), education and experience requirements, and instructions about how to apply for positions.

Projects

40. Have students who are interested in retailing as a career look up locations and curriculums of different schools that offer fashion merchandising or retailing. Students may use the Internet or look in *The College Handbook* and *Index of Majors*. Ask students to obtain course catalogs and admission information from the schools that sound best for them. Also, the National Retail Federation has a list of colleges and universities that offer degrees in various areas of retailing.

41. Have students write an essay that discusses a subject of their choice relating to this chapter. Examples might include the following: why a fashion merchandising employee must be well groomed and have a fashionable appearance; how the positions of fashion director in the textile and retail industries are similar and different; and how good physical stamina, enthusiasm, and self-assurance can help people in jobs within fashion retail careers. Students should show thought and analysis beyond what was presented in the chapter. Essays can be read to the class or turned in to the teacher.

42. Invite a retail store employee to speak to the class about the job responsibilities of several different retailing positions. Maybe a buyer could tell about a recent trip to market, including the pre-planning, selections made, and orders placed.

43. Have students contact the human resources offices of local large retail stores about job openings, requirements, pay levels, opportunities for advancement, and other specifics.

Answer Key

Text

Fashion Review, pages 587

1. fashion merchandising
2. because of industry consolidation and the use of new technology that has automated some retail tasks
3. a promotion manager
4. They should be outgoing, well organized, and able to handle figures and details well. They need energy and stamina as well as the ability to move and think quickly. They must be able to get along well with others and work under stress. Good grooming and a sense of fashion are important. Good leadership abilities and self-confidence enable advancement.
5. merchandise management track concerned with merchandise planning and buying; operations management track concerned with salesforce management and store operations
6. large specialty chains, department stores, mass merchandisers
7. salesperson
8. because they meet the public and represent that company and its image to the outside world
9. on an hourly wage, commission, or a combination of the two
10. at a central headquarters buying office of the retail company
11. manufacturer's representatives, coworkers, and customers

12. to interpret and react to trends indicated by the data
13. supervisor of the preparations and commentator
14. assistant department manager
15. the department manager
16. receiving goods, protecting them, and controlling their movements
17. because it involves a lot of lifting, bending, and pushing
18. college graduate, stock clerk, salesperson
19. office work, teaching, and promotional activities
20. evaluate merchandise to determine if quality standards have been met as established by the retail firm

Student Workbook

Retail Employment Differences,
Activity A

1. A two-functional organization is a retail company structure that has one manager employed to oversee all merchandising duties and another manager in charge of operations, both reporting to the owner/operator. A three-functional organization has merchandise, operations, and financial managers all reporting to a general manager.
2. A departmental buyer is a traditional department store employee who plans and purchases goods for only one department and is responsible for the sales and profits of the department. A classification buyer plans, chooses, purchases, prices, and promotes one classification for all the branches in a chain or large retail organization.
3. Central buyers are the same as classification buyers. Category managers oversee business units that customize merchandise and service for individual branches to better satisfy local needs.
4. Product managers develop, coordinate, execute, and deliver private label corporate programs. Product sourcers identify, research, open, and develop production sourcing markets and vendors that meet the company's long-term product supply needs.
5. An executive trainee, also called management trainee, is a new retail employee with a college degree who receives a general orientation. The training supervisor is the retail employee who gives the orientation classes to the new salespeople.
6. A buyer's clerical is a retail employee who keeps records, schedules appointments, answers phones, and does follow-up work for a buyer. A merchandise manager is an employee who coordinates the merchandise of several retail departments.
7. A DMM is a retail executive who supervises a group of buyers and/or coordinates the merchandise of several related departments, divisions, or stores.

A GMM is a higher retail executive who is responsible for the total retail merchandising operation.
8. A retail fashion director makes sure all buyers, fashion departments, and stores of a large retail business are kept updated on the latest trends. A fashion consultant, also known as a personal shopper, chooses merchandise in response to customers' requests or accompanies customers to offer fashion advice and selection help.
9. A department manager runs a retail department or group of departments, working with both the buyers and the sales staff. A store manager is the top employee of a specific store, in charge of every aspect of the store's operations.
10. Branch coordinators with large retail organizations keep tabs on all the branches to see that their stock, selling techniques, and general operations coordinate with the main store or headquarters' policies. Distribution planners are retail stockkeeping employees who keep track of all units of merchandise through computerized records.
11. A district manager for a chain store is responsible for growth and volume of up to a dozen stores. A regional manager oversees several districts.
12. The head of stock is in charge of the merchandise for a given department or area. The customer service manager serves as an intermediary between the store and its customers.

Teacher's Resources

Retail Careers Review, reproducible
master 28-9

1. because many of the duties are combined
2. (Name five:) product planning and development, marketing, sales promotion, fashion buying, merchandise math, consumer motivation, retail operations, business law, computer science, small store management
3. between six months and two years
4. from turnover of employees
5. low to medium
6. classification buyer
7. oversee business units that customize merchandise and service for individual stores to better satisfy local needs
8. product development trainee
9. assistant buyer, fashion magazine work, or responsible jobs with fabric or apparel manufacturers
10. divisional merchandise manager
11. vice president of merchandising
12. to help the fashion director with details, set up appointments, make telephone calls, book models, run errands, help put on fashion shows, write fashion bulletins, and observe market trends

13. up to 12 and up to 75 or 80, respectively
14. checking incoming goods against the numbers of each item ordered, assessing quality, making any necessary adjustments, checking or attaching tags, and authorizing payment of invoices
15. takes in, lets out, and reshapes garments that do not fit the consumer properly
16. personal shopper

Chapter 28 Test

1. A	11. T	21. B
2. D	12. F	22. D
3. G	13. F	23. C
4. B	14. T	24. B
5. E	15. T	25. A
6. H	16. T	26. D
7. I	17. T	27. D
8. C	18. F	28. B
9. F	19. T	29. D
10. J	20. T	30. A

31. A merchandise manager and an operations manager work for an owner/operator.
32. The merchandise management track is concerned with merchandise planning and buying. The operations management track is concerned with sales-force management and store operations.
33. receiving goods, protecting them, and controlling their movements

Pros and Cons of Retail Jobs

Advantages of Retail Jobs

- Opportunities to work with the newest merchandise

- Opportunities in every geographic location

- Store discount on merchandise

- Good financial rewards after skill is proven through sales/profits

- Company-paid travel to markets

Disadvantages of Retail Jobs

- Low starting pay

- Long hours plus weekends/holidays

- Seasonal work peaks and valleys

- Tough competition

Expressing Retail Career Interest

Name_____ **Date** _____ **Period** _____

Read the list of activities related to retail careers and place a check in the column that best represents your level of interest about each. Then analyze your score according to the directions that follow. (You will not be graded on your score.)

Activities	Interested	Unsure	Not Interested
Helping customers coordinate total fashion looks			
Predicting fashions that will be popular in the future			
Creating new products by observing customer preferences			
Deciding on merchandising concepts for the selling floor			
Learning about store management, hiring, training, and scheduling			
Working under pressure to make important decisions			
Studying and interpreting sales and inventory computer data			
Traveling to a domestic or foreign market center to do buying			
Staying within a budget when buying merchandise for a store			
Helping promote merchandise you have bought to sell			
Deciding the prices for each item placed on the floor of a store			
Negotiating with apparel manufacturers about cost and delivery			
Opening your own apparel store			
Working with customers who like the items available in the store			
Trying to sell more goods than last month or than another branch			
Subtotals =			

Total score _____

For each Interested response checked, give yourself 3 points. For every Unsure response checked, give yourself 1 point. For every Not Interested response checked, give yourself 0 points. If your total score is between 31 and 45, you have a high interest in going into retailing as a career. If your total score is between 15 and 30, you are interested in some aspects of retailing but may not succeed in a retail career. If your score is less than 15, you are not interested in retailing as a career.

How does your score correspond with your previous thoughts about retailing as a career?_____

_____

_____

Skills Needed by Retail Employees

Ability to...	Description
• Listen	"Hear" while actively listening
• Question	Clarify as much information as possible
• Understand	Try to see the customer's point of view
• Resolve	Create options and work out solutions
• Respond	Defuse customer tension while satisfying wants
• Be flexible	Adjust to varieties of tasks and adapt to changing needs

Creating Superior Retail Staffs

1. Hire good people.

2. Educate and/or train them continuously.

3. Set measurable, realistic goals.

4. Evaluate employees' progress.

5. Reward quality performance.

6. Receive and acknowledge feedback.

7. Challenge complacency.

Tasks of Store Merchandising Personnel

- Determine future quantity and timing demand for styles, colors, prices, and fashion emphasis.

- Plan how to meet the demand while assuring a profit.

- Source, buy, and price the merchandise.

- Coordinate sales promotion/advertising to draw customers.

- Project company image through all activities.

- Strategize/establish merchandising policies for success against the competition.

Buyers' Knowledge Needs

Retail buyers must have knowledge of

- fashion trends

- customer preferences

- sources of supply

- management policies

- computer programs

- business math

How Buyers Are Evaluated

Sales results—based on setting and beating realistic goals of total dollars, units of merchandise sold, and sales per square foot of selling space

Inventory results—based on stock turnover, stock shortages, and proportion of prior stock versus new goods in inventory

Profit results—based on initial markup, maintained markup, gross margin, and operating profit by dollars or percentages

Industry comparisons—based on previous records of the department/classification and similar areas of other stores and firms

Tasks of Store Operations Personnel

- Recruiting and training store employees

- Supervising store employees

- Organizing store traffic flow

- Maintaining store facilities

- Carrying out customer service

- Ensuring store security

- Planning and implementing information systems

Retail Careers Review

Name_____ **Date** _____ **Period** _____

As you review the chapter, answer the following questions.

1. Why do employees of smaller stores have a greater variety of job responsibilities and tasks to perform? _____

_____

_____

_____

2. Name five courses usually taken in a college program in fashion merchandising._____

_____

_____

_____

_____

_____

3. How long do executive trainee programs last?_____

_____

_____

4. How are many retail salesperson job openings created?_____

_____

_____

_____

5. What is the usual level of pay for apparel sales work?_____

_____

_____

6. What is another name for a central buyer?_____

_____

7. What do category managers do? _____

_____

_____

8. With what job title might college graduates in apparel design or apparel production start their retail-related careers?_____

_____

_____

(Continued)

Name_____

9. What job or types of work might people do before becoming buyers?_____

_____

_____

_____

_____

10. In small retail organizations, what is another name for the job of merchandise manager? _____

_____

_____

11. What is the equivalent title for a general merchandise manager in a small firm?_____

_____

_____

12. What are the job duties of an assistant fashion director?_____

_____

_____

_____

_____

_____

13. For how many stores might a district manager and regional manager have responsibility, respectively?

_____

_____

_____

14. What stockkeeping tasks are involved with receiving merchandise? _____

_____

_____

_____

_____

15. What does an alterations expert do? _____

_____

_____

_____

_____

16. What is another name for a fashion consultant? _____

_____

_____

_____

Extra Thoughts About Retail Careers

Name_____ Date _____ Period _____

Read these statements, think about each one, and comment on them in a class discussion.

1. Almost all retail employees say that one of the best advantages of their work is the store discount on merchandise purchased at the store. However, some also say they buy too much merchandise because it seems like such a good deal.

2. Buyers take small laptop personal computers to market when doing retail buying. The buyers take notes and write purchase orders directly on their laptops rather than having to transfer the information later. Final orders can be transmitted directly to vendors.

3. Retail buyers can now dial up electronic catalogs that show collections of available merchandise. After quickly viewing the assortments of many suppliers, they can put in orders from their computer, thus saving the time and money of another trip to market.

4. It has been said that the retail industry will not see an increase in the number of buying jobs in the future. However, the level of professionalism will increase as buying is based on information rather than just instinct.

5. Assistant buyers have become "computer system jocks," using technology to track goods that have been ordered, handle questions, execute merchandise promotions, and follow up on price changes. The challenge for them is to learn the merchandising side of the business.

6. Because retailers can't afford to be wrong with their merchandise, some firms are using specialized three-member teams of planners (to decide on quantities to order and distribute), buyers (to make selections in the market), and store managers (to react to customer and store needs).

7. Because different retail companies have their own methods and computer systems and have long-term partnerships with suppliers, buyers who know their jobs are difficult to replace. It is also hard for these buyers to move to another company or be promoted because they do their current jobs so well!

8. With so many young people working in retail settings for their first jobs, it is important to offer retail education in high schools, trade schools, and colleges.

9. Automatic replenishment systems reorder the same goods as long as they continue to sell. Buyers with good intuition and experience are needed to recognize new trends and match them with the needs of their customers to add new, fashionable variety to the store's stock.

10. Customers often don't like salespeople who are paid by commission because they tend to push too hard to sell merchandise.

11. Labor scheduling software, developed especially for retail stores, provides an automated system to improve sales and customer service with the right number of employees.

12. Some retail companies offer work-study programs for college students that cover selling, stock supervision, and management training. At graduation, participants are assistant store managers.

13. Large chains must have an additional division for real estate, with employees who oversee location planning, rental leases, building construction, and other physical site activities.

Successful Retail Personalities

Name_____ **Date** _____ **Period** _____

Choose one from the following list of previous or present heads of successful retail companies. Research the person's background and career, including current details about the retail business with which the person is associated. Prepare a report to present to the class.

- **R. H. Macy:** pioneered fixed retail prices and other retailing policies in the mid-1800s.
- **John Wanamaker:** revolutionized the department store business in the late 1800s.
- **Marshall Field:** started the Chicago company that beared his name, purchasing inventory with cash. He believed "the customer is always right."
- **Andrew Saks:** a peddler in the early 1900s who eventually started Saks Fifth Avenue.
- **Sam Walton:** the founder of Wal-Mart.
- **Martin Bloom:** retired head of May Department Stores International.
- **Allan Questrom:** past chairman and CEO of Federated Department Stores. He turned the company around in bad times and also served as chairman of the National Retail Federation. Then he became CEO of JCPenney.
- **Donald G. Fisher:** founder and chairman of The Gap, Inc.
- **William R. Howell:** presided over the transformation of JCPenney from mass retailer to national department store.
- Other of your choice with the approval of the teacher.

_____
_____
_____
_____
_____
_____
_____
_____
_____
_____
_____
_____
_____
_____
_____
_____
_____
_____
_____
_____

Retail Careers

Name_____

Date_____ **Period**_____ **Score**_____

Chapter 28 Test

Matching: Match the following terms and identifying phrases.

_____ 1. An employee of a large retail organization who keeps tabs on all the branches to see that their stock, selling techniques, and general operations coordinate with the main store or headquarters' policies.

_____ 2. A retail stockkeeping employee who keeps track of all units of merchandise through computerized records.

_____ 3. An employee who coordinates the merchandise of several retail departments.

_____ 4. A central buyer who purchases only one classification of merchandise.

_____ 5. A chain store employee responsible for the growth and volume of up to a dozen stores.

_____ 6. A chain retailer executive who oversees several districts.

_____ 7. The top employee in charge of every aspect of a store's operations.

_____ 8. A traditional department store employee who plans and purchases goods for only one department and is responsible for the sales and profits of the department.

_____ 9. A college graduate hired to train with a company for future management positions.

_____ 10. A retail employee who gives orientation classes to new salespeople.

A. branch coordinator

B. classification buyer

C. departmental buyer

D. distribution planner

E. district manager

F. executive trainee

G. merchandise manager

H. regional manager

I. store manager

J. training supervisor

True/False: Circle *T* if the statement is true or *F* if the statement is false.

T F 11. Fashion merchandising will always be necessary because consumers need to buy apparel.

T F 12. The three-functional organization is a two-functional organization with a human resource manager added.

T F 13. Most large retailers offer management training programs for people with high school diplomas.

(Continued)

Name_____

T F 14. Retail salespeople sell goods directly to customers.

T F 15. An advantage of retail work is the employee discount on merchandise bought at the store.

T F 16. Most classification buyers work at a central headquarters buying office of the retail company.

T F 17. Retail buying is changing because of QR partnership linkages and private label manufacturing.

T F 18. Resident buying office buyers are responsible for retail sales and profits of the goods they choose.

T F 19. Assistant store manager jobs are often available with specialty chains.

T F 20. The job of stock clerk is an entry-level position for someone without college training.

Multiple Choice: Choose the best response. Write the letter in the space provided.

_____ 21. Fashion merchandising careers .
A. are available only with large retail firms
B. combine fashion with business
C. usually lead to top store operations jobs
D. All of the above.

_____ 22. People who want to pursue a career in fashion retailing should _____.
A. be outgoing, well organized, and able to handle figures and details well
B. have energy, stamina, and the ability to move and think quickly
C. have good grooming, be able to get along well with others, and work under stress
D. All of the above.

_____ 23. Retail salespeople _____.
A. must know every aspect of the company's management structure
B. must be able to analyze point-of-sale data to detect trends
C. are important because they meet the public and represent the company to the outside world
D. All of the above.

_____ 24. A checkout cashier _____.
A. helps to sell merchandise in the store
B. rings up customers' purchases, makes change, and bags the items
C. receives a medium level of pay
D. All of the above.

_____ 25. Category managers oversee business units that _____.
A. customize merchandise and service for individual stores to better satisfy local needs
B. order all the merchandise for one category of goods to be sold by the retail company
C. sell to the same category of customers in each branch or chain store of a retail company
D. are concerned with financial matters of the company rather than merchandise buying or selling

(Continued)

Name_____

_____ 26. Employees responsible for developing, coordinating, executing, and delivering private label corporate programs have the job of _____.
A. product sourcers
B. product designers
C. merchandise managers
D. product managers

_____ 27. Extremely large firms have buyer's clericals, who _____.
A. keep records, schedule appointments, and answer phones for buyers
B. must be organized and have the ability to carry out jobs accurately and quickly
C. receive low to medium pay
D. All of the above.

_____ 28. A retail executive who supervises a group of buyers and/or coordinates the merchandise of several related departments, divisions, or stores to maximize profits has the job of _____.
A. general merchandise manager (GMM)
B. divisional merchandise manager (DMM)
C. fashion director
D. vice president of merchandising

_____ 29. A retail department manager _____.
A. runs a retail department according to the framework of the company's overall plan
B. is the liaison between the buyer and sales staff, providing feedback about department sales and inventory
C. trains, supervises, and schedules salespeople for a department and handles customer complaints
D. All of the above.

_____ 30. A fashion consultant is a _____.
A. personal shopper who selects merchandise requested by customers
B. comparison shopper who checks and reports back about goods and services of competitors
C. garment fitter who marks or pins changes for needed alterations to customers' fashions
D. customer service manager who serves as an intermediary between the store and its customers

Essay Questions: Provide complete responses to the following questions or statements.

31. Describe or draw an organization chart for a two-functional organization.

32. Briefly describe the two main career paths for professional retail employees.

33. Name the three general tasks or responsibilities of stockkeeping employees.

Promotion Careers

Objectives

After studying this chapter, students will be able to

- explain how fashion is communicated by models, photographers, writers, illustrators, audiovisual workers, and Web site designers
- describe visual merchandising careers.
- give examples of fashion advertising employment.
- explain public relations job opportunities.

Teaching Materials

Text, pages 588–602
  Fashion Terms
  Fashion Review
  Fashion in Action
Student Workbook
  A. *Promotion Review*
  B. *Promotion Career Fill-In*
  C. *Career Groupings*
  D. *A Fashion Interview*
Teacher's Resources
  The Relationship of Promotion to Supply and Demand Situations, transparency master 29-1
  Merchandise Promotion Tasks, transparency master 29-2
  Retail Promotion Structure, transparency master 29-3
  Promotion Employee Goals, transparency master 29-4
  Modeling Career Pros and Cons, transparency master 29-5
  Expressing Visual Merchandising Interest, reproducible master 29-6
  Tasks of Advertising Personnel, transparency master 29-7
  Advertising Planning Sources, transparency master 29-8
  Promotion Careers Review, reproducible master 29-9
  Chapter 29 Test

Introductory Activities

1. *The Relationship of Promotion to Supply and Demand Situations*, transparency master 29-1. Use the transparency to emphasize how important promotion employees are to every fashion company. Discuss how fashion promotion is the indirect selling function of merchandising, creating market demand for products among the buying public. Discuss that this chapter describes auxiliary "supporting" enterprises, which are not technically part of the soft goods chain, but without which the chain would not be successful. Explain that many companies throughout the chain, from fiber to retail, have internal promotion staffs in addition to using outside agencies.
2. *Merchandise Promotion Tasks*, transparency master 29-2. Use this transparency to introduce employment tasks involved in merchandise promotion.
3. *Retail Promotion Structure*, transparency master 29-3. Use this transparency to discuss how the internal sales promotion of large retail companies is divided.
4. *Promotion Employee Goals*, transparency master 29-4. Use the transparency to discuss promotion goals from an employee's perspective.
5. Go through slides of a PowerPoint CD with the class to discuss the flair of many different fashion promotion careers. *Careers in Fashion* is available from D.E. Visuals

Communicating Fashion

6. **RT** Ask different students to describe the job duties and personal requirements of runway models, fit models, and photographic models.

7. **RF** *Modeling Career Pros and Cons*, transparency master 29-5. Use the transparency to discuss the advantages and disadvantages of a modeling career.

8. **ER** Ask students if they have any knowledge about famous past and present models (such as Christie Brinkley, Kim Alexis, Bridget Hall, Cindy Crawford, Kate Moss, Naomi Campbell, Carolyn Murphy, Linda Evangelista, Claudia Schiffer, Gisele Bundchen, Elsa Benetiz, Heidi Klum, Tyra Banks, Kathy Ireland, Adriana Lima, Elle Macpherson, Sofia Eng, Nina Flag, Stella Tennant, and Christy Turlington) they can share with the class. Create a resource folder for pictures of these and new top models. Show the pictures to the class as a group or have the folder available for students to look through when they have time.

9. **RF** Discuss the increased use of models that present a more realistic perspective of the buying public, including people with average to large proportions, older people, and people with disabilities.

10. **RT** Discuss the requirements and duties of fashion photographers, assistant photographers, and photo stylists.

11. **EX** Show students a video about fashion promotion. *Fashion Careers*, which discusses the world of modeling and fashion shows, is available from D.E. Visuals, VMS, Inc., and Meridian Education Corporation. *Fashion Illustration: Sketching* is available from Insight Media and D.E. Visuals. *Young Models Growing Up Fast* is available from Teacher's Media Company.

12. **RT** Ask four students to stand in front of the class. The first student should explain the job of fashion journalists or members of the fashion press, as well as their importance to fashion manufacturers and retailers. Each of the other three students should explain one of the following jobs: fashion reporter, copywriter, and editor.

13. **RF** *A Fashion Interview*, Activity D, WB. Students are asked to write out five questions they would ask a fashion expert, do research to determine answers to the questions, and hold an actual interview with a classmate in front of the class.

14. **RT** Describe the job of a fashion illustrator. Discuss the duties of an illustrator, personal talents required, and places an illustrator might work.

15. **EX** Show students a video about audiovisual work. *The Arts, Audio Visual Technology & Communications* is available from Cambridge Educational. Several videos about photography and videography are available from VMS, Inc. Finish with a discussion of the opportunities and requirements for fashion video work.

Visual Merchandising

16. **RF** *Expressing Visual Merchandising Interest*, reproducible master 29-6. Students are asked to read and respond to statements that will help them evaluate their interest in a visual merchandising career.

17. **RT** Ask the students to explain the job duties of and personal qualifications necessary for display managers, display designers, and window dressers. Discuss the different approaches to displays taken by small shops (in which the manager and salespeople may do displays as best as they can), medium-sized stores (which may hire a freelance design specialist), and large retail stores (which have their own display departments).

18. **EX** Show students a video about visual merchandising work. *Visual Merchandising* and *Visual Coordinator* are available from Cambridge Educational. *Fashion Display Skills* and *Pinning and Flying in Fashion Display* are available from Insight Media.

19. **RF** Ask students to look at and take notes about fashion displays in store windows and interiors, as well as merchandise presentation. Then have them report their observations to the class, noting what they thought were excellent examples of visual merchandising and what improvements could be made.

20. **EX** Ask students to check Internet sites for visual merchandising resources. They might search and follow links on the following Web sites: www.retailreporting.com (for Retail Design & Visual Presentation), www.stpubs.com (for *Visual Merchandising & Store Design Magazine*), www.ddimagazine.com (*Display & Design Ideas Magazine*), and www.visualstore.com (for trade shows and journals).

Fashion Advertising

21. **RF** Have a group of seven students form a mock advertising group. One student should act as the advertising director and another should act as an account executive. Others in the group should role-play a media buyer, art director, graphic

designer, layout artist, and paste-up/mechanical artist (or computer graphic designer). The students should do additional study about their job assignments. As a group, they should plan a presentation to show how they would create an advertisement for a particular fashion item or line of merchandise. If time permits, the group might even prepare a sample ad on poster board to use as an example of how the jobs are accomplished.

22. **RT** Have a class discussion about collateral materials. Have students bring any collateral materials they have at home to class.
23. **RF** *Tasks of Advertising Personnel*, transparency master 29-7. Ask students how they might accomplish each of the tasks listed on the transparency if they had a job in fashion advertising.
24. **EX** *Advertising Planning Sources*, transparency master 29-8. Use the transparency to discuss how fashion advertising professionals use each of the resources listed to help them plan their advertising.
25. **RT** *Promotion Review*, Activity A, WB. Students are asked to write answers to questions as they review the chapter.
26. **EX** Show the class a video about fashion advertising. *Newspaper Advertising* is available from D.E. Visuals.
27. **RT** *Promotion Careers Review*, reproducible master 29-9. Students are asked to answer questions as they review the chapter. The activity can be used as a practice exercise for students who need review or as an extra credit assignment for those who wish to raise their grades.

Public Relations

28. **RT** Ask students to discuss public relations activities and the job of a publicist.
29. **EX** Show students a video about all aspects of promotion and public relations. *Promotion: Solving the Puzzle* is available from D.E. Visuals.
30. **RT** *Promotion Career Fill-In*, Activity B, WB. Students are asked to complete the puzzle using vocabulary terms from the chapter.
31. **RF** *Career Groupings*, Activity C, WB. Students are asked to choose a general promotion category that interests them. Then students are to form groups with others in the class who have chosen the same career category, discuss that career option with the group, and respond to given statements. Finally, students are to respond to additional statements strictly from their own points of view.
32. **ER** Show the class a video that reviews careers in this chapter. *Communication* is available from The School Company.

Additional Enrichment Activities

Research

33. Ask students to pick one of the jobs (other than modeling) described in this chapter. Have them do research about the job or career using resources from the library, Internet, and school guidance counselors. They might also interview people who work in the chosen field. Students should then prepare a written report about the job including necessary qualifications, type of company or organization for which they would work, and tasks they would perform. Students should also mention the salary range and fringe benefits they could expect as well as opportunities for advancement.
34. Ask students to research modeling careers, schools, ways to avoid scams, portfolio needs, appointment procedures, conventions, and modeling agencies. Books they might consult are *The Madison Avenue Handbook*, *The Fashion & Print Directory*, *The International Directory of Model and Talent Agencies and Schools*, and *The New York Model and Talent Agency Directory*. These books list magazines, photographers, schools, agencies, portfolio needs, appointment procedures, and interviewing tips. Also, many books and videos are listed in the free catalog from Models Mart. Students might search Internet Web sites such as www.models-mart.com, www.fashioncenter.com, www.fashion.about.com, www.mlamtc.com, www.imta.com, www.maai.org, www.pgdirect.com, and others.

Projects

35. Make "Opportunities in..." books available for students to use in preparing reports and presentations to the class. *Modeling*, *Writing*, *and Journalism* are all available from Cambridge Educational. Other books are *Careers in the Fashion Industry* by John Biacobello (available from the Social Studies School Service), and *Fashion Careers* by Wendy Samuel (in book stores).
36. Accumulate a collection of fashion magazines, such as *Glamour*, *Mademoiselle*, *Elle*, *Vogue*, *Harper's Bazaar*, and *GQ*. Encourage the students to study all the magazines. Then form a panel of students to do more study about fashion magazines, give a report to the class, and conduct a discussion about the different "personalities" and markets the magazines have.

37. Invite a retail advertising employee to speak to the class. Ask the speaker to tell what persons are involved in preparing the advertising budget, how far in advance the advertising budget is planned, how the store's advertising expenditures compare with the national average for similar businesses, the store's primary types of advertising, what merchandise is usually advertised, when and where most advertising is run, the target market to whom the store's advertising is directed, and the duties performed by various advertising staff members. Also have the speaker discuss the interaction between merchandising people and advertising people so the right merchandise is advertised properly.

38. If you feel students are mature enough to evaluate books (mostly fictional) objectively that may exaggerate aspects of fashion promotion careers, suggest they read one of the following books, available at bookstores or on the Internet: *Model: The Ugly Business of Beautiful Women* by Michael Gross, *The Devil Wears Prada* by Lauren Weisberger, *Fashionistas* by Lynn Messina, and *In Full Bloom* by Caroline Hwang. Nonfiction books written by models to tell their experiences and give advice are *Everything About ME Is Fake and I'm Perfect* by Janice Dickenson and *Tyra's Beauty Inside and Out* by model Tyra Banks.

39. Have students record all textile/apparel advertisements they see or hear within one week. Have students write down the time and media of newspaper, radio, TV, bill inserts, outdoor ads, or any other types of advertising. Have students bring in as many ads as possible. Then have the class show and discuss the ads they have recorded. Place the ads on the bulletin board for others to look at and compare.

Answer Key

Text

Fashion Review, page 602

1. It builds the company's fashion image, increases store traffic, fosters goodwill with the community, and sells merchandise.
2. visual merchandising, advertising, and public relations departments
3. to fit the proportions of the company's clothing
4. because photos make the model's body look heavier than it really is
5. name, address, age, height without shoes, weight, and body measurements
6. photo studios, advertising agencies, publications, and large retailers
7. (List three:) test the lighting, take sample photos, help prepare sets and props for backgrounds, help develop pictures
8. photos along with descriptions or short articles about a company's latest designs
9. Then you can take appropriate samples of your writing with you and point out your specific qualifications that blend well with that publication.
10. high prestige and high to extremely high pay (depending on the job level and publication)
11. seams and trimming details of the apparel to give the sewer an idea of the construction required
12. to catch the attention of viewers and tempt them to buy what is shown
13. (Name three:) planning programs, writing scripts, getting props, and producing the presentations
14. a broadcast station, advertising agency, marketing firm, or video production company
15. Plans are drawn up at central headquarters and sent with needed props, signage, and instructions to local store managers for implementation.
16. the company's buyers and merchandise managers, and advertising and public relations people
17. marketing specialist
18. because large retailers have their own in-house advertising departments
19. newspapers, magazines, direct-mail flyers, radio, television, signs, and outdoor media
20. publicity and special events

Student Workbook

Promotion Review, Activity A

1. in design areas and showrooms of designers or manufacturers
2. to represent the way people really are
3. get plenty of sleep, eat balanced meals, and exercise regularly
4. accredited modeling schools and modeling employment agencies
5. one full-length, one close-up, and one smiling
6. mainly for newspapers and fashion magazines, and sometimes for trade journals
7. a college degree in journalism, combined with merchandising, apparel, and advertising courses
8. in large cities
9. fashionable uses for their company's line of fabrics
10. writing, speech, drama, and the use of equipment

11. what merchandise is available and how items can be combined and accessorized
12. (Name three:) holiday seasons, a new color, a fashion trend, a community event (Students may justify other responses.)
13. They can contract with a freelance service to do their displays at scheduled times.
14. (Name three:) selling aids, labels, and signs (Students may justify other responses.)
15. They bargain for the lowest rates and make deals for good advertising broadcast times and the best positions in publications.
16. because the work is being done by graphic designers directly on computers that also automatically execute the printing through software
17. Large companies have their own public relations departments; chain organizations have PR planning departments at headquarters that coordinate activities with local stores; small stores may hire independent PR agencies to oversee important news or events.

Promotion Career Fill-In, Activity B

1. fit
2. photographic
3. stylists
4. graphic
5. publicists
6. reporters
7. managers
8. copywriters
9. advertising
10. layout
11. media
12. journalists
13. directors
14. audiovisual
15. account
16. runway
17. collateral
18. mechanical
19. editors
20. designers
21. relations
22. illustrators
23. dressers

Teacher's Resources

Promotion Careers Review,
reproducible master 29-9

1. Ideally, a typical model should be young, tall, and thin.
2. about 10 years and 20 years, respectively

3. how to stand, pose, and move properly, as well as posture, speech, hairstyles, and makeup
4. photographs and a résumé listing training, experience, and personal specifications
5. take pictures that show fashionable clothes and accessories looking their best
6. write a daily or weekly column or periodic feature stories about fashions seen at important social and cultural events
7. examples of his or her written copy
8. trends or garment features being described by the fashion writers
9. from personal interviews, phone calls, fashion events, and wire services
10. sell products, educate consumers or students, train or update industry people, or entertain
11. a broadcast station, advertising agency, marketing firm, or video production company
12. the merchandise and effective approaches to reach the right consumers
13. (List five:) advertising, psychology, fashion, business, writing, English, printing, photography, art
14. (List five:) basic design, drawing, painting, lettering, photography, typography, advertising, promotion, typesetting/printing, audiovisual, computer graphics
15. for broadcasting commercials on radio and TV, publishing ads in newspapers or magazines, or mailing promotional materials directly to the public
16. layout artist and paste-up/mechanical artist

Chapter 29 Test

1.	I	16.	T
2.	D	17.	T
3.	A	18.	F
4.	E	19.	T
5.	F	20.	T
6.	B	21.	D
7.	G	22.	B
8.	J	23.	D
9.	C	24.	C
10.	H	25.	A
11.	T	26.	C
12.	T	27.	D
13.	F	28.	C
14.	F	29.	D
15.	T	30.	D

31. visual merchandising, advertising, and public relations departments
32. They book models, accessorize apparel, obtain props, pin up hems, iron garments, and pick up and return merchandise.
33. (List three:) planning programs, writing scripts, getting props, producing presentations, filming, editing (Students may justify other responses.)

The Relationship of Promotion to Supply and Demand Situations

- **When supply is greater than demand**—promotion should try to increase demand to prevent prices and profits from falling.

- **When demand is greater than supply**—promotion can continue to keep demand strong and growing while companies try to quickly increase the supply.

- **When supply and demand are equal**—promotion should try to continue the growth of demand, which keeps prices and profits strong. This will also lead to a growing supply.

Merchandise Promotion Tasks

- Planning special events

- Creating promotional displays

- Devising advertising strategies

- Selecting advertising media

- Preparing advertisements

- Gaining favorable publicity

- Following a promotion calendar

- Working within a promotion budget

Retail Promotion Structure

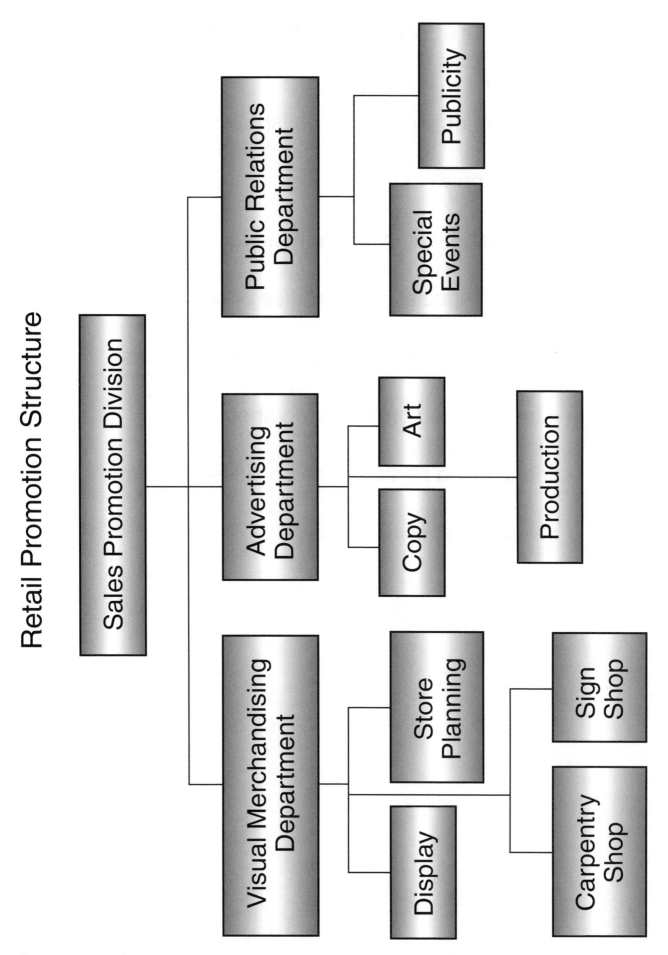

Promotion Employee Goals

Promotion employees establish plans to

- attract new customers

- establish fashion authority and image

- present special merchandise or prices

- introduce new products, services, or ideas

- stress related products together

- identify and reinforce the qualities of a brand

- introduce special events

Modeling Career Pros and Cons

Advantages of Modeling	Disadvantages of Modeling
• Might earn high pay • Glamour and excitement • Opportunity to travel • Work with the latest fashions • Public recognition	• Unsteady work—lack of job security • Short career span • Must always look good • Stiff competition causes frequent rejection for jobs • Unhealthy lifestyle influences (such as eating disorders, drugs, etc.)

Expressing Visual Merchandising Interest

Name_____ **Date** _____ **Period** _____

Read the list of activities related to visual merchandising. Place a check in the column that best represents your level of interest about each. Then analyze your score according to the directions that follow. (You will not be graded on your score.)

Activities	Interested	Unsure	Not Interested
Learning how store windows and interior displays are assembled			
Learning how displayed merchandise can entice customers to buy			
Showing customers different ways of coining fashionable outfits			
Selecting the clothing, accessories, and props for displays			
Cleaning, building, and painting the sets for window displays			
Arranging objects according to design elements and principles			
Putting promotional thoughts into actual visual form			
Creating a theme or atmosphere within a retail store			
Following orders from the head of the display design team			
Thinking of new display techniques to increase sales			
Comparing the window displays of two stores			
Seeking display input from retail buyers and store managers			
Organizing the storage of display props and equipment			
Using lighting techniques to emphasize fashion trends			
Arranging merchandise in wall areas and on tables and racks			
Subtotals =			

Total score _____

For each *Interested* response checked, give yourself 3 points. For every *Unsure* response checked, give yourself 1 point. For every *Not Interested* response checked, give yourself 0 points. If your total score is between 31 and 45, you have a high interest in becoming a visual merchandiser. If your total score is between 15 and 30, you are interested in fashion display, but not as a career. If your score is less than 15, you are not interested in a career in visual merchandising.

How does your score correspond with your previous thoughts about being a visual merchandiser?_____

_____

_____

Tasks of Advertising Personnel

- To interest consumers in products before they enter the store by preselling

- To introduce new merchandise to customers

- To inform customers about the merchandise offered for sale

- To remind customers about goods and their availability

- To reach out to specific age groups, ethnic groups, and others

- To increase sales by appealing to consumer desires and needs

- To promote the store's image

- To build goodwill with customers and the community

Advertising Planning Sources

- Records of past ads and their results

- Financial conditions of the economy and company

- Goals of management

- Promotions planned by manufacturers, competitors, and publications

- Success or failure of types of ads by other retailers

- Input from the resident buying office, merchandising division of the company, National Retail Federation, trade publications, and fashion magazines

Promotion Careers Review

Name_____ **Date** _____ **Period** _____

As you review the chapter, answer the following questions.

1. What attributes of typical models does our society consider "ideal"? _____

   _____

   _____

   _____

2. What are the average working times for female and male models, respectively? _____

   _____

   _____

3. What might a person learn at an accredited modeling school? _____

   _____

   _____

   _____

4. When applying for modeling jobs, what information should models provide? _____

   _____

   _____

   _____

5. What do fashion photographers do? _____

   _____

   _____

   _____

6. What might a fashion reporter or editor for a newspaper do? _____

   _____

   _____

   _____

7. What should a copywriter's portfolio contain? _____

   _____

   _____

   _____

8. What might be emphasized when fashion illustration work is done for fashion magazines or trade publications?_____

   _____

   _____

(Continued)

Name_____

9. When fashion writers do their own research for fashion articles, from what sources do they gather material? _____

_____

_____

_____

10. For what purposes might audiovisual productions be used? _____

_____

_____

_____

11. For what types of companies might an audiovisual professional work?_____

_____

_____

_____

12. To succeed in selling products, what must advertising people know? _____

_____

_____

_____

13. List at least five subjects in which fashion advertising directors have probably taken courses in college.

_____

_____

_____

14. List at least five college course subjects that might be taken by someone who aspires to be an art director._____

_____

_____

_____

_____

15. For what forms of advertising do media buyers handle arrangements?_____

_____

_____

_____

16. What are the job titles of two entry-level graphic design positions?_____

_____

_____

_____

Promotion Careers

Name_____

Date_____**Period**_____ **Score**_____

Chapter 29 Test

Matching: Match the following terms and identifying phrases.

_____ 1. A model who poses in front of cameras for pictures used in press releases or advertisements.

_____ 2. An employee who does interior merchandise displays.

_____ 3. An advertising agency employee in charge of selling to and handling specific advertising accounts.

_____ 4. The supervisor of fashion writers and copywriters.

_____ 5. A design room or showroom model who tries on and models samples for the company's management and retail buyers.

_____ 6. A retail employee who supervises the advertising department and publications.

_____ 7. An advertising employee who comes up with the visual representation for advertisements and collateral materials.

_____ 8. A model who works in front of live audiences.

_____ 9. An advertising designer who conceptualizes ads for newspapers, magazines, direct-mail flyers, radio, TV, signs, and outdoor media.

_____ 10. An advertising employee who selects and buys the best media for clients' ads.

A. account executive

B. advertising director

C. art director

D. display designer

E. editor

F. fit model

G. graphic designer

H. media buyer

I. photographic model

J. runway model

True/False: Circle *T* if the statement is true or *F* if the statement is false.

T   F   11. Fashion promotion is the indirect selling function of merchandising.

T   F   12. Modeling is a combination of advertising and performing.

T   F   13. "Mannequin work" is done by photographic models.

T   F   14. The average working time for male models is about 10 years.

T   F   15. A modeling employment agency arranges job opportunities and interviews for models.

T   F   16. Fashion journalists write, edit, and pass along fashion information through the mass media.

T   F   17. Computer skills are essential for fashion writers.

(Continued)

Name_____

T   F   18. Most fashion journalism and illustration jobs are located in small towns.

T   F   19. Marketing specialists are essentially advertising directors who work for manufacturing firms.

T   F   20. Layout artists specify the typefaces and do sample renderings that show what finished ads will look like when printed.

Multiple Choice: Choose the best response. Write the letter in the space provided.

_____ 21. For retailers, fashion promotion _____.
    A. builds the company's fashion image
    B. increases store traffic and sells merchandise
    C. fosters goodwill with the community
    D. All of the above.

_____ 22. Slimness is especially important for photographic models because _____.
    A. photos make the figure look shorter than it really is
    B. photos make the figure look heavier than it really is
    C. photos make the background look farther away than it really is
    D. All of the above.

_____ 23. At an accredited modeling school, prospective models learn _____.
    A. how to stand, pose, and move properly
    B. about posture and speech
    C. about hairstyles and makeup
    D. All of the above.

_____ 24. Assistant photographers _____.
    A. take pictures that show fashionable clothes and accessories at their best
    B. try to make pictures look like models are in motion
    C. test the lighting and help prepare sets and props for backgrounds
    D. All of the above.

_____ 25. A fashion reporter for a newspaper may _____.
    A. write a daily or weekly column or periodic feature stories
    B. be a boss of several copywriters and photographers
    C. prepare press kits that are sent to magazines about fashion news from the paper
    D. All of the above.

_____ 26. Fashion illustrators _____.
    A. design original fashions for companies that don't have their own designers
    B. sketch accessorized outfits that have been sold by retail stores
    C. draw garments that have been designed and produced by others
    D. take pictures of fashionable apparel being worn by models

(Continued)

Name_____

_____ 27. Audiovisual productions are produced to _____.
   A. sell products and entertain audiences
   B. educate consumers or students
   C. train or update industry people
   D. All of the above.

_____ 28. Display managers _____.
   A. are also known as window dressers
   B. work for advertising agencies, fashion publications, and retailers
   C. are the head employees of retail display staffs and oversee all display work
   D. All of the above.

_____ 29. Collateral materials are _____.
   A. all the parts of advertisements, such as the illustration, copy, headline, and logo
   B. extra photos, headlines, and copy that are not used in the final version of an advertisement
   C. secondary versions of advertisements that are presented to clients in case the top choice is rejected
   D. brochures, annual reports, packaging, hangtags, and other corporate image projects

_____ 30. Publicists _____.
   A. are public relations agents who try to anticipate problems a company might have with the public
   B. tell the story of a firm or its products through various media
   C. try to gain public information media space with newsworthiness
   D. All of the above.

Essay Questions: Provide complete responses to the following questions or statements.

31. Internal sales promotion of large retail companies is often divided into what three departments?

32. Describe the job tasks of photo stylists.

33. List three job activities in audiovisual work.

Entrepreneurship and Other Fashion-Related Careers

Objectives

After studying this chapter, students will be able to

⊖ describe the personal traits needed and opportunities available for entrepreneurs.

⊖ explain fashion careers in the home sewing industry.

⊖ tell about the field of theatrical costuming.

⊖ summarize clothing care and preservation careers.

⊖ describe careers for those who want to teach.

Teaching Materials

Text, pages 603–619
  Fashion Terms
  Fashion Review
  Fashion in Action
Student Workbook
  A. *You as an Entrepreneur*
  B. *Job Qualifications*
  C. *A Retail Start-Up*
  D. *Read About Real Life*
  E. *Match the Terms*
Teacher's Resources
  The Entrepreneurial Thought Pattern,
    transparency master 30-1
  Small Business Success Criteria, transparency
    master 30-2
  Keeping a Small Business Growing,
    transparency master 30-3
  Rules for New Retail Ventures, transparency
    master 30-4
  Tips for Good Teaching, transparency
    master 30-5
  Last Chapter Review, reproducible master 30-6
  The New Generation of Leaders, transparency
    master 30-7
  Freelancing or Consulting, reproducible
    master 30-8

Evaluating a Franchise Opportunity,
  reproducible master 30-9
Chapter 30 Test

Introductory Activities

1. Ask students to write a one-page report on their ideas about the work of one of the following:
   - the owner of a small fashion-related business
   - someone who works professionally within the home sewing industry
   - a theatrical costumer
   - someone who works in clothing care or preservation
   - a fashion educator
   Use these reports to introduce subjects as they are presented in the text.
2. Ask students to look for newspaper and magazine articles that describe people who work in small businesses, the home sewing industry, theatrical costuming, clothing care or preservation, and education. Have students bring the articles to class, discuss the contents, and pass them around for the other students to read.

Strategies to Reteach, Reinforce, Enrich, and Extend Text Concepts

Entrepreneurship

3. **RT** Ask students to define the term entrepreneur. Have students discuss the personal traits needed to succeed as an entrepreneur and specific factors to consider when starting a business.
4. **ER** *The Entrepreneurial Thought Pattern*, transparency master 30-1. Use the transparency to discuss each point in the entrepreneurial thought process. Ask students to give examples illustrating each point.

5. **RT** Have the class look at Chart 30-3 in the text. Have students read the points of the chart and explain them more fully in their own words. Continue by having the class discuss the points of Chart 30-4.

6. **RT** Hold a class discussion about home-based businesses and independent sales representatives. Emphasize the pros and cons of each as they are discussed.

7. **ER** Find out if any local trade schools or community colleges offer courses that prepare people to start small or home-based businesses. Get information about the courses to share with the students.

8. **EX** Show students a video that teaches them more about entrepreneurship. *Entrepreneuring Skills* is available from The School Company. *The Entrepreneur* is available from Nasco and The Curriculum Center for Family and Consumer Sciences. *Your Own Business: Getting Started, How to Write a Business Plan, Setting Up a Home-Based Business*, and many other videos are available from the American Institute of Small Business. *Entrepreneurship: Starting a Small Business, Up & Running, Selecting a Form of Business Ownership, Highlighting Small Business, Hispanic Entrepreneurs, Entrepreneurship for the New Millennium, Entrepreneurship: Marketing Strategy for Small Business*, and *Your Own Business: Getting Started*, and others are available from D.E. Visuals.

9. **RF** *Small Business Success Criteria*, transparency master 30-2. Ask students to explain why each of the points on the transparency is important in the success of a small business.

10. **RF** Have students play a board game to learn what it takes to start and run a retail or other business. *You're the Boss* is available with teacher's guide from Sunburst Communications. *We Mean Business! An Adventure in Entrepreneurship* is available from Nasco.

11. **RF** Have students work with business plan software or see and discuss business plan PowerPoint slides, available from D.E. Visuals. *Cash Compass* and *Business Plan Pro* are computer CDs. *Aspects of Business Plan* and *Vision & Mission Statements* are in slide format

12. **ER** Show students a video about writing a business plan and promoting and running a small fashion business. *The Business Plan, The Business Plan and Beyond*, and *Promotional Strategy for Small Business* are available from D.E. Visuals.

13. **EX** *You as an Entrepreneur*, Activity A, WB. Students are asked to calculate their nerve and urge for achievement to indicate the extent of their entrepreneurial aptitude.

14. **ER** *Keeping a Small Business Growing*, transparency master 30-3. Have students discuss each of the points presented on the transparency and explain why each would be important to the strength of an entrepreneurial venture.

15. **ER** Show students guidebooks that would help entrepreneurs establish their businesses. Kalorama Information offers many directories of mailing lists, trends, industrial outlooks, and other data.

16. **EX** Show the class a video about franchising. *Franchises: Making Their Dream Your Dream, Franchising*, and *Find the Right Franchise* are available from D.E. Visuals.

17. **RF** *Rules for New Retail Ventures*, transparency master 30-4. Have students discuss the importance of each point presented on the transparency. (These "rules" may also assist students with Activity C of the WB.)

18. **RT** Ask students to research and discuss the retail store start-up costs listed in Chart 30-5 of the text. Continue by having the class discuss the points in Chart 30-6 of the text.

19. **RT** Hold a class discussion about the duties and personal requirements of owning a dressmaking or tailoring shop, being an apparel producer, or owning a trading company or mail-order business.

20. **ER** Offer students extra information about specific types of entrepreneurial ventures. The video *Developing an Apparel Line* is available from Meridian Education Corporation. The video *Cutting Their Own Cloth: Entrepreneurial Clothing Designers* is available from D.E. Visuals. Teaching materials and color collars for color analysis work, from Nasco, is called *Color Collar*.

21. **EX** Have students do their own research about resources that offer help to entrepreneurs, such as training, support, formulating their ideas, writing business plans, applying for licenses and permits, obtaining financing, etc. Web sites to search are www.entrepreneur.com, www.inc.com, www.bizmove.com, www.retailowner.com, www.sewing.org, www.vfinance.com, and others. Guide books for small apparel store entrepreneurs are on www.tjreid.com.

22. **RF** Ask students to discuss the employment opportunities in fashion-related freelancing and consulting.

23. **RT** Create a bulletin board depicting the many kinds of entrepreneurial opportunities related to fashion.

Other Fashion-Related Careers

24. **RT** Hold a class discussion about jobs in the home sewing industry.

25. **RF** Take apart an old sewing pattern and distribute parts of it to twenty students in the class. Then have those students stand in front of the class. Each student should take on one of the following identities: commercial pattern company marketing employee, fashion director, merchandise director, designer, pattern maker, seamstress, fit model, pattern grader, checker, marker, fabric editor, accessories editor, technical writer, diagram artist, illustrator, layout designer, printing plant employee, retail coordinator, copywriter, or educational representative. In character, the students should explain what their job is, list qualifications necessary for that job, and point out the results of their work on the finished pattern.

26. **RF** Ask students if they would like a career in theatrical costuming. Have them explain why or why not. Then have students watch a particular TV show or movie. Discuss the costuming coordination and wardrobe challenges as a class.

27. **RT** Have the class discuss careers in clothing care and preservation. You may ask students to visit a dry cleaner to observe how various jobs are done. The students should write a short description of each job observed and give an oral report to the class.

28. **RF** Have the class discuss the pros and cons of a teaching career related to fashion. If possible, have your local county extension agent speak to the class on that day.

29. **EX** Show the class a video about careers in consumer education, school education, and various extension services. *FACS Careers* is available from Cambridge Educational. *Career Encounters: Teaching* is available from Meridian Education Corporation.

30. **ER** *Tips for Good Teaching*, transparency master 30-5. Use this transparency to discuss the importance and seriousness of teaching fashion-related courses.

31. **RF** *Job Qualifications*, Activity B, WB. Students are asked to match each of the given job titles with the person in the descriptions whose qualifications meet it best. Then students are to tell which job in the descriptions appeals to them the most and why.

32. **RT** *Last Chapter Review*, reproducible master 30-6. Students are asked to answer given questions as they review the chapter. Use this as a practice exercise for students who need review or as an extra credit assignment for those who wish to raise their grade.

Gaining Success in the Fashion Industry

33. **RT** Hold a class discussion about what it takes to succeed in the fashion industry.

34. **EX** *The New Generation of Leaders*, transparency master 30-7. Use this transparency to show the results of a study among current college graduates. As you go through each of the points with the class, discuss how the soft goods industry must provide opportunities for these new leaders or fashion companies will lose good talent.

35. **EX** Use a video or computer software program to extend students' understanding of gaining success in a career. *How to Be a Success at Work Video Series* and *Start Your Job: Promptness and Other Skills Employers Seek* are available from JIST Publishing. *Business Etiquette* is available from The Curriculum Center for Family and Consumer Sciences. Many videos about business etiquette and gaining success are available from D.E. Visuals.

36. **ER** *A Retail Start-Up*, Activity C, WB. The class is asked to start a small retail store. Students in facility, finance, personnel, merchandise, and promotion groups are to answer the questions given to help them solidify their thinking, coordinate their ideas, and write up a business plan. This is a comprehensive project that involves all students and reviews material from the entire course. A professional presentation is to be given at the completion of the project.

37. **ER** *Read About Real Life*, Activity D, WB. Students are asked to find an article in a newspaper or magazine about someone in a career related to the content of this chapter. Students are to attach the article to the page and answer given questions.

38. **RT** *Match the Terms*, Activity E, WB. Students are asked to match chapter terms with definitions.

Additional Enrichment Activities

Research

39. *Freelancing or Consulting*, reproducible master 30-8. Students are asked to research an area of freelancing or consulting work that interests them. Questions are provided to help them complete their research. You may choose to have students do research in groups by interest category and report their findings to the class.

40. Have students do research about the U.S. Small Business Administration. They may obtain information by contacting the office closest to your location or checking the Web site www.sba.gov. Have students find out what books, speakers, and other resources are available to help people start and succeed with small businesses. Then have students obtain and read some of the booklets offered. Some booklets pertaining to retailing

include *Preventing Retail Theft, Stock Control for Small Stores, Reducing Shoplifting Losses, Outwitting Bad-Check Passers, Marketing Checklist for Small Retailers, A Pricing Checklist for Small Retailers, Improving Personal Selling in Small Retail Stores,* and *Advertising Guidelines for Small Retail Firms.* Additionally, SBA videos include *The Business Plan: Your Roadmap to Success* and *Home-Based Business: A Winning Blueprint.*

41. Have students do research about the Service Corps of Retired Executives (SCORE), a group of retired businesspeople who volunteer to help troubled businesses gain success. Students may want to start their research on the Web site www.score.org.

42. Have students do research about business plans. Then have groups of students prepare sample business plans for specific small fashion-related businesses and assemble their worksheets into a booklet. Have students show and explain their business plan booklets to the rest of the class.

Projects

43. *Evaluating a Franchise Opportunity,* reproducible master 30-9. Students are asked to use the form to interview the owner of an apparel franchise. They may also evaluate a franchise opportunity they or someone they know is planning to purchase.

44. Have students study a book about the content of this chapter. Examples available from www.amazon.com are *The "Business" of Sewing: How to Start, Maintain, and Achieve Success* by Barbara Wright Sykes; *The Business of Teaching Sewing: How to Be a Great Teacher* by Marcy Miller, Pati Palmer, and Ann Price Gosch; *Sew to Success: How to Make Money in a Home-Based Sewing Business* by Kathleen Spike; *How to Start & Maintain a Profitable Sewing Business: Making Money with Your Sewing Skills* by Becky Reed; *Marketing Your Sewing Business: How to Earn a Profit* by Barbara Wright Sykes; *The Fashion Designer Survival Guide: An Insider's Look at Starting and Running Your Own Fashion Business* by Mary Gehlhar and Zac Posen; *Start and Run a Retail Business* by James E. Dion; *The Business Startup Checklist and Planning Guide* by Stephanie Chandler; *Start and Run a Craft Business* by William G. Hynes; *How to Start and Run Your Own Retail Business* by Irving Brustiner; and others. There are also many "small business" books available from Crisp Learning and the American Institute of Small Business. After reading one of the books, have students give an in-depth report to the class.

45. Have students talk with an entrepreneur who has started a business. Without asking personal or sensitive (such as financial) questions, have students try to discover the following: kinds of products offered by the business; previous work experience of the entrepreneur; how the entrepreneur started or gained ownership of the company; what help was gained from courses, agencies, or trade groups; if a comprehensive business plan was written; what was done right or wrong; how long it was before a profit was realized; specific advantages and disadvantages of owning/running the company; what the biggest challenges and rewards have been; personal traits that have contributed to success; the hours worked per week or month; any advice to those thinking of being entrepreneurs. Have students write a "Diary of an Entrepreneurial Venture" as if it had been their own experience. Students may turn the reports in or read them to the class.

Answer Key

Text

Fashion Review, page 619

1. more than half
2. lack of experience, poor planning, and inadequate capital
3. the idea (proposal), operations, financial forecast, product, market opportunities, competition, and strategy
4. If one doesn't sell well, commission income can still be made from the other lines.
5. Body scanners will enable manufacturers to make customized garments.
6. cutting and sewing equipment, rent, utilities, and wages and training for workers
7. product line expertise and contacts with international suppliers and domestic retailers
8. There is no sure way of knowing how many orders will be received.
9. (Name three:) advising them on personal images, wardrobe coordination, accessorizing, color analysis, wedding consultants
10. to design, produce, package, and sell patterns for home sewers
11. look over patterns to see if notches line up, facings match their corresponding garment parts, and other cutting and sewing markings are properly included
12. to write clear sewing directions that are easy to read and follow
13. a theater company, movie or television studio, or costume shop
14. high pay, industry recognition
15. a high school education and training under skilled workers

16. electronic scanning microscopes
17. instructional plans follow a master curriculum but, as fashions change and different students enroll in the classes, the specific content of the courses vary
18. (Student response for one advantage and one disadvantage.)
19. promote their firms' products by teaching about them
20. to participate in professional organizations, take advanced courses and seminars, and read trade journals and other publications

Student Workbook

Job Qualifications, Activity B

1. D	6. J
2. I	7. A
3. H	8. F
4. E	9. G
5. B	10. C

Match the Terms, Activity E

1. E	11. I
2. K	12. Q
3. M	13. B
4. A	14. H
5. P	15. O
6. G	16. L
7. D	17. R
8. T	18. N
9. J	19. C
10. F	20. S

Teacher's Resources

Last Chapter Review, reproducible master 30-6

1. (List three:) innovation, flexibility, creativity, drive, self-confidence, ambition (Students may justify other responses.)
2. two
3. a business plan
4. (List four:) Family matters can be distracting and disruptive. It is too easy to work evenings and weekends without taking time off to relax. Clients may intrude on personal time or not take the business seriously. Neighbors may object to having a business near them.

5. Buy a business or partnership in a business that is already in operation, start a new retail business, or buy a franchise.
6. because body scanners will enable production companies to make customized garments
7. retail buyers, fashion editors, suppliers, and contractors
8. figure out what the company's customers will want in patterns and anticipate sales
9. research and obtain the latest available styles of buttons, jewelry, shoes, scarves, and belts for the accessories room
10. operas, ballets, stage plays, circuses, movies, advertisements, television shows, and parades
11. soil that could prematurely age and damage the fabrics, hanging strain, discoloration or fading, and insects such as moths
12. museums, libraries, and universities
13. textiles, fashion, grooming, clothing selection and care, sewing construction, and careers
14. Instructional plans follow a master curriculum but the specific content of the courses vary.
15. at a school or community center

Chapter 30 Test

1. E	16. T
2. G	17. T
3. I	18. T
4. A	19. T
5. C	20. T
6. D	21. D
7. B	22. C
8. J	23. B
9. H	24. A
10. F	25. B
11. F	26. D
12. T	27. C
13. T	28. B
14. T	29. A
15. F	30. C

31. (List four. See illustration 30-5 in the text.)
32. Freelancing is the selling of expert skills to accomplish particular tasks, and consulting is the selling of a person's expert ideas and advice as a service business.
33. Consumer education combines teaching with business promotion. Consumer educators teach people about their companies' products.

The Entrepreneurial Thought Pattern

- Where is the opportunity?

- How do I capitalize on it?

- What resources do I need?

- How do I gain control of the resources?

- What organizational structure is best?

Small Business Success Criteria

- A promising business opportunity

- An appropriate ownership structure

- A good business plan

- Adequate financing

- Effective management

Keeping a Small Business Growing

- Seek out mentors to offer insight.

- Respect your instincts.

- Gain direction from the marketplace.

- Maintain a strong outside network.

- Learn the art of being a boss.

- Touch base with your customers regularly.

- Avoid procrastinating. Tasks can pile up.

- Take time off periodically.

- Admit your mistakes and learn from them.

- Have fun!

Based on work by Susan Peterson of Susan Peterson Productions, Inc.

Rules for New Retail Ventures

- Identify a market niche with sufficient volume potential.

- Seek a location with little or no direct competition.

- Create an inexpensive but interesting store.

- Establish reasonable, achievable sales goals.

- Buy goods that can have a good original markup.

- Live with less inventory than you really want.

- Monitor the operating expenses carefully.

- Change the format as conditions warrant.

Based on work by Bill Pearson, Retail Analysis & Planning, Pasadena, CA

Tips for Good Teaching

- Set goals for material to cover.

- Communicate what is expected and why.

- Understand the subject matter thoroughly.

- Follow instructional materials closely.

- Accept responsibility for student achievement.

Adapted from a study by the U.S. Department of Education Office of
Educational Research and Improvement.

Last Chapter Review

Name_____ **Date** _____ **Period** _____

As you review the chapter, answer the following questions.

1. List three attributes a successful entrepreneur needs to launch a business operation. _____
   _____
   _____
   _____

2. How many years does it usually take to start making a profit in a new business? _____
   _____
   _____

3. What main document is needed for an entrepreneur to borrow money from lending institutions when starting a business? _____
   _____
   _____

4. List four disadvantages in operating a home-based business._____
   _____
   _____
   _____
   _____

5. What are the three main ways to become an owner of a retail shop? _____
   _____
   _____
   _____
   _____

6. Why might it become harder to make a good living as a dressmaker/tailor in the future? _____
   _____
   _____
   _____

7. Apparel production entrepreneurs who leave large firms to start their own businesses should be acquainted with what types of professional people? _____
   _____
   _____
   _____

(Continued)

Name_____

8. What do commercial pattern company merchandising directors do?_____

_____

_____

_____

9. What do commercial pattern company accessories editors do? _____

_____

_____

_____

10. For what types of productions is theatrical costuming done?_____

_____

_____

_____

_____

11. In textile/apparel preservation, against what are garments protected? _____

_____

_____

_____

_____

12. Costume conservators care for the historic costume collections of what types of organizations?

_____

_____

_____

13. What subjects might family and consumer sciences teachers teach in relation to apparel? _____

_____

_____

_____

_____

14. What is meant by the phrase "teaching provides a routine with variety"? _____

_____

_____

_____

_____

15. Where are adult education courses usually taught?_____

_____

_____

_____

_____

The New Generation of Leaders

- are ambitious, optimistic, energetic

- are open-minded, culturally varied, value diversity

- mesh with the global market (speak foreign languages, are willing to live in other countries)

- seek companies with strong, open managerial structures that offer flexible work schedules, empowerment, and rewards for accomplishments

- are excited about new technology and ongoing training

Freelancing or Consulting

Name_____ **Date** _____ **Period** _____

Define *freelancing*.

_____

_____

_____

Define *consulting*.

_____

_____

_____

Check which career in freelancing or consulting would interest you the most for your future:

_____ Freelance fashion designer   _____ Bridal consultant

_____ Freelance fashion illustrator   _____ Color analysis consultant

_____ Freelance promotion specialist   _____ Wardrobe consultant

_____ Freelance fashion photographer   _____ Image consultant

_____ Freelance display designer   _____ Other freelancer or consultant (specify)

Research the freelancing or consulting career you checked and answer the following questions.

1. What education would you need?_____

   _____

   _____

   _____

   _____

2. What preparatory work experience would you seek? _____

   _____

   _____

   _____

   _____

3. How would you establish the rates you would charge? _____

   _____

   _____

   _____

   _____

(Continued)

Name_____

4. How would you keep records and do billing? _____

_____

_____

_____

5. How would you negotiate contracts with clients? _____

_____

_____

_____

6. Are there any other legal aspects you should consider? _____

_____

_____

_____

7. How would you develop leads for jobs and market your services? _____

_____

_____

_____

8. What kind of a portfolio would you assemble to promote your work?_____

_____

_____

_____

9. What other important information did you discover from your research? __

_____

_____

_____

_____

_____

_____

_____

Evaluating a Franchise Opportunity

Name_____ Date _____ Period _____

Use this form to interview the owner of an apparel franchise or to evaluate a franchise opportunity you or someone you know is planning to purchase.

Franchisor Company:	How long has the company been in business?
	How strong is it financially?
	What plans are there for future development?
	What is the rating with the Better Business Bureau?
	Is the company selective in choosing franchisees?
Product:	What is the quality of the company's products?
	Are items commodity, fad, luxury, or seasonal?
	How well do products sell?
	To whom do products sell?
	How long have items been on the market?
	Would you buy the products?
	Are items competitively priced?
	Are items attractively presented?
Sales Area:	Is there a well-defined, exclusive territory?
	Is the area large enough for good sales potential?
	What are growth possibilities?
	What is expected income?
	Are there income fluctuations?
	What competition is present?
	How are different nearby franchises doing?
Contract:	Is the contract complete?
	Are the responsibilities, liabilities, benefits, and protection of both parties clearly defined?
	Can the contract be renewed, terminated, or transferred?
	What are the conditions for obtaining or losing the franchise?
	Must a certain size and type of operation be maintained?
	What payments and merchandise purchases are required?
	Can franchisee return merchandise for credit or perform other business activities?

(Continued)

Name_____

Continuing Assistance:	Does franchisor provide fast, continuing assistance?
	What training is offered?
	What manuals, sales kits, and accounting systems are supplied?
	Who selects store location, design and layout, displays, and opening inventory?
	Who handles lease arrangements?
	What help is provided for purchasing and financing?
	What assistance is provided concerning inventory control methods, market surveys, and financial analysis?
	What general promotion is provided by franchisor and advertising aids to franchisee?

Evaluation of the franchise opportunity

Advantages:

_____

_____

Disadvantages:

_____

_____

General analysis:

_____

_____

_____

Entrepreneurship and Other Fashion-Related Careers

Name_____

Date_____ Period_____ Score_____

Chapter 30 Test

Matching: Match the following terms and identifying phrases.

_____ 1. Educators hired and paid by state land grant universities to work as family and consumer scientists in various counties or an entire state.

_____ 2. The expenses to turn a new business venture into reality.

_____ 3. Wardrobing for operas, ballets, stage plays, circuses, movies, advertisements, television shows, and parades.

_____ 4. Instructional courses held for adults at night.

_____ 5. Theatrical wardrobe helper who organizes the costumes and accessories by character and scene.

_____ 6. Expert sewers who make custom garments or do apparel alterations and repairs.

_____ 7. People who locate, identify, and determine the age of textiles, apparel, and accessories from the past.

_____ 8. Heads of theatrical costume departments.

_____ 9. The giving of special attention to long-term care of fabrics and clothing.

_____ 10. People who give instruction in school clothing and merchandising classes, extension work, and adult and consumer education courses.

A. adult education

B. costume curators

C. costume technicians

D. dressmakers/tailors

E. extension agents

F. fashion educators

G. start-up costs

H. textile/apparel preservation

I. theatrical costuming

J. wardrobe designers

True/False: Circle *T* if the statement is true or *F* if the statement is false.

T   F   11. It takes about four years for most new businesses to start making a profit.

T   F   12. Before starting a company, experience should be gained with the same type of product or service.

T   F   13. A business plan should define the idea, operations, and financial forecast of a proposed company.

T   F   14. Independent sales reps often handle several different lines for small manufacturers that are not in direct competition with each other.

(Continued)

Name_____

T F 15. A cottage industry is people in rural towns who gather together to make crafts and simple garments.

T F 16. A trading company imports or exports goods, usually specializing in a certain product category.

T F 17. Freelancers and consultants work independently on individual, short-term jobs or on a contractual basis.

T F 18. Businesses in the home sewing industry deal with nonindustrial sewing machines, notions, fabrics, and patterns.

T F 19. The clothing care industry includes commercial laundries and dry cleaning establishments.

T F 20. Educational representatives promote their firms' products by teaching about them.

Multiple Choice: Choose the best response. Write the letter in the space provided.

_____ 21. Entrepreneurs are people who _____.
   A. organize, launch, and direct new business ventures
   B. assume the financial risks and uncertainties of new business ventures
   C. are able to turn innovation, flexibility, and creativity into functioning business operations
   D. All of the above.

_____ 22. Most small business failures are due to _____.
   A. the wrong location and not enough employees
   B. worsening economic conditions and labor strikes
   C. lack of experience, poor planning, and inadequate capital
   D. All of the above.

_____ 23. The U.S. Small Business Administration (SBA) is a _____.
   A. division of the U.S. Chamber of Commerce, with offices in most major cities
   B. government agency that offers helpful counseling, workshops, videotapes, and free publications
   C. nonprofit organization, supported by member companies, that offers services and publications
   D. trade organization that uses retired executives to help entrepreneurs start new companies

_____ 24. Advantages of working from home include _____.
   A. no commuting time or parking expenses and lower wardrobe costs
   B. no expenses for legal, accounting, and other professional fees
   C. the ability to visit with neighbors during the day and to work evenings and weekends
   D. All of the above.

_____ 25. Buying a franchise store rather than starting a retail operation from scratch usually _____.
   A. costs less money because the format is already established
   B. has a lower failure rate since the parent firm gives some guidance and promotional assistance
   C. takes more time because training must be done by the franchisor organization
   D. All of the above.

(Continued)

Name_____

_____ 26. The owner of a small retail shop should know how to _____.
   A. establish and maintain advantageous vendor relationships
   B. assure proper inventory levels with good sales/stock ratios
   C. analyze POS and financial data to improve business performance
   D. All of the above.

_____ 27. Inventory planning for a mail-order business can be tricky because _____.
   A. competitors might send out twice as many catalogs
   B. computer technology is less effective since no store POS information is gathered
   C. there is no sure way of knowing how many orders will be received
   D. the company's location usually affects how fast goods come in and go out

_____ 28. A commercial pattern company employee who figures out what the customers will want in patterns and anticipates sales is the _____.
   A. fashion director
   B. merchandising director
   C. marketing researcher
   D. designer

_____ 29. In the home sewing industry, technical writers _____.
   A. create sewing directions for pattern guide sheets that are easy to read and follow
   B. do technical drawings to show sewing methods on the guide sheets
   C. produce the finished pattern pieces, guide sheets, envelopes, and counter catalogs
   D. provide press releases and publicity for the media

_____ 30. Classroom teachers in career/technical high schools give training that _____.
   A. prepares students for college curriculums
   B. will provide a routine with variety
   C. can lead students directly to gainful employment
   D. prepares students to be clothing specialists at the local or state level

Essay Questions: Provide complete responses to the following questions or statements.

31. List four retail start-up costs.

32. What is the difference between freelancing and consulting?

33. Describe consumer education.